Social Work Services in Schools

SIXTH EDITION

Paula Allen-Meares
University of Illinois, Chicago

Allyn & Bacon

Boston   Columbus   Indianapolis   New York   San Francisco   Upper Saddle River
Amsterdam   Cape Town   Dubai   London   Madrid   Milan   Munich   Paris   Montreal   Toronto
Delhi   Mexico City   Sao Paulo   Sydney   Hong Kong   Seoul   Singapore   Taipei   Tokyo

Senior Acquisitions Editor: *Patricia Quinlin*
Editorial Assistant: *Carly Czech*
Senior Marketing Manager: *Wendy Albert*
Production Editor: *Karen Mason*
Manufacturing Buyer: *Debbie Rossi*
Cover Administrator: *Kristisna Mose-Libon*
Editorial Production and Composition Service: *Laserwords*

Library of Congress Cataloging-in-Publication Data

Social work services in schools / Paula Allen-Meares. — 6th ed.
    p. cm.
  Includes bibliographical references and index.
  ISBN 0-205-62712-9
 1. School social work—United States.   I. Allen-Meares, Paula
  LB3013.4.A45 2010
  371.7—dc22

                               2009020281

10 9 8 7 6 5 4 3 2 1 [HAM] 13 12 11 10 09

Allyn & Bacon
is an imprint of

www.pearsonhighered.com

ISBN-10: 0-205-62712-9
ISBN-13: 978-0-205-62712-7

Contents

4 An Ecological Perspective of Social Work Services in Schools   65

5 Student Rights and Control of Behavior   88

6 Violence in Schools   125

Foreword

American schools are on an innovation streak. Although our level of commitment and rate of change are not all that is needed, the recent course of reform now seems to be lasting and expanding. Public schools are implementing new assessment and accountability measures, charter schools are growing in number and diversification (e.g., residential charter schools and same-gender charter schools), and new technologies are becoming routinely integrated into every facet of school life.

This powerful sixth edition of *Social Work Services in Schools* offers a timely and important guide to developing the optimal use of social work in schools in this rapidly changing environment. The information contained herein offers a clear road map for enhancing the success of schools, and school social workers, in delivering human services that improve educational outcomes. *Social Work Services in Schools* continues to keep pace with the conceptual, empirical, practice, and program changes in school social work practice and offers a vision for its future.

This sixth edition has its origins in the first edition, written entirely by Paula Allen-Meares, Robert Washington, and Betty Welsh, and builds on the strong frame of that work to offer the field an integrated view of school social work practice. In the third edition, key chapters were written by experienced school social work practitioners (including Cynthia Franklin, who is joined by Mary Beth Harris and Christine Lagana-Riordan, MSW, in this edition). The fourth edition integrated important additional content from several more of the nation's leading school social work and education scholars (e.g., Ron Astor—joined here by Rami Benbenishty and Roxana Marachi, Gary Bowen, Mary Beth Harris, and John Sipple—joined by Hope Casto in the sixth edition). The fifth edition added specialized knowledge on new policy (e.g., No Child Left Behind), program, and practice fronts (e.g., evidence-based practice).

The sixth edition is most notable for bringing greater depth and precision to the discussions of evidence-based practices—from the accumulation of new work that is reviewed—and also adds new material on technology in the schools (including advances like social networking and untoward implications like cyberbullying) and updates information on relevant legal rights, challenges, and outcomes from Sandra Kopels. Bruce Thyer also joins as an author, adding his perspective to Siri Jayaratne's insights on evaluation and its increasing importance to service delivery.

Befitting their longstanding involvement in schools, communities, and with school social work, the authors cast the net broadly for topics that are critical to school social work practice, both present and future. Several discussions address changes larger than the school (e.g., charter schools, homeschooling, and major initiatives in school financing), but most of them are focused on issues directly addressing services in schools. No Child Left Behind has a new and central place in this volume, and the authors address such national issues such resegregation, legal reform regarding bilingual education, ethics, and Title IX.

These authors offer unique and engaging treatments of many of these topics because they have been involved in the development and implementation of these efforts. The book is clearly from an insider's perspective. The writing is strong and sprinkled with insights that show that these authors have been lead actors in the evolution of school social work services, not just observers of its unfolding. The text draws strength and richness from their participation in the changes about which they write. The analyses are crisp and telling. The policy content is remarkably vivid and helps readers go well beyond the common critiques of such emerging forces as the expansion of standardized testing and the emergence of vouchers and charter schools to a more nuanced understanding of what elements of these innovations are concerning and how to address them.

This is not to suggest that the authors have taken the easier path and written a policy book or a book for middle managers, who are implementing reforms. Although this text offers something for readers operating to influence a multitude of school-related ecologies and their interdependence, this is fundamentally a volume dedicated to enhancing the performance of direct practitioners. The practice content has been strengthened with more cases and with attention to evidence-based interventions. The latter treatment is careful and captures the promise and challenges of implementing such services in the schools. Additional seasoned school social work practitioners provide a broader and deeper well of school social work practice knowledge. The excellence of prior volumes has been extended, and the field is the benefactor.

Richard P. Barth
Professor and Dean
University of Maryland, Baltimore
School of Social Work

Preface

During recent elections around the nation, education, the economy, and health-care policy rose to the top of the list of many political candidates. Some cited the past and current failure of the public educational system to achieve its historic and ongoing objectives—educating the diverse masses for effective participation and leadership in our great society and the larger global society. Proposals ranged from zero to five plans that would quadruple the number of eligible children in early Head Start programs; an increase additional learning time in schools; encouraging schools to develop strong relationships among parents and students; promoting evidence-based models that would decrease dropout rates; supporting summer learning opportunities for disadvantaged children through partnerships between local schools and community organizations; and improving assessment models that would provide educators and students with feedback in real time and that would extend beyond standardized tests. *Social Work Services in Schools* has much comment and insight to supplement these agenda items.

Consequently, we are excited about the sixth edition of *Social Work Services in Schools.* In this book, we discuss historical and contemporary concepts, policies, and evidence-based interventions in the field of social work in schools. Along with these important concepts, new ones, such as integrated service or full-service schools, violence in schools and preventive interventions, and issues of education and welfare reform, are addressed. It is a basic book for persons specializing in social work services in schools, as well as for those who are preparing to work in related agencies of the community and find it necessary to understand school policies, educational practices, social services, and groups of pupils who are at risk of educational failure. Social workers who are now providing services will find the book a valuable resource about the state of this field and new forces shaping its future.

In recent years school social workers have grown in number and have become a well-organized and vocal group. Many have completed their professional education and are seeking to increase their competence by acquiring knowledge about new aspects of educational policy, evidence-based intervention, and alternative models of social work services in schools.

The materials integrated in this book include empirical findings described in professional literature, case illustrations of social work practice in schools, and interviews. Social work practice is examined in relation to the present emphasis on improving the quality of education, charter schools, school reform, and full-service schools. Major educational policy issues, societal conditions that impact upon or affect the quality of life of pupils and their families, and the strategic position of the school in attempting to solve critical problems of children and young people are also brought into focus. The chapter authors believe that social workers who are unfamiliar with major educational policies and practices and with the societal conditions that affect pupils cannot deliver responsive, quality social services in schools. A sound background and an understanding of the interdisciplinary nature of this field and how to collaborate are also required.

The major objectives of this textbook are the following: (1) to consider the conceptual framework of social work as currently developed by the professional and the application of those concepts to school social work; (2) to examine the roles and responsibilities of school personnel and of the children and parents served, as well as the legal framework for the establishment, financing, and governance of the school, and the unity and complexity of its interacting personalities and their functions; (3) to explain the major problem areas of public school education and to analyze the resultant sociological policy issues that affect the quality of education; (4) to identify target populations of school schoolchildren for whom social work services are indicated at critical points of the life cycle; (5) to understand social work intervention and prevention in relation to the ecology of the schoolchild; and (6) to present a basis for assuming the responsibility to design, deliver, and evaluate the effectiveness of school social work services within a multicultural context. The chapter on evaluation includes topics such as different approaches to evaluation and design and implementation issues, examples of studies that embellish the discussion of approaches, and ethical and human subject issues.

Although the order of the chapters lends itself to the construction of a coherent course and teaching outline, each chapter is written to stand alone so that, if desired, the chapters can be ordered to reflect individual preferences. Each chapter begins with a brief introduction that identifies the substantive content and provides unifying ideas.

Questions for study and discussion, suggestions for projects, and additional references for further study appear at the end of each chapter. Relevant Internet Web sites are identified. The notes within each chapter are a source for additional exploration of ideas discussed in the text. Illustrations of school–community–pupil problems and appropriate interventions are intended to help the reader become familiar with the school setting within which social work takes place. Assessment instruments are discussed, and the appendices contain rich practice-relevant resources.

We continue to be grateful to Lela B. Costin (deceased), who, more than two decades ago, developed the original prospectus, which has been modified and expanded by chapter authors. Additionally, we would like to acknowledge the wonderful contributions of Bob Washington (deceased) and Betty Welch to previous editions of this book. This sixth edition is in their honor.

Paula Allen-Meares
Chancellor and Professor,
University of Illinois at Chicago;
Dean Emeritus, Professor Emeritus
of Social Work and Education
at the University of Michigan, Ann Arbor

Contributors

Paula Allen-Meares is currently Chancellor and John Corbally Presidential Professor at the University of Illinois at Chicago, and Dean Emeritus/Professor Emeritus of Social Work and Education at the University of Michigan, Ann Arbor. Her research interests include school social work, the tasks and functions of social workers employed in educational settings and the organizational variables that influence service delivery; improving the mental health/health of poor children and adolescents of color; adolescent pregnancy, including repeat births among adolescents and young adults; health care utilization, and social integration factors which influence sexual behavior and parenthood; and maternal psychiatric disorders and their direct and indirect effects on parenting skills and developmental outcomes of offspring. In addition, she has published on such topics as conceptual frameworks for social work and research methodologies. She has served as Principal Investigator on a W. K. Kellogg Foundation Grant, entitled *Global Program for Youth,* and was Co-Principal Investigator of the NIMH Center on Poverty, Risk, and Mental Health. Dr. Allen-Meares serves as a board member of the New York Academy of Medicine and is a member of the Institute of Medicine of the National Academies (IOM).

Sally Atkins-Burnett, Ph.D., is a Senior Researcher at Mathematica Policy Research, Inc. Her research interests include assessment, early childhood development, dual language learners, and children with disabilities. Her background in teaching children with disabilities and in teacher preparation of special educators, as well as her personal experience as a parent to individuals with disabilities, informs her writing and research.

Ron Avi Astor, Ph.D., is the Richard M. and Ann L. Thor Professor in Urban Social Development. He holds appointments in the schools of Social Work and Education at the University of Southern California. His professional interests include children's understanding of violence, large-scale, city-wide youth empowerment monitoring systems, and school violence interventions. He has been awarded a Senior Scholar Fulbright Fellowship, National Academy of Education/Spencer Fellowship, William T. Grant foundation projects, and an H. F. Guggenheim Fellowship. He has authored over 100 scientific publications and has numerous research projects on school violence. His work has won numerous awards including best book and two best research article awards from the American Educational Research Association and the American Psychological Association.

Rami Benbenishty, Ph.D., is a Professor of Social Work at Bar Ilan University in Israel. He is a leading international expert on school violence. He was the Principal Investigator of one of the largest school violence studies conducted in any country to date. He is currently exploring how different forms of violence are manifested in different cultures and different school contexts. He works with the Israeli Ministry of Education and local school districts on the monitoring of school violence.

Gary L. Bowen, Ph.D., MSW, is William R. Kenan, Jr., Distinguished Professor at the University of North Carolina at Chapel Hill School of Social Work. His professional interests include social work with families, work and family linkages, the military family, research and evaluation, and family values.

Cynthia Franklin, Ph.D., LCSW, LMFT is a Professor, holder of the Steirnberg/Spencer Family Professorship in Mental Health, at the University of Texas at Austin, and the coordinator of clinical social work concentration. She is an internationally known leader in school social work and school mental health practice. Professor Franklin has authored over 100 publications about dropout prevention, clinical assessment, the effectiveness of solution-focused therapy in school settings, and adolescent pregnancy prevention. She has also served as past Editor-in-Chief of the National Association of Social Worker's (NASW's) journal *Children in Schools.*

Mary Beth Harris, Ph.D., LCSW, is a Clinical Associate Professor at the University of Southern California. She has conducted numerous clinical studies and authored a number of seminal publications on adolescent mothers in the school environment. Dr. Harris was a family therapist and administrator in family and school-based services for more than two decades.

Srinika D. Jayaratne, Ph.D., is a Professor at the School of Social Work, University of Michigan. He has been studying the effects of work stress on the health and well-being of mental health practitioners, client violence toward social workers in the workplace, and professional practice standards.

Sandra Kopels, J.D., MSW, is a Professor at the University of Illinois, Urbana-Champaign School of Social Work, where she teaches both law and social work policy courses. Professor Kopels has authored numerous articles and book chapters primarily focusing on the law's impact on the rights of vulnerable clients and the responsibilities of social workers who work on their behalf. She has specifically focused on ethical and legal issues related to confidentiality and the disclosure of information in situations where clients are viewed by practitioners as being in danger from their actions or those of others.

Christine Lagana-Riordan, M.S.W., is a doctoral student at the University of Texas at Austin School of Social Work. Before beginning doctoral education, Ms. Lagana-Riordan was a school social worker in Baltimore, Maryland serving students with special cognitive and mental health needs. Her research interest areas include school social work practice, interventions for students with developmental disabilities, and education policy.

Roxana Marachi, Ph.D., is an Assistant Professor of Education at San José State University. Her research explores how interpersonal climates in schools relate to school violence and student victimization. She has presented her work at national and international conferences and is currently co-chair of the *Safe Schools and Communities Special Interest Group* for the American Educational Research Association.

John W. Sipple, Ph.D., is an Associate Professor in the Department of Education at Cornell University. His research interests include school reform, organizational studies, and the equity implications of the implementation of education policy.

Bruce A. Thyer, Ph.D., LCSW, is a Professor and former Dean with the College of Social Work at Florida State University. He is the Editor of the journal *Research on Social Work Practice,* published by Sage Publications, Inc. His professional interests related to the fields of applied behavior analysis, evidence-based practice, and program evaluation.

1

Major Issues in American Schools

JOHN W. SIPPLE & HOPE CASTO
Cornell University

Introduction

Public education continues to play a complex role in American society. This role is associated with hope, sharp criticism, and incessant calls for change. Most Americans view the educational system as the heart of the quest to form a more perfect nation, a nation that provides unparalleled opportunities to all children, no matter what their background. Schooling is the springboard for the American Dream; with equal access to education, goes the belief, there is equal access to the dream. Yet, schools are also the recipients of continual criticism and blame for economic woes; socioeconomic, racial and gender disparities; and unfavorable international comparisons. It is in this context that we wish to introduce the major issues in American education in hopes of motivating a discussion and analysis of the role that social work plays in the betterment of individuals and society as well as the future of American education.

We suggest that the future of public education rests in the struggle between three sets of competing—and sometimes overlapping—responses to the aforementioned expectations' uncertainty: government involvement; free markets, and professionalism. Throughout the remainder of this chapter, we will explore each of these responses.

The past century has witnessed a steady increase in the centralization of decision making and funding at both the state and federal levels. The early half of the 20th century brought about standardized school organization and the standardized role and preparation of teachers. The latter half witnessed dramatic increases in state funding and involvement in curriculum and accountability standards. More recently, we have witnessed the creation of school choice programs in steadily increasing numbers and an expansion of alternatives to the traditional model of university-based teacher preparation. We are at the brink of major change in federal education policy, change that will press for greater (1) federal funding (and influence) and/or (2) market pressures and school choice. Not unrelated to these two fundamental directions is the set of policies that will affect who is educating our children and just how much autonomy and professional knowledge is demanded or allowed.

We suggest the various policies and programs discussed in this chapter can be located in this framework in one of the circles or at the nexus of two or even three of the competing pressures (Figure 1.1). For instance, increasing federal financial support for charter schools would intersect government involvement and free markets, whereas deregulating teacher education (e.g., removing the near-monopoly of university-based teacher education and state certification) would link free markets with the press for professionalism.

1

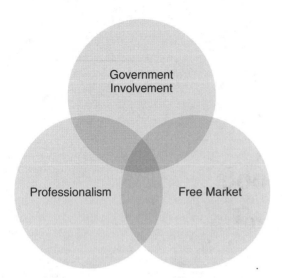

FIGURE 1.1   Overarching Pressures on the K–12 Educational System

Purposes of Public Education

Posing a question to parents about what they want their local school to provide for their child will likely reveal an array of interests, needs, purposes, and goals for their local schools. Posing the question to community members (i.e., taxpayers) without a formal link to the local schools reveals a different though overlapping set of expectations, purposes, and goals.[1] These multiple purposes are not new. There is much historical evidence that schools (public and private) have, from their inception, fulfilled multiple and competing purposes (Kaestle, 1983; Ravitch, 2000; Rury, 2005; Tyack & Cuban, 1995). These purposes encompass religious, social, political, economic, racial, and scientific interests. Remarkably, contemporary public schools attempt to provide for most of these interests by offering a range of academic subject area courses, remediation courses, advanced placement offerings, interscholastic athletics, art and music, student government, health and sex

education, college advising, and—for too many children—the best nutrition and care they receive all day. The modern, comprehensive high school has even been compared to a shopping mall in that it caters to such a variety of interests and needs so that most consumers can find at least something they like (Powell, Farrar, & Cohen, 1985). Of course, there is great variation across schools, school districts, and states in their ability or interest in providing what Kozol (1991) termed the "savage inequalities" between poor and wealthy schools, opportunities, and outcomes.

A central outcome of the socially determined purposes of public schools is the relative opportunity afforded each child. There is no debate that children arrive in kindergarten with very different levels of preparation and require a unique set of services to succeed.[2] What is debated are the nature of the educational services offered, how such services are provided, and who is responsible for the provision of such services. The history of American public schools provides a richly decorated canvas for further discovering and understanding the tensions and debates of what social services are provided, by whom, and to whom.

David Labaree (1997) offers a set of alternative goals for American education and how these goals have been at the center of conflict since the founding of this nation. He writes that schools are in an "awkward position" between what "we hope society will become and what we think it really is" (p. 41). Labaree argues that the core problems with American schools are not pedagogical, organizational, social, or cultural, but rather "fundamentally political." The philosophical and pragmatic dilemma between Thomas Jefferson's political idealism and Alexander Hamilton's economic realism (Curti, 1935/1959, cited in Labaree, 1997) has outlasted two centuries of school reforms. Labaree suggests that schools promote equality while at the same time adapting to inequality; hence schools promote excellence for all children, though they are

---

[1]See, for example, Rose & Gallup (2001) *The 33rd Annual Phi Delta Kappa/Gallup Poll of the Public's Attitudes Toward the Public Schools,* and U.S. Department of Education (1999), NCES, *Digest of Education Statistics*, Table 23.

[2]The National Center for Education Statistics' *Early Childhood Longitudinal Study* (ECLS) is one of the first nationally representative studies to allow examination of early childhood and early educational experiences (see http://nces.ed.gov/ecls/).

often organized to provide differential services to different students. In doing so, schools translate these contradictory purposes into three goals:

1. *Democratic equality*—A democratic society cannot persist unless it prepares all of its young with equal care to take on the full responsibilities of citizenship in a competent manner.... [S]chools must promote both effective citizenship and relative equality...Education is seen as a public good, designed to prepare people for political roles.

2. *Social efficiency*—[Society's] economic well-being depends on our ability to prepare the young to carry out useful economic roles with competence.... [S]ociety as a whole must see to it that we invest educationally in the productivity of the entire workforce...Education is seen as a public good designed to prepare workers to fill structurally necessary market roles.

3. *Social mobility*—Education is a commodity, the only purpose of which is to provide individual students with a competitive advantage.... Education is seen as a private good designed to prepare individuals for successful social competition for the more desirable social roles (Labaree, 1997, p. 42).

How government policy decisions and legal decisions affect these goals, free market pressures, and educator professionalism should be of great interest to readers of this volume. Specifically, are we more apt to achieve democratic equality with greater government intervention, free market pressures, or real improvements in the professionalism of educators and support personnel in schools?

Over the course of the last 50 years, American schools have faced a variety of external pressures that have elicited responses embedded in one or more of the purposes of schooling. The pressures have come from the early industrialists (see Bowles & Gintis, 1976), the scientific managers of early corporate America (see Callahan, 1962), more contemporary business and political leaders (Chubb & Moe, 1990; National Commission on Excellence in Education, 1983), and research-based instructional methods and programs required

by President Bush's Leave No Child Behind Act of 2001 and the Individuals with Disabilities Education Improvement Act of 2004 (IDEA, 2004).

The *Brown v. Board of Education* decision in 1954 signaled a dramatic shift in how American society was to view and use its public schools. Stating that separate schools are inherently unequal, the Supreme Court overturned its 58-year-old doctrine affirmed in *Plessy v. Ferguson* (1896) of separate but equal. The implication of this decision was that de jure segregation of schools was unconstitutional, though de facto segregation continued, and some argued it has expanded (see Orfield, 1978; Orfield & Eaton, 1996; see Chapter 9 for a more comprehensive discussion of *Brown* and school desegregation).

After the launching of *Sputnik* in 1957 by the Soviet Union, Congress passed the National Defense Education Act (NDEA) to promote increased attention and scrutiny of math and science education. The law used schools as a central agent to increase the technical capacity of the country and counter the perceived scientific superiority of the Soviet Union. It was commonly perceived that the American way of life was being threatened, and the schools were a major part of the solution to regain international superiority.

Robert Kennedy trekked with the media through Appalachia serving to bring the issue of rural poverty into the living rooms of middle-class America. Furthermore, President Johnson's Great Society initiative included the passage of the Elementary and Secondary Education Act of 1965 (ESEA). For the first time, this act called for federal dollars to be given to public schools in an effort to improve the educational opportunities of economically and academically disadvantaged children. This began a new era of increased government intervention and state support for academic opportunity for poor children and provided new resources for schools. Along with the new resources, however, came heightened expectations and broader obligations for local educators.

Whereas the ESEA began the flow of federal dollars into schools to enhance the education of poor and underperforming children, the passage of Public Law 94–142 (1975) marked a watershed moment in the education of handicapped children. While guaranteeing handicapped children a federal statutory right to an education, the law (in 1990, the law was renamed the Individuals with Disabilities Education Act, known as IDEA) provided guidelines, federal funding, and local accountability in promoting the education of children with handicaps (see Chapter 7 for more on this). Reauthorized in 2004, IDEA 2004, now the Individuals with Disabilities Improvement Act, established a higher standard for the requirement of a free and appropriate public education. Namely, the federal law now demands an education for children that will prepare them for "successful post-school employment or education" (20 U.S.C. Section 1400(c)(14)). No longer is the goal for teachers and social workers to just "get students through" school. Now, they are charged with preparing all special-needs students for additional schooling and work beyond high school.

A selection of other court cases has also dramatically shaped the purposes of public schools, along with the opportunities and responsibilities of local educators and social workers. Among them are *Lau v. Nichols* (1974), in which the Supreme Court ruled that schools must provide native-language instruction to children whose native language is not English (see Chapter 9). This, like the inclusion of special education children, requires schools to provide a wide range of services to an increasing number of children. In light of the tremendous exodus of white families from inner cities that took place between the 1950s and the 1970s, the *Milliken v. Bradley* (1974) decision had a profound effect on the ability of schools to provide an integrated educational experience for their students. Twenty years after *Brown,* and just three years after *Swann v. Charlotte-Mecklenburg* (1971), which allowed forced busing as a strategy to integrate schools, the *Milliken* decision disallowed the inclusion of suburban communities in city desegregation plans. Two decisions that were handed down by the Supreme Court in 2007 (*Parents Involved with Community Schools v. Seattle School District No. 1* and *Meredith v. Jefferson County Board of Education*)

have now made it unconstitutional to use race as a deciding factor when assigning students to public schools to achieve desegregation. These decisions limited the role of government intervention in desegregating schools and left desegregation issues to be influenced by local housing choices. The fallout from PL 94–142 and the *Brown, Lau,* and *Milliken* cases is that the public schools are required to educate all children, though they typically do so in highly segregated communities (by race/ethnicity and wealth) and school buildings.

Less than a year after President Carter promoted the U.S. Office of Education to a federal department with cabinet-level status, newly elected President Ronald Reagan set out to abolish the Department of Education. The prevailing belief within the new Republican administration was that the federal role was unnecessary and that a return to more local control was what was needed to promote the improvement of public schools. To do so, the president established a blue-ribbon commission to report on the state of U.S. public education. The commission submitted their report (National Commission on Excellence in Education, 1983), and rather than reduce the federal role in education, they stated that the nation was at risk and stressed the "imperative" for educational reform. This time the threat was economic, suggesting, "If an unfriendly foreign power had attempted to impose on America the mediocre educational performance that exists today, we might well have viewed it as an act of war" (p. 1). Rather than reducing the federal role in education, the report stirred so much interest that the federal government felt compelled to maintain its involvement.

The Goals 2000 Act, first promoted by President George H. W. Bush and then signed into law by President Clinton, exemplifies Labaree's statement that schools both reflect what "we hope society will become and what we think it really is" (Labaree, 1997, p. 41). Among its many components, it called for the United States to be first in the world in math and science (reminiscent of the NDEA in 1958) and called for all children to be "ready to learn" by the time they entered kindergarten by the year 2000.

On January 3, 2002, President George W. Bush signed into law the No Child Left Behind Act of 2001 (NCLB), which reauthorized the ESEA. This 670-page bill is the most recent attempt to use the power and authority of the federal government to improve the performance of American public schools. This law, however, ties together many themes and reflects the confounding nature of the multiple and competing purposes of public schools. The full title of the act signals the attempt to promote each of the goals: "An act to close the achievement gap with accountability, flexibility, and choice, so that no child is left behind." This accentuates the need to reduce the achievement gap while also preserving the American commitment to liberty. In addition, this act has influenced and prompted all three of the reactions mentioned in the introduction of this chapter. It increases government intervention in schools by requiring the reporting of achievement data. Moreover, it allows a greater influence of free markets by encouraging reforms like charter schools and limited intradistrict school choice, which are discussed in further detail later in this chapter. Finally, NCLB calls for highly qualified teachers who are not only state certified but who also possess degrees in their area of instruction, which affects the level of professionalism of the field. The future of this act is unclear at the time of this writing, as the outcome of the 2008 election will determine how federal education policy will be addressed.

A final point of emphasis is warranted on the continued growth and political complexity in pushing for higher educational expectations for all children. On August 22, 2005, the state of Connecticut filed suit against the U.S. Secretary of Education. The plaintiffs argued that the federal government is imposing an unfunded mandate on states by requiring annual testing (in grades 3–8) to assess student performance and progress. Although the suit is unlikely to derail the NCLB, it does signal a growing tension between states' rights and federal control of local schools.

Each of these major events in the past 50 years promotes one or more of the aforementioned purposes of American schools. Some press for increased equality and the preservation of democracy, whereas others promote competitiveness found in the free market and the gain of some at the expense of others. Later in this chapter, some major reform models are reviewed, the goals they support or contradict highlighted, and the challenging position of educators and social workers is discussed.

The seemingly ubiquitous relationship between students' social class or race/ethnicity and school performance is a continual challenge for educators, policymakers, and communities. Whether comparing SATs, reading aptitude, or science achievement, the relationship holds. This relationship is not new, however, nor has it been ignored. Researchers have documented the relationship for nearly 40 years while schools, communities, and governments have undergone multiple attempts to reform; at least some of which have targeted the achievement gap.

The Inexorable Link Between Poverty and School Performance

On Saturday July 2, 1966, then-U.S. Commissioner of Education Harold Howe held a press conference to release a report in response to Section 402 of the Civil Rights Act of 1964.[3] The act called for the commissioner to conduct a survey "concerning the lack of availability of equal opportunities for individuals by reason of race, color, religion, or national origin in public educational institutions at all levels in the United States." This report intended to document the unequal opportunities afforded minority students in the segregated and underfunded schools that

[3]The report was released on the Saturday of July 4th weekend with the hope of minimizing media coverage. See Grant (1973) for the "best treatment" of the Coleman Report (personal communication with Harold Howe, Hanover, NH, February 1998).

existed at that time. Specifically, the report addressed four questions: (1) To what extent are racial and ethnic groups segregated from one another in public schools? (2) Do schools offer "equal educational opportunities" to students of different races? (3) How much do students learn in different schools as measured by standardized exams? (4) What is the relationship between students' achievement and the kinds of schools they attend? In conducting the study, Coleman and his colleagues surveyed approximately 600,000 students (roughly half white and half minority), 67,000 teachers, and 4000 principals. This study, entitled *Equality of Educational Opportunity* (Coleman, 1966), later came to be known as the Coleman Report.

The report itself was lengthy, more than 700 pages, and exceedingly complex in its design, conclusions, and politics (Grant, 1973). The danger with such complexity lies in its interpretation by the media, policymakers, citizens, and educators. The desire for a simple message is natural, and yet this study did not lend itself to such simple messages and conclusions.

To the surprise of most, the results of the massive Coleman Report did not support the conventional wisdom that minority students were at a significant disadvantage, compared with white students, because of the "kind" of schools they attended. The summary report attempted to capture the essence of the study's findings.

- *Segregation:* Four in five white students attended schools that were at least 90% white. Sixty-five percent of Negro[4] students attended schools that were at least 90% Negro. In the South, most students attended schools that were either 100% Negro or white.
- *Teachers:* Sixty-five percent of the teachers in the average Negro elementary school were Negro. In the South this was close to 100%.
- *Facilities:* "There is not a wholly consistent pattern—that is, minorities are not at a disadvantage in every item listed" (p. 9; e.g., age of building, class size, librarian, free textbooks, textbooks under four years old, chemistry laboratory), though the disadvantage exists most consistently with facilities more closely related to students' learning (e.g., laboratories and numbers of books in libraries). This relationship is stronger in the South than in other regions of the country.
- *Programs:* Children attending Negro schools had slightly less access to curricular and extracurricular programs more related to academic learning (e.g., college preparatory curriculum, debate teams), though, again, the inequality was much greater in the South than elsewhere.
- *Achievement:* "The minority pupils' scores are as much as one standard deviation below the majority pupil's scores in the first grade. By 12th grade, the gap of average test scores between races is larger."

Finally, in what may be the most important and talked about finding from the study:

> It appears that a pupil's achievement is strongly related to the educational backgrounds and aspirations of the other students in the school" (p. 22). Further analyses suggest "if a white pupil from a home that is strongly and effectively supportive of education is put in a school where most do not come from such homes, his achievement will be little different than if he were in a school composed of others like himself. But if a minority pupil from a home without much educational strength is put with schoolmates with strong educational backgrounds, his achievement is likely to increase. (p. 22)

The repercussions from this study were felt across the country and still reverberate today. The study had a profound impact on policy decisions on matters of school reform, racial desegregation and busing plans, and school finance litigation. The most common interpretations from the Coleman Report were that "money doesn't matter" and that "schools don't matter." Coleman and his

---

[4]"Negro" was the term used in this 1966 report.

associates refuted these claims, but in part due to the complexity of the study and its complicated and contextualized findings, the simple interpretations held. One immediate implication was that there was no tangible infusion of funds into minority schools as was anticipated with the passage of the Civil Rights Act. Rather, attention turned toward efforts at racial integration programs, typically through voluntary or forced busing of minority children into predominantly white schools (see *Swann v. Charlotte-Mecklenberg,* 1971, and Chapter 9).

Despite many attempts to refute the findings (e.g., Jencks, 1972; Jencks & Phillips, 1998), the consistent relationship between student background and academic performance is inescapable. Although billions of federal dollars have been spent through the ESEA, Head Start, and IDEA programs and many other major efforts at local, state, and national levels, current academic assessments reveal a similarly strong and consistent achievement gap. Whether it is educational attainment, dropout rates, or SAT scores, the disparities hold. Some measures suggest a closing of the gap between Black Americans and whites, particularly in dropout rates, though disparities between Hispanics and whites remain great. The so-called *Nation's Report Card,* the National Assessment of Educational Progress (NAEP), provides the best measure of state and national progress in increasing educational performance. In a 2002 report on Raising Achievement and Reducing Gaps (Barton, 2002) using NAEP data, the author stated

> No significant progress has been made [since 1994] in reducing the performance gaps experienced by minority and economically disadvantaged children. This is the *fundamental challenge* that must be the focus of the next phase of the education reform and improvement. (p. 7, emphasis added)

In 2007, *The Nation's Report Card* found that White, Black, and Hispanic students all scored higher on the fourth- and eighth-grade reading tests than in 1992; however, this did not reduce the overall achievement gaps except in the White–Black fourth-grade reading scores, between which the gap was narrower than it was in 1992 or 2005. A 2007 National Center for Education Statistics (NCES) report, *Status and Trends in Education of Racial and Ethnic Minorities* (KewalRamani, Gilbertson, Fox, & Provasnik, 2007), highlights the differential school experiences of students by race:

- In 2005, half of all Black and Hispanic students were enrolled in schools with more than 75% of the students eligible for free or reduced-price lunch, whereas only 5% of White students were enrolled in such schools.
- In 2005, 52% of all Black students and 58% of all Hispanic students were enrolled in schools with more than 75% minority enrollment, whereas only 3% of White students were in schools with high minority enrollment.
- From 1999 to 2005, the number of number of minority students taking AP exams increased by 81%, whereas it increased 71% among White students; however, Black students have the lowest mean score.
- In 2003, 8% of White, 17% of Black, and 11% of Hispanic students had ever repeated a grade.
- In 2003, 9% of White, 20% of Black, and 10% of Hispanic students had ever been suspended from school.
- In regard to school safety, 7% of White, 8% of Black, and 10% of Hispanic students reported having been threatened or injured with a weapon in school in 2005.
- In 2005, 12% of White, 17% of Black, and 18% of Hispanic students reported having been engaged in a physical fight in school.

Schools, Their Students, and Their Communities

Given what we know about the link between race, ethnicity, poverty, and student achievement and academic outcomes, it is especially important to examine the changing demographic makeup of the school-age population. As a result of recent immigration, migration, and fertility patterns, an increasing proportion of school-aged children are African, Asian, and Hispanic American.

Demographic and Population Changes. The population of school-aged children closely reflects the changes in the U.S. population and is becoming increasingly diverse in terms of race, ethnicity, language, and religion. The number of children in elementary and secondary schools increased from 35 million children in 1960 to 45 million in 1970. This number fell back to less than 40 million by 1985, but then increased steadily through 2005, returning to approximately 49 million students. Despite the fluctuations in the overall population, there has been a steady increase in prekindergarten education. The number of children enrolled in prekindergarten programs has increased dramatically from less than 100,000 in 1980 to over 1 million in 2006 (Digest of Education Statistics, 2008, Table 37). The percentage of 3- and 4-year-olds enrolled in preschool programs has grown from 10% in 1965 to more than 55% in 2006. In

addition the older students, 18- and 19-year-olds, enrolled in high school has grown from 10% to nearly 20% from 1970 to 2006. And the percentage of 18- and 19-year-olds in higher education has increased from 37% to 46% over the same time period. (Digest of Education Statistics, 2007; Figure 1.2).

The national trends, however, mask important state-level differences in K–12 enrollments. From 2000 to 2005, four states had an increase in enrollment of more than 10% including Nevada, Arizona, Texas, and Georgia. Over the same time period, nearly 20 states had decreasing enrollments, including the northeast and other regions. Ten states, mainly in the southwest and Rocky Mountain regions, are forecast to increase their enrollments by more than 5%, whereas 12 states, predominantly in the northeast, will likely experience a decrease of at least 5% (Digest of Education Statistics, 2007). The population growth is overrepresented by increases in minority populations, in particular growth in the number of Hispanic children.

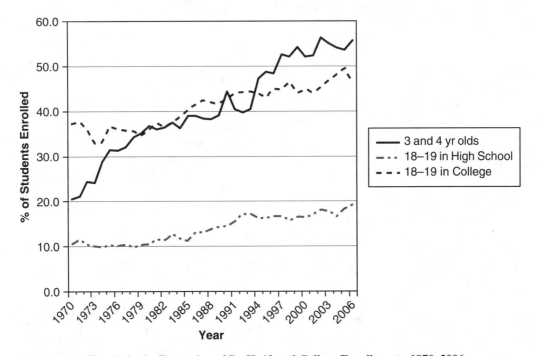

FIGURE 1.2   Trends in the Expansion of PreK–12 and College Enrollments, 1970–2006

Such demographic changes create both an opportunity and demand for the provision of additional social work services. Given the achievement gap and the disproportionate growth of minority children, it is particularly important that greater numbers of children receive appropriate educational, social work, and health-care services before and during their formal schooling. The integration of children and family services, economic development, and educational opportunities, all of which are sensitive to the particular needs of greater proportions of minority children and families, is critical.

School Reform

Among the myriad efforts at improving school performance, reducing the achievement gap, and increasing the effects of schooling, a number of reforms warrant further attention. These reforms offer an interesting blend of government intervention, market forces, and professionalism.

As schools, the communities they serve, and state and federal governments all seek new and improved strategies to improve the education of all children, a number of old ideas have been thrust to the forefront of the conversations on school improvement. Some of these ideas have been school based (e.g., improved curriculum, testing, staff development) and others have been community based (e.g., child care, health care). However, we are now witnessing an exciting and challenging blurring of the boundaries between school- and community-based reforms aimed at improving the lives of children, their families, and the broader community.

Standards-Based Reform

The most visible and controversial reform shaping schools in recent decades has been the dramatic change in K–12 curriculum standards and accountability systems. Of course, the headliner in this push is government intervention in the form of the federal law, The No Child Left

Behind Act of 2001. Although the NCLB has garnered much attention and criticism, the law sometimes reinforced state initiatives already underway and pushed other states into the age of school-based accountability.

Several states initiated heightened graduation requirements, state testing at specific grades or exit exams, and school accountability systems prior to NCLB. These systems were often the result of public pressure to produce tangible results, given the dramatic increase in state funding of local schools (see Figure 1.5). Moreover, when teacher grades are the only assessment of student performance, parents and students pressure teachers to reduce rigor (Hart, 1995 cited in Bishop, 2004; Figlio & Lucas, 2004).

The most aggressive of the pre-NCLB state initiatives took place in Kentucky, Louisiana, Maryland, and New York. These states were in front of the push to externally control curriculum variation and accountability measures. In New York, the state required all fourth- and eighth-grade students to be tested in mathematics and English/language arts beginning in 1996. Beginning in 2000, any student wanting to graduate from high school in New York State would have to meet a set course of requirements and end-of-course examinations established by the state. Similarly, Michigan began its MEAP testing program in the mid-1990s, Texas the TAAS, Massachusetts the MCAS, Florida the FCAT, and too many other states to mention. So when the NCLB was passed, these states already had testing programs in place, though often they had to increase the number of grades involved in the testing program from typically two grades to all children in grades 3 through 8 and one grade in high school.

In other states, however, the federal testing requirements brought them into the fold of standardized school accountability. Most often, states purchased the tests from private companies, with the curriculum material often tailored to the individual state curriculum frameworks.

It is important to note that although the federal government has spurred interest in school-based

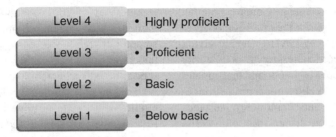

FIGURE 1.3   NCLB Proficiency Levels for State-Level Examinations

accountability systems, there is no national curriculum, testing program, or even a common standard of "proficiency." Under current law, the states are responsible for creating (or adopting) state curriculum standards and a testing program and use the four-level rubric to assess performance (Figure 1.3). Schools are held accountable for annual gains in student performance as measured by gains in their performance index from one year to the next.

Performance Index = (% of students scoring at level 2 + ((% scoring at level 3 + % scoring at level 4)*2))

If all students in a school are graded as proficient then a school's performance index would be 200. Current law requires all districts to be on a performance trajectory to reach a PI of 200 by 2014. Although this federal pressure is clearly pushing schools to improve the preparation of students to move toward this goal, the actual standard for proficiency varies from state to state.

A study in 2005 (NCES) comparing student performance on state exams using the state definition of proficiency to the results of the National Assessment of Educational Progress (NAEP) is instructive. NAEP is a federal set of exams administered to a sample of districts in a sample of states each year. Although there are no true national exams given to every school and every student, the goal of NAEP is to take a snapshot of student performance across the country each year. The comparison of the NAEP results to the state assessments of proficiency was revealing and concluded

> There is a strong negative correlation between the proportions of students meeting the states' proficiency standards and the NAEP score equivalents to those standards, suggesting that the observed heterogeneity in states' reported percents proficient can be largely attributed to differences in the stringency of their standards. (p. iii)

In other words, on average, students' scores on the NAEP were sometimes well below where the performance on state exams would have predicted they would score (e.g., Mississippi, Tennessee, Georgia). Conversely, in states such as Massachusetts, South Carolina, and Wyoming, student performance on the NAEP was above where they performed on the state exams. What this means is that in some states, the state standard for proficiency is dramatically below the NAEP standard for proficiency, and in others the state standard is higher than that of the NAEP. Political pressures to maintain a truly federalized system of education (e.g., state and locally set standards) have thus far carried the day in Washington, D.C. As the new administration takes over, this decision may be revisited.

Market-Based Reforms

Allowing market forces to enter the environment of public education is not a new idea. In fact, in the early decades of the republic, that is all there was. But with the growth of the bureaucratic educational system throughout the last century (see Meyer, Scott, Strang, & Creighton, 1988; Tyack, 1974), market-based reforms have taken a prominent position among some school reformers (see Belfield & Levin, 2005; Chubb & Moe, 1990). An interesting mix of conservative and liberal reformers have called for the break-up of the public school "monopoly"—conservatives because of their inherent beliefs in the efficiency and productivity of free markets, and liberals because of the need to provide any kind of choice alternatives for those parents and children left with no options other than the local school infested with academic apathy and violence. Those with economic means typically have choices for their children. These choices may take the form of paying private school tuition or, in growing numbers, the decision to homeschool their children. In addition the growing number of charter schools provides a free and public option for many families. A parent's freedom and ability to choose from these market-based options is often greatly limited by their time and financial resources.

Vouchers.   Access for all parents, regardless of income, to school choice is at the heart of a voucher program upheld by the U.S. Supreme Court in 2002 (*Zelman v. Simmons-Harris,* No. 00-1751). In what may be the most important K–12 education-related case argued before the high court in decades, the Court decided 5–4 that the Cleveland (OH) voucher plan is constitutional. The plan offers a voucher worth $2500 toward the tuition at any public or private school to students living in the city of Cleveland. The vouchers presumably offer choice options for children and parents who are not satisfied with their assigned public school in the city of Cleveland. In practice, however, the plan is restricted by the fact that not a single suburban district chose to participate in the voucher program. The result is that 97% of the students taking advantage of the vouchers are attending private or religious schools in and around Cleveland.

The Court's decision rested on whether the program violates the establishment clause of the federal Constitution. This clause prohibits the state from promoting or inhibiting the establishment of religion and thus violating the separation of church and state. There was precedent for state money to be given to religious schools; however, these funds were typically restricted to textbooks and transportation. The argument is that government payments for books and busses narrowly

assists the education of children, thus benefiting the child, and does not more broadly benefit the religion or church. In *Lemon v. Kurtzman* (1971) the Court established guidelines for such state involvement in religious schools in the form of a three-part "Lemon" test: "a statute or other government policy (1) must have a secular legislative purpose, (2) must have a principal effect that neither advances nor inhibits religion, (3) and must not foster 'an excessive government entanglement with religion' " (*Lemon v. Kurtzman,* cited in Zirkel, Richardson, & Goldberg, 1995).

Two other voucher plans have also received much attention. The Milwaukee plan is the oldest, having begun in 1991 and hence has received the most study and scrutiny. This plan differs from Cleveland's in that it offers vouchers only to poor families. There is no widespread agreement as to whether this program is effective, as both proponents and opponents find data to support their positions.

A more recent plan in Florida uses school performance to determine who qualifies for participation. Each school in the state is assigned a grade (A, B, C, D, F) based on the achievement of its students on state exams. If a school receives a grade of an F twice in a 4-year period, the students attending that school are given a voucher to use toward the cost of enrolling in another public or private school. Given the tremendous growth in the school-aged population in recent years, the elasticity of the market in Florida is in question. In other words, as more schools receive Fs, will other public and private schools have enough available seats to enroll the students from the failing schools? Preliminary analyses are skeptical on how much of a market is available in south Florida (Diaz de La Portilla, 2002). The future of voucher programs depends greatly on the political officials in office at the time because it is a politically contested element of the role of the free market in the education sector.

Charters.   A second type of school reform founded on free market principles, though avoiding the litigious nature of voucher programs, is

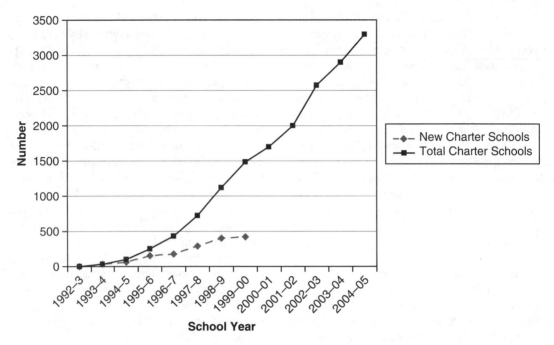

FIGURE 1.4   Growth in the Number of Charter Schools in the United States, 1992–3 Thru 2004–5

the creation of charter schools.[5] Charter schools are publicly funded schools without attendance boundaries and are free of at least some state regulation or local work rules. Depending on the strength of the authorizing state statue, some charter schools are free of most regulation that governs the public schools, whereas others are constrained in their effort to be different from the public schools (see Education Commission of the States at http://mb2.ecs.org/reports/Report.aspx?id=65).

The first charter school law was passed in 1991 in Minnesota, and since that time the numbers have grown exponentially (Figure 1.4). As of 2008, 41 states have passed a law allowing the creation of charter schools, and within these states the number of charter schools varies widely. Although approximately 4,147 charter schools were in operation in

2007, California (710) and Arizona (4509) are the states where charter schools are most prevalent (Center for Education Reform [CER], 2008). The total enrollment in charter schools in the 2007–08 school year was 1,241,706, which is about 2.5% of the total public K–12 enrollment. In 2007, 347 new charter schools opened their doors to students across the county. Since 1992, 560 schools have closed, and although the reasons vary, they may include, but are not limited to, financial troubles and declining enrollments.

The Center for Education Reform (CER, 2004), an organization that publicly supports the charter school movement, categorizes state charter school legislation into strong and weak laws. Strong laws "foster the development of numerous, genuinely independent charter schools... available to a wide array of children and families"

[5]See a special report in *Education Week,* "Changed by charters." This three-part report can be found at www.edweek.org/sreports/special_reports_ardcle.cfin?slug—charters.htm.

(p. 1). Weak laws are described as those that "provide fewer opportunities for charter school development." More specifically, CER assesses the strength of charter school laws in 10 major categories, including the number of charter schools allowed, whether there are multiple chartering authorities, whether schools may be started without evidence of local support, whether there is an automatic waiver from state/local laws, the degree of fiscal autonomy, and whether the schools are exempt from collective bargaining agreements. According to the CER (2008), Arizona, Minnesota, Washington, D.C., Delaware, Michigan, California, Florida, and Indiana have enacted the strongest laws and received a grade of "A." On the other end of the continuum are Wyoming, Hawaii, Alaska, Rhode Island, Virginia, Kansas, Iowa, and Mississippi, which received a grade of "D" or "F."

Key questions abound for voucher and charter-school programs. For whom are they created? Whom do they serve? Are they effective? No doubt it is easier to document who they serve than how effective they are. Charter schools, on average, serve students that closely mirror the populations that attend the surrounding traditional public schools. The fear that charter schools will promote additional white flight from the public schools is largely unfounded. A proportional number of poor and minority children are attending charter schools and using vouchers (Gill, Timpane, Ross, & Brewer, 2001). Concerning the effectiveness of voucher programs or charter schools, the research is still inconclusive (Carnoy, Jacobsen, Michel, & Rothstein, 2005). A Rand study, attempting to measure the effectiveness of vouchers and charters, concluded that there is simply not yet enough evidence to make a clear determination as to whether vouchers or charters are more or less effective than the traditional public schools (Gill et al., 2001).

One obstacle to the growth in the number of charter schools (beyond the authorizing legislation) is the start-up cost of opening a charter school. Building the infrastructure for charter schools requires a great amount of capital. A Government Accounting Office report (Government Accounting Office [GAO], 2000b) identified three major issues in charter school development: (1) the degree to which charter schools have access to traditional public school facility financing, (2) whether alternative sources of facility financing are available to charter schools, and (3) potential options available to the federal government if it were to assume a larger role in charter school facility financing.

A recent addition to the charter school movement has been the growth of networks of schools sharing names, methods, and curriculums. In the early days of charter schools, the for-profit model, exemplified by Edison Schools, seemed to be expanding; however, running schools did not appear to be profitable, as nonprofit entities, like KIPP seem to be succeeding more recently. KIPP, which stands for the Knowledge for Power Program, was started by two teachers who had worked with Teach For America and decided to start a school in Houston based on the goal of helping minority students succeed. There are 57 KIPP schools in 16 states serving more than 14,000 students as of 2008 (www.kipp.org). These schools share a set of principles referred to as the Five Pillars, which include high expectations, choice and commitment, more time, the power to lead, and a focus on results. For example, the pillar of more time is typically enacted at a KIPP school by having students in school from 7:30 a.m. until 5 p.m. every weekday, every other Saturday, and for 3 weeks during the summer. KIPP claims that this is 60% more time in school than a typical public school student in the United States (www.kipp.org). Reforms such as charter schools and KIPP in particular exemplify the role of the free market system within the public K–12 educational system. They also call into question the role of professionalism, as alternative routes to certification and programs like Teach For America are placing an increasing number of uncertified teachers in classrooms. Many of these programs offer support to the new teachers and require that they pursue certification while teaching; nonetheless, these programs hint at the potential overlap between the role of the free market and of professionalism in education.

Homeschooling. Time magazine featured a question on its cover: "Is homeschooling good for America?" (August 27, 2001). This is a new wrinkle on the typical question of whether homeschooling is good for the homeschooled child or the local school and serves as another free-market pressure in schools. Homeschooling has come of age in the last two decades. It is now more publicly acknowledged in many circles as acceptable and is exhibiting significant growth in the numbers of homeschooled children. Researchers have begun to study the phenomenon, policymakers are paying attention, and educators are beginning to feel the effects of greater numbers of children staying at home to go to school. More recently, homeschooling has benefited from increasing legal, political, and social support (Cooper & Sureau, 2007). The movement has been politicized and draws strength from its grassroots organization, lobbying strategies, and organizations like the National Home Education Research Institute, the Home School Legal Defense Association, and the Christian Homeschool Association of Pennsylvania (Cooper & Sureau, 2007).

A report published by the National Center for Education Statistics (NCES), using data collected from the 2003 Parent Survey of the *National Household Education Surveys Program,* provides a comprehensive portrait of the extent of homeschooling, by who homeschools and for what reasons (Princiotta and Bielick, 2006).

> In 2003, an estimated 1.1 million students nationwide were being homeschooled. This amounts to 2.2% of U.S. students, ages 5 to 17, with a grade equivalent of kindergarten through grade 12. Data from 1999 and 2003 estimates that four out of five homeschoolers were homeschooled only (82%), and one out of five homeschoolers were enrolled in public or private schools part time (18%). Parents give a variety of reasons for homeschooling their children. In 2003, 31% of parents said the most

> important reason they homeschooled was because of their concern about the environment of schools, and another 30% said the primary reason was to be able to provide religious or moral instruction. Sixteen percent cited dissatisfaction with the academic instruction, and 14% referred to either physical or mental heath problems or to other special needs. (U.S. Department of Education, 2004)

These data clarify some of the assumptions surrounding who is being homeschooled. What remains unclear is whether children in need of special education services or other social services are disproportionately kept in schools to receive the services, or whether schools must provide such services for homeschooled children. A clear concern with at-risk children being homeschooled is the separation or isolation from the school and services provided therein. Just how social service agencies can find and track at-risk children if they are homeschooled remains to be seen.

The School as Community Hub

Schools and communities have been inextricably linked over the history of American education. In many areas schools provide a town or neighborhood center, where school plays and athletic events may be the main source of entertainment. As previously mentioned in this chapter, the role of schools and purpose of education is debated. Increasingly, schools are home to services beyond the traditional realm of education, including school-based health centers, public libraries, community centers, and others. Time will tell if this centralization of the services will help to meet the needs of students and in turn prepare them for academic success, or if this arrangement of services is a distraction from academic goals.

Early Childhood Care and Pre-K Education

Long an eclectic web of care in homes, centers, nursery schools, and government-sponsored organizations (i.e., Head Start), the early care and education of children ages birth to 4 is being thrust into a relationship with K–12 public educational systems. Motivating this marriage are calls for public schools to provide prekindergarten education to 4-year-olds through what are now commonly called universal pre-K programs.

Universal pre-K (UPK), the notion of making publicly funded prekindergarten available to all children via government intervention in the form of the K–12 system, is becoming more popular in many states across the nation (Zigler, Gilliam, & Jones, 2006). Whereas Head Start and Even Start (two federally funded programs supporting poor families) have need-based eligibility standards, the new trend is to make pre-K available to all children, regardless of family income. In most states this takes place in elementary schools, though some states allow contracting with local community-based organizations. In West Virginia and New York, school districts are even required to subcontract with community-based organizations (CBOs) as a condition of receiving the state grant to help fund the local programming. The partnering with entities outside schools is meant to preserve the free market of the early child care system and to ensure a variety of choices for parents within a community and to not snuff out the financial viability of CBOs. The subcontracting relieves space constraints in schools allowing some or all of the UPK services to be offered off the school site. In small and rural communities, the context is different. In these communities, there are few if any CBOs with which to partner, and hence the school districts become fully responsible for hosting the pre-K programming (Sipple, McCabe & Ross-Bernstein, 2007; Sipple, McCabe, Ross-Bernstein & Casto, 2008).

Of import is the meshing of services provided by two distinct systems: early care and education and the K–12 system. For instance, Head Start is financed and regulated through the federal Department of Health and Human Services (DHHS) and has shown to have consistent though modest effects (DHHS Head Start Impact Study, 2005). Federal aid for schools comes

through the Department of Education. At the state level, state departments of health and/or offices of children's and family services often regulate early care programs. Regulations for schooling are rooted in state boards of education and state departments of education. Moreover, counties play a key role in the regulation and funding of these early care and education services. In some states (e.g., Maryland, Florida) the county and school district boundaries are one in the same. In these states, the linking of early care and K–12 governance is markedly easier than in those states where there is no relationship between district and county boundaries and governance (e.g., New York).

Given the broad attention given to the state-level investments in UPK in recent years, obvious questions of effectiveness arise (Zigler et al., 2006). Whereas most research has cited the long-term benefits of early education based on the High/Scope Perry Preschool project in Michigan and the Abecedarian program in North Carolina, these programs were full-day, year-round and enrolled children for at least 2 years. Furthermore, the short-term positive outcomes from these programs were more noncognitive (i.e., attendance and growth–motor development) than cognitive. It was argued that such direct noncognitive benefits are essential to successful cognitive development. These programs, however, are in contrast to most of the current UPK programming across the country that are typically half day and only during the 9-month school year. Precisely how effective these less-intensive programs are is less well understood (Cunha & Heckman, 2006), though recent research suggests that the benefits of UPK accrue to not only poor children but to middle-class children as well (Gormley, Phillips, & Gayer, 2008).

Children's Health and Schools

It is common knowledge that healthy children learn more than unhealthy ones, and that schools are the one place that all children (by law) must attend on a regular basis. Merging these two sectors results in a fast-growing trend of linking schools with other social and health services. Originating in the 1970s in Minnesota and Texas, school-based health centers (SBHCs) are growing in popularity. The National Assembly of School-Based Health Centers (NASBHC)[6] conducts a regular census tracking the location, services provided, and state and national trends. Although only 600 SBHCs existed in 1994, the most recent census accounted for approximately 1,700 such health centers located in schools (NASBHC, 2008).

The range of services provided by SBHCs varies greatly as state regulations vary dramatically from state to state. According to the census, the majority of the centers are located in urban areas, though there are a growing number in rural areas. Nearly 4 in 10 are in high schools, and nearly 1 in 4 are in elementary schools.

The research on the effectiveness of SBHCs has been slower to surface. There is strong evidence that SBHCs provide greater access to health care for poor and minority children than tradition health-care agencies. And although greater attendance rates seem to correlate with the presence of an SBHC, longer-term academic outcomes and positive cost-benefit analyses remain unclear (Geierstanger & Amaral, 2005). However, the Health Care Safety Net Act of 2008 (a reauthorization of the Community Health Center Program) calls for the General Accountability Office (GAO) to conduct a cost-benefit study of federal investment in SBHCs and an assessment of the impact on student health at these centers.

Finance

By any measure, Americans spend a great deal of money educating their children. While debate continues as to whether we spend too much or too little, there is also much debate about how current education revenues are raised and how the money is spent. At the heart of the issue are issues of equity, equality, excellence, and accountability. The financing of American education is derived from local, state, and federal sources, with expenditures for the 2005–2006 school year totaling $529 billion dollars (NCES, 2008, Table 32). This amounts to more than $11,350 per pupil, up from $137 billion (or $213 billion adjusted for 2000 dollars) and $5,500 per student ($3,400 in current dollars) in 1989–1990 (NCES, 2008, Table 32). Expenditures per pupil, however, vary greatly by state, with some states spending nearly three times as much as others (NCES, 2007; see Figure 1.5).

Given that there is no mention of education in the U.S. Constitution and that the Tenth Amendment delegates all rights and privileges not included in the Constitution to the states or to the people, states are granted the plenary authority for the provision of public education. Following *San Antonio Independent School District v. Rodriguez* (1973) in which the U.S. Supreme Court declared that there is no federal right to a public education, the state courts have been the locus of the debate on the equality, equity, and adequacy of school finance practices. The debates involve the distribution of local and state resources to school districts within each state. Specifically, the debates involve the degree to which state funding formulas *equitably* redistribute dollars from wealthy to poor communities and whether the absolute number of dollars spent on public education is *adequate.* Since the first state-court (California) school finance case was decided in 1971 (*Serrano v. Priest*), at least 38 states have had their funding formulas reviewed by their state supreme court, with about one half being found unconstitutional. Muddying this fiscal debate is the lack of agreement among policymakers and researchers on how important additional dollars are to improving school performance (see, e.g., Ladd, Chalk, & Hansen, 1999).

[6]http://www.nasbhc.org/

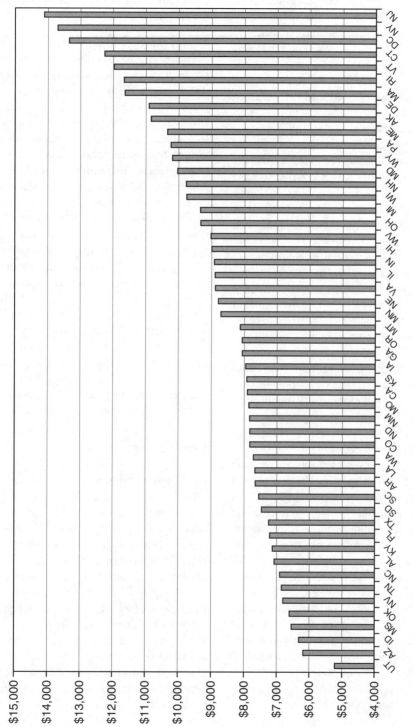

FIGURE 1.5   U.S. School Expenditures Per Pupil by State

Federal Priorities. The federal government has long had a minor role in the financing of public education. The federal role has hovered at around 5% of local district revenue for nearly three decades (NCES, 2001a). The largest source of federal money is the ESEA. Although the IDEA and the free and reduced-price lunch/ breakfast programs also contribute to local revenues, the bulk of federal funding for most school districts, particularly those serving a greater percentage of poor students, is found within the ESEA. With the 2001 reauthorization of the ESEA, federal funding is less restrictive and hence less targeted than it has been since the early years of the Reagan administration when the Education Consolidation and Improvement Act of 1981 consolidated dozens of categorical programs into a block grant. Unfortunately, for many schools this meant a reduction in the absolute number of federal dollars received. How the new act will support schools is at this time unclear.

In further trying to promote equity, excellence, and adequacy, the federal government began requiring states to collect and report assessment data by disaggregated groups of students. According to a 2000 GAO report, only one third of the states were collecting disaggregated data. Not reporting disaggregated results "can mask the results of disadvantaged students and prevent the states and the districts from identifying schools that may not be meeting the educational needs of disadvantaged students" (GAO, 2000a). It remains to be seen what happens to the flow of dollars and federal commitment to reducing the achievement gap, though the controversial testing in grades 3–8 will provide vast amounts of data with which to measure the status of the achievement gap.

Mirroring the purposes and language of the NCLB, the reauthorization of the IDEA now emphasizes the preparation for "further education" in addition to employment and independent living for students with disabilities (20 U.S.C. Section 1400(d)Ia). This supports the widespread mantra among many policymakers that schools must ratchet up their standards and expectations for all students.

Local Effort. Although the local proportion of the cost of public education has diminished since the 1970s, the absolute number of local dollars being spent on local schools has steadily increased. Targeted state and federal programs supplement local funds, but often are not allowed to supplant local effort. Therefore, as the expectations for public schools continue to increase (e.g., educate all children to high levels, provide additional social services, provide more meals, ensure a safe environment, provide extracurricular activities and character/citizenship education), the money to provide such services is stretched thin and often requires additional local effort. This leaves local community and school leaders few choices. Options include increasing local property taxes, reducing services, and sometimes consolidation with other school districts. Each of these options are likely to improve the short-term fiscal picture, though the resultant effect on at-risk children can be harsh. These decisions, however, must be weighted carefully if children are to be adequately and equitably served by their public schools.

Conclusion

In reviewing the major issues in American schools, one is struck by the remarkable successes and failures of the American public educational system; success in that we have achieved universal participation for school-aged children and continue to increase the number of very young children who are now provided with social and educational services. We have come to some sort of agreement that schools must serve all children in various ways, that no child should be left behind. Consistent efforts have been made at altering structural arrangements in schools in the name of improving the social and educational services. There are increasing intersections of the role of government intervention, free markets, and professionalism in the light of school reforms of varying types. Schools are becoming a hub for a wide range of services for children, especially with the rise of universal pre-K programs and school-based health centers. There are steady increases in funding from the local, state, and federal levels to pay for, at least part of, the cost for the additional services.

The public educational system has also been described as being in an "awkward position" between what "we hope society will become and what we think it really is" (Labaree, 1997, p. 41). The achievement gap documented so starkly in the mid-1960s remains to this day. The current rhetoric of federal and state education policies are aimed at reducing this gap; however, it remains to be seen to what degree

schools alone can minimize these achievement discrepancies based on socioeconomic and racial differences. Although schools appear very similar to the red brick schoolhouses we envision from more than a century ago, they are increasingly being asked to serve multiple purposes and solve larger societal problems. Although schools look similar to one another and to those from the past, they are greatly affected by the political shifts at the national level, especially in relation to those issues discussed herein. With ever-increasing market forces and the related tension with increased professionalism on the part of educators, and ever-increasing government intervention, time will tell how education and schools can and will serve individual students and assist to create the more perfect union in the first half of the 21st century.

Case for Class Discussion

The following case illustrates the many forces influencing the work of schools and the numerous opportunities and obstacles associated with partnering with community organizations to better serve students:

Trevor has worked as a social worker in the Woodville School District for 5 years and has recently been asked to move from the high school to the elementary school. Woodville is a geographically large district in an isolated rural area with a small student population of 600 being served by only one elementary, one middle, and one high school. At the high school level, Trevor worked with students from a range of socioeconomic backgrounds, some of whom struggled to balance work and school. He was constantly trying to keep many of his students from dropping out of high school. As he began at the elementary school, he secretly thought the job would be easier without the threat of dropouts.

The elementary school had been offering preschool for 25 years using local funds to children of low-income families, as well as targeted prekindergarten. However, the district had recently taken a state grant, which would make it possible for them to allow students of all economic backgrounds into the program, provide universal prekindergarten, and expand

it to a full-day program. In addition, this would make it possible for the school to identify children with special needs before they entered kindergarten. Trevor had been peripherally involved in this decision, but felt the earlier families were connected with the school, the more easily he could serve the needs of the children.

In his first week of work before the school year began, Trevor attended a meeting of a countywide network of organizations that, although separate from the school district, had been instrumental in the shift to universal prekindergarten. Trevor met the Even Start coordinator, who was connected with several low-income families with children from birth to 3 years old. The director said she would be able to connect him to a few families who were terrified to send their children back to the school from which they had dropped out. She hoped he would be able to convince them to enroll in prekindergarten because if they aged out of Even Start and were not in school, then they would have no formal connection to the district.

He also met the director of the county Head Start, which served three school districts, but did not have any children enrolled from Woodville. She hoped Trevor would convince some of the local families to apply for Head Start so that additional 0- to

3-year-olds could be served. In addition, the state universal prekindergarten grant required the school to coordinate its services with community organizations, and Head Start was one of the few available. However, the children in Woodville would need to be transported 45 minutes, one way, on a bus.

Next, Trevor spoke with the coordinator of the county special-needs services for students needing physical or speech therapy or other services. She mentioned that although the county identified and provided services to pre-school-age children, he would need to coordinate with her to enable the students enrolled in prekindergarten at the school or at Head Start to be served during their program so the county therapists no longer had to drive across the county to serve them in their homes.

Trevor met a number of other representatives from local organizations like the United Way, the food bank, the library, and the health clinic. After walking out of the meeting, he wondered if getting children into school at age 4 and matching all their needs with the appropriate services was going to be just as hard, if not tougher, than keeping 16-year-olds from dropping out.

For Study and Discussion

The challenge for social workers, whether they work in schools or in community agencies that interface with schools, is to build on past successes and learn from the failures. Thoughtful provision of services that meet the individual needs of children is more likely when social workers have an enriched understanding of the broader issues at play in schools. This chapter, coupled with the more detailed chapters that follow, should provide the reader with knowledge necessary for improved practice and understanding of school social work and the remarkable organizations in which the work takes place.

1. Interview several teachers, administrators, parents, and policymakers inquiring about their expectations for their local school and the purposes of the broader public educational system. How (dis)similar are the responses, and what are the implications for practice?

2. Given the growth in homeschooling and market-based reforms (e.g., voucher programs and charter schools), how might free market forces shape the professional knowledge requirements of those working in the charter schools and their public school neighbors?

3. Efforts are often hampered by the overburdened agencies and educators due to two distinct, though related, issues: lack of sufficient resources and the ever-increasing need for schools to provide more and better services for all children. Consequently, does the practice of social workers need to change? What new services must be provided?

4. Labaree (1997) argued that the core problems with schools are political and not technical. Do you agree? How do local and national politics affect the services provided to different children? What technical services can be provided regardless of politics?

5. Researchers have documented the differential levels of school success for different groups of children for more than 50 years. What can be done to interrupt the reproduction of society's social and economic strata?

6. Discuss the concept of equality of educational opportunity. How do the different types of school reform enhance or inhibit educational opportunity for poor or minority children?

7. What role does the current financing of public education play in the provision of equal educational opportunity?

Additional Readings

Achinstein, B., Ogawa, R. T., & Speiglman, A. (2004). Are we creating separate and unequal tracks of teachers? The effects of state policy, local conditions, and teacher characteristics on new teacher socialization. *American Educational Research Journal, 41*(3), 557–603.

Belfield, C. R., & Levin, H. M. (2007). *The price we pay: Economic and social consequences of inadequate education.* Washington, DC: Brookings Institution Press.

Brewer, C. A., & Suchman, T. A. (2001). *Mapping census 2000: The geography of U.S. diversity* (CENSR/01-1). Washington, DC: U.S. Census Bureau.

Business Roundtable. (1992). *The essential components of a successful education: Putting policy into practice.* Washington, DC: Author.

Coleman, J. (1968). The concept of equality of educational opportunity. *Harvard Educational Review, 38*(1), 7–22.

Collins, R. (1979). *The credential society: An historical sociology of education and stratification.* New York: Academic Press.

Comer, J. P., & Haynes, N. M. (1992). *Summary of school development program effects.* New Haven, CT: Yale Child Study Center.

Conant, J. B. (1959). *The American high school today.* New York: McGraw-Hill.

Cuban, L. (1993). *How teachers taught: Constancy and change in American classrooms, 1890–1990* (2nd ed.). New York: Teachers College Press.

Cuban, L. (1998). How schools change reforms: Redefining reform success and failure. *Teachers College Record, 99*(3), 453–477.

Dewey, J. (1938). *Experience and education.* New York: Collier.

Dewey, J. (1943). *The school and society* (Rev. ed.). Chicago: University of Chicago Press.

Engel, M. (2000). *The struggle for control of public education: Market ideology vs. democratic values.* Philadelphia: Temple University Press.

Epstein, J. L. (2001). *School, family, and community partnerships: Preparing educators and improving schools.* Boulder, CO: Westview Press.

Firestone, W. A., Bader, B. D., Massel, D., & Rosenblum, S. (1992). Recent trends in state educational-reform: Assessment and prospects. *Teachers College Record, 94*(2), 254–277.

Gamoran, A. (2007). Standards-based reform and the poverty gap: Lessons for No Child Left Behind. Washington, DC: Brookings Institution Press.

Goldhaber, D., & Hannaway, J. (2004). Accountability with a kicker: Observations on the Florida A+ accountability plan. *Phi Delta Kappan, 85*(8), 598–606.

Gordon, D. T. (2003). *A nation reformed? American education 20 years after A Nation at risk.* Cambridge, MA: Harvard University Press.

Hanushek, E. A., & Raymond, M. E.. (2005). Does school accountability lead to improved student performance? *Journal of Policy Analysis and Management, 24*(2), 297–327.

Harding, H. (2005). Why is corporate America bashing our public schools? *Teachers College Record, 107*(7), 1427.

Jencks, C. (1992). *Rethinking social policy: Race, poverty, and the underclass.* Cambridge, MA: Harvard University Press.

Killeen, K., & Sipple, J. W. (2005). Mandating supplemental intervention services: Is New York state doing enough to help all students succeed? *Education Policy Analysis Archives, 13*(19), Retrieved March 10, 2005, from http://epaa.asu.edu/epaa/vl3nl9/

Kozol, J. (1995). *Amazing grace: The lives of children and the conscience of a nation.* New York: Crown.

Ladd, H. F., & Fiske, E. B. (2008). *Handbook of research in education finance and policy.* New York: Routledge.

Lareau, A., & Horvat, E. M. (1999). Moments of social inclusion and exclusion: Race, class, and cultural capital in family-school relationships. *Sociology of Education, 72,* 37–53.

Levin, H. (2001). *Privatizing education: Can the marketplace deliver choice, efficiency, equity, and social cohesion?* Boulder, CO: Westview Press.

Louis, K. S., & Smith, B. A. (1992). Cultivating teacher engagement: Breaking the iron law of social class. In F. M. Newmann (Ed.), *Student engagement in American secondary schools* (pp. 119–152). New York: Teachers College Press.

Orfield, G., & Kornhaber, M. L. (2001). *Raising standards or raising barriers? Inequality and high-stakes testing in public education.* New York: Century Foundation Press.

Pedroni, T. C. (2007). *Market movements: African American involvement in school voucher reform.* New York: Routledge.

Plank, D. N., & Sykes, G. (2003). Choosing choice: School choice in international perspective. New York: Teachers College Press.

Ravitch, D. (1974). *The great school wars, New York City, 1805–1973; A history of the public schools as battlefield of societal change.* New York: Basic Books.

Ravitch, D., & Viteritti, J. P. (2001). *Making good citizens: Education and civil society.* New Haven, CT: Yale University Press.

Roosevelt, G. (2006). The triumph of the market and the decline of liberal education: Implications for civic life. *Teachers College Record, 108*(7), 1404–1423.

Sipple, J. W., Killeen, K., & Monk, D. H. (2004). Adoption and adaptation: New York State school districts' responses to state imposed high school graduation requirements. *Educational Evaluation and Policy Analysis, 26*(2), 143–168.

Valenzuela, A. (1999). Subtractive schooling: U.S.-Mexican youth and the politics of caring. Albany: State University of New York Press.

Weiss, L. (2008). The way class works: Readings on school, family, and the economy. New York: Routledge.

Zigler, E., Gilliam, W. S., & Jones, S. M. (2006). A vision for universal preschool education. New York: Cambridge University Press.

2

School Social Work: Historical Development, Influences, and Practices

PAULA ALLEN-MEARES

University of Illinois at Chicago

Children are important. Education and schools are important. The child who comes to school must be accepted as he is. School social work has a philosophy, a discipline, and a service to offer that is good in meeting the needs of children.

—Ray Graham[1]

Introduction

The history of school social work is interesting and rich. In 1906 social conditions, life struggles, and a growing immigrant population were forceful factors that supported the development and expansion of education and, in turn, school social work. As education became increasingly regarded as a right for every child, the importance of linking school and community took on more significance. It was during this period that school social workers (then known as visiting teachers) recognized that their role should be more in tune with the social conditions and social movements of the day, and they sought changes in school policies that adversely affected the lives of children. Essentially, they served as the link between the school and the home.

Unfortunately, as this field of practice grew, the role of liaison received less emphasis. School social workers, concerned about their identity, sought a more specialized role, one that they believed would link their efforts more closely to the central purpose of education. The 1940s and 1950s were primarily dominated by the social casework approach. The emphasis on establishing a liaison between home and school was not considered as important. However, by the late 1960s and 1970s, the literature once more demanded a broader, more responsive role definition and approach to practice.

Presently, legislation and mandates to a large degree determine role definitions. Reactions from school social workers have been mixed. Some fear that mandates may cripple the search for different approaches that began during the 1970s. Others feel

[1]© 1952, National Association of Social Workers, Inc. Reprinted with permission. Ray Graham, "The Development of School Social Work Practice: Trends toward the Integration of a Social Work Function within an Education Setting," in *Bulletin of the National Association of School Social Workers*, 28(1), p. 8.

that what school social workers should contribute to the educational process is clear for the first time in the history of education.

The Establishment of School Social Work

School social work began at about the same time (during the school year 1906–07), although independently, in three cities: New York, Boston, and Hartford. The development originated outside the school system; private agencies and civic organizations in these three localities supported the work (Costin, 1969b). It is important to note that at this same time, a similar program was being established in London, the outcome of which forms a striking contrast to U.S. school social work services (Lide, 1959).

As in the development of social work generally, school social work was first intended to benefit the so-called underprivileged. In New York City, settlement workers from the Hartley House and Greenwich House thought it was necessary to know the teachers of children who came to the settlements, and they assigned two workers to visit schools and homes to work more closely with schools and community groups, for the purpose of promoting understanding and communication (Lide, 1959).

In Boston, a similar development was taking place. The Women's Education Association placed visiting teachers in the schools to bring about more harmony between school and home, to make the child's education more effective.

The director of the Psychological Clinic in Hartford initiated the first visiting teachers' program in that area. The director of the clinic recognized the help that could be derived from such a program. This person would assist the psychologist in securing histories of children and implementing the clinic's treatment plans and recommendations.

It was not until 1913, in Rochester, New York, that the first board of education initiated and financed a "visiting teacher program." The board of education stated,

This is the first step in an attempt to meet a need of which the school system has been conscious for some time. It is an undisputed fact that in the environment of the child outside of school are to be found forces which will often thwart the school in its endeavors. The appointment of visiting teachers is an attempt on the part of the school to meet its responsibility for the whole welfare of the child . . . and to maximize cooperation between the home and the school. (Oppenheimer, 1925, p. 5)

The Rochester Board of Education took an active role in the development of the service. The board placed visiting teachers in special departments of the school, under the administration and direction of the superintendent of schools. This arrangement drew attention to the necessity of avoiding separation of the school social worker from the whole school system and the community.

A national professional association had emerged—the National Association of Visiting Teachers. It held its first meeting in New York City, where concern was expressed about the organization, administration, and role definition of visiting teachers.

Early Influences

The early twentieth century was a fertile period for the development of school social work. Important influences in its early development were

■ Passage of compulsory school attendance laws. A concern for the illiteracy of immigrant children and then the illiteracy of American-born children brought attention to the child's right to at least a minimum education and the states' responsibility for securing this for all children and gave support to the enactment of compulsory attendance statutes in some states. However, statutes were often circumvented both by parents, who wished their children to work to supplement inadequate adult wages, and by factory owners, who wished to use the cheap labor of children. Without compulsory birth registration to make a child's age a matter of public record, it was easy for children to secure working papers before they were legally of age. This situation was aggravated by the failure of school districts to provide facilities for children who were ready and willing to attend school.

The lack of effective enforcement of school attendance laws led to such studies as that of Abbott and Breckinridge (1917) on the nonattendance problem in the Chicago schools. The findings of this study supported the need for school attendance officers who understood the social ills of the community, such as poverty, ill health, and lack of secure family income, and their effects on attendance (Abbott & Breckinridge, 1917). Abbott and Breckinridge held that this responsibility should be assigned to the school social worker, someone knowledgeable about the needs of children and the effects of such conditions. Further, they indicated that some poverty-stricken families had not come to the attention of community social service agencies, implying that the school was an important institution in the lives of these families. The first compulsory attendance laws in the United States were those of Connecticut and Massachusetts during the colonial period. By 1918 each state had passed its own compulsory attendance law, a situation that in effect proclaimed that each child had not only the right to benefit from what the school had to offer but an obligation to secure these advantages. This marked a new era in education, especially for parents, who were now forced to send their children to school.

As legislatures in various states extended the scope of compulsory education laws, schools were required to expand their facilities to provide for larger numbers of children with a greater range of individual abilities and backgrounds. School social workers played an important role—one of clarifying and sensitizing school personnel to the out-of-school lives of children and how they are affected.

- Knowledge of individual differences. As the scope of compulsory education laws expanded, states were forced to provide an educational experience for a variety of children. Simultaneously, new knowledge about individual differences among children and their capacity to respond to improved conditions compelled school personnel to look to other fields for an understanding of these differences.

Previously there had been no real concern about whether children had different learning needs; those who presented a challenge were not enrolled. Compulsory attendance laws changed this situation very quickly. Teachers concerned about these "different and/or excluded" children sought knowledge about individual differences so that they would be better prepared to address the educational needs of such children.

Again, the role of school social workers was one of sensitizing both teachers and other school personnel to the life conditions and forces that affect learning. Some social workers sought adaptations in the school program. The Henry Street Settlement, under the auspices of the New York City Board of Education and with social work leadership, formed the first class for upgraded pupils (children who suffered from mental defects). This settlement provided the necessary equipment and instructional resources so that these children could be educated. This was one of the first attempts to adapt instructional materials and resources to meet the special needs of students (Wald, 1915).

- Realization of the strategic position of education. Social workers of the early 20th century were keenly aware of the strategic place of school and education in the lives of children and youths and were impressed by the opportunities presented to the school. S. P. Breckinridge, addressing the National Education Association in 1914, stated,

> To the social worker the school appears as an instrument of almost unlimited possibilities, not only for passing on to the next generation the culture and wisdom of the past, but for testing present social relationships and for securing improvement in social conditions. (Breckinridge, 1914)

She begged for a closer inspection and study of failures of the school and of the consequent loss in social well-being for children and their future happiness.

■ Concern for the relevance of education. Simultaneously, social workers in the settlement houses were expressing the need for the school to relate itself more closely to the present and future lives of the children. Oppenheimer (1925) noted that during the early twentieth century the influence of the social settlement on the development of school social work was very strong, "both in respect to the type of methods used and in respect to the development of [the] social center in the schools" (Oppenheimer, 1925, p. 2). Social workers in the settlements expressed concern about "the insufficient number of visiting teachers to bring the school and home together" (Lide, 1959, p. 109).

Early Definitions

In 1916, Jane Culbert defined the role of school social worker as follows:

> Interpreting to the school the child's out-of-school life; supplementing the teacher's knowledge of the child ... so that she may be able to teach the whole child ... assisting the school to know the life of a neighborhood, in order that it may train the children for the life to which they look forward. Secondly, the visiting teacher interprets to the parents the demands of the school and explains the particular difficulties and needs of the child. (Culbert, 1916, p. 595)

The principal activity in school social work continued to be as a home–school–community liaison. In 1925, Julius Oppenheimer carried out a study to obtain a more detailed list of tasks than had been delineated in the 1916 definition of function. The study involved the analysis of 300 case reports; it resulted in a list of 32 core functions of the visiting teacher service. An appraisal of the nature of these tasks affirmed the emphasis on school–family–community liaison as the main body of school social work activity. Not found in the study were tasks involving a one-to-one, ongoing relationship of a visiting teacher with individual children to help them with their personal problems. One of the most important functions of the school social worker, Oppenheimer stated, "was to aid in the reorganization of school administration and of school practice by supplying evidence of unfavorable conditions that underlie children's school difficulties and by pointing out needed change" (Oppenheimer, 1925). According to Oppenheimer, the visiting teacher was the one person in the school who was knowledgeable about the outside life and social environment of children.

Expansion in the 1920s

The number of school social workers increased, largely as a result of a series of 3-year demonstrations, under the auspices of the Commonwealth Fund of New York, which were aimed at the prevention of juvenile delinquency (Oppenheimer, 1925).

The Commonwealth Fund gave the National Committee of Visiting Teachers financial support for a countrywide demonstration and for experimentation in the field of school social work. Thirty school social workers were placed in 30 different communities, both rural and urban, throughout the country for a demonstration project.

Each local community shared in the payment of the salaries of these visiting teachers. When the Fund withdrew its support in 1930, 21 of the communities that had served as demonstration sites continued the programs. Meanwhile, other cities were busily implementing their visiting teacher programs. By this time, there were about 244 school social workers in 31 states.

It was the massive demonstration project initiated by the Commonwealth Fund that gave social service in school its visibility. Boards of education, noting the value of the service, responded to the program by establishing visiting teacher programs in other communities. In turn, the National Association of Visiting Teachers grew and focused its efforts on establishing professional standards and direction for its membership.

The school was viewed as a strategic center of child welfare work, linking children and their families with resources, so that learning and growth would not be hindered.

Influence of the Mental Hygiene Movement

The literature of the 1920s reflects the beginning of a therapeutic role for school social workers in the public schools. The mental hygiene movement brought about an increasing emphasis on treating the individual child. According to Lela Costin, the increasing recognition of individual differences among children and interest on the part of the mental hygienists in understanding behavior problems led to an effort on the part of visiting teachers to develop techniques for the prevention of social maladjustment. (Costin, 1978, p. 4)

Mental hygiene clinics sprang up in almost every community. Their central purpose was to diagnose and treat nervous and difficult children. Such questions as, "How can we help the emotionally disturbed child through the school experience?" and "How can we help all children to find in their lives at school an emotionally enriching and stabilizing experience?" guided both school social workers and mental hygienists at this time.

Jessie Taft wrote,

> The only practical and effective way to increase the mental health of a nation is through its school system. Homes are too inaccessible. The school has the time of the child and the power to do the job. It is for us who represent mental hygiene and its application through social casework to help the school and teacher to see their vital responsibility for an education which shall mean the personal adjustment of the individual through the activities of the group. (Taft, 1923, p. 398)

Shifting Goals of the 1930s

The development of social work service in the schools was greatly retarded during the Depression of the 1930s, as were other social service programs for children. Services provided by visiting teachers were either abolished or seriously cut back in volume (Areson, 1923.) The provision of food, shelter, and clothing preoccupied much of what activity there was. As the Depression worsened, federal aid was made available to hard-pressed families. At this time visiting teachers began to

view their role differently. The early image of law enforcer and attendance officer was essentially replaced by the role of social caseworker. Abandoning their earlier commitment to change adverse conditions in the schools and linking home, school, and community, school social workers sought a more specialized role of providing emotional support for troubled children (Hall, 1936).

Many of these workers were anxious to improve their image. The role of attendance officer was not viewed as "professional." Further, because some were being used as "errand boys," school social workers were eager to have a more well-defined role—one with more specialized skills and less stigma.

Gladys Hall and Edith Everett saw the primary role of visiting teachers as supporting "wholesome childhood." Hall noted that the role of the school social worker was changing from one of school–community liaison to preventing poor mental health among children, a duty that later became associated with social casework. Everett stated,

> My own feeling as a result of a good many years of experience in connection with a city school system is that we can be most helpful by limiting our professional responsibility to doing as well as we humanly can our casework job within the school itself. (Everett, 1938, p. 58)

Everett further spoke against the practice of some visiting teachers, who took on a community responsibility outside the field of casework. On the other side, Bertha Reynolds was one of the first to recognize that not all problems experienced by the "troubled child" were inherent in his or her personality or background and that the school could be the source of the child's problem.

> It is clear that the contribution of social casework is to supplement the basic public administrator, not to struggle to make up for mistakes of a poor one. If a faulty school curriculum is causing every year thousands of school failures, it would be stupid to engage visiting teachers to work individually with the unsuccessful children. Why not change the curriculum and do away with that particular problem at one stroke? (Reynolds, 1935, p. 238)

Others, such as Charlotte Towle, raised similar concerns, urging school social workers to see the potential of social casework from a broad social perspective. She wrote,

> We are coming not only to recognize the futility of persisting in situations which are beyond the scope of casework help, but to realize also our social responsibility for revealing the inadequacy of social work in these instances, in order that interest and effort may be directed toward social action. (Towle, 1936)

Emphasis on Social Casework 1940–1960

By 1940, school social workers' roles as home–school liaisons and attendance officers had been virtually forsaken for a more specialized role. The literature, which had grown markedly during this period, called attention to "an appropriate function" of school social work: social casework. No longer were social change and neighborhood conditions seen as targets of intervention. Instead, the profession now had a clinical orientation. The personality needs of the individual child took on primary attention.

Ruth Smalley described the role of the school social worker as being a "specialized form of social casework, a method of helping children use what the school offers" (Smalley, 1947, p. 22). Swithun Bowers described social casework as "an art in which knowledge of the science of human relations and skill in relationship are used to mobilize capacities in the individual" (Bowers, 1949, p. 417). Joseph Hourihan, in a study of the duties and responsibilities of the visiting teachers in Michigan, recommended limiting work to those duties and responsibilities that are related to assisting individual emotionally maladjusted children (Hourihan, 1952).

A book entitled *Helping the Troubled School Child: Selected Readings in School Social Work, 1935–1955,* dealt extensively with the provision of social casework services to different groups of children. "Casework Method: An Elementary School Child" and "The Child and the Social Caseworker in the Schools" are typical tides of the chapters contained in this volume. The introduction to the chapter on the practice of school social work begins

> More and more state and local systems of education are providing specialized casework services for children who are showing by their failure to use the school experience effectively that they have social and emotional difficulties. This is a skilled method of working with individual children and their families.... The school social worker is responsible for individual children who show that they need an additional and different kind of help from that provided in the classroom.... Through casework skills the worker develops a relationship with an individual child through which he may be enabled to gain a better understanding of himself, the school situation, and the problem that is hindering his use of the school experience to his potential capacity. (Lee, 1959, p. 231)

In the same volume, Poole (1949) wrote,

> Social casework with the child in school has certain characteristics that are specific to the setting and that must be understood and related to the generic principles of the social casework process. The school is a setting which, to the child, is very much his own and one in which he is very much on his own. He assumes a major part of the responsibility for the use which he will make of his school experience. When he encounters some difficulty in this setting, the worker helps him to take responsibility for solving it. She helps him to understand the difficulty as it appears to the school and to clarify the problem as it exists for him. (Poole, 1949, p. 416)

Ruth Smalley wrote,

> The psychological base for social work is found in the social worker's appreciation of the psycho-biological organizing force which characterizes and is the essence of every living being .... The method which social work has developed to discharge its responsibility is a casework method, which comes alive as skill, and is made available and used, within an individual-to-individual relationship. (Smalley, 1955)

Mildred Sikkema's study of types of referrals made to school social workers confirmed that, in all community studies, behavior or personality problems far outnumbered any other type of referral

(Sikkema, 1953). In contrast, Jane Culbert found that the largest number of referrals stemmed from maladjustment in scholarship and deficiency in lessons (Culbert, 1923, p. 28). The literature of the 1950s also confirmed that indeed a transition had taken place. Descriptions of casework practice led the reader to believe that the transition was fully completed and that a new era had emerged.

In addition to the casework method, another social work method used in the schools was group therapy. Paul Simon undertook a study on the assumption that although school social work consisted primarily of casework with children and parents, with concomitant relationships with teachers and others, children might also be helped to resolve some of their problems in interpersonal relationships through the use of selected group experience. The primary objective was to help the child in his relationship to his peers and teachers (Simon, 1955).

Work with Others to Promote Social Casework Goals. The social worker recognized that the casework approach relied on communication with the parents of troubled children. A varying amount of casework was spent with parents, with the intent of helping the parent to perceive and share the school's concern and to support the child's casework relationship. Anna Braunstein stated that "the social worker's objective in interviewing the parent is to understand the child and his behavior in order to learn the probable cause of it. She can then offer assistance in providing better conditions for the child" (Braunstein, 1959, p. 268). Also, the potentiality of working with parent groups was acknowledged by Aline Auerbach (1955). The goal of these group sessions was to educate parents about their children, the school, and various developmental behaviors.

In the 1940s and 1950s, social workers consulted with teachers frequently to interpret the child's emotional difficulties and to aid them in an early recognition of personality difficulty (Alderson, 1952). Social workers' collaboration with other school personnel concerning changes in the educational program received minimal attention in the literature; the importance of

differentiating the casework relationship from the interprofessional relationship was stressed to some degree. Sikkema attempted to broaden the bases of collaboration by stressing the point that the school social worker could aid other school personnel in understanding human behavior and then translating it into practice in curriculum planning (Sikkema, 1949). John Nebo cited one instance in which school social workers, after two years of conferences, were instrumental in changing the unsound administrative practice of allowing uniformed police officers to come to the school and take children to the police station for questioning without the consent of their parents. However, it should be understood that social work influence in changing school policies was not a "typical professional activity" (Nebo, 1955).

Still we find concern expressed about who the school social worker was.

> Who is the school social worker? ... He may be "visiting teacher," "visiting counselor," "school counselor," "school social worker," or any of the other several titles. This lack of uniformity seems to reflect to some extent the confusion as to the purpose and function of service. (Kozol, 1967; National Advisory Committee on Civil Disorders, 1968; Silberman, 1970; Task Force on Children Out of School, 1970)

Changing Goals and Methods in the 1960s

Public schools were under attack from all quarters during the 1960s. There were those who argued that public education was not educating the pupils. Further, there was considerable discussion about the need for change in the public school as well as change in the practices of various pupil personnel staff: social workers and guidance counselors. Several studies of public education documented adverse school policies. It was claimed that inequality in educational opportunity existed as a result of segregation; that public schools were reinforcing the myth that minority children and those youths from low-income backgrounds could not perform as well as their middle-class white counterparts, with the result that the educational staff expected poor performance from these students; that the school was essentially a repressive institution, hindering the development of creativity and the desire on the part of some pupils to learn. Some parents claimed that they felt alienated from the school and that they wanted more voice in the education of their children (Lide, 1959).

In the midst of all of these critical issues confronting public education, many school social workers remained somewhat entrenched in their emphasis of individual work with emotionally disturbed children, even though the literature at this time was calling for a broader view of the role of the school and of social work services: the school as a "social system" was widely discussed in the writings of educators as well as in those of some social workers (Wessenich, 1972; Willis, 1969).

Some experimentation with different methods of social work was also cited in the literature. Virginia Crowthers spoke strongly in support of "school social workers using group work for parents and students, stressing the importance of understanding the individual and his behavior in relationship to the group" (Crowthers, 1963). In a research progress report, Robert Vinter and Rosemary Sarri described the effective use of group work in dealing with such school problems as high school dropouts, underachievement, and academic failure. According to these authors, pupil malperformance was a result of both pupil characteristics and school conditions. This report led the researchers to conclude that school social workers should address themselves more to the conditions of the school and not limit their efforts to contact with pupils; that school social workers are in a strategic position to identify school policies and arrangements that adversely affect children; and that social workers in the schools should have a dual function—they should assist specific individuals and simultaneously deal with the sources of pupil difficulties within the school (Vinter & Sarri, 1965).

Accompanying a growing interest in the use of group work in the schools was attention to new ways of working with the community. A broader kind of community work was recognized, aimed at bringing the school community and geographical community closer together. Hourihan, in describing community work in Detroit, emphasized "the two-way communication established by such a relationship in helping troubled children" (Hourihan, 1965). A project in the Detroit public schools, sponsored by the Ford Foundation, also provided evidence that the community was taking on more importance. The thrust of this project was to bring the inner-city community and school closer together. Because inner-city children were not achieving, and in fact were far behind other students, school–community agents were appointed whose job was to connect school and community as partners in education (Deshler & Erlich, 1972).

Confusion of Roles. As school social workers began to use different methods to deal with problems in the public schools, there were those who were systematically investigating how others viewed the social work role and the role of related disciplines. The school social worker generally operates as a team member, working in collaboration with other school personnel—principal, psychologist, nurse, special educator, and so forth. Robert Rowen conducted a study in New Jersey to determine the differences in the perceptions of the function of school social workers by school superintendents and school social workers, respectively. He found significant disagreement or confusion existed in about one out of every four tasks performed by the school social worker. The superintendent saw the school social worker's role as encompassing more tasks than most of the workers actually performed. These tasks included investigation of the child's home, neighborhood, and environment; assistance in the collection of background materials on the child and family for the psychologist when mental retardation was suspected; and service on community committees and other social agencies (Rowen, 1965).

John Fisher's study of role perception of various school specialists (attendance coordinators, psychologists, and social workers) found that each specialist group believed that its members were more highly involved in various sample situations presented than anyone else thought they were (Fisher, 1966).

Merville Shaw, in a study of role delineation among the guidance professionals, found that their functions overlapped significantly with those that the school counselors, school social workers, and school psychologist wanted to carry out (Shaw, 1967). Richard J. Anderson found that the confusion among roles was not confined to the school, but that it was reflected in ineffective working relationships of school personnel with community agencies. He studied the process and problems of referring maladjusted schoolchildren to mental health clinics in Illinois and concluded that troubled children suffer because of the inability of professional personnel working in clinics and school personnel to cooperate with each other. Only the highly motivated child and parent would be willing to blunder through the lack of communication and coordination (Anderson, 1968). In 1969, Costin assessed the importance that a national sample of school social workers attached to specific tasks and sought to determine whether their practice was in tune with changes in social conditions and problems affecting public schools and youths (Costin, 1969a). Her findings revealed that the social workers' description of social work reflected the clinical orientation of the social work literature of the 1940s and 1950s, showed little response to the concerns expressed in both education and social work literature, and ranked leadership/policy making tasks as least important. Furthermore, these practitioners were not willing to delegate school social work tasks to individuals with less and/or different levels of education and training than their own. Based on these data and a review of issues in education, Costin later stated,

> It is apparent that if social workers in the schools are to meet their professional obligations and account for their claim on education resources, then they must move with speed to provide part of the remedy for problems of the school and its pupils. The first step is to reassess the objectives of a school social work service.... In today's world the focus of social work with pupils must be shifted away from a major emphasis on emotion, motivation, and personality and toward such cognitive areas as learning, thinking, and problem solving. Goals should center upon helping pupils acquire a sense of competence, a readiness for continued learning, and a capacity to adapt to change. (Costin, 1972, p. 350)

John Alderson and Curtis Kirshef undertook a partial replication of Costin's study, asking a population of Florida school social workers who had varying levels of professional training and preparation to indicate the importance of social work tasks and their willingness to delegate them (Alderson & Kirshef, 1973). This population ranked leadership and policy making as either first or second in priority. In Costin's study, it had been ranked least important. Also, this group demonstrated greater readiness to experiment with different staffing patterns, suggesting a positive move not evidenced in Costin's study. However, caution should be used in comparing these studies: Costin analyzed a national random sample of social workers with master's degrees; Alderson and Kirshef analyzed professionals with different backgrounds and levels of training in only one state.

Robert Bruce Williams investigated the extent to which the behavior of the school social worker reflected the climate of the individual school and the professional acts of the school social worker in compatible (receptive to school social work) and incompatible (not very receptive) schools (Williams, 1970). This research was based on the assumption that the principal primarily determined the administrative policies and practices of each school and thus played a key role in determining social work practice. The results of this study suggested that the performance or nonperformance of the social worker was attributed to attitudinal and behavioral aspects of the principal–social worker relationship.

John P. Flynn studied how other school personnel perceive social work tasks (Flynn, 1976). Pupil personnel service workers, teachers, principals, and instructional specialists were asked to rate the importance and performance of 107 school social work tasks. The results were as follows. (a) Each professional group differed in its perception of task importance and task performance. (b) Only a few of the tasks were viewed as shared with other groups, either in terms of task importance or task performance. (c) These groups also ranked casework and clinical service as most important and a policy-making role as least important.

Expansion in the 1970s: The Call for Leadership

The 1970s were a time of great expansion. The number of school social workers increased, and more emphasis was placed on family, community, teaming with workers in other school-related disciplines, and pupils with disabilities. Social conditions were also changing rapidly.

A document that significantly influenced public education during this time was the Kerner Report (National Advisory Committee on Civil Disorders, 1968). It analyzed the racial violence of the 1960s and placed much of the blame on public schools and their failure to educate minority children. The report recommended that racial segregation in the nation's schools be eliminated and that opportunities for parental and community participation in the public schools be expanded. Sarri and Maple believe that school social work was greatly influenced by the Kerner Report:

> The Kerner commission report virtually placed on the doorsteps of the schools much of the responsibility for the race riots of the 1960s. In reaction to that report, as well as being aware of the need to strengthen school social work's contribution to American education, the NASW [National Association of Social Workers] Council on Social Work in Schools undertook a three-year project to expand the school community linkage role .... Jointly funded by the National Institute of Mental Health and NASW; the project produced a national workshop and twelve regional institutes. (Sarri & Maple, 1972, p. 5)

"Social Change and School Social Work in the 1970s" was the theme of the national workshop held at the University of Pennsylvania in June 1969. The thrust of the workshop was to "stimulate innovation and change in school social work throughout the United States and to encourage school social workers to assume leadership roles" (Sarri & Maple, 1972). Proceedings of these national and regional meetings were later incorporated in a book entitled *The School in the Community*.

Linda Wessenich, Helen Nieberl, Betty Deshler, and John Erlich were among the contributors to *The School in the Community*. Wessenich studied systems analysis, proposing that systems theory be used as a basis for school social work problem solving (Wessenich, 1972). Nieberl urged focusing away from the microcosm of the individual child to the wider world of the school and community (Nieberl, 1972). This approach required the collection of data about the school and its community to determine the various factors that affect student learning. Deshler and Erlich reported on a demonstration project in Detroit in which social workers were used as agents to extend the links between school and community (Deshler & Erlich, 1972).

Other writers also denounced the stagnation gripping the field. Spitzer and Welsh called for a problem-focused practice approach rather than method orientation, delineating specific steps to be included in the problem-solving process (Spitzer & Welsh, 1969). Benjamin and Lois Gottlieb concluded that there were essentially three constraints inhibiting a more responsive approach to practice: (a) the educational preparation of school social workers focused too much on individual casework and a method orientation; (b) this training was based on a medical orientation, which focused on intrapsychic factors rather than environmental conditions; and (c) the traditional expectations held by educational administrators encouraged practitioners to be caretakers of deviants (Gottlieb & Gottlieb, 1971).

Models of Practice. As school social work practice has evolved, so have different practice models. A practice model can be defined as the "representation or statement of essential facts, central ideas and concepts and their interrelationships within the domain established for the expository model. Constructed simplification of a complex of phenomena which can be perceived" (Johnson, 1972, pp. 95–96). William Reid and Laura Epstein stated that a model is "a coherent set of directives which state how a given kind of treatment is to be carried out. A model is basically definitional and descriptive. It usually states what a practitioner is expected to do or what practitioners customarily do under given conditions" (Reid & Epstein, 1972, pp. 7–8). Peter Kettner identified several components for analyzing and comparing models: theoretical underpinning, level of intervention, target group or system, roles and responsibilities of the worker, goals and objectives, methods of assessment, and strategies employed, to name a few (Kettner, 1975). Models are developed to fit a particular practice need, which, of course, is designed in context to environmental conditions of the time.

Alderson has done considerable work in this area and has offered four models of school social work practice: the traditional clinical model, the school change model, the social interaction model, and the community school model (see Table 2.1) (Alderson, 1972).

The best-known and most widely used model described by Alderson is the traditional clinical model, which focuses on individual students with social and emotional problems that interfere with their potential to learn. This model uses psychoanalytic and ego psychology as its primary theoretical base. A major assumption of the model is that the individual child (and/or the child's family) is dysfunctional and is experiencing difficulty. Thus, the school social worker provides casework services to the child and/or the child's family. The school system itself is not the focus of the worker's activity. School personnel become involved in the assessment process only to share their perspectives and insights on how the child operates in school.

A second model identified by Alderson is the school change model. The target for this model is the school and its institutional policies and practices; the school in its entirety—all persons and subgroups—is viewed as the client. This model encourages changes in institutional policies that are seen as causing student malperformance.

The third model, the community school model, focuses primarily on deprived or disadvantaged communities. Its thrust is to educate these communities about what the school has to offer, to organize support for the school and its programs, and to explain to school officials the dynamics of the community and the operant societal factors.

A fourth model, the social interaction model, has as its emphasis reciprocal influences of the acts of individuals and groups. The target of intervention is the kind and quality of exchanges between parties (the child, groups of children, families, the school, and the community). The social worker is a mediator, a clarifier, and a facilitator of better understanding between and among the parties. This mediation involves identifying "common and shared ground": The worker points out the mutual interests of the parties to help them define a specific goal or objective.

Costin's Model. An important model that grew from a demonstration project of a multiuniversity consortium for planned change in pupil personnel services is Costin's school–community–pupil relations model (Anderson, 1974; Costin, 1975; Vargus, 1976). This model emphasizes the complexity of the interactions among students, the school, and the community (see Table 2.2). Its primary goal is to bring about change in the interaction of this triad and thus to modify to some extent harmful institutional practices and policies of the school. Attention is given to the characteristics of groups of pupils and of their school. The focus is on the situation of student groups, not on the personality development of individual group members.

Each problem involves groups of students who are similarly situated (truants, pregnant teenagers, or children with similar learning needs) and who form a dysfunctional unit as their unique characteristics interact with conditions in the school and community. The problem is not viewed as springing entirely from the group; the school and the community are viewed as contributors.

TABLE 2.1 Alderson's Practice Models for School Social Work

	Traditional Clinical Model	School Change Model	Community School Model	Social Interaction Model
Focus	Pupils identified as having social or emotional difficulties	The milieu of the school (especially school norms and conditions)	Deprived and disadvantaged communities that misunderstand and mistrust the school	Reciprocal interaction between pupils and the school; identify problems in interaction
Goals	Enable the pupil identified as having a school-related social or emotional difficulty to function more effectively	Alter dysfunctional school norms and conditions	Develop community understanding and support; develop school programs to assist pupils who are poverty victims; alleviate deprived conditions	Foster development of mutual aid system; remove barriers to reciprocal interaction
Target system	Pupil-clients and their parents	Entire school	Community and school become targets as well as other systems	Interactional field
View of sources of difficulty	Child's emotional or psychic difficulty, stemming primarily from family, especially parent-child problems	Dysfunctional school norms and conditions	Poverty and other social conditions; school personnel lack full understanding of cultural differences and effects of poverty	Difficulty of pupil-clients, and the various systems within which social interaction occurs, to communicate and to mutually assist
Worker tasks and activities	Casework, primarily with pupils and parents; some work with groups and with family as a group; liaison functions between and among pupils, parents, and educational staff, including teachers	Identify school norms and conditions which are dysfunctional; some direct work with pupils, especially group work; consult with teachers and administrators, individually and in groups	Involve self in activities of community; enable community to ask questions and raise issues; assist community in understanding school and vice versa; encourage community involvement in school programs	Identify and highlight commonalities; establish assist communication; establish mutual aid system; direct work with individuals, groups, and community
Major workers' roles	Enabling supportive collaboration and consultation	Advocacy, negotiation, consultation, mediation	Mediation, advocacy, and outreach	Mediation, consultation, enabling
Conceptual and theoretical base	Psychoanalysis, psychosocial, ego psychology, and casework theory and methodology	Social science theory, especially theories of deviance; organizational theory	Community-school concept, communication theory	Systems theory, social science theory, communication theory

Source: From John Alderson in Rosemary Sarri and Frank F. Maple, eds., *The School in the Community*, pp. 57–74, excerpts; Fig. 1. Copyrighted material reprinted with permission from the National Association of Social Workers, Inc.

TABLE 2.2   Costin's School–Community–Pupil Relations Model

Focus: On school and community deficiencies and specific system characteristics as these interact with characteristics of pupils at various stress points in their life cycles

Goal: To bring about change in school–community–pupil relations that will alleviate stress upon target groups of pupils

Assessment Procedures: Study and evaluate pupil characteristics and school and community conditions that affect equality of educational opportunity for target groups of pupils; assess needs and identify problem situations that form a problem complex; consult with administrators, teachers, other school personnel, and the affected group—pupils and their parents

Development of a Service Plan: Requires continuing consultation with administrators, teachers, and other school personnel, and with concerned individuals; submission of written plan to administrators and others whose participation and support are essential; agreement on time-limited contract for service; and control of the workload of those who have responsibility for carrying out the service plan

Worker Tasks and Activities: Help student groups diagnose and articulate the problems they see as critical in their school; serve as ombudsman, as individual or group, for student grievances; set up informal groups of teachers, students, and administrators to voice concerns and settle conflicts; form change-agent or problem-solving teams; act as an advocate, consultant, mediator, and negotiator with teachers, administrators, families, and agencies; address the conditions of the school rather than limiting efforts to contacts with students; assist teachers and administrators in identifying those school practices and arrangements that inadvertently hinder learning and adjustment; assess the functioning of target groups of children in relation to the general characteristics of the school

Development of Personnel: Establish a member of a pupil specialist team that is optionally interdisciplinary; maintain maximum flexibility within the team to allow for differentiation of skills, but implement a unified approach to problem-solving and team authority; emphasize open sharing of information and ideas among team members and other persons who can help

Supporting Theories: Social learning theory; systems theory and some of its derivatives (organization development, situation theory, classification of role, and system problems)

Source: From *Social Work,* 20:2 (March 1975), pp. 135–139, excerpts. Copyrighted material reprinted with permission from the National Association of Social Workers, Inc.

Frequently, the school social worker may provide casework, group work, and crisis intervention on behalf of individual children who are members of a particular target group. However, social casework is not the major social work task, according to this model. Instead, the school social worker may assist in the development of new programs, consult and collaborate with school officials regarding policies and practices that contribute to malperformance, and work with community agencies to provide services for the pupils and their families. Interdisciplinary teamwork and cooperation between school social workers and auxiliary school personnel are necessary components of this model.

Replication of Costin's Study: The 1970s. In the late 1970s, Allen-Meares replicated Costin's 1969 study to assess the status of social work practice in schools (Allen-Meares, 1977). Stimuli for this investigation were the social work literature calling for new roles and models of practice; the *NASW Manpower Policy Statement* (Willis & Willis, 1972), which brought renewed attention to teaming; the unfavorable social conditions and rapid social change (inflation, drug abuse, child abuse and neglect, poverty, and high dropout rates) confronting public schools; and support for a new, humanistic approach to education, which had positive implications for school social work.

Allen-Meares modified Costin's original questionnaire to incorporate activities that were currently being described in the literature. The final questionnaire was mailed to a randomly selected national sample of school social workers. As in Costin's study, respondents rated task importance and indicated their willingness to delegate tasks to persons with less and/or different educational preparation than their own.

Factor analysis of the data yielded seven factors. In rank order of importance, these are (a) clarifying the child's problem with others, (b) tasks preliminary to the provision of social work services, (c) assessing the child's problem, (d) facilitating school–community–pupil relations, (e) educational counseling with the child and parents, (f) facilitating the utilization of community resources, and (g) leadership and policy making. The five highest-ranked factors led to the conclusion that school social work practice was in transition, away from the predominantly clinical casework approach found in Costin's study to one of home–school–community liaison and educational counseling with children and their parents. However, leadership and policy making were still considered least important. These conclusions fell between the traditional casework approach and the systems-change models, or those involving school–community relations. They did not indicate a strong emphasis on identifying target groups of children, changing adverse conditions of school and community, or responding to the crises in schools. These practitioners also remained reluctant to delegate and assign tasks, apparently maintaining that they were the only professionals within the school system who could perform these functions—a result that conflicted with literature findings that supported experimentation with teaming.

The NASW Study. The NASW Council on Social Work in Schools met for the first time in the fall of 1973 and identified numerous issues facing school social workers. Because inflation and budget cuts were threatening public education and other school personnel were claiming roles similar to those provided by school social

workers, it became imperative for the council to assess the current status of practice. To bring attention to these issues and to secure the opinions of practitioners, the council published an open letter in an issue of the *NASW News,* inviting school social workers to share their perceptions (Watson, 1975). The response was overwhelming; letters from all over the United States reinforced the council's concerns. Later in 1974, the council made a report to the Midwest Conference on School Social Work. At this meeting it became clear that national standards were needed to clarify the nature of services and to explain the parameters of the services to other personnel in the school setting.

Before embarking on this task, the council sought additional information on the status of practice, the educational preparation of school social workers, and the structure of school social work systems throughout the United States. The survey was done in the summer of 1975. Representatives of each of the 50 state departments of education were interviewed, and questionnaires were mailed to a random sample of school social workers and to graduate and undergraduate departments in schools of social work.

Almost all the school social workers surveyed at the time (88.4%) were employed by a local school district, and their positions were funded by state or local agencies or a combination of both (*Summary of the Preliminary Report on the Survey of Social Workers in the Schools,* 1978). Most (88.8%) had a master's degree in social work (MSW) and were eligible for tenure and collective bargaining. One fifth reported that they were directly responsible to a social work supervisor, and about 90% were members of an interdisciplinary team. Professional practice was defined primarily as direct service. Typical problems were those of parent–child relationships involving emotionally disturbed pupils. Almost half of these children came from low-income areas, and two thirds were white. The most often identified work-related problems were too many referrals, excessive caseloads, and school personnel who did not understand the social workers' role and functions.

Fifty states reported that school social workers were employed by school districts, but only six states required the employment of school social workers. About two thirds of the states required that school social workers have an MSW degree.

At the undergraduate level (230 schools), less than one third of the schools offered a specialized curriculum in school social work, but the school setting was frequently used as a fieldwork placement: Almost all reported that there was little collaboration between them and the department of education on the same campus.

At the master's-degree level, only eight graduate schools (of 82 contacted) reported a special curriculum in school social work, and 19 offered some graduate courses in school social work. As at the undergraduate level, the departments of education and the schools of social work had minimal, if any, collaborative arrangements.

When the findings of the NASW study were compared to Allen-Meares'study, several similarities became apparent. Both found that the practice was described as focusing on the individual child and his or her parents rather than on helping target groups of children or changing adverse educational policies and practices, although Allen-Meares did find that practice was in transition.

1980s: The Interface of Social Work and Education

School Social Work: Practice and Research Perspectives (Constable & Flynn, 1982) captures the thrust of the service in the 1980s and some of the important research endeavors and educational issues of the future. Representative topics are "An Ecological Perspective on Social Work in the Schools," "School Social Work Practice and P.L. 94-142," "Implications of Legal Mandates for Schools and School Policy," "Social Work in Regular and Special Education," "The School as an Organization," "Research Processes for System Change," "Practical Approaches to Conducting and Using Research in the Schools," and "Program Evaluation and School Social Work."

A content analysis of school social work literature over the period 1968 to 1978 indicated several important shifts in practice. School social

work focused on pupil groups (specifically children with disabilities) and on work with other school personnel. The liaison role was emphasized, as was the role of promoting change in the school policies (Allen-Meares & Lane, 1982). Another research project confirmed these findings. This project sought information about school social workers' perceptions of P.L. 94-142 (The Education for All Handicapped Children Act) and its impact on their practice. Consultation, learning, diagnosing disabilities, a move away from long-term clinical treatment, and an organizational role that assisted the school in its primary function were found (Timberlake, Sabantino, & Hooper, 1982).

Interestingly, this book reflects the impact of changes both in social work and in education. Presently in social work there is a strong push for adopting an ecological perspective of practice. And the evaluation of practice is advocated (Constable & Flynn, 1982; Germain, 1979; Tripodi & Epstein, 1980; Winters & Easton, 1983). During the 1980s, school social workers grew in number, and so did their state associations. In response to this growth, NASW held a number of special conferences to address the needs of this group. For example, in 1988 the school social work conference was held in Philadelphia, and in 1990 a special school social work track was held as a part of the NASW annual meeting. These special conferences primarily focused on expanded roles (e.g., work with infants, the role of the school social worker in early childhood special education, school reform and how the school social worker could enhance cultural diversity, and mainstreaming children with learning disabilities), new populations (e.g., chemically exposed infants and youth infected with AIDS), and how to respond to the increasing number of homeless children and their families. In response, the need for literature about the practice escalated. Social Work Services in Schools, published in 1986, was the first comprehensive text that dealt with this subject matter (Allen-Meares, Washington, & Welsh, 1986). Some state associations of school social workers published their own journals and newsletters.

Educational legislation continued to play a major role in shaping and expanding school and social work services. For example, school social workers were included as "qualified personnel" in Part H of the Education of the Handicapped Act Amendments of 1986, P.L. 99-457, Early Intervention for Handicapped Infants and Toddlers; in P.L. 100-297, the Elementary and Secondary School Improvement Amendments of 1988; and in P.L. 101-476, the Individuals with Disabilities Education Act.

The debate about the quality of education and the challenge to reform the system led to a national study of state departments of education to ascertain reform initiatives and conditions that were barriers to excellence. Allen-Meares (1987) maintained that the impetus for the study also evolved from concern about the erosion of federal support for social welfare programs for children and their families (Allen-Meares, 1987). The call for excellence in education ignored such barriers as poverty, inadequate health care, race and gender discrimination, and their interaction with schooling. Her study found that excellence was defined by having an effective school administrator, maintaining high expectations for students and staff, involving students in learning, and eradicating school problems. Reform initiatives were to appoint blue ribbon committees, pressure the legislature to increase funding, increase the scholastic requirements for teachers and pupils, and give attention to math and science. Barriers to excellence in education were parental apathy, poverty, child abuse and neglect, family crisis, poor parenting skills, economic deprivation, poor parent–teacher relationships, lack of dropout prevention programs and teamwork among school personnel, and lack of financial resources.

1990s–Present

In 1994 (known as the Year of Education Reform) school social workers were once more included in a major piece of legislation—the American Education Act, P.L. 103-227. This act was signed into law on March 31, 1994. Eight national goals were outlined, including those related to school readiness, school completion, student achievement and citizenship, teacher education and professional development, achievement in math and science, goals related to adult literacy and continuing education, safety and discipline in schools, and parental involvement with their student's learning. The major objectives of the act were to promote research, consensus building, and systemic change to ensure equality of educational opportunities for all students.

Though this major piece of legislation targets reform initiatives particular to schools, major social, technological, and economic changes in the broader society may prevent it from achieving equity in educational opportunity. For example, an increasing number of children and female-headed households live in poverty (Danziger & Gottschalk, 1993), technological advancements require a more sophisticated labor force, reform in welfare and health care are still topics of debate without firm proposals for real change, there is a call for more community control of schools, and violence in the community and in schools is at an all-time high. It is important to relate this state of affairs to the conceptual framework of this book. The school is influenced by its larger community and societal context. If social supports are not present for children and their families to buffer the consequence of poverty and other problems, even with the implementation of school reform proposals, educational success is highly unlikely.

The Growth of State Associations of School Social Workers and a New National Organization. Since the early 1970s, the number of state associations of school social workers has risen. Many NASW chapters now have school social work committees. There are four regional councils: Midwest School Social Work Council, formed almost three decades ago; the Southern School Social Work Conference; the Western Alliance; and the Northeastern Alliance. In 1994, spearheaded by the school social work leadership, a National Association of School Social Workers was formed independent of the NASW (National Association of Social Workers Commission on Education, 1991).

In many state offices of education there are persons who assume administrative responsibility for school social work services. These individuals are known as school social work state consultants. There is a National Council of State Consultants in school social work.

These state, regional, and national organizations are providing their members with educational opportunities for professional growth, yearly workshops, job networks, continuing education credit, and legislative advocacy. As state associations increase and develop, it will be essential for them to form linkages with NASW and other related school-based progressive groups. It would be detrimental to the profession if these independent membership groups isolated themselves from the national organization. In 1994, NASW identified school social work as the first section under its then newly organized structure. The NASW School Social Work Section has celebrated several anniversaries. The section provides members with national leadership for school social workers, a newsletter, professional development opportunities at the national conference, lobbying at the national level and comment on federal education legislation and regulations, and advocacy to influence relevant policies. The section is producing a series of minipublications on school social work effectiveness (NASW Steering Committee, 1997).

School Social Work Credentials. States are now taking a more active role in specifying education requirements for practice in the school. For example, in Illinois, practitioners seeking certification must complete an approved graduate social work program that includes special coursework on school social work (e.g., educational legislation, exceptional children, models of practice, and state and school laws) and take the two special exams (a test of knowledge specific to school social work and a test of basic skills in math, reading, and other subjects). For those practitioners who completed their coursework prior to the implementation of these requirements, procedures are in place to certify them. Because so many states are adopting credentialing procedures for all school employees as a way to upgrade the quality of personnel, NASW, in consultation with Allen-Meares and the Education

Testing Service, Princeton, New Jersey, developed the first School Social Work Credential Exam. This exam was first administered in 1992.

The School Social Work Specialist (SSWS) credential was, at one time, voluntary and not required for state social work certification. This credential recognized school social workers who had

- Met nationally established standards of knowledge and practice by achieving a passing score on the National Teacher's Exam's (NTE) School Social Worker Specialty Area Test
- Demonstrated 2 years of paid post-MSW social work experience and professional supervision in a school setting
- Provided a professional evaluation from a social work supervisor and a reference from a colleague

However, in 1999 the National Teacher's Exam decided to remove the social work portion of the exam due to declining interest. Because the National Teacher's Exam was one of the requirements for a school social work credential, NASW responded by creating the Certified School Social Work Specialist (C-SSWS) designation to replace the credential program in 2000 (NASW, n.d.). Like the School Social Work Credential Exam, the C-SSWS recognizes the holder of the certification as a professional in the field of social work and that the holder meets national standards in the field. Although the C-SSWS certifies the holder as a professional in social work, it does not replace any license or certification that individual states require of school social workers (NASW, n.d.). Licensing remains under the control of the state, and school social work requirements vary accordingly.

The move to test and review the credentials of those seeking employment as school social workers holds important implications for the educational preparation offered by schools of social work.

Standards for Social Work Services in Schools. In 1976 the first standards for school social work services were developed. These standards were grouped into three areas: (a) attainment of competence, (b) organization and administration, and (c) professional practice.

The standards included a taxonomy of school social work tasks. An important theme running throughout the standards was prevention.

In 1992 the standards for social work services in schools were revised by the Education Task Force and again in 2002 (NASW, 2002). The standards were divided into three sections: (a) competence and professional practice, (b) professional preparation and development, and (c) administrative structure and support. Appropriate ratios for social worker–student populations are determined by the populations of the student body and its needs. For example, a school consisting of a large number of handicapped pupils would need more workers.

Future Directions and Challenges.   Questions about the quality of schooling, reduced tax base, increased demand to serve a more diverse student population, increased poverty among children and families, and increased violence will challenge the profession to think creatively and differently about their services. The capacity of the community to devote its resources to enhance the availability and scope of social and economic supports will be a decisive factor. Building integrated school and community service models will be important if we are to achieve success.

What does this mean for school social work services? With the new emphasis on developing integrated service-delivery systems (or full-service schools) involving collaboration between schools and community agencies, the challenge will be to redefine school social work to meet this paradigm shift.

A recent trend in school social work has been to embrace technology as a tool to continually evaluate social work interventions in the school setting (Pahwa, 2003; Redmond, 2003). Pahwa (2003) noted that the use of technology and consistent data collection helped to support the positive impact that school social workers had with students who had not been documented otherwise at one school. Other social workers have developed guides for school social workers to work within their existing system to create and implement a new information system and database using the School Social Work Information Systems (SSWIS) as a model (Redmond, 2003). Technology has also been examined as a missing component in the connection between other social services in the schools and communities and the school social worker. However, more research is needed to see how this network of social services would affect student interventions in the schools.

Conclusion

Since the early twentieth century, school social work has been preoccupied with essentially three questions: Who are the school social workers? What services can such individuals provide? To whom must they relate? To do full justice to the historical development of the service, we should trace the history of education in the United States. Table 2.3 summarizes some of the key forces in society and education that have shaped social work services in schools. School social workers should be conscious of the changes in approaches to education and in those social conditions that education responds to. By doing so, school social workers can be proactive rather than reactive in the determination of their role.

TABLE 2.3   Historical Development of and Influences on School Social Work, 1800–21st Century

Social Trends and Movements	Public Education	Social Work	School Social Work
1800–1919			
Age of progressiveness: liberalism, social Darwinism.	Crusade for public education; expansion of public education at elementary, secondary, and collegiate levels (1875–1900) in northern and western states.	Movement from volunteer to paid employment.	Outside agencies provided social work services to students in schools in Hartford, Boston, and New York City, 1906–1907.
Immigrant population increase.		Growth of the immigrant population leads to the first settlement house in the United States, 1887.	First school system to finance school social work service: Rochester, New York, 1913.
Development of social science as a body of knowledge.	Influence of John Dewey and "progressive education."	Beginning of social work education with an emphasis on method of practice; social science theory predominant.	
Growth of labor movement and child labor movement; concern for working conditions.	Concern for the development of the individual child.		
Establishment of juvenile courts.	Compulsory attendance required in all 48 states (first: Massachusetts, 1852; last: Mississippi, 1918).	Beginnings of establishing practice theory with the publication of Mary Richmond's *Social Diagnosis* (1917).	
World War I ("Make the world safe for democracy").	Smith-Hughes Act for the support of vocational education.	Development of practice in specialty areas.	
Nativists believe that the new wave of immigrants from Europe was destroying the "fabric of society and the race."	Emergence of nonpublic schools.		
Development and influence of psychology and Freudian theory.			
1919–1929			
Prosperity: national income high, unemployment low.	Establish that nonpublic schools may be an acceptable alternative to public schools, 1925.	Marked increase in philanthropic foundations.	Commonwealth Fund, a private foundation, supported 30 school social workers in 20 communities.
Reduction in immigration; deportation of alien radicals.	Increase in student population and growth of school programs reflective of prosperity.	Formation of community chests and reorganization of private charities.	Increase in the number of visiting teachers.
Increase in racial intolerance; upsurge of the Ku Klux Klan.		Rise of "child guidance," and character-building agencies; concern for the prevention of delinquency.	National Association of Visiting Teachers established 1919.
		Emphasis on function rather than on social cause; emphasis on the adjustment of individuals.	

(continued)

TABLE 2.3   Continued

Social Trends and Movements	Public Education	Social Work	School Social Work
1930–1945			
Great Depression; solutions sought for economic and social ills in action by the federal government.	Development of the Civilian Conservation Corps (CCC); education programs were developed in each CCC camp; significant influence on the youth.	Federal government became involved in social welfare, relief programs, and public works programs.	Services provided by visiting teachers either abolished or significantly reduced in 1930s.
New Deal; the entrance of the federal government into relief programs.	National Youth Administration (NYA) provided employment for students in high schools and colleges.	Federal funding; state administration of assistance for children, the elderly, and the disabled.	Movement to a more specialized role in social casework.
Mass population shift from rural to urban settings.		Group work became a part of social work; formation of the National Association of the Study of Groups, 1936.	Michigan first state to pass legislation for State Department of Education reimbursement of social work services in schools, 1944.
Fair labor standards, continued development of labor movement.			
World War II: Revolt against totalitarianism and emphasis on national unity.		Lane Report on Community Organization as a method; fewer settlement houses established.	
Social Security Act of 1935.			
1946–1960			
Postwar prosperity.	Expansion of schools; crowded schools; half-day sessions.	Growth of the National Institute of Health.	Emphasis on collaboration with other school personnel; development of pupil personnel services.
Population explosion with the baby boom.	*Brown v. Board of Education* (1945): "Separate but not equal education."	Concerns about juvenile correctional institutions and delinquency.	Increase in visiting teacher programs.
Growth of metropolitan communities; migration of minorities from cities.	National Science Foundation developed (1950) to promote basic research and education in the sciences.	Growth in community chests and councils; establishment of United Foundation.	NASW by-laws provide for the establishment of School Social Work, 1955.
Television promoting image of the happy home.	Establishment of the U.S. Department of Health, Education, and Welfare, 1954.	Establishment of the U.S. Department of Health, Education, and Welfare, 1954.	
	Passage of a bill creating and funding position of elementary school counselor.		

42

1961–1970

High employment. Minority rights issues moved from civil rights to black power.	Vocational Education Act of 1963.	War on poverty; Great Society programs.	Great Cities Project funded by the Ford Foundation—developed community–school programs in 13 urban cities to bridge the gap between school and community; social workers employed as "community agents."
Women's liberation movement.	Elementary and Secondary Education Act of 1965 and the title program.	Growing ADC roles; AFDC, 1962.	Move to change name from visiting teacher to school social worker.
Report of the National Advisory Commission on Civil Disorders, 1968.	Civil Rights Act of 1964 and the Coleman Report.	Development of community social work with an emphasis on politics, social planning, and advocacy.	Recognition in literature that the school environment contributes to student learning.
Space Program.	National assessment of educational progress, 1963.	Concern with manpower issues.	Integration of group work method in school social work casework practice.
High-profile assassinations.	Supreme Court calls for immediate termination of dual school systems.	Growth of social workers in many new agencies created by the Great Society programs.	
Vietnam War and student demonstrations and protests.	Increased federal support for education.	Increased emphasis on "social systems" theory.	
Gault decision (1965), adjudicated the right of juveniles to legal representation.	Child abuse legislation in many states making school personnel, including social workers, responsible for reporting.	National Institute of Mental Health and NASW funded project entitled "Social Change and School Social Work in the '70s."	
	Move toward community control of schools.		

1971–1989

Inflation, fiscal retrenchment.	Section 504, Vocational Rehabilitation Act of 1973.	Accreditation of Bachelor of Social Work programs; development of doctoral programs; diversity of educational programs.	Increase in number of school social workers and development of new programs.
Concern for law and order; Watergate; consumerism; conservative trend.	P.L. 94-142, Education for all Handicapped Children Act.	NASW accepts BSWs for membership; new NASW code of Ethics, 1979.	Shift of service to disabled students.
Unemployment climbs.	Family Rights and Privacy Act.	Proliferation of new practice modalities.	Evaluation and accountability stressed.
Rights of people with disabilities recognized.	Drop in student enrollment; closing of school buildings.	Emphasis on research and theory development.	Emergence of ecological approach to practice in schools.
Influence of computer in business, education, and scientific advances in all areas.	Dismissal of school personnel, including some tenured persons.	Growing emphasis on the ecological perspective.	NASW task force on social work.
Continued recession with high unemployment at all levels of society.	Emphasis on accountability.		*School Social Work Journal* (NASW).
	Development of student codes of conduct.		National Conferences on School Social Work.
			NASW Committee on Social Work in Schools (1976).

(continued)

TABLE 2.3 Continued

Social Trends and Movements	Public Education	Social Work	School Social Work
Reduction in social programs and aid to the poor.	Violence in schools becomes more prevalent.	Development of integrated or generalist methods.	Provisional Council on Social Work Services in Schools created (1979).
Conservative national policies.	Concern about illiteracy at graduation.	Growth of state licensing laws.	NASW Board creates Practice Advancement Council on Social Work Services in Schools.
Beginning of the PC era and other technological advances.	Bilingual education programs.	Increases in number of social work journals.	Commission on Education created by NASW, 1985.
	Development of preschool public education.	Development of specializations in graduate social work programs.	First comprehensive book published on School Social Work, 1986.
	Increased number of private schools.	Emphasis on prevention of social and mental health problems.	Decrease in number of social workers in schools because of economic situation and decrease in enrollment.
	Continued reduction of school programs.	Continued rise of "clinical social work" movement and private practice.	School Social Work track in NASW conferences (1988, 1990)
	Reduced federal support to education.	Increased emphasis on the evaluation of practice and accountability.	National Survey of School Social Workers, in collaboration with Allen-Meares, ETS, and NASW.
	Development of Office of Education.	Integration of research and practice.	Links with related National organizations take on more importance (e.g., National Association of School Psychologists, Council on Exceptional Children).
	Threat to eliminate the Office of Education.		
	Increased development of vocational education.		
	Evaluations of education urge an overhaul to the system.		
1990–present			
Increase in children and families living in *extreme* poverty, particularly in single-parent and minority homes.	Increased pressure for choice and alternative schools as a result of a decrease in confidence in the public schools	In 1993, a new structure was adopted by the NASW Board of Directors, which created optional specialty practice sections. The first section is School Social Work.	A trend exists that creates integrated collaborative services in which schools and community agencies provide health, mental health, and social services to children and families in or near schools. School social workers are the "glue-factor" for the collaboratives.
Continuing concerns of substance abuse, homelessness, domestic violence, unemployment, and underemployment.	Many states move toward statewide academic standards and assessments in an attempt to increase performance standards of students and schools.	Increased community-based vs. residential-based services.	

Continuing transition from Industrial to Technological Age.	Increase in public preschool, day care programs, and after-school care.	Call for a better understanding of the influence of chronic urban violence on teens.	Increase in school-based linked services.
Political emphasis on welfare and health-care reform.	Increase in violence in schools.	Continued increase in private practice.	School social workers serve more populations (e.g., Head Start, children with disabilities, alternative education).
Increasingly diverse U.S. population. Highest immigration rates since the 1920s.	Call for more school–community partnerships to improve school and student performance.	Increased development of social work services in business and industry.	School social work becomes NASW's first Section—more than 16,000 signed the petition.
Shift in immigrant countries of origin from Europe to Asia, Latin America, the Caribbean, and Africa. Attention to new immigrants.	Continued debate on public vs. private education.	A call for more political action.	Some states adopt competency requirements for practice. New standards for School Social Work Services, 1992, revised in 2002.
Increase in violence as a means of resolving conflict.	Increased pressure to fully include special education students in general education classes.	More emphasis on research to undergird evidence-based practice.	Increased emphasis on coordination of family, school, and community—an ecological approach.
Debates of gay and lesbian issues and rights.	Pressure comes from the courts, statutes, and advocacy groups.	NIMH research centers focus on mental health of children and families.	Provides services to reduce or eliminate substance abuse and violence in schools.
Awareness of precarious economy in light of federal deficit.	Extension of school services to at-risk and disabled children prior to them beginning kindergarten.	Emphasis on family preservation.	Increased emphasis on multidisciplinary work.
Increased U.N. and U.S. involvement in international conflicts and issues.	Comprehensive Health Education, which includes sex education and other concerns, such as HIV/AIDS.	Increase in number of specializations.	Position statement on the School Social Worker and Confidentiality.
HIV/AIDS reached epidemic proportions.	Debates on teaching human sexuality.	Move toward solution-focused, short-term interventions.	Elimination of NASW Commission on Education.
Passage of the Americans with Disabilities Act (ADA).	American Education Act passes, 1994.	Social workers support the view that homosexuality is not a mental health disorder, but is a normal form of sexuality.	School social workers required to have active role in early childhood special education, and in some states are the lead agency in the delivery of services.
Increase in school-age population, reaching record number of students each year until 2017.	Increased emphasis on technology in schools.	NASW involved in legal developments for LGBT rights and Supreme Court decisions.	Development of National School Social Work Association.
Increase in self-advocacy and empowerment among varied groups.	Charter schools.	With the aging baby boom generation, there has been a greater need for social workers with specialized knowledge in aging.	
An increased move toward inclusion in all sectors.	Wraparound services for children with complex needs.	NASW Code of Ethics highlights that social workers will not discriminate on the basis of sexual orientation.	
People first language (i.e., child with disabilities, not disabled child).	Increasing recognition of need for developing community in schools.		
	Growing home school movement.		

(continued)

TABLE 2.3 Continued

Social Trends and Movements	Public Education	Social Work	School Social Work
Elimination of entitlements to welfare; passage of welfare reform.	No Child Left Behind Act, 2001.	Social workers embrace technology for ongoing evaluation and database management.	National NASW School Social Work Specialist credential issued in 2002.
Research on brain development focuses new emphasis on the importance of early development.	Mental health services contracted out to other agencies.	Social work has become one of the fastest-growing careers in the U.S., expected to increase by 30% between 2002 and 2010.	Guidelines for HIV/AIDS student support services.
More grandparents and other nonparental family members parenting children.	Increase in the use of schools of choice for student enrollment.		Transition planning for special education students.
	Increase in public school enrollment.	There are now 42 different specializations in social work.	In some states, the social worker acts as advocate/parental surrogate for children in residential facilities.
Increased homelessness as housing becomes a larger percentage of income.	Students from low-income areas are more likely to drop out of school.	Social workers are the largest groups of mental health service providers; there are more social workers than psychiatrists, psychologists, and psychiatric nurses combined.	School social workers continue to work with lawmakers to reauthorize the Elementary School Counseling Act.
Decreasing teen pregnancy rates across the U.S. Teen pregnancy is still an issue for concern.	The Safe Schools/Healthy Students initiative created to reduce violence in schools.		
Child care continues to be debated in Congress on funding allocations.	Overall increase in academic performance in mathematics and the sciences.	Social work is recognized by law as one of the five core mental health professions.	Promote safe schools and positive environments for LGBT students.
Child abuse remains an underestimated issue in the U.S.	Increased demand for bilingual education due to immigration.		Improved use of technology for database management and intervention evaluation.
The aging baby boom generation and lengthening life span has increase the proportion of older people in the population.	Increase in emphasis on accountability through standardized testing.		Work to promote positive intervention to reduce problems associated with bullying in schools.
			Legal encouragement for evidence-based practice in schools.

Source for the discussion on education comes largely from Ronald F. Campbell et al., *The Organization and Control of American Schools*, 3rd ed. (Columbus, OH: Charles E. Merrill, 1975) reprinted with permission and Livingston, A., & Wirt, J. (2004). *The condition of education 2004: In brief*, National Center for Education Statistics (NCES 2004-076); the source for the discussion on social work and societal trends in Louise C. Johnson, *Social Work Practice: A Generalist Approach*. Copyright © 1983 by Allyn and Bacon, Inc., reprinted with permission and the National Association of Social Workers (2005). *School social work profession*. Retrieved from http://naswdc.org on August 15, 2005; the source for the discussion on recent immigration comes largely from Lauterbach, S. (Ed.). (2004). *The United States in 2005: Who we are today. Society & Values, 9*(2), 1–46; and the source for the discussion on school dropout and socioeconomic status come from Crowder, K., & South, S. J. (2003). Neighborhood distress and school dropout: The variable significance of community context. *Social Science Research, 32*, 659–698.

For Study and Discussion

1. Identify positive and negative vestiges of the historical development of social work services that exist in schools today.
2. Identify and discuss reasons why social workers in schools have been so preoccupied with role definition.
3. Visit a local school and talk with administrators, other school personnel, and the social worker about their roles and tasks. Find out how they "team" and what factors undermine teaming. Also obtain their opinions about what each discipline contributes to the education of children. Is there overlap?

4. Identify several social forces or conditions that presently have a direct bearing on education in the United States. What are the implications for social work practice in the schools? What are the implications for the educational preparations of social workers?
5. Obtain a copy of the *NASW Standards for Social Services in the Schools.* Evaluate these standards in light of contemporary educational issues and concerns. What targets of service would you give most attention to? Why?

Additional Readings

Allen-Meares, P. (1992). International and multicultural themes relevant to school social work. *Social Work in Education, 14*(3)

Allen-Meares, P. (1996). The new federal role in education and family services: Goal setting without responsibility. *Social Work, 41*(5), 533–540.

Allen-Meares, P., Hudgins, C. A., Engberg, M. E., & Lessnau, B. (2005). Using a collaboratory model to translate social work research into practice and policy. *Research on Social Work Practice, 15*(1), 29–40.

Browne, G., Gafni, A., Roberts, J., Byrne, C., & Majumdar, B. (2004). Effective/efficient mental health programs for school-age children: A synthesis of reviews. *Social Science & Medicine, 58*(7), 1367–1384.

Daly, B. P., Burke, R., Hare, I., Mills, C., Owens, C., Moore, E., et al. (2006). Enhancing No Child Left Behind—school mental health connections. *The Journal of School Health, 76*(9), 446–451.

Eyal, O. (2008). Caught in the net: The network-entrepreneurship connection in public schools. *International Journal of Educational Management, 22,* 386–398.

Ford Foundation. (1989). *The common good: Social welfare and the American future.* New York: Ford Foundation.

Franklin, C. (2005). The future of school social work: Challenges and opportunities. *Advances in Social Work, 6*(1), 139–160.

Gelman, C. R., & Tosone, C. (2008). Teaching social workers to harness technology and inter-disciplinary collaboration for community service. *British Journal of Social Work,* doi:10.1093/bjsw/bcn081.

Killeen, K. (2007). How the media misleads the story of school consumerism: A perspective from school finance. *Peabody Journal of Education, 82*(1), 32–62.

Kozol, J. (1995). *Amazing grace: The lives of children and the conscience of a nation.* New York: Crown Publishers.

Magolda, P., & Ebben, K. (2007). From schools to community learning centers: A program evaluation of a school reform process. *Evaluation and Program Planning, 30*(4), 351–363.

Mitra, D. L. (2008). *Student voice in school reform: Building youth–adult partnerships that strengthen schools and empower youth.* Albany: State University of New York Press.

Pahwa, B. A. (Ed.). (2003). *Technology-assisted delivery of school based mental health services.* Binghamton, NY: Haworth Press.

Parton, N. (2008). Changes in the form of knowledge in social work: From the "social" to the "informational"? *British Journal of Social Work, 38*(2), 253–269. doi:10.1093/bjsw/bcl337.

Radin, N. (1989). School social work services: Past, present, and future trends. *Social Work in Education, 11*(4), 213–225.

Rubin, L. J., & Borgers, S. B. (1991). The changing family: Implications for education. *Principal, 71*(1), 11–13.

Smokowski, P. R., & Hartung, K. (2003). Computer simulation and virtual reality: Enhancing the practice of school social work. *Journal of Technology in Human Services, 21*(1/2), 5–30.

Vernon, R. (2005). Technology convergence and social work: When case management meets geographic information. *Advances in Social Work, 6*(1), 91–96.

Weist, M. D., Goldstein, J., Evans, S. W., Lever, N. A., Axelrod, J., Schreters, R., et al. (2003). Funding a full continuum of mental health promotion and intervention programs in the schools. *Journal of Adolescent Health, 32*(6S), 70–78.

3

Social Organization and Schools: A General Systems Theory Perspective

GARY L. BOWEN

The University of North Carolina at Chapel Hill

Introduction

Social workers bring a perspective to practice in schools that focuses on the transactions between people and their social environments as the primary unit of analysis in planning and implementing social interventions (Richman, Bowen, & Woolley, 2004). This transactional or person–environment fit perspective emphasizes the environments forming children's ecosystem (e.g., school, community, family), the system-level interfaces between the environments in which children live and function (e.g., schools and neighborhoods, schools, and families), and the larger institutional forces that frame and shape environments for children and youth at all levels (e.g., funding for social work services in schools). Social work interventions should and can occur within any system, or any combination of systems, that impinge negatively on students' functioning at the microlevel or the performance of schools at the macrolevel.

School social workers must have a working understanding of the collective processes that influence student functioning and learning outcomes. For example, if the social climate of the school lacks warmth, support, and incentives, then learning and teaching become difficult. If the neighborhood in which the student lives is unsafe

and lacks supportive adults to monitor the behavior of children and youth who live there, the student may not have a safe route between home and school. Consequently, the students may be less prepared to learn when they arrive at school. The school social worker is in a position to intervene directly or to collaborate with others to change the quality of these collective processes.

This chapter focuses on the school as a social system. In particular, I focus on social organizational processes in schools that distinguish high-performing from low-performing schools. Also, I examine the functioning of schools in the broader community and how the local environments in which students are embedded influence their school performance. General systems theory provides concepts that are useful for understanding and analyzing the functioning of schools and the broader context in which they function. I focus specific attention on the general systems theory concept of social organization and the application of this concept to the schools that students attend and the neighborhoods in which they reside.

Schools are a specific type of social system that sociologists label *formal organization*. Unlike informal organizations that are more voluntaristic and typically less organized networks of personal and collective relationships, formal organizations are social systems that have been "planfully instituted" to accomplish specific objectives and typically have more rigidly enforced rules and norms that govern social interaction and performance (Bertalanffy, 1968, p. 9). As stated in Chapter 1, schools in America exist to prepare children and youth to participate as citizens in a democratic society and to develop specialized abilities to function successfully as workers in the economy.

A General Systems Theory Perspective

General systems theory, which has been used as an integrative perspective in social work education since the mid-1950s, provides an organized means for studying schools as dynamic environments and for studying the multifaceted interactions between schools and other segments of society. General systems theory uses assumptions and concepts from the systems paradigm to study living beings and their interrelationships at multiple levels (Barker, 1999).

Using an organismic metaphor to describe formal organizations (e.g., schools) with the same principles and concepts used to describe biological organisms, general systems theory is most closely associated with Ludwig von Bertalanffy (1968), whose work in the 1920s and 1930s captured the dynamic relationship between biological organisms and their environment. A Viennese biologist, Bertalanffy brought together the common principles of an evolving "systems" approach in such diverse disciplines as biology, the social sciences, and economics under the rubric of general systems theory. Bertalanffy defined a system as "sets of elements standing in interrelation" (p. 38). Social systems theory applies a general systems perspective to humans, individuals, or groups of individuals standing in interrelation (Bausch, 2001).

General systems theory shares a close kinship with Lewin's (1951) psychological field theory and ecological theories (Bronfenbrenner, 1979; Lerner, 1995). Structural concepts from ecological theory (microsystems), which are reviewed in Chapter 4, may be combined with dynamic concepts from general systems theory (e.g., positive and negative feedback) to create an ecosystems perspective for social work practice (Szapocznik & Williams, 2000; Van Wormer, Besthorn, & Keefe, 2007).

As a core perspective in the knowledge base of school social work (Freeman, 1995), general systems theory helps the school social worker to understand that schools are social systems with complex properties and subsystems (parts of the larger whole) and suprasystems (environmental contexts). As open systems with permeable boundaries, schools function in dynamic equilibrium with their environments; that is, they have both internal and external inputs and outputs. Open systems tend to maintain themselves in steady states through feedback processes (positive and negative feedback loops) that operate through the dynamic interplay of subsystems and suprasystems.

A major assumption of general systems theory is that all systems are purposeful and goal directed. Human or social systems are self-aware in their purposefulness, whereas other types of living systems are simply self-monitoring (Whitchurch & Constantine, 1993). As a social system, a school exists to achieve objectives through the collective effort of individuals and groups in the system. For example, student achievement as reflected in grades, end-of-grade and end-of-course performance evaluations, and graduation rates are major purposeful goals of schools as social systems.

Schools as Goal Oriented

The simplest example of a school as a social system is a single school with a student body, teachers, and an administration. Edgar Schein (1985) has described two major goals of social systems, such as schools, that interact in a highly interdependent state: (a) external adaptation, which addresses the mission and purpose of the system, and (b) internal integration, which addresses the internal functioning of the system. Although it is possible that a school could evidence high levels of internal integration without achieving a similar level of external adaptation, the converse is unlikely. A school without internal bonds of commitment, supportive cohesion, and a sense of caring and support is unlikely to achieve its mission. Yet, according to Schein, internal integration is promoted by successful performance or by high levels of external adaptation. We may have all felt the highly positive emotion of being part of a winning team. In addition, schools may achieve similar levels of external adaptation and internal integration in different ways. General systems theory uses the concept of *equifinality* to describe the ability of social systems to arrive at the same end point from different starting points and from the use of different strategies and combinations of strategies.

In the context of managing the problems of external adaptation and internal integration, social systems develop group boundaries that define insiders and outsiders and rules for behavior that regulate interactions and exchanges. Over time, they also develop cultures, which Schein (1985) defined as "a pattern of basic assumptions—invented, discovered, or developed by a given group as it learns to cope with its problems of external adaptation and internal integration—that has worked well enough to be considered valid and, therefore, to be taught to new members as the correct way to perceive, think, and feel in relation to those problems" (p. 9). A less complex description of culture is simply "how we do things around here." Cultures may be overt or covert, positive or negative, and supportive or unsupportive in achieving the system-level goals of external adaptation and internal integration.

Learning organizations are a special type of organizational culture, which are consistent with schools as goal-oriented social systems (Hiatt-Michael, 2001; Senge et al., 2000). Bowen, Rose, and Ware (2006) associated learning organizations with "a core set of conditions and processes that support the ability of an organization to value, acquire, and use information and tacit knowledge acquired from employees and stakeholders to successfully plan, implement, and evaluate strategies to achieve performance goals" (pp. 98–99). Importantly, this description expands the organizational boundary to include not only employees, but also those served by the organization. In the case of schools, this would include students, their parents, and community members. Schools that function as learning organizations operate flexibly, make decisions in a decentralized manner, embrace trial-and-error learning, focus on achievable goals in a limited number of high-priority areas, and remain open to new ways of working in the context of organizational goals (Argyris, 1992; Hiatt-Michael, 2001; Orthner & Bowen, 2004). The collective expressions of positive regard and support among employees that reinforce internal integration and social harmony are also important to the functioning of schools as learning organizations (Bowen, Ware, Rose, & Powers, 2007). Principals set the tone for development of learning cultures in schools by accepting challenges to their authority; seeking involvement from students, parents, and community stakeholders; and encouraging new ideas from teachers and school staff (Leithwood, Jantzi, & Steinbach, 1998; Lick, 2006).

In a recent study in middle schools (Bowen et al., 2006), the more the employees of a school affirmed the operation of the school as a learning organization, the more likely they were to report better health, higher job satisfaction, greater likelihood to continue their employment at the school for another year, greater belief in their capacity to make a positive difference in the school's ability to meet its performance objectives for students, and more positive views about both the actual performance and the potential performance of the school in addressing the educational needs of all students. Recent efforts to train school employees in organizational learning have shown promise, as demonstrated by Orthner, Cook, Sabah, and Rosenfeld (2006) in a cross-national pilot-test of training in organizational learning for staffs of after-school programs in Israel and the United States. The framing of a learning question as a starting point for discussion was a key component of this training. Sabah and Orthner (2007) emphasized the importance of schools continually posing and addressing learning questions to improve performance.

Subsystems

The success of a school in achieving its goals depends in large part on the facilitating effects of several subsystems within the system. Subsystems, which include classrooms, teachers, and social workers, are designed to achieve order and organization in the face of environmental demands. Subsystems represent a division of labor and are designed to promote the external adaptation and internal integration of social systems. The classroom, and the functioning of teachers within the classroom, is one of the most defining subsystems in schools.

Component subsystems do not usually all have equal power—some individuals and subgroups have greater power than others. *Power* is defined as the ability to make decisions and to influence the actions and behavior of others. Like businesses, schools are typically hierarchical social systems. The principal and his or her management team are the sanctioned leaders in a school. Teachers and other professional staff members, such as school social workers, operate under the authority of the principal and the management team, and students are at the bottom of the hierarchy (see Figure 3.1). Student groups may be more or less organized in schools to exercise more influence and control over decisions and to gain access to scarce resources (see Waller's 1965, classic discussion of the ways in which student groups may wield power and influence in schools).

James Coleman (1997) described schools as an example of an "administratively-driven organization" (p. 16). These highly centralized organizations have long feedback loops from the top of the organization (e.g., the principal) to each component subsystem (e.g., teachers, students). Coleman contrasted "administratively-driven organizations" with "output driven organizations," which he described as allocating power and decision-making authority at multiple levels (p. 16). Coleman considered schools with decentralized authority structures and norms of accountability and social support as

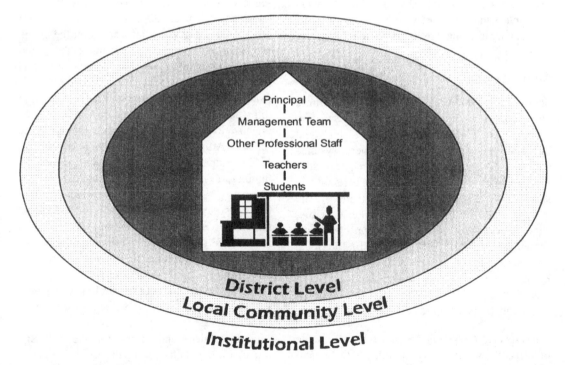

FIGURE 3.1 The Organizational Structure of Schools: Subsystems and Suprasystems *Source:* Author

having more promise than those with traditional bureaucratic forms for increasing teacher and student performance.

Subsystems may be examined either as parts of a larger system or as social systems in their own right. Central to understanding this idea is that any system is by definition both part and whole. General systems theory uses the concept, *holon,* to describe this ability to see the same entity from either perspective. For example, a single classroom may be studied as a social system. Its inputs and processes, however, are tied to the operating processes of the entire school. Pupils and teachers leave and enter the classrooms; materials and physical facilities are provided; even social relationships are regulated in terms of classroom norms as well as products of the larger school, the school district, and educational establishment. Conversely, the social system of the classroom is composed of an intricate network of interactions and relationships composed of physical seating arrangements, status hierarchies, racial differences, authority structures, and differences in learning histories, ability, sex, and age. Members of the class may alternately be studied as systems based on dyads, small groups, or as a holon.

Suprasystems

Schools are open systems; they operate within a larger context with which they exchange matter, energy, and information through formal and informal feedback processes. In general systems terminology, *environment* is defined as the totality of physical and social factors that are external to a system's boundaries and exert an influence on the system. Three levels of external influence are discussed next as providing a context for school performance: (a) the district level, (b) the local community level, and (c) the institutional level. From a general systems theory perspective, a school functions in dynamic *interaction* with its larger context (see Figure 3.1).

The District Level. Typically, schools operate in a larger complex of school units, both elementary and secondary, each with its own administrator

and teaching staff, overlaid with a systemwide administrative cadre. In moderately complex systems, this administrative cadre consists of a chief administrator (superintendent), who is responsible for the direction of all system activities, and his or her immediate staff. In more complex systems, there may also be administrative echelons for directing instructional activities (e.g., directors of elementary or secondary education), multiple hierarchies for providing supportive professional and nonprofessional services (e.g., a director of personnel), and a large number of individuals holding staff positions in agencies attached to the superintendent's office. School reform at the district level may focus on policies about the allocation of scarce resources to individual schools, including decisions about teacher–student ratios and about the employment of school social workers.

The Local Community Level. Schools also operate in a local community context, which includes community structure and processes. *Community* is defined as "the proximate spatial setting in which schools are located and in which students reside" (Bowen & Richman, 2002, p. 68). This local setting includes a physical infrastructure; the quality and kind of community resources; the demographic and social profile of the community, which varies according to social class, age, and racial and ethnic composition; the community power structure; and community norms that influence the organizational structure and functioning of the school (Arum, 2000; Furstenberg & Hughes, 1997). Employers, places of worship, neighbors, families, peer groups, and public and private community agencies are all part of this local community ecosystem, which includes schools. Many of the entities at the local community level may be classified as *constituencies* of the school system—people and organizations with a vested interest in school and student-level performance.

An important focus of research from a general systems theory perspective is the effects of structural features (e.g., availability and access to support services and programs) and collective processes (e.g., behavioral patterns) in both communities and schools on school-related outcomes.

School reform at the local community level may focus attention on building and strengthening the networks of relationships among institutions and community members that support student achievement (Timpane & Reich, 1997).

The Institutional Level. Schools also are situated in larger, nonlocal, institutional contexts—a focus that will resonate well with many social workers involved in management and community practice. Arum (2000), who distinguished these broader contexts from local community structures and processes, defined these contexts as "organizational fields" (p. 395).

These organizational fields, which influence policies and practices at the local community and school levels, include federal and state public welfare policies, mechanisms for financing and administering health and social services, court decisions, policies from state boards of education, the functioning of labor unions and teacher associations, training curriculums in schools of education, and marketplace dynamics. For example, changes in federal and state policies, such as the No Child Left Behind Act (NCLB) of 2001, have led to stringent testing standards that have compelled school systems to experiment with new policies and practices to promote student achievement and attain substantial year-to-year improvements in rates of proficiency. Federal funding, as part of the NCLB Act, for development of 21st Century Community Learning Centers has stimulated new partnerships between schools and local community agencies and organizations in support of student achievement (Anderson-Butcher, 2004). The education initiative also describes the need for implementing research-based practices in schools to meet the higher standards of accountability (Christensen, 2004; Issacs, 2003). More specifically, the NCLB policy states more than 100 times that educators should support their practices by utilizing "scientifically based research" (Raines, 2004).

Research by Orthner, Cook, Rose, and Randolph (2002) demonstrated the value of assuming such a broad perspective in examining school-related outcomes. Combining administrative data

from school and public agency sources on both adults and children who received public welfare, the authors examined the relationship between children's performance in school and the recent implementation of more aggressive welfare reform strategies. The results suggested higher rates of school dropout for successive ninth-grade entry cohorts of children (1993–1994 to 1999–2000) living in poverty whose families received cash assistance through Temporary Assistance to Needy Families (TANF). Although the authors were careful to assert the limitations of their data, the findings suggest that the goals of welfare reform and the goal of school success for children from poor families may need some reconsideration. The authors recommended that welfare reform legislation reflect more of a family perspective—strategies that are attentive to the needs of both parents and children.

School reform from a neoinstitutional perspective addresses these larger political, social, and professional forces. Such forces shape the opportunity structure and the normative environment for school success either directly or indirectly through local community structure and processes.

Social Organization

Schools and communities across this nation generally consider students' academic performance as the primary indicator of school success. However, the latest statistics about educational outcomes are not encouraging. In the context of structural shifts in the American economy that have increased the importance of educational success and postsecondary education (Vernez, Krop, & Rydell, 1999), many students are failing to complete high school; many others are finishing school with limited skills in reading and mathematics and without the academic qualifications to further their education (Amos, 2008). Generally, American students perform lower in math and science than their counterparts in other developed nations, and the relative performance standing of American students falls significantly from grade 4 to grade 12 (Haycock & Huang, 2001; Organisation for Economic Co-operation and Development, 2004). Students from low-income homes and African-American and His-panic/Latino students are particularly likely to face challenges in meeting performance standards at each grade level, demonstrating the requisite academic skills for promotion from one grade to the next, completing high school, graduating from high school with the qualifications necessary to attend a four-year college, and pursuing and com-pleting some form of postsecondary education (Gladieux & Swail, 1998; Haycock & Huang, 2001; KewalRamani, Gilbertson, Fox, & Provasnik, 2007; Richman et al., 2004). The academic gap between income and racial/ethnic groups looms large, and trends in low achievement and school failure start early.

This chapter is based on the premise that social organizational processes in school and community systems can be understood and con-trolled in the interest of promoting outcomes associated with successful school performance and that the primary function of school social work is to help in that process. *Social organization* is a dimension of social systems that refers to net-works of relationships among people, their pat-terns of exchange and levels of reciprocity, and the degree to which they provide instrumental and expressive support to one another in achieving their individual and collective goals (Mancini, Martin, & Bowen, 2003). Social organization also includes accepted standards and norms that inform and regulate individual and collective behavior, such as expectations for social responsi-bility and mutual support for one another, and the content and extent of shared values that support these standards and norms (Furstenberg & Hughes, 1997; Sampson, 2001).

It is important to note several caveats in this definition of social organization. First, social orga-nization is not a property of an individual; it is an emergent and collective property of a social system that is associated with individual and collective outcomes. The emergent property of social organi-zation is captured in the concept of *wholeness* from general systems theory.

Second, as defined earlier, the concept of social organization is closely related to the concept of internal integration, which was defined earlier as a critical goal of social systems. In discussing the concept of internal integration, Schein (1985) made the following statement: "What keeps a group together, its 'reason to be,' or what I have called the 'external adaptation function,' is quite different from the processes of creating that togeth-erness, processes that make groups capable of accomplishing things that individuals alone cannot accomplish" (p. 65). The internal integration or the cohesion of a group is considered a component of social organization, which is a broader and more encompassing concept. Social organizational proc-esses may also include dimensions of external adaptation or performance expectations, which is exemplified later in the discussion of academic press in school environments.

Third, it is important to distinguish social structure from social process. In their review of neighborhoods as a context for child develop-ment, Furstenberg and Hughes (1997) distin-guished social organization from structural features of social systems, which they describe with regard to their physical infrastructure, social and demographic features, and institutional resources. These structural features operate as a context for social organizational processes in schools and communities; they influence out-comes for children and youth indirectly through their direct influence on these collective processes (Lee, Dedrick, & Smith, 1991; Sampson, 2001).

In the sections that follow, examples of social organizational processes in schools and communi-ties are provided that are associated with student achievement. In schools, research is reviewed that examines the influence of *academic press* and *sense of community* on student achievement. In commu-nities, attention is focused on the burgeoning research related to influence of neighborhoods on school-related outcomes. Attention is focused on two key social organizational processes in neigh-borhoods: *social control* and *social support.*

The discussion of social organizational proc-esses in schools and communities is informed by the work of a number of behavioral and social scientists who have examined how dimensions of social organization influence outcomes for children and youth (Croninger & Lee, 2001; Furstenberg, Cook, Eccles, Elder, & Sameroff, 1999; Leventhal & Brooks-Gunn, 2000). The seminal research of James Coleman (1997) in examining schools as social institutions anchors the analysis. Coleman's (1988) concept of social capital is a theoretical cornerstone in the analysis of social organizational processes in schools and communities. As discussed by Coleman (1988), social capital is an enabling resource emanating from social relations that allows individuals to achieve otherwise unattainable outcomes. Coleman identified three forms of social capital that are consistent with the present conceptualization of social organization: reciprocal obligations, information sharing, and social norms. Framed by this social capital perspective, attention is turned first to social organizational processes in schools.

Schools

The Coleman Report (1966), *Equality of Educational Opportunity,* which was published by Coleman and his associates more than 40 years ago, is a useful starting point in discussing social organizational processes in schools that are associated with student outcomes (see Shouse, 2002, for a brief overview of this report and its major findings). In examining gaps in academic achievement across racial/ethnic and socioeconomic groups, Coleman and his associates included in their investigation a focus on the influence of school-level factors on student-level achievement. A number of important findings emerged from the analysis. Perhaps the most surprising finding in the context of this review was the general weak effect of teacher characteristics (e.g., education and experience) and school resource factors (physical facilities, curricula, per-pupil spending) on student achievement. Although the findings of Coleman and his associates have been the target of numerous methodological critiques, their findings have prompted researchers to look beyond structural correlates of student achievement to

examine social organizational processes within schools that may help account for differences in achievement across racial/ethnic and socioeconomic groups. From a general systems theory perspective, researchers are attempting to identify the *throughputs* that connect *educational inputs,* such as average pupils per class, to *educational outputs,* such as student achievement (Shouse, 2002, p. 520).

Academic Press and Sense of Community.   A significant body of research has established two key social organizational processes in schools as important correlates of student achievement: academic press and sense of community (Bryk & Driscoll, 1988; Bryk, Lee, & Holland, 1993; Lee & Smith, 1999; Phillips, 1997; Royal & Rossi, 1996; Shouse, 1997). Shouse defined the first, academic press, as "the degree to which school organizations are driven by achievement oriented values, goals, and norms" (p. 61). According to Shouse, schools with high academic press provide students with diverse and challenging courses, recognize and reward high performance, expect students to attend school and complete homework, provide an attractive and safe environment for students, and employ teachers that use innovative teaching strategies, make assignments meaningful and challenging, and have high expectations for student learning and performance.

Sense of community is the second key social organizational feature associated with student achievement. Although definitions of sense of community are often fairly abstract and elusive, the most central feature of schools with a strong sense of community is a spirit of caring that governs social interactions within and between all levels of the school organization. A central feature of communality is the nature of the relationship between teachers and students, such as the degree to which students perceive teachers as caring about them and respecting and appreciating them as individuals (Bowen, Rose, & Bowen, 2005; Crosnoe, Johnson, & Elder, 2004).

As described by Bryk et al. (1993), this *ethic of caring is* reinforced by two additional components of sense of community: *shared values* that promote a common agenda and encourage social responsibility and *shared activities* that offer opportunities for social interaction and reinforce communal norms (pp. 277–278). In schools that evidence these two additional components of communality, there is a crystallization of values and norms among adults at school about academic goals and school priorities, and all students are encouraged and afforded opportunities to participate fully in school-related activities. Royal and Rossi (1997) see respect for diversity as an additional component of sense of community.

Research Findings.   From this discussion, student achievement would be expected to be highest in schools with both high academic press and a high sense of community. On the other hand, student achievement would be expected to be lowest in schools in which academic press and sense of community are both low. School-level research by Shouse (1997) suggests a more complex relationship between these two features of social organization. First, in examining the mathematics test scores of a national sample of high-school students, Shouse reported that academic press had a positive and significant effect on student mathematics achievement. On the other hand, the positive influence of sense of community was virtually eliminated once academic press was entered into the predictive equation. In other words, in the context of academic press, school sense of community did not have a statistically significant influence on student math achievement. In an examination of the mathematics achievement and attendance of middle school students, Phillips (1997) reported a similar finding.

In combination, these findings might bring into question the impact of sense of community on student achievement. However, Shouse (1997) took his analysis a step further by examining the influence of academic press and sense of community by the average socioeconomic status (SES) of students attending schools in the sample (low, mid, and high). He also subdivided both school-level academic press and sense of community into low, mid, and high categories for purposes of this interactive analysis. His findings revealed that the influence of sense of community on student achievement must be considered in the context of both academic press and the school's socioeconomic level.

Academic press had its strongest effect on student achievement in low-SES schools. In low-SES schools, sense of community enhanced student achievement when academic press was high. However, at low-SES schools with a low level of academic press, higher levels of sense of community actually lowered student achievement. Math achievement was lowest for those students who attended schools with low academic press and a high sense of community. In a subsequent publication, Boyd and Shouse (1997) described the paradigmatic motto of these schools as "No one fails here who shows up" (p. 149). In examining these findings, Shouse drew the following conclusion: "For low-SES schools, a strong academic context serves as a prerequisite for communality's positive achievement effects" (p. 73).

In middle-SES schools, sense of community enhanced student achievement at all three levels of academic press (low, mid, and high). The combined effects were particularly pronounced at those schools with both high academic press and high sense of community. Sense of community played an even more important role in high-SES schools. In these schools, student achievement was more dependent on sense of community than academic press. Academic press had little influence at high-SES schools with a high sense of community. Shouse (1997) argued that students from more affluent families are more likely than students from lower-income families to have ties with adults outside the school who stress academic achievement. Consequently, they have less dependence on school as a source of academic press.

Discussion.   These findings are perhaps both illuminating and frustrating for school social workers. On one hand, they reinforce what many school social workers already know: Social interventions must be tailored to reflect the uniqueness of each school. On the other hand, they indicate the power of research to identify social organizational processes that are leverage points in promoting student achievement. The findings have particular relevance for schools in which school social workers are most likely to be employed—schools with a high proportion of low-income students. In these schools, the development of a caring and nurturing school environment is likely to have greater positive consequences on student achievement when academic press is high. Promoting a high sense of community in low-SES schools with low academic press may actually have a counterproductive effect on student achievement. As Shouse (1997) stated, the educational experiences of students in these schools may be more "socially therapeutic" than "academically challenging" (pp. 64–65).

The challenge for social work practitioners is to develop empirically based intervention strategies for influencing these outcomes. School-based interventions, such as Project Peace (de Anda, 1999) and Project ACHIEVE (Knoff & Batsche, 1995), are cases in point. Project Peace works to promote a safer and more supportive school climate, greater student confidence in adults at school, and more affirming peer interaction. Project ACHIEVE, which is designed to assist schools in increasing academic press, includes school-level planning and problem-solving techniques, staff and curriculum development, social and behavioral interventions, and parent training. However, as noted earlier, schools do not exist in isolation from the broader community in which they are situated. Successful interventions to promote students' academic outcomes require not only an understanding of the school environment, but also the community environment in which the school is located. We now shift our attention from the school to the community social environment.

Communities

As in schools, it is also possible to examine social organizational processes in the communities in which schools are located. For our purpose, we are interested in how these processes spill over to influence both student outcomes and social organizational processes at the school level. Durkheim was one of the first scholars to discuss the interdependency between schools and the surrounding community (Boocock, 1973); in the tradition of Durkheim, Benbenishty and Astor's (2005) heuristic model of school violence depicts the spillover of neighborhood factors (e.g., crime rates) on student victimization at school.

Although schools mirror the larger community of which they are a part, researchers and practitioners often treat schools as if they were insular. However, relatively few students attend boarding schools where they live on campus and where faculty function as surrogate parents. (And even these students are not captives in school-based enclaves with no contact with the external world.) Most students live in family households, and these households are located in residential communities or neighborhoods. The distance of the school from the students' residences may vary from a few blocks to many miles, and students at a school may be drawn from multiple locations in the community. Irrespective of the distance traveled from home to school and the number of locations from which students are drawn, from a general systems theory perspective, students transport matter, information, and energy across the boundaries of systems in which they participate. Events and situations in one setting have implications for events and situations in other settings, and the respective cultures in the settings may have more or less similar rules for engagement, interaction, and success.

Both researchers and practitioners increasingly recognize the local community as an important setting for child and youth development (Booth & Crouter, 2001). This attention has been spurred in part by Coleman's (1988) work on social capital as a resource that exists within and between multiple microsystems, social work's adoption of the ecological theory as a guiding framework for practice (see Chapter 4), and a renewed emphasis on community practice in social work (Bowen, Martin, Mancini, & Nelson, 2000; Johnson, 1998; Sviridoff & Ryan, 1997). Social workers today realize that schools cannot solve the complex challenges faced by many students in succeeding academically at school (Bowen & Richman, 2002). As concluded by Turner (1998), human service professionals today increasingly search for "the holy grail of community and neighborhood" in an attempt to strengthen the effectiveness of their interventions (p. ix).

Social Control and Social Support.   This section addresses two interrelated social organizational processes in neighborhoods: social control and social support. Recent studies are highlighted as illustrative of neighborhood effects that demonstrate the negative influence of crime and disorder (lack of social control) and the positive influence of support from neighbors (presence of social support) on the educational behavior and academic achievement of middle- and high-school students. Neighborhoods are defined from a geographical perspective as the spatial settings in which children and youth reside. This definition is conceptually similar to the one proposed by Sampson, Raudenbush, and Earls (1997): "a collection of people and institutions occupying a subsection of a larger community" (p. 919).

Researchers have used the level of crime and violence reported by residents as an indicator of neighborhood social control. Crime and violence are likely to be higher in neighborhoods where residents have little influence over the behavior of others and where norms for looking out for one's neighbors and for children in the neighborhood are low. Research by Bowen, Bowen, and Cook (2000) and Brodsky (1996) suggests that living in neighborhoods with threatening characteristics, like crime and violence and negative youth behavior, may increase the level of social isolation among residents and decrease supportive patterns of exchange and reciprocity.

High rates of community crime and violence may not only spill over directly into the school and increase the probability of school crime and violence (Bowen & Van Dorn, 2002), but also may negatively influence the educational engagement and academic performance of students who live in these communities. Only recently have researchers begun to examine the influence of indicators of social control in the neighborhood, such as crime and violence, on school-related outcomes. The work of Bowen and Bowen (1999) is a case in point, which will be used to focus our discussion that follows.

Research Findings.   Using a nationally representative sample of middle- and high-school students, Bowen and Bowen (1999) examined the effects of crime and violence in neighborhoods and schools on the school behavior and performance of adolescents. Bowen and Bowen's analysis was preceded by earlier work that indicated that more than one third of the students in their national sample reported one or more than one personal experience with neighborhood crime and violence in the past 30 days (Bowen, Bowen, & Richman, 1998). In addition, almost one in three teens in the earlier analysis reported either feeling unsafe in their neighborhood, afraid on the *way* to school, or both—findings that are very similar to those from the 2003 National Survey of Children's Health for non-Hispanic black and Hispanic children under 18 years of age (Child Trends, 2003). As expected, Bowen and Bowen found that the greater students' confrontation with personal threats to their safety in the neighborhood, the lower their attendance at school, the greater their involvement in problem behaviors, and the lower their academic performance. Not surprisingly, students who experienced personal threats in the neighborhood were also more likely to face threatening situations at school. This finding indicates that some students may not have any place that they can consider a safe zone.

In a study of 4,772 middle- and high-school students who had been identified by school personnel as at risk of school failure, Nash (2002) provided further support for the link between students' exposure to crime and violence in the neighborhood and school outcomes. Nash reported that students' reports of crime not only directly and negatively influenced their educational behavior (e.g., attendance, avoidance of problem behavior, and grades), but also indirectly influenced these outcomes by decreasing the likelihood that they found school meaningful, manageable, and comprehensible. Nash labeled this last domain "sense of school coherence." Recent longitudinal self-report data from 4,071 middle-school students also support the link between neighborhood safety and school outcomes—students who reported lower rates of crime and violence in their neighborhoods at Time 1 reported greater trouble avoidance at school and higher grades 12 months later (Bowen, Rose, Powers, & Glennie, 2008).

When neighborhoods evidence high social control, as indicated by low rates of crime and violence, they are also likely to evidence positive relationships among neighbors. Personal relationships among neighbors operate as a lubricant for their willingness to get involved on each other's behalf and to monitor the behavior of children and youth (Sampson et al., 1997). These positive relationships help explain why communities with stable populations often have low crime rates. Consequently, researchers have combined measures of social control and social support, like neighbor support, into a single construct. Sampson et al. used the term *collective efficacy* to describe neighborhoods with high social control and high social support, which they defined as "social cohesion among neighbors combined with the willingness to intervene on behalf of the common good" (p. 918). Bowen, Bowen, and Ware (2002) described the flip side of this situation, neighborhoods with low social control and low social support, as socially disorganized neighborhoods.

In a recent analysis, N. K. Bowen et al. (2002) reported that neighborhood social disorganization (i.e., lack of neighbor support, negative peer behavior, and high crime and violence) exerted a strong and negative effect on middle- and high-school students' reports of positive education behavior, including grades. Neighborhood social disorganization had not only a direct effect on students' education behavior but also an indirect effect through its negative effect on supportive family behaviors. These findings, based on a national sample of middle- and high-school students, are consistent with other studies that show how social control and social support components in neighborhoods directly and indirectly spill over to influence child and adolescent adjustment and their experiences and outcomes at school (Bowen & Chapman, 1996; Nash, 2002; Powers, Bowen, & Rose, 2005). Darling and Steinberg (1997) surmised that students in well-functioning neighborhoods might benefit less from their experiences

with adults as agents of social control and social support and more from their peer relationships that are more likely to be affirming and supportive in such neighborhoods.

Discussion. These findings suggest the importance of building bridges between schools and the neighborhoods in which students and their families reside. From a general systems theory perspective, the success of schools in educating our children and youth requires interventions that target the multiple environments in which students and their families live and work. Evidence-based interventions exist to help schools address neighborhood and community issues. Creating Lasting Family Connections is one such program, which is designed to strengthen families and communities by reducing drugs and violence (Johnson et al., 1996). Through a comprehensive curriculum, including teaching families how to access community resources, families are empowered to remain resilient in the face of environmental risk factors. School social workers can also work as partners with law enforcement agencies and neighborhood groups to develop strategies for increasing neighborhood safety. For example, community involvement in a neighborhood block watch program may decrease some types of crime (Williams, Ayers, & Arthur, 1997). Consistent with central assumptions from Maslow's (1954) hierarchy of needs theory, it will be difficult to develop connections between neighbors without first attending to their safety needs. Bowen and Van Dorn (2002) stressed the importance of involving parents and youths in discussions about community-based interventions. As concluded by Daniel Yankelovich ("An Interview," 1992), "If you include people in the dialogue, they will struggle with the hard issues. They will take the responsible positions. If you exclude them, the opposite happens" (p. 14). The work of Nelson (2000) in facilitating community "self-governance" dialogues demonstrates the willingness of citizens to come together and tackle the tough problems like crime and violence. School social workers can work as catalysts in supporting school and community stakeholders to sponsor community dialogues for purposes of strengthening community ties and mobilizing community efforts on behalf of children and youth.

Conclusion

General systems theory offers school social workers a familiar perspective. From this perspective, schools must be understood as dynamic systems that are embedded in larger community and institutional settings. The concept of social organization brings social workers to a touchstone of practice—a focus on people and collective processes. Findings presented in this chapter clearly note that collective processes in schools and communities can overpower the detrimental effects of place.

This chapter has offered a broad perspective, and we have been judicious in discussing only a few of the many social organizational processes in schools and communities that may influence student achievement. For example, the influence of parent involvement in schools on student achievement (e.g., Bowen & Bowen, 1998), the powerful effect of prosocial and academically engaged peers on the school-related attitudes and behavior of middle- and high-school students (e.g., Darling & Steinberg, 1997), the role of school-linked services in schools on the coordination and delivery of support services to students (e.g., Jozefowicz-Simbeni & Allen-Meares, 2002), and the contribution of school-based multidisciplinary planning teams in designing system-level interventions (Phillippo & Stone, 2006) are also important topics of discussion. The aim of this chapter has been illustrative with regard to the application of general systems theory rather than either comprehensive or definitive.

General systems theory provides school social workers with a broad lens through which to view schools as organized, complex, and dynamic entities. A body of highly integrated concepts helps them to address the school's effectiveness as a social system committed to achieving the optimal development of children.

One of this theory's greatest contributions lies in translating the participation of many scientific disciplines into a common theoretical formulation or set of constructs that allows communication across disciplines. Such communication has done much to broaden the conceptual and empirical foundation for effective social work practice in schools.

Implications for Social Work Practice in Schools

Since the publication of the Coleman Report in 1966, researchers have made significant progress in identifying social organizational processes in schools and communities that separate effective schools from ineffective ones. This chapter has addressed a few of these influential processes, using the concept of social organization as a conceptual umbrella. Yet, schools continue to struggle to meet academic goals, and too many students remain unprepared and ill-equipped to meet the economic and social realities of the 21st century. If social work is to contribute to solving the challenges faced by our nation's schools, social interventions are needed that target social organizational leverage points in schools and communities.

What is the *science* of social work practice in schools? A great deal of discussion in social work today centers around the issue of evidence-based practice (EBP) (Gambrill, 1999), and a few evidence-based (EB) programs have been highlighted in earlier sections of this chapter. According to Gambrill (2001) and Gibbs (2003), practicing from an EBP perspective requires practitioners to look at the evidence before choosing an intervention. For school-based clinicians, this task includes evaluating existing practices to identify the most effective services in the context of current student needs and interests, and constraints of the school practice setting.

In a recent book, *Community programs to promote youth development,* which was published under the auspices of the National Research Council and the Institute of Medicine (2002), the interdisciplinary committee identified the role of "supportive relationships" as a key feature of effective programs to promote youth development. Programs, such as Teen Outreach, Quantum Opportunities, and Big Brothers and Big Sisters, were included as examples of programs in which social relationships are a key focus of social intervention and as examples of promising initiatives on the basis of the evidence reviewed. School social workers can play an important role in working with both school-based partners and community agencies to offer such evidence-based program initiatives in schools and local communities.

New easy-to-use, Web-based reference guides for EB programs are an important resource for school practitioners. An example of this type of reference guide is found under the Best Practices link on the School Success Profile (SSP) Web site (http://www.schoolsuccessonline.com). Presented for both elementary-school-age children and middle- and high-school students and organized by target dimension (e.g., teacher support), information is provided on a number of programs whose efficacy has been demonstrated by previous research. Programs are organized into three categories, according to their level of prevention: (a) universal programs that target all students, (b) selective/indicated programs that target students who are reported to be at risk, and (c) multicomponent programs, which include both universal and selective/indicated components. For each program, a detailed program description, program objectives, target group, location of services, number and duration of sessions, implementation requirements, program cost, contact information, and evaluation references are provided. Such Web-based reference guides provide school practitioners with the information necessary to practice within an evidence-based practice framework. Powers et al. (2005) proposed a two-step intervention planning process in the context of their discussion of the SSP Best Practices link for middle- and high-school students that rests on an intervention matrix between 14 dimensions of the students' social environment and 8 dimensions of their individual adaptation, including school-related attitudes and behavior. Other best practice

Web sites also are available for informing school social work practice. For example, Child Trends offers a comprehensive data bank of programs in support of positive youth development and school success called *What Works: A Guide to Effective Programs* (http://www.childtrends.org). Communities In Schools (CIS), the nation's largest prevention organization to keep students in school, in partnership with the National Dropout Prevention Center at Clemson University, recently published a technical report on dropout risk factors and exemplary programs (Hammond, Linton, Smink, & Drew, 2007). The report is available on the CIS Web site (www.cisnet.org).

Despite calls for EBP in schools, the increasing number of EB programs, and the availability of Web sites for learning about these programs and their application in schools, school-based practitioners have been slow to incorporate these programs into their practice. A recent dissertation by Powers (2005) sheds light on this situation. In examining the characteristics of 51 EB programs targeted to school-aged youth, study findings suggest that resource requirements (staffing, time, training, and cost) were extensive for the majority of the EB programs in the sample. The resource requirements may function as barriers to EB program adoption in schools because the finances, training, staffing, and time required to implement most of them in schools are sizeable. Another potential barrier identified by the study was the high level of difficulty in locating basic information about many of the programs highly recommended as effective for schools. A lack of information about resource requirements and the effectiveness of EB programs also represents a major barrier to their use in schools. It is not practical to expect that school clinicians have the time or the access to search peer-reviewed journals and other data sources that are primarily available to researchers and academics. As long as basic information about EB programs remains unavailable and inaccessible to practitioners, EBP will not materialize in most schools.

One critical next step in better promotion of EBP in schools is to ensure that information is more easily accessible about commercially available

EB programs, about the extent of resources they require, and about their documented effectiveness. This would allow practitioners to be informed consumers of EB programs, as is dictated by models of evidence-based practice. The EBP reference guide on the SSP Web site is a step in the right direction for school-based practitioners. Importantly, adoption of EBPs in school settings requires more than increased access to information about these programs; it requires a willingness on the part of school-based practitioners to critically examine their practices and to embrace those that align with the best available evidence (cf. Gioia, 2007). The functioning of schools as learning organizations, as discussed earlier, offers a supportive context for school social workers to engage in this critical thinking process about the link between social problems and evidence-based interventions. Such learning organizations are more likely found in schools with an administrative team that combines what Jim Collins (2001), in his book *Good to great,* labels "professional will" (e.g., results-focused) and "professional humility" (e.g., provides opportunities for all employees to be part of the success equation) (p. 36).

A special challenge for school social workers is to develop the knowledge, attitudes, and skills for working effectively as change agents within a highly centralized bureaucracy to develop the types of administrative and support structures that optimize the preparation of students for adult roles. Effectiveness in their roles as change agents also requires that school social workers practice in the context of broader community, including the neighborhoods in which students and their families reside. School social workers must understand that like individuals and families, schools and communities *vary* in their demographic and social profiles and have developmental rhythms that must be appreciated in designing interventions (The Harwood Group, 1999).

Unfortunately, in many cases, school social workers work in relative isolation from one another. Not all schools have school social workers; other schools may have only one social worker who, in some cases, works across several schools. In their roles as change agents, school social workers may increase their leverage and gain professional support by forging strong alliances of support and collaboration with other school social workers. Powers and Bowen (2006) identified several strategies by which school social workers can reduce their isolation and function as a community of practice, including the development of peer support groups and the use of Internet technology to establish online practice exchanges.

From a general systems theory perspective, social organizational processes in schools and communities do not exist independently of their structural and institutional context. For example, as reviewed earlier, Shouse's (1997) research described how the impact of academic press and sense of community on student achievement varied, depending on the average socioeconomic status of students attending the school. Research by Sampson et al. (1997) and Cantillon (2006) depicts how structural conditions in neighborhoods, such as concentrated disadvantage and residential instability, may adversely influence the probability of community social organization and informal social control among residents. Many other structural variables influence social organizational processes in schools and neighborhoods. For example, the research on school size suggests the challenge of developing academic press and sense of community in large schools (Bowen, Bowen, & Richman, 2000). Other research suggests how social relations for school-age youth may be especially restricted in neighborhoods in which socioeconomic inequality is linked to race (Blau, Lamb, Stearns, & Pellerin, 2001). School social workers may influence social organizational processes through structural interventions, such as advocating for smaller schools or for the start-up of community development corporations in neighborhoods that are ecologically disadvantaged.

Some policy makers and researchers believe that nothing less than a fundamental shift in the way schools are organized and governed will result in significant educational progress for students (see Boyd & Shouse, 1997, for a discussion of this point). In the absence of such changes, serious attempts at school reform to promote student achievement are likely to be thwarted or limited at best (Willower, 1991). Others believe that the answer to American students' poor performance lies less in the institutional and organizational structure of schooling and more in the nature of their personal, family, and community lives outside schools (Steinberg, 1996). As employees of the school and as advocates on behalf of students and their families, school social workers have an important voice in debates about school reform and about the design and implementation of interventions to address the support needs of students and their families.

Cynthia Franklin (2000), former editor of *Children & Schools,* discussed the future of school social work as involving more attention to community networking and coordination of services between schools and local community agencies. Winters and Gourdine (2000) added the role of community organizer to the expanding job description of school social workers, a role that is consistent with promoting a more positive interface between the neighborhood and the school. A special focus of this expanded role for school social workers is increasing the community connections between racial and ethnic groups in an attempt to promote more cultural appreciation and to reduce the cultural disconnect that minority students and their parents may feel in schools where the majority of administrators and teachers are white (Lee & Bowen, 2006; Ogbu, 1978).

In their book, *The dance of change: The challenges to sustaining momentum in learning organizations,* Peter Senge and associates (1999) encouraged managers to stop thinking of themselves as *mechanics,* whose role is to fix something, and to begin thinking of themselves as *gardeners,* whose role is to grow something. This metaphor is as pertinent for school social workers as it is for managers. As stated by Senge in a subsequent interview, "The most universal challenge that we face is the transition from seeing our human institutions as machines to seeing them as embodiments of nature" (Webber, 1999, p. 179). The view of schools as living entities in a broader context is undergirded by general systems theory, consistent with a focus on social organization in schools and communities, and supportive of the expanded practice roles and responsibilities of school social workers.

For Study and Discussion

1. The statement, "The whole is greater than the sum of its parts," is associated with the systems paradigm. Although we did not discuss this statement explicitly in the chapter, explain why this statement is consistent with a general systems theory perspective, and identify an example of this phenomenon in schools and in neighborhoods.
2. Of all the concepts that were introduced and discussed in this chapter, what single concept had the most influence on your thinking about school social work practice? Please discuss the implications of this concept for social work practice with a colleague.
3. What are some strategies that school social workers may use to gain entry to working with neighborhoods as a context for practice?
4. Many school social workers work in relative isolation. What are some strategies that school social workers can use to build a professional network of peer support and collaboration?

Additional Readings

Arum, R., & Beattie, I. R. (2000). *The structure of schooling: Readings in the sociology of education.* Mountain View, CA: Mayfield.

Bidwell, C. E. (2001). Analyzing schools as organizations: Long-term permanence and short-term change. *Sociology of Education Extra Issue,* 100–114.

Blum, R. W., McNeely, C. A., & Rinehart, P. M. (2002). *Improving the odds: The untapped power of schools to improve the health of teens.* Minneapolis, MN: Center for Adolescent Health and Development, University of Minnesota.

Bowen, G. L., Richman, J. M., & Bowen, N. K. (2000). Families in the context of communities across time. In S. J. Price, P. C. McKenry, & M. J. Murphy (Eds.), *Families across time: A life course perspective* (pp. 117–128). Los Angeles: Roxbury.

Coleman, J. S., & Hoffer, T. (1988). *Public and private high schools: The impact of communities.* New York: Basic Books.

Dornbusch, S. M., Glasgow, K. L., & Lin, I.-C. (1996). The social structure of schooling. *Annual Review of Psychology, 47,* 401–429.

Kozol, J. (1991). *Savage inequalities: Children in America's schools.* New York: Crown.

Miller, J. (1978). *Living systems.* New York: McGraw-Hill.

National Association of Secondary School Principals. (2002). *What the research shows: Breaking ranks in action.* Reston, VA: Author.

Putnam, R. D. (2000). *Bowling alone.* New York: Simon & Schuster.

Rosenfeld, L. B., Richman, J. M., & Bowen, G. L. (2000). Social support networks and school outcomes: The centrality of the teacher. *Child and Adolescent Social Work Journal, 17,* 205–226.

Skytmer, L. (2001). *General systems theory: Ideas and applications.* Singapore: World Scientific.

Traub, J. (2000, January 16). What no school can do. *New York Times Magazine,* pp. 52–67.

Wehlage, G. G., Rutter, R. A., Smith, G. A., Lesko, N., & Fernandez, R. R. (1989). *Reducing the risk: Schools as communities of support.* Philadelphia: Falmer Press.

Woolley, M. E., & Bowen, G. L. (2007). In the context of risk: Supportive adults and the school engagement of middle school students. *Family Relations, 56,* 92–104.

Woolley, M. E., & Grogan-Kaylor, A. (2006). Protective family factors in the context of neighborhood: Promoting positive school outcomes. *Family Relations, 55,* 95–106.

Woolley, M. E., Kol, K. L., & Bowen, G. L. (2009). The social context of school success for Latino middle school students: Direct and indirect influence of teachers, family, and friends. *Journal of Early Adolescence, 29,* 43–70.

4

An Ecological Perspective of Social Work Services in Schools

PAULA ALLEN-MEARES

University of Illinois at Chicago

Ecology ... Because it emphasizes the interdependence of organism and environment, ecology is especially suitable as a metaphor for social work, given our historic commitment to the person-in-environment concept. The ecological metaphor helps the profession enact its social purpose of helping people and promoting responsive environments that support human growth, health, and satisfaction in social functioning.

—Germain & Gitterman[1]

An ecological metaphor for practice can respond to the dual function in a way that the traditional medical or disease metaphor cannot do.

—Carel Germain[2]

Introduction

An important theme in most social work literature has been the search for a unifying conceptual framework for useful guiding practice. In recent years, considerable progress has been made in this regard, and some agreement has been reached. As indicated in Chapter 2, the literature seems to recommend that the social work profession adopt an ecological perspective of practice. Such a perspective is most useful for attaining social work goals and for directing practice. This chapter is concerned with this perspective, the concepts and elements that distinguish social work from other professional practices, and its application to social work in schools. We view social work in schools as a specialized field of practice within the profession. In this chapter, we present examples and illustrations of professional social work values and their special relevance for school social work.

The Profession of Social Work

Throughout its history and development, the social work profession has sought a schema that conceptualizes its practice. But how do we conceptualize practice when social work is so diverse in methods, clients, settings, funding sources, and focus? What is the common base? The profession has spent considerable time and energy studying these questions. The milestones in this process are

---

[1]Germain, C. B., & Gitterman, A. (1996). *The Life Model of Social Work Practice*, p. 5. New York: Columbia University Press.

[2]Germain, C. B. (2006). An Ecological Perspective on Social Work in the Schools. In R. Constable, C. R. Massat, S. McDonald, & J. P. Flynn (Eds.), *School Social Work: Practice, Policy, and Research* (6th ed., p. 30). Chicago: Lyceum Books.

65

(a) the 1929 Milford conference, which confirmed that the various specialty interests had enough in common to validate the idea that all social workers are part of one profession; (b) the 1951 Hollis-Taylor report, which attempted to define what social work was and what it was not; (c) the 1958 meeting of a subcommittee of the National Association of Social Workers (NASW) Commission on Practice, which devised a definition of social work practice that included an explanation of social work value, purpose, sanction, knowledge, and method; and (d) the 1959 curriculum study of the Council on Social Work Education (CSWE) (*Special Issue*, 1977; Brieland, 1977). The curriculum study offered the following definition of social work:

> Social work seeks to enhance the social functioning of individuals, singly, and in groups, by activities focused upon their social relationship which constitute the interaction between man and his environment. These activities can be grouped into three functions: restoration of impaired capacity, provision of individual and social resources, and prevention of dysfunction. (Werner, 1959, p. 54)

In the late 1970s, the NASW convened a task force on specialization. The consensus of the task force was consistent with Werner's definition:

> Social work focus is on the interaction between people and their environments. . . . The fundamental zone of social work is where people and their environments are in exchange with each other. Social work intervention aims at the coping capabilities of people and the demands and resources of their environments so that the transactions between them are helpful to both. Social work's concern extends to both the dysfunctional or deficient conditions at the juncture between people and their environments, and the opportunities there for producing growth and improving the environment. It is the duality of focus on people and their environments that distinguishes social work from other professions. (NASW Task Force on Specialization, 1978, p. 3)

The fifth milestone in this process was the publication in 1977 of a special conceptual frameworks issue of the NASW journal, *Social Work* (*Special Issue*, 1977). In this issue, such scholars as A. Minahan, A. Pincus, W. Reid, W. Gordon, and S. Cooper examined existing perspectives and raised some serious but crucial questions concerning the context of contemporary problems: What is the mission of social work practice? What are the skills, values, and commonalities of the profession? What are the practical and educational implications of these dynamics? The same types of questions were considered more fully in a second special issue of *Social Work* (*Conceptual Frameworks II*, 1981). We have learned from these efforts that certain concepts or elements distinguish the various specializations of social work from other professional practices. These include values, purpose, knowledge, sanction, and methods of intervention.

Values

In general, the profession of social work has a unique value system. Values, in this context, are defined as ethical concepts or principles that provide a philosophical foundation for a profession. It is their values that determine how social workers relate to people and provide services to them. According to Harriett Bartlett, values are frequently divided into ultimate (or ideal) values and instrumental values (the means to achieve ultimate values). That every human being is entitled to liberty and self-realization is an example of an ultimate value. An example of an instrumental value, which is more specific, is that every individual has a right to self-determination and equal educational opportunity. The second level of values refers to the valued qualities of a well-functioning person; and the third level focuses on operational values, which are the means to achieve the higher value (Bartlett, 1970). Ultimate and instrumental values are to be distinguished from cultural values, which are concerned with societal mores and expectations for social behavior in society. Some primary social work values and examples of applications in school social work follow.

Social Work Values

1. Recognition of the worth and dignity of each human being.
2. The right to self-determination or self-realization.

3. Respect for individual potential and support for an individual's aspirations to attain it.
4. The right of each individual to be different from every other and to be accorded respect for those differences.

Applications to Social Work in Schools
1. Each pupil is valued as an individual, regardless of any unique characteristic.
2. Each pupil should be allowed to share in the learning process and to learn.
3. Individual differences (including differences in rates of learning) should be recognized; intervention should be aimed at supporting pupils' educational goals.
4. Each child, regardless of race and socioeconomic characteristics, has a right to equal treatment in the school.

Examples of other values compatible with those of the profession as a whole but having special relevance to school social work are (a) that children are entitled to equal educational opportunities and to learning experiences adapted to their individual needs, and (b) that the process of education should not only provide the child with tools for future learning and skills to use in earning a living, but also be an essential ingredient of the child's mental health.

These social work values highlight the central position of the individual pupil in social work. This does not mean that casework or work with the individual is the preferred way of offering school social work services. Other forms of intervention can also contribute to the realization of these values. The practitioner should keep in mind that although the child may be the identified client, that child may actually be signaling for help for the family or the class or bringing attention to an area of injustice in some other system. However, the focus on the individual reflects the democratic commitment to the welfare of each individual in society and to the assumption of social responsibility by citizens.

In situations involving one or more persons, some values appear to weigh more heavily or even

to conflict. When this is the case, school social workers must then search for an acceptable balance. The "best interest of the child" should guide these deliberations. One example of conflicting values, taken from school social work practice, is a gifted child whom the father wants to be just average because the child, who is showing signs of stress from underachievement, "will be happier that way." Another example is secondary-school students whose excessive absenteeism shows that alternative forms of education are needed, even though the community and school do not recognize such need. Ultimate value should guide practice. Additionally, the school social worker's course of action should profit the client(s), but not at the expense of another person.

Purpose

School social workers contribute to improving the quality of life by adding their efforts to the school's attempt to achieve its central purpose—to provide a setting for teaching and learning in which children and young persons can acquire a sense of competence, a capacity for problem solving and decision making, and a readiness to adapt to change and to take responsibility for their own continued learning.

Just as the values of the profession determine its purpose, knowledge makes some purposes and goals more practical and attainable than others. Thus, values and knowledge interact to determine the dominant purposes of social work.

Knowledge

According to Bartlett, a profession's strongest foundation is its body of knowledge (Bartlett, 1970; Gordon, 1962). Newly attained knowledge drawn from research and study results in verifiable propositions that can be confirmed. Knowledge can be distinguished from value assumptions—propositions that do not appear confirmable, although they may become so later. Most important, all knowledge building is guided by the ultimate values of the profession.

The knowledge base of social work and school social work is as broad as human behavior. This characteristic has led social workers to borrow knowledge from other fields such as education, behavioral and biological sciences, psychiatry, medicine, law, and political science. The borrowed knowledge includes concepts and principles selected for relevance to social work, then tested in practice, and sometimes reformulated in social work terms. Such clusters of borrowed knowledge are useful and legitimate if appropriately integrated with social work purpose. Essentially, the concepts of the social work profession guide in the selection of knowledge.

Examples of Knowledge Applicable to School Social Work Practice.   School social workers can find support for their purpose and concerns in new knowledge about the development of an individual's intelligence. As a result of research conducted by educators and child psychologists, we now know that the belief in fixed intelligence is not tenable. Development can no longer be viewed as predetermined as it once was. The brain's intellectual processes may be viewed as comparable to the information processes programmed into computers for problem solving. Because experience is the "programmer" of the human brain, the early experiences of young children are highly important for perceptual, cognitive, and intellectual functions. Learning is motivated by the intrinsic effects of information processing, among other factors.

Further, we now know that the home environment affects the level of a child's measured intelligence and success in school. Important characteristics of the home that are conducive to school learning are learning materials (e.g., books, toys), models of language and behavior, help in language development, and parental stimulation and concern for achievement.

As a result of the historic research of educator Benjamin Bloom, we have learned that differences found among racial and socioeconomic groups of children are not inherent or fixed, but can be explained by widely differing amounts and kinds of environmental stimulation. Also, early

school achievement is essential for later school achievement or for obtaining employment and being successful in a career. Further, although family and social factors are critical, most pupil failures can be overcome through adjustment of the learning conditions in schools. According to Bloom, most children can learn; it is important to analyze the entry-level skills and motivation of each child and to make certain that appropriate instruction is given (Bloom, 1976).

Sanction

The authority to act is granted to school social workers by the state (in many instances), the community, the school, the profession of social work, and the record of competent performance of individual professional social workers. Sanction does not define school social work in the same sense that value, purpose, and knowledge do; nevertheless, sanction is a necessary condition for professional practice.

Sanction from the community comes through federal and state legislation that provides for social work services in schools, systems of licensure and certification, and allocation of resources. The sanction of the school is indicated by the hiring policies of the school board and by consultations and negotiations with school administrators.

The NASW *Code of Ethics and Professional Standards* provides professional sanctioning for certain kinds of ethical behaviors and the basic values and principles undergirding social work. A unique characteristic of social work is the focus on the empowerment of people who are vulnerable, oppressed, and living in poverty. The focus on individual well-being in a social context and environmental forces that create and contribute to problems in living also distinguishes social work from other professions. The core professional values are service, social justice, dignity and worth of the person, importance of human relationships, integrity, and competence. It is truly this constellation of values from which concern about balance between context and the complexity of the human experience is derived (National Association of Social Workers [NASW], 1999). Clients are individuals, families, communities, groups, and organizations, which exist in culturally diverse contexts. Social workers are sensitive to cultural and ethnic diversity and strive to end discrimination, oppression, poverty, and other forms of social injustices.

The 2002 revision of the standards for social work services in schools served as the guide for the development of school social work. The Standards have been revised to reflect changes within the profession and current social work policies and practices. These Standards were originally created in 1978, revised for the first time in 1992, and revised again in 2002. Overall, past and current Standards reinforce the traditions and current practices of this field of practice, and the goals and objectives of the school systems. However, for some school systems these Standards provide a challenge, or goals, to be achieved in the best interest of pupils, the educational process, and the desired outcomes. The Standards underscore the importance of interdisciplinary team work, ethics and how the service is to be organized to accomplish its objectives (NASW, 2002).

School social workers obtain sanction from the clients they serve. One illustration is parental permission to provide social services to young children and participation by parents in determining appropriate intervention. Also important is the sanction acquired through competence in the performance of school social work tasks, which brings respect for the profession and for the individual social worker. However, school social workers should be alert to hazards to schoolchildren and young persons when services become involuntary and limits of authority are exceeded.

Intervention Methods

Professional intervention in school social work most often refers to the interface between the child and his or her appropriate environment as the unit of attention. This act is "guided and carried out through the conscious use of social work knowledge and values and thus is consonant with the idea of their priority" (Bartlett, 1970, p. 72). *Intervention* is an umbrella term comprising a variety of acts to select from according to their pertinence to various situations.

> Intervention—1. Interceding or coming between groups of people, events, planning activities, or an individual's internal conflicts. 2. In social work, the term is analogous to the physician's term "treatment." Many social workers prefer using intervention because it includes "treatment" and other activities to solve or prevent problems or achieve goals. Thus, it refers to psychotherapy, advocacy, mediation, social planning, community organization, finding and developing resources, and many other activities. (Barker, 2003, pp. 226–227)

The Ecological Perspective

Social workers must be aware of the effect the many institutions have on the social functioning of the child. One perspective for examining the transactions between and among the child and various institutions and systems is the ecological perspective. As discussed in Chapter 3, general systems theory provides tools to help social workers examine and understand the organization of the public school and its subsystems. This theory maintains that environments do have boundaries, structures, and maintenance systems. The concepts of this theory are useful for conceptualizing, gathering, and organizing data about and from the various institutions and systems in which the child functions (the school, family, and community). Based on the seminal work of Urie Bronfenbrenner (1979), an ecological perspective provides the framework for understanding the nature of the transactions between the person and different institutions and systems. It helps the social worker to identify and consider all systems contributing to the pupil's situation or difficulty. Further, it recognizes that resolution may be more effective when intervention takes place within more than one system. Ecological theory is a theory of interaction and transaction. It deals with the broad, complex reciprocal transactions between organisms and their environments. It is not based on static units of pupil behavior encompassed in the labels "dropout," "emotionally disturbed" or "slow learner." It is concerned with dynamic transactions of which the child's behavior is but one part.

There are several underlying assumptions of the ecological perspective. They are

- Behavior has a value specific to the setting. In other words, a pupil's behavior is defined within the setting. Behavior of a pupil that may be culturally appropriate in his or her home and community could be viewed as deviant in the classroom (See Appendix III).
- Deviancy refers to behavior that is conflicting with the values of its setting.
- It is important to consider the fit of the person to the setting.
- People within the setting make the value judgement.
- There is a bidirectionality to interactions within a setting. For instance, there are two transactions between the teacher and the student. The teacher responds positively to a child who adapts positively to the classroom, which in turn reinforces the child's behavior.
- Ecological systems, rather than people, may need to be changed. In other words, altering the environment/ecosystem could be one target of intervention. Changing the expectations/belief systems/behaviors of teachers, parents, and peer groups could result in a better fit for the pupil.
- Ecological interventions are heuristic and eclectic. There is no prescribed intervention or set of ascribed assumptions about a specific situation (Swartz & Martin, 1997).

The ecological perspective is the most appropriate perspective for viewing social work practice in schools and for locating the target(s) of intervention. It is appropriate in that it directs attention to the whole system and the client's place in it, and not to any one part or aspect of the client's situation to the exclusion of the rest (see Appendices I and II). The focus is on the social process of interaction and the transactions between a child and that child's environment.

The environment is defined as the aggregate of external conditions and influences that affect and determine a child's life and development. In addition to the family, some of these determinants are schools, courts, neighborhoods, hospitals, clinics, and the mass media. As Carel B. Germain stated,

> Actually, school social workers stand at the interface not only of the child and the school, but of family and school, and community and school. Thus, they are in a position to help child, parents, and community develop social competence and, at the same time, to increase the school's responsiveness to the needs and aspirations of children, parents, and community. (Germain, 2006, p. 31)

The social worker's function is to work at the interface of the person and the environment to bring about a match between the client's needs (indicated by coping behaviors) and environmental resources. Person–environment match is the actual fit between an individual's or a collective group's needs, rights, goals, and capacities and the qualities and operations of their physical and social environments within particular cultural and historical contexts. The match can be favorable, somewhat adequate, or dysfunctional (Monkman, 2006). In a book entitled *The Bell Curve,* the authors argued that persons are genetically different at birth and that it is this variable that determines intellectual growth and thus achievement (Herrnstein & Murray, 1994). These authors virtually ignored the role of environment in the determination of coping behaviors for growing and achieving (Monkman, 1978, 2006). Social workers can achieve a good match only if they have fully assessed each side of the interface. An analysis of the components of each side of the interface begins with an analysis of the coping behaviors of the individual (see Figure 4.1). Coping behaviors are defined as behaviors that are directed toward the environment, including the individual's efforts to exert some control over his or her own behavior. To use the "self" purposefully, social workers deal with three categories of coping behaviors.

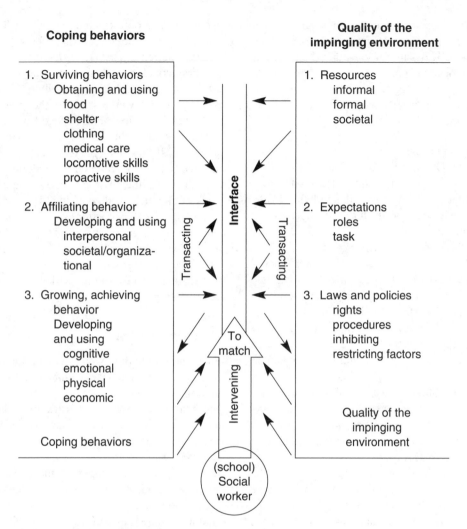

FIGURE 4.1 A Framework for Social Work Practice *Source:* Marjorie McQueen Monkman, "The Specialization of the School Social Worker and a Model for Differential Levels of Practice," in *Differential Levels of Student Support Services,* Minnesota Department of Education, 1982, p. 139. Reprinted by permission from the Minnesota Department of Education.

■ *Coping behaviors for surviving* enable the person to obtain and use resources and make it possible to continue life activity—for example, the effort to obtain food, shelter, and medical treatment. In school social work practice, we often assess the pupils, their families, and significant others in terms of their capability to provide essential life needs. A child cannot survive in an environment that is physically and emotionally abusive.

■ *Coping behaviors for affiliating* enable individuals to unite in close connection with others in their significant environments. Subcategories of affiliating behavior are the capacity to develop and maintain intimate personal relationships (social skill functioning) and the ability to use organizations and organizational structures (such as clubs, school, family, and social services).

■ *Coping behaviors for growing and achieving* enable the person to pursue intellectual and social activities useful for self and others. Subcategories of coping behaviors for growing and developing are cognitive functioning and development of physical, economic, and emotional capacities.

The coping behaviors of individuals develop over a lifetime. Often, behaviors displayed by an individual or group of individuals are related to an accumulation of information that individuals have about themselves or feedback from significant environments.

In the ecological perspective, the child is viewed as a member of a social system. There is equal emphasis on the pupil and the social systems, which can be thought of as environments. Martin and Swartz-Kulstad (2000) identified five target areas for intervention: "youth cognitive process, the family system, the peer network, the school or vocational arena, and the environment" (p. 14). Intervention planning is grounded in information about the aspects of the ecosystem in terms of culture and social class. These ecosystems contain both supporting and inhibiting factors. They place demands on the pupil in terms of expectations and ways of behaving.

Some environments may be stressful for children. Stress is the experience of "an imbalance between a perceived demand and perceived capability to meet the demand through the use of available internal and external resources," which can be characterized by troubled emotional or psychological states (Gitterman & Shulman, 2005, p. 5). Life stressors are generated by critical life issues that people perceive as exceeding their personal and environmental resources for managing them. Life stressors include difficult social or developmental transitions, traumatic life events, and any other life issues that disturb the existing fit (Gitterman & Shulman, 2005). For example, consistent negative information and feedback from family and school to a child about that child's academic abilities could result in and maintain poor academic performance. Monkman (1978) defined *environment* as those qualities and

characteristics of the situation with which the individual is in direct contact. Environments in which children of poverty-level urban families function could be characterized as dense and often lacking appropriate cognitive stimuli. In practice, social workers assess the individual's capacities to obtain what is needed from the environment for surviving, affiliating, and growing or achieving. If they discover that what the individual needs to improve social functioning is not available from the environment and the expectations of significant others or that there is a mismatch in the transactions, the environment becomes the target of change. The social worker may attempt to restructure the environment so that the child or groups of children receive positive feedback to encourage self-worth and academic performance.

Case Illustration

A number of children who lived in a multifamily dwelling in an inner-city neighborhood were not turning in homework, an expectation of the fifth- and sixth-grade teachers. Further exploration of the situation by the social worker revealed that the apartments (the living environment) were small, and there were no areas where the children could study quietly. A meeting with the manager and interested residents resulted in formulation of a plan to provide a quiet place. The manager of the building offered use of the community room, evenings from 6:00 to 8:00 p.m., when it was not used much by the residents. Volunteers were found in the building who would supervise the study hours on Tuesdays and Wednesdays. Teachers agreed to give homework only on those nights. Students were involved in each phase of the plan.

In the attempt to change the environment, the emphasis is on determining quality (availability of assistance, degree of stress, and responsiveness). Additional dimensions of the environment include resources, expectations, and laws and policies. *Resources* are people, family, organizations, or institutions that can be turned to for support or help, as needed or desired. Resources may be available supplies. Informal resources may provide support, affection, advice, and concrete services. Formal resources include membership organizations, businesses, schools, and social service agencies. These resources are drawn into the development of social service plans and often are coordinated to assist pupils and families. *Expectations* are the patterned performances and normative obligations that are grounded in established societal structures (see Figure 4.1). Expectations can involve roles and tasks. For example, a child may have several roles—class member, student-learner, family member, and member of organizations such as boys' clubs and Boy Scouts. The pupil performs specific tasks in meeting the expectations of persons in the environment and fulfilling role requirements. *Laws and policies* are defined as binding rules of conduct created by controlling authorities at national, state, and local levels. Laws and policies dictate institutional policies and practices and govern individual behaviors. The Education for All Handicapped Children Act (P.L. 94-142), the forerunner of today's Individuals with Disabilities Education Act (IDEA), discussed in Chapter 7, changed the roles, tasks, and functions of school staff and parents and has to some degree restructured the educational process (by emphasizing individual educational programs, due process, and nondiscriminatory testing) and the learning environment of handicapped pupils (by emphasizing the least-restrictive environment).

Social work intervention can seek change in either the coping behaviors of the individual (surviving, affiliating, growing, and achieving), the quality of the environments (policies and practices, resources, and expectations), or both. For example, crack babies and pupils classified as attention deficit disordered, may need one-on-one intervention. If a local school policy discriminates against one pupil group because of the pupils' inability to pay a certain fee, and the activity is identified as an important educational experience, the school social worker should seek to change the policy (See Appendices I & II for examples of urban and rural interventions).

Because school social workers are located at the interface, they are in an excellent position to prevent problems before they arise. Prevention is frequently advocated by social workers. The research of Felner, Phillips, DuBois, and Lease (1991) was early in the development of ecologically based preventative efforts. They developed preventive intervention efforts that wed ecological theory and research in the school setting to assist at-risk pupils. They adopted a developmentally ecological model to maximize school achievement and healthy developmental outcomes. Preventative ecological interventions in schools have also been developed for adolescent pregnancy (Corcoran, Franklin, & Bennett, 2000), HIV/AIDS (Latkin & Knowlton, 2005), bullying (Limber, 2006), and dropout prevention (Jozefowicz-Simbeni, 2008).

SAFEchildren is an example of a preventative program based on ecological theory, which was designed and shown to help understand the risk of antisocial behaviors in children from families who live in low-income inner-city areas and the prevention of such behaviors. The sample included 424 families with children entering first grade from five Chicago schools located in inner-city neighborhoods. Forty-three percent of the sample group was African American, and 57% was Latino. Driven from a developmental–ecological perspective, the SAFEchildren families were involved in a family-focused prevention group that met regularly for 20 sessions and were involved in academic tutoring for their children. The family group helped to create a supportive network of families in the community, while the tutoring worked to promote academic success. Due to the nature of an ecological approach, this study controlled for several moderators and covariates, including marital status, family income, gender, ethnicity, and specific school. The experimental group displayed an overall improvement in school performance and parental involvement from their participation in the SAFEchildren prevention program (Tolan, Gorman-Smith, & Henry, 2004; Gorman-Smith, Tolan, Henry, Quintana, Lutovsky, & Leventhal, 2007).

To employ a preventive approach, practitioners must be aware of and understand the role of the significant ecological environments (the school, community, relevant resources, and unique needs of different pupil groups). Then, and only then, can they have insight to prevent problems through collaborative efforts and advocacy. Collaboration and consultation with the school's significant actors are fundamental tasks of school social workers.

To attain the objectives of school social work, intervention tasks must be defined in terms of dysfunctional transactions or discord: Such tasks are generated by the interaction and transactions between schoolchildren and their environments. Schoolchildren and their family-neighborhood-school-community environment make up a complex system. A first task of the practitioner is to try to locate children's difficulty at the point of "misfit" between their needs and the qualities of their environment and to recognize the difficulty in the transactions. In locating the point of misfit, the practitioner must examine the structure of the school and community. Which ones are detrimentally affecting large numbers of pupils? Norma Radin, an advocate of structural assessment, suggested that one course of action is to develop in-school alternatives and community services and to modify policies that reinforce the misfit. According to Radin, optimum effectiveness and efficiency can be achieved by school social workers if they analyze the variables that hinder the development of many children rather than those that hinder a single child. By doing so, practitioners can pin an understanding of some of the blocks to children's growth and increase their own visibility and credibility, while simultaneously developing healthy environments (Radin, 1975).

Case Illustration

School and Community Interface.   A school social worker, concerned about the poor attendance and lack of interest in school in one geographical area, decided to collect additional information about the situation. The worker held informal discussions with the pupils and their parents and learned that they felt isolated and ignored by the school's officials. The area, characterized as low income and racially mixed, with municipal housing, had a community center that

was rarely used by the residents. The worker secured permission from the management of the housing project to utilize the center for parent–school meetings.

The worker then described the parents' and pupils' sentiments regarding the school to key school administrators and found that they were very concerned about these residents' apathy and lack of involvement in school activities. They had assumed that these parents were just not interested in the school that served their children.

After considerable discussion with the parents and school administrators, agreement was reached that a meeting of parents, pupils, and school officials to exchange information would benefit all parties. The worker then contacted parents and administrators to discuss the possibility of meeting at the community center (as part of a plan to develop an outreach program to promote communication). The meeting was well attended, and parents freely shared their impressions, criticisms, and concerns. Specific concerns were that their children had to cross a dangerous intersection on the way to and from school without supervision, and that there was no bus service. Administrators, unaware of these concerns, responded positively and promised to investigate. They explained some of the changes in curriculum that they were developing and described the opportunities for parents and pupil involvement that existed in the school. This effort opened up lines of communication between the school and a section of the community it served. Results of the project included improved attendance and a significant increase in the number of parent–school contacts (Midwest Center Satellite Consortium for Planned Change in Pupil Personnel Programs for Urban Schools in Indiana, 1974).

Family–school relations and connections are essentially the cornerstone of school social work practice. The characterization of family–school relations is described in a variety of ways in the literature: family–school collaboration or partnership or alliance or family-centered priorities. If you consider the family and the school as two nurturing systems in the lives of children, their importance takes on considerable significance as targets of intervention. These relationships are indeed very complex. Building functional relations, helping each to solve problems, finding a common ground between the two when there are differences, and linking each with other community and statewide resources is all about building mutual support that advances the development and education success of the youth. When there are inconsistencies and poor communication between the family and school, the consequences can be devastating.

In 2002, with the passage of the No Child Left Behind Act, schools were encouraged to focus on meaningful parental involvement in the classroom and school. The NCLB requires that schools include parents in all levels of program development and implementation. This goes beyond "traditional" forms of involvement such as open houses, parent–teacher conferences, and fund-raising. Davies (2002) indicated that for the most part, schools have hardly caught up with the flourishing rhetoric that schools should reach out to parents and form partnerships to promote and support the academic success of pupils. According to Davies, the culture of school still remains at arm's length in terms of parent involvement: Too few parents are truly involved in meaningful ways, though there is rhetoric calling for their involvement. In reality, we see "the tried-and-true" forms of parent involvement: an open house, two or three short parent conferences a year, and parents attending sports events, fairs, and as partners in fund-raising. Too few parents are involved in efforts to change the school curriculum, school policies, and innovations. The traditional separateness remains, and even when partnerships are developed with families and community groups, input is too limited. Yet, the literature suggests that school success and reform is linked to community success and vice versa. In other words, school and community success are linked, and parents are indeed significant stakeholders and components of the community. The NCLB, when its implementation required more meaningful interaction between school and community, did not provide a road map for how to do this (Mandel, 2007). The school social worker has many skills that would be useful in facilitating

this involvement, precisely because the social worker stands at the interface of the school and the community.

In a review of existing literature, Durlak et al. provides optimism regarding school–family–community partnerships. Though the literature is still growing, there were more than three hundred studies targeting family–school, community–school, or family–community–school relationships. Of these, only 79 conducted quantitative assessments of their efforts, but, encouragingly, all but two of these studies had medium to large effect size, meaning that the efforts to change the systems had positive effects on the subjects (Durlak et al., 2007).

Case Illustration

Pupil and School Interface.   A social worker in a small Midwest school district, concerned about the large number of high school students who were spending their days in a local park and shopping center, sought to understand their lack of interest in schooling. The worker held discussions with these youths and found that they were bored and restless, they cut classes regularly, and they felt that the school offered neither challenge nor satisfaction. Though many of them had some of the cognitive skills necessary for success in school, they were not committed to learning, given the school environment.

The worker took this information to the superintendent and other school officials. After much discussion with them and with the pupils, the worker developed a proposal for an alternative educational program for that high school. This proposal was submitted to the school board and was approved. The cost of starting the program was low because the new school would be held in a frame building already owned by the school district. Twenty-five students enrolled in the 9-week pilot program. Students, volunteers, parents, and administrators who were interested in the program held a retreat to discuss the new school's educational program, policies, and procedures. The students described how thoroughly disillusioned they were with the existing school framework.

The school social worker asked such questions as: What do you see in your school now? What would you like to see? What are our mission objectives? The school met the requirements of the Illinois School Code, including the course requirements. The students established the goals, assisted in the design of the curriculum, and interviewed prospective teachers.

The creation of this program is an excellent illustration of how to bring about change in transactions between a pupil group and the school. The identification and analysis of an imbalance, followed by implementation of a carefully thought-out plan of intervention that facilitates healthy exchange, exemplifies an ecological approach to school social work practice.

According to Rappaport,

> The ecological viewpoint should be regarded as an orientation emphasizing relationships among persons and their social and physical environment. Conceptually the term implies that there are neither inadequate persons nor inadequate environment, but rather the fit between the persons and environment may be in a relative accord and/or discord. (1977, p. 7)

Another example of the student and school interface is the implementation of the Olweus Bullying Prevention Program in classrooms across the United States (Limber, 2006). The first bullying prevention program was initiated in Norway in 1983 by Professor Dan Olweus. This program responded to increasing problems with bullying and victimization that students are faced with both in and out of school and revealed an overall significant reduction in student bullying and victimization in and out of school. The Norwegian design takes effect at three different levels: schoolwide, the classroom, and the individual. Olweus originally used schoolwide interventions such as a schoolwide questionnaire to assess the severity of a bully/victim problem, creation of new school rules and implementation of those rules, a "kickoff" session to explain and introduce the new program to the student body, and coordinated adult supervision at popular teen hangouts throughout the community (Limber, 2006).

Following its success, the Olweus Bullying Prevention Program was brought to the United States. With a sample of about 6,400 South Carolina students, the Prevention Program again significantly showed reduced problem behaviors and instances of victimization. The South Carolina program went one step further, partnering with several people and groups in the community, to implement an ecological perspective. The program branched out from the classroom to also involve popular youth hangouts and services like camps, playgrounds, transportation services, and churches with the school, thus creating effective relationships that helped stop problem behaviors (Limber, 2004). Although the program displayed an overall success, there were several differences that the South Carolina group had to adjust for from the original Norwegian method. Some of these barriers included resistance from staff and parents to accept that an issue existed with bullying and victimization within the school system, an increased effort to change the mind-set away from short-term solutions to a more permanent one, and the need to move away from a zero-tolerance rule completely removing bullies from the school without intervention (Limber, 2006).

The ecological perspective also makes one aware of relationships that exist among systems—for example, relationships between family and school, and between peer group and community. According to Carel Germain, one major advantage of the ecological perspective of social work is that it

> contributes scientific knowledge concerning the delicate relationships of human beings to the rapidly changing physical and social environment. At the same time, it fosters a passionate concern for human aspirations and for the development of milieus to promote them. An ecological perspective enables us to reach toward a complementarity between our scientific and humanistic concerns, between cause and function. (1979, p. 326)

Risk and Resiliency

According to Werner (1986), Bernard (1992), and Fraser (2004), a pupil's risk when viewed from a developmental perspective changes with the social context (environments) in which he or she lives. Risk can be defined as the likelihood of an individual developing a certain problem or difficulty in functioning, over a specific period of time. For example, infants and toddlers deprived of early cognitive and physical stimuli may be at risk of various developmental delays. A set of predisposing factors (in this case, the lack of stimuli) places the child at risk. Risks can be buffered or minimized if the appropriate resources and protective factors are provided at critical stages of development. These protective factors reduce or eliminate risk and, in some instances, promote competence. In the literature, there is mention of children who appear to triumph over adversity (Gitterman & Shulman, 2005). They are beset with problems (e.g., poverty, dysfunctional homes, parents who may suffer from mental illness), yet they appear to be resilient or less vulnerable than others with similar situations. Perhaps informal environmental factors, caregiving, and social relations act as protective factors or buffers for these children and increase their stress resistance.

According to Gitterman and Shulman (2005), resilience is defined as

> a concept that entered the literature in studies of "at-risk" children who were hardy and "stress resistant" in extreme adversity. It was initially thought to be a personality trait. However, the concept anchored in the transactional arena as the fields of psychiatry, psychology, and social work appreciate and utilize perspective in viewing and intervening in human phenomena. (pp. 586–587)

Resilience is a set of behaviors and, as internalized capacities, represents positive outcomes when risks are present. Research has found two such positive outcomes, which help to predict a child's resilience: academic success and positive self-identity (Spencer, Fegley, Harpalani, & Seaton, 2004). Behaviorally, resilience means coping with, recovering from, or overcoming adversity. Persons who are resilient respond better to difficult life transitions, environmental stressors, and crisis situations (Gitterman & Shulman, 2005).

Protective factors are assets that individuals use to cope with, adapt to, or overcome vulnerability or risks. Protective factors can include residence within a family, social group, or community; peer applications and a healthy relationship with parents; adequate financial resources to provide a decent standard of living; external social supports (e.g., relatives and friends); and positive social competencies (Gilgun, 1996).

Resilience can be fostered in all children as a preventative intervention. Programs that teach children skills such as problem solving, coping, affect regulation, empathy, and impulse control can foster resilience by providing the child with a toolbox for stressful situations. The Promoting Alternative Thinking Strategies (PATHS) program, which is a multiyear elementary school curriculum, has been successful in promoting social, emotional, and behavioral competence in a variety of populations, including children exposed to high neighborhood adversity (Kam, Greenberg, & Walls, 2003). Resilience in children can also be encouraged through work with the family to improve parenting practices and communication patterns. Several programs have been shown to be effective in improving child outcomes over a control group. These include the Iowa Strengthening Families Program for rural families and the New Beginnings program for divorced women with children (Winslow, Sandler, & Wolchik, 2005). Organizationally, the goals to increase resilience are classroom management and changing school ecologies to be more supportive of students. Examples of effective intervention in this sphere are the Olweus Bullying Prevention Program, discussed earlier, and School Transitional Environment Project, which is aimed at easing the transition between middle and high school (Winslow et al., 2005).

Ecological Environments

Figure 4.2 shows the significant environments and systems in which the child interacts and with which the child transacts (Allen-Meares, Lane, & Oppenheimer, 1981, and modified in 2002).

The ecological environment is a nested arrangement of structures, each of which is contained

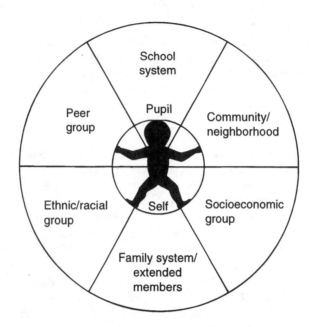

FIGURE 4.2   A Child's Natural Habitat   *Source:* Allen-Meares, Lane, and Oppenheimer, 1981, and updated 2002.

within the next (see Figure 4.3). The definitions of these structures are as follows:

- Microsystem: adults that nurture and teach children; peers and siblings who play and socialize with them; and the settings such as day care, home, and school.
- Mesosystem: interactions and relationships between and among individuals and settings that comprise the microsystem. The mesosystem represents the degree of connection, coordination, and continuity across a child's microsystems.
- Exosystem: the contexts that influence the child indirectly. The exosystem exerts its influence on the child via its impact on individuals and institutions in the child's microsystems (e.g., the workplaces of the child's parents).
- Macrosystem: broadest level of influence and is comprised of political systems, social policy, culture, and economic trends.
- Chronosystem—represents the element of time, both in the individual's life trajectory (e.g., infancy, childhood, adolescence, adulthood) and in the historical context (Weiss, Kreider, Lopez, & Chatman, 2005, pp. xiv–xv; Bronfenbrenner, 1979).

One can apply this four-level ecological systems perspective to design gang prevention programs. However, all four levels must be addressed if the intervention is to be effective at reducing the impact such groups have on society (Williams, Rivera, Neighbours, & Reznik, 2007). At the microlevel, each gang member's personality, academic skills, cognitive ability, physical characteristics, and family relationships must be addressed. At the mesosystem level, various systems in the environment of gang members must be addressed (e.g., schools, neighborhood programs, and recreational centers). At the exosystem level, the attitudes, practices, and actions of leaders could influence gang members' access to mental health and youth services. Community business leaders, the police department, and neighborhood constituencies must work together to provide support where needed. The outermost level—the macrosystem—which represents values, laws, and policies of society, affects the other three levels. Legislative action resulting in programs and policies has a bearing on opportunities to reintegrate gang members into society, as well as developing programs to prevent delinquency. All too often, gang members have lost

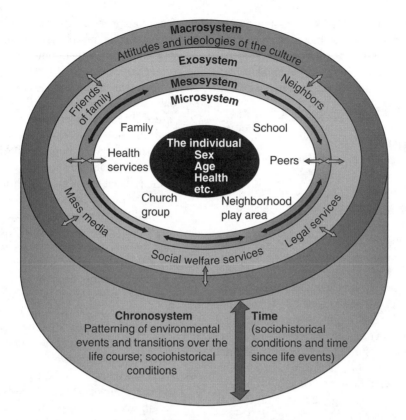

FIGURE 4.3 The Ecological Environment *Source:* Santrock, J. W., *Life-Span Development,* 9th ed. New York, NY: McGraw-Hill, 2004, p. 55. © Copyright The McGraw-Hill Companies, Inc. Reprinted with permission.

their connections with constructive relationships, and the gang itself has become a closed mesosystem in which antisocial behaviors are reinforced. Clearly schools, civic leaders, religious institutions, concerned citizens, social and human service agencies, and the justice system will need to work together to address this problem.

The nested arrangement that characterizes the ecological environment is described as follows:

It seems useful to picture the ecological network as consisting of three nested systems or levels. The first level and the most basic environmental unit or system is the behavior setting.... The behavior setting consists of a physical milieu, a program of activities, inhabitants, and a location in time and space. A child in a behavior setting (such as a classroom) is a component of the setting and is also significantly influenced by the expectations, constraints and opportunities available in that setting. Behavior settings can be described with various degrees of inclusiveness: the kindergarten class or the whole school; the family at breakfast or the home.

The second level of analysis in this nested model is patterns of behavior across settings. At this level, behavior settings comprise the building blocks for studies of more complex child–environment interactions, including, for example, the behavior of the same child at home and school or the behaviors of children labeled disturbed and nondisturbed in different settings.

The community and culture influence the design and meaning of simple behavior settings and the relationships among them. Community and culture as the third and most complex level of analysis includes formal and informal structures as local and supra-local levels as well as characteristics of the physical environment. (Swap, 1978, pp. 186–196)

Components of the ecological system of the school and the place of the learner in it are depicted in Figure 4.2. Every pupil or learner is considered unique, and thus his or her transactions and interactions with the school and its subsystems are unique.

Ecological Assessment. Applied Ecological Psychology for Schools within Communities: Assessment and Intervention (Swartz & Martin, 1997), is an excellent book that describes assessment and interventions in the primary microsystems in which pupils live: home, community, and school. No other book has been published in the last decade that describes assessment for schools as well. The authors provide a useful framework for assessment that is consistent with the perspective advocated in this book. Specifically, assessment must include attention to individual physiological factors and aspects of environment. A poor fit between pupil characteristics and demands of the environment can result in a disturbance of child adjustment. For example, a pupil may not be capable of performing certain academic and behavioral tasks considered to be normative for his or her age group and thus is perceived to be deviant by the teacher. This is known as the ecological perspective of deviance. Allen-Meares and Lane (1987) offered a framework for ecological assessment. Rooted in the ecological perspective and systems concepts, it facilitates the isolation of three major dimensions of assessment as well as relevant data sources (see Figure 4.4). By breaking the three-dimensional block into its component cells, one can begin to identify the assessment components represented by each cell. Figure 4.4 represents an ideal framework. In our daily practice, it may be impossible to address every cell, and in some cases perhaps there is no need to do so. Many constraints prevent practitioners from conducting comprehensive assessments (e.g., agency policy, time, large caseloads, client or family resistance).

Six practice principles are derived from this framework:

1. A comprehensive ecosystems assessment requires that data be collected about multiple ecosystems (e.g., school, home, and community). Questions to consider include: What are the educational opportunities of the community and family? Are there unique ethnic and cultural characteristics?

2. Assessment should include data from all three data sources (person, significant others, and direct observations of the pupil in his or her environment). The school social worker may want to observe a pupil in the home, classroom, and an informal setting. The practitioners may want to speak with different persons about the pupil's behavior in different contexts and at different times of the day.

3. The third principle advocates for assessment data on all the critical data variables that describe the person (cognitive, affective, behavior, physical attributes) and the situational context. For example, if a pupil's intellectual functioning on standardized tests suggests above-normal capacity, but the teacher reports underachievement and sleeping in the classroom (even though there is no illness).

4. A comprehensive assessment should include as many components as is possible. For example, to understand a pupil's inability to make friends, a school social worker would also want to assess the child's social skills across settings, obtain information from a number of persons, and perhaps draw on objective techniques such as sociometric ratings from peers.

5. The assessment data must be integrated into a comprehensive picture of the pupil's situation. Each variable is one piece of a total picture. It also helps the practitioner to locate the source of difficulty (in the pupil, the environment, or both).

6. The sixth principle deals with connecting the assessment with an elective and effective repertoire of intervention strategies. The school social worker would need to know about interventions that target the person and the environment(s).

Adaptive behavior is considered "the ability of a person to function in society, in a group or in a classroom according to specific standards of behavior and ability" (Allen-Meares, 2008). In research on the assessment of adaptive behavior of pupils for possible placement in special education

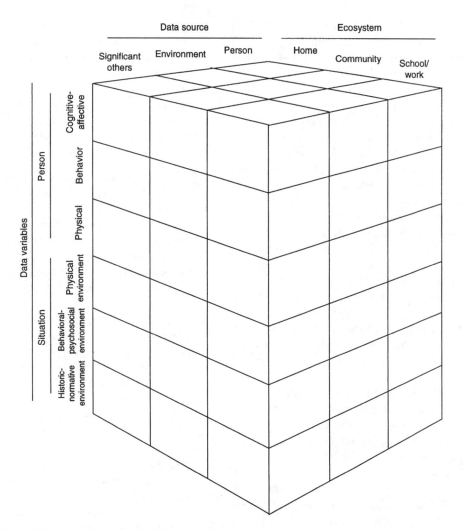

FIGURE 4.4   Ecosystems Assessment Framework   *Source:* Allen-Meares, P., and Lane, B., "Grounding Social Work Practice in Theory: Ecosystems," *Social Casework*, 68, no. 9 (November, 1987), p. 519. Used with permission from Families in Society: The Journal of Contemporary Social Services, published by the Alliance for Children and Families (www.FamiliesinSociety.org).

classes, a case is made for the inclusion of standardized assessment measures (Allen-Meares, 2008; Allen-Meares & Lane, 1983). This article draws on the same perspective and theoretical constructs presented in this chapter (See Appendix III).

Standardized measures have an important role to play in our practice; however, their use should be based on a set of criteria consistent with our theory, values, and what we know about the empirical validation of assessment measures.

There are a number of ecologically sensitive assessment instruments and techniques. According to Martin and Swartz-Kulstad (2000), a good ecological assessment should investigate

(a) the individual adolescent with whom they are working (including cognitive, affective, and behavioral attributes), (b) the contexts in which the adolescent is functioning (e.g., home, peers, school, work), and (c) the "fit" between the individual adolescent and the various contexts. (p. 48)

Though it is beyond the scope of this book to elaborate on each of these instruments, a few will be described. There are several different methods of assessment from which to choose. Martin and Swartz-Kulstad (2000) reported seven different methods: interviews, eco-maps, self-report *objective* measures, projectives, family interactive tasks, enactments, and assessment for intervention planning. There are three widely used self-report *objective* measures: the Family Environment Scale (a 90-item true/false test that measures social and environmental characteristics of families for both children and parents), the Life Stressors and Social Resources Inventory–Youth Form (addresses additional family concerns and issues dealing with adolescence), and Family Adaptability and Cohesion Evaluation III (a 20-item Likert-style questionnaire that measures adaptability and cohesion of both children and parents) (Martin & Swartz-Kulstad, 2000). The psychometric properties of these instruments are well documented. Of course, school social workers rely on informal sources of data to complement data gathered from standardized instruments. For example, a review of pupil records, teacher and parent interviews, observational data, and various rating scales provides useful information for ascertaining a comprehensive ecological perspective of the pupil.

Another area that requires specific attention in ecological assessment is culture (Martin & Swartz-Kulstad, 2000). Culture has a great effect on a person's identity formation, values, habits, customs, beliefs, and self-esteem, which can explain behavior patterns. For instance, Allen, Elliott, Kataoka, Morales, Hambarsoomian, and Schuster (2007) conducted a study of more than 250 Latino eighth graders, measuring the acculturation and family characteristics of the children. Their conclusion is that acculturation contributes to poor mental health of Latino adolescents, but the presence of extended family members and parental monitoring are moderating factors.

Ecological Intervention.   School social workers intervene in transactions. Their intervention can be aimed at a perceived cause of imbalance existing outside the school environment or within

the school system, at the child, or at a combination of these. Targeting intervention at the pupil or at groups of pupils is just one strategy that the school social worker can use. To promote change in the various transactions, Apter (1982) suggested that school social workers build strong ecosystems and link the various aspects of each child's world. A school social worker might seek to achieve the following goals:

- To build new social skills or competencies on the part of adults, parents, and children.
- To identify new resources and social service agencies that will assist children and their families and to develop new programs in the school and community.
- To change the perceptions of adults (such as teachers who may have a negative view of a pupil).
- To increase knowledge and understanding (for example, provide in-service training to educators about child abuse and neglect).
- To restructure activities (for example, develop modified educational schedules for children who have difficulty functioning in an all-day setting).
- To develop new ties with relevant community agencies (such as mental health and adolescent services) and school-based services.
- To develop new roles for teachers, parents, and community agency personnel (for example, teacher as group work leader, parent as volunteer, agency personnel as a school resource).
- To develop new and innovative programs where a need exists (such as alternative programs, flexible scheduling, in-school programs for pregnant girls, after-school programs for children whose parents are employed, modified physical education programs for those with physical handicaps). (Apter, 1982, pp. 70–71)

The case or need for environmental and/or school change is highlighted by research, which suggests that children with behavior disorders are more likely to be rejected and victimized by their peers than are other pupils (Martin & Swartz-Kulstad, 2000). School social workers must work to change the attitudes of peers and teachers as well as the overall climate of the school. Too often social workers will focus on the individual pupil, perhaps by enhancing his or her social skills, while ignoring the need to change the climate of the classroom and the attitudes of peers.

We know that a pupil's school experiences are shaped not only by the classroom setting but also by the larger school environment. To prevent problems and stress for pupils, school social workers must understand what the social environment is like and its influence on those who occupy it (Bowes, 2004).

The organizational climate of the school has been the subject of considerable empirical investigation. Though there is no standard definition of organizational climate and some use the terms *climate* and *culture* interchangeably, attempts to measure it continue. The notion of organizational health and healthy environments focuses attention on how schools conduct their business and on the nature and quality of the interactions among those within the system. Climate assessment tools include the Organizational Climate Description Questionnaire, which was revised by Hoy and Clover (2007) to a more precise measure of school climate where the object of inquiry is principally the teachers and administration, and the Organizational Health Inventory, developed by Hoy and Feldman (2007). The OHI measures the health of the school on seven dimensions of student–teacher, teacher–teacher, and teacher–administrator interactions (Hoy & Feldman, 2007).

A growing body of literature on systemic interventions for promoting safe schools is congruent with the theoretical framework espoused in this chapter (Conoley & Conoley, 2001). Schools are located within a context that makes them an important location for mounting preventive interventions to reduce violence (see Chapter 6) and for linking with important service providers. Approaches that change the systems and relationships of the school, community, and classrooms are important for effective interventions to reduce violence. Whatever approach is adopted for prevention, a critical variable is early and comprehensive intervention. Interventions such as parent training (that focuses on how to handle early

childhood oppositional behavior), social cognitive skills training (which focuses on the promotion of functional social skills, anger management, and conflict resolution), and multisystemic therapy (which focuses on highly structured, intensive family and community-based treatment that targets inappropriate and violent behaviors) are promising. The promotion of positive identification with the social context or one's community also acts as a buffer against violence (which means that there must be a good fit between the child and the school's culture, policies, and practices). And there must be in place, within the school, ways for assisting pupils with academic performance (e.g., tutoring, self-monitoring, and time delay procedures, the method of transferring stimulus control by changing the temporal interval between the natural cue and the teacher's prompt). Singularly or in combination, the aforementioned interventions offer promising approaches for responding to different graduations of violence.

One role that practitioners can play as they promote change in linkages and ecosystems is the role of advocate. Advocacy on behalf of pupil groups can take place on several levels: in school and community committees organized to develop and plan programs for pupils; at the state and national levels (supporting the rights of high-risk pupil groups); and within the school and community systems (identifying adequate services and unfair policies and practices). Examples of those skills that are relevant include

1. Collecting appropriate information to document aspects of the biological, medical, psychological, cultural, sociological, emotional, legal, and environmental factors that affect the learning process of school pupils
2. Collaborating with community agencies in school-linked service projects or other programs to solve specific problem situations or develop new resources for children and their families
3. Identifying and developing resources within and outside the local education agency and the community

4. Making systematic observation and assessment of needs and characteristics of pupils, parents, school system, neighborhood, and community and evaluating the effects of the interaction of these characteristics with pupil characteristics

5. Analyzing and influencing policy at local, county, state, and national levels

6. Consulting with persons in the client system to clarify situations, give or receive information, monitor progress in an intervention plan, or mediate among points of view

7. Assessing the influences operating in school–community–pupil–parent relations and interpreting these influences (*NASW Standards for Social Work Services in Schools,* 2002)

A Framework for Specialization in School Social Work

Essentially, school social work is one of the specialized fields of social work practice. According to Bartlett, defining the characteristics of a field of practice makes it possible to define desirable educational input. Bartlett specified five characteristics of social practice: (a) a central problem, (b) a system of organized services, (c) a body of knowledge, (d) sociocultural attitudes, and (e) characteristic responses and behavior of the persons served (Bartlett, 1970). We would add a sixth characteristic: contemporary forces of change, both inside and outside the field of practice.

1. *Central problem.* The primary function of the public schools is education. When the interaction between the school and the child results in a dysfunctional relationship for both—in particular, when pupils are not learning and adapting and the school is experiencing difficulty in helping them to achieve—then there is a problem.

2. *System of organized services.* The school is a highly departmentalized bureaucracy. It has levels of achievement and advancement that operate to categorize children; it has specialized personnel such as regular classroom teachers, psychologists, reading teachers, counselors, social workers, and administrators at various levels to oversee specific areas. The school's rules of operation are intricate and well established to enhance performance and conformity.

3. *Body of knowledge.* The field of education contains a variety of teaching materials and methods as well as ideologies concerning how and under what conditions children learn best. Differences in opinion range from the humanistic approach to the more structured behavioral approach. The fundamental knowledge base and the methodologies for preparing educators are different from those used in the preparation and training of social workers. The educator focuses on mastery of cognitive and affective skills and on the child's in-school performance. The social work profession also values these dynamics, but its focus is broader in that it includes the "total child" (family, school, community, and culture) and the quality of interaction among these components. Skills and other elements of competencies for working with this population of schoolchildren have been identified in the *NASW Standard for Social Work Services in Schools.* These skills emerge from a substantial body of knowledge. This knowledge is translatable into social work intervention in the transactions between schoolchildren and their home–school–community environment.

4. *Sociocultural attitudes.* Our society highly values the function of the public schools. It gives the schools responsibility for developing the population's functional skills and preparing children for career opportunities and citizenship—all of which enhances and perpetuates the society. Academic success in our society is often considered one of the keys to upward mobility and self-respect.

5. *Characteristic responses of the person served.* The general response of the majority of children to the school setting is one of adaptation. However, there are children who are anxious and

whose fear of failure undermines their potential for learning. There are also children who do not adapt to the structure of the institution and its environmental, social, and psychological demands, and thus are rejected or assigned to various specialized or remedial programs.

6. *Forces of change.* Because of innovations, laws, and community pressure, the public school system has periodically changed its methodology and has frequently altered its theories of how children learn. Historically, legislation has played a significant role in shaping our educational system, and it still does. The interplay among legislation, innovations in education, and developments related to social work services in the schools should be analyzed periodically (Allen-Meares, 1981).

Conclusion

In this chapter the reader was introduced to the profession of social work: its values, purposes, goals, and sanctions; the search for a conceptual framework; and the application of social work in the school setting. An ecological perspective of practice was advocated, for it offers a comprehensive view of pupils, school, community, and parents and of the transactions and interactions among them that can cause pupil malperformance. The goal of school social workers is to change the pupil, the environment, or both—to promote the healthy social functioning of pupils. This chapter also made clear the unique contribution of the social work profession to schools and the profession's dual perspective of person and environment. No other discipline in the school works at this interface. The school social worker recognizes that the quality of pupils' transactions with environments outside the school, as well as those within the school system, has much to do with the pupils' academic performance and the development of competencies required for successful societal adjustment. As Bernard stated, "The challenge … is the implementation of prevention strategies that strengthen protective factors in our families, schools, and communities" (Bernard, 1992, p. 3).

For Study and Discussion

1. List several positive aspects of an ecological perspective of social work practice in schools. Who do you think advocates this perspective? Some have questioned whether the ecological perspective is sufficient to inform and direct social work practice. Can the ecological model guide social work practice? What is your opinion?

2. In the school we often find school psychologists, counselors, and other supportive service staff. Describe some of the tasks that might be shared by these individuals and that they might share with the school social worker. Then describe the unique contributions of, and tasks performed by, the social worker.

3. Why has it been so difficult for the profession of social work to define and adopt a conceptual framework? Identify several factors unique to the profession that may contribute to this situation.

4. Write your state department of education and request the certification requirements for school social workers.

5. Cite several hypothetical case illustrations of a poor "fit" or "match" between any of the following combinations: school, community, pupil group, and parents (note the case illustrations in this chapter). What would be the practitioner's role or service plan? How should the practitioner proceed to achieve a better match?

6. Secure a copy of the *NASW Standards for Social Work Services in Schools.* Why is this document important to school social workers? What standard(s) would you add and why?

7. Why is the study of risk, resiliency, and protective factors so important for social work practice in schools? Identify and discuss a list of protective factors for pupils in an urban setting.

Additional Readings

Aisenberg, E., & Herrenkohl, T. (2008). Community violence in context: Risk and resilience in children and families. *Journal of Interpersonal Violence, 23*(3), 296–315.

Allen-Meares, P., Hudgins, C. A., & Engberg, M. E. (2004). The global program on youth: Lessons learned from collaboratories in action. *Journal of Technology in Human Services, 22*(4), 39–53.

Anthony, E. K. (2008). Cluster profiles of youths living in urban poverty: Factors affecting risk and resilience. *Social Work Research, 32*(1), 6–17.

Beck, B. M. (1959). School social work: An instrument of education. *Social Work, 4*(4), 87–91.

Benbenishty, R. (2005). *School violence in context: Culture, neighborhood, family, school, and gender.* New York: Oxford University Press.

Brindis, C. D., Klein, J., Schlitt, J., Santelli, J., Juszczak, L., & Nystrom, R. J. (2003). School-based health centers: Accessibility and accountability. *Journal of Adolescent Health, 32*(6S), 98–107.

Clancy, J. (1995). Ecological school social work: The reality and the vision. *Social Work in Education, 17*(1), 40–47.

Comer, J. P. (1984). Home-school relationships as they affect the academic success of children. *Education and Urban Society, 16*(3), 323–327.

Frey, A. J., & Dupper, D. R. (2005). A broader conceptual approach to clinical practice for the 21st century. *Children & Schools, 27*(1), 33–44.

Germain, C. B., & Bloom, M. (1999). *Human behavior in the social environment: An ecological view.* New York: Columbia University Press.

Goldstein, S., & Brooks, R. B. (2005). *Handbook of resilience in children.* New York: Springer.

Haber, M. G., & Toro, P. A. (2004). Homelessness among families, children, and adolescents: An ecological-developmental perspective. *Clinical Child and Family Psychology Review, 7*(3), 123–164.

Haynes, K. S., & Mickelson, J. S. (2005). *Affecting change: Social workers in the political arena* (6th ed.). Boston: Allyn & Bacon.

Heath, M. A., Money, K., Annandale, N., Fischer, L., & Young, E. L. (2007). Crisis intervention for students of diverse backgrounds: School counselors' concerns. *Brief Treatment and Crisis Intervention, 7*(1), 12–24.

Jakes, S. S., & Brookins, C. C. (Eds.). (2004). *Understanding ecological programming: Merging theory, research, and practice.* Binghamton, NY: Haworth Press.

Jaycox, L. H., McCaffrey, D. F., Ocampo, B. W., Shelley, G. A., Blake, S. M., Peterson, D. J., et al. (2006). Challenges in the evaluation and implementation of school-based prevention and intervention programs on sensitive topics. *American Journal of Evaluation, 27*(3), 320.

Jozefowicz-Simbeni, D. M. H., & Allen-Meares, P. (2002). Poverty and schools: Intervention and resource building through school-linked services. *Children and Schools, 24*(2), 123–136.

Khoury-Kassabri, M., Astor, R. A., & Benbenishty, R. (2007). Weapon carrying in Israeli schools: The contribution of individual and school factors. *Health Education & Behavior, 34*(3), 453–470.

Langsford, J. E., Deater-Deckard, K., & Bornstein, M. H. (Eds.). (2007). *Immigrant families in contemporary society.* New York: The Guilford Press.

Lee, L. J. (1983). The social worker in the political environment of a school system. *Social Work, 28*(4), 302–307.

Maynard, B. R. (2007). To EBP or not to EBP?: Social work's dilemma with evidence based practice. *Praxis, 7,* 5–15.

Michals, A. P., Cournoyer, D. E., & Pinner, E. E. (1979). School social work and educational goals. *Social Work, 24*(2), 138–144.

Miller, T. W. (2008). *School violence and primary prevention.* New York: Springer.

Pardeck, J. T. (2006). *Children's rights: Policy and practice.* Binghamton, NY: Haworth Press.

Payne, M. (2002). The politics of systems theory within social work. *Journal of Social Work, 2*(3), 269–292.

Popham, W. J. (2006). Assessment for learning: An endangered species? *Educational Leadership, 63*(5), 82–83.

Popham, W. J. (2007). *Classroom assessment: What teachers need to know* (5th ed.). Boston: Allyn & Bacon.

Raines, J. C. (2004). Evidence-based practice in school social work: A process in perspective. *Children & Schools, 26*(2), 71–85.

Sanders, M. G. (2006). *Building school-community partnerships: Collaboration for student success.* Thousand Oaks, CA: Corwin Press.

Sarason, S. B. (1971). *The culture of the school and the problem of change.* Boston: Allyn & Bacon.

Schwartz, S. J., Pantin, H., Coatsworth, J. D., & Szapocznik, J. (2007). Addressing the challenges and opportunities for today's youth: Toward an integrative model and its implications for research and intervention. *The Journal of Primary Prevention, 28*(2), 117–144.

Sheidow, A. J., & Henggeler, S. W. (2008). Multisystemic therapy for alcohol and other drug abuse in delinquent adolescents. *Alcoholism Treatment Quarterly, 26*(1/2), 125.

Sheridan, S. M., & McCurdy, M. (2007). Ecological variables in school-based assessment and intervention planning. In R. Brown-Chidsey (Ed.), *Assessment for intervention: A problem solving approach* (pp. 43–64). New York: The Guilford Press.

Sosin, M., & Caulum, S. (1983). Advocacy: A conceptualization for social work practice. *Social Work, 28*(1), 12–17.

Vanderbilt-Adriance, E., & Shaw, D. S. (2008). Conceptualizing and re-evaluating resilience across levels of risk, time, and domains of competence. *Clinical Child and Family Psychology Review, 11*(1), 30–58.

Vinter, R. D., & Sarri, R. C. (1965). Malperformance in the public school: A group work approach. *Social Work, 10*(1), 3–13.

5

Student Rights and Control of Behavior

SANDRA KOPELS

University of Illinois, Urbana-Champaign

In our system, state-operated schools may not be enclaves of totalitarianism. School officials do not possess absolute authority over their students. Students in school as well as out of school are "persons" under our Constitution. They are possessed of fundamental rights which the State must respect, just as they themselves must respect their obligations to the States.
—U.S. Supreme Court in Tinker v. Des Moines

Teacher don't you fill me up with your rules. Everybody knows that smokin' ain't allowed in school.
—Motley Crue, "Smokin' in the Boys Room"

Introduction

In this chapter, we explore the broad issues that pertain to student rights and the problems associated with student control as a requirement for carrying out the goals and functions of the school. As we pointed out in Chapter 3, schools as social systems have certain boundary maintenance functions that must be reconciled with the guarantees of the First, Fourth, and Fourteenth Amendments. Achieving this balance often presents a dilemma because school officials have the right and responsibility to control what occurs within the schools, although their control must be balanced against students' rights to be treated fairly.

The U.S. Supreme Court first acknowledged this dilemma in *West Virginia State Board of Education v. Barnette* (1943). It affirmed school officials' right to prescribe and control conduct but said that school officials do not have total authority over pupils. The Court upheld the notion that students' freedom of expression must be

protected, but that students also must understand the principles on which the government stands. It also noted that schools as microcosms of society must also be a "marketplace of ideas," where truth can be discussed through the "robust exchange of ideas and not by enclaves of totalitarianism."

In *Stanley v. Northeast Independent School District* (1972), the Court observed: "One of the great concerns of our time, is that our young people, disillusioned by our political processes, are disengaging from political participation. It is most important that our young people become convinced that our Constitution is a living reality, not parchment preserved under glass."

Although the courts have expressed concerns regarding the need for children to develop into politically aware citizens, during the late 1980s and 1990s, societal problems such as drugs, weapons, and violence became almost commonplace in the schools. Incidents such as school shootings, wherein children bring weapons into the schools and cause grave injuries and death to other students and teachers, have affected the philosophies behind decisions about control of student behavior and the maintenance of school safety. Even the terrorist attacks on the United States on September 11, 2001, have affected certain educational provisions regarding safe school environments.

These issues have had impact on the courts as well. As society has passed new laws targeted to reduce drugs, weapons, and violent incidents within the schools, court decisions over the past half-century regarding the control of student conduct have vacillated in their attempts to balance the rights of school officials against students. The balance is between schools' needs to control the conduct of students and safety for all with the rights of students to behave in ways that express themselves as individuals. As you will see, the decisions reflect the tenor of the times.

The primary aim of this chapter is to impress on social workers in schools that democracy and the values that social workers hold inviolable must be preserved and that the role of social workers is to assist society in balancing the rights of children, the interests of parents in raising their children, and the duty of the schools to maintain an orderly learning environment.

The chapter begins with an overview of the principles that provide the legal authority to maintain control over children within the school. Next, we discuss rights students have as persons under the Constitution. We then turn to issues related to the punishment or discipline of students when they challenge the control of school officials and the requirement that they attend school. Throughout this discussion, we present leading cases that reflect the balance of the competing interests. Finally, we offer some suggestions and imperatives for school social workers to bridge the gap between student rights and the responsibilities of school districts.

Sources of School Districts' Authority

In this section, we discuss the sources of the authority that school officials have to maintain a learning environment that is both orderly and safe. These sources include the *in loco parentis* doctrine, the common law of the schools, and the legal authority of the state.

The *In Loco Parentis* Doctrine

The legal concept of *in loco parentis* is a Latin phrase that means "in place of the parents." It describes a relationship similar to that of a parent to a child, in which an individual assumes the status of a parent and the rights and responsibilities of a parent for an individual, usually a child, without formally adopting the child. Although *in loco parentis* can be applied to other contexts, such as the relationship between a guardian and a ward, the most common usage of the doctrine relates to teachers and their students.

The classroom teacher has a closer association with and understanding of the pupil than other school personnel and thereby enters into a special legal relationship. In fact, one of the basic legal principles regarding student control is that the teacher, by virtue of his or her position, has legal authority over a pupil, analogous to a parent's authority over a child, at least for purposes of necessary control and correction.

Initially, this doctrine gave power to school officials to exercise the same control over students at school (or even when students were going to and from schools) that parents could exercise at home. Technically, however, this principle still left open the question of just what powers parents have over children, although generally such power has been interpreted as being extensive, almost unlimited, short of obvious, gross abuse. Thus, when *in loco parentis* was applied to the schools, the result was to give teachers, principals, and other administrators enormous control over students. This control extended not only to formal studies but also to clothing, hairstyles, speech, manners, morals, organizational membership, and even behavior away from school. For example, from the late 1800s to the late 1950s, courts upheld the authority of public school officials to expel pupils for joining a social fraternity (*Smith v. Board of Education,* 1913), going home for lunch (*Bishop v. Houston School District,* 1931), having a venereal disease (*Kenny v. Gurley,* 1923), smoking off campus (*Tanton v. McKenney,* 1924), and violating a school rule against going to the movies on weeknights (*Mangum v. Keith,* 1918). Courts have also held that pupils can be expelled for speaking against school policy at a student body meeting (*Wooster v. Sunderland,* 1915), wearing a fraternity insignia to school (*Antell v. Stokes,* 1934), expressing offensive sexual views (*Morris v. Nowotny,* 1959), arranging for a communist speaker to speak off campus (*Zarichney v. State Board of Agriculture,* 1949), and even for refusing to tell who wrote "dirty words" on the school wall (*Board of Education v. Helston,* 1889). As we will see later in this chapter, some of these court decisions would no longer be decided in the same way.

The protest movements of the 1960s and the growing tide of civil rights advocacy gave impetus to the decline in the use of the *in loco parentis* doctrine. Despite the shift in the application of the doctrine, school officials still have broad powers in exercising discipline in schools. However, a lot depends on the circumstances in individual cases. For example, courts have given schools wide discretion in punishing pupils as long as their actions are reasonable and connected to the educational process (*Neuhaus v. Federico,* 1973). Courts have sanctioned punishments for using tobacco, alcohol, and drugs on the grounds that "an effort to maintain and inculcate habits designed to preserve good health among pupils is a legitimate element of an educational system" (*Rando v. Newberg Public School Board,* 1975).

In general, over the last 40 years, the courts have placed limits on the types of behavior that schools can punish. The most important limit is that pupils *may not* be punished for asserting their First Amendment rights (of free speech, press, or association) unless students substantially disrupt the existing conditions for learning.

Common Law of the Schools

Another closely related concept to *in loco parentis* is the common law of the schools. This concept derived from the colonists as they developed the colonial American schools. The colonists borrowed the English ideal that schools not only have an educational but also a moral responsibility for students. Accordingly, both the teachers and the pupils have mutual responsibilities and obligations. The mutuality of the relationship is predicated on society's expectations of the school in the advancement of the common good of the community (Alexander & Alexander, 1998).

Thus, the common law of the school, as prescribed by extensive judicial precedent, reflects a synthesis, characterized by the school, wherein the highest interest of the individual and the preeminent interest of the community coincide. The individual, in pursuing his or her own interest, pursues that of the community, and in promoting the interest of the community, promotes his or her own. This harmony of interests is defined and furthered by the common law of the public school. Therefore, the reasoning of the common law, which conveys to the teacher the authority to maintain an orderly atmosphere of learning, as a benefit to both the student and the community, may be understood in the context of both law and philosophy (Alexander & Alexander, 1998).

The Legal Authority of the State

Within constitutional limits, state legislatures have plenary (i.e., complete, absolute, and unqualified) authority with respect to school policy and control. However, the language of statutes dealing with the control of pupils is usually rather general. Much of the legislation concerning student control is permissive in nature, thereby delegating to school districts the authority and responsibility to determine the specifics of such control. Experts consider this proper because a school district is a territorial subdivision of the state, and thus school board members are state officials overseeing the state function of education. Moreover, most authorities argue that the school may be thought of as similar to a legislative body, enacting rules and regulations that govern student control within the boundaries of the school district.

Although legislatures are given general authority to govern schools, they cannot violate the pupils' basic constitutional rights. Where legislators fail to fulfill constitutional requirements, the courts may invalidate their acts. The fact that education is specifically set out in state constitutions as a required state function gives education a "preferential position" relative to other state governmental functions that are not specified (Alexander & Alexander, 1998).

Because of the very broad authority that schools have under any of these principles, within the last decade "zero-tolerance" policies have developed. Under zero tolerance, a school district will enact a policy that allows for no deviations from a rule. In other words, the school will not tolerate any breach of a school rule, regardless of how good the reason or how minor the deviation. As we will discuss later in this chapter, newspaper articles are replete with stories about children being suspended or expelled from school for violating their schools' zero-tolerance policy. The authority of the school is not without limits, however.

Basic Constitutional Rights

Before we begin to talk about balancing the rights of schools to maintain order and provide a safe learning environment against the constitutional rights of students, it is necessary to have a basic understanding of certain constitutional principles and constitutional rights.

Due Process

According to the Fifth and Fourteenth Amendments to the U.S. Constitution, before there can be any governmental deprivation of life, liberty, or property, due process must be afforded. Under the concept of substantive due process, the idea is that there are limitations on the substance of what governments may do. Therefore, if the government wants to place restrictions on certain rights of individuals that are considered to be fundamental

(i.e., derived from the Constitution), then the government has to have compelling reasons to abridge these rights, and the reasons for the abridgement must be tailored narrowly to accomplish the governmental objectives (Kopels, 1998). For example, if a school district wants all its students, no matter how young, to have body cavity searches every day to prevent drugs from coming into the school, school officials would have to justify how their interest in drug-free schools outweighs students' privacy rights. The schools would also have the burden of proving that there would be no less intrusive way (e.g., searching backpacks or purses) to reach their goal.

Under the concept of procedural due process, procedural rights must be afforded to individuals before their rights to life, liberty, or property are taken away. If the governmental purpose is proper, then procedural due process requires that before there is a deprivation of rights, the individual is to be given whatever procedures are required constitutionally before the deprivation occurs. Using the same example, if the schools were to conduct body cavity searches, they would be required, at a minimum, to let parents and students know that the searches were going to occur and how objections could be mounted, before the searches began.

The right to an education, although incredibly important to individuals and the nation, has been determined not to qualify as a fundamental right under the Constitution (*San Antonio Ind. Sch. Dist. v. Rodriguez*, 1973). However, education has been determined to implicate liberty and property rights under the Constitution (*Goss v. Lopez*, 1975). Courts have determined that liberty or property rights are involved in short-term suspensions, corporal punishment, transfers from one school to another for disciplinary reasons, grade reductions, and expulsion from school or extracurricular activities (Eisenman & Fischer, 1994). Accordingly, schools must develop careful policies and proper procedures that address students' constitutional rights when the results of the official decisions affect students' educational rights.

Other Constitutional Rights

Many of the protections of the Bill of Rights to the U.S. Constitution have been applied to the school context. Among the rights that we will discuss are ones that derive from the First, Fourth, and Eighth Amendments to the Constitution. The First Amendment places prohibitions on the government from making laws that restrict individuals' freedom of speech and expression, freedom of the press, the right to assemble, or the right to the free exercise of their religion. The Fourth Amendment places prohibitions on the government against unreasonable searches and seizures, and the Eighth Amendment prohibits the government from inflicting cruel and unusual punishment on its people. The issues that we will discuss later all find their basis in the constitutional principles of due process and implicate at least one of the aforementioned constitutional rights. Public school officials, as representatives of the government, must ensure that the policies they create do not impermissibly violate students' constitutional rights.

Freedom of Speech and Expression

The First Amendment states that the government shall make no law abridging the freedom of speech. Until 1969, the Supreme Court did not have the opportunity to address the application of this constitutional principle to the public schools.

The *Tinker* Case

The landmark decision in *Tinker v. Des Moines School District* (1969) established three general principles regarding freedom of expression in schools: (a) the First Amendment protects the freedom of speech of students in public schools; (b) symbolic speech, such as the wearing of armbands, buttons, or other symbols, is protected as is actual speech; and (c) no right, not even the right to speak, is absolute, and the right to free speech and other student rights may be limited under certain circumstances.

In December 1965, a group of adults and students in Des Moines held a meeting at the Eckhardt home. The members of the group decided to publicize their objections to the hostilities in Vietnam and their support for a truce by wearing black armbands during the holiday season and by fasting on December 16 and on New Year's Eve. The petitioners in the case were John F. Tinker, 15 years old, and Christopher Eckhardt, 16 years old, who attended high schools in Des Moines, Iowa, and Mary Beth Tinker, John's sister, a 13-year-old student in junior high school. The children previously had engaged in similar activities with their parents and decided to participate in this protest at school.

The principals of the Des Moines schools became aware of the plan to wear armbands. On December 14, 1965, they met and adopted a policy that pupils wearing armbands to school would be asked to remove them; if they refused to do so, they would be suspended until they returned without the armbands. Aware of the regulation that the school authorities had adopted, Mary Beth Tinker and Christopher Eckhardt wore black armbands to their schools on December 16; John Tinker wore his armband the next day. They were all sent home and suspended from school until they returned without their armbands. They did not return to school until after New Year's Day, 1966.

A complaint was filed in the U.S. District Court by the petitioners, through their fathers, under Section 1983 of Title 42 of the U.S. Code. It asked for an injunction restraining the school officials and the members of the board of directors of the school district from disciplining the petitioners, and it sought nominal monetary damages. After an evidentiary hearing, the court dismissed the complaint, upholding the constitutionality of the school authorities' action on the grounds that it was reasonable in order to prevent disturbance of the school environment.

The case was later brought to the U.S. Supreme Court. On behalf of the Court, Justice Abe Fortas reviewed the history of the case, including the decision by the district court and the legal principles on which the district court judge had relied.

The Court ruled that in the absence of any facts that may have led school officials to forecast a substantial disruption of or material interference with school activities, or any showing that disturbances on school premises, in fact, occurred when students wore black armbands on their sleeves, prohibiting students from wearing armbands to schools and suspending them for failing to remove the armbands was an unconstitutional denial of students' rights to expression of opinion. In his ruling, Justice Fortas made his oft-quoted statement, "It can hardly be argued that either students or teachers shed their constitutional rights to freedom of speech or expression at the schoolhouse gate" (*Tinker* at 736).

The decision in *Tinker* made it clear that restricting a student's right to freedom of expression, for example, is unconstitutional unless there is evidence to show that the forbidden conduct would "materially and substantially interfere" with the smooth running of the school. The decision left to future courts the determination of what circumstances posed "the potentiality and imminence of disruption."

Almost 15 years later, the Supreme Court again faced an issue of freedom of speech. In *Bethel School District No. 403 v. Fraser* (1986), a high school student made a nomination speech at a school assembly and referred to his candidate using explicit and graphic terms, full of sexual innuendos. The school suspended him, and he appealed. The U.S. Supreme Court upheld the school's imposition of discipline and concluded that this student's speech was not constitutionally protected. The court wrote that the fundamental values that are essential to a democratic society must include tolerance of divergent political and religious views, even when the views are unpopular. However, the court stated that these values

> must also take into account consideration of the sensibilities of others, and, in the case of a school, the sensibilities of fellow students. The undoubted freedom to advocate unpopular and controversial views in schools and classrooms must be balanced against the society's countervailing interest in teaching students the boundaries of socially appropriate behavior. (*Fraser* at 683)

The court found that a highly appropriate function of public school education is to prohibit the use of vulgar and offensive terms in public discourse.

Soon after, in *Hazelwood School District v. Kuhlmeier* (1988), the Supreme Court upheld the decision of a high school principal to omit two pages from a student newspaper on stories about three students' experiences with teenage pregnancies and about the impact of divorce on students. Student members of the school newspaper's editorial staff had sued the school on the grounds that withholding the pages of the stories violated their First Amendment rights to free speech. The Supreme Court focused on school-sponsored publications that might be considered to bear the imprimatur of the school. The Court held that a school did not have to tolerate students' speech that is inconsistent with its basic educational mission. Accordingly, the Court stated that educators do not offend the First Amendment by exercising editorial control over style and content of student speech in school-sponsored expressive activities so long as the actions are reasonably related to legitimate pedagogical concerns. Therefore, a school may control speech that is biased or prejudiced, vulgar or profane, unsuitable for immature audiences, or appears to be sanctioned by the school.

For almost 20 years, *Tinker*, *Fraser*, and *Hazelwood* controlled how courts interpreted students' free speech rights. In 2007, the Supreme Court sided with the school administration in a case where a student's expression of speech was considered inconsistent with school policy. In *Morse v. Frederick*, students unfurled a large banner at a school event which read, "BONG HiTS 4 JESUS." The school principal demanded that the students take down the banner, believing that the banner advocated and promoted illegal drug use. All but one student complied. The principal confiscated the banner and suspended the student from school. The student sued, claiming that his speech was a political expression and therefore protected by the First Amendment. In its opinion, the Supreme Court ruled that school officials may restrict student speech at a school event when that speech is reasonably viewed as promoting illegal drug use. Citing the importance of the schools' role in educating students against the dangers of drug use, the Supreme Court ruled that the First Amendment does not require schools to tolerate at school events students' expressions that contribute to those dangers.

The important points in *Tinker* are that (a) for the state (the school) to prohibit such an expression of speech, it must be able to show that the forbidden conduct will interfere with the discipline required to operate the school; and (b) the test to determine whether a child has gone beyond protected speech is whether she or he materially or substantially interferes with the requirements of appropriate discipline in the operation of the school.

The important points made by *Fraser*, *Hazelwood*, and *Morse* show that not all student speech is protected. Taken together, the holdings in *Tinker, Fraser, Hazelwood,* and *Morse* establish that although students do not shed their constitutional rights to freedom of speech and expression at the schoolhouse gate, students' offensive speech or expression in school, inappropriate student speech or expression identified with a school, or promotion of illegal drugs will not violate the First Amendment. However, limitations on political expression may violate the First Amendment. School officials can regulate expressions of opinions that materially and substantially interfere with the requirements of appropriate discipline in the operation of the school or that collide with the rights of others. The imposition of disciplinary sanctions to point out to students that vulgar speech and lewd conduct is inconsistent with the fundamental values of public school education may be appropriate (Simpson, 2001).

School social workers promote cultural diversity and respect for the values and beliefs of others. Some states or school districts within states have begun experimenting with the use of antiharassment policies that prohibit the use of demeaning language or actions against vulnerable minorities. For example, in 2007, Iowa passed legislation that required all public schools and accredited private schools to adopt a policy declaring harassment or bullying in schools, school functions, school-sponsored activities, and school property to be against state and school policy. At a minimum, prohibited actions included electronic, written, verbal, or physical actions toward others based on traits or characteristics of other students based on their "age, color, creed, national origin, race, religion, marital status, sex, sexual orientation, gender identity, physical attributes, physical or mental ability or disability, ancestry, political party preference, political belief, socioeconomic status, or familial status" (Iowa Code, 2008). In 2008, New York City unveiled its "Respect for All" program, which prohibits students from bullying other students for any reason and includes taunting and intimidation through the use of epithets or slurs involving race, color, ethnicity, national origin, religion, gender, gender identity, gender expression, sexual orientation or disability. The policy applies on school grounds, on school buses, and at all school-sponsored activities, programs, and events (Respect for all, 2008).

One interesting case that may have implications for school social work practice concerns a Pennsylvania school district that enacted an antiharassment policy in which students were required to treat members of the school community with mutual respect. The policy defined harassment as verbal or physical conduct based on actual or perceived race, religion, color, national origin, gender, sexual orientation, or disability. The policy prohibited conduct that offends, denigrates, or belittles an individual because of any of the aforementioned characteristics and further prohibited harassment based on things such as clothing, social skills, intellect, educational program, hobbies, or values. Students who violated the policy were subject to punishment including warnings, counseling, suspension, expulsion, and transfer. Certain students, who were worried that their views on morality, including their beliefs regarding the harmful effects of homosexuality, would subject them to reprisals under this policy by the school, challenged the policy in court. The Third Circuit Court of Appeals struck down the school district's antiharassment policy, ruling that it violated the students' rights to free speech (*Saxe v. State College Area School District,* 2001). McCarthy (2002) noted that the appellate court lost sight of the mission of the public school to instill civil behavior, citizenship values, and respect for others as well as the need to prohibit harassing and disrespectful behavior in light of school violence. In other cases around the country, when there have been racial incidents or evidence of racial tensions in the school, courts have upheld antiharassment policies that discipline students for displays of Confederate flags or other emblems associated with racial conflicts (McCarthy, 2008). Issues of sexual harassment, while not discussed here, are addressed in Chapter 9.

As should be clear, not all issues ultimately will be resolved by the Supreme Court. A variety of factors in different cases change the situation and the balance between the competing interests of schools and students. For example, if a student says, "I understand how being bullied can cause one to snap under the pressure like those kids at Columbine did," can this student be disciplined for his or her speech? Is this a threat? Does it materially and substantially interfere with school discipline? How does Internet usage, at home and at school, affect free speech? Clearly, if a student uses the school library to look at pornographic Web sites banned by the school, the school can punish him for his usage, because his actions will substantially interfere with school discipline. What if a student creates a Web site, at her home, that is critical of teachers and demeaning to other students and she shares the Web site address with students from her school? Is this an issue of freedom of speech, and how will it be resolved? What if that same student shares her Web site only with one or two friends, but her friend distributes the Web site to many other classmates? Would the student who made the Web site be punished? What about students who brag in their MySpace and Facebook pages about engaging in illegal activities off-campus? Can they be disciplined for these activities by school officials? Student speech may occur in many locations and forms, from a variety of sources. Whether these activities

can be considered to cause material disruption in school and subject the student to discipline will pose a challenge to school personnel. School social workers can play an instrumental role in ensuring that school policies consider students' rights as these policies are developed.

Freedom of Dress and Appearance

Freedom of expression includes speech, both political and expressive. Freedom of expression includes more than the freedom to speak as one wishes and has been extended to govern personal appearance. As part of their self-expression, students, male and female, may wear their hair long or very short, in unusual styles or colors, have facial and body piercings, and/or have their own sense of the clothing that constitutes fashion and style.

Questions regarding the school's authority to control students' dress and appearance have led to a variety of cases and court opinions. For example, in 1921, Pearl Pugsley was suspended from a public school in Clay County, Arkansas, because she broke a rule that prohibited the use of talcum powder on a student's face. Her teacher told her to wash it off and not to return with it on. Defiant, Pearl later returned to school with powder on her face and was denied admission until she obeyed the rule. Pearl refused to return to school and asked the court to set aside the school's restriction (*Pugsley v. Sellmeyer,* 1923). The court dismissed her case. She then appealed, and the Arkansas Supreme Court, in a split decision, ruled in favor of the school board. One of the court's reasons was that although schools are not without limits, they have a wide range of discretion in matters of school policy and administration.

Almost a half-century later, Chelsey Karr, a 16-year-old pupil, petitioned the courts for a decision against an El Paso high school that refused to enroll him because his long hair violated the school's dress code. After a 4-day trial, the U.S. District Court ruled that the denial of a public education to Karr on the basis of the school regulation violated the due process and equal protection guarantees of the U.S. Constitution. The court ruled that "one's choice of hair style is constitutionally practiced" and that the burden was on school authorities to demonstrate that long hair disrupted the educational process (*Karr v. Schmidt,* 1972).

However, the El Paso School Board appealed the decision, and the appellate court concluded that because the case did not raise constitutional issues of fundamental liberty, the regulations would be presumed valid. Judge Morgan, writing on behalf of the court, rejected arguments based on the First and Fourteenth Amendments and the equal protection clause. He emphasized that the court's ruling did not indicate an indifference to the personal rights of Chelsey Karr, but rather reflected the "inescapable fact" that neither the Constitution nor the federal judiciary had been conceived to be a keeper of the national conscience in every matter "great and small."

Circuit and appellate courts have been divided with regard to grooming issues. The Supreme Court has refused on several occasions to review the question of whether student dress or hairstyles are constitutionally protected.

Why do schools feel the need to govern students' appearance? Some districts believe that learning occurs better in an environment in which appearance is controlled. In *Phoenix Elem. Sch. Dist. No. 1 v. Green* (1997), students challenged the school dress code policy because they felt that it violated their First Amendment rights. The Arizona appellate court upheld the policy and cited with approval the reasons the school district gave for having its dress code. These reasons were (a) promotes a more effective climate for learning, (b) creates opportunity for self-expression, (c) increases campus safety and security, (d) fosters school unity and pride, (e) eliminates "label" competition, (f) ensures modest dress, (g) simplifies dressing, and (h) minimizes cost to parents.

Other school districts enact dress code policies to attempt to deal with the rising problems of gangs. Because gang members are often identified with certain clothing colors or items of clothing,

such as hats worn backward, some schools create dress code policies to eliminate the wearing of certain types of clothing for all students. Other schools have created school uniform policies that require all students to wear the same type of clothing. In these schools, for example, all children wear certain school-sanctioned clothing such as blue jeans and a white shirt. Still other schools may ban clothing that the officials consider immodest, overly sexual, or inappropriate to the school environment. In these cases, the school officials believe that the presence of the clothing may lead to an unhealthy school atmosphere.

Despite the fact that these policies may be well intentioned and, more important, are designed with school safety in mind, dress code policies are not without challenges. For example, in *Chalifoux v. New Carey Indep. Sch. Dist.* (1997), school district police officers told two students that they could not wear white plastic rosaries on the outside of their clothing. The students explained that they wore these rosaries as an expression of their Catholic faith. The school district policy prohibited the wearing of "gang-related apparel" in school or in school-related functions, and the school police officers had information that members of the "United Homies," a gang present in that school, also wore rosaries as a means of identifying themselves. Pursuant to the analysis in *Tinker,* the court ruled that the students' religious expression did not materially or substantially disrupt the school environment so they were allowed to wear their rosaries.

In some school districts, students have been suspended or expelled for refusing to remove their religious headscarves or hijabs as a violation of the schools' dress codes. For example, an Oklahoma school district's dress code prohibited "hats, caps, bandannas, plastic caps, and hoods on jackets inside the [school] building." Although other students were permitted to wear head coverings for nonreligious purposes, a 12-year-old student was suspended twice. She sued the school district, and the Department of Justice intervened on her behalf. She later testified before the Oklahoma Senate on the hostility she faced by wearing her headscarf, stating that it sparked a "battle between being obedient to God by wearing my hijab to be modest in Islam versus the school dress code policy." The policy was later amended (Moore, 2007).

School social workers may be asked to participate in the development of school dress code policies for their school districts. Dress codes are governed under the same principles as speech; students should be free to express themselves so long as they do not materially or substantially disrupt the school environment. Although schools appear to have the authority under *Fraser, Kuhlmeier,* and *Morse* to prohibit speech that is lewd, vulgar, could be perceived to be sanctioned by the school, or promotes illegal drug use, it is also clear that *Tinker* allows speech that is an expression of someone's religious beliefs, so long as those beliefs do not cause material disruption to the school. School social workers can assist schools to develop policies that are respectful of cultural diversity, religious beliefs, and student rights while protecting the safe environment of the schools. Gilbert (1999) offered nine principles for drafting a dress code that will take into account factors considered by the courts. He argued that the keys to a successful dress code policy are common sense, the ability to compromise, and the desire of all persons involved to work through their differences. School social workers are uniquely skilled in these issues and can mediate these differences to help arrive at a policy that balances the desires of school officials with those of students.

Freedom of Religion

The questions related to freedom of religion in the public school context are especially complicated because the First Amendment has two clauses related to religion. One clause prohibits the government from interfering with individuals' rights to worship as they choose, and the other clause prohibits the government from taking action that could be considered as the establishment of a religion. Both of these clauses often overlap in their application to specific facts. The underlying idea is that the government should be neutral toward religion by neither advancing religious causes nor inhibiting their private exercise. Because public schools are part of government, schools must be careful not to take actions that violate the First Amendment's religious prohibitions.

One of the first cases to reach the Supreme Court regarding the exercise of religion in the public schools was *Minersville School Dist. v. Gobitis* (1940). In this case, the petitioners, who were Jehovah's Witnesses, sought an injunction to alter the requirement that participation in the salute to the flag was a condition for attending school in the Minersville, Pennsylvania, school district on the grounds that it violated their freedom of religion.

The Supreme Court, by an eight-to-one vote, upheld the compulsory flag salute, but did acknowledge freedom of religion as a "precious right." This thought was expressed eloquently in the dissenting opinion of Justice Harlan F. Stone:

> The Constitution may well elicit expressions of loyalty to it and to the government which it created, but it does not command such expression or otherwise give any indication that compulsory expressions of loyalty play any such part in our scheme of government as to override the constitutional protection of freedom of speech and religion. And while such expressions of loyalty, when voluntarily given, may promote national unity, it is quite another matter to say that their compulsory expression by children in violation of their own and their parents' religious convictions can be regarded as playing so important a part in our national unity as to leave school boards free to exact it despite the constitutional guarantee of freedom of religion. (*Minersville* at 605)

The issue of school prayer in the public schools first reached the Supreme Court in *Engle v. Vitale* (1962). In *Engle,* parents of 10 students challenged the constitutionality of a new practice within the New York school system for students to recite a short daily prayer created by school officials. The parents contended that the official prayer was contrary to their beliefs, religions, and religious practices and those of their children. In ruling that the prescribed prayer was in violation of the establishment clause, the Supreme Court focused on the fact that even if a prayer is denominationally neutral or its observance on the part of students is voluntary, the prayer could not be freed from violation of the Constitution. The following year the court struck down provisions of laws from Maryland and Pennsylvania that required daily reading of Bible passages or the recitation of the Lord's Prayer as unconstitutional violations of the establishment clause (*Sch. Dist. of Abington Twp., Pa. v. Schempp,* 1963).

During the 1970s and 1980s, the courts consistently held that prayer, whether at football games or at graduation, violated the establishment clause. However, the trends of the 1990s and this decade show that the courts are wavering on this issue more frequently than in the past.

In *Lee v. Weisman* (1992), the Supreme Court struck down a Rhode Island school district's policy that allowed principals to invite clergy members to deliver invocations and benedictions at middle- and high-school graduation ceremonies. School officials had attempted to avoid the church–state conflict by providing clergy with a pamphlet that provided guidelines that were considered appropriate for nondenominational prayer. The Court found that the policy had a coercive effect. Even though the school district argued that graduation ceremony attendance was voluntary, the Court believed that students would feel pressured to participate in the prayers if they were part of the graduation ceremonies. Because the principal chose the clergy and decided that an invocation and a benediction would be given, the Court found that the involvement of the school system created a state-sponsored and state-directed religious exercise in the public school.

The Supreme Court's decision in *Lee* created a backlash. Certain school authorities and students have identified creative ways to include prayers in graduation ceremonies (McCarthy, 2000). For example, in two cases decided after *Lee,* the issue before the courts was whether

prayer is permissible if students freely vote to choose a nonsectarian, nonproselytizing prayer at graduation. When school officials include a prayer, it is considered an unacceptable violation of the establishment clause. On the other hand, if students have the choice and vote to include a prayer, that choice may be acceptable because it is protected by the free speech and free exercise clauses of the First Amendment (Condon & Wolff, 1996).

For example, in *Harris v. Joint Sch. Dist. No. 241* (1993), a case originating from Idaho, the school district allowed its senior class to vote on whether it wanted prayer at graduation and to decide who would say the prayer. A group of pupils challenged the ceremonial prayer as a violation of the separation of church and state. The court found that because the senior high school students in School District No. 241 were free to choose whether any prayer would or would not be included in their graduation programs, the mere fact that graduation ceremonies in the district were supervised by faculty and administrators did not begin to constitute the kind of state involvement present in *Lee.*

In another case that upheld student initiated and voted on prayer, *Jones v. Clear Creek Indep. Sch. Dist.* (1992), the court questioned why so many people attach importance to graduation ceremonies. The court stated,

> If they only seek government's recognition of student achievement, diplomas suffice. If they only seek God's recognition, a privately sponsored baccalaureate will do. But to experience the community's recognition of student achievement, they must attend the public ceremony that other interested community members also hold so dear. By attending graduation to experience and participate in the community's display of support for the graduates, people should not be surprised to find the event affected by community standards. The Constitution requires nothing different. (*Jones* at 973)

The court ruled that student-initiated prayer at a public school graduation is allowable because the students made the prayer decision. The court recognized that a majority of students have the ability to do what the state acting on its own cannot do—to incorporate prayer in public high school graduation ceremonies.

In addition to issues related to prayer in the classroom and at graduation ceremonies, the courts have grappled with many other issues related to the establishment clause in public schools. These have included (a) distributing Gideon Bibles to fifth-grade public school students (*Berger v. Rensselaer Cent. School Corp.,*1993); (b) posting the Ten Commandments in every classroom (*Stone v. Graham,* 1980); (c) requiring the teaching of evolution science with creation science or not at all (*Edwards v. Aguillard,* 1987); (d) beginning school assemblies with prayer (*Collins v. Chandler Unified School District,* 1981); (e) teaching a transcendental meditation course that includes a ceremony involving making an offering to a deity (*Malnak v. Yogi,* 1979); (f) refusing to allow the formation of a Christian Club at the school (*Board of Educ. of Westside Comm. Sch. v. Mergens,* 1990); (g) limiting the officers of a Bible Study Club to Christians only (*Hsu by and through Hsu v. Roslyn Free School Dist. No. 3,* 1996); and (h) allowing student-initiated, student-led invocation or message before varsity football games (*Santa Fe Independent School District v. Doe,* 2000).

One of the newest and most controversial issues that relates to the freedom of religion and public schools concerns school vouchers. The concept of school vouchers is that the government gives parents a voucher, stipend, or credit that can be used to pay for tuition at the schools of the parents' choosing. In some circumstances, the vouchers can be used at private, religious schools. Although the implementation of school vouchers takes on a variety of forms in different locales, its proponents argue that it will bring greater choice and accountability to the schools, whereas its opponents believe that vouchers, if used for religious schools, violate the establishment clause.

The U.S. Supreme Court recently upheld the constitutionality of a case that concerned school vouchers in the Cleveland, Ohio, public school system (*Zelman v. Simmons-Harris,* 2002). As recounted in the U.S. Supreme Court's decision, more than 75,000 children were enrolled in the Cleveland City School District. The majority of these children were from low-income and minority families and were unable to send their children to any school other than an inner-city public school. Cleveland's public schools were among the worst-performing public schools in the United States. The district had failed to meet any of the 18 state standards for minimal acceptable performance. Only 1 in 10 ninth graders could pass a basic proficiency examination, and students at all levels performed at a dismal rate compared with students in other Ohio public schools. Because of this, Ohio enacted, among other initiatives, its Pilot Project Scholarship Program to provide financial assistance to families in any Ohio school district that was under federal court order requiring supervision and operational management of the district.

The pilot program provided two basic kinds of assistance to parents of children in a covered district. First, the program provided tuition aid for students in kindergarten through third grade, expanding each year through eighth grade, to attend a participating public or private school of their parent's choosing. Second, the program provided tutorial aid for students who chose to remain enrolled in public school. Because parents could use the vouchers at private religious schools, the voucher system was attacked as being a violation of the establishment clause of the Constitution.

The U.S. Supreme Court ruled that the program passed constitutional muster because it was neutral and did not advance religion. The court stated that:

> We believe that the program challenged here is a program of true private choice . . . and thus constitutional . . . [t]he Ohio program is neutral in all respects toward religion. It is part of a general and multifaceted undertaking by the State of Ohio to provide educational opportunities to the children of a failed school district. It confers educational assistance directly to a broad class of individuals defined without reference to religion, i.e., any parent of a school-age child who resides in the Cleveland City School District. The program

permits the participation of all schools within the district, religious or nonreligious. Adjacent public schools also may participate and have a financial incentive to do so. Program benefits are available to participating families on neutral terms, with no reference to religion. The only preference stated anywhere in the program is a preference for low-income families, who receive greater assistance and are given priority for admission at participating schools. (*Zelman* at 2470)

Because the Supreme Court has ruled that the use of vouchers does not offend the establishment clause, proponents of religious education may advocate for other school districts to adopt a voucher program. If parents can use vouchers to pay for private or religious schools, there is concern about how this will affect the public school system in the United States.

Other Privacy Issues

Although not based on the First Amendment, the notion of privacy guaranteed by the First Amendment contributed to the passage of a student records law. Congress gave students and their parents new rights when it passed the Family Educational Rights and Privacy Act of 1974 (FERPA), also known informally as the Buckley Amendment.

The Family Educational Rights and Privacy Act of 1974

Congress passed the Family Educational Rights and Privacy Act (FERPA) as a rider to the 1974 education amendments. This act denied federal funds to any school system that refused to show the contents of students' records to their parents or, if the students were 18 years of age or older, to the students themselves. This legislation was significant because it established two principles: (a) Parents (until the student reaches 18 years of age) have the right to see their children's records; and (b) parents may not examine the records of any other pupil. This amendment, combined with the Department of Health and Human Services implementing regulations issued in 1976, have

forced significant changes in record-keeping policies and procedures at virtually all institutions that receive federal financial assistance. This includes public elementary, secondary, and post-secondary education.

At least six points contained in FERPA and the implementing regulations are important for school social workers: (a) Parents of a pupil (or the 18-year-old student) must be shown the records no more than 45 days after requesting to see them; (b) any item in the records may be subject to a validity challenge; (c) items inserted before January 1, 1975, need not be shown; (d) a pupil may waive his or her right to see confidential letters such as letters of recommendation; (e) the right of a school to release personal information about a pupil to a third party is restricted to specified purposes and to specified persons/ organizations; and (f) pupils and parents are to be notified annually of their rights with regard to access to records.

The law specifies that any educational institution receiving federal funds will lose those funds unless it provides parents with access to and the right to challenge their child's full educational records, the right to have inaccurate or misleading records changed, and the right to give consent before any records can be shown to outside parties. Unfortunately for parents, the loss of federal funding for the schools is the only remedy provided to them by FERPA. Court cases have routinely determined that FERPA does not provide a private right of action for parents. Courts have determined that Congress did not intend for parents to be able to sue for violation of students' privacy rights if schools wrongly disclose student records or mishandle student information. Instead, courts believe that Congress intended that the Department of Education would pursue recovery of an educational institution's federal funding if the institution improperly violated students' rights.

Students who are 18 years old or over, or any person attending a postsecondary institution, must be given the same rights with regard to their records. In addition, all affected school agencies and institutions must notify parents and pupils

18 years old and over of these rights, must establish hearing procedures in the event of disagreements, and must keep on file all requests for school records from outsiders.

Parents and authorized individuals can "inspect and review" at will the "official records, files and data, including all material that is incorporated into each pupil's cumulative record folder and intended for school use" (FERPA, 1974). Educational records, which include information directly related to a student and that are maintained by or for an educational agency, may be shared with parents, their representatives, and other authorized persons. These records include academic work completed, grades, standardized achievement test scores, attendance data, aptitude and psychological tests, health and family background information, and verified reports of serious behavior patterns. The act also puts a near absolute clamp on distribution of individual records without written consent from a parent or the student, depending on the pupil's age.

Sharing Student Information

Recent changes to FERPA and its companion regulations shed new light on just how far schools can go to cooperate with local agencies or other persons that share a common interest in serving and protecting children. As we have already noted, FERPA protects the privacy of a student's educational record primarily by requiring that educators obtain written consent before disclosing information contained in the record to agencies or personnel outside the school district. However, not all releases of information between schools and other agencies require prior written consent.

In fact, the increased violence in schools, such as the Columbine and Virginia Tech school shooting tragedies, as well as the enactment of the USA Patriot Act of 2001, created after the September 11 terrorist attacks, have increased the number of situations in which student records can be released without prior consent. There are now 16 exceptions to the requirement of prior written consent. We will discuss a few points that are important for school social workers to know.

- Schools can share information with other school officials, including teachers and administrators within the school if these persons have legitimate educational interests.
- FERPA does not distinguish between custodial or noncustodial parents. Accordingly, no matter who has custody of a child, either parent has the right to access their child's records and consent to their disclosure. However, if a valid court order concerning divorce or custody of a child has a provision related to access to the child's records, the court order will control.
- Schools can share directory information with other agencies. Directory information is information "which would not generally be considered harmful or an invasion of privacy if disclosed." It includes, but is not limited to, the student's name, address, telephone listing, date and place of birth, major field of study, participation in officially recognized activities and sports, weight and height of athletic team members, dates of attendance, degrees and awards received, and the most recent previous educational agency or institution attended. Parents must be given prior notice when schools adopt a policy of releasing directory information. Parents who object to directory information disclosures may prohibit them by requesting so in writing.
- Educators can communicate orally with other agencies based on their personal knowledge and observations of a juvenile that do not derive from the educational record. Communications based on independent knowledge of students are outside the reach of FERPA.
- A school may communicate without prior written parental consent when it shares the content of records of its law enforcement unit. A law enforcement unit is an individual, division, department, or other component of a school district that is officially authorized to enforce any federal, state, or local law, or to maintain the physical security and safety of the school. Under the regulations, a law enforcement unit

"does not lose its status as a law enforcement unit if it also performs other, non–law enforcement functions for the agency or institution, including investigation of incidents or conduct that might lead to disciplinary action or proceedings against a student." The exempt records include only those that are created and maintained by the unit for the purpose of law enforcement. Internal disciplinary records are not included in this category.

- FERPA permits educational agencies to disclose, without the consent or knowledge of the parent or student, personally identifiable information from the student's record in response to an ex parte order from the U.S. attorney general or designee in connection with the investigation or prosecution of terrorism crimes. The school official does not need to record the fact of this disclosure in the student's records.
- Schools are permitted to disclose, without consent, information contained in student records to comply with lawfully issued subpoenas. This includes grand jury subpoenas and law enforcement subpoenas. The courts that issued the subpoena may order the educational institution not to disclose to anyone the existence or contents of the subpoena.
- In contrast to the grand jury and law enforcement subpoenas, schools may share information with other agencies without obtaining prior written consent when acting in compliance with a court order or lawfully issued subpoena. In these cases, the regulations do require that schools make a reasonable effort to notify the parent prior to compliance with the court order.
- Schools may share information with other agencies without obtaining prior written consent when acting "in connection with an emergency if knowledge of the information is necessary to protect the health or safety of the student or other individuals." These situations now specifically include substantial health risks to the general population like in the case of smallpox, anthrax, or other bioterrorism activities or other physical safety concerns.

In 2003, Congress passed HIPAA, the Health Insurance Portability and Accountability Act, which applies to protecting the privacy and confidentiality of health information (Kagle & Kopels, 2008). HIPAA has very strict rules that covered entities, which include social workers, must follow when protected health information is revealed. Education records under FERPA, were specifically exempted from the definition of protected health information. When HIPAA became law, most schools largely ignored HIPAA, believing that it did not apply to the school context. One of the increasingly complicated issues for school social workers, however, is how to handle situations when the school records contain information that is generated by outside sources, like hospitals, mental health facilities, or other clinical providers. These other providers are considered to be covered entities under HIPAA, and their records are, in fact, covered by HIPAA. More and more schools are becoming aware that HIPAA may have an impact on school records, although the extent of the impact is as yet unknown.

School social workers should be aware of the laws of their own states as well as those provided by the federal government to ensure confidentiality in the schools (Kopels, 1992; Kopels & Lindsey, 2006; NASW, 2001). Certain state laws contain other provisions regarding confidentiality of school records. For example, in Illinois, in domestic violence situations, persons may be prohibited by orders of protection from inspecting or obtaining school records of a student (Illinois School Student Records Act, 2008). School personnel with knowledge of such an order must prohibit access to or inspection of the student's school records. Among other reasons, a perpetrator should not be able to look at his/her child's records and locate the address where the child is now residing.

Reasonable Search and Seizure

As we have seen, the rights of students to freedom of speech, expression, and religion find their basis in the First Amendment. Students also have certain rights in the educational setting that stem from the Fourth Amendment.

The Fourth Amendment of the U.S. Constitution states that "the right of the people to be secure in their persons, houses, papers, and effects, against unreasonable searches and seizures, shall not be violated." This guarantee has generally been interpreted to mean that an adult or his or her property can be subjected to a police search only after issuance of a warrant and after a finding of probable cause.

Minors, particularly students, have not had these protections. Generally, it has been held that school officials may search a pupil's locker, without the consent of the pupil and without a search warrant, if they have cause to believe the locker contains an item, the possession of which would be a criminal offense or would present harm to another individual (*People v. Overton*, 1969). The legal basis for such action is that the school, not the student, owns the locker and that, at best, they share possession of it. The public notion that the school has the responsibility to provide for and protect the welfare of the entire school is so strong that this responsibility has been allowed to overshadow the intent of the Fourth Amendment.

In *New Jersey v. T.L.O.* (1985), the Supreme Court attempted to delineate the power of public school officials to conduct searches of a student. In *T.L.O.*, a teacher discovered two girls smoking in the bathroom and took the students to the vice-principal's office. One of the girls admitted to smoking in the bathroom but the other, T.L.O., did not. Because the vice-principal believed that T.L.O. had violated the school's rule against smoking at school, he opened her purse and saw a package of cigarettes. When he reached into the purse to get the cigarettes, he discovered rolling papers that he thought were related to marijuana use. He continued the search, believing there might be marijuana, and he discovered a small quantity of the drug, a pipe, empty plastic bags, money, and an index card that listed names of persons who owed T.L.O. money. T.L.O. was suspended and found to be a delinquent under state law. The issue presented to the Supreme Court was the constitutionality of the search of her purse.

The court ruled that to determine the reasonableness of a search, there had to be a twofold inquiry. First, school officials had to decide whether the search was justified at its inception and second, whether the search that actually took place was reasonably related in scope to the circumstances that justified the search in the first place. In other words, to determine the reasonableness of searches by school officials, courts must consider the suspicion underlying the search and the scope of the search in light of the reasons for the suspicions. In the context of reasonableness of searches in the public school, the court focused on the schools' need to control students, the special relationship between school officials and students, and the mission of the school to educate students in a disciplined learning environment. Because of the special needs of the school, the Court pitted the child's legitimate expectations of privacy against the school's legitimate need to maintain a learning environment. Discipline tipped the balance in favor of school officials (Urbonya, 2001). The following recent cases illustrate the courts' attempts to balance these principles.

In *People v. Dilworth* (1996), a police liaison officer at an Illinois alternative high school searched a student and found nothing suspicious. Right after, he saw the student laughing and making mocking gestures with his friend. Believing something was amiss, the liaison officer noticed the student had a flashlight, and thinking a flashlight was strange in school, searched the flashlight and found five bags of cocaine. In upholding the conviction, the court decided that a reasonable suspicion was all that was necessary for the liaison officer to conduct a search, rather than the probable cause standard that would be required for police.

A student who was adjudicated a juvenile delinquent and placed on probation for possessing a knife in school claimed that the search that led to the discovery of the weapon was invalid. The pupil alleged that the search was inappropriate because it was not based on an individualized suspicion of him. An appellate court in Pennsylvania disagreed (*In re S.S.*, 1996). The court upheld the action as reasonable because officials searched all students in the same minimally intrusive manner on entering school (a metal detector and pat-down search of belongings), and that the search was justified due to the high rate of violence in area schools.

A school board in Florida hired an independent security firm to conduct random searches in their schools. As the search team was explaining the procedures to the selected class, the assistant principal noticed a coat being passed to the back of the room, searched it, and found a gun. The pupil who owned the coat denied that the gun was his and claimed that the search was unlawful. An appellate court reversed in favor of the state (*State of Florida v. J.A.*, 1996). The court upheld the search on the grounds that it was minimally intrusive and involved the legitimate school concern for safety.

In *Covington County v. G. W.* (2000), the principal of a Mississippi school was informed by another student that G.W., a 17-year-old student, had been drinking in the school's parking lot. The principal and a school security officer went to the parking lot and saw several empty beer cans in the back of G.W.'s truck. They then asked G.W. if they could search his truck. He unlocked his truck and allowed them to search. They found seven, unopened beer bottles in a locked tool box. G.W. admitted they were his and that he had purchased the beer. He did not appear to be under the influence. The school suspended him for 5 days and then expelled him for the remainder of the school year. His parents protested the legality of the search, stating that a search warrant needed to be obtained before the school district searched his vehicle and that there is a greater expectation of privacy in an automobile than there is in a student locker. On appeal, the appellate court applied the *T.L.O.* standards to the facts of the case. The court ruled that the search was justified at its inception when the principal was informed that G.W. was drinking and then saw beer cans in the back of

G.W.'s car, and that the search of G.W.'s car was reasonable in its scope. The court also ruled that the principles set forth in *T.L.O.* clearly state that search warrants are not required when school officials conduct a search. Moreover, although there may be a greater expectation of privacy in one's vehicle when driving down the road, the same is not true when the car is parked on school property.

Ten years after the *T.L.O.* decision, the U.S. Supreme Court decided the case of *Vernonia Sch. Dist. v. Acton* (1995), which concerned the legality of a school district's drug testing policy for athletes. After noticing that student athletes were rude and used profane language in class and because school officials believed that athletes were role models for other students, the Vernonia school district in Oregon adopted a policy of drug testing its student athletes. The athletes were not allowed to participate in sports unless they first signed a form consenting to weekly urine testing during their sport's season to detect amphetamine, cocaine, and marijuana. One seventh-grade student, Acton, refused to sign the consent form and was prohibited from playing on the football team. His parents sued the school district, believing the urine testing policy was unreasonable under the Fourth Amendment. In its decision, the court mentioned the common law power of the schools, the *in loco parentis* concept, and the special needs doctrine. To determine whether the drug testing was within the special needs of the school, the court examined four factors: (a) the nature of the student's privacy interest, (b) the character of the intrusion, (c) the nature and immediacy of the governmental concern, and (d) the efficacy of the selected means for meeting it. After balancing these factors, the court held that drug-testing athletes under the facts of the case was reasonable under the Fourth Amendment.

More recently, the Supreme Court expanded this ruling to uphold an Oklahoma school district's policy of requiring drug testing for any middle- or high-school students who chose to participate in any competitive, extracurricular activities (*Bd. of Educ. v. Earls*, 2002). These activities included the Academic Team, Future Farmers of America, Future Homemakers of America, band, choir, pom pom, cheerleading, and athletics. The Court found that although there was no proven drug problem within the school, testing students who participate in extracurricular activities is a reasonably effective means of addressing the school district's legitimate concerns in preventing, deterring, and detecting drug use.

T.L.O. involved searches directed at the activities of a particular student. *Vernonia* involved a group of students, athletes, who were not under suspicion. However, both decisions heavily relied on the presumption of diminished constitutional protection for students and characterized schools as places with special needs in determining the reasonableness of searches under the Fourth Amendment (Urbonya, 2001). By allowing random drug testing of students who participate in any extracurricular activities, the Supreme Court made it clear that the school's interest in drug prevention and control outweighs the individual's right to privacy. In the future, whether the Supreme Court will allow random drug testing to be conducted on any student who attends public school is an open question.

Sometimes, school officials use extremely poor judgment and conduct strip searches of students as they look for missing property or drugs. Strip searches can range from requiring students to strip down to their undergarments or to become completely naked while their bodies are inspected for the sought-after items. Not surprisingly, strip searches can be psychologically damaging to children, especially very young children or developing adolescents.

In some cases, the items searched for are not extremely valuable or dangerous. For example, junior high school students in Indiana filed a civil rights action claiming that a principal and teachers conducted an illegal strip search for four dollars and fifty cents that was missing from a locker room after a physical education class. Although the specifics of the searches varied for each girl, each search involved searching the girl's bra. A federal trial court reasoned that

because the principal was not the policy maker for the board, the board could not be held liable for his behavior (*Hines ex rel. Oliver v. McClung*, 1995). At the same time, however, the court decided that because the search was not reasonable under the circumstances, the educators were not entitled to qualified immunity from the civil rights action and could be held responsible for the illegal search.

In several cases, strip searches of students have been held to be legal. Most of these cases concerned older adolescents who were accused of hiding illegal drugs on their bodies, often with the intention of selling the drugs. For example, in *Cornfield v. Consolidated High School* (1993), school officials had strong reason to believe that a 16-year-old student, Cornfield, was hiding drugs in the crotch of his pants because he seemed too "well-endowed." There had been recent incidents of drug-related activity reported by teachers and personal observations of bulges in the student's crotch area. Information from third parties buttressed this observation, including another student's report that Cornfield had brought drugs onto campus and a teacher's report that Cornfield admitted he had previously dealt drugs as well as "crotched" drugs during a police raid at his mother's house. Moreover, the local police had reported to the school that they received information that Cornfield was selling marijuana to other students. The information provided a basis to believe that a strip search was necessary to reveal the contraband. Cornfield was taken into a locker room and told to remove his pants. However, he was allowed to put on his gym uniform during the search. These factors—teacher observations indicating the contraband was hidden in Cornfield's underwear, tips from impartial students, police reports, and the student's previous admissions—convinced the court that the search was justifiable at its inception and was not unduly intrusive.

In another case, *Widener v. Frye* (1992) a 15-year-old student challenged the reasonableness of his strip search. The court, in reviewing the facts, stated that the school officials had reasonable grounds to believe that the search would turn up evidence that the student was violating the law or the rules of the school. Several school officials detected what they believed to be the odor of marijuana emanating from the student, and they testified that the student was acting "sluggish" and "lethargic," or in a manner otherwise consistent with marijuana use. Furthermore, when they questioned the student about their suspicions, they were not satisfied with his explanation.

The court found that the search conducted by the school officials was reasonable in its scope in light of the age and sex of the student and the nature of the infraction. The student was removed from the classroom. He was asked to remove his jeans only and not his undergarments. The search was conducted in the presence of two male security guards. He was never threatened in any way, nor touched at all while his trousers were down.

In 2008, the National Association of Social Workers filed a friend of the court brief in a case that involved a strip search of a 13-year-old honors student, Savana. Based on a tip from another student (who was the actual wrongdoer), the assistant principal of a middle school in Arizona removed Savana from class, brought her to his office and questioned her about items that he had confiscated from the other student. Because he was dissatisfied with the results of his questioning, he asked Savana if he could search her belongings. She agreed. He rummaged through her backpack and found nothing. Even though the search of Savana's backpack supported her statements and despite her discipline-free history at the school, he asked his assistant to take Savana to the nurse's office for a second, more thorough search. There, at his request, the assistant and the school nurse conducted a strip search of Savana. They had Savana peel off each layer of clothing, in turn. First, Savana removed her socks, shoes and jacket for inspection. Then, they asked Savana to remove her T-shirt and pants. Embarrassed and scared, Savana complied, sitting in her bra and underwear while the two adults examined her clothes. Again, nothing was found. Next, Savana was instructed to pull her bra out to the side and shake it. Her naked breasts were exposed

during this process. Savana was next told to pull out her underwear at the crotch and shake it, revealing her pelvic area. In the affidavit that accompanied her lawsuit, Savana described the experience as "the most humiliating experience" of her life and said she felt "violated by the strip search."

What was the school searching for? To go to such extreme lengths, one would imagine that they must have suspected that Savana possessed some serious, illegal, and dangerous drug. Instead, they were searching for prescription-strength ibuprofen.

The appellate court that handled the appeal concluded that the school officials who strip-searched Savana acted contrary to all reason and common sense, trampling over her legitimate and substantial interests in privacy and security of her person. Not only did the court rule that the search was not justified at its inception, it stated that the search was unreasonable in its scope. The court stated that the scope of a search can only be permissible if the measures adopted are reasonably related to the objectives of the search and are not excessively intrusive in light of the age and sex of the student and the nature of the infraction. The court wrote that the school authorities adopted a disproportionately extreme measure to search a 13-year-old girl for violating a school rule prohibiting possession of prescription and over-the-counter drugs. The court believed that rather than strip-searching a 13-year-old, a more commonsense approach would have been to keep the child in the principal's office until the parent arrived or to send the child home because the alleged possession of ibuprofen posed no imminent danger to anyone.

Importantly, the court recognized that the psychological trauma intrinsic to strip searches of adults is magnified when strip searches are performed on schoolchildren. The appellate court referred to the amicus curiae brief filed by the National Association of Social Workers (Brief of Amici, 2008) which cited psychological research that describes the serious emotional damage that can happen to young victims of strip searches. The court noted that when strip searches are used, the "overzealousness of school administrators in efforts to protect students has the tragic impact of traumatizing those they claim to serve" (*Redding* at 1086). The United States Supreme Court recently agreed to review the school district's appeal of the *Redding* case; the privacy rights of children versus those of adults will certainly be a significant issue.

The discipline cases described are typical but by no means exhaustive. In some ways, these children are the "lucky" ones, regardless of the outcomes of their cases, because they had someone, parents or advocacy organizations, to challenge the actions of the schools. In many more cases, children are subjected to discipline by schools that go unchallenged.

The growing violence and increase in students' use of weapons and drugs have made reasonable searches and seizures essential to the orderly operation of the schools. The question remains as to what is considered to be a reasonable search. Schools have used strip searches, metal detectors, drug and weapon sniffing dogs, Breathalyzers, pat downs, and other techniques to ensure safety and discipline in the schools. The reasonableness of these searches will always vary based on the scope of the search, its intrusiveness, the age of the child, the seriousness of the items being searched for, and other contextual factors. Beckham (2000) provided recommendations that school officials should consider in striking the balance between the maintenance of a safe learning environment and the student's expectation of privacy. School social workers should ensure that school policies are developed regarding searches that respect the privacy of students as well as concerns for school safety. School social workers should encourage their schools to develop policies that are based on more positive disciplinary approaches. They should avoid any personal involvement in as well as actively discourage their schools from using strip searches on school-age children.

Discipline in the Schools

As we have seen, schools have a legitimate need to maintain order to provide a safe and effective learning environment. School officials have the responsibility to instill into students the desire to be good citizens and productive members of society. Part of being a member of society is following appropriate rules. Students who misbehave or do not follow rules of conduct set by the school or by society can be punished in a number of ways. Among the methods schools use to discipline children are corporal punishment and suspension and expulsion from school.

Corporal Punishment

Corporal punishment is the infliction of physical pain on individuals for their misconduct. Corporal punishment in the school is in part an outgrowth of the *in loco parentis* concept and the tradition of early colonial schools, which practiced corporal punishment in conjunction with their religious philosophy, which focused on character development and morality. Increased litigation and adverse court decisions have led to less frequent use of such punishment as a primary form of student control.

For corporal punishment to be legal, it must be reasonable in the eyes of the judiciary. Courts invariably have based their decisions on the reasonableness of the rules, on the one hand, and the reasonableness of the penalties, on the other hand.

Courts had discussed the idea of reasonableness as early as 1859, in *Lander v. Seaver* (1859). An 11-year-old boy was herding his cow past a teacher's house when, in the presence of other pupils, he called the teacher "Old Jack Seaver." The next morning when the boy arrived at school, he was reprimanded and whipped for his use of "insulting language." The father of the boy insisted that the teacher had no authority to punish the child for an act committed out of and away from school, but the court rejected the father's contention. The reasoning was that because the boy was in the presence of other pupils, his "contemptuous language" had "a direct and immediate tendency to injure the school, to subvert the master's authority, and to beget disorder and insubordination."

The application of the *in loco parentis* doctrine in the early 1970s led to different court interpretations. In *Baker v. Owen* (1975), the Supreme Court affirmed, without comment, a decision of the federal district court in North Carolina that allowed teachers to administer corporal punishment without the approval of the parents. For the person who administered corporal punishment to be protected from liability, certain guidelines were to be observed. These guidelines included that children must be warned in advance regarding what behaviors could be punished, that less drastic measures had to be tried first, that a second staff member be present to witness the punishment, and on request, parents be furnished a written statement of the paddling, the reasons for it, and the names of witnesses who observed it.

In 1977, the Supreme Court decided its only corporal punishment case to date. In *Ingraham v. Wright* (1977), two junior high school students sued their school district for damages they received from being struck with a wooden paddle. The school district's policy was that students could be struck for violating school rules, although the teachers were to consult with the school principal before they hit the students. Both of the students had received large bruises from repeated strikes from a wooden paddle. One student was beaten more than 20 times with a two-foot-long wooden paddle. He suffered a bruise that kept him out of school for 11 days. Another student complained that he was struck twice on the arm, which resulted in the loss of its full use for a week. The plaintiffs argued that the school's punishments violated the Eighth Amendment and represented cruel and unusual punishment as well as the denial of due process. The Court ruled that the Eighth Amendment only applies to criminals in custody, and not to children in schools. As for due process, the Court said it was impractical to hold a hearing each time a teacher wanted to use corporal punishment. It said that abuses were not common, that schools

were open to public scrutiny, and that teachers and other pupils were there to keep a watch over excessive force.

The court did acknowledge that only such corporal punishment that is reasonably necessary for the proper education and discipline of a child would be allowed. Punishments that go beyond what is reasonable may subject the school or teacher to civil or criminal liability. In other words, parents who do not believe that the corporal punishment of their children is within reasonable limits may pursue criminal prosecution of the teacher or civil lawsuits after the fact to challenge the propriety of the actions.

Although parents have the right to sue for injuries inflicted on their children, the problem in many cases is proving that the punishment was not reasonable in light of the situation. For example, in a Georgia case, the parents of a middle-school student sued the teacher and school, alleging that the teacher had physically restrained and choked their son, causing him to have physical and emotional injuries. In her response, the teacher stated that the child had been causing problems and when he would not respond to her attempts to get him to behave, she reached up to him, grabbed his face with her fingers splayed across his cheeks, and turned his face toward her to get his attention. The court ruled against the parents, finding that not all physical contact between a teacher and a child is considered to be punishment and that the teacher was simply exercising her responsibilities to regain control and supervise her class (*Daniels v. Gordon*, 1998).

In *Saylor v. Board of Education* (1997), a 14-year-old boy got into a "wild" fight with another child at the school. As punishment for the fight, both boys received five licks with a wooden paddle. The Kentucky school district had a policy in place in which parents could tell the school that they did not want their children subjected to corporal punishment. The parents claimed that they had told the school district that they did not want the school to use corporal punishment on their child. The schoolteacher and administrators stated that the father had told them at a meeting that they could discipline the child as needed. Despite the factual dispute, the court ruled in favor of the school district. The court saw no violation of substantive due process because the child was fully clothed when he was hit on his buttocks and the beating was not so severe or disproportionate as to shock the conscience of the court.

Other cases have found the conduct by school personnel to be shocking. For example, in *Neal v. Fulton County Bd. of Ed.* (2000), Durante Neal, a 14-year-old freshman and member of a Georgia high school varsity football team, got into a fight with another student, Griffin. Neal reported the fight to the assistant coach who told him to learn to handle his own business. Neal took a metal weight lock from the coaches' office and put it in his gym bag. After practice, Griffin again approached Neal. Neal took the weight lock and hit Griffin in the head. The two boys started fighting. The coach and the principal came running over to Neal and the coach hit Neal with the weight lock in the left eye, knocking the eye out of the socket and destroying it, leaving Neal blind in one eye. In *Neal,* the Fifth Circuit Court of Appeals, in reviewing principles created by other courts with respect to corporal punishment, found that constitutional principles protect a student from corporal punishment that is excessive, intentional, and creates a foreseeable risk of physical injury. The court stated that many corporal punishment cases involve what might be called traditional applications of physical force, such as where school officials, subject to an official policy or in a more formal disciplinary setting, mete out spankings or paddlings to a disruptive student. However, the court stated that not all corporal punishment cases arise under those circumstances and may involve less traditional, more informally administered, and more severe punishments. The *Neal* court cited the cases of *London v. Directors of DeWitt Pub. Schs.* (1999; school official's acts of dragging student across room and banging student's head against metal pole was corporal punishment); *P.B. v. Koch* (1996; school principal's conduct in hitting student in mouth, grabbing and squeezing student's neck, punching student in chest, and throwing student headfirst into lockers

was corporal punishment); *Metzger v. Osbeck* (1988; official's conduct consisting of grabbing student in choke hold, causing student to lose consciousness and fall to the pavement, resulting in student breaking his nose and fracturing teeth, met corporal punishment framework); *Carestio v. School Bd. of Broward County* (1999; school employees' conduct in ganging up on student and beating him ruled to be corporal punishment); and *Gaither v. Barron* (1996; teacher's head butting of student described as corporal punishment). In *Neal,* the court, in deciding that Neal's eye loss was a severe form of punishment that constituted corporal punishment, did not delineate what other types of corporal punishment were excessive or serious enough to support a claim. The question remains, however, whether corporal punishment should *ever* be used to discipline children.

Hyman and Rathbone (1993), strong advocates against corporal punishment, explored the arguments in favor of and in opposition to the use of corporal punishment in the schools. They noted that some educators who are proponents of corporal punishment believe that when a student learns to associate inappropriate behavior with strong negative consequences, the student will learn quickly to modify the undesirable behavior to conform to educational and social norms. For other proponents, corporal punishment is seen as a useful, moral, and acceptable way to teach children proper behaviors, often in line with religious beliefs. Hyman and Rathbone also delineated arguments used by opponents of corporal punishment. Opponents claim that corporal punishment does more harm than good and is psychologically damaging to those who receive it. Opponents also argue that rather than teaching a preference for cooperation and respect for the thoughts and feelings of others, it teaches the value of aggression and force as a means of settling problems. These arguments remain today.

Although it does appear that corporal punishment is becoming less accepted as an educational practice throughout the country, its use still remains. At the time of the *Ingraham v. Wright* decision in 1977, 23 states addressed corporal punishment through legislation. Of those states, 21 authorized the use of corporal punishment in public schools, and only two, New Jersey and Massachusetts, prohibited its use. Today, however, 21 states still permit corporal punishment (Human Rights Watch, 2008). More promising is the continuing reduction in the reported number of paddlings of students. In the 1979 to 1980 school year, 1.4 million paddlings were inflicted compared to 365,000 in 1997 to 1998, with 90% of these incidents coming from Louisiana, Mississippi, and Texas (Wigoren, 2001). In the 2006 to 2007 school year, the number of paddlings was further reduced to 223,190 students nationwide who received corporal punishment at least once during that school year (Human Rights Watch, 2008).

Even though the number of incidents of corporal punishment is decreasing throughout the country, certain groups of students are subjected to corporal punishment at disproportionate rates. In the 2006 to 2007 school year, African-American students comprised approximately 17% of the U.S student population, but received almost 36% of the paddlings (Human Rights Watch, 2008). Boys are subjected to corporal punishment at a much higher rate than girls, with boys receiving approximately 78% of the paddlings. Although girls of all races were paddled less than boys, African-American girls were physically punished at more than twice the rate of their white counterparts in the 13 states that most frequently used corporal punishment (Human Rights Watch, 2008). Students with mental or physical disabilities also received corporal punishment at a higher proportionate rate than their percentage to the total student population (Human Rights Watch, 2008).

School social workers understand that students who receive corporal punishment from adults at school will not find the school to be a safe and nurturing environment. For some of those children, the school becomes a replication of their home, rather than a safe harbor. More than 40 national organizations in the United States oppose the use of corporal punishment, including the National Association of Social Workers (NCACPS, 2008). Worldwide, many countries oppose corporal punishment, and multiple organizations from around the world work toward its abolition (Gershoff & Bitensky, 2007). School social workers should work to abolish the use of corporal punishment in the 21 states where its use is still permitted. Additionally, social workers should work with school personnel to find more positive ways to achieve resolution for disciplinary infractions.

Suspensions and Expulsions

As already mentioned, schools possess the broad authority to establish and maintain the learning environment of the school. Accordingly, schools have the authority to discipline a student in a variety of ways. We have explored the topic of corporal punishment, a very harsh form of discipline. In some cases, schools use milder forms of punishment, such as taking away privileges, assigning special duties, denying the right to participate in graduation exercises, and lowering students' grades. Schools also possess the authority to remove from school, through suspension and expulsion, students whose conduct disrupts or defies the operation of the school and its rules, as well as students whose behavior poses a threat to other students, school personnel, or school property.

A suspension is usually considered to be a removal from the school environment for a short period of time, usually less than 10 days, whereas an expulsion is a longer-term removal from school. When students are suspended, it is likely that they will return to school. With suspensions, children are usually excluded from school, school activities, or school transportation for a short term.

With expulsion, the student's status is much more questionable. In some cases, students may be expelled from school for up to the remainder of the school year. In other cases, the expulsion may result in the student's permanent exclusion from school. The permanent exclusion would be more likely to occur with a child who is older than the age requirement for compulsory school attendance in the state.

Instead of removing the child temporarily from the classroom, some schools use different forms of suspensions. For example, some schools suspend a student until the parent comes into the school to discuss the child's situation. This may be burdensome for some parents who have different work schedules, who have difficulty arranging transportation or child care, or who lack the motivation, interest, or ability to come to the school. In these cases, the school may resort to in-school suspensions, where the pupil remains in school but is not allowed to attend classes for a period of time. In many school districts, state statutes dictate the length of the suspension.

The landmark case involving suspension occurred during the 1970s in Columbus, Ohio. It involved nine pupils, who were suspended for 10 days for a variety of infractions. In *Goss v. Lopez* (1975), the Supreme Court ruled that students had both property and liberty constitutional interests related to school attendance. The court held that the students' rights to a free public education cannot be taken away by suspensions, even temporarily, without due process of law. The Court found that for short suspensions, defined as less than 10 days, students must be given informal notice, including a statement of the charges and evidence against them, as well as an opportunity to tell their side of the story. In *Wood v. Strickland* (1975), the Court expanded the *Goss* ruling to state that school officials may be sued for monetary damages if they know or reasonably should have known that their disciplinary actions would violate the constitutional rights of pupils.

Although *Goss* protected the child's procedural due process rights, the court noted that suspensions are "considered not only to be a necessary tool to maintain order but a valuable education device" (*Goss* at 580). Therefore immediate suspension is sometimes appropriate to protect other pupils and to preserve the decorum of the school. Students whose presence imposes a continuing danger to persons or property or constitutes an ongoing threat of disrupting the academic process may be immediately removed from school.

From the limited case law available on the subject, it is not entirely clear whether a pupil can be expelled from a public school permanently. However, there is no doubt that a pupil can be expelled from public school if the board of education then places the student in an alternative school. Generally, however, expulsion of a student by a board of education does not extend past the end of the current school year.

Another area that remains unclear is the types of incidents that can trigger an expulsion. State law varies on the types of infractions and what procedures are required to be given to students before they can be expelled. Some courts treat expulsions and long-term suspensions as equivalent. Most hold that pupils facing expulsion or long-term suspension have the right to additional due process practices, including a written statement of the charges, enough time to prepare a defense, and an impartial hearing on the evidence. Many states delineate in their legislation the procedures for expelling children from school and the rights students have in these hearings, before the expulsion can occur. The rights may include presenting and cross-examining witnesses, a hearing before a hearing officer, an appeal to the school board, the right to a transcript of the proceedings, and court review.

The concept of removing children from school on a short-term or permanent basis has been further complicated by two recent developments. One of these developments is the passage of the Gun-Free Schools Act, and the other is the overwhelming increase in zero-tolerance policies.

In 1994, Congress passed the Gun-Free Schools Act, which was reauthorized and recodified in 2002. The Gun-Free Schools Act mandates that all local educational authorities have a policy in place that requires a 1-year expulsion from school for any child who brings a firearm to school or possesses a firearm on school property. The Act, in defining what constitutes a firearm, refers to the federal Criminal Code (20 U.S.C. 921(a) (2002)). Under the criminal code, a firearm is defined as any weapon, including a starter pistol, that is designed or modified to expel a projectile (like a bullet) by the action of explosives. A firearm also includes "destructive devices" like bombs, grenades, rockets, missiles, and mines. As a result of the Gun-Free Schools Act, school districts must create a policy that children can be expelled from school for bringing a firearm, broadly defined, to school. Many school districts or state laws have broadened the concept of firearms to include other weapons, such as knives. Other districts also have expanded on the length of the punishment for infractions (e.g., requiring an expulsion to last for the remainder of the school year and the entire following year).

The Gun-Free Schools Act also requires that school districts refer a case to the criminal justice or juvenile delinquency systems when a student brings a firearm or weapon to school. The law does allow for some discretion. Congress attempted to give discretion to school officials by allowing that the gun-free expulsion policy can be modified on a case-by-case basis. Additionally, there is nothing in the federal law to prevent a school district from choosing to provide education in an alternative setting to an expelled student.

Although federal law allows for case-by-case discretion, many school districts have passed zero-tolerance policies that allow none. Within the last decade, "zero-tolerance" policies have developed throughout the country. Zero-tolerance policies proscribe behaviors that will not be accepted and mandate predetermined consequences or punishments for specific offenses. As they first developed, zero-tolerance policies focused on truly dangerous and criminal behaviors by students that required mandatory expulsions.

Today, zero-tolerance policies not only include weapons but may also govern drugs and alcohol, gang activities, tobacco offenses, fighting and other disruptive activities, sexual harassment, threatening speech, and other prohibited incidents (Ballard, 2002). Proponents of zero-tolerance policies believe that the policies increase safety in the school and have the support of educators and parents. The critics of zero-tolerance oppose its one-size-fits-all mentality; in other words, no matter whether there are legitimate reasons or justifications why students break policy, nor how minor the violation, they are all treated in the same way. Punishment is meted out in accordance with a stated policy, with no allowance for any mitigating circumstances.

Henault (2001) reported a number of incidents in which students were suspended or expelled from school because of seemingly innocuous violations of their schools' policies. Among her examples, Henault cited situations that occurred in West Virginia and Louisiana. For example, in West Virginia, a seventh grader who shared a zinc cough drop with a classmate was suspended for 3 days pursuant to the school's antidrug policy because the cough drop was not cleared with the office. In Louisiana, a second grader brought his grandfather's watch to school for show-and-tell; attached to the watch was a 1-inch-long pocketknife. Because the school viewed this as a violation of its weapons policy, the child was suspended and sent to an alternative school for a month.

The media, seemingly amused by the newsworthiness of these stories, often report instances in which children were suspended or expelled pursuant to zero-tolerance policies. For example, in Georgia, an 11-year-old girl was suspended for 2 weeks for bringing her "Tweety Bird" wallet to school. The school considered it to be a weapon because it had a short chain connecting the wallet to her key ring ("Georgia Girl," 2000). In Ohio, a 13-year-old honor student was suspended for 10 days for accepting two Midol pills, given to her by a friend, for menstrual discomfort. After she agreed to go to drug awareness classes, she returned to her classroom, and her suspension was reduced to 3 days in her school records (Midol Suspension, 1996). More recently, a high-school student was suspended for 10 days for refusing to end a cell phone call with his mother, a soldier who called him from her deployment in Iraq ("Call from Mother," 2005). Because the incident attracted national news media attention and prompted a flood of e-mail to the school, the student's suspension was shortened to the 2 days he had served.

Parents, angry about their children's suspensions and expulsions, have successfully challenged their districts' zero-tolerance polices. In a Pennsylvania case (*Lyons v. Penn Hills Sch. Dist.,*

1999), a 12-year-old, seventh-grade honor student was seen filing his fingernail with a miniature Swiss army knife he had found in a school hallway. The instructor requested the child to turn over the penknife, and the student complied without incident. The knife was ultimately brought to the school's associate principal, who questioned the child about it. Lyons told the associate principal that he had found the knife and had intended to turn it over to his instructor. The school informed the parents that the child had violated the school's zero-tolerance policy and that there would be an expulsion hearing before a hearing officer. The school board adopted the hearing officer's recommendation that the student be expelled from school for 1 year. The parents sued the school district, and the appellate court affirmed the trial court's ruling against the district. The court found that the school district, in enacting its local zero-tolerance policy, exceeded its authority because it did not give the superintendent case-by-case discretion as provided in Pennsylvania law. In a Tennessee case, a student was expelled for having a knife in his car on school property. He claimed that he was unaware of the knife's presence, due to his transporting some of his friends. The Sixth Circuit ruled that if the student unknowingly possessed the weapon, then suspending or expelling him for weapons possession was irrational (*Seal v. Morgan*, 2000). These cases may be the beginning of a trend that will impose a reasonableness standard in zero-tolerance policies.

Studies have shown that zero-tolerance policies not only increase the numbers of students who are suspended and expelled, but also are differentially enforced against African-American and Latino students. For example, the U.S. Department of Education (2000) reported that in 1998, more than 3.1 million students were suspended, with another 87,000 students expelled. However, although African-American children represented only 17% of public school enrollment nationally, they made up 32% of out-of-school suspensions. In contrast, white students, who comprised 63% of the national enrollment, made

up only 50% of the suspensions and 50% of the expulsions. Another study interviewed attorneys who represented children facing disciplinary actions based on zero-tolerance policies. It found that the attorneys believed that racial profiling played a large part in determining which students were subjected to harsh penalties (Harvard Project, 2000). The attorneys reported that African-American and Latino students were more likely to be disciplined for offenses such as defiance or disrespect of authority. The attorneys believed that the subjectivity of what is considered "disrespect" could lead to a racial bias in student discipline.

School social workers would be invaluable members of a school disciplinary team and should help develop reasonable disciplinary policies. School social workers should suggest that schools avoid using zero-tolerance policies and, instead, consider the totality of the circumstances under which the breaches of the policies occur. Additionally, social workers should assist other members of the school to recognize that some students' cultural differences may be mistaken for disrespect or defiance. Those students can be taught the schools' behavioral expectations, rather than be unnecessarily punished for their unintentional disobedience of school rules.

Discipline of Children with Disabilities

As you will see in Chapter 7, students with disabilities have the right to a free and appropriate public education that is appropriate to their needs. Prior to the passage of the Education for All Handicapped Children's Act in 1975 (EAHCA, P.L. 94–142), now known as the Individuals with Disabilities Education Improvement Act of 2004 (P.L. 108–446), or (IDEA 2004), school officials often used disciplinary measures to purposefully exclude children with disabilities from education. As a result, safeguards were incorporated into the EAHCA, so that expulsions or long-term suspensions would trigger procedural protections for children with disabilities from being excluded from education.

Many children with disabilities exhibit behaviors that put them in conflict with school rules. For example, a child that has difficulty sitting still may disrupt the learning environment. A child with behavior problems may defy school rules. A child who has difficulty reading may exhibit frustration and low self-esteem that may trigger attention-getting behaviors. Because children with disabilities are entitled to receive a uniquely designed education to meet their needs, discipline that involves removing the child from the educational environment is considered to be a change of placement and requires a reconvening of the Individualized Education Program (IEP) team to look at the child's behavior. If the parents object to any proposed plan, a child with a disability will "stay-put" in the current educational placement, regardless of the seriousness of the child's behavior, while the dispute is pending. In *Honig v. Doe* (1988) a California school district attempted to expel children with disabilities from school because they exhibited behavior that the school considered dangerous. The U.S. Supreme Court found that no exception to the stay-put requirement exists for children exhibiting dangerous behavior. If a school district believes that a child poses a real and serious risk to others, the Supreme Court suggested that the district go to its local court and seek an injunction to remove the child. Otherwise, the child had statutory rights to remain in the school environment, regardless of concerns regarding his or her behavior.

As should be clear by now, changes in society have made the schools less safe learning environments. When the Gun-Free Schools Act was enacted in 1994, an exception to the "stay-put" aspect of IDEA was included so that students with disabilities who brought weapons to school could be removed from the educational environment. However, removals were limited to reasons of weapons only and not for behavioral issues, and the child could not be removed for more than 45 days. The child would still receive educational services in an interim alternative educational setting.

In 1997, the Individuals with Disabilities Education Act Amendments of 1997 (P.L. 105–17) changed many of the provisions of IDEA. In the new law and the 1999 regulations that interpreted it, rules regarding discipline of children with disabilities became part of legislation for the first time. When IDEA 2004 reauthorized IDEA '97, it maintained the discipline provisions for children with disabilities. However, the regulations that were promulgated in 2006 allowed schools to remove children with disabilities from school under additional circumstances, as long as procedural safeguards were provided to them.

Under IDEA, public schools are authorized to remove a child with a disability for 45 days to an alternative education setting for possession of not only guns, but for all dangerous weapons or for the use, possession, or sale of illegal drugs or controlled substances on school grounds, or if the child has inflicted serious bodily injury on another person. Additionally, a child with a disability can be removed for up to 45 days if the child is substantially likely to cause injury by remaining in the current educational environment. Schools are not required to provide any services to a child with a disability for the first 10 days of any removal. If a child is removed for more than 10 consecutive schooldays, a disciplinary "change of placement" occurs. In that case, the school district must convene an IEP meeting to determine whether the problematic behavior is actually a manifestation of the child's disability. If it is a manifestation, the IEP team must conduct a functional behavioral assessment and implement a "behavioral intervention plan" to create specific interventions designed to address the problematic behaviors. If the child needs to be removed from school on subsequent occasions, the IEP team must review the plan to determine what modifications are necessary. If the behavior is not a manifestation of the child's disability, the child can be disciplined to the same extent as a nondisabled child. However, appropriate educational services still must be provided to enable the child with a disability to progress appropriately in the general curriculum and advance toward the goals set out in the child's IEP (Altshuler & Kopels, 2003).

Children with disabilities have heightened legal protections with respect to being suspended or expelled from school, and at the same time, schools have more limits placed on their powers to discipline them. Therefore, with respect to the discipline issues we have discussed, children with disabilities have a legal advantage over children who do not have disabilities. Children with disabilities have a right to a free, appropriate public education, even if they are expelled from school. Children without disabilities can be expelled permanently from school without receiving any education. As we have seen, however, protections for all children seem to be eroding. For any child, being removed from the school environment has very serious consequences.

School Attendance

It may seem obvious, but children have the right to attend school. However, unlike many of the rights mentioned previously in this chapter, the right to attend school is not guaranteed through the U.S. Constitution or federal law. In *San Antonio Independent School District v. Rodriguez* (1973), a case that challenged Texas's school financing system that provided more funding to schools in districts with higher property taxes, the Supreme Court specifically held that there is no fundamental constitutional right to an education. Instead, the right of a student to attend school derives from individual state laws and state constitutions. In *Goss v. Lopez* (1975), mentioned earlier in the discussion of suspensions and expulsions, the Supreme Court recognized that education can be viewed as a property right. The Court stated that protected interests in property normally are not created by the Constitution. Rather, property rights are created and their dimensions are defined by an independent source such as state statutes or rules. In *Goss*, the Supreme Court ruled that although Ohio may not have been constitutionally obligated to establish and maintain a public school system, it had nevertheless done so and had required its children to attend, thereby creating constitutionally protected property rights for those students. Therefore, the right to attend school is actually a mandate placed on children that requires their attendance. All states compel students between certain ages to attend school.

Compulsory Education

The notion of compulsory school attendance is based on the belief that democracy requires an educated citizenry and that it is both inefficient and impractical to leave the education of future citizens to the family. In *Brown v. Board of Education of Topeka* (1954), in which the U.S. Supreme Court ruled that racial segregation in public schools deprives school children of equal educational opportunities, the court stressed the importance of education to the nation's children and society as a whole. The Court stated that

> . . . education is perhaps the most important function of state and local governments. Compulsory school attendance laws and the great expenditures for education both demonstrate our recognition of the importance of education to our democratic society. It is required in the performance of our most basic public responsibilities, even service in the armed forces. It is the very foundation of good citizenship. Today it is a principal instrument in awakening the child to cultural values, in preparing him for later professional training, and in helping him to adjust normally to his environment. In these days, it is doubtful that any child may reasonably be expected to succeed in life if he is denied the opportunity of an education. Such an opportunity, where the state has undertaken to provide it, is a right which must be made available to all on equal terms. (*Brown v. Board of Education* at 493)

Although education is not a fundamental constitutional right, all states provide education to the children residing within their borders.

By 1918, all 48 states then in the Union had compulsory school attendance laws. Today, compulsory attendance laws are found in all 50 states, the District of Columbia, and Puerto Rico. The original Compulsory School Attendance Act was passed in Massachusetts in 1852 and served as the model for most states. It required public school attendance of all able-bodied children of a certain age, unless the parent could demonstrate that the child was receiving equivalent instruction elsewhere. Parents could educate their children in private schools so long as the state judged the private school as able to provide an adequate education to the children.

Typically, state laws require attendance but delineate certain conditions or circumstances that excuse compulsory attendance. For example, Illinois requires that students attend public school unless (1) they attend private or parochial schools that meet certain educational requirements; (2) they are physically or mentally unable to attend school as certified by a physician (schools cannot exclude pregnant students simply because they are pregnant or have given birth to children); (3) they are children who are lawfully and necessarily employed pursuant to child labor laws; (4) they are between 12 and 14 and are attending confirmation classes; or (5) the tenets of his or her religion forbid secular activity on a particular day or days or at a particular time of day (Illinois School Code, 2008). In California, a pupil shall be excused from school when the absence is due to (1) his or her illness; (2) being in quarantine under the direction of a county or city health officer; (3) having medical, dental, optometrical, or chiropractic services rendered; (4) attending the funeral services of a member of his or her immediate family; (5) jury duty; (6) the illness or medical appointment during school hours of a child of whom the pupil is the custodial parent; (7) justifiable personal reasons, including, but not limited to, an appearance in court, attendance at a funeral service, observance of a holiday or ceremony of his or her religion, attendance at religious retreats, or attendance at an employment conference; or (8) serving as a member of a precinct board for an election (California Education Code, 2008). Although states vary on the types of absences that will be excused in their laws, they uniformly excuse absences based on

mental, emotional, or physical disability. Jones (1997) analyzed the state and federal cases in which the courts discussed whether, or under what circumstances, the conditions at a particular public or private school justified or excused noncompliance with a state's compulsory attendance laws. She found that courts generally excused absences that were reasonably necessary on the grounds of the child's health and welfare. In cases where parents do not send their children to school based on religious grounds, courts are not routine in their rulings. Several courts have recognized that a pupil's absence arising from dismissal, expulsion, or threatened expulsion for refusing, on religious grounds, to participate in a pledge of allegiance and flag-salute ceremony was, or would be, excused or justified. However, other allegedly religious reasons, such as objections to "race mixing" or being present where music was played or meat was eaten, were held not to constitute an excuse for nonattendance. Similarly, parents who objected to reading of the Bible or the recitation of the Lord's Prayer in a public school were also held not to justify the parents' failure to have their children attend school. Finally, Jones noted that in jurisdictions that require by law that public transportation be provided, absence has generally been held not to be excused if the child lives less than 2.5 miles from the school or less than 1 mile from the transportation provided by the school district. Where hazardous conditions en route to the school or bus stop, or other danger to the health and well-being of the child due to lack of public transportation, are alleged, the courts have found the child's absence to be excused in some cases (Jones, 1997).

Compulsory attendance is dependent on the age of the student. In other words, states regulate the minimum and maximum ages that students must attend school. For example, many states set 6 years of age as the age by which a child must be enrolled in school. Parents may send their children to school for kindergarten, typically at age 5. Once they enroll their children, parents are required to send them to school. However, until the children reach the age of compulsory attendance, the parents have a choice on whether they want their children to attend. States also vary on how long they require children to attend school. The most common age until which a student must remain in school is 16 years of age. At 16, the child or his or her parents can choose whether the child will continue to attend school or "drop out" of school. Some states have extended the maximum age by which children must attend school. California requires children to attend school from the ages of 6 until 18 (California Education Code, 2008), and Illinois recently revised its law to require children to attend school from 7 until 17 years of age, rather than the previous requirement of 16 years of age (Illinois School Code, 2008).

Attendance and Certain Groups of Children

Although all states have compulsory attendance laws, certain groups of children have had problems surrounding their ability to attend school. Some of these children are members of groups who historically have been excluded from school, and others are children who have personal reasons that keep them from attending public schools. These groups include children who are homeless, children who have disabilities, children whose religious beliefs or those of their parents are in conflict with the teachings or environment of the public schools, and children who refuse to attend school.

Children Who Are Homeless

As you will learn in other chapters, children who are homeless have additional problems when it comes to enrolling, attending, and succeeding in school. Homeless children are not exempt from compulsory education laws and have the same rights to attend school as do other children. In fact, the recent reauthorization of the McKinney-Vento Homeless Education Assistance Improvements Act of 2001 requires schools to ensure that each child of a homeless individual has equal access to the same free, appropriate public education as is provided to other children and youth.

The McKinney-Vento Act requires any state that has a residency requirement as a component of its compulsory school attendance law to review and undertake steps to revise its policies that act as a barrier to the enrollment, attendance, or success of homeless children. These steps include immediately enrolling the homeless child or youth, even if he or she is unable to produce the records normally required for enrollment (such as previous academic records, medical records, proof of residency, birth certificates, or other documentation).

Students are afforded other rights under the McKinney-Vento Act. Students are allowed to attend the same school they attended before they became homeless (their school of origin), or the school in the district where they are temporarily staying. Children who are homeless are also entitled to transportation to school until they obtain permanent housing. Homeless children are automatically eligible for any free breakfast and lunch programs provided by the school as well as free textbooks, tutoring, or Title I services. Additionally, homeless children have the right to attend school and extracurricular activities with their classmates and cannot be segregated from the mainstream school environment.

Children with Disabilities

As you will see in Chapter 7, children with disabilities were routinely excluded from public school attendance because of their disabilities. When P.L. 94-142, the Education of All Handicapped Children's Act (EAHCA) was enacted in 1975, Congress found that more than one half of the children with disabilities in the United States were not receiving appropriate educational services and that one million children with disabilities were entirely excluded from public education. It must be stressed that children with disabilities have the right to attend school and to receive a free and appropriate public education under federal law. State compulsory education laws, which often exempt children from attendance because of physical or mental disability, cannot be used as a justification to exclude children with disabilities from receiving an education. Instead, the compulsory attendance laws that exempt children from school attendance because of their disabilities usually relate to children's inability to be present in school because of their temporary illnesses or conditions. These conditions may include children who are presently contagious, children who are hospitalized, or children who are otherwise too ill to come to school. For example, a child who has been in an automobile accident and is in traction in the hospital may be excused from compulsory attendance because he or she physically cannot attend school. However, a child who has been in an automobile accident, is hospitalized for several months, recovers, and is left with severe cognitive deficits, should not be excused from compulsory school attendance. That child has the right to attend school. That child is a child with a disability and has the right to receive a free, appropriate public education.

Children with Religious Objections to Public School Attendance

Certain children and/or their parents hold religious beliefs that are at odds with public school attendance. Some parents who believe the public schools promote an environment that is contrary to their religious holdings send their children to private religious schools or homeschool their children. In this way, the parents feel they can keep their children safe from what the parents see as harmful or immoral situations and keep the children from learning ideas that are inconsistent with their religious beliefs.

Since 1925, the Supreme Court has recognized that parents can send their children to private, religious schools, rather than being forced to send them to public schools. In *Pierce v. Soc'y of Sisters* (1925), a private religious school challenged an Oregon law that required students to attend public schools. The Court noted that the state had shown no failure on the part of the private schools and no extraordinary circumstances existed as the impetus for such a law. The Court concluded that the Oregon law unreasonably interfered with the liberty of parents and guardians to

direct the upbringing and education of children under their control; the state had no power to standardize its children by forcing them to accept instruction from public teachers only.

In *Wisconsin v. Yoder* (1972), members of the Amish religion were convicted for violating Wisconsin's compulsory school attendance laws. Wisconsin law required attendance at public or private school until the age of 16. However, the Amish community made it a practice to pull their children from the public educational system after the eighth grade. The Amish community's rationale was that its children needed basic education to be good citizens, but that the influence of public high school would conflict and threaten the Amish community's way of life and have detrimental psychological consequences for their children. Balancing the state's responsibility to educate its citizens and the parental interest in the religious upbringing of their children, the Court found that the sincere religious convictions of the Amish were severely threatened by the compulsory school attendance law. Moreover, the Court found that foregoing 2 years of compulsory education would not impair the physical or mental health of Amish children, result in their inability to be self-supporting, to discharge the duties and responsibilities of citizenship, or in any way materially detract from the welfare of society.

Parents who send their children to private schools or who homeschool their children are still required to provide an educational program that follows the educational prerequisites set by the state. Homeschools are often defined as private schools under state law. Homeschools and private schools are regulated by the laws of the states and are considered to be an appropriate form of education so long as the schooling meets curriculum and other standards set by the state. One of the main issues today between parents who homeschool their children and school districts is the extent to which the homeschooled children, who are not enrolled in the school district, are allowed to participate in school district extracurricular activities, such as sport teams or musical activities.

Children Who Do Not Attend School

Certain children have problems attending school. These problems may include being tardy to school, being absent for days or certain portions of the day, or being truant from school. Truancy typically means an unexcused absence from school or class. New Hampshire enacted a law in 2005 that defined the concept of "truancy" as an unexcused absence from school or class without parental or administrative permission (New Hampshire Revised Statutes Annotated, 2008). Illinois's laws pertaining to who is truant have been in existence far longer. Illinois defines a "truant" as a child subject to compulsory school attendance who is absent without valid cause from such attendance for a school day or any portion thereof. Illinois's law goes further to define a chronic and habitual truant as being absent without valid cause from such attendance for 10% or more of the previous 180 regular attendance days (Illinois School Code, 2008). These children may be referred to the juvenile court for intervention.

States vary in their approaches to encouraging children to attend school. In some states, truant officers are paid employees of school districts whose job functions include investigating unexcused absences and locating children who do not attend school. Truant officers are often empowered to send notices to parents, conduct hearings on absent children, and refer cases to the juvenile court for prosecution. Although many state laws require that each school district should employ at least one truant officer, in large urban school districts there may be an insufficient number of truant officers to ensure attendance. In North Carolina, the legislature has assigned school social workers the responsibility to investigate unexcused absences and to report and prepare documents for criminal prosecution of children or their parents related to nonattendance at school (North Carolina General Statutes, 2008).

To encourage school attendance, states have begun putting the onus on parents or on other persons who have control over or responsibility for a child to ensure that the child goes to school. If the person with the responsibility does not send the child to school, then the parent or the responsible adult can be criminally prosecuted. For example, in a Missouri case, *State v. Self* (2005), Brenda Self's 15-year-old child, Jennifer, missed approximately 40 days of school in a 6-month period. The school reported these absences to the prosecuting attorney, who charged Ms. Self with the class C misdemeanor of failing to cause her child to attend school on a regular basis. Ms. Self agreed to the prosecutor's recommendation that the court impose a sentence no greater than 15 days in jail, execution of which would be suspended, and 2 years' probation. Ms. Self appealed her conviction. The appellate court overturned the conviction because the state had not proved that the mother acted knowingly or purposely to cause her child not to attend school regularly.

Additional actions have been taken against parents or others who fail to exercise their responsibilities to send children to school. Criminal prosecutions against parents and other persons who encourage children not to attend school have increased. Additionally, when children do not attend school, juvenile court petitions may be filed under state law that allege the minor is a neglected minor, educationally neglected, dependent, truant, or delinquent. In this way, juvenile courts may become involved to provide additional oversight or pressure on parents to make sure their children go to school. Juvenile court involvement has the added benefit of ordering the provision of social services, including counseling, skills training, budgeting, and other needed services to parents and children.

In addition to pressuring the parents, juvenile courts often coerce children to attend school. In *Commonwealth of Virginia v. May* (2003), April was adjudicated a child in need of supervision (CHINS) because she had an extreme history of absences from her Virginia public school. When she was adjudicated, she had missed 29 out of 69 school days with 28 absences. Among the orders of the court was the requirement that April attend school every day and participate in community service. She continued to miss school, and on five separate occasions, the juvenile court found her in contempt of court and sentenced her to detention. During her last court appearance, the court sentenced April to a period of 10 days in jail. April appealed the jail sentence, saying it was not within the juvenile court's power to sentence her to jail for not attending school. The appellate court disagreed, believing that it was within the power of the juvenile court to hold April in contempt for disobeying its orders.

School districts have tried other strategies to reduce truancy. These options include reducing grades, not granting high school diplomas, restricting driving privileges, and providing incentives to attend school. In *State ex rel. Barno v. Crestwood Bd. of Educ.* (1998), Jennifer sued her school district for its refusal to issue her a high school diploma because the district believed Jennifer did not complete the "curriculum" as defined by the Board of Education. The Board had enacted a strict attendance policy requiring each student to attain a 93% attendance rate to receive academic credit. A student could be absent for approximately 13 days and still graduate. Jennifer was absent a total of 18 $\frac{1}{2}$ days her senior year. All but two of these were excused, but under the terms of the policy, both excused and unexcused absences would count against the student when figuring the final attendance rate. Although Jennifer had a 3.966 grade point average out of a 4.0 and had passed all required proficiency exams, the principal of the school informed Jennifer that she would not be allowed to graduate because of her poor attendance. The appellate court reviewed the school's refusal to grant the diploma and stated that

> the choice between competing attendance policies is generally committed to the sound discretion of the boards of education, which are free to select a policy that provides incentives for good attendance, disperses punitive, administrative consequences for bad attendance, such as detentions and suspensions, lowers grades when a predetermined number of absences is reached, or the like. (*Barno* at 508)

The court went on to say that if the school district had chosen one of those policies, the court would have deferred to the school board's discretion. However, the court found the district's policy to be unreasonable and an abuse of power because the district counted excused absences against a student and did not define extenuating circumstances.

Some states try to encourage attendance by tying attendance and/or school performance to driving privileges. Twenty-three states have such policies, although they vary in what they require (Burke, 2005). Nine states require attendance in school to receive a license; 5 states have minimum academic performance standards for initially obtaining a driver's license; 10 states designate truancy or lack of academic progress as a cause for suspension of a license; and 5 states have policies that require attendance for both the initial issuance and maintenance of a license (Burke, 2005).

Negative Consequences for Absent Children

It should be apparent that some children, because of their behaviors, may not be part of the learning environment of the school. This may be because children have engaged in behaviors that have caused school officials to remove them from the school environment or because children have problems that cause them not to attend school. In any case, children who are absent from the learning environment of the school suffer serious negative consequences. These negative consequences are borne both by the student and by the overall community, which each suffer when children do not receive an education.

Being absent from school because of suspensions, expulsions, or nonattendance has immediate and long-range effects that have both direct and indirect impacts on students, the school staff, and the larger community. Removals and absences also interrupt the pupils' instructional programs. Because many suspended, expelled, and truant students experience academic difficulty, the lost instructional time may determine their academic success for the semester. If the school does not permit the pupils to make up exams and homework, the lost grades may automatically mean that no matter how high their previous or subsequent grades, the students may receive failing marks. Consequently, they might not attempt to complete course work or attend school for the remainder of the semester. Additionally, students who are expelled for the remainder of the school year or longer, especially if they are beyond the age of compulsory school attendance, may decide to drop out of school permanently. Punitive discipline policies reject students; these students are often "pushed out" of the school environment (Dupper, 1994).

Another consequence of suspension, expulsion, and nonattendance is that other staff members in the school may label students as problems because the behaviors have been recorded in official school records and because knowledge of their occurrence has circulated among the staff. This may have informal as well as formal consequences. For example, informally, due to some vague, preconceived perceptions that they are "problem students," staff members may be quicker to refer pupils who have been suspended previously. In a formal sense, a suspension is almost always considered in subsequent disciplinary incidents and usually influences the school to impose a longer suspension the next time.

In fact, in some states, newer laws pertaining to school records permit the disclosure of prior disciplinary reports when students transfer to a new school district. In this way, a student who has been suspended or expelled cannot escape serving a long-term suspension or expulsion by beginning anew in a different school district. For example, in Illinois, the student temporary record includes information regarding serious disciplinary infractions that resulted in expulsion, suspension, or the imposition of punishment or sanction. Parents cannot challenge the references to expulsions or out-of-school suspensions if the challenge is made at the time the student's school records are forwarded (Illinois School Student Records Act, 2008). When the new school receives the student's records, they may be more likely to perceive the child as a discipline problem. At the same time, the child does not really have a chance to have a fresh start, with no prior negative expectations following him or her.

Suspensions, expulsions, and nonattendance also isolate students from an important, structured environment. For most children, school is their first formal relationship with the government (Losen & Edley, 2001). Although some students may view absence from school as a welcome vacation and may consciously manipulate the system to bring about this vacation, to others it represents the equivalent of solitary confinement. For this latter group, school represents a dynamic and important social setting that is a comfortable balance between structured routines and new and exciting experiences. Suspensions separate these pupils from an important part of their lives and isolate them psychologically from their social families.

Suspensions, expulsions, and nonattendance often lead to high levels of parent and community resentment because of the perception of the school's failure to meet the needs of pupils through less intrusive means. This resentment may cause open hostility that results in a refusal of parents to believe in or to support the schools, not only with regard to issues of discipline but also regarding more general issues that affect education.

Perhaps the most important role social workers can play in matters of student absence is to help the school, family, and community appreciate the reality that excluding children from schools has very direct economic consequences for the school and community. For schools that receive state aid based on average daily attendance, suspensions, expulsions, and truancy may result in a significant loss of state funds. Even for districts that receive state aid based on yearly enrollment, there is a loss in the sense that the schools have structured their instructional programs and services for a larger number of pupils than will actually receive those services.

The personal consequences of absences for the students can also make them extremely costly for society. If students are unable to acquire suitable employment because of their school record, or they lack basic skills for entry-level jobs, or to continue their education, the cost to society is extremely high. Until skills are developed, society may have to provide public assistance, health insurance and other subsistence benefits. Another societal cost resulting from expulsions is the resultant increase in juvenile delinquency and, ultimately, criminal activity. The cost of increases in delinquency and criminality can be measured in terms of increased fear and suffering as well as by the increased financial costs for police, courts, detention facilities, hospitalizations, and insurance costs for the accompanying property and personal damages.

Because of these factors, the uneducated youth in a community remain in their community and influence its development. Most communities want their youth to improve their situations with increased opportunities. Absences and removals from school decrease opportunities for these students. Given the potential consequences and costs of absences for the student, the school, and society, it seems clear that schools should find ways to avoid school expulsions as often as possible and to reduce their negative consequences. A variety of other disciplinary tools including behavioral modification, rewards, and behavior contracts can be tried, depending on a student's age group. Hopefully, the recent emphasis on positive behavioral interventions and supports (PBIS) may change the educational climate of the school to support all students to remain in school.

Conclusion

During the last half-century, schools have experienced significant changes in the control of student behavior and student rights. Changes in the application of the principle of *in loco parentis* and the ebb and flow of liberal versus conservative public sentiments have influenced court decisions and, in turn, the actions of students, parents, and school administrators.

Fundamentally, what the various courts' decisions have established is that the school has jurisdiction over the child when the child is under the reasonable control of the school. The courts have held, however, that the school's right to control a child is not the same general right as that of parents; it is limited because teachers cannot exceed their responsibilities. The courts have attempted to balance the constitutional rights of students to demonstrate their individuality—politically, religiously, and expressively—with the growing need of school personnel to control the learning environment and to keep the schools safe.

The courts have become very instrumental in assisting schools to develop commonsense approaches to discipline, notwithstanding school officials' broad discretionary power to decide when punishment is appropriate and necessary. Social workers bring broad insights and social science knowledge in assisting administrators on this subject. For example, the social worker's understanding of frustration and aggression offers a theoretical base for helping school officials to mitigate students' aggressive impulses. Social workers can strongly advocate at IEP meetings for the formulation of behavioral assessment plans that connect behavior problems to the students' disabilities (Altshuler & Kopels, 2003).

Earlier work by Schimmel and Eiseman (1982) found that one important consideration in punishing children is that they must believe that whoever is selecting and inflicting punishment does so equitably. In other words, the pupil must believe that the school official would inflict the same punishment on anyone else who committed the same offense or who engaged in a similar pattern of disruptive behavior. Hearings play a central role in promoting fairness, and the more elements of due process that are included in the hearing, the harder it is for the student to maintain a perception that the official is being unjust.

To that end, social workers should insist that students know exactly what they are being accused of before any disciplinary action occurs. For example, the typical suspension letter from a principal to a student's parents merely states that the pupil is charged with "violating school rules" or "serious misconduct." It does not adequately inform them of what specific act or conduct the student engaged in. Without knowing this, the student cannot adequately refute the charges, if he or she is not guilty of the wrongdoing. Just as important, students cannot begin to reflect on their conduct and consider whether the school selected punishment that is reasonable under the circumstances.

Unfortunately, the increased use of zero-tolerance policies may whittle away any opportunity for self-reflection. Students may not have the opportunity to present their sides of the story when infractions are equated with automatic punishments. Instead, the lesson they may learn is that the government, in the form of the school, can take away their rights or privileges for often trivial violations without first listening to or considering their reasons or explanations regarding their actions. Social workers should provide leadership in opposing zero-tolerance policies and, instead, allow both sides of the story to be told. Serious punishments, such as suspensions or expulsions, should not be imposed for minor rule breaking and should never be imposed unfairly by racial or gender characteristics.

Drawing on general systems theory and the ecological perspective, social workers have a solid foundation from which they can help school personnel understand the problems of absenteeism and the effect of the environment on the truant. The social worker's goal is to enhance the student's social functioning. Social workers, in helping students with their school adjustment or attendance problems, may be required to assist school personnel in exploring and identifying school and nonschool factors that contribute to adjustment and/or attendance problems, to assist school officials in determining the severity of these problems, and to refer pupils to appropriate social services and supports, both within and outside the school.

Social workers in schools can play an important role in creating a positive learning environment for children that respects their rights as well as ensures that schools remain a safe place to learn. They can assist in the development of policies and procedures for securing and maintaining records; they can consult with school officials regarding basic human rights; they can provide firm, constructive counsel to students about their responsibilities and remind them to have respect for others; and they can take leadership in developing and refining student codes of conduct, and the penalties for their violation. Social workers are well equipped by training and by their value orientation to organize committees composed of school officials, parents, pupils, and community leaders to prepare written guidelines and policy statements governing student behavior, due process, suspensions and expulsions, and other matters related to the orderly operation of schools.

The U.S. Constitution requires that government agencies treat all persons fairly. Specifically, the Fourteenth Amendment states that the government may not "deprive any person of life, liberty, or property, without due process of law." Social workers, who are often mediators in matters of student behavior, can play an important role in reminding principals, teachers, coaches, security guards, and all other employees of the school that they, too, are employees of the government and, under the Fourteenth Amendment, have a legal duty to treat all students fairly.

Following are eight specific ways in which school social workers can assist the school and community to resolve problems related to student rights and student control.

1. Work with the local school board and lobby for restrictions on corporal punishment.
2. Assist state lobby groups.
3. Work with school officials and administrators to develop school code handbooks specifying reasonable expectations for pupils and teachers.
4. Assist and act as advocate for students who have been unjustly or improperly punished.
5. Provide in-service training to teachers on classroom management and suggest alternatives to corporal punishment and harsh discipline policies.
6. Advocate against zero-tolerance and strip search policies.
7. Work to ensure alternative educational programs for students who have been expelled.
8. Identify factors, inside and outside the school, that operate as barriers to students' school attendance.

For Study and Discussion

1. The concept of *in loco parentis* has been practiced for a long time. Discuss its pros and cons in a society that has moved from rural-agrarian culture to one now characterized as postindustrial and litigious.

2. What is your opinion regarding the adage, "Spare the rod and spoil the child"?

3. How would you assist school officials in discovering options to suspensions and expulsions? What specific roles could you play?

4. What are your opinions about prayer in schools?

5. What factors should you consider in developing a zero-tolerance policy?

6. What are the negative implications for students who do not receive an education?

7. Should a student be allowed to wear a T-shirt that says "Osama bin Laden had the right idea"?

6

Violence in Schools

RON AVI ASTOR

University of Southern California

RAMI BENBENISHTY

Bar Ilan University, Israel

ROXANA MARACHI

San Jose State University

Introduction

Violence prevention in schools is becoming a major focus of practice for school social workers (Astor, 1998; Astor, Behre, Fravil, & Wallace, 1997; Astor, Behre, Wallace, & Fravil, 1998; Astor & Meyer, 1999; Astor, Pitner, Meyer, & Vargas, 2000; Klein, 2002). Social work as a profession has contributed to the national and international dialogue concerning violence intervention programs (for example, Astor, Benbenishty, & Estrada, 2008; Astor, Benbenishty, Marachi, & Pitner, 2008; Astor, Benbenishty, & Meyer, 2004; Astor, Meyer, Benbenishty, Marachi, & Rosemond, 2005; Benbenishty & Astor, 2005; Benbenishty, Astor, & Estrada, 2008; Benbenishty, Astor, & Zeira, 2003; Benbenishty Astor, Zeira, & Vinokur, 2002; Khoury-Kassabri, Benbenishty, Astor, & Zeira, 2004; Zeira, Astor, & Benbenishty, 2002, 2004; Zeira, Benbenishty, & Astor, 2004) and school social workers play an increasingly important role in shaping and implementing policy, interventions, and procedures that make U.S. schools safer. To be effective, school social workers need to be aware of current philosophical, empirical, and practice issues surrounding school violence. Several intervention approaches have demonstrated significant reductions in school violence, and overall national trends have indicated declines in school violence rates (Astor et al., 2005; DeVoe et al., 2004; Dinkes, Cataldi, & Lin-Kelly, 2007). Social workers could be very effective in creating an accurate national awareness regarding the tremendous strides schools have made on this issue over the past 10 years. By providing accurate information on school violence, they may help counter some harmful misperceptions that exist in the media and among the general public (Astor, Rosemond, Pitner, & Marachi, 2006). In this chapter, we review some of the major trends in U.S. school violence and explore potential areas in which school social workers could make an impact, at both conceptual and practical levels.

Major Trends and Issues

Expanding School Violence Definitions and Behaviors. During the past 30 years, many physically and psychologically harmful behaviors have been subsumed under the term *school violence.* The concept of school violence now spans an array of behaviors that includes physical harm, psychological harm, and property damage. Currently, the term *school violence* could include behaviors that vary in severity and frequency such as bullying, verbal threats, and intimidation (Batsche & Knoff, 1994; Benbenishty & Astor, 2005; Olweus, 1993; Olweus, Limber, & Mihalic, 1999); cyberbullying (Ybarra & Mitchell, 2007); vandalism (Goldstein, 1996); school fighting (Boulton, 1993; Schafer & Smith, 1996); corporal punishment (Benbenishty, Zeira, & Astor, 2002; Benbenishty, Zeira, Astor, & Khoury-Kassabri, 2002; Youssef, Attia, & Kamel, 1998); sexual harassment (Stein, 1995; Zeira et al., 2002); gang violence (Kodluboy, 1997; Parks, 1995); the presence of weapons (Astor, Benbenishty, Meyer, & Rosemond, 2004; Pittel, 1998); violence directed at school staff (Zeira et al., 2004; Benbenishty, Zeira, & Astor, 2000); rape (Page, 1997); hate crimes geared at students from ethnic/religious groups or at gay, lesbian, bisexual, and transsexual students (Berrill, 1990; Pitner, Astor, Benbenishty, Haj-Yahia, & Zeira, 2003); dating violence (Burcky, Reuterman, & Kopsky, 1988; Cano, Avery-Leaf, Cascardi, & O'Leary, 1998); and murder (Bragg, 1997; Hays, 1998). Many of these types of behaviors have evolved into separate research and practice literatures. In this chapter, we present an overview of the trends and prevalence rates of select types of school violence in the United States. We have focused mainly on the kinds of violence (e.g., violent crimes, weapon carrying, school fatalities, school fights) that have nationally representative data.

One potentially harmful myth about school violence is that it is currently on the rise in U.S. schools. However, contrary to what most of the U.S. public perceives, empirical data indicate steady declines in the rates of school violence (Dinkes et al., 2007). In the next section, we outline the reductions in violence in detail.

The Myth of a Continual Rise in School Violence Rates

Fatal Victimization on School Grounds. It is important for school social workers to know that media perceptions and national norms surrounding school violence deaths are not entirely accurate (Cornell, 2006). This understanding is especially important because many of the misperceptions center on issues of race, socioeconomic status, and gender. Furthermore, the efforts of school personnel may go unacknowledged by the media and the general public due to the perception that violent school deaths and shootings are on the rise.

The intense public attention on school violence is most likely associated with the widespread media coverage given to the late 1990s mass homicides on school grounds. This nationwide attention to violent deaths in schools reflects a normative shift in U.S. cultural attitudes regarding violent deaths on school grounds. However, research suggests that such incidents existed at comparable or higher rates before the intense media coverage of the late 1990s. For example, according to government statistics from the Departments of Education and Justice (DeVoe et al., 2004; Dinkes et al., 2007), there were 28 to 34 violent deaths of students (not including suicide) on school grounds in each of the years 1992 to 1999. If we examine the number of fatal events, government data show that the actual number has decreased and the latest figure of student homicides on school grounds is 14 (2005–2006). One might argue that we now have a greater awareness about school deaths and should not tolerate even 5 deaths (we support such a position). However, empirical evidence suggests that U.S. schools have seen more than 40% *reduction* in violent deaths on school grounds since 1992 to 1993 (to 2005–2006; see Dinkes et al., 2007; Figure 1.2 for details). We emphasize this reduction in order to acknowledge that efforts at violence prevention may be making an impact and that there is reason to hope that violence rates can decline even further.

Due to the intensified media coverage of the school shootings, many in the general public are now under the incorrect impression that violent deaths in schools are a relatively new phenomena and that fatalities are increasing on school grounds in the United States. We suspect that many in the general public have distorted perceptions of the frequency of school fatalities and may not be aware of how rare school fatalities actually are in the United

TABLE 6.1   Guiding Questions for School Social Workers Regarding Culture and School Violence

A social work practitioner or researcher might ask themselves a series of questions to guide their critical thinking on culture as it relates to violence in schools.

1. What are the norms surrounding the acceptability of violence or retribution within the culture I'm working with? Is there a *range* of perspectives within the culture surrounding these norms? Do the norms within a culture vary by religiosity, gender, age, education, assimilation, or generation? Or, are the norms fairly uniform across these variables? School social workers should be aware of the symbolic meaning of certain behaviors, such as carrying a weapon, and the preference for certain types of weapons. These kinds of preferences vary from culture to culture and within subgroups of cultures.

2. Am I aware of how the culture sees the school and how the school sees the culture? School social workers should be aware and sensitive to the way the culture perceives the school, teachers, and their authority—to what extent the culture values academic achievement, identifies with the school, accepts the authority of teachers/principals, compared with the authority of parents. Are the school staff and workers aware of these dynamics?

3. Can I distinguish between "culture" and economic issues? To what extent is the violence in the community related to political, social, or economic conditions surrounding this culture?

4. Do I know who has authority within the culture? School social workers should be aware of who may have influence within a given culture as potential partners to school intervention—in certain cultures it may be parents, in others elder brothers, religious leaders, political activists, leading gang members, sports leaders, and other types of leaders/celebrities that may have influence. Are there culturally accepted ways or structures of dealing with conflict peacefully? Are there culturally relevant themes that may be used, such as religious teaching, traditional proverbs/legends/stories, political agendas (protect our group against others), cultural role models, etc.?

5. Is there a history of oppression and prejudice that could help account for the violence seen? Do the interventions proposed match the historical themes and cultural norms surrounding oppression?

6. Does the school staff understand the various aspects of the culture? Do they understand the language, history, politics, arts, music, food, and economic hardships faced by students and families?

7. Are there economic underground subcultures that interact with cultural norms?

8. Is there a historical sense of privilege, entitlement, and hierarchy that could help account for violence seen?

9. To what extent is parental or community education a part of the intervention?

10. Are there language-based, religious, holiday music, literature, or arts communities within the culture that support peace? Are they being used? Are the schools aware of them? In some cultures there are formal mechanisms to deal with violence and peace. Can they be fit to the school or programs being used?

11. Does this culture have a media or arts group targeting it, and is the school violence program/effort part of the media/arts effort?

12. Do the interventions used appear familiar and appropriate to the parents, students, community or do they feel foreign, oppressive, and unnatural?

13. Are members of the school community/culture involved in planning the antiviolence events? Are there teachers/administrators within the district that can serve as liaisons and leaders within the school district?

States compared with other contexts in our society (DeVoe et al., 2004). Government data indicate that violent deaths are not common occurrences on school grounds when compared with other settings (such as neighborhoods and homes). Thus, the percentage of youth homicides occurring at school remained at less than 2% of the total number of youth homicides over all available survey years even though the absolute number of homicides of school-age youth at school varied to some degree across the years (Dinkes et al., 2007). This evidence suggests that students may be safer from violent crime when they are in school than when they are out and further illuminates the stark difference between public perception and actual violence rates in U.S. schools.

In addition to the misperceptions about overall violence rates, many misunderstandings exist around issues of race, religion, and violence. Patterns of fatal student victimization fluctuate over time, vary across areas, and also differ among ethnic groups. These variations occur in our society in general (Ash, Kellermann, Fuqua-Whitley, & Johnson, 1996; Gray, 1991; Hammond & Yung, 1993; Issacs, 1992; Prothrow-Stith & Weissman, 1991) and also on school grounds (Astor, Pitner, & Duncan, 1996; Kachur et al., 1996; Kaufman et al., 1998).

One of the common public myths of the post-Columbine era is that school fatalities are for the first time occurring in suburban areas, whereas prior to Columbine, fatal school deaths were occurring primarily in urban settings. Another contradictory media myth is that recent violent deaths (especially those involving shootings) have not occurred in inner-city/urban schools in the past and that shootings are associated with a new phenomenon of alienated angry White suburban males. These myths are unsubstantiated. The data suggest that a significant proportion of violent deaths occurred in *both* settings before and after the late 1990s shootings. Kachur et al. (1996) reported that in 1992 to 1993 (prior to the Columbine shootings), 30% of the school fatalities occurred in suburbs, 62% occurred in urban areas, and 8% occurred in rural settings. These statistics raise serious questions as to why the media and public continue to perpetuate unsubstantiated and potentially harmful myths that serve as "proxies" for racial and economic stereotyping. School fatalities occurred in both urban *and* suburban areas during the early 1990s. Urban and suburban media coverage of violent deaths in the early 1990s was not as much as the national media coverage of those occurring in the late 1990s in the suburbs. Furthermore, the perception that violence in the late 1990s is exclusive to "angry White males" ignores the actual rates of school fatalities of other ethnic groups.

For example, in 1998 during the peak of the intense media coverage, Hispanic students were five times more likely and African-American students nine times more likely than White students to suffer a school-related lethal event (Kaufman et al., 1998).

Weapons on School Grounds. The *potential* for lethal violence in schools remains quite high due to the availability of weapons. Nevertheless, the U.S. public and school personnel are not aware generally of the impressive declines in the presence of weapons on school grounds in recent years. This lack of awareness is particularly problematic because many federal, state, and district policies have been focused on the reduction of weapons on school grounds (Dinkes et al., 2007; U.S. Departments of Education and Justice, 2000). It is possible that the policies implemented have had a dramatic effect. For example, between 1993 and 2006, the Department of Education reported that the percentage of students in grades 9 to 12 who reported bringing a gun on school grounds during the 30 days preceding the survey dropped from 12 to 6%. This is an astonishing 50% nationwide reduction in the number of students who report bringing weapons on to school grounds. There are also significant gender differences in rates of weapon carrying, with male students being more than three times more likely to carry a weapon on school property than female students (10 vs. 3%, respectively) (Dinkes et al., 2007). Asian students were less likely than students from all other racial/ethnic groups, except for African Americans, to report carrying a weapon on school property, but no differences were detected among African-American, White, and American-Indian students. Hispanic students were more likely than African-American students to report carrying a weapon during the previous 30 days on school property in 2005 (8 vs. 5%; Dinkes et al., 2007). Nationally, multiracial students are twice as likely to carry a weapon on campus than White and African-American students (Dinkes et al., 2007). More should be done to explore the reasons behind these cultural and racial differences.

This accomplishment should be tempered with the knowledge that the national percentage of students in grades 9 to 12 who report being threatened and/or injured by someone using a weapon on school grounds has remained very constant (between 7 and 9%) from 1993 to 2005 (Dinkes, 2007). In 2005, racial differences in rates for threat and injury on school grounds were not large, and the only measurable difference was a higher rate among Hispanic students compared with White students (10 vs. 7%). From a social work perspective, education surrounding both dramatic reductions and similarities/disparities between ethnic groups should be a primary goal because national policy is often influenced by inaccurate stereotypes.

Expulsion for Weapons and Zero Tolerance. Some are crediting the zero tolerance gun laws as the major cause for the decline of overall weapons on school campuses. Due to national and state zero-tolerance laws, many students have been expelled for bringing weapons on school grounds in recent years. However, consistent with the other data presented in this chapter, expulsion rates have also gone down. Rates of expulsion for firearms dropped from 5,724 in 1996 to 1997 to 3,658 in 1998 to 1999. Although it is true that these school expulsions may be reducing the number of students with weapons, there ought to be serious social concern over where these expelled and potentially violent students are going after they are expelled (U.S. Departments of Education and Justice, 2000).

From a social work and public policy perspective, it is unwise to deprive a potentially violent and armed youth of an education. To the detriment of society as well as the lives of these youth, current policy does not (a) provide alternative programs, (b) track the success of these programs, or (c) track the expelled students' whereabouts. According to current U.S. government data, 44% of students expelled were referred to alternative programs; however, we do not know how many students actually went or stayed in those programs and how successful those programs were. This problem is a serious public health/safety gap in the current zero-tolerance laws that needs to be addressed. School social workers' advocacy and education of the public could play a vital role in this policy issue.

As a corollary to the zero-tolerance laws, some advocacy groups and academicians have argued that these laws should be administered more judiciously to create a "safe" climate rather than a punitive climate of fear (Noguera, 1995). It has been argued that what has been defined as "security" does not necessarily translate into a safe environment (Benbenishty & Astor, 2005; Noguera, 1995). Hyman and Snook (2000) suggested that these kinds of extreme measures have created an authoritarian and punitive environment that may be inconsistent with the public schools' overall goals of creating democratic citizens.

In a study conducted through the National Center for Education Statistics, Heaviside, Rowand, Williams, and Farris (1998) examined some of the effects of tough zero-tolerance policies. They found that schools relying too heavily on zero-tolerance policies continue to be less safe than schools that implemented fewer components of zero tolerance. A study by Mayer and Leone (1999) used structural equation modeling to predict the incidence of school violence. They found that overreliance on physical security procedures appeared to be associated with an *increased* risk of school disorder. Also qualitative research has suggested that misuse of school security measures such as locker or strip searches may create emotional backlash in students (Hyman & Perone, 1998). In light of these findings, it becomes increasingly important not only to assess the violence that occurs in schools, but also to examine how the school climate may be affected by procedures that are enacted to curb violence. Oftentimes, measures intended to remedy a problem may inadvertently exacerbate it. School social workers should add their voices to this kind of debate about what "security" means to students.

Physical Fights on School Grounds. Serious physical school fights are perhaps one of the most familiar forms of school violence. Teachers and administrators could use social workers' guidance in developing response procedures to school fights from an ecological and school community perspective. Annual rates of fights on school grounds for students in grades 9 to 12 from 1993 to 2003 did not change much over the years (16 to 13%). Overall, male students were more likely to report that they had been involved in a physical fight on school property in the past 12 months (18% of males vs. 9% of females). Rates of being involved in a physical fight on school property also varied by grade level, with students in lower grades reporting that they had been involved in more fights on school property than students in upper grades. More specifically, approximately 19% of ninth graders reported being involved in a physical fight in the past year, compared to only 9% of twelfth graders (Dinkes et al., 2007). There were significant differences by race/ethnicity in students' involvement in fights on school property. Specifically, in 2005, Asian students were less likely than students from all other racial/ethnic groups to report being in a fight on school property (6 compared with 12 to 24% of students from other racial/ethnic groups). Between 2003 and 2005, the percentage of Asian students who reported having been in a fight on school property declined from 13 to 6%.

We caution, however, about the interpretation of fight statistics. "School grounds" was not defined in these studies, and it is unclear whether students included fights that occurred immediately after school just off school grounds. This issue of school vs. community fights is important because Department of Justice statistics indicate that the highest rates of student/youth fights and assaults occur mainly on school days between 3 and 4 p.m. (much closer to 3 than 4) near school grounds. We believe that many of these kinds of fights emanate from school social dynamics (i.e., are potentially controllable by the school) and should be categorized as school fights (rather than community or elsewhere). Currently, fights occurring after 3 p.m. are most likely not counted as school fights. Hence, the number of school-related fights is probably much higher than the percentages listed earlier.

Given this caveat, and as a way of understanding the possible total amount of fights, according to the Centers for Disease Control and Prevention (CDC) in 2005 (Eaton et al., 2006), 36% of secondary-school-aged students were involved in serious fights (anywhere, not on school grounds) during that year (43% of males and 28% of females). Again, the vast majority of these occurred just after 3 p.m. and only on school days. If school social dynamics were *not* a key component, we would see much higher rates on nonschool days and more variation in the after-school hours. In fact, the rate of fights on nonschool days is very low and does not include the afternoon spike in events that accounts for most fights (Snyder & Sickmund, 1999). These overall fight percentages have also slightly declined since 1993.

Other Nonfatal Forms of Violence.   Between 1992 and 2005, the total crime victimization rates for students ages 12 to 18 generally declined both at school and away from school; this pattern held for the total crime rate as well as for thefts, violent crimes, and serious violent crimes (Dinkes et al., 2007). If the total number of student victimization events are examined (including nonfatal crimes such as rape, sexual assault, robbery, theft, aggravated assault, and simple assault), there were significant declines in victimization between 1992 (144 crimes per 1,000 students) and 2005 (57 per 1,000 students). This accounts for approximately a 60% reduction in school crime nationwide. These data add more evidence that we are in the midst of a profound decline in student victimization rates (DeVoe et al., 2004; Dinkes et al., 2007; Kann et al., 1998; Kaufman et al., 2000; U.S. Departments of Education and Justice, 2000).

Gang Activity at School.   Between 1995 and 1999, there have been reductions in reported gang activity in schools. With all the media hype of the late 1980s and early 1990s on the influence of gangs on school violence, these reductions have gone virtually unnoticed in the national media and by the public. Overall, the percentage of students who reported gang presence in their school dropped from 1995 to 2005 (from 29 to 24%). The reductions of gang activity in schools have been strong across all settings and ethnic categories (DeVoe et al., 2004; Kaufman et al., 2000; U.S. Departments of Education and Justice, 2000). This is yet another area where the media and general public have not acknowledged positive societal change and improvements in historically oppressed groups of students. According to Dinkes and colleagues (2007), students in public schools were many times more likely to report the presence of gangs than were students in private schools, regardless of the school's location (25% versus 4%), and Hispanic and African-American students were more likely than White students to report gangs in their schools in 2005 (38 and 37%, respectively, vs. 17%).

Student Perceptions of Safety at School/on the Way to and from School.

The U.S. Departments of Education and Justice report indicated declines in the percentages of students ages 12 to 18 who reported that they avoided one or more places in school in the previous 6 months due to fear of attack from 1995 to 2005 (9 to 4%, respectively, Dinkes et al., 2007). The reductions of fear were greater in urban settings (12 vs. 6% in 1995 and 1999, respectively) and for Hispanic students (13 vs. 6% for 1995 and 1999, respectively). In 1995, students in urban settings were more likely to be fearful at school, whereas in 1999 fear among urban students dropped so significantly that urban and suburban students were equally likely to be fearful of violence at schools. Students were also less likely to fear that they would be attacked while traveling to and from school from 1995 to 1999 (7 to 4%, respectively). Across all years, trends suggest that younger students (grades 9 and 10) were more likely than older students (grades 11 and 12) to fear being attacked while traveling to and from school. These trends have not changed significantly between 1999 and 2003 (DeVoe et al., 2004; Kann et al., 1998; Kaufman et al., 2000; U.S. Departments of Education and Justice, 2000). There are no gender differences in avoiding places in school due to fear of attack.

Bully/Victim Rates.

The United States participated in a cross-national research project coordinated by the World Health Organization on the prevalence of bullying and victims on school grounds. This first U.S. representative sample consisted of students in grades 6 to 10. Nansel and colleagues (2001) found that 10.6% of the sample reported bullying others sometimes (moderate), and 8.8% admitted to bullying others frequently (once a week or more). Reports on victimization were slightly lower—8.5% of students reported being bullied sometimes and 8.4% once a week or more. About 30% of the sample reported being involved in school bullying either moderately or frequently, as bullies (13.0%), victims (10.6%), or both (6.3%). Reports from the U.S. Department of Education also found similar results for the years 2001, 2003, and 2005 (DeVoe et al., 2004; Dinkes et al., 2007). In 2005, 28% of students ages 12 to 18 reported having been bullied at school during the previous 6 months (79% of them inside the school). Of these students, 53% said that the bullying had happened once or twice, 25% once or twice a month, 11% once or twice a week, and 8% said they had been bullied almost daily. Nineteen percent of students said that they had experienced bullying that consisted of being made fun of; 15% the subject of rumors; and 9% said that they were pushed, shoved, tripped, or spit on (Dinkes et al., 2007). There is an inverse relationship between age and bully victimization. The grade decline in victimization is sharp with 37% of sixth graders reporting being bullied in school versus 20% of 12th graders being bullied (Dinkes et al., 2007).

Cyberbullying.

In recent years there are growing concerns over new forms of interpersonal youth violence that involve electronic media. This kind of violence is alternately called *cyberbullying*, *online aggression*, *Internet-based harassment*, *cyberstalking*, and *cyberviolence*.

Media-related violent behaviors, include a range of willful attempts to inflict harm, such as making threats, spreading malicious rumors or lies, and making public humiliating pictures and other information (either of a private nature or falsified). It can be carried out using multiple means (e.g., cellular phone text messaging, e-mail, and Internet instant messaging) and can take place in multiple cyberlocations (e.g., chat rooms, personal Web sites, social networking sites such as

MySpace, Internet bulletin boards, and in other Web-based environments).

There are many indications that victimization by electronic violence has a significant negative impact on youth. For example, Patchin and Hinduja (2006) found that over 42% of victims were frustrated, almost 40% felt angry, and over one fourth (27%) felt sad. The negative effects of online victimization extended beyond cyberspace, as 31.9% and 26.5% of respondents revealed that they were negatively affected at school and at home, respectively. Mitchell, Ybarra, and Finkelhor (2007) reported that virtually all types of online and offline victimization were independently related to depressive symptomatology, delinquent behavior, and substance use. Sexual solicitation messages were especially distressing. Youth who report being victims of Internet harassment are significantly more likely to concurrently report depressive symptomatology, life challenges, interpersonal victimization, deficits in social skills, and harassing others online themselves (Ybarra, Alexander, & Mitchell, 2005; Ybarra, Mitchell, Wolak, & Finkelhor, 2006). Further, there are several indications that youth at high risk are victimized more by online harassment (Wells & Mitchell, 2008; Ybarra et al., 2007).

Currently, media-related violence is not included in national representative studies that monitor other indicators of youth and school violence (such as Dinkes et al., 2007). Nevertheless, available studies suggest that such violence is quite prevalent. The most recent Growing Up with Media, a national cross-sectional online survey of 1,588 youth between the ages of 10 and 15 years old, indicates that 35% of youth (ages 10 to 15) reported being targeted by Internet harassment; 8% reported frequent harassment (i.e., being targeted monthly or more often). The Second Youth Internet Safety Survey, a national telephone survey of youth between the ages of 10 and 17 years ($N = 1,500$) found that 6% of youth reported frequent Internet harassment perpetration, an additional 6% reported occasional perpetration, and 17% reported limited perpetration of Internet harassment in the previous year (Ybarra & Mitchell, 2007).

Similarly, Patchin and Hinduja (2006) conducted a pilot study of 384 adolescent Internet users to assess experience with various forms of cyberbullying, including bothering someone online, teasing in a mean way, calling someone hurtful names, intentionally leaving persons out of things, threatening someone, and saying unwanted sexually related things to someone. Approximately 29% of youth reported being the victim of such behavior, 11% reported engaging in such behavior, and almost half (47%) reported witnessing such behavior. Comparable rates were reported in other large-scale surveys (Patchin & Hinduja, 2006; Kowalski & Limber, 2007).

Teacher and School Social Worker Victimization. Teachers are also the victims of both theft and violent crimes. Many school violence interventions ignore the fact that teachers and school staff also need support. Even so, overall teacher victimization rates have been dropping. Between 1992 and 1996, the annual average rate of victimization (combining theft and physical violence) for teachers was 76 incidents per 1,000 teachers (Kaufman et al., 1998, p. 71, Table 9.1). Between 1998 and 2003 the annual average rate of victimization was 51 per 1,000 teachers. This represents approximately a one fourth reduction in teacher victimization (DeVoe et al., 2004). Also, a smaller percentage of teachers were threatened with an injury or an attack in 2003 to 2004 compared with 1993 to 1994 (7% versus 12%; Dinkes et al., 2007). The community setting of the schools appears to influence teachers' victimization as well. Teachers in urban schools were more likely than in suburban and rural schools to report being the victim of violent acts. For instance, in 2003 to 2004 5% of teachers in city schools were physically attacked by students, compared to 3% of teachers in suburban and town schools, and 2% of teachers in rural schools. (Dinkes et al., 2007, p. 44). We do not have national data indicating how many teachers are threatened or attacked by other adults such as parents, teachers, or school outsiders such as gang members in the community. However, we do have such data on school social workers.

In a national study, 35% of school social workers in the United States reported being physically assaulted or physically threatened during the past year (Astor et al., 1997, 1998, 2000). Of those who reported being threatened or assaulted, 77% identified the assailant as a student, 49% identified the attacker as a parent, and 11% identified the perpetrator as a student gang member (some social workers were attacked more than once and by more than one type of perpetrator, therefore the total percentages are higher than 100%). Not surprisingly, many school social workers feared for their personal safety. In fact, one third of school social workers reported that they feared for their personal safety about once a month or more. However, there were differences in the proportion of social workers in each community setting that reported fear. Compared with social workers in urban (36%), suburban (37%), and rural (31%) schools, more social workers in inner-city schools (71%) reported that they feared for their personal safety. The Astor et al. studies (1997, 1998) suggest that their fear may be related to a lack of training on how to handle or prevent violent situations. In the Astor et al. studies (1997, 1998), few school social workers received formal university training to deal with school violence, and the vast majority stated that they wished they had more (Astor et al., 1998). School social workers also expressed strong beliefs that school violence needed to be dealt with from an ecological point of view (Astor et al., 1998, 2000).

Is School Violence Still a Problem? Based on the declining overall frequencies regarding school violence, some might conclude that school violence is no longer a problem (or only a small one). We believe this conclusion, if based only on frequencies, would be a mistake. Clearly, school violence rates have declined across multiple forms of victimization, but these rate reductions do not address how society *should* determine when school violence is a problem. When does a specific school cross the threshold from having an average level of school violence to having a "high" level? Conversely, how do we know when

a school is considered a "model" safe school? These are not abstract, moral, or academic issues alone. Several state and national politicians, organizations, and task forces have declared publicly that punitive measures should be taken against schools that are "unsafe" (shut them down, hire new staff, etc.). Despite these movements, no one yet has put forth a clear set of criteria on what would constitute an unsafe school district or school. Social work participation in these philosophical discussions could add to the national dialogue because as a society, as practitioners, and as researchers, we must have agreed on ways to understand what is a safe or unsafe school. Without a clear sense of what is considered safe or unsafe, it will be difficult to assess the success or failure of prevention and intervention programs.

Types of Interventions

Characteristics of Ineffective Interventions

A Singular Focus on the Source of the Problem. Most practitioners and researchers would agree that school violence is associated with a wide array of individual, family, community, and societal variables. Figure 6.1 presents select examples of correlates commonly mentioned in the school violence practice and research literatures; these correlates are presented at different ecological levels. The outside circles represent many of the variables outside the school that influence behaviors in the school, such as the family, culture, and peer group. It also presents factors within the school that can either increase violence or help prevent it, such as the school climate and student/teacher relationships. Given the number of variables associated with school violence, one would expect school violence interventions to target multiple factors both inside and outside the school. Instead, most school violence interventions focus only on one or two variables or ecological levels (e.g., the child, the family, or the classroom) and tend to ignore the complex interplay of multiple variables. Consequently, it is not surprising that most

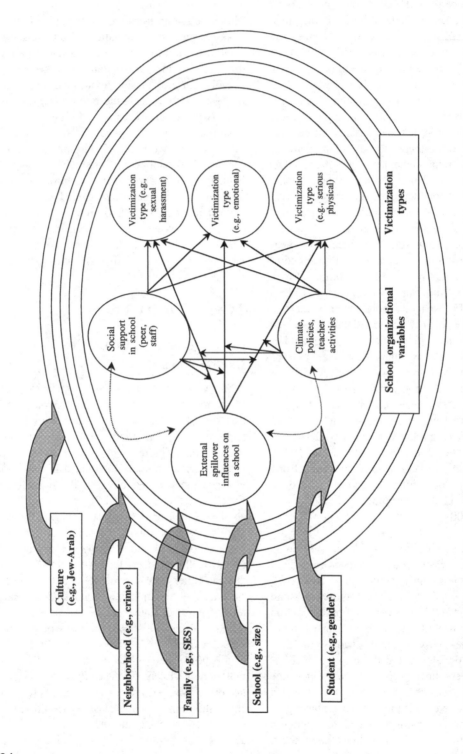

FIGURE 6.1 A Model of Social-Ecological Influences on Student Victimization   *Source:* Benbenishty, R. & Astor, R. A. (2005). *School violence in context: Culture, neighborhood, family, school, and gender.* Oxford University Press.

programs that address only one variable tend not to be effective in reducing levels of school violence. Figure 6.1 also represents our theoretical conceptualization of how, with the help of programs or self-initiated interventions, the school could buffer or exacerbate outside influences that come from factors external to the school environment. As shown in Figure 6.1 (Benbenishty & Astor, 2005), the school policies/procedures and social supports could affect various forms of student victimization differently. Based on our assessment of the research, we believe that successful programs strengthen the school infrastructure/social environment to buffer students from many risk factors external to the school and ultimately reduce overall rates of victimization in the school (see Benbenishty & Astor, 2005, for a discussion on community/school influences). We suspect that less successful programs tend not to focus on the *school social environment* at the core of the interventions.

A Psychological/Behavioral Focus.   The most popular school violence interventions are psychological and behavioral interventions (e.g., anger-management, conflict mediation, peer counseling, curriculum-based programs). Historically, psychology has focused on identifying cognitive, emotional, and social-relational reasons why individual children become violent (American Psychological Association, 1993). Consequently, school-based psychological interventions have focused mainly on psychological variables. These types of interventions have been geared primarily toward individual children (or their families) with very little focus on the interplay between social contexts such as schools and violence in the school setting (Hudley, Britsch, Wakefield, Demorat, & Cho, 1998). Unfortunately, with few exceptions, research suggests that narrowly focused social skills interventions, peer counseling/mediation, and other kinds of psychological interventions have been ineffective in reducing levels of school violence and in some cases (e.g., peer mediation groups and programs like DARE) may even increase aggression and violence levels in schools (see Astor et al., 2005, for a review of

these programs). Overall, psychological programs have been effective only when used conjointly with other interventions that target the organizational or social system of the school (Olweus, 1993).

Conceptual Underdevelopment and Underuse of the School Context.   Generally, many "packaged" programs tend to be "add-on" programs (Larson, 1998). Often, these types of programs are unrelated to the academic curriculum and social goals of the school. This situation is due, in part, to the fact that the social variables associated with the context of schools and school violence have not been conceptualized clearly (see Astor & Meyer, 2001, for a discussion of these issues). For example, researchers have conducted very few studies regarding the social dynamics surrounding a hallway fistfight or sexual harassment on school grounds. Moreover, until very recently, researchers or practitioners have not distinguished carefully between the concepts of school violence and youth violence (Astor, 1998; Astor & Meyer, 2001; Benbenishty & Astor, 2005). Instead, many articles and analyses of youth violence are presented with a strong assumption that the youth is the "carrier" of violent behavior and that dynamics within settings play a small or tangential role in violent behavior.

Focus on "Deficits" in Children.   Many school violence interventions are based on either formal or implicit theoretical assumptions of deficits surrounding what is causing violent behavior in individual children or subpopulations of children. For example, most social skills programs are based on the theoretical assumption that due to a lack of social exposure and practice, aggressive children are lacking in either social-cognitive or behavioral skills needed to deal with conflict appropriately. Without these more complex skills, it is believed that children naturally gravitate toward using aggression as a solution to social conflict. Consequently, these types of programs systematically target specific deficits in cognitive and behavioral skills within specific children or entire schools. What these deficit perspectives ignore is the powerful influence of contextual factors in the school environment that may influence student behavior.

Characteristics of Successful Programs.   Based on our review of programs, it appears that successful schoolwide intervention programs have the following core implementation characteristics:

- They raise the awareness and responsibility of students, teachers, staff, and parents regarding the types of violence in their schools (e.g., sexual harassment, fighting, weapon use).
- They create clear guidelines and rules for the entire school.
- They target the various social systems in the school and clearly communicate to the entire school community what procedures should be followed before, during, and after violent events.
- They focus on getting the school staff, students, and parents involved in the program.
- The interventions often fit easily into the normal flow and mission of the school setting.
- They utilize faculty, staff, and parents in the school setting to plan, implement, and sustain the program.
- They increase monitoring and supervision in nonclassroom areas.
- They are culturally sensitive, culturally competent, and immersed within the community/culture of the students.

Cultural Considerations

Another important lens through which social workers might view violence is to take account of the social and cultural contexts through which tensions may emerge in schools. This focus on culture is outlined by Soriano, Soriano, and Jimenez (1994), who suggest that the study of school violence must incorporate issues of culture and background. The authors do not necessarily consider culture or cultural membership as causes of violence, but rather suggest that they may reveal patterns of differential treatment that can reveal important information for prevention efforts. Soriano and his colleagues suggested a greater likelihood of violent outcomes when "increasingly diverse cultures come together in social, economic, and cultural contexts that afford easier access and privilege to some, while excluding others. Racism, classism, sexism, and racial privilege are believed to be related to school violence" (p. 217). The authors suggested that the tensions created by inequalities, as well as increasing divides in terms of communication and understanding of cultural differences between homes, communities, and schools may serve to fuel aggressions and further create divisions among groups.

This perspective is increasingly important to consider as several studies note extreme disproportional rates of disciplinary measures employed against minority students in comparison to nonminority students, even after controlling for socioeconomic status and actual student behavior (McCarthy & Hoge, 1987; McFadden, Marsh, Price, & Hwang, 1992). Bowditch (1993) contended that regardless of the conscious nature in which this disproportionality might occur, overrepresentation of exclusionary strategies that target those of lower socioeconomic status ultimately leads to increased racial and economic stratification in schools and society.

Epp and Watkinson (1997) echoed the focus on culture to emphasize how school structures can provide varying experiences for students from culturally different populations. Epp and Watkinson defined systemic violence as "any institutional practice or procedure that adversely impacts on individuals or groups by burdening them psychologically, mentally, culturally, spiritually, economically, or physically. Applied to educational settings, it means practices and procedures that prevent students from learning, thus 'harming them'" (Epp & Watkinson, 1997, p. 1). Examples of this type of systemic violence in the schools include exclusionary practices, overly competitive learning environments, toleration of abuse, school disciplinary policies rooted in exclusion and punishment, and discriminatory guidance policies. Again, although the school itself is not commonly thought of as the violence-inducing agent (more commonly, individual students are viewed as the culprits), this idea seems particularly salient in Epp and Watkinson's conceptualizations of the proposed roots of tensions between students. This framework, although not explicitly discussed in the prevention literature, has clear links to various efforts that are often put forth that involve changing school structures to provide more equity among students from diverse populations (Soriano et al., 1994). Several culture-based models of prevention highlight the inequalities faced by minority students and suggest these as areas for increased attention and change (Baker, 1998; Delva-Tauili'ili, 1995; Soriano et al., 1994; Ward, 1995). This type of framework provides a different perspective in that it does not focus as closely on characteristics/developmental patterns of individuals, but, rather, examines social contexts in school settings that may contribute to violence.

Social Work Research Contributions to Cultural Understandings of School Violence

Understanding and honoring culture is one of the cornerstones of social work practice. In addition to values, research is often helpful in better sifting through aspects of culture, economics, and violence. For example, it is commonly assumed among the American public that school violence varies by culture, and that cultural practices contribute to high/low rates of violence within and between cultures. Research by Benbenishty and Astor (2005) recently showed that although base rates may *vary* across cultures, the patterns contributing to many forms of school violence are common across many diverse cultures (Bedouins, Druze, Orthodox Jewish, African Americans, Secular Israelis, Hispanic Americans, and White Americans). Variables outside the schools, such as poverty, parental education, and employment, as well as variables in the school, such as school climate, teacher–child relationships, and school mission, appear to function similarly in creating safe schools across different cultures.

Forms of victimization such as physical assault appear to have mainly age and gender patterns (younger children and boys higher in victimization), with culture playing a relatively small role in patterns for those forms of violence. With other forms of victimization related to sexual assault or harassment, culture plays a prominent role in school violence patterns and in its potential solutions (e.g., with issues of sexual harassment and sexual assault in schools, culture appears to be a dominant influence; Benbenishty & Astor, 2005). Trying to distill aspects of socioeconomics and culture is an ethical obligation for social workers. For example, at first glance, some cultures appear to have great differences in their violence rates. However, it is possible that different cultures and subcultures have vastly different economic, social, and educational conditions. Consequently, in many of their analyses comparing different cultures, Benbenishty and Astor (2005) found that poverty and parental education appeared to be accounting for a large percentage of differences between cultures. When socioeconomic variables are accounted for, most if not all of the differences between cultures disappeared or became insignificant. Therefore, carefully distinguishing between economic, historical, and education-related factors and "cultural factors" becomes a key to culturally sensitive practice, as well as scholarly and theoretical thinking on the role of culture and schools. Table 6.1 (p. 127) includes questions that school social workers might consider in exploring how culture relates to school violence.

Common Types of Interventions That Schools and School Social Workers Are Using

The Scope of Programs. Nationwide, approximately 78% of principals reported that they have programs addressing violence in their schools (Kaufman et al., 1998). Eleven percent of the schools had programs that lasted only 1 day or less, 24% reported that they had only ongoing violence programs, and 43% indicated that they had both ongoing and 1-day programs designed to address school violence. It is unclear what types of programs principals consider to be violence interventions. However, school social workers reported that there is a wide array of violence intervention programs and services, which includes counseling services, crisis intervention, skill training, peer programs for students, community programs, teacher-based programs, and security measures.

Table 6.2 presents the percentage of social workers who reported in Astor et al. (1998) that their school has such a program or service and the percentage of social workers who are involved with various programs. The vast majority of services, method-based interventions (e.g., counseling, crisis intervention, and home visits), and programs implemented have not been evaluated extensively as violence reduction strategies.

TABLE 6.2   Percentage of School Social Workers (N = 576) Reporting Specific Violence Programs and Services in Their Schools

Type of Program or Service	% of Schools with Program	% of Social Workers Involved in Program
Counseling services		
Violence crisis intervention	50	40
Victim assistance and support services	30	24
Individual or family counseling	53	46
Posttraumatic stress groups for observers or victims	15	12
Services targeting ethnic, religious, or racial conflicts	24	13
Child abuse education	58	41
Skills training		
Conflict management	63	43
Social skills training	66	53
Pro-social behavior curriculum	53	35
Skill streaming	35	25
Groups for aggressive children	54	43
Leadership training	41	19
Peer programs for students		
Positive peer culture	39	24
Friendship clubs	31	15
After school sports or clubs	75	15
Community programs		
Antigang program	22	8
Services that address community violence	15	6
Police antiviolence program	38	7
Parent support group	21	14
Church group or youth group	15	3
Teacher-based programs		
Teacher support groups or training on violence	26	14
Classroom management	60	34
Antibully campaign	14	9
Academic programs aimed at aggressors, victims, or witnesses	8	3
Physical plant changes		
Metal detectors	14	3
Security guards	37	6

Source: Adapted from Astor et al., 1998.

For example, in Astor et al. (1998), many school social workers said that they conducted home visits personally to help reduce aggressive behaviors. Ninety-one percent of social workers endorsed home visits. Nevertheless, there is a paucity of data on the effectiveness of the home visits as an intervention.

Common Interventions. Few evaluations have been conducted assessing the effectiveness of interventions normally used by schools (such as expulsion, suspension, referral to special education, sending the child to the principal's office, during- and after-school detention, parent conferences, and counseling). However, interventions such as expulsion, suspension, and school transfer are common responses to acts of school violence. In the latest report, Dinkes et al. (2007) provided the following information: Forty-eight percent of public schools (approximately 39,600 schools) took at least one serious disciplinary action against a student—including suspensions lasting 5 days or more, expulsions, and transfers to specialized schools. Of the 830,700 serious disciplinary actions taken during the 2005 to 2006 school year, 74% were suspensions for 5 days or more, 5% were removals with no services, and 20% were transfers to specialized schools. Similarly, other common interventions such as contacting parents, parent–school meetings about aggressive behaviors, or school-based consequences such as staying after school, better adult supervision in the school yard, and better monitoring of the routes to and from school and violence-prone school areas should be researched further. Data from Europe and Australia suggest that these types of interventions are easier to implement and may be highly effective in reducing some types of school violence such as bullying (Olweus, 1993; Sharp & Smith, 1994; Smith & Sharp, 1994).

Special Education and Violence. Another response schools commonly have to persistent and chronic aggression in individual children is special education referral, assessment, and placement. Unfortunately, the school violence literature has not examined closely the relationships between special education and violence reduction in schools. Nevertheless, it is likely that many children receive services for aggressive behavior through special education. These interventions often include services such as counseling, parent training, contained classrooms, specialized curriculum, and day treatment facilities. This area of research should be developed further because it is possible that social workers, psychologists, counselors, and teachers view the special education process as an important strategy with some aggressive children.

Program Interventions

In the next section, we will discuss various types of interventions that are used to address school violence. Some of the interventions discussed are used commonly but have very little research documenting their effectiveness. Other interventions have undergone evaluation procedures and have research studies that support their effectiveness. Had this chapter been written 10 years ago, we would most likely conclude that very few interventions show any positive results. Within the past 10 years, however, many new programs and curricula have emerged with multiple studies to support their effectiveness.

Promising Prevention and Intervention Programs

In this section, we present some examples of prevention and intervention programs available to schools and practitioners. The programs discussed here do not represent an exhaustive list of programs available. Table 6.3 includes an abbreviated list of some of the most commonly used programs that have had strong empirical evidence of effectiveness across a variety of evaluative sources. In the text, we describe several programs that either show promise or have demonstrated a degree of effectiveness in at least one study.

TABLE 6.3 Model Violence Prevention Programs and Evaluating Sources

Program	Grade	Participants	Program Components	Outcome Measures	Results
Bullying Prevention Program	4th–7th grades	2,500 students in 42 primary and secondary schools in Norway. (The program is now international and is being applied in 15 countries. The materials are translated in over 12 languages.)	Core components of the program are implemented at the school level, the class level, and the individual level. Including: ■ Distribution of anonymous student questionnaire assessing the nature and prevalence of bullying ■ Development of positive and negative consequences for students' behavior ■ Establishing a supervisory system ■ Reinforcement of schoolwide rules against bullying ■ Classroom workshops with video and discussions to increase knowledge and empathy ■ Interventions with children and victims of bullying ■ Discussions with parents	Student self-report measures collected at introduction of the program, 4 months after introduction, 1-year follow-up, and 2-year follow-up. ■ Reports of incidents of bullying and victimization ■ Scale of general youth antisocial behavior ■ Assessment of school climate—order and discipline ■ Measure of social relationships and attitude toward school	The results show a 33–64% reduction in the levels of bully and victim incidents. The author found a 30–70% reduction in aggregated peer rating variables. In addition there was no displacement of bullying to before or after school. There was also a significant reduction in antisocial behavior such as fighting, theft, and truancy. The school climate showed marked improvement with students reporting an increase satisfaction with school in general, positive social relationships, and positive attitude toward schoolwork and school * rated: Effective–1, 2, 3, 4, 6, 7, 8, 9

Child Development Project	3rd–6th grades	4,500 students in 24 elementary schools from 6 diverse districts throughout the United States	This is a comprehensive model focused on creating a cooperative and supportive school environment. Classroom components include ■ Staff training in cooperative learning ■ Implementation of a model that fosters cross-grade "buddying" activities ■ A developmental approach to discipline that fosters self-control ■ A model to engage students in classroom norm-setting and decision-making Schoolwide community-building activities are used to promote school bonding and parent involvement activities such as interactive homework assignments that reinforce the family–school partnership.	Data were collected after 1 year and 2 years of intervention. Teachers were assessed through four 90-minute observations and annual teacher questionnaires. Student assessments were self-report surveys of drug use and delinquent behavior.	Results showed that students experienced a stronger "sense of community" and more motivation to be helpful, better conflict-resolution skills, greater acceptance of people who are different, higher self-esteem, stronger feelings of social competence, less loneliness in school, and fewer delinquent acts. Statistically significant effects were found for marijuana use, vehicle theft and carrying a weapon. By the second year of implementation, students in schools showed significantly lower rates of skipping school, carrying a weapon and vehicle theft ($ps < .01$). * rated: Effective–3, 4, 5, 6, 7, 9

* Rated by (1) American Youth Policy Forum, (2) Blueprints for Violence Prevention, (3) Center for Mental Health Service, (4) CSAP, (5) DOE Safe Schools, (6) Communities that Care, (7) Sherman, (8) Surgeon General Report, (9) OJJDP, (10) Hamilton Fish.

(continued)

TABLE 6.3 Continued

Program	Grade	Participants	Program Components	Outcome Measures	Results
FAST Track—Families and Schools Together	Long-term program. Three cohorts of students. Grade 1–10. (ongoing)	At-risk kindergartners identified based on combined teacher and parent ratings of behavior (CBCL). Highest 10% recruited for study. N = 445 intervention children N = 446 control group children	Multiple program components. Weekly enrichment program for high-risk children and their parents. Students placed in "friendship groups" of 5–6 students each. Discussions, modeling stories and films, role-plays. Sessions focused on reviewing and practicing skills in emotional understanding and communication, friendship building, self-control, and social problem solving. Parents met in groups led by Family Coordinators to discuss parenting strategies, then 30-minute parent–child cooperative activity time. Biweekly home visits. Academic tutoring provided by trained tutors in 30-minute sessions 3x/week.	▪ *Externalizing Scale of CBCL*—oppositional, aggressive, and delinquent behaviors—parents. ▪ *Parent Daily Report*—degree to which child engaged in aggressive and oppositional behaviors during previous 24 hrs (Given 3x) ▪ Child Behavior Change ▪ Teacher assessment of acting-out behaviors in school (Teacher Report Form, Achenbach 1991) ▪ Scale from the TOCA-R (Teacher Observation of Classroom Adaptation—Revised) ▪ Authority Acceptance Scale ▪ Peer rating of aggressive and hyperactive-disruptive behaviors.	Intervention group had higher scores on emotion recognition, emotion coping, and social problem solving compared to control group. They also found lower rates of aggressive retaliation compared to control group. Direct observation results: ▪ Intervention group spent more time in positive peer interaction than did the control group. ▪ Intervention group received higher peer social preference scores than control group. ▪ Intervention group had higher language arts grades than control group. * rated: Effective–2, 3, 6, 8, 9, 11

FAST Track—Families and Schools Together PATHS curriculum	1st–5th grades over three cohorts (Results from grade 1 findings only are reviewed here)	198 Intervention Classrooms 180 Control Classrooms matched by school size, achievement levels, poverty, and ethnic diversity. 7,560 total students 845 students were in high-risk intervention or control conditions. (6,715 students non-high-risk children.)	PATHS (Promoting Alternative Thinking Strategies). Administered to classrooms. 57 lessons (1/2 hr sessions, 2–3x/week) ■ Skills related to understanding & communicating emotions ■ Skills related to increase of positive social behavior ■ Self-control and social problem-solving. Presented through direct instruction, discussion, modeling stories, or video. Teachers attended 2.5 day training and received weekly consultation from FAST Track staff. Quality of implementation was assessed by observer rating of teacher's ■ Skill in teaching PATHS concepts ■ Managing the classroom ■ Modeling and generalizing PATHS throughout day ■ Openness to consultation	1. Teachers were interviewed about behavior of each child in class. (Fall/Spring of 1st Gr.) 2. Sociometric assessments (peer nominations made by students) collected to assess ■ Peer aggression ■ Peer hyperactivity/ disruptiveness ■ Peer social status 3. Quality of classroom atmosphere was assessed by observer ratings assessing the following: ■ Level of disruption ■ Ability to handle transitions ■ Ability to follow rules ■ Level of cooperation ■ Use of problem-solving skills ■ Ability to express feelings ■ Ability to stay focused on task ■ Criticism vs. supportiveness	Hierarchical Linear Modeling (Accounting for gender, site, cohort & intervention) Intervention classrooms had lower ratings of hyperactivity/disruptive behavior, aggression, and more favorable observer ratings of classroom atmosphere. Three cohorts of intervention, so teachers administered curriculum, 1, 2, or 3 times. When "teacher experience" was included in analyses, teachers who taught more cohorts had higher classroom atmosphere ratings (by neutral observer). Quality of implementation Teacher skill in program implementation was also related to positive outcomes. * rated: Effective–2, 3, 6, 8, 9, 11

(continued)

TABLE 6.3 Continued

* Evaluating sources:

1. American Youth Policy Forum: *Less Hype, More Help: Reducing Juvenile Crime, What Works–and What Doesn't* by Richard A. Mendel. American Youth Policy Forum, Washington, DC, 2000. Programs are categorized as *Effective* (refer to www.aypf.org).

2. Blueprints for Violence Prevention: Programs are divided into *Model* and *Promising* (refer to www.colorado.edu/cspv/blueprints).

3. Center for Mental Health Services, U.S. Department of Health and Human Services, Prevention Research Center for the Promotion of Human Development: Programs are divided into *Effective* and *Promising* (refer to www.prevention.psu.edu).

4. Center for Substance Abuse Prevention, Substance Abuse and Mental Health Services Administration, Department of Health and Human Services, National Registry of Effective Programs: Programs are divided into *Model, Promising,* and *Effective* (refer to www.modelprograms.samhsa.gov).

5. Department of Education: Safe and Drug Free Schools: Programs are divided into *Exemplary* and *Promising* (refer to www.ed.gov/about/offices/list/osdfs/index.html?src=mr).

6. Communities that Care: Posey, Robin, Wong, Sherry, Catalano, Richard, Hawkins, David, Dusenbury, Linda, & Chappell, Patricia (2000). Communities That Care Prevention Strategies: A Research Guide to What Works. Programs are categorized as *Effective* (refer to www.preventionscience.com/ctc/CTC.html).

7. Sherman et al. (1998): ***Preventing Crime: What Works, What Doesn't, What's Promising.*** University of Maryland Department of Criminology and Criminal Justice. NCJ 165366. Programs are categorized as *Effective* (refer to www.ncjrs.org/works/).

8. Youth Violence: A Report of the Surgeon General: Programs are divided into *Model* and *Promising: Level 1-Violence Prevention; Level 2-Risk Prevention* (refer to www.surgeongeneral.gov/library/youthviolence).

9. Title V (OJJDP): Effective & Promising Programs Guide. Washington, DC: Office of Juvenile Justice and Delinquency Prevention, Office of Justice Programs, U.S. Dept. of Justice. Programs are divided into *Exemplary, Effective,* and *Promising* (refer to www.dsgonline.com).

10. Center for Disease Control: National Center for Injury Prevention and Control—Division of Violence Prevention. *Best Practices of Youth Violence Prevention: A Sourcebook for Community Action* 2002. Programs are categorized as *Effective* (refer to www.cdc.gov/ncipc/dvp/bestpractices.htm).

11. Hamilton Fish Institute on School and Community Violence. Programs are divided into *Effective* and *Noteworthy* (refer to www.hamfish.org/programs/).

Sources: Benbenishty, R., Astor, R. A., & Zeira, A. (2003). Monitoring school violence at the site level: Linking, national, district, and school-level data. *Journal of School Violence,* 2(2), 29–50. Reprinted by permission of Taylor & Francis Group, http://www.informaworld.com; from Olweus Web site by Hazelden. Copyright 2008 by Hazelden Foundation. Reprinted by permission of Hazelden Foundation, Center City, MN; Battistich, Schaps, Watson, & Solomon (1996) www.devstu.org/; Conduct Problems Prevention Research Group, www.fasttrackproject.org.

High-Quality Early Childhood Education.
From a primary prevention perspective, high-quality preschools may help in reducing violence rates. Data from the Perry Preschool High/Scope study suggest that a high-quality preschool education can be highly effective in reducing violence throughout the life span (Schweinhart, Barnes, & Weikart, 1993). In this longitudinal study, researchers found that children who were randomly assigned to participate in a high-quality preschool environment were far less likely to have been involved in criminal and violent activity through development than those who were assigned to a lower quality preschool program. These longitudinal data are important because they suggest that the effects carry through early development into adulthood (age 27 was the latest follow-up). Furthermore, the effects are wide ranging and pronounced. By age 27, students who were assigned to low-quality preschool programs were five times more likely than the high-quality preschool students to have been arrested five or more times (many for violent acts). In addition, children in the high-quality classes were significantly more likely than children in low-quality classes to earn more money, own a house, and graduate from high school. Alternatively, they were significantly less likely to have used social services.

A cost-benefit analysis suggested that participation in a high-quality preschool saved the general public *$57,585* per child on issues related to crime and victimization alone (in 1992 dollars). Researchers (Schweinhart et al., 1993) believe that the preschools' focus on social responsibility, empowerment, decision making, and conflict resolution is an important contributor to the reductions in violence. Also, the Perry Preschool High/Scope program emphasized parent education and involvement around parenting issues and in-depth teacher training regarding issues of conflict and discipline. Schweinhart and colleagues believe that the tripartite focus on students, parents, and teachers accounts for the lower levels of violence throughout development. At the "macro" level, several *very* large cities (such as Los Angeles) and states (California) are planning universal preschool programs (www.first5.org/).

Not surprisingly, law enforcement agencies such as the police, sheriffs' departments, and probation organizations are endorsing this social policy as a preventative way to reduce overall crime in our society. Social workers should support these efforts and ensure that these programs have the high-quality components mentioned in the Perry Preschool study.

School-Based Bully and Victim Intervention Programs. During the 1970s, surveys in Norway found that bullying was a considerable problem for students in Norwegian schools. In an effort to reduce bully and victim problems, Dan Olweus, a Norwegian professor, developed a comprehensive nationwide antibullying program for children in grades 1 to 9 in Norway. The program has many simple interventions and is aimed at students, teachers, and parents in schools, classrooms, and individual settings. Strategies that were offered to reduce bullying included the establishment of clear class rules against bullying, contingent responses (praise and sanctions), regular class meetings to clarify norms against bullying, improved supervision of the playground, and teacher involvement in the development of a positive school climate. Also, a booklet defining and listing ways to counteract bullying was distributed to school personnel, a video illustrating the problem was made available, and parents were sent a booklet with information and advice. Findings from 42 schools that participated in the program showed a 50% reduction in rates of bullying and victimization. Furthermore, the positive effects of the program appeared to increase over time, and there was an increase in student satisfaction with school life (Olweus, 1993). Similar antibullying programs have been developed in Great Britain (see Sharp & Smith, 1994; Smith & Sharp, 1994, for empirical evaluations and detailed practical procedures for educators) and Australia (Rigby, 1996). Evaluations of those programs also show significant reductions in aggressive behaviors and increases in student satisfaction with school life (for more discussion and international reviews, see Astor, Benbenishty, Pitner, & Meyer, 2004; Benbenishty & Astor, 2003).

Second Step.   Based on the "habit of thought" model that posits that violence can be unlearned, the Second Step program targets children in preschool through kindergarten, grades 1 to 3, and grades 4 to 5. Second Step is a curriculum-based approach that attempts to prevent aggressive behavior by increasing prosocial behavior through competence in peer interactions and in interpersonal conflict resolution skills. The curriculum is administered twice a week with an average of 50 to 60 lessons. The specific lessons include activities to help youth acquire empathy, impulse control, problem-solving, and anger management skills. An evaluation of the program found it to have some level of impact on participants (Grossman et al., 1997). After taking the 30-lesson curriculum, an evaluation of participants illustrated that Second Step decreased the amount of physical aggression of youth and increased positive and prosocial behaviors both on the playground and in the lunchroom (Grossman et al., 1997). Another study that trained elementary and middle-school teachers with the curriculum also suggested that teachers and administrators reported considerable respect for the capacity of the curriculum (Milwaukee Board of School Directors, 1993).

Practitioners should be aware that other similar curriculum-based conflict resolution programs have not performed well when evaluated intensively (Webster, 1993). For example, the popular Violence Prevention Curriculum for Adolescents (Prothrow-Stith, 1987) has little empirical support suggesting that it actually reduces violence (Larson, 1998; Tolan & Guerra, 1994).

Positive Adolescents Choices Training.   The Positive Adolescents Choices Training (PACT) program was "designed to teach African-American youth social skills to aid in prevention of violence" (Hammond & Yung, 1991, 1993; Yung & Hammond, 1998). A unique aspect of PACT is that it is culturally relevant and aimed at reducing aggression and victimization in high-risk youth. The program components include anger management, prosocial-skills training, and violence risk education. The sessions are built around videotapes that demonstrate culturally sensitive social situations. Participants learn specific skills needed to solve the situation peacefully. Participants in the program increased an average of 33.5% in the areas of giving feedback, problem solving, and resisting peer pressure. Teachers also observed a significant improvement in the targeted skills of trained youth (30.4%) compared to untrained youth (–1.1%). In addition, whereas students perceived their greatest improvement in their ability to provide negative feedback, they felt they had the least gain in problem solving. Most important, students demonstrated a significant reduction of physical aggression at school, and their overall aggressive behavior was improved during the training and maintained when they graduated from the program (Yung & Hammond, 1998).

Cyberbullying Interventions.   Media-related violence presents schools with new major challenges. Some of the media-related violence is perpetrated on school grounds (e.g., through sharing negative instant messages during school time or using cell phones to spread rumors or sexually charged images). However, many other forms of victimization take place after school hours. Nevertheless, schools cannot ignore this form of violence. Often it is difficult to separate between violence that overflows from school grounds to after-school time and vice versa. The consequences of such victimization are felt at school, through mental health and academic problems and engagement in retaliatory violence.

Currently there are many efforts to design responses and policies to address this form of violence. It should be noted that whereas some forms of media violence share much in common with non-electronic bullying (such as spreading rumors) and may be included in existing interventions, there are some differences that may have important conceptual and practice implications. For instance, media violence may target victims that the perpetrator does not even know.

Many schools and organizations responded by enacting clear policies that address media violence, even when perpetrated not on school grounds. According to the National Conference of State Legislatures, several states have enacted legislation that included cyberbullying in existing school antibullying legislation (http://www.ncsl.org/programs/educ/SchBullyingEnactLeg.htm). The California School Boards Association provides a detailed policy brief that details policy considerations for school boards on cyberbullying (*Files/Services/PolicyServices/SamplePolicies/Cyberbullying.ashx*). Many Web sites that address school violence now include specific references to media violence. For instance, the extensive and most helpful Australian site, Bullying No Way! has a special treatment for cyberbullying (http://www.bullyingnoway.com.au/talkout/spotlight/cyberBullyingSchools.shtml). There are also Web sites dedicated to provide information and programs to help stop this type of violence (e.g., http://www.stopcyberbullying.org).

Additionally, schools provide opportunities to acquire new skills to practice safe surfing in the Internet. For instance, the Canadian Teacher Federation published cyberbullying policy guidelines that provide clear definitions, principles of coordinated educational action, and a range of activities that can improve students' and teachers' "cyberconduct" and prevent cyberbullying (http://www.ctf-fce.ca/e/resources/cyberbullying).

How to Select the Right Program for a Specific School or Document the Success of Grassroots Programs.

We believe that school social workers can make a significant impact nationally and locally if they demonstrate with data how they adapted programs (like the ones listed earlier) or created "grassroots" interventions. Most practitioners are aware that each school is unique and may have different kinds of problems, thus necessitating different kinds of approaches. For example, one school may have a problem with sexual harassment among the younger male students, whereas another school in the same district may have a problem with weapons on school grounds, primarily with older students. These two types of problems may necessitate very different kinds of programs. Instituting a singular "antiviolence" program across schools with different needs is unlikely to address effectively the specific problems that might exist in each school.

As obvious as this may seem, some schools select a "promising program" (such as the ones listed in the earlier section) and never collect data to assess if they initially had a problem in that area or if the intervention program the school adopted actually worked. Furthermore, from a social work and intervention perspective, it is philosophically problematic that most current "school violence interventions" and "programs" *are moving away from developing grassroots and community-generated interventions.* How can school violence interventions reflect social work values of community, parent participation, and student/teacher voice? Can school interventions reflect a social work belief in democracy and participation in the definition of the problem and the creation/implementation of the interventions? How do social workers empower school communities to deal with their own specific kinds of school violence problems? How do school social workers know when programs work or fail? The following sections on monitoring and school mapping are presented as potential responses to these challenges.

Monitoring and Mapping as Methods and a Process

This monitoring and data-based approach assumes that successful programs stem from the following: (a) a belief that the efforts to "fit" a program to a school involves *grassroots* participation, (b) a belief that students and teachers in the school need to be *empowered* to deal with the problem, (c) a belief that *democracy* is at the core of a good violence program, and (d) a belief that schools should demonstrate *a proactive vision* surrounding the violence problem in their school. The implementation of interventions could be slightly different for each school site because it is assumed that the social dynamics of each school site are unique. Each school is expected to adapt the program to its unique demographic, philosophical, and organizational needs.

We believe that *data are necessary* for the successful adaptation of safety programs to schools (Astor & Benbenishty, 2005; Astor et al., 2004; Benbenishty et al., 2003; Benbenishty & Astor,

2007; Benbenishty, Astor, & Estrada, 2008). Hence, an important element of successful violence prevention programs is the use of data in an ongoing and interactive manner. Figure 6.2 represents our interpretation of the cycle of monitoring and how data should be used to maintain successful programs. This perspective proposes that the ongoing analysis and interpretation of data is an essential part of the intervention process. Data are used to create awareness, mobilize different school constituents, assess the extent of the problem, plan interventions, implement programs, and evaluate effectiveness. Information is provided continually to different groups in each step of the intervention process.

We argue that the *process of introducing school-specific data* to each of the school groups allows each school to identify its specific needs, limitations, strengths, and resources so that the school community can choose and debate which program fits their needs best. Moreover, this approach assumes that the process of building and implementing programs is continuous and cyclical, always changing to respond to new circumstances and emerging needs. The following sections on monitoring and school mapping are presented as quantitative and qualitative processes that (a) help create a "whole-school response," and (b) help the school identify, create, and/or adapt programs to the site.

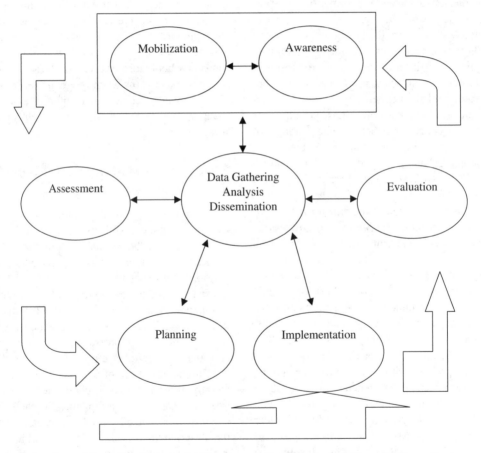

FIGURE 6.2   The Role of Data in the Development and Implementation of Interventions
Source: Astor, R. A., Benbenishty, R., & Meyer, H. A. (2004). Monitoring and mapping student victimization in schools. *Theory into Practice, 43*(1), p. 41. From the theme issue Conflict Resolution and Peer Mediation. Copyright 2004 College of Education and Human Ecology, The Ohio State University. Reproduced by permission of the publisher and authors. All rights reserved.

Quantitative Monitoring of Violence-Prone Locations: Example of School A. School A was a secondary school with about 1,500 students. The vast majority of students came from immigrant and low-income families. The school was slowly turning itself into a "high-technology" school setting with courses focusing on computer programming, the sciences, and a business incubator philosophy. Still, there was a sense among the administrators and teachers that more could be done to address the issue of violence in their school. The school decided to adopt a monitoring system method as outlined by Benbenishty et al. (2003).

The students, teachers, and administrators participated in developing and administering a questionnaire about school violence, school climate, and what could be done to address the violence. The entire student body filled the anonymous questionnaire as a form of "voice" and "democracy." The school wanted to raise awareness and involvement of the teachers, students, and parents. In this particular school, they worked out a system where the students and staff were scanning surveys and distributing their own data. Much of this was done through class work under the direction of teachers and administrators. This allowed the school to add their own questions and to carry out analyses to explore specific questions.

These data were shared systematically with the student body in their classrooms, with the teachers in teachers' meetings, and with the PTO. The data were used to create an awareness and generate collaborative solutions, but more importantly (at the first stage), they were used to anchor the dialogue between staff, students, administration, and parents. The process of continual dialogue about the data between the students and the teachers created a sense of personal and school-wide investment in the interventions adopted.

As one example, the school chose to use this monitoring system to identify where the violence problem exists in their school. They wanted to know where violence was occurring most. Table 6.4 shows the percentage of students in this school rating areas in their school as dangerous. The findings indicated that the school gate at the end of the school, the locker room, and the school yard were

areas about which students were most concerned. Girls in the school were twice as likely to be fearful of the school gate after school and the locker room. Boys, on the other hand, were more likely to rate the school gate before school and the school yard as more dangerous. The student surveys showed that the school gate after school, the locker room, and the school yard were particular problems for the 10th and 11th graders and not as severe for the 12th graders. These kinds of reports and site-specific data were distributed to all the students, teachers, and parents. Dialogue groups were also formed in classes to talk about the problem and to generate possible student, teacher, and principal solutions to this particular issue.

The staff and students made extraordinary efforts to target violence-prone locations. They even moved the vice principal's offices closer to the bathrooms and reorganized the physical structure of the school to improve social interaction and staff monitoring of student behaviors. The school implemented school beautification projects, produced multiple student-led mural projects, and created a Web site devoted to peace and school discipline where students could voice concerns to the administration and peers. The follow-up monitoring survey showed improvement with school morale/school spirit and subjective feelings about school. Monitoring surveys conducted by the students and staff a year later (see Figure 6.3) showed that the school was successful in reducing a sense of danger in certain locations. However, the data suggested that more work needed to be done to make those locations even safer. Although this feedback was disappointing initially to the staff and students (even though it was their own self-reported data), it prompted them to focus more on reductions of violence rates and new approaches. The staff and students in this school had data suggesting what was working and not working. The data did not always coincide with their subjective feelings of "total success." Therefore, the monitoring surveys served as an anchor whereby the students and teachers could talk about ways to make those locations even safer. This approach fit well within a social

TABLE 6.4   Examples of Actual Tables Given to Principals Regarding Dangerous Times and Places in School

How dangerous are times and places in school

	Not at all	A little	Quite dangerous	Dangerous	Mean
	1	2	3	4	
	%	%	%	%	
Class	70	20	7	3	1.43
School yard	35	30	25	10	2.10
School gate, when school starts	70	15	12	3	1.48
School gate, when school ends	30	24	26	20	2.36
Locker room	32	22	25	21	2.35

How dangerous are times and places in school—by gender

	Boys	Girls
	%	%
Class	8	12
School yard	42	28
School gate, when school starts	20	10
School gate, when school ends	30	62
Locker room	33	59

Entries are percentages of students saying the place is either "quite dangerous" or "dangerous."

How dangerous are times and places in school—by grade

	10th	11th	12th
	%	%	%
Class	11	11	8
School yard	42	40	23
School gate, when school starts	12	17	16
School gate when school ends	53	58	27
Locker room	55	57	26

Entries are percentages of students saying the place is either "quite dangerous" or "dangerous."

Note: The original figures provided to staff were translated, shortened, and modified to be presented in this figure.
Source: Benbenishty, R., Astor, R. A., & Zeira, A. (2003). Monitoring school violence at the site level: Linking, national, district, and school-level data. *Journal of School Violence, 2*(2), 29–50. Reprinted by permission of Taylor & Francis Group, http://www.informaworld.com

work, democratic, grassroots, empowerment perspective without compromising the role of comprehensive schoolwide data.

Qualitative Mapping of Violence-Prone Locations: Example of School B.   The second school was a high school with approximately 1,000 students from mainly middle- and upper-middle-income families. This school was

not interested in conducting schoolwide surveys but wanted to involve staff and students in the process of violence prevention. They also wanted to adapt the interventions to their specific school. Like the quantitative survey monitoring process, this qualitative mapping process was designed to document (a) the locations and times within each school where violence occurred for that term, and (b) the perspectives

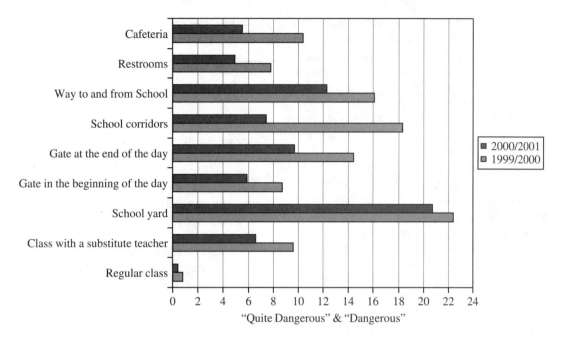

FIGURE 6.3   Specific Places Perceived by Students to be Dangerous in a School   *Source:* Benbenishty, R., Astor, R. A., & Zeira, A. (2003). Monitoring school violence at the site level: Linking, national, district, and school-level data. *Journal of School Violence, 2*(2), 29–50. Reprinted by permission of Taylor & Francis Group, http://www.informaworld.com

of students, teachers, staff, and administrators regarding the school's organizational response (or nonresponse) to violent events in these locations. The main goal was to use qualitative data to generate clarity about the nature of the problem and diverse perspectives on possible causes and solutions to the problem.

Students, teachers, and staff (e.g., administrators, hall monitors, cafeteria workers) were interviewed in four to five separate *focus groups* about the physical spaces where violence had been committed and what time of day the violence had occurred. Each group was given an empty map of their school and asked to identify the areas where the events occurred and areas of the school that felt unsafe for them (see Astor, Meyer, & Pitner, 1999; Astor, Vargas, Pitner, & Meyer, 1999, for an in-depth description of the mapping process). After students and teachers individually identified these places, they were

interviewed in focus groups as to why they thought violence occurred where it did and what could be done to improve the situation.

All the individual maps were consolidated into one large school map. Transferring all the reported events onto one large map of the school enabled students and staff to locate specific "hot spots" for violence and dangerous time periods within each individual school. For example, events tended to be clustered by time, age, gender, and location. In the case of older students (11th and 12th graders), events were clustered in the parking lot outside the auxiliary gym immediately after school, whereas for younger students (9th and 10th graders), events were reported in the lunchroom and hallways during transition periods. For this school, the map suggested that interventions be geared specifically toward older students, directly after school, by the main entrance, and in the school parking lot. Students and teachers agreed that increasing the visible presence of school staff in and around the parking lot for the 20 minutes after school had great potential for reducing many violent events. Younger students were experiencing violence mainly before, during, and after lunch, near the cafeteria. Many students expressed feelings of being unsafe between classes in the hallways.

Teachers suggested interventions such as all the teachers and support staff standing in hallways during transitions and positively greeting "by name" as many students as possible. Many staff felt this was a different and more positive message to students than "security guards" and yet provided a high level of supervision. Students also suggested a role in monitoring the hallways. Some student leaders suggested that they could do more in their student groups to prevent fights. They especially felt they could do more to discourage their peers from forming the large circles that often formed when a fight occurs.

The focus groups also identified organizational issues that could improve the violence situation in the school. Themes from teachers included a sense of "being caught in the middle." Some teachers expressed a personal desire to prevent violence but did not possess the skills or knowledge of how to intervene. Many staff members were unclear about their professional role in nonclassroom locations (see Astor, Meyer, & Behre, 1999, for a detailed description of what types of themes can be anticipated from each group). Tables 6.5 and 6.6 show examples of the kinds of issues that were the focus of discussions about organizational issues and potential interventions.

Nonteaching staff also revealed important information in the focus groups, including very specific interventions associated with their areas of the school. For example, cafeteria workers revealed that only two or three adults were expected to supervise nearly 1,000 children during the lunch period. Additionally, secretaries had very clear suggestions for interventions regarding children who were sent to the office for fighting during less supervised periods (such as recess, lunch, or transitions between classes).

Conclusion

We believe that school social workers can play an important role in school violence interventions at the local, state, and national levels. One important role they could play is educating the public, students, and staff and providing accurate data on school violence. Currently there are many myths surrounding gangs, students of color, suburban White students, and specific forms of violence. These stereotypes about the rates of violence and groups associated with violence are potentially harmful to students *and our society.* These inaccurate perceptions may also be harmful because they do not reflect the possible efforts schools have invested and successes that they have had in reducing school violence. School social workers could initiate important conceptual dialogue in their schools and school districts regarding the categorization of a violence problem in schools. We strongly encourage school social workers to adopt the approach that the *entire school* setting be the focus of violence prevention strategies. School data should serve as the basis for interventions and their subsequent evaluations. One method we endorse is creating a comprehensive survey-based *dialogue group* monitoring system that could help to generate grassroots interventions and adapt existing programs that have been found to be effective. Furthermore, we suggest an alternative school violence procedure that integrates school maps (to locate violent "hot spots" in the school) and focus groups with students, teachers, school staff, and administrators (to identify reasons why violence is occurring in certain places and potential solutions). Information obtained through either the monitoring or the mapping process could (a) increase the dialogue between students, teachers, and school staff on issues of school violence; (b) serve as an evaluation of school violence interventions already used in a school setting; and (c) increase school involvement in violence interventions.

TABLE 6.5 Core Student, Teacher, and Administrator Comments Related to Organizational Response

Domain	Students	Teachers	Administrators
Organizational Response	"I wouldn't actually jump in there either because these, like, goons up here they don't care about a teacher and they fight and they not concerned about the teacher. If the teacher gets hit, most likely they going to say they shouldn't be in the way. So it's not they job to break up fights."	"Two young ladies were going at it outside of my door, and I went to pull one off. She started punching me … and she was swearing. We ended up on the floor. I'll never forget. I looked up and two male teachers were standing there, not doing anything."	"We've told the teachers they can take any level of activity they feel comfortable taking. They can intervene physically if they feel they have to. And I've had some teachers do that."
	"Because I've seen a lot of people who get suspended and, you know, you see them a few weeks later getting in-school suspension. I mean what's the difference?"	"I have a call button … they don't answer, they don't respond. I have to run next door and tell my department head. She would pick up the phone and try to locate security … the kid would be back in my class in three days."	"If you're in the immediate area, you've got to break that fight up. You're to do what you can … state law requires teachers to be responsible in that situation."
	"[A]nd she told me to go to the hallway. We went to the hall. The girl came out into the hall … Then you know the teacher is still in the classroom, but she knows all this time that we are arguing and it is going to be a conflict. Why didn't she stop when we were having words?"	"I can remember a few years back, we had a convicted rapist who was in classes at this school. The teachers were not told that this student was convicted of rape … he was scheduled with a number of young women teachers … and the principal never said a word …"	"There's a liability issue here. It's something that a lot of teachers don't seem to understand … it means that they must at least give a verbal command to stop."
	"That's like when the tuition office got held up. Don't you know, I was walking down the hall and I didn't even know what happened. Can you imagine how I felt? I could have got shot for no reason …. I think they should let us leave at least when the police came. Evacuated out one of these doors."	"I think that some teachers probably would not like to get involved. In fact, I saw one (a fight) about nine months ago where the teacher walked away from it and didn't want to get involved."	"And, many times we would just transfer a student who had one fight. You could say anyone who fights in this building is gone."

Source: Adapted from Astor, Meyer, & Behre, 1999.

153

TABLE 6.6 Student-Reported Violent Events and Suggested Interventions

Location of Event	Nature of Violent Event	Suggested Interventions by Students
Hallway	<ul><li>pushing</li><li>fighting</li><li>gun pulled</li><li>gang fights</li><li>assault</li></ul>	"There's so many people that you can understand that the hallways are crowded. That's our number one problem—the hallways are too crowded." "Have a rule that if you surround a fight you're helping … so you would get the same punishment as the people fighting, because you're helping people fight." "… they (security) should know what is going on in their hallway instead of like two or three of them going down the same way."
Parking Lot	<ul><li>physical fights</li><li>weapons</li><li>shooting</li><li>stabbing</li><li>physical threats</li><li>racially motivated fights</li></ul>	"Well where there's not supervision (parking lot) there's always going to be trouble … the principal. He should be out there."
Abandoned or Unmonitored Spaces	<ul><li>physical fights or assault</li><li>sexual assault or rape</li><li>strangers entering</li><li>weapons</li><li>robbery</li></ul>	"Maybe if we had regular security guards, like they had a 70-year-old man security guard, and like that guy can't even move." "People walk in at like 7 o'clock. No guards anywhere. It's just quiet—nobody anywhere." "When we have a weapon search, they supposed to check you. There's some people they don't check." "More lights … or have a monitor. Have somebody down there." "I mean lock the school doors … the back door is always open and people come in." "I think we need to have IDs to show … and then like a speaker at the door."
Cafeteria	<ul><li>physical fights</li><li>food fights</li><li>throwing chairs</li><li>gang scuffles</li></ul>	"They should have at least 5 teachers in there … a minimum of five teachers. Because now there's only two teachers." "It's too crowded … our lunch hour is only 25 minutes." "I think you should go basically anywhere during lunch, as long as you clean up after yourself, because keeping a lot of people together kind of generates fights."

Source: Adapted from Astor, Meyer, & Behre, 1999.

For Study and Discussion

1. This chapter documents dramatic reductions in various forms of school violence. What social variables do you believe account for these reductions? Discuss specific variables at the cultural "macro" level, but also at the family and individual levels. What kinds of school-related policies and practices could account for these reductions in school violence?

2. Currently, there is a national attempt to create safe schools. Discuss which variables you would focus on or measure to determine if a school was safe or unsafe. Is the safety of a school related to the number of violent events per year in that school? If so, how many violent events would it take in a high school of 1,000 students for you to call it an "unsafe school"? What types of violent behaviors would you consider qualitatively more salient? How many of these kinds of behaviors would constitute an unsafe school during a 1-year period? What measures or outcomes would you use as a school social worker to determine whether a school has a school violence problem?

3. Discuss several ways that school social workers could educate their school community about the reality of school violence. Generate three types of processes that could involve students, teachers, and parents to own school violence as a problem.

4. What types of empowerment activities should students be responsible for in an effort to reduce school fights?

5. Describe one effective intervention in detail and indicate in what circumstances this intervention may be most appropriate.

6. Discuss the specific social dynamics in discrete school contexts such as the school restroom, schoolyard, hallways, lunchrooms, and routes to and from school (including buses). Are there dynamics unique to each setting that would make grassroots interventions work better than packaged programs? If so, what are they? As an example, discuss the routes to and from school and ways the school/families can define responsibility for monitoring the safety of those routes more effectively.

7. Do you believe there are cultures/countries where school violence is low? If so, which cultures/countries do you think have low school violence rates? Why do you think they are low in those countries? Could the United States learn from programs in those countries? Explain why or why not. As a follow-up, explore cross-cultural articles/chapters (e.g., Smith, Morita, Junger-Tas, Olweus, Catalano, & Slee, 1999, *The nature of school bullying: A cross-national perspective.* Routledge: London & New York) to see if your assumptions of those countries were correct or not correct.

8. What kinds of steps would a school social worker take to prepare their school to respond to crisis? (For comprehensive guides and best practices, see Brock, Lazarus, & Jimerson (Eds.), (2002). *Best practices in school crisis prevention and intervention.* Bethesda, MD: NASP Publications).

Suggested Class Activities

1. Imagine that you participated in a school board meeting that is convened because parents complained about severe violence in the school. You were asked to present a step-by-step plan of how to deal with these complaints. Provide an outline of the document you would submit to the school board. Would this document vary if the school is situated in an upper-class suburban area, a farm area in the South, or is an inner-city school with mostly minority students?

2. Provide a mock set of findings from a quantitative assessment of a school; explain what you learned from this set of findings. What are the implications for intervention?

3. Imagine that you are making a school-level qualitative assessment. Describe, step by step, how you will conduct such an assessment, provide examples of findings, and analyze them. What do they teach you, and what are the implications for practice?

Additional Readings

American Association of University Women. (2001). *Hostile hallways: Bullying, teasing, and sexual harassment.* Washington, DC: Author.

Arnette, J., & Walsleben, M. (1998). *Combating fear and restoring safety in schools* (NCJ167888). Washington, DC: Office of Juvenile Justice and Delinquency Prevention.

Artz, S. (1998a). *Sex, power and the violent school girl.* New York: Teachers' College Press.

Artz, S. (1998b). Where have all the school girls gone? Violent girls in the school yard. *Child and Youth Care Forum, 27,* 77–109.

Astor, R. A., & Meyer, H. (2001). The conceptualization of violence prone school sub-contexts: Is the sum of the parts greater than the whole? *Urban Education, 36,* 374-399.

Astor, R., Meyer, H., & Pitner, R. O. (2001). Elementary and middle school students' perceptions of violence-prone school subcontexts. *The Elementary School Journal, 101,* 511–528.

Baker, J. A. (1998). Are we missing the forest for the trees? Considering the social context of school violence. *Journal of School Psychology, 36,* 29–44.

Benbenishty, R., & Astor, R. A. (2003). Violence in schools: The view from Israel. In P. K. Smith (Ed), *Violence in schools: The response in Europe* (pp. 317–331). London: Routledge Falmer.

Bosworth, K., Espelage, D., & Simon, T (1999). Factors associated with bullying behavior in middle school students, *Journal of Early Adolescence, 19,* 341–362.

Cane, A., Avery-Leaf, S., Cascardi, M., & O'Leary, K. (1998). Dating violence in two high school samples: Discriminating variables. *Journal of Primary Prevention, 18,* 431–446.

Cornell, D. G. (2006). *School violence: Fears versus facts.* Mahwah, NJ: Erlbaum.

Errante, A. (1997). Close to home: Comparative perspectives on childhood and community violence. *American Journal of Education, 105,* 355–400.

Everett, S. A., & Price, J. H. (1995). Students' perceptions of violence in the public schools: The MetLife Survey. *Journal of Adolescent Health, 17,* 345–352.

Finkelhor, D. (1995). The victimization of children: A developmental perspective. *American Journal of Orthopsychiatry, 65,* 177–193.

Hyman I. A., & Snook P. A. (2000). Dangerous schools and what you can do about them. *Phi Delta Kappan, 81*(7), 488–501.

Jimerson, S. R., & Furlong, M. J. (Eds.). (2006). *Handbook of school violence and school safety: From research to practice.* Mahwah, NJ: Erlbaum.

Kaufman, P., Chen, X., Choy, S., Ruddy, S., Miller, A., Fleury, J., et al. (2000). *Indicators of school crime and safety, 2000.* Washington, DC: U.S. Departments of Education and Justice. NCES 2001-017/NCJ-184176.

Klipp, G. (2001). *Resallying quids: Resilience of queer youth in school.* Unpublished doctoral dissertation, University of Michigan, Ann Arbor.

Kodluboy, D. (1997). Gang-oriented interventions. In A. Goldstein (Ed.), *School violence intervention: A practical handbook* (pp. 189–214). New York: Guilford Press.

Meyer, H. A., & Astor, R. A. (2002). Child and parent perspectives on routes to and from school in high crime neighborhoods. *Journal of School Violence, 1*(4), 101–128.

Pellegrini, A., & Bartini, M. (2000). A longitudinal study of bullying, victimization, and peer affiliation during the transition from primary school to middle school. *American Educational Research Journal, 37,* 699–725.

Price, J. H., & Everett, S. A. (1997). Teacher's perceptions of violence in the public schools: The MetLife survey. *American Journal of Health Behavior, 21,* 178–186.

Rose, L., & Gallup, A. (2000). The 32nd annual Phi Delta Kappa/Gallup poll of the public's attitudes toward the public schools. *Phi Delta Kappan, 82,* 41–66.

Stein, N. (1999). *Classrooms and courtrooms: Facing sexual harassment in K–12 schools.* New York: Teachers College Press.

Sullivan, K. (2000). *The anti-bullying handbook.* New York: Oxford University Press.

Vossekuil, B., Reddy, M., Fein, R., Borum, R., & Modzeleski, W. (2000). *U.S.S.S. Safe School Initiative: An interim report on the prevention of targeted violence in schools.* Washington, DC: U.S. Secret Service, National Threat Assessment Center.

Web Sites with School Violence Prevention Information and Links to Many Other Useful Sites

Colorado Center for the Prevention of Violence: www.Colorado.edu/cspv

Compendium of Assessment Tools for Measuring Violence among Youths: http://www.cdc.gov/ncipc/pub-res/measure.htm

Department of Justice: www.ojp.usdoj.gov/bjs

National Association of School Psychologists: www.nasponline.org/index2.html

National Center for Educational Statistics: nces.ed.gov

National Resource Center for Safe Schools: www.safetyzone.org

National School Safety Center: www.NSSCI.org

The Hamilton Fish Institute: www.hamfish.org/

7

Children with Disabilities

SALLY ATKINS-BURNETT
Mathematica Policy Research, Inc.

Introduction

On December 3, 2004, the Individuals with Disabilities Education Improvement Act of 2004, the ninth reauthorization of what is commonly known as IDEA, became law. Originally known as Education for All Handicapped Children Act (P.L. 94-142), this legislation mandates the rights of children with disabilities to a free and appropriate education in the least restrictive environment. How to best ensure these rights has been discussed at length through the years and has been the focus of many court cases. Multiple pieces of legislation and litigation (see Boxes 7.1A and B) influenced current practice. Special education services continue to evolve amid a climate of strong accountability. This chapter summarizes the major influences and the ongoing debates surrounding the provision of a free and appropriate education to infants, children, and youth with special needs. Key provisions of legislation are described and current issues are explored. IDEA recognizes the role that social workers play in facilitating the education of children. It lists social work services among the related services that should be available to children with disabilities. IDEA 2004 specifically mentions roles for social workers in preparing a developmental or social history, group and individual counseling with the child with disabilities and/or the child's family, forming partnerships with the family and others to work on problems that affect the child's adjustment in school, mobilizing the resources in both the school and the community to enable the child to benefit

from the educational program, and assisting in the development of positive behavioral intervention strategies (300.34 (c) (14)). Different aspects of these roles will be discussed in this chapter. Throughout the chapter are short stories (in italics) of how school social workers serve children with disabilities.

Background and Early Influences

The confluence of civil rights and education litigation and legislation has shaped special education policy and practices since the 1960s (see Boxes 7.1A and B). Prior to 1970, it is estimated that millions of children with disabilities were excluded from schools or educated inappropriately (U.S. Department of Education, 2000). The 1954 Supreme Court decision in the civil rights case *Brown v. Board of Education* ruled to end racial segregation in U.S. schools. Advocates for children with disabilities purported that the court's ruling on the unconstitutionality of segregation and exclusion should be extended to children with disabilities. However, as late as 1969, a North Carolina statute allowed children to be labeled as "uneducable" and made it a crime for parents to challenge the school's designation (Palmaffy, 2001). Civil rights advocates feared that minority children would be labeled "uneducable" or mentally retarded in an effort to exclude them from schools and worked to challenge laws that excluded children.

BOX 7.1A • *Summary of Important Educational Legislation*

Trying to broaden the base of support and for all types of individuals with disabilities, two groups organized in the early 1950s:

- The National Association for Retarded Citizens (NARC)
- The Council for Exceptional Children (CEC)

1965 Elementary and Secondary Education Act (ESEA) P.L. 89-10

- Provided limited federal support in organizing and maintaining special education in public schools, but no support services to make it possible.

1996 Amendments to ESEA, P.L. 89-750

- Added Title VI. This was the first time federal money had been allocated for support services for children with disabilities, but no specific guidelines.
- Established the Bureau of Education for the Handicapped and the National Advisory Committee on the Handicapped.

1970 Education of the Handicapped Act (EHA), P.L. 91-230

- Repealed Title VI of the ESEA.
- Authorized funding but no criteria.
- Did not dictate which, if any, social services could participate in the education of children with disabilities.

1973 Rehabilitation Act Section 504, PL. 93-112

Extended the protections implied in the *PARC* and *Mills* judicial decisions to individuals in any institution that receives federal funds (Palmaffy, 2001). It affirmed the principle that students with disabilities have a right to be educated in regular classrooms to the maximum extent possible. Any agency receiving federal money must end discrimination in offering services to individuals with disabilities. Section 504 and ADA offer more remedies to parents and were a main vehicle for special education litigation in the 1990s (Martin, Martin, & Terman, 1996). Students may qualify for protections under Section 504 without qualifying under the IDEA. Section 504 and ADA define an individual with a disability as someone who has an impairment that "substantially limits one or more life activities of such individual"; or has a history of impairment, or is considered by others as having an impairment (Turnbull, Turnbull, Shank, & Smith, 2004, p. 35).

1975 Education of All Handicapped Children Act (EAHCA), P.L. 94-142[1]

- Kept in place as the allocation formula for FY1976–77. It was the allocation formula used in FY 1975, which granted states $8.75 for each child in the state to be used specifically to educate children with disabilities.
- Established a new grant formula based on the number of children with disabilities (aged 3 through 21) being served multiplied by a percentage of the national per pupil expenditures.
- Stipulated that no state could count more than 12% of its children aged 5–17 as handicapped.
- Required each state to provide a free and appropriate education to all its children with disabilities, aged 3–21, unless federal law was contrary to state law or court order.
- Encouraged states to provide education for children with disabilities aged 3–5 by authorizing incentive grants of an additional $300 for each child receiving educational services.
- Required that federal funds supplement, not supplant, state and local funds. States and Local Education Authorities (LEAs) must pay as much for each child with disabilities as they do for typically developing children.
- Required the LEA, in consultation with the teacher and the parents, "if appropriate"; to establish an IEP for each child with disabilities.
- Required, where appropriate, the education of individuals with disabilities in the least restrictive environment.
- Strengthened existing due process procedures to guarantee the rights of individuals with disabilities, including due process, in all matters regarding identification, evaluation, and placement of the child, assurance that testing materials and procedures would not discriminate racially or culturally, and assurance that information gathered by the state would be kept confidential.

1977 Amendments to EAHC, P.L. 95-49 1983 Amendments to EAHC, P.L. 98-199

1986 Education of the Handicapped Act (EHA), P.L. 99-457[2]

- Amended EHA to authorize an early intervention program for infants and toddlers with disabilities and their families mandated by 1991.

- Established a new grant program for state development and operation of early intervention services for infants and toddlers with disabilities from birth to age 2 by the fifth year of participation.
- Required preparation and review of individualized family plans by local service providers.
- Repealed state exception for children aged 3–5 from state special education requirements.
- Mandated free public education for all children with disabilities beginning at age 3.
- Authorized appropriations for Department of Education grants to state, local, and private-sector agencies for education programs, including
  - Education services for individuals with disabilities at preschool, elementary, secondary, and postsecondary levels and vocational training.
  - Services at education regional resource centers.
  - Development of demonstration programs for extended school year services to children and youth with severe disabilities.
  - Special education research, teacher training, and support personnel recruitment and training program.

1988 Amendments to EHA, P.L. 100-630

1990 Individuals with Disabilities Education Act (IDEA), P.L. 1010-476[3]
- Revised and extended through FY 94 Department of Education discretionary special education programs.
  - Included grants to states for research, demonstration projects, personnel training, and information dissemination on special education and related services to children and youth with disabilities.
- Denied states immunity from lawsuits for violations of the act.
- Authorized a new discretionary grant program for the education and related needs of children and youth with emotional impairments.

1991 Amendments to IDEA, P.L. 102-119[4]
- Amended IDEA to authorize appropriations for FY 92–94 Department of Education grants to states for early educational services for infants and toddlers with disabilities.

- Improved services to children with disabilities on Indian reservations.
- Expanded training programs for paraprofessionals, special education teachers, and parents of children with disabilities.

1997 Amendments to IDEA, P.L. 105-17
- Added categories of disability: developmental delay.
- Greater emphasis on access to general curriculum and accountability.
- Related services added to transition services.
- Required the provision of services to children who have been suspended or expelled from the public school.
- Reduced the requirement for testing every 3 years.

No Child Left Behind Act of 2001 (NCLB)
- This reauthorization of ESEA emphasized need for more preventative services and research-based practices.
- Allowed states to use funds for prekindergarten programs.
- Strong emphasis on applying the same *academic* standards to all schools and children.
- Strong emphasis on ensuring children are taught by highly qualified teachers.
- Requires that students with disabilities be included in the accountability procedures. Schools must show adequate yearly progress (AYP) for each subgroup. Children with disabilities are one of the subgroups. Ninety-five percent of each group of students are required to participate in state assessments beginning in grade 3. Regulations of 1% have been relaxed to allow up to 2% of student with disabilities to take assessments based on modified standards (U.S. Department of Education, 2005).
- Requires use of the regular diploma as the new standard for calculating graduation rates (Council for Exceptional Children, 2003).

Individuals with Disabilities Education Improvement Act of 2004 (IDEA 2004)
- Aligned IDEA with NCLB including increased accountability when using alternative assessments, definitions of highly qualified special

(continued)

BOX 7.1A • Continued

---

education teachers, and increased emphasis on sanctions for noncompliance.

■ Increased parental responsibilities for due process and instituted a statute of limitations on filing complaints and appeals.

■ Allowed 15% of funds for early intervening.

■ Increased involvement of Vocational Rehabilitation agencies in transition planning and required postsecondary goals beginning at 16 years of age.

[1]Congressional Quarterly Almanac, 94th Congress, 1st Session, 1975, Vol. XXXI, 1976, pp. 651–652,
[2]Congressional Information Service Annual Legislative Histories for U.S. Public Laws, 1986. Congressional Information Service, Inc.: Washington, DC, 1987.
[3]Congressional Information Service Annual Legislative Histories for U.S. Public Laws, 1990. Congressional Information Service, Inc.: Washington, DC, 1991.
[4]Congressional Information Service Annual Legislative Histories for U.S. Public Laws, 1991. Congressional Information Service, Inc.: Washington, DC, 1992.

BOX 7.1B • *Summary of Important Special Education Litigation*

1971 *Pennsylvania Association for Retarded Children (PARC) v. Commonwealth of Pennsylvania*

On behalf of 13 children with mental impairments, PARC contested a state law that allowed public schools to deny services to children whose mental age was determined to be below 5 years. State agreed to provide full access to a free public education; established standard of appropriateness—each child to be offered education appropriate to his/her learning capacities; established a clear preference for least restrictive placement.

1972 *Mills v. Board of Education, District of Columbia*

Class-action suit on behalf of children who were refused enrollment, suspended, or expelled on the basis of their disability; school district admitted an estimated 12,340 children with disabilities would not be served in 1971–72 school year due to budgetary constraints; court ruled the problem of finance could not be allowed to bear more heavily on children with disabilities than on other children. Prohibited schools from budgeting special services in advance and offering only on a "space available" basis. Based primarily on the Equal Protection Clause and Due Process Clause of the U.S. Constitution (Fifth and Fourteenth Amendments), this case granted children with disabilities full procedural protections when a change in status (e.g., suspensions, expulsions, transfers out of regular classrooms, or reassignment) is considered, including notice of proposed changes, right to be heard and legal counsel at hearings to

determine changes in program access to school records, and regularly scheduled status reviews.

1972 *Diana v.* State *Board of Education*

Charged that Mexican-American children whose primary language was Spanish, had been assessed improperly. Intelligence tests administered in English qualified them for placement in an educable, mentally retarded classroom. Retest results indicated seven of nine children involved were not mentally impaired. Court ordered all Mexican-American and Chinese-American students reevaluated in their native language and inappropriate placements rectified. The misuse of tests had been raised initially in *Hobson v. Hansen* (1967).

1972 *Larry P. v. Riles*

Questioned the assignment of Black students to Educationally Mentally Retarded (EMR) classes based on psychometric testing. Although only 28.5% of district's students were Black, 66% of the students in district EMR classrooms were Black. Court prohibited district from using IQ scores as primary criteria for EMR placement.

1982 *Rowley v. Board of Education, 458 U.S. AT 203,102 5. CT. at 3049*

Supreme court interpreted "appropriate" education; a state satisfies the requirement to provide a free and appropriate public education (FAPE) by provision of services and instruction, at public expense, that meet the state's educational standards and are consistent with the child's Individualized Education Program (IEP).

1988 Honig v. Doe

Supreme Court ruled schools could discipline students with disabilities using traditional procedures as long as it did not result in a change in placement. In cases of immediate threat to the well-being of students, a child with a disability could be suspended for up to 10 days. A pattern of suspensions (totaling more than 10 days during a single school year) constitutes a change in placement.

1989 Daniel R. R. v. State Board of Education, 874 F.2d 1036 (5th Cir.)

Spelled out two-part inquiry in determining child's placement. First, could regular placement be satisfactorily achieved with supplementary services? Has school taken steps to modify regular education? Can child benefit from modifications? Will detriment to child result from placement in regular education? What effect will child have on the regular classroom environment? Second, if the decision is made to remove the child for any portion of the day, has the child been mainstreamed to the maximum extent possible? It is not an all or nothing proposition.

1994 Sacramento City Unified School District, Board of Education v. Rachel H., 12 F.3D 1398 (9th Cir.)

The Ninth Circuit Court offers a slightly different standard for determining placement using four factors: (a) educational benefits available in the regular classroom to this child, (b) the nonacademic benefits of interaction with children who are typically developing, (c) effect of the presence of the child with disability on the teacher and other children in the classroom, and (d) the cost of mainstreaming (IDEA does not allow cost to be considered in placement—where a service is necessary, cost considerations would not excuse a school district from providing the service. However, when more than one service or program is appropriate, school district may be allowed to consider costs.)

1999 Board of Education of LaGrange School District No. 105 v. Illinois State Board of Education and Ryan B., 184 F.3d 912 (7th Cir.)

The U.S. Court of Appeals ruled in favor of the family of a preschool child with Down syndrome. The parents wanted the child educated in a preschool for typically developing children, but the district did not have a preschool and refused to pay for private tuition, offering instead a placement in a Head Start or in a special education classroom. The court awarded the parents reimbursement of tuition at the private preschool and held that the LRE decision needed to take into account the special needs of the child.

Two pieces of litigation in 1972 set the stage for later legislation establishing three guiding principles (Palmaffy, 2001). The *PARC v. Commonwealth of Pennsylvania* and *Mills v. Board of Education of District of Columbia* decisions ruled that (a) the exclusion of students from schools based solely on disability is a violation of the Constitution's guarantees of equal protection and due process; (b) parents of children with disabilities should have available a range of legal remedies (including impartial hearing and access to the courts) for challenging schools regarding the educational programming; and (c) cost is not an acceptable excuse for excluding children from the public school system. These principles have continued to guide later legislation.

Ambiguity regarding what constitutes a free and appropriate education and what the least restrictive environment is for a given child has led to numerous court cases. Is lack of progress in school adequate evidence that a student is not receiving a free and appropriate education? Can a district consider other students' needs when determining programming, some of which may be costly? Case law continues to provide a broad set of protections for children and youth with disabilities (Palmaffy, 2001). (See Box 7.1B for a brief description of some of the major court decisions affecting special education.) The court decisions support the education of children with disabilities alongside their peers in the regular classroom to the maximum extent possible. Students may be excluded only if the school demonstrates that they have attempted a range of interventions and the student's behavior continues to seriously disrupt the learning or endanger the students in the classroom. Cost considerations are not acceptable reasons for removing a child to an alternative placement (Palmaffy, 2001). The Individualized Education Program (IEP) must be "reasonably calculated to enable the child to receive educational benefits" (458 U.S. 176 at 207).

Landmark Legislation: The Education for All Handicapped Children Act of 1975 (P.L. 94-142)

In 1975, Congress passed P.L. 94-142, which historians consider the most important and far-reaching piece of federal legislation in the area of special education (Education for All Handicapped Children Act, 1975). This law can be considered the "bill of rights" for children with disabilities. For the first time, Congress authorized federal money to be spent by state educational agencies so that local school districts could provide education to children with disabilities who needed it. The passage of P.L. 94-142 impacted social work services in schools profoundly. Social workers were named specifically as one of the related services required to help individuals with disabilities benefit from special education. For the first time, social workers were given legislative recognition for their contribution to the educational process.

P.L. 94-142 was intended to (a) ensure that all children with disabilities, aged 3 through 21, have available free, appropriate public education (FAPE) in the least restrictive environment (LRE), which includes special education and related services to meet their unique needs; (b) ensure that the rights of children with disabilities and their parents are protected; (c) assist states and localities in providing for the education of all children with disabilities; and (d) ensure the effectiveness of efforts to educate these children. P.L. 94-142 significantly expanded children's rights and placed substantial responsibility on the educational agencies that serve children with disabilities. At the time of its passage, there were over 8 million children with disabilities in the United States; of this group, about 1.75 million were receiving no formal education, and 2.5 million were estimated to be receiving inadequate education. By fall 2007, almost 7 million children and youth with disabilities from birth to 21 years old were being served by IDEA. The number of children and youth being served from 6 to 21 years old has begun to level off since 2004 while the number of children served before age 5 has continued to increase gradually.

One of the challenges of IDEA has been funding. The promise of federal funding for 40% of the costs of special education has never been realized. By the year 2000, federal funds were supporting approximately 12% of the costs of educating individuals with disabilities. At the same time, amendments to the law and increased identification of individuals with disabilities have expanded the scope of special education, and the costs have mushroomed. The IDEA has been reauthorized every 5 to 7 years and has expanded educational opportunities to infants and preschoolers with disabilities, and to students with autism, traumatic brain injury, deaf-blindness, or attention deficit disorders. It is estimated that educating children with disabilities costs approximately twice what it costs to educate a typically developing student (Palmaffy, 2001). Until the increased emphasis on early intervening in NCLB and IDEA 2004, the number of identified children continued to rise (see Figure 7.1). In the 1976-1977 school year, a little over 8% of all enrolled children were identified as disabled. By the turn of the century, more than 13% of the students were identified as disabled (U.S. Department of Education, 2000). In 2007, approximately 9% of all students from ages 6 to 21 and 2.5% of the nation's infants and toddlers received services under IDEA.

No Child Left Behind Act of 2001

The 2001 bill reauthorizing the Elementary and Secondary Education Act (ESEA) was signed into law on January 8, 2002. Named the No Child Left Behind (NCLB) Act, it includes changes that are intended to prevent reading problems and increase academic achievement for all children. Children identified as having learning disabilities represent approximately half of children with disabilities. The majority of these students are identified due to a failure in learning to read. Provisions were made in

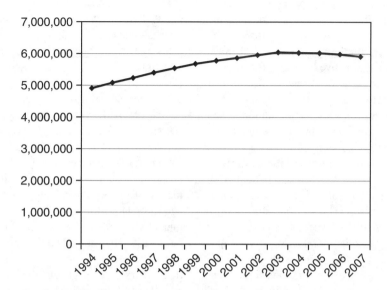

FIGURE 7.1   Children with Disabilities Aged 6–21   *Source:* U.S. Department of Education (2008) and U.S. Department of Education, Office of Special Education Programs, Data Analysis System (DANS), OMB #1820-0043 Data updated as of July 15, 2008.

the NCLB to allow states to use some of the funding for prekindergarten programs and for additional paraprofessionals in the classroom. It relies on four principles to bring about the anticipated results: emphasis on researched, proven teaching methods, stronger accountability focused on results, increased flexibility and local control, and more options for parents. Among the accountability provisions, the NCLB requires greater than 95% participation in standards-based assessments beginning in grade 3, and that children and youth in all subgroups, including those with disabilities, make Annual Yearly Progress (AYP) toward having all children reach proficiency on grade-level achievement standards by 2014. If even one subgroup does not meet AYP, the entire district is considered as not meeting AYP. Schools and districts do not have to report by subgroups if the number of the children in the subgroup is small. States define small in different ways from as few as five to as many as 50 students. Schools with fewer children identified with disabilities do not have to report AYP for that subgroup. The NCLB allows testing accommodations and for a small percentage of students (2%), an alternative assessment with modified or alternate standards. However, states struggle with the creation of reliable, valid assessments that are aligned with the standards and with providing children the opportunity to learn what will be assessed. In fact, some teachers report cases where students are asked to complete an assessment that is so far beyond the students' capability that it causes emotional distress. In an effort to ensure that schools meet AYP, the NCLB requires that schools strive to have *highly* qualified teachers (HQT) in every classroom. For special educators, this means that they need to be highly qualified not only in strategies for intervention, but also in the content for any core academic subjects that they teach. The NCLB has had a strong impact on the landscape of education.

The Individuals with Disabilities Education Act (IDEA) Today

The IDEA has been refined and expanded during subsequent reauthorizations (see Box 7.1A for a summary of legislation). The IDEA has brought about many positive changes. Every state in the nation now has laws ensuring the provision of a

FAPE to all individuals with disabilities. In the IDEA 2004, legislators noted that almost 30 years of experience in implementing this law have demonstrated that effective services to children with disabilities include (a) strong involvement of parents and partnerships between parents and schools; (b) high expectations for children and access to mainstream curriculum to the maximum extent possible; (c) alignment of special education efforts with state and local improvement efforts so that individuals with disabilities can benefit from the improvements (legislators included a reminder that special education is a service rather than a place); (d) provision of special education and related services (such as social work) in the regular classroom to the maximum extent possible; (e) provision of incentives for prereferral interventions to reduce the need to label children disabled to meet their behavioral and learning needs, specifically mentioning early reading programs, positive behavioral interventions, early intervening, and use of response to intervention; (f) a focus on provision of resources for teaching and learning while reducing paperwork demands; (g) support for high-quality intensive preservice and professional development for everyone (e.g., paraprofessionals, teachers, adjunct staff) who works with children with disabilities to ensure that the knowledge and skills necessary to effectively assist children are attained by all pertinent personnel; and (h) maximizing accessibility for children by supporting the development and provision of assistive technology devices and services. IDEA 2004 also shifted accountability efforts to focus on stronger student academic outcomes and align with the requirements of NCLB. In addition, IDEA 2004 aligns with Child Abuse Prevention and Treatment Act (CAPTA: as amended in 2003 in the Keeping Children and Families Safe Act) by requiring referral for services under Part C of any child under the age of 3 years with a substantiated case of child abuse or neglect, including those with withdrawal symptoms resulting from prenatal drug exposure.

IDEA has a positive effect on the lives of children with disabilities. Almost twice as many individuals with disabilities are employed as young adults, and the quality of life has improved for many. Students with disabilities are completing high school at a much higher rate than they were 20 years ago. According to the National Longitudinal Transition Study (Wagner, Newman, Cameto, & Levine, 2005), in 1987 only 53.5% of youth with disabilities completed high school and by 2003, 70.3% of youth with disabilities completed high school. In 2007 less than 15% of youth with disabilities aged 14 to 21 who exited from special education dropped out, compared with more than 27% dropping out ten years earlier. Children are being identified and begin receiving services at a younger age (U.S. Department of Education, 2008). Unfortunately, for others the promise of IDEA has not been fulfilled. Students who are minorities are overrepresented in separate special education settings, marking special education as a new form of racial/ethnic segregation (see Figure 7.2). In 2007 a greater percentage of students with limited English proficiency (LEP) and disabilities (18%) dropped out of school than their English proficient counterparts (15%) (DANS, 2008). Identification of disability is more challenging for students who have LEP, particularly for a language-based learning disability (Klingner & Harry, 2006; Lesaux, 2006).

Early Intervening.   Prior to IDEA 2004, students needed to qualify for special education prior to receiving services. This meant that children had to experience repeated and continuing failure before receiving special education services and supports. The IDEA 2004 recognizes the importance of addressing learning problems as soon as possible. The IDEA 2004 allows schools to use up to 15% of the IDEA money to support children in regular education who exhibit academic or behavioral problems, but have not been identified as disabled. To differentiate this from Part C, the legislation refers to it as *early intervening*. In many school districts, these funds are used for Response to Intervention (RTI) approaches (see "Evaluation and Eligibility").

Highly Qualified Teachers.   The IDEA 2004 supports the highly qualified teacher requirements of NCLB. However, most states and districts were interpreting this section of NCLB to mean that teachers needed to be qualified to teach the children whom they served, that is, to hold certification

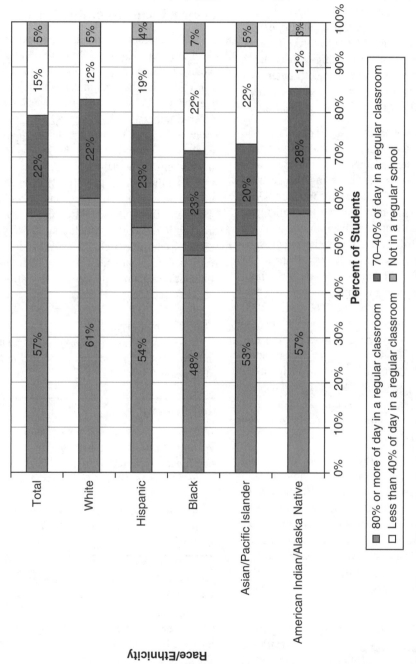

FIGURE 7.2 Students with Disabilities: Percentage Distribution of Students ages 6–21 Served by IDEA, by Placement in Educational Environment and Race/Ethnicity: Fall 2007

in the area of the children's disabilities. The IDEA 2004 requires that a teacher also be qualified in all the subject areas in which they provide core instruction. They can either hold appropriate licensure in these areas or pass a test indicating expertise in the subject matter. The U.S. Department of Education encourages team teaching with a teacher who is highly qualified in the subject matter as a way to provide services when the special educator is not qualified in all the necessary subject areas.

Increased Responsibility for Parents. The IDEA 2004 responded to concerns from districts regarding placement changes for children with behavioral challenges and regarding the costs of litigation. In response to these concerns, the IDEA 2004 puts the focus on the parents to challenge a change of placement for disciplinary reasons when the school determines that the behavior is not the result of the child's disability. Prior to the current legislation, the burden was on the school district to sue for change of placement if the parents disagreed with the change. The IDEA 2004 requires that parents and districts meet and discuss complaints before the parent can begin the due process involving lawyers and hearings. In addition, parents can now be held responsible for some litigation costs, potentially discouraging parents from pursuing complaints. In addition, a statute of limitations for complaints and appeals has been included in the IDEA.

Paperwork Burden. Professionals and school districts voiced concern about the amount and burden of the paperwork required by the IDEA. The IDEA reduces some of the burden of IEPs by eliminating the requirement of short-term objectives and benchmarks. In addition, the IDEA 2004 allows up to 15 states to demonstrate ways to reduce the burden by allowing 3-year IEPs, relieving those states of the requirement for yearly IEP meetings.

Transition to Adulthood. The IDEA requires that postsecondary goals (adult living, vocational plans, postsecondary education) be addressed in the student's IEP beginning at age 16. The student must receive a summary of progress toward those goals and ongoing transition needs when they leave secondary school.

Critical Elements of the IDEA

The IDEA is founded on the provision of a FAPE to all children with disabilities. No child may be excluded on the basis of a disability. Even when a district decides that a child is ineducable or disruptive, the district must provide services if the child is covered under Part B of the IDEA (for children younger than age 3, states decide which infants and toddlers to serve). Part B is the section of the law that pertains to the delivery of services to children with disabilities from age 3 to 21. The zero-reject principle has been challenged and upheld in court (Turnbull, Turnbull, Shank, & Leal, 1995). Children with disabilities (including those who are homeless) have a right to a FAPE in the least restrictive environment. The least restrictive environment is explained further in this section.

This section will describe the critical elements of the IDEA (Martin, Martin, & Terman, 1996; Turnbull et al., 1995) and explore some of the ways in which social workers contribute to the enactment of the principles embodied in this legislation.

Kelly's story

Kelly was a 17-year-old young man who had a learning disability. He was also an "unaccompanied homeless youth" as defined in section 725(6) of the McKinney-Vento Homeless Assistance Act (42 U.S.C. 1143a(6)). Since it was time for his annual IEP meeting, his social worker contacted the local regional resource area to find someone to fill the role as surrogate for Kelly.

Child Find. States must ensure that all children with disabilities, regardless of severity of disability, who are in need of special education and related services are identified, located, and evaluated. Children who are eligible for services (see Box 7.2 for eligibility definitions) must be offered appropriate educational and related services. This includes children who are homeless

BOX 7.2 • *Federal Definitions of Eligibility Categories*

- *Autism* means a developmental disability significantly affecting verbal and nonverbal communication and social interaction, generally evident before age 3, that adversely affects a child's educational performance. Other characteristics often associated with autism are engagement in repetitive activities and stereotyped movements, resistance to environmental change or change in daily routines, and unusual responses to sensory experiences. The term does not apply if a child's educational performance is adversely affected primarily because the child has an emotional disturbance, as defined in paragraph (b)(4) of this section. (ii) A child who manifests the characteristics of "autism" after age 3 could be diagnosed as having "autism" if the criteria [above] are satisfied.

- *Deaf-blindness* means concomitant hearing and visual impairments, the combination of which causes such severe communication and other developmental and educational needs that they cannot be accommodated in special education programs solely for children with deafness or children with blindness.

- *Deafness* means a hearing impairment that is so severe that the child is impaired in processing linguistic information through hearing, with or without amplification, that adversely affects a child's educational performance.

- *Developmental delay is a* discretionary category that includes children aged 3 through 9 who experience developmental delays, as defined by the state and as measured by appropriate diagnostic instruments and procedures, in one or more of the following areas: physical development; cognitive development; communication development; social or emotional development; or adaptive development; and (ii) who, by reason thereof, needs special education and related services.

- *Emotional disturbance* is defined as follows: (i) The term means a condition exhibiting one or more of the following characteristics over a long period of time and to a marked degree that adversely affects a child's educational performance: (A) An inability to learn that cannot be explained by intellectual, sensory, or health

factors. (B) An inability to build or maintain satisfactory interpersonal relationships with peers and teachers. (C) Inappropriate types of behavior or feelings under normal circumstances. (D) A general pervasive mood of unhappiness or depression. (E) A tendency to develop physical symptoms or fears associated with personal or school problems. (ii) The term includes schizophrenia. The term does not apply to children who are socially maladjusted, unless it is determined that they have an emotional disturbance.

- *Hearing impairment* means an impairment in hearing, whether permanent or fluctuating, that adversely affects a child's educational performance but that is not included under the definition of deafness in this section.

- *Mental retardation* means significantly subaverage general intellectual functioning, existing concurrently with deficits in adaptive behavior and manifested during the developmental period, that adversely affects a child's educational performance.

- *Multiple disabilities* means concomitant impairments (such as mental retardation-blindness, mental retardation-orthopedic impairment), the combination of which causes such severe educational needs that *they* cannot be accommodated in special education programs solely for one of the impairments. The term does not include deaf-blindness.

- *Orthopedic impairment* means a severe orthopedic impairment that adversely affects a child's educational performance. The term includes impairments caused by congenital anomaly (e.g., clubfoot, absence of limb), impairments caused by disease (e.g., poliomyelitis, bone tuberculosis), and impairments from other causes (e.g., cerebral palsy, amputations, and fractures or burns that cause contractures).

- *Other health impairment* means having limited strength, vitality, or alertness, including a heightened alertness to environmental stimuli, that results in limited alertness with respect to the educational environment, that (i) is due to chronic or acute health problems such as asthma, attention deficit disorder or attention

(continued)

BOX 7.2 • Continued

deficit hyperactivity disorder, diabetes, epilepsy, a heart condition, hemophilia, lead poisoning, leukemia, nephritis, rheumatic fever, and sickle cell anemia; and (ii) Adversely affects a child's educational performance.

- *Specific learning disability* is defined as follows: (i) General. The term means a disorder in one or more of the basic psychological processes involved in understanding or in using language, spoken or written, that may manifest itself in an imperfect ability to listen, think, speak, read, write, spell, or to do mathematical calculations, including conditions such as perceptual disabilities, brain injury, minimal brain dysfunction, dyslexia, and developmental aphasia. (ii) Disorders not included. The term does not include learning problems that are primarily the result of visual, hearing, or motor disabilities, of mental retardation, of emotional disturbance, or of environmental, cultural, or economic disadvantage.

- *Speech or language impairment* means a communication disorder, such as stuttering, impaired articulation, a language impairment, or a voice impairment, that adversely affects a child's educational performance.

- *Traumatic brain injury* means an acquired injury to the brain caused by an external physical force, resulting in total or partial functional disability or psychosocial impairment, or both, that adversely affects a child's educational performance. The term applies to open or closed head injuries resulting in impairments in one or more areas, such as cognition; language; memory; attention; reasoning; abstract thinking; judgment; problem solving; sensory, perceptual, and motor abilities; psychosocial behavior; physical functions; information processing; and speech. The term does not apply to brain injuries that are congenital or degenerative, or to brain injuries induced by birth trauma.

- *Visual impairment* including blindness means an impairment in vision that, even with correction, adversely affects a child's educational performance. The term includes both partial sight and blindness. (Authority: 20 U.S.C. 1401(3)(A) and (B); 1401(26)).

Source: 34 C.F.R.§ 300.7 Retrieved October 14, 2008 from http://frwebgate.access.gpo.gov/cgi-bin/get-cfr.cgi

and protected by the McKinney-Vento Homeless Assistance Act (42 U.S.C. 11434a). Earlier identification and delivery of services has occurred (U.S. Department of Education, 2007). A greater percentage of infants and toddlers are being served under IDEA each year, whereas the percentage of children from ages 3 to 21 served each year leveled out around 2004. Ten years ago less than 1.5% of children under 3 years were served (U.S. Department of Education, 2007). By 2007, 2.5% of infants and toddlers were reported receiving services under IDEA, whereas 9% of school-age children and almost 6% of preschool children received services under IDEA in 2007 (U.S. Department of Education, DANS, 2008). The percent of school-age children served under the IDEA in the categories of Other Health Impaired, Developmental Delay, and Autism have increased in the last 10 years, whereas other categories have decreased or leveled out. These categories continue to represent a small proportion of the children and youth with disabilities (see Figure 7.3).

The school social worker can assist in the development of community-based referral procedures that can be utilized by parents, agencies, doctors, child-care workers, and others to locate children needing services. The social worker can explain the school's programs and the referral procedure to important groups in the community. A part of this role is maintaining open communication between the school and the various community groups. The social worker can also provide in-service training to classroom teachers and relevant groups concerning the identification of children with special needs. A school social worker with an early intervention program may screen the child in the home and obtain the social developmental history.

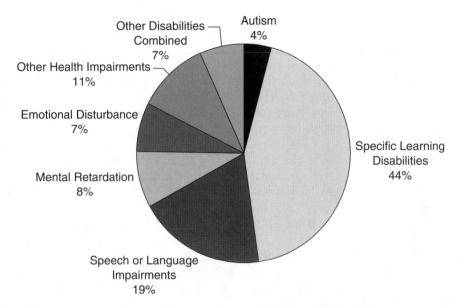

FIGURE 7.3 Disability Distribution of Children from 6-21 Years of Age Receiving Services Under IDEA: Fall 2007 *Source:* U. S. Department of Education, Office of Special Education Programs, Data Analysis System (DANS), OMB #1820-0043. Unpublished Author Tabulations based on Table 1-3: "Students ages 6 through 21 served under IDEA, Part B, by disability category and state: Fall 2007." Data updated as of October 14, 2008.

Notes: Other Disabilities Combined category includes: Multiple Disabilities (2.2%), Developmental Delay (1.5%); Hearing Impairments (1.2%); Orthopedic Impairments (1.0%); Visual Impairments (0.4%); Traumatic Brain Injury (0.4%); Deaf-Blindness (0.02%)

Aaron's story

Aaron had difficulty learning. Though a very cheerful, personable child, he frustrated his teachers by his inability to read, by frequently repeating the same errors, and continually breaking the same rules, despite promises not to do so. When his social worker, Rita, came to observe in the classroom, she recognized the distinctive facial features of fetal alcohol syndrome (FAS). She provided the teacher with research on FAS and made an appointment to meet with the family to discuss the evaluation process.

Evaluation and Eligibility—Use of Valid, Reliable, Nondiscriminatory Procedures. Students who are being considered for specialized services must be evaluated by a multidisciplinary team that is knowledgeable about the specific disability. The IDEA 2004 requires that evaluations "... are provided and administered in the language and form most likely to yield accurate information on what the child knows and can do academically, developmentally, and functionally, unless it is not feasible to so provide or administer" (IDEA, 2004).

To prevent inappropriate referrals, factors in the child's culture, language proficiency, learning style, and experiential background (especially the classroom context) must be considered when evaluating (Klingner & Harry, 2006). Although many improvements have been made in psychometric assessment, continued attention to potential biases in and interpretation of nationally standardized tests is needed, particularly on instruments that measure language (Suzuki, Short, Pierterse, & Kugler, 2001; Valencia & Suzuki, 2001; Washington & Craig, 1992). The examiner needs to consider whether the sample used to validate the test included children who are similar to the child being assessed. The evaluation should include an assessment of the child's adaptive behavior in his or her natural environments (home, community, and playground). No single test can be used as the sole criterion for determining placement into special programs (see Appendix III for more information on adaptive behavior).

The first three steps are screening procedures, prereferral procedures, and referral. Students who go through a prereferral process may never need to be referred because appropriate accommodations can be recommended. The IDEA 2004 allows evaluation of the response to research-based interventions (RTI) as a criterion for establishing eligibility as a child with a specific learning disability. This approach is considered particularly helpful for children who are English language learners (ELL) (Rinaldi & Samson, 2008). RTI is typically discussed in terms of three to four tiers. Tier 1 is the primary prevention of disability by using evidence-based curricula and instructional practices in teaching and universal screening for disability. The first tier may include progress monitoring for some children who are borderline. The second tier involves small-group tutoring or more intensive instruction—usually for about 15 weeks. The response to this tutoring is evaluated. Children who do not make gains with the tutoring are referred for individualized programming and monitoring and/or referred for a multidisciplinary evaluation (Tiers 3 and/or 4). Tier 2 may employ a specific intervention approach for all the children or may use a problem-solving model using data-based decision making to determine the most effective instruction (Cummings, Atkins, Allison, & Cole, 2008; Division for Learning Disabilities, 2007; Fuchs and Fuchs, 2007). Although RTI is intended for identification of learning disabilities, it is sometimes applied to early intervening with children suspected of emotional impairments. Several programs to teach specific social and emotional skills are available for preschool and early elementary classrooms. In addition, many elementary schools have begun adopting schoolwide positive behavior intervention and support (PBIS) systems (see www.pbis.org for more information).

Student evaluations must include a variety of assessment tools and strategies to gather functional and developmental information that may help in determining the presence of a disability and the content of the child's IEP. The IDEA 2004 establishes a 60-day timeline for this. If the parent does not assure that the child is available for the evaluation, the district is excused from this timeline. The assessment should include information provided by the parent. A single procedure is insufficient for determining whether the child has a disability or the appropriate educational program. The education agency must use technically sound instruments that assess cognitive and behavioral factors in addition to physical or developmental factors. The education agency must also assess the child in all areas of suspected disability and utilize assessment tools and strategies that provide information to assist in determining the educational needs.

The IDEA amendments of 1997 reduced unnecessary testing costs by relieving districts of the requirement to conduct a reevaluation testing every 3 years. Section 614(c) allowed the evaluation team to decide to dispense with tests to determine the need for continued eligibility, if the team determines that such testing was unnecessary and the parent agreed with this decision. The team needs to notify the parent if they decide that testing is unnecessary and explicate their decision. The team must still review existing evaluation data and identify additional data that may be necessary to determine eligibility and current level of functioning and any data needed to recommend any modifications to services and appropriate educational plans. The school social worker can provide observational data, a social developmental study (see Box 7.3), an adaptive behavior assessment, and an ecobehavioral assessment. This information is essential for a total picture of the child's functioning in significant environments both in and out of the school. When this information is combined with other data (such as psychological testing), a comprehensive profile can be formed.

BOX 7.3 • *Social and Developmental History*

- Prenatal influences (Tell me about your pregnancy)—listen for problems in pregnancy, sickness, bleeding, weight gain, use of substances, stressful experiences. exposure to viruses, unplanned pregnancy, concerns about potential hereditary disorders
- Perinatal influences (Tell me about his first days of life)—probe for difficulty of delivery, jaundice, anoxia, seizures, illness, medications, gestational age (prematurity, on time, late), and birth weight
- Infancy and early childhood (What was he like as an infant?)—probe developmental milestones, colic, illnesses, hospitalizations, ear infections, seizures)
- Parent perception of problems (Tell me about your first concerns about his/her learning or development)
- Family history (Has anyone in the family had a disability or learning problems?)
- Parent perceptions of strengths (Tell me about his/her strengths and interests. What is easy for him/her? What does he/she enjoy?)

- Family strengths and supports (see Beach Center Family Research Toolkit for some new measures)
- Adaptive Behavior Assessment (commonly used tools include the Vineland Adaptive Behavior Scales–II (Sparrow, Balla, & Cicchetti, 2005; the Adaptive Behavior Assessment System–Second Edition (Harrison & Oakland, 2003)
- Social-emotional development (utilize a parent report measure such as the *Ages and Stages Questionnaires-Social emotional* (Squires, Bricker, Twombly, Yockelson, Davis, & Schoen; 1995); *Temperament and Atypical Behavior Scale* (Neisworth, Bagnato. Salvia, & Hunt, 1999); *Vineland Social-Emotional Early Childhood* Scales (Sparrow, Balls, & Cicchetti, 1998); *Preschool Kindergarten Behavioral* Scales 2 (Merrell, 1994); *Social Skills Rating System* (Gresham & Elliott, 1990); *Achenbach System of Empirically Based Assessment [Child Behavior Checklist]* (Achenbach, 2001); *School Social Behavior Scales*, 2nd ed. (Merrell, 2002); *Devereux Behavior Rating Scale-School Form* (Naglieri, LeBuffe, & Pfeiffer, 1993).

Social workers can also help other professionals on the team to understand the role of culture in development. Very few teachers have received training in understanding cultural influences on learning and development. Some children may be inappropriately referred to special education due to their use of nonstandard English or behaviors that are inconsistent with the mainstream culture (e.g., avoiding eye contact with adults or those in authority).

Chaiya's story

Chaiya recently moved to PS 3. Chaiya's first-grade teacher suspected that Chaiya had an attention deficit. During independent work, Chaiya was frequently out of her seat going to help other children when her own work was not finished. Chaiya's teacher reported that she could not get Chaiya to stay focused on her. Chaiya would not make eye contact for more than a few seconds, even when the teacher demanded it. Chaiya's teacher said she was hesitant to impose consequences because Chaiya's mother had recently died, necessitating the family's move to the area. Mark, the social worker, reviewed Chaiya's school file and noted that Chaiya had attended a BIA Reservation school prior to her mother's death. Mark helped the teacher to understand the cultural differences and the effects of grieving on the learning process. He recommended that the teacher incorporate more cooperative learning and group projects.

Parental Input. Parents are entitled to participate in placement and programming decisions. The IDEA involves parents in the placement decisions. Even when the child has been made a ward of the state and placed in foster care, the IDEA 2004 requires that informed consent be obtained from the parents unless the court has ruled otherwise.

Parents have the right to an impartial hearing if they disagree with the final placement decision. If a parent does not agree to services, the school district may not provide them. The school district must obtain informed parental consent in writing prior to the formal evaluation of the child. Parents must also be informed about the multidisciplinary staff conference, which should be held at a time and place that allows parental participation. If necessary, school districts should assist parents to utilize the hearing process if they are not in agreement with their child's placement. The social worker can be instrumental in ensuring parental participation. The worker can make home visits to explain and clarify the nature of parental participation and its benefits. He or she can help foster collaboration among parents and school personnel. The social worker may also explain parental concerns to the educational staff before such concerns develop into problems. This liaison function is important in that it facilitates parental involvement in the education of their child and enables educators to be aware of family stressors that may compromise the success of some interventions, as well as alert the team to strategies that the family has found useful. Home and school are the major microsystems for the child. If both are working in synergy, everyone will benefit. Input from the social worker is particularly critical for the involvement of families who are not from the mainstream culture and who are marginalized in society (Harry, 1998; Harry, Allen, & McLaughlin, 1995; Harry, Kalyanpur, & Day, 1999).

Developing a posture of culture reciprocity (Harry, Kalyanpur, & Day, 1999; Kalyanpur & Harry, 1999) will help in forming partnerships with families. The steps involved in developing this posture include examining the cultural values that are implicit in your interpretation of the child's disability and the recommendations that you make, sharing your underlying assumptions with the family and discovering whether they value these assumptions, providing explicit respect for any cultural differences that you discover and explaining to the family the basis of your beliefs, and collaborating with the family in adapting your recommendations

to be more consistent with the value system of the family (Harry, Kalyanpur, & Day, 1999; Kalyanpur & Harry, 1999). Developing relationships with families will be discussed in the section on parent–professional relationships.

Due Process. Parents of children with disabilities must be given prior notice of preplacement evaluations. This notice must include an explanation of the procedural safeguards available to parents, a description of the proposed action and reasons for it, and a description of the evaluation procedures. Written consent from parents is also required before an evaluation can be made and before children can be placed in special education programs. Parents who disagree with the IEP can request a hearing if they have met with the local educational agency (LEA) and were unable to resolve the disagreement. Due to the high cost involved in litigation, the most recent amendments to the IDEA require that the parent and the LEA meet and attempt to solve the problem before a due process hearing can occur. IDEA 2004 also establishes a 2-year statute of limitations on the parents' ability to complain and a 90-day limitation on appeals. Hearing officers must decide cases based on FAPE rather than procedural errors. In prior legislation, the school district was responsible for legal costs involved in hearings. The IDEA 2004 provisions allow districts recover the costs of attorney fees from parents in cases of *frivolous* or unfounded complaints. In addition, the question of who bears the burden of proof in hearings (the LEA or the parent) was not clearly defined in the law and will be determined by litigation (National Council on Disability, 2005).

The social worker can inform the parents of their rights and prepare them for the process. He or she can act as an intermediary when there are misunderstandings between parents and school officials. The worker can arrange meetings between parents and the educational staff to facilitate further clarification. The social worker can also help locate informal supports (e.g., other parents who have struggled with similar challenges, parent advocates) who may assist and support the parent in problem solving and in their quest for appropriate services.

Least Restrictive Environment. To the maximum extent possible, children should have their educational needs met in natural environments (for infants and toddlers) and/or regular education programs. The LRE is often implemented through the practice of inclusion. Inclusion involves the openness of the school system to include *all* students, even those severely impaired, in general education by making accommodations, adaptations to the curriculum, and changes within the regular classroom. Advocates of inclusion argue for greater use of cooperative learning, peer tutoring, differentiated curriculum, and varied teaching strategies. However, without training for students in the social skills associated with these approaches, these techniques will fall short of their intended purposes. Currently, the LRE is not implemented equally across racial/ethnic groups (see Figure 7.2).

The social worker may assist with the transition plan between environments, assist regular education teachers in classroom behavior management and positive behavior interventions, help with teaching social skills, and support the collaboration process among administrators, teachers, paraprofessionals, and parents.

Kim's story

Kim was adopted at age 6 when she was in the first grade. Her early years were marked by severe neglect and suspected sexual abuse, followed by a series of homes as a preschooler. Kim was recommended for retention in the first grade due to great difficulty reading. Kim was very withdrawn in school. She was quiet and did not form friendships with the other children. She continued to struggle with school during her second year in first grade. Although Kim was exceedingly compliant and volunteered to help with any chore in the classroom, the teacher was also concerned about Kim's mood in school. Kim seldom smiled and still did not talk much with other children. In addition, the teacher suspected her of stealing food and other things from the other children in the class. The teacher requested a meeting with the school's Intervention Assistance Team to discuss how to help Kim.

With the parent's permission, the social worker met with Kim. She asked Kim to draw her some pictures. Kim began drawing very happy pictures with flowers and sunshine and offering them as gifts to the teacher and social worker. As the worker talked with Kim about the pictures, it became clear that Kim was concerned about upsetting the authority figures in her life. Her helpfulness and pictures were an attempt to keep the adults in her life happy and pleased with her. The social worker began to ask Kim to draw what she would like her day at school to be like and what a happy day would be for her. The drawings were used to enable Kim to communicate her dreams and later to communicate about the early abuse. Kim learned to read and write and continued to use a journal throughout her life as a means of dealing with depression.

Individualized Education Program (IEP). Every student identified as needing education services must have a written statement concerning his or her education that includes the present level of educational performance, annual goals, and specific educational and related services to be provided to the student, and the extent to which the student will be able to participate in regular curriculum and classroom. Prior to the 2004 revision, the IEP included short-term instructional objectives and benchmarks. As noted earlier, this was eliminated in an effort to reduce the burdens of paperwork for teachers. The IDEA 2004 only requires these benchmarks for children who take alternative assessments that are based on alternative standards. The IDEA 2004 also eliminated the requirement that parents of children with disabilities receive progress reports at least as often as parents of nondisabled children.

The appropriate education principle further requires that the education services benefit the student. Nonmedical-related services (such as social work) that are necessary for the provision of FAPE must be provided. When related services are all that are needed, they may be considered the special education services received.

When a child moves from one school district to another, the IDEA 2004 requires that the new district provide the child a FAPE in accord with the previous IEP until a new IEP is developed. When moving from one state to another, the IDEA requires a presumption of eligibility, and the IEP is to be implemented as closely as possible until the district evaluates eligibility. Additional changes to the IEP process in the IDEA 2004 include the provision for amending or modifying an IEP without convening an IEP meeting. A revised copy of the amended IEP will be provided to the parent upon request.

A more controversial change to the IEP in the IDEA 2004 is the proposal to allow up to 15 proposals from states to permit LEAs to develop multiyear (up to 3 years) IEPs, rather than annual IEPs. With written parental consent required, the multiyear IEP will include measurable goals and should be designed to enable the child to continue to make progress in the general education curriculum. The goals and current levels of performance are to be reviewed at natural transition points, at least once a year. Parents may request a review of the child's multiyear IEP. The intent of the multiyear IEP is to reduce paperwork, an area that is an issue for special educators (Study of Personnel Needs in Special Education, 2002). Concern about the effectiveness of multiyear IEPs led to the compromise of allowing only 15 proposals and monitoring effectiveness. It remains to be seen whether multiyear IEPs will maintain adequate attention to goals and whether it will indeed reduce paperwork burdens.

For children younger than age 3, an Individualized Family Service Plan (IFSP) describes the goals and services to be provided to the family. In recognition of the critical importance of the family to the child's development, the IFSP targets the provision of services that facilitate the family's ability to encourage further development of their child. Part C includes a wider range of services and more collaboration with other agencies.

Unlike Part B, in some states parents may be asked to pay for some services, often on a sliding fee scale.

At the multidisciplinary staff conference with the parents, the social worker can collaboratively discuss goals and recommendations and assist in the formulation of overall instructional goals. The worker can provide summaries of the child's cultural, family, and community life resources and identify additional resources for the family. The worker may specify the nature of the work with the student (casework, group work, family intervention, behavioral intervention) and how the outcome will be evaluated. The worker may also facilitate parental involvement in the IEP by explaining the process to the parents prior to the conference, helping them to identify their goals and concerns about their child, as well as the child's strengths and interests, and actively seeking their input during the conference.

Teachers may need assistance with developing social skills and adaptive behavior skills, particularly for learning-disabled and emotionally impaired children. The social worker may recommend and implement a social-emotional program (Kuche & Greenberg, 1995; McGinnis & Goldstein, 1997, 2003; Walker et al., 2004; Webster-Stratton, n.d.) or a positive behavioral intervention and supports system (www.pbis.org), or utilize a Circle of Friends or a similar program in facilitating social relationships for included children.

George's Story

Mr. Kamin came to the Child Study Team to discuss the problems he was having with George, a fourth grader. By the time classes started each day, George had already been involved in several fights—pushing or hitting other children as he came down the hall to the classroom. The students who had lockers next to George's tended to leave the area when they saw George arriving. Mr. Kamin said that he had changed lockers around so that the children on either side of George's locker were some of his most compliant students. Mr. Kamin commented that George "seemed to have so much anger" and "always has a bad attitude." He said that he had tried talking with George and disciplining him by keeping George's desk separated from the other students. None of the other students wanted to work with George anyway.

Mrs. Burke, the social worker, scheduled a morning to observe George's behavior. She watched George get off the bus. As the children approached the doorway, they began to crowd closer together. Whenever someone bumped into George, he would turn and shove them away or hit them. Before things escalated further, Mrs. Burke intervened and asked George to stand with her for a few minutes. George began defending his behavior, "He pushed me." George interpreted the jostling that occurred in narrow spaces as aggressive moves by his peers. Mrs. Burke asked George to watch with her for awhile. She pointed out that other students were also getting bumped when an area became crowded. When the number of students was dwindling, Mrs. Burke directed George to walk to his locker and said that she would meet him there in a minute. She watched him walk calmly down the hall to his locker without being bumped and without hitting or pushing anyone himself. She joined George at his locker and complimented him on walking so nicely to his locker keeping his hands to himself. George smiled at the compliment, but said that the other children in the hall were nice to him today "probably 'cause you were watching."

Mrs. Burke responded that she thought it was because there were not as many people in the hall and so they were not bumping into him. She made a plan to meet him when he got off the bus the next day, and they would watch the other students going in. Mrs. Burke again pointed out to George that other students were bumped. When the number of students dwindled enough, she again suggested to George that it was time to walk to his locker, but she would not be able to stay and watch. She said she would see him at lunchtime, and she turned and walked to her car. When she went to meet George for lunch, Mr. Kamin said that George had had the best morning ever. There had been no fighting at all that morning. Mrs. Burke shared that news with George and complimented him on his self-control. During

lunch together, they talked about how he managed to walk calmly to his locker and planned how he could do this every day. After school, Mrs. Burke met with Mr. Kamin and explained that George attributed aggressive intentions to students who bumped against him in crowded places. George would need help in attributing different intentions to peer actions. Mrs. Burke asked Mr. Kamin if he could recommend some children in the class who might provide a circle of friends for George. She would have lunch with the group of them in her counseling room once a week and help George to form positive relationships with some of his peers.

The social worker may assist in the development of behavioral contracts with children, do an ecobehavioral evaluation and plan, or identify other means of assisting with prevention and management of problem behaviors.

The social worker may also help the team to take a more strengths-based and solution-focused approach to designing an IEP, eliciting input from the teachers, parents, and students themselves in designing a program that utilizes the strengths and resources in the students' personal repertoire and ecosystem.

Early Intervention. Beginning with the amendments in P.L. 99-457, the IDEA is the most important legislation enacted for young children who are developmentally vulnerable (Richmond & Ayoub, 1993). This legislation calls for statewide, multidisciplinary, comprehensive, coordinated, interagency programs of early intervention for all infants and toddlers with disabilities and their families. Although these services are not mandated by law, all states have elected to participate in this program, referred to as Part C. Initially, services were required to be delivered by the highest-level professional, but the recent legislation allows for use of paraprofessionals in service delivery. In order to coordinate among agencies, each state appoints a lead agency. The lead agency for early intervention differs according to the state. Most states assigned either education (15 states) or health departments (20 states) as lead agencies

(Trohanis, 1994). Currently, more than 30 of the states involve the health department as at least one of the lead agencies (www.nectac.org/partc/ptclead .asp?text=1).

The IDEA operationalized the central role of the family through the use of IFSP in place of IEPs for this age group. Although programs have struggled with how to develop and implement IFSPs that are responsive to families, the lessons learned from the process itself have been helpful in increasing our understanding of how to provide comprehensive and coordinated interagency services to families.

The focus of intervention in the early years has shifted from child to family. Reviews of research about the effectiveness of early intervention (Guralnick, 1997a, 1997c) offer convincing evidence that early intervention produces important positive effects for children when programs identify and address the many stressors affecting families. The shift to family-centered care has been so successful in the early years that professionals are advocating its implementation in the preschool years and beyond. In reflecting on the chapters presented in his book, Guralnick asserted that the most important theme identified is that "the field of early intervention appears to be coalescing in *a systems* and *developmental* sense" (Guralnick, 1997b, p. v).

When a child has a disability or is at significant biological risk of developing a disability, families experience a variety of additional stressors, including interpersonal or family distress (e.g., redefinition of roles, realignment of family resources, possible changes in the family support system particularly when a stigma is attached to the disability, reassessment of long-term expectations and goals), increased need for information (e.g., about expected progress, medical and therapeutic interventions, identification of sources of information about disability or intervention approaches, about how to access and navigate the different community resources, advice on behavior management or assistance with parent–child interaction), need for additional resources (e.g., respite care, financial or insurance needs, sources for therapeutic

interventions and equipment), and parental concerns about their ability to fulfill primary caregiving roles. Family patterns of interactions including parent–child transactions (e.g., reciprocity, nonintrusive scaffolding) and family–community interactions (shopping, visiting friends, child-care arrangements), and family sense of control of child's experiences (developmentally appropriate toys and materials, level of structure in home environment, increased intrusion of professionals into family life) can be altered by the added stress. With an increase in the percentage of the families with children with special needs falling below the threshold for low income (Bowe, 1995; U.S. Department of Education, 2002), limited financial resources add to the stress of many of the families. In addition, some children are at additional risk due to environmental stressors such as parental mental illness, unrealistic child-rearing attitudes or beliefs, strained marital relationships, or lack of social supports. Although we have much to learn about the complex interactions of stressors, family characteristics, services, and developmental outcomes, we have already learned about the importance of attending to the stressors affecting families if we wish to effectively serve them (see Shonkoff & Phillips, 2000, and research briefs at www.developingchild.net for further discussion of what we now know about the connections among stressors, patterns of interaction, and child developmental outcomes). Provisions in the Child Abuse Prevention and Treatment Act (CAPTA, 2003) and the IDEA 2004 recognize the effects of abuse and neglect on children and require that infants and toddlers who have substantiated claims of abuse and neglect be referred to Part C for a developmental assessments (and services if they qualify).

Services to infants and toddlers include statewide, multidisciplinary, comprehensive, coordinated interagency programs of early intervention for all infants and toddlers with disabilities and their families. Some states elected to also serve high-risk populations. The IFSP epitomizes the increased emphasis placed on family involvement. Social workers may be case managers or primary interventionists, or they may provide supportive and consultative services. In some states, mental health, public health, or social services are the lead agency rather than education.

Transition Planning. Transition planning involves a coordinated set of activities designed to promote movement from school to postschool activities, including postsecondary education, vocational training, supported employment, integrated employment, independent living, community participation, leisure and recreational involvement, and continuing adult education.

Beginning with the 1997 amendments, the IDEA mentions social work as one of the services available for transition planning. Prior to the IDEA 2004, schools needed to consider issues around transition but were not held accountable for establishing or reaching clear goals for postschool. The IDEA 2004 requires that transition goals be set starting at age 16. The law stipulates involvement of the vocational rehabilitation agency in the transition planning. When leaving a secondary school, students with disabilities are to receive a summary of the transition plan and accomplishments. Social workers can be helpful in coordinating person-centered planning meetings, as well as helping students with setting goals and learning self-advocacy, self-determination, and socially responsible and adaptive behavior (Kaiser & Abell, 1997; Miner & Bates, 1997). The worker may be the liaison with the vocational rehabilitation agency and other community supports.

Related Services. Related services include transportation and developmental, corrective, and other supportive services required to assist a child in benefiting from special education, including audiology, speech therapy, physical therapy, occupational therapy, rehabilitative counseling, assertive technology, school health services, psychological services, and social work services.

As noted in the Introduction, social work services in the schools under the IDEA 2004 include

1. Preparing a social or developmental history on a child with a disability;
2. Group and individual counseling with the child and family;
3. Working with those problems in a child's living situation (home, school, and community) that affect the child's adjustment in school; and
4. Mobilizing school and community resources (for example, community recreation, financial resources for instructional technology, and home adaptations) to enable the child to learn as effectively as possible in his or her educational program (34 C.F.R. Section 300.16).

Section 504 Plans

Section 504 of the Rehabilitation Act of 1973, as amended 29 U. S. C. § 794 (Section 504), is a civil rights statute that prohibits discrimination against individuals with disabilities and provides that "No otherwise qualified individual with a disability in the United States . . . shall solely by reason of her or his disability be excluded from the participation in, be denied the benefits of, or be subjected to discrimination under any program or activity receiving Federal financial assistance . . ." Unlike IDEA which is a grant statute, Section 504 does not provide any type of funding. Some students who do not qualify for funding under IDEA are eligible for protection under Section 504. To be protected under Section 504, an individual needs to have an impairment that limits substantially a major life activity. These are defined as including "functions such as caring for one's self, performing manual tasks, walking, seeing, hearing, speaking, breathing, learning, and working" (34 C. F. R. 104.3(j)(2)(ii). Elementary and secondary schools are required to provide FAPE to students who qualify for protections under Section 504. However, students who use drugs illegally are excluded from the protection under section 504. If a student is eligible under IDEA, the IEP meets the requirements of Section 504, and a separate plan is not necessary. If a student is not eligible under IDEA, but is protected under Section 504, a Section 504 plan is developed to document the appropriate educational program for the student, including any accommodations, aids, or services that are needed to provide a student with a disability an equal opportunity to participate in the educational program. General education teachers are required by law to implement the provisions of Section 504 plans. Similar to an IEP, the school district is required to obtain parental consent for initial evaluations under Section 504, but the consent does not need to be in writing. A variety of sources such as assessments and professional reports are considered in determining eligibility for protection under Section 504. Placement decisions need to be made by a group of people such as doctors, therapists, and teachers, including someone knowledgeable about the student. If a school provides preschool education to typically developing children, the requirements of Section 504 apply also to preschoolers. Section 504 requires that private schools may not exclude students with disabilities if, with minor adjustments, they can provide an appropriate education.

Issues in Implementation

Renewed Attention to the Primacy of Emotional Development

The importance of mental health and the primacy of emotional development have received increased attention from researchers and policy makers (Raver, 2002; Shonkoff & Phillips, 2000). Mental illness is one of the most frequent causes of disability for individuals from ages 15 to 44 (Insel, 2005). Suicides are the cause of more deaths each year than either AIDS or homicide (Insel, 2005). Violence in schools has continued to be an additional concern (see Chapter 6 for more information). Programs have been designed to identify children with mental health problems at a younger age (Sugai et al., 2000; Walker et al., 1997) and to provide both prevention (Collaborative Dissemination for Prevention

Programs Group, n.d.; Devereaux Foundation, n.d; Domitrovich, Cortes, & Greenberg, 2007; Kuche & Greenberg, 1994) and intervention (Center for Social and Emotional Foundations for Early Learning, n.d.; Gettinger & Stoiber, 2006; Guralnick, Connor, Neville, & Hammond, 2006; Gray, n.d., 2000; Gray, White, & McAndrew, 2002; Knoff & Batsche, 2001; McGinnis & Goldstein, 1997, 2000; Walker et al., 1997, 1998; Webster-Stratton & Reid, 2006). In keeping with the NCLB, these programs are based on practices with a research base or have established their own research base. The *What Works Briefs* and the *Training Modules* at the Center on the Social and Emotional Foundations for Early Learning (n.d.) provide a good resource for social workers to use in training classroom teachers in how to support positive social and emotional development. These materials, including video clips, are available free of charge.

Jamal's story

Jamal was born at 28 weeks gestational age and experienced seizure and intraventricular hemorrhaging in the first 3 days of life. When assessed at 2 years of age, his IQ score was 52, and he was diagnosed with cerebral palsy. Despite these challenges and chronic ear infections, Jamal had a very nurturing home environment and a parent that advocated for him strongly. By the time that he was in middle school, Jamal was reading close to grade level and was included into some general education classrooms. He was able to walk independently, though his gait was not normal and he had poor balance. Jamal had great difficulty understanding social situations and responding appropriately. He did not interpret body language well and would often stand too close to other children. He began getting into fights at school. His mother immediately requested an IEP and asked for a social skills training program and the support of the social worker to help Jamal learn how to read body language and behave in different social situations.

Special Education Philosophy and Early Intervention

The philosophy guiding early intervention services is more consistent with the tenets of social work than many of the other services offered through special education. As special education evolved, the hope that this philosophy would guide the delivery of services in elementary and secondary schools has not been realized. With increased emphasis on accountability (meeting AYP) and the cognitive areas of development, the emphasis on K–12 has moved back toward a deficit view of disability and away from systems and strengths-based approaches.

The developmental domains have been the organizing principle for determining ability/disability. The entire labeling system attempts to classify students into homogenous groups so that services can be efficiently delivered. Typically, however, educational interventions for different categories of students have been more alike than different. Most effective programming utilizes the same principles and often the same procedures (intensive individual instruction, along with close monitoring and feedback), regardless of whether the student is classified as learning disabled, mildly mentally retarded, seriously emotionally disturbed, a slow learner, or educationally disadvantaged. (Reschly, 1996, p. 47). Research examining aptitude by treatment approaches has little empirical support. This includes approaches using disability categories, modality preferences, cognitive processing, learning styles, and neuropsychologically intact areas (Reschly, 1996).

Our placement of children into categories of disability assumes an underlying attribution of the problem as something inherent in the individual child. Research has attempted to find the cause of different disabilities (to prevent recurrence) and to develop appropriate remediations or compensatory strategies when remediation was not possible. This view of disability has been helpful in identifying and preventing further incidences of a number of disabilities, for example, identifying the effects of alcohol on the fetus, identifying the connection between folic acid deficiencies in early pregnancy and spina bifida. However, it is not a helpful paradigm for increasing our understanding of how to help children with the challenges they have.

Unlike the services offered in the school-age population, early intervention embraces family-generated goals and needs, includes recognition of the child and family strengths, views parents as planners and participants, and evaluates family outcomes, as well as developmental skills and milestones. Some theorists in early intervention propose a new paradigm that moves from development to the centrality of relationship as the organizing principle. Under this new paradigm, relationship is viewed as the organizer of development, and family–provider relationships form the medium for the intervention process. Intervention involves a flexible blending of discipline-specific (e.g., education, occupational therapy, physical therapy, audiology) and nondiscipline-specific relationship and process issues. Outcomes focus on parent–child interaction, family functioning, child adaptive capacities, and parent understanding, confidence, and satisfaction (Weston, Ivins, Heffron, & Sweet, 1997). Relationship as the organizer in development is gaining increasing support in research examining brain development, resilience, and infant mental health (Greenspan, 1997; National Scientific Council on the Developing Child, 2004; Shore, 1997; Sroufe, 1996). Social workers are uniquely suited to helping early intervention teams and educators to focus more on relationships.

Functional Behavioral Assessment

Beginning with the 1997 amendments, the IDEA requires that *when* a student's behavior impedes learning—his or her own or that of other students—the IEP team should consider positive behavioral strategies to address the negative behaviors before they reoccur. Many districts address this requirement by developing Functional Behavioral Assessments. These assessments attempt to understand why a student behaves in a certain way by examining both the antecedents to the behavior and the consequences that may be reinforcing the behavior. The steps in completing a functional behavioral assessment include (a) identifying the behavior(s) most in need of change, (b) identifying the context in which the behavior occurs and what contexts may contribute to the behavior, (c) collecting data on the student's behavior from a variety of sources to determine the function of the behavior and any contributing factors, (d) developing a hypothesis about the function of the behavior and where and why it is most likely to occur, (e) identifying alternative behaviors that can serve the same function more appropriately and can be taught to the student, (f) trying out the behavioral intervention plan, and (g) evaluating the success of the behavioral intervention (Jordan, 2001). The intervention plan may include teaching the student appropriate social skills, changing the environment to support positive behaviors (e.g., reducing clutter or noise, redirecting traffic patterns), providing a means for the student to meet their needs in a more positive manner, and providing reinforcement and support for the student to utilize the appropriate behaviors (e.g., preventive cueing reminding a child to use appropriate behaviors; Jordan, 2001). Social workers may be called on to help develop the functional behavioral plan, to help collect data on the student's behaviors, to recommend behavioral intervention strategies, to teach social skills and strategies to the student, and/or to provide support for the student as part of the behavior intervention plan. Social workers may also help in selecting and implementing a schoolwide positive behavioral intervention system to prevent problem behaviors before they get to the point that they impede learning.

Discipline

Despite much debate in the negotiation of the 2004 legislation, 1997 amendments on discipline were retained in the IDEA 2004. The law allows school personnel to order a change in the placement of a child with a disability to an appropriate interim alternative education setting (IAES), a change to another setting, or suspension for up to 10 days in any school year (to the extent such an alternative might be applied to children without disabilities). A child who carries a weapon to school or a school function, or who is involved in possession, use, or solicitation or sale of a controlled substance at school or a school function, or who has committed serious bodily injury can be assigned to an IAES without a hearing officer ruling for the same amount of time a child without a disability would be subject to discipline, up to 45 school days, but would continue to receive services. The legislation further requires that, either before or within 10 days of disciplinary action, an IEP meeting be convened to develop an assessment plan to address the problem behavior (if a functional behavior assessment has not already taken place and a behavior intervention plan implemented); or if the student already has a behavior implementation plan, the IEP team will review the plan and modify it as necessary to address the behavior. The IEP team will review the relationship between the child's disability and the behavior subject to disciplinary action (manifestation determination review) and whether the behavior was the direct result of the LEA's failure to implement the IEP. If the behavior was not a manifestation of the child's disability, the same disciplinary procedures that would be applied to a child without a disability may be utilized, with the exception that the child will continue (in whatever setting) to receive a FAPE. To determine that the misbehavior is not a manifestation of the disability, the team must decide (a) that the child's IEP and placement were appropriate; (b) that supplementary aids, services, and behavior intervention strategies were provided according to the IEP; and (c) that the child's disability did not impair the ability of the child to understand the impact and consequences of the behavior or to control the behavior. The law places the burden on the parent to appeal change of placement decisions when they disagree about the determination that the misbehavior was not a manifestation of the disability. An educational agency may report a crime committed by a child with a disability, but must ensure that copies of special education and disciplinary records of the child are sent for consideration by the authorities.

Placement may be changed to an IAES for not more than 45 school days by order of a hearing officer if the officer determines that the public agency has substantial evidence to support an argument that current placement will likely result in harm to the child or others and the agency has already made reasonable efforts to minimize risk of harm in the current placement (including the use of supplementary aids and services). The officer must also consider the appropriateness of the current placement and determine whether the IAES meets the requirements. The IAES must be determined by the IEP team and selected to enable the child to continue to participate in the general curriculum and to receive services and modifications that assist the child in meeting the goals of the IEP, and it must include services and modifications designed to address the problem behavior.

Despite these provisions, the National Longitudinal Transition Study (Wagner, Newman, Cameto, & Levine, 2005) found that more than half of the recent cohort of youth with disabilities had experienced disciplinary actions or other negative consequences for their behavior, compared to only one third of the 1993 cohort of students. In the 2004 to 2005 school year, more than 65 thousand students with disabilities were suspended from school for more than 10 days in the school year. Almost half (47.5%) of those students are black (non-Hispanic).

Fayette's story

P.S. 27 had a high incidence of emotional impairments, bullying, and violence. Spurred by the option of using some of their IDEA funds for preventative programs, the school decided to implement a prevention program. Fayette, the social worker, was assigned the task of investigating and making recommendations about the Fast-Track (Conduct Problems Prevention Research Group, 1992, 2004), First Step to Success (Walker et al., 2004), Skillstreaming (McGinnis & Goldstein, 1997, 2003), and the OSEP-funded programs (Collaborative Dissemination for Prevention Programs Group, n.d.).

Accountability

The standards movement in education and the move to high-stakes testing for schools affected not only general education, but also the delivery and evaluation of special education. In the last century, the monitoring process for the IDEA focused on compliance with procedures rather than positive outcomes for children. McLaughlin (2002) argued that, until recent years, most special education legislation developed relatively independent of the general education and called for a more cohesive policy. Until the turn of the century, students with special education needs were excluded from program evaluation testing. This resulted in schools being evaluated only on children who did not struggle to learn. It encouraged overidentification of low-performing students. The momentum from the standards and accountability movements changed the focus of parents, advocates, and legislators from the identification of special needs and provision of programs to evaluation of educational results. The NCLB Act requires that all but the most severely impaired students be included in statewide assessment programs. Accommodations are allowed for students who require them according to state-developed guidelines. For those students who experience severe impairments, alternative assessments may be used if recommended by the IEP, but the IEP must then include benchmarks and short-term objectives. The alternative assessments must be "aligned with the state's challenging student academic achievement standards and if the state has adopted alternate academic achievement standards permitted under the [NCLB] regulations, measure the achievement of children with disabilities against those standards" (IDEA, 2004). The 1997 and 2004 amendments to the IDEA aligned with NCLB and changed the focus of accountability to results. Advocates of this change assert that this entails a shift to a higher standard than the "educational benefit" standard endorsed in the Rowley decision (Palmaffy, 2001). However, some advocates consider the application of the general curriculum to all students (rather than the individualized curricula encouraged by the original legislation) a death knell for special education (Lieberman, 2001). The IDEA 2004 recognizes the need to address *functional* goals as well as academic goals, but it is not clear how districts will interpret that when the pressure to achieve AYP for students is so strong and the stakes for districts are high. Districts and states are struggling to meet AYP for students with disabilities.

The accountability efforts surrounding higher standards also represent a cause for concern (Lieberman, 2001; McDonnell, McLaughlin, Morison, et al., 1997). With the application of high stakes to the performance of individual students, assurances are needed that those students are given the opportunity to acquire the skills and knowledge that is expected. The current testing and measurement system addresses the higher end of the continuum, but does not assess well the progress of children who struggle (McDonnell et al., 1997). One encouraging aspect of the alignment of the IDEA and the NCLB is the increased attention to prevention, early intervention, and an emphasis on response to research-based interventions (RTI) as a criterion for evaluating eligibility. However, this does not address the needs of students who have more severe disabilities.

By definition, children who qualify for the IDEA have difficulty learning. Expecting this subgroup to make AYP penalizes areas that have a higher concentration of children with disabilities. The link between poverty and disability is well documented (Shonkoff & Phillips, 2000; Sherman, 1997). As poor urban areas with high incidences of children with disabilities struggle to

ensure that students can *pass the test,* the curriculum offered to children is increasingly focused on memorization skills that can be assessed easily by multiple-choice tests, even though NCLB requires that higher-order thinking skills also be addressed. The NCLB focused initially on literacy and mathematics. Science may soon be added to the areas included in the AYP reports. Sanctions are imposed on schools that do not meet AYP so, in many schools, the majority of the school day is devoted to explicitly addressing the content that will be assessed. Opportunities for students to experience the arts, physical education, and even social studies are becoming more limited, especially in low-income areas. Elementary classrooms in areas of higher SES with lower concentration of minorities and with fewer children with disabilities typically have longer school days with more exposure to the arts, physical education, and social opportunities (Allington, 2005; Roth, Brooks-Gunn, Linver, & Hofferth, 2003).

The National Research Council cautions that unintended consequences may occur from the implementation of high standards and accountability procedures. They advise that parents of students with disabilities be given information that allows them to make informed choices about their child's participation in standards-based reform and the potential consequences (McDonnell et al., 1997). Parents are again encouraged to be the primary regulators. This is problematic for many economically disadvantaged and minority families (McDonnell et al., 1997). Advocacy takes time, energy, knowledge of the law and regulations, and assertion in communication. For some families, just meeting the demands of daily life is already burdensome. The addition of an advocacy role is not feasible. Social workers may need to be the voice of these families.

Minority Representation in Special Education

African-American students are disproportionately overrepresented and Hispanic students underrepresented in special education. Among school-age students, more Black students than White students are labeled as having mental retardation (U.S. Department of Education, 2008).

The IDEA 2004 has provisions that require each state to examine data to determine if there is significant disproportionality of race in the identification of children with disabilities or in the placement of children. When such disproportionality occurs, the state must provide for review and, as necessary, revision of policy and practices. Black students are overrepresented in the special education categories most directly related to school performance: mental retardation and emotional impairment. Some of this overrepresentation may be explained by the effects of poverty. Minority children are disproportionately poor, and poverty is associated with lower birth weight, greater exposure to harmful toxins early in development, and fewer environmental supports for learning (Donovan et al., 2002). More persistent poverty increases the number of risk factors for child development. More than three risk factors early in life affects the development of the brain (Shonkoff, 2008). In addition, schools in areas of high poverty are less likely to have experienced, well-educated teachers (Westat, 2002) and more likely to have shorter school days (Roth et al., 2003).

Despite the higher risks associated with poverty, black children are not overrepresented in the low incidence disability categories (e.g., physical and sensory impairments; Donovan, Cross, & Committee on Minority Representation in Special Education, 2002; U.S. Department of Education, 2002). Is the higher incidence of mental retardation and emotional impairments truly disability or societal failure to care for the well-being of children? Inequities in background knowledge are already evident when children arrive in kindergarten (Bowman, Donovan, & Burns, 2001; Lee & Burkham, 2002; West, Denton, & Germino-Hausken, 2000), but instead of decreasing once schooling begins, those gaps increase over time. The higher proportion of identified children among minority populations would be less troubling if identification of a disability brought adequate supports to enable the children to be successful in school. Unfortunately, no evidence is available to support such a statement. Schools in areas that are likely to serve large percentages of minority children are usually in poor urban areas. The Study of Personnel Needs in Special Education (SPeNSE) documented a greater shortage of trained special educators in schools that were urban or in higher poverty areas (SPeNSE, 2002). Children identified with disabilities who are Black are more likely than their White counterparts to spend the majority of their school day in a segregated setting. The NCLB and IDEA 2004 legislative mandates for early intervening, monitoring results, use of RTI, and ensuring highly qualified teachers are intended to try to address inequities. However, concern has been voiced that the RTI has not been researched adequately over time to be able to clearly define methods, and the impact on children from diverse backgrounds has not yet been investigated (Council for Exceptional Children, 2004). IDEA 2004 requires that states continue to monitor the proportionality by race/ethnicity of children by impairment category. The NCLB also requires that states examine AYP by subgroups to ensure that all children benefit. We should not assign potentially stigmatizing labels to students who would benefit more by remaining in the regular education classroom. As much as possible, attention should be paid to supporting the general education program to meet the needs of all children, rather than sort and label children to provide specialized services outside the mainstream.

Social workers can advocate for children particularly in high poverty areas. Social workers serve as members of the prereferral teams and can recommend different approaches to supporting the positive behavior and development of the child in the classroom. Social workers can communicate with families about how they might support children at home. Social workers can also help teachers understand the cultural differences that may lead to problems for students. As noted earlier, social workers can recommend and implement schoolwide PBIS and social-emotional curricula that will support more positive behavior and opportunity to learn for all children.

Research in Special Education

In an effort to gain more information about the outcomes of special education, the Center for Special Education Research in the Institute for Education Sciences (IES) has funded longitudinal studies designed to document the services provided to children with disabilities and the academic and social performance of children receiving these services. These studies were initiated under the auspices of the Office of Special Education programs, but the IDEA 2004 moved research on individuals with disabilities to the IES and created a center dedicated to special education research within the IES. The longitudinal studies are designed to capture information from birth through postsecondary outcomes. The National Early Intervention Study (NEILS) collected information on more than 3,300 children receiving services through Part C of IDEA. The study began in September 1997 and concluded with the collection of follow-up data when the children were 5 to 7 years old in 2006. The PreElementary Education Longitudinal Study (PEELS) is a 7-year study that began data collection in 2003 and follows children from preschool through early elementary school. The Special Education Elementary Longitudinal Study (SEELS) began collecting data in 1999 on approximately 13,000 elementary and early middle school students and followed them until 2008. The National Longitudinal Transition Study-2 (NLTS2) is a 10-year study of approximately 13,000 students as they transition from secondary schools into adulthood. It will describe the characteristics of the students and their families, their school programs, related services, extracurricular activities, postsecondary services received, and the outcomes of all these experiences, including academic, social, and vocational accomplishments.

The initial results of this study have already begun to inform public policy (U.S. Department of Education, 2002; Wagner et al., 2005).

Preschool Inclusion

Services to children from birth to 5 years old have evidenced the most change in the last decade. Americans with Disabilities Act (ADA, P.L. 101-336) bars discrimination against individuals on the basis of disability. ADA requires child-care facilities and nursery schools to be accessible to children with disabilities unless "undue burden" or "direct threat to health/ safety" can be substantiated (Americans with Disabilities Act, 1990) (42 U.S.C. 12101-12213). The issues of "undue burden" and "threat to health/safety" have begun to be tested in the courts. If the struggles to include children with special needs in public schools are mirrored in the preschool population, then medically fragile children and children with behavioral problems will encounter more difficulty in inclusion than other children (Craig & Haggart, 1994). With the increase in the number of state preschool programs (Barnett et al., 2008), opportunities for preschool inclusion are more numerous. However, research indicates that preschoolers are expelled at a rate more than three times the expulsion rate found in elementary schools (Gilliam, 2005). Helping families in advocating for their children by increasing community awareness of the benefits of inclusion, helping with transitions, and offering ongoing support for placements are roles that may be assumed by social workers, particularly for children with social–emotional and behavioral difficulties or environmental challenges.

Inclusion in preschool programs and community child care offers many potential advantages for children with special needs and their families:

- Relief from caregiving responsibilities.
- Possibility of increased social support through contact with other families with young children.

Community child care represents one of the social support networks for families of young children.

■ Redefinition of child behaviors. If the parents have not had much experience with young children, they may not be aware of the spectrum of behaviors that fall within the range of normal development. Observation of other children in care may help them to recognize that many behaviors exhibited by their child are typical behaviors for young children and help them to focus on the child rather than the disability. Alternatively, if the child's abilities are markedly delayed, observation of other children in care might lead parents to experience increased grief and sorrow.

■ Development of cognitive and language skills. Interaction with other children could increase the child's abilities in areas important to the parent. Children are often great imitators of other children.

■ Opportunity for the child to develop social and peer-interaction skills. This may be dependent on the skills of the teacher or child-care provider. Research with preschoolers has demonstrated that when teachers/caregivers scaffold social skills, children increase their use of social strategies. However, it has also been noted that many early childhood teachers devote the majority of their attention to cognitive and academic areas of development, neglecting the social aspects.

■ Providing an outlet for mastery for parent. If a child is not making progress developmentally, some parents cope by seeking mastery in other areas. Child care would allot parents time to develop such mastery (File & Kontos, 1992).

These advantages depend on the availability of high-quality care for these young children. As noted in Chapters 1 and 8, quality of care is a problem for even typically developing infants and toddlers receiving care in centers. Poor child care represents a risk factor for children—one that

children already identified with special needs can ill afford.

Ecological perspectives of child development emphasize the importance of the interplay among the different systems surrounding the child (see Chapter 4). Those systems closest to the child (microsystems) and the relationships among these systems (mesosystems) have the strongest direct effect on development (Garbarino, 1990). "The quality of a microsystem depends upon its ability to sustain and enhance development and to provide a context that is emotionally validating and developmentally challenging" (Garbarino, 1990, p. 81). The home environment, especially parent–child interactions, the child care or preschool environment, and the early intervention interactions constitute major microsystems in the lives of young children with disabilities.

Angie's story

Angie taught a preschool special education classroom. She came into the teacher's lounge one day very angry about the mother of one of the children in her classroom. The parent did not bring in an extra set of clothes for her child. The extra change of clothes was typical for early childhood classrooms and designed to be used for spills and accidents that might occur with young children. This child's mother had been asked repeatedly to bring in the clothes. The child spent a lot of the day in either child care, Head Start, or the preschool classroom for children with special needs. His mother worked long hours at McDonald's. The day came when the child had an accident and needed to be changed in the middle of the school day. The teacher went to the classroom closet for the extra clothing. The only pair of pants that fit the child had a rip in the knee. At the end of the day, the teacher received a call from the mother, who was absolutely irate that her child came home in a pair of pants that were ripped. Maria, the social worker, who worked in the classroom, explained to Angie the realities that the mother was dealing with, the possible reasons for the mother's anger, and alternative ways that Angie could address the problem. Maria also obtained a list of resources for Angie to include for all the families in the next class newsletter.

Parent–Professional Relationships and Collaboration

Researchers focusing on parent–professional relationships have emphasized family-centered principles and the development of partnerships that enable or empower parents. Partnerships between parents and professionals that are empowering are purported to reduce stress and increase functioning of families (Dunst, Trivette, & Deal, 1994b). Good partnerships are most often characterized as involving trust and open, honest communication among partners; active listening; reciprocity; mutually agreed goals; flexibility; openness; caring; understanding; shared responsibility; mutual support and respect; strengths-based, proactive, solution-focused stance; future orientation; and enabling competence (Dinnebeil, Hale, & Rule, 1996; Dunst, Trivette, & Deal, 1994a, 1994b; Turnbull & Turnbull, 1996). Respect for cultural diversity is implicit in these partnerships. The knowledge and expertise of the family needs to be respected on an equal footing with the expertise that professionals bring to the table (Turnbull, Turnbull, Shank, & Smith, 2004).

With the strong focus on the family in Part C of IDEA, early intervention and early childhood has led the field in new approaches to collaborating with families. Attention is being given to training personnel in coaching and consultation using models that involve collaborations rather than hierarchical relationships (Hanft, Rush, & Shelden, 2004), and that are respectful of the family culture (Harry, Kalyanpur, & Day, 1999; Kalyanpur & Harry, 1999; Lynch & Hanson, 1998). These approaches have also been applied to collaboration with preschool and general education teachers.

Empowering partnerships with parents are guided by a philosophy that emphasizes

a. recognizing and strengthening of child and family capabilities using a proactive rather than a deficit approach,
b. enabling and empowering parents with the necessary knowledge, skills, and resources needed to perform family and parenting functions in a competent manner, by
c. using partnerships between parents and professionals as the means to strengthen, enable, and empower families (Dunst, Trivette, & Thompson, 1994, p. 209).

Zeanah and McDonough (1989) outlined practice principles for forming a working alliance with families: (a) sensitivity to the family's unique situation; (b) assigning a positive connotation to parent and child behavior; (c) sensitivity and responsivity to the family's needs (information content is less important than the sharing process and how intervention is delivered, e.g., physical accessibility, emotional availability); (d) nonjudgmental attitude (accept and show respect for the parents' current adaptation, "even as we entertain the possibility that the parents can acquire new ways of thinking, behaving, feeling, and coping in the future" (p. 520); and (e) willingness to monitor intense feelings aroused by the family (impatience, aversion, rescue, burden—may mean overinvolvement, i.e., working too hard to impose your agenda on the family or an inappropriate role with the family).

Waters and Lawrence (1993) advocated a competence approach to family intervention. Their framework is useful to collaboration as well. They define competence as encompassing an inborn striving for mastery and growth. In congruence with the Turnbulls (Turnbull, 1994; Turnbull & Turnbull, 1996), they advocate developing visions, which they distinguish as a mind-set moving toward mastery and belonging, rather than some "castle in the air" (p. 107). Less focus is placed on a single vision and more on the envisioning process. To proceed toward a vision, one needs courage. Waters and Lawrence are clear about stating that the "road to courage is paved with competence, not just challenge" (p. 107). The professional's role involves encouraging the individual by helping him or her to identify and develop competencies as well as develop a vision to move toward.

Conclusion

An overall evaluation of current special education services recognizes that large gains have been made in the provision of services to children with disabilities and in the availability of services to a broader group of children. The laws are attempting to encourage more preventative programming and to foster more inclusion of children with disabilities. Awareness of the inequities of services is heightened. Schools are being held accountable for results. However, threats to special education services abound. The rising cost of delivering special education services continues to be a grave concern. The application of general education curriculum standards may place such a heavy emphasis on academics that some children with disabilities will not gain the adaptive behavior and social skills that are necessary for positive life outcomes. Current sentiment regarding students who become discipline problems may threaten access to free and appropriate education for students, particularly those who experience social and emotional disabilities. The increased percentage of students who have been suspended is troubling. The number of special education teachers graduating each year is insufficient to meet the needs of schools and children. Vacancies are filled with teachers who are not trained to work with the students whom they serve. General education teachers are asked to provide instruction to students with disabilities, often with no supports and with no training in how to meet these students' needs. Although the NCLB

and the IDEA 2004 call for a highly qualified teacher in every classroom, it is not clear where districts will find those teachers. Special education teachers are asked to provide consultative support for students, though they may have never been taught about consultation models or how best to approach the task of consultation. Families are burdened with the job of monitoring their child's educational programming. For families already burdened by multiple stressors, this task is more than they can handle. With an increased percentage of children with disabilities in poverty (U.S. Department of Education, 2002), there is greater likelihood that families will need support in navigating the special education system. More and more children with health problems are surviving and being served in special or general education (U.S. Department of Education, 2008), but they need the support of the health and medical profession to enable participation. Strong collaboration and interdisciplinary educational preparation is necessary to enhance the provision of services to children and families.

Implications for Social Workers

The social work literature reveals that since the passage of P.L. 94-142, the roles and tasks of school social workers have expanded to assist children with disabilities. For example, besides participation in the multidisciplinary team conferences and consultation, social workers coordinate IEP and IFSP conferences, serve as trained mediators, act as advocates, lead parent education and informational groups, function as case managers, and facilitate the development of relationships that link the services of the school with those found in the community.

However, to function in the public school and to serve this target population, a social worker must stay informed about legislation and litigation that affect the school and other service providers' responsibility to this group as well as their roles and those of others. Social workers will need to be advocates for many of the children and their families.

The school social worker will need specialized knowledge in human development, disabilities, positive behavior interventions, case management, evaluation of outcomes, how to work across disciplines, and how to link services and build support systems for families (because the number of agencies that could become involved with the population continues to grow), and as stated earlier, knowledge of special education litigation and legislation. In the chapter on the

history of social work (Chapter 2), it is made clear that since our beginnings, we have served as the liaison/link between school and home/community.

The social work profession is founded on democratic and humanitarian ideals. It is committed to protecting the right of individuality, self-respect, and the opportunity for development, without discrimination. Legislation that grants children and youths the right to an appropriate education in the least restrictive environment is consistent with these ideals.

For Study and Discussion

1. Read "Understanding the differences between IDEA and Section 504" (deBettencourt, 2002) or the Department of Education's explanation of Section 504 (http://www.ed.gov/about/offices/list/ocr/504faq.html) and create a presentation of the important points discussed and how they apply to social workers.

2. Learn more about conducting a Functional Behavioral Analysis by visiting http://cecp.air.org/fba/default.asp

3. The Center for Effective Collaboration and Practice (CECP) offers a series of monographs addressing the challenges of serving children with special needs. CECP is focused on improving the services to children with emotional and behavioral problems. Review some of the articles and topics such as learning from families, promising practices in early childhood mental health, and wraparound stories from the field by visiting the Web site http://cecp.air.org/promisingpractices/default.asp

4. Read "Eliminating Ableism in Education" by Thomas Hehir (2002). Identify ways in which ableism is manifested and interferes with the education of children with physical, emotional, and mental impairments. Retrieved October 5, 2008 from http://www.hepg.org/her/abstract/64

5. Analyze your state's rules and regulations governing special education programs and services. What are the implications for social work tasks and services? What changes need to be made to enable students with disabilities?

6. Interview the parents of students in a classroom that includes students with moderate to severe disabilities. What are the advantages and disadvantages perceived by parents of typically developing students? What are the advantages and disadvantages perceived by parents of the students with disabilities?

7. Visit the Technical Assistance Center on Social Emotional Intervention for Young Children, also known as TACSEI, at http://www.challengingbehavior.org/ and learn about positive behavior support and other evidence-based strategies for supporting social and emotional development. This five-year grant is made possible by the U.S. Department of Education, Office of Special Education Programs.

8. Visit a program designed to assist infants and toddlers with disabilities. Find out what services are typically provided to families of children with differing disabilities. Ascertain how these services are incorporated into the Individualized Family Service Plan and what roles, if any, are carried out by the school social worker.

9. Talk with teachers who have children with disabilities included in their classrooms. From a teacher's perspective, what are the challenges to providing appropriate education for all the children in their class?

10. Programs have been designed to prevent social and emotional problems in schools. Visit the Web site http://cecp.air.org/preventionstrategies/Default.htm to compare information about the

OSEP-funded prevention programs: Achieving Behaving Caring (ABC) Program, Behavior Prevention Program, Conflict Resolution/Peer Mediation Program, Improving the Lives of Children, Linkages to Learning Program, and Project Success.

11. Learn more about the various disability categories and ways to assist students with disabilities by visiting the Web sites for the National Clearinghouse for Children and Youth with Disabilities <www.nichcy.org/>, IDEA Practices, funded by the U.S. Office of Special Education Programs, <www.ideapractices.org/>, or the Educational Resources Information Center (ERIC) digests available on the Department of Education Web site www.eric.ed.gov

12. Explore the most recent findings of the OSEP-funded longitudinal studies of children with disabilities: NEILS <www.sri.com/neils/>, PEELS <www.peels.org/>; SEELS <www.seels.net/>, NLTS-2. http://www.nlts2.org/

13. Parents share their struggles and success stories online. Visit some of the following Web sites and read the stories written by parents to increase your understanding of the joys and challenges of parenting children with disabilities (Retrieved September 1, 2005): www.fathersnetwork.org/.

http://www.specialchild.com/index.html, http://tell-us-your-story.com/ (use the search term "parent").

14. Family Village sponsored by the Waisman Center is one of the top-rated resources available to families. Browse the Web site to see the types of resources available for parents (Retrieved October 5, 2008): http://www.familyvillage.wisc.edu/

15. To understand more about teens with disabilities, visit Web sites in which they tell their stories such as viewing parts of the video *What's Normal?: Overcoming Obstacles and Stereotypes* on the PBS Web site (Retrieved October 5, 2008): http://www.pbs.org/inthemix/shows/show_whatsnormal.html

16. View the parent guides and resources for understanding IEPs and participating in IEP meetings. See the links included in the NICHY Web site: http://www.nichcy.org/EducateChildren/IEP/Pages/overview.aspx

17. It is critical to intervene early when children are showing signs of autism or pervasive developmental disorders. Learn more about this disability area and examine different screening tools for early identification of children with autism. Visit http://www.ninds.nih.gov/disorders/autism/detail_autism.htm and http://www.firstsigns.org/screening/tools/rec.htm

Additional Readings

Atkins-Burnett, S., & Allen-Meares, P. (2000). Infants and toddlers with disabilities: Relationship-based approaches. *Social Work, 45*(4), 371–379.

Center for Effective Collaboration and Practice (1998). *Addressing student problem behavior-Part II: Conducting a functional behavioral assessment.* Washington, DC: Authors.

Center on the Social and Emotional Foundations for Early Learning. (n.d.). *Training modules.* Retrieved October 17, 2008, from http://www.vanderbilt.edu/csefel/modules.html

Fecser, F. A., & Long, N. J. (1998). *Life space crisis intervention.* Retrieved September 5, 2005, from http://cecp.air.org/interact/authoronline/april98/1.htm.

Gettinger, M. & Stoiber, K. C. (2006). Functional assessment, collaboration and evidence-based treatment: Analysis of a team approach for addressing challenging behaviors in young children. *Journal of School Psychology, 44*(3), 231–252.

Guralnick, M. J., Connor, R. T., Neville, B., & Hammond, M. A. (2006). Promoting the peer-related social development of young children with mild developmental delays: Effectiveness of a comprehensive intervention. *American Journal on Mental Retardation, 111*(5), 336–356

Gorman, S. (2001). Navigating the special education maze: Experiences of four families. In C. E. Finn, A. J. Rotherham, & C. R. Hokanson, Jr. (Eds.), *Rethinking special education for a new century* (pp. 233–257). Dayton, OH: Thomas B. Fordham Foundation and the Progressive Policy Institute. Retrieved October 19, 2008, from http://www.edexcellence.net/doc/special_ed_final.pdf

Hanft, B. E., Rush, D. D., & Shelden, M. L. (2004). *Coaching families and colleagues in early childhood.* Baltimore: Paul H. Brookes.

National Council on Disability. (2005, August 9). *Schaffer v. Weast pending in the Supreme of the United States: Position statement.* Washington, DC: Author.

Retrieved September 5, 2005, from www.ncd.gov/newsroom/publications/2005/burdenofproo£htm

Roncker v. Walters. (1983). 700 F 2d 1058 (6th Circuit 1983), cert. den. 464 U.S.864, 1045. Ct. 196, 78 L. Ed. 2d 171.

Silverstein, R. (2005). A *user's guide to the 2004 IDEA reauthorization (P.L. 108–446 and the conference report).* Washington, DC: Consortium for Citizens with Disabilities. Retrieved June 1, 2005, from www.cec.sped.org/pp/IDEA120204.pdf

U.S. Department of Education. (July, 1997). *The inclusion of students with disabilities and limited English proficient students in large-scale assessments. A summary of recent progress.* National Center for Education Statistics, Doc\#97-482. Washington, DC: Author.

Wagner, M. (1995). Outcomes for youths with serious emotional disturbance in secondary school and early adulthood. *The Future of Children, 5*(2), 90–112.

8

Some Target Groups of Children

PAULA ALLEN-MEARES

University of Illinois at Chicago

America's future will be determined by the home and the school. The child becomes largely what he is taught; hence we must watch what we teach, and how we live.

—Jane Addams, social worker and founder of Hull House

The failure of a person to display competencies is due not to deficits within a person, but to the failure of social systems to provide opportunities for competencies to be acquired or displayed. When new competencies are needed, the optimal way of providing them is through experiences that allow people to make positive self-attributions regarding their ability to influence important life events.

—Rappaport, 1981[1]

What do you love about these people? It is often the key to finding a way in to a level of collaboration that can make a difference. If the answer is nothing, then we are not joined with them. We do not have enough appreciation of how they came by their problems honestly and we do not see past those problems to their strengths. We believe that every problem has a caring side but that side will remain imperceptible until one finds a way to care about the person.

—Waters and Lawrence, 1993, p. 117[2]

Introduction

School social workers play a variety of roles in relation to different target groups of pupils. First and most important is the identification of pupils who are at risk of school failure or experiencing difficulty in learning and meeting school requirements. Their vulnerability may be attributed to numerous factors: their stage of psychosocial development and approaching developmental transition, a unique characteristic (such as their minority status, family background, or poverty); academic ability or the lack thereof, and an inability to behave according to school policies and expectations. A part of the role identifying these children is assessing the quality of transactions between the students, the family, the school, and the community. Are school policies and practices fair? Does staff provide equal support and assistance to these groups? If not, why? What factors interfere with engaging these children in learning? Are community values in conflict with those of the school? Social workers must make referrals, file petitions with the court, assist in the development

[1]Rappaport, J. (1981). In praise of paradox: A social policy of empowerment over prevention. *American Journal of Community Psychology, 9*(1), 1–25.

[2]Waters, D. B., & Lawrence, E. C. (1993). *Competence, courage and change:* An *approach to family therapy.* New York: W. W. Norton.

of policies and programs within the school and community, work with the parents of these children, and advocate changes to unfair institutional policies and practices. In other words, the practitioner should seek changes in the pupil or in the quality of the impinging environment, or both.

In this chapter we call attention to the concept of pupil life tasks, and we discuss several types of vulnerable pupils. We recognize that there are many more vulnerable pupil groups, but discussion of all of them is beyond the scope of any one text. This chapter will focus on such pupil groups as disadvantaged preschool children, children from low-income areas, migrant children, homeless children, school-age pregnant girls and school-age parents, youth with HIV/AIDS, gay and lesbian youth, abused and neglected children, children living with relatives other than their parents, and children involved with gang violence and delinquent behavior such as nonattendance and drug and alcohol abuse (see Table 8.1). Finally, this chapter will also examine the challenges of children who are gifted and talented.

Enrollment and Staffing

Though there was evidence of a decline in enrollment in both public and private schools in the 1970s, enrollment has been increasing every year since 1985, setting a new all-time high record in 2004. The enrolled population increased 15% between 1991 and 2004 and is projected to increase another 9% between 2004 and 2016 (see Table 8.2). According to the U.S. Department of Education (2008), these increases have been influenced by legal and illegal immigration and the high birth rate in the 1990s. In 1980 there were 46.2 million pupils in prekindergarten through grade 12; by 2008 there will be 56.0 million, and by 2016 it is projected there will be 59.8 million.

The percentage of minority students increased from 24% in 1984 to 38% in 1999 and to 42% in 2004. Hispanic and Asian/Pacific Islander students increased in both time periods, with increases in Native American students between 1984 and 1999, while the percentage of African-American students remained stable in both periods.

TABLE 8.1   Moments in America for All Children

Every second	a public school student is suspended.*
Every 11 seconds	a high school student drops out.*
Every 19 seconds	a child is arrested.
Every 20 seconds	a public school student is corporally punished.*
Every 21 seconds	a baby is born to an unmarried mother.
Every 33 seconds	a baby is born into poverty.
Every 35 seconds	a child is confirmed as abused or neglected.
Every 39 seconds	a baby is born without health insurance.
Every minute	a baby is born to a teen mother.
Every 2 minutes	a baby is born at low birthweight.
Every 4 minutes	a child is arrested for a drug offense.
Every 7 minutes	a child is arrested for a violent crime.
Every 18 minutes	a baby dies before his or her first birthday.
Every 44 minutes	a child or teen dies from an accident.
Every 3 hours	a child or teen is killed by a firearm.
Every 5 hours	a child or teen commits suicide.
Every 6 hours	a child is killed by abuse or neglect.
Every 14 hours	a woman dies from complications of childbirth or pregnancy.

* Based on calculation per school day (180 days of seven hours each).
Source: Children's Defense Fund, *Moments in America for Children.* Washington, DC: Children Defense Fund, 2009.

TABLE 8.2   Actual and Projected School Enrollment in the United States 1970–2016 (in thousands)

	All Schools	**Public Schools**			**Private Schools**		
Year	*Pre K–12*	*Pre K–8*	*9–12*	*Total*	*Pre K–8*	*9–12*	*Total*
1970	51,257	32,558	13,336	45,894	4,052	1,311	5,363
1980	46,208	27,647	13,231	40,878	3,992	1,339	5,331
1985	44,979	27,034	12,388	39,422	4,195	1,362	5,557
1990	46,864	29,878	11,338	41,216	4,514	1,134	5,648
1995	50,759	32,341	12,500	44,841	4,906	1,264	6,170
2000	53,373	33,688	13,515	47,203	4,906	1,264	6,170
2001	53,992	33,938	13,734	47,672	5,023	1,296	6,319
2002	54,403	34,116	14,067	48,183	4,915	1,306	6,221
2003	54,639	34,202	14,338	48,540	4,788	1,311	6,099
2004	54,928	34,178	14,617	48,795	4,773	1,376	6,149
2005	54,224	34,387	14,983	49,370	4,779	1,375	6,154
2006*	55,524	34,387	14,983	49,370	4,779	1,375	6,154
2007*	55,762	34,592	15,018	49,610	4,784	1,368	6,152
2008*	55,966	34,870	14,939	49,809	4,805	1,348	6,153
2014*	58,486	37,271	14,864	52,135	5,088	1,262	6,350
2015*	59,147	37,578	15,155	52,733	5,133	1,281	6,414
2016*	59,780	37,917	15,382	53,299	5,179	1,301	6,480

* projected
Source: U.S. Department of Education, National Center for Education Statistics. (2008). *Digest of Education Statistics, 2007* (NCES No. 2008-022): Table 3.

The teaching staff in our nation's schools is about 74% female, whereas 59% of the public school principals are male. Among private schools, 62% of the principals are male. About 83% of the public school teachers are white, 8% African American, 6% Hispanic, and just over 1% Asian. Almost 83% of public school principals are white, 11% are African American, and approximately 5% are Hispanic. This is startling when compared to the percentages of minority students in U.S. schools. Although there was some decrease in the percentage of minority teachers in the mid-1990s, there have been gains since then (see Table 8.3; Strizek, Pittsonberger, Riordan, Lyter, & Orlofsky, 2006).

TABLE 8.3   Racial and Ethnic Representation among Public School Teachers between 1976 and 2003

	1976	**1981**	**1986**	**1991**	**1996**	**2000**	**2003**
White	90.8	91.6	89.6	86.8	90.7	84.6	83.1
Black	8	7.8	6.9	8	7.3	7.3	7.9
Other	1.2	0.7	3.4	5.2	2	8.1	9

Source: U.S. Department of Education, National Center for Education Statistics. (1998). *Digest of Education Statistics, 1997* (NCES No. 98-015): Table 69. Strizek, G. A., Pittsonberger, J. L., Riordan, K. E., Lyter, D. M., & Orlofsky, G. F. (2006). *Characteristics of Schools, Districts, Teachers, Principals, and School Libraries in the United States: 2003–2004* (NCES No. 2006-313). U.S. Department of Education: Table 67.

In 2003, 26% of students in grades 1 through 12 attended schools chosen by their families. Less than half of these students (10% of all students) attended a private school (see Figure 8.1). Fifteen percent attended a public school of choice. As the charter school movement continues to grow (discussed in Chapter 1), the number of options is likely to increase (Tice, Princiotta, Chapman, & Bielick, 2007).

Family income differences are apparent in options for schooling. Students whose families had incomes at or above twice the federal poverty level (FPL) were significantly more likely to attend a school of choice than were the students from families with incomes below the FPL, and more of the wealthier students attended private schools (15%). Parents of students in private schools indicate more satisfaction with the school, teachers, academic standards, and disciplinary policy (Tice et al., 2007). A comparison of class size of public and private school teachers found that the former taught about 4.9 periods a day with about 24 students in class, whereas the latter taught 4.6 periods with about 20 students in a class. The average basic salary for public school teachers in 2003 was $43,671, and for private school teachers, it was $29,030 (Strizek et al., 2006).

In personal conversations with teachers employed in private institutions, several themes emerge. Though their salaries are substantially lower in many cases, they maintain that the working conditions are much better. Work conditions were operationalized as smaller class size, fewer

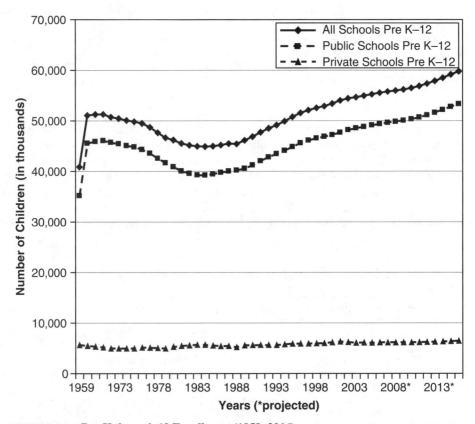

FIGURE 8.1   Pre-K through 12 Enrollment (1959–2016)   *Source:* National Center for Education Statistics. (2008). *Digest of Education Statistics, 2007* (NCES No. 2008-022): Table 3.

students in class, fewer behavioral problems, more constructive parental involvement and support of education, better-prepared students who are interested in learning, and more flexibility and support for innovation in instruction. In personal conversations with educators in public institutions, it is evident that the public educators believe in the historical mission of the schools to serve as the foundation for democracy; students and parents are too often judged unfairly because they represent the wide spectrum of racial, ethnic, and economic groups; the diversity of creativity among these pupils needs to be recognized and developed; and the isolation of pupils by economic and racial lines is not congruent with the fact that the population of the 21st century will be more diverse than ever before. This increasing diversity is seen by public educators as one cause of "white flight" to private schools, in an attempt to avoid certain groups (African Americans and Latinos), and a factor in the decline of city centers all over the country.

Will public education, as we know it, exist in the future? Will public education come to serve only one class or only those pupils of minority status? Will we have an educational system that encourages class and economic separation? Most urban areas have fewer resources available to support the schools, and yet enroll children whose needs for educational support are greater due to lack of resources, overburdened families that are unable to provide experiences that would be supportive of academic achievement, or language barriers.

The Concept of Pupil Life Tasks

During the 1950s and 1960s, the dominant view of why some pupils failed and others progressed was believed to be genetics. Decades later, this controversial position returned with the publication of Herrnstein and Murray's *The Bell Curve* (1994), in which the authors suggested that intelligence, as determined by intelligence quotient (IQ) tests, is less a function of environment and more a function of genes. Furthermore, success in

life is tied to "good genes" that yield a higher IQ. With the successful mapping of the human genome, this perspective is once again gaining the attention of the media.

According to Herrnstein and Murray, low intelligence is a good predictor of poverty, school failure, criminality, high divorce rates, and poor parenting. Their theory ignores the critical role environment plays in prenatal and later developmental stages. They ignored institutional racism, sexism, cultural bias, and other stresses that affect intelligence and influence its development. There is little debate over the existence of "raw" test score differences between Whites and minorities, raw meaning test scores before economic and family considerations are taken into account.

Subsequent research demonstrates Herrnstein and Murray's errors by showing that IQ differences between Black and White children are significantly reduced when you control for the effects of family poverty, neighborhood economic conditions, mother's education, and prior learning experiences (Todd & Wolpin, 2007).

Furthermore, it has been shown that, contrary to Herrnstein and Murray's notion of "inequality of endowments," including intelligence and other conclusions, the level of inequality and privilege in America is determined by social conditions and national policies, not by nature (Card & Rothstein, 2007; Fischer et al., 1996; Jacobs, 1999). Moreover, according to Fryer and Levitt (2007), there is such a small difference in intelligence scores before the age of 2 that genetic differences are not likely to be the cause of the test score gap.

All children are vulnerable to stress at various stages of their pupil life cycle, that is, at one or more of the normal points of progression through the education system. Stress can be produced during the initial entry into the education system: the separation of children from their families for extended periods during the day and/or when children are required to enter a new or different school at any point of their school career. As children pass from preschool to elementary school and then to secondary school, specific biological, maturational, and psychosocial changes occur. As they attempt to respond to their own developmental changes, they must simultaneously respond to the expectations of significant others and to different environmental conditions. However, some degree of stress (e.g., a stimulating environment) is essential for human growth and for developing the skills required to cope with life tasks. The adaptability of individual pupils to certain stages of the educational process varies and is in part related to the availability of resources and sources of support that can be drawn on in making such adjustments (see Table 8.1).

Many children can do what is required of them without experiencing excessive stress, but others cannot, for various reasons, including the following. (1) They lack access to an appropriate remedy. A child who has a special learning need on entering elementary school might find adjustment problematic unless the appropriate educational service is not provided. (2) They experience stress associated with a traumatic event or an unbalanced combination of stressful conditions (for example, the loss of a parent who had been relied on for emotional support or a violent episode at school) or are physically or emotionally abused by parents. (3) Some children lack adequate skills to cope with pupil life tasks and environmental demands. Their social skills are poorly developed; their self-confidence is low; their exposure to different or strange environmental conditions has been limited; and the interactional patterns within their own family are maladaptive, resulting in maladaptive social interaction with peers, which then becomes exacerbated by the demands placed on them by the social environment and the staff. (4) Other pressures may arise from subtle but powerful community forces, such as the idiosyncratic philosophy of a juvenile court judge, characteristics of the foster care system, health-care policy, and sociocultural attitudes regarding delinquency, mental retardation, and poverty.

Such stress in a child's life can lead to a crisis if resources are fragmented or limited. Such crises generally take two forms: situational or developmental. A situational crisis may be the loss of a parent or sibling or abuse and neglect by a significant other. Frequently, with the appropriate social work intervention, such children can be helped to restore or develop adequate coping mechanisms and experience minimal (if any) long-term harm. A developmental crisis may occur as the child moves into adolescence or when a preschool child is separated from his or her family for the first time. Some children adjust better than others to such changes. When adjustment is problematic, the child often exhibits specific symptomatic behaviors. The school social worker can identify different target groups of pupils that share particular stress-inducing characteristics and can work with such children individually and in small groups. The social worker should determine whether the stress felt by these pupils can be attributed to another system (school, family, community, or peer group) and whether change or supports for that system are warranted.

Pupils Who Are at Risk of School Failure

During the early 1960s, concern was expressed about the disadvantaged child and the educational implications of such deprivation. The word *deprived* has come to mean, or is used interchangeably with, *disadvantaged, educationally deprived, culturally deprived,* and *lower class* (today referred to as "child-at-risk"). Today some refer to these children as "children of promise," indicating that they have strengths that can be nourished, given a fertile environment. Alternatively, these talents are wasted if the environment does not provide even the most basic needs for food, safety, and relationships.

At-Risk Preschoolers

The United States has the highest rate of child poverty of any developed nation, with 17.4% counted as poor (Children's Defense Fund, 2007;

see Table 8.4). As stated in Chapter 1, the child who lives in poverty and whose parents find the fulfillment of basic needs difficult often enters the school system lacking some of the prerequisite skills. Academic handicaps are in large part attributable to overburdened home situations in which acquisition of the basic necessities (food and shelter) takes priority over books, health care, and educational experiences. A developmental lag may begin at birth, and these experiences may become more difficult to make up as time passes.

Preschoolers from households lower in socioeconomic resources have less well developed language and mathematics skills and are more likely to have behavioral problems. This results in a less effective educational experience, making the original disadvantage more difficult to overcome and compounding the problem as the

TABLE 8.4 Children under 18 Living Below the Poverty Level in Types of Families, by Race/Ethnicity, 1960–2005

Race/ Ethnicity	Year	Number of Children Under 18 (in thousands)		Percentage of Children Under 18	
		All Families	*Single-Mother Families*	*All Families*	*Single-Mother Families*
All Races	1960	17,288	4,095	26.5	68.4
	1970	10,235	4,689	14.9	53.0
	1980	11,114	5,866	17.9	50.8
	1990	12,715	7,363	19.9	53.4
	1995	13,999	8,364	20.2	50.3
	2000	11,005	6,116	15.6	39.8
	2005	12,335	7,210	17.1	42.8
White	1960	11,229	2,357	20.0	59.9
	1970	6,138	2,247	10.5	43.1
	1980	6,817	2,813	13.4	41.6
	1990	7,696	3,597	15.1	45.9
	1995	8,474	4,051	15.5	42.5
	2000	6,834	2,955	12.3	33.0
	2005	3,973	2,158	9.5	33.1
Black	1960	5,022	1,475	65.5	81.6
	1970	3,922	2,383	41.5	67.7
	1980	3,906	2,944	42.1	64.8
	1990	4,412	3,543	44.2	64.7
	1995	4,644	3,954	41.5	61.6
	2000	3,495	2,830	30.9	49.4
	2005	3,743	2,993	34.2	50.2
Hispanic	1975	1,619	694	33.1	68.4
	1980	1,718	809	33.0	65.0
	1990	2,750	1,314	37.7	68.4
	1995	3,938	1,872	39.3	65.7
	2000	3,342	1,303	27.6	48.3
	2005	3,977	1,774	27.7	50.2

Source: U.S. Department of Education, National Center for Education Statistics. (2008). *Digest of Education Statistics, 2007* (NCES No. 2008-022): Table 21.

children grow up (Duncan & Brooks-Gunn, 1997; Barbarin et al., 2006).

With increased demand for more rigorous standards in education, the expectations of the public schools in regard to kindergarten skills have steadily increased. Yet the diversity of skill level found among children entering kindergarten is extensive—ranging from children who do not know their last name to children who are already reading proficiently.

The Head Start Program was established in 1965 as part of President Johnson's War on Poverty. The goal was to provide disadvantaged children with preschool experiences that were not available to them in their home and community environments to develop these children to their maximum potential. Designed as the first comprehensive intervention, the hope was that if these children could be better prepared to enter school, their future educational achievement would be comparable to that of their middle-class peers. Head Start programs (both summer and full-year programs) funded by the federal government sprang up all over the United States—in large, medium, and small urban areas; in suburban and rural communities; in migrant camps; and on Indian reservations. Such programs provided medical, dental, and nutritional services; they involved parents and mobilized social service and community resources. The Head Start program has enrolled more than 24 million children since it was developed in 1965 (Office of Head Start, 2007).

The goals of the Heat Start Program were well accepted until 1969, when the Westinghouse evaluation of the program indicated that the educational gains of those children who participated were not permanent; in fact, the momentum gained by children was generally lost in a few years (Kean, 1970). Such findings raised considerable doubt that the effects of poverty could be eliminated by large-scale social programs, either because the theory was flawed or because of poor implementation (Haskins, 2004). Though the research methodology of the Westinghouse study was questioned, its findings were well publicized and generally accepted. Advocates of Head Start questioned the narrow measurement used to evaluate the program

and argued that one could not expect a single year of even the most comprehensive program to reduce the effects of many years of poverty.

In 1995, Head Start began an effort to develop and report on its accountability for services to children and their families each year, via an evaluation process. This effort was in response to a specific legislative mandate, strategic planning for the program, and more emphasis on accountability and results-oriented evaluations. The conceptual framework for these evaluations includes attention to input/process and outcome measures. The framework was driven by the ultimate goal of the program, which is to promote the social competence of children by enhancing their health and development; to provide education, health, and nutritional services; to link children and families to community resources; and to involve parents in decision making (Office of Head Start, 2005a).

These recent evaluations of the Head Start Program's performance have included a wide spectrum of input and outcome measures (i.e., program quality and its link to classroom performance; characteristics of the teachers; cognitive, social, emotional, and physical development of the child; and characteristics, well-being, and accomplishments of the families). A recent impact study found that Head Start helped narrow several achievement gaps between 3- and 4-year-olds in the Head Start Program and the nation's norms after the first year (Office of Head Start, 2005b). For 3-year-olds, the prereading gap was reduced by 8%. The 4-year-olds also experienced a reduction in the prereading gap by 45%, and the prewriting gap was reduced by 28%. The data collected showed that the first year of Head Start had a more positive impact on the group of first-year students who were 3 years old than it did for those who were 4 years old in the following four domains: cognitive, social-emotional, health, and parenting practices (Office of Head Start, 2005b).

Research on brain development has led policy makers to begin Head Start at birth rather than waiting until the child is age 3 or 4. The Head Start Act Amendments of 1994 established Early Head Start, programs that provide "family-centered services for low-income families with very young children designed to promote the development of the children, and to enable their parents to fulfill their roles as parents and to move toward self-sufficiency" (42 U.S.C. § 9840a). The four cornerstones of Early Head Start programs are child development, family development, community building, and staff development. The program seeks to enhance the child's development and help parents meet their own goals, while assisting parents to be better caregivers and teachers to their children. In the fiscal year 2002, Early Head Start funds were over 650 million dollars, an increase of over 400% from the 1997 allocation of 150 million dollars.

A rigorous national evaluation of Early Head Start Programs, which included 3,000 children and families in 17 sites and began in 1995, found that after a year or more of program services, when compared with a randomly assigned control group, 2-year-old Early Head Start children performed significantly better on a range of measures of cognitive, language, and social-emotional development. Their parents scored significantly higher than the control group parents on many of the measures of the home environment, parenting behavior, and knowledge of infant-toddler development. Early Head Start families were more likely to attend school or job training and experienced reductions in parenting stress and family conflict. Although these impacts are generally modest in size, the pattern of positive findings across a wide range of key domains important for children's well-being and future development is promising. For example:

- Early Head Start children, at 2 years of age, scored higher on a standardized assessment of infant cognitive development than the control children and were reported by their parents to have larger vocabularies and to use more grammatically complex sentences. On the assessment of cognitive development, Early Head Start children were less likely to score in the at-risk range of developmental functioning; Early Head Start is moving some children out of the low-functioning group, perhaps reducing their risk of poor cognitive outcomes later on.
- Early Head Start 2-year-olds lived in home environments that were more likely to support

and stimulate cognitive development, language, and literacy, based on researcher's observations using a standard scale. Their parents were more likely to read to children daily and at bedtime (Office of Planning, Research, and Evaluation, 2002).

Although Head Start's long-term consequences have been debated in the political and scientific arenas, today there are over 50,000 Head Start Classrooms in the United States serving more than 900,000 children, with a budget of over six billion dollars annually (Office of Head Start, 2007). Head Start and Early Head Start give the Administration for Children and Families, in collaboration with the National Institutes of Health and the National Academy of Sciences, the opportunity to develop strong research on young children and families over time.

The welfare reform of the 1990s prompted an expensive change in the Head Start Program. Before the reforms, most Head Start programs were half-day programs. With the work requirement inherent in the reforms, fewer parents were able to continue to be involved in the parental component of Head Start, and children would have to be shifted from one environment to another (child care to Head Start), or receive Head Start services. Faced with this new obstacle, many Head Start programs have begun to provide full-day programs, and families in programs that are still half-day had to make other arrangements. More than half a million families in Head Start needed full-day, year-round child care in 2005. Forty-seven percent of these families received services directly from Head Start, 30% received care from an adult in their home, and 15% received care from publicly subsidized or fee-for-service child care. The remaining families made other arrangements for their children, including public-school pre-Kindergarten programs, family child care homes, or other arrangements (Office of Head Start, 2007)

With the extension of the Individuals with Disabilities Education Act to include infants, toddlers, and preschoolers with developmental disabilities and those at risk of developing disabilities (known as Part C), the screening and interventions for these disorders begins earlier. The numerous roles for the school social worker in this process include social, developmental, and functional assessments of the child; group and individual counseling with the child and family; problem solving with the child's family and others on issues that relate to the child's functioning in school; accessing school and community resources that can enable the child to learn as effectively as possible in his or her educational program; and assisting in the development of positive behavioral intervention strategies (34 CFR 300.34(c)(14)). A part of the individualized education program must be concern for developmental transitions (e.g., from infancy to the toddler stage and from the toddler stage to the preschool stage). The social worker must engage in long-term planning and understand the individualized needs and required interventions. Support groups for parents can be a part of the service planning to facilitate adaptations in their behaviors in accordance with the needs of the child. School social workers can also be instrumental in the development of community-service networks.

Children from Low-Income Areas

The Federal Poverty Level (FPL) for 2008 was $21,200 for a family of four (Federal Register, 2008). In almost all areas of the United States, a family of four would only begin to be able to provide basic necessities for twice the FPL (Bernstein, Brocht, & Spade-Aguilar, 2000). Research on poverty has begun to call people who make less than twice the FPL "low-income." Children from low-income families make up about 39% of children, and almost half of those live below the poverty level. Fifty-two percent of children in low-income families live with a single parent. Young children are disproportionately low-income, with 43% of children under age 6 living in low-income families. Almost two thirds of American Indian children and three of every five Latino or Black children live in low-income families, whereas about one in four White or Asian children live in low-income families (Fass & Cauthen, 2007).

Poverty places children at a much greater health and developmental risk. They are disproportionately exposed to more adverse social and environmental conditions than their middle- and high-income peers. They experience more family turmoil and violence and are more likely to be separated from their parents (spend time in foster care; Evans, 2004). These children are also three times more likely to die in childhood and at greater risk of disability, academic failure, and adolescent pregnancy (Children's Defense Fund, 2005). They are more likely to be exposed to environmental hazards such as lead and toxic substances and to substandard housing (Kozol, 1995), and the air and water that they intake is more polluted than their peers' (Evans 2004).

Children from impoverished families are more likely to have poor attendance records and to fall behind in achievement. Children in poverty are at additional risk if the mother's education is also low. Poverty and low maternal education exert independent negative effects on children's development. As one would anticipate, the effect of low maternal educational levels on children's achievement increases as children become older (Smith, Brooks-Gunn, & Klebanov, 1997). In addition to a high incidence of poverty, 44% of all Hispanic children live in a home in which neither parent is a high school graduate (Children's Defense Fund, 2005). This places Hispanic children at higher risk of school failure and dropout.

According to the U.S. Department of Agriculture Economic Research Service, 10.9% of U.S. households (12.6 million) had some food insufficiency in 2006. This means that they had trouble providing food for the family based on their own resources at some point during the year. About one third of these households were very food insecure, meaning that the food intake of one or more adults was reduced, and their eating patterns were disrupted at times during the year due to a lack of resources and coping mechanisms. Children are usually shielded from food insecurity, but in 2006, 210,000 households (0.6%) had children that experienced food insecurity as well as the adults (U.S. Department of

Agriculture, 2007). Effects of hunger in children are often subtle: frequent headaches, fatigue, difficulty concentrating, dizziness, irritability, and frequent illness.

The Migrant Child

The migrant child, often another victim of poverty, moves from place to place as the family searches for work in farming communities. The fact that their exact number is unknown is proof of how isolated these families are. These migrant families include Latinos, including Mexicans, Mexican Americans, and Puerto Ricans, as well as other nationalities and heritages, such as African Americans, Afro Caribbeans, and Whites. Compensation for their labor is not controlled, and many labor regulations, including workmen's compensation, are not guaranteed to them. These families must often tolerate inhumane living conditions; housing is generally substandard and very crowded.

The 2001 No Child Left Behind Act made amendments to the Migrant Education Program (MEP), Title I, to provide formula grants to states to improve the education of migrant children. Title I MEP defines eligible students as "... those children of migratory workers who have, within the last 36 months, moved across school district boundaries in order to obtain temporary or seasonal employment in agriculture or fishing" (20 U.S.C. § 6399).

In the school year that began in the fall of 2004, more than 500,000 migrant students were enrolled in public schools. This is just over 1% of total enrollment. Over 40% of migrant children in school were enrolled in California, where migrant students make up almost 4% of total enrollment. The Migrant Education Program also provides for students to be enrolled in the summers, and in the summer of 2005, almost 250,000 migrant students were enrolled in these programs (U.S. Department of Education, 2006).

The Migrant and Seasonal Head Start programs are one attempt to help these families. In addition to the typical Head Start services, Migrant Head Start centers have a unique emphasis on serving infants and toddlers, as well as preschool children, so that these children need not be cared for in the field or left in the care of very young siblings. Migrant centers provide extended day services up to 12 hours a day and 6 days a week when harvest season is at its peak. In 2006, Migrant Head Start served over 33,000 children in 37 states in every region of the country (National Migrant and Seasonal Head Start Association, n.d.).

Since passage of the Elementary and Secondary Education Act of 1965, funds are available to states to assist in developing educational programs for children of migrant workers. The effects of poverty, constant migration, poor health care, and tenuous ties with schools make this population clearly at risk. Children are often taken into the fields to assist with work so the parents can work more efficiently. It is not uncommon for a 12-year-old child to be working 16 to 18 hours a week. Most children that should be entering high school are in the fields as full-fledged workers (Green, 2003).

In a recent cross-sectional, partially random sample of migrant families in North Carolina, 44% of the children had visited a doctor in the preceding 3 months, but 53% of the children had an unmet medical need in the past year. This study found that income was not a significant factor to the use of health services, but a family member receiving WIC, female gender, and young age are associated with use of health services. Unlike other, largely anecdotal evidence, this study found that use of health services was largely illness-driven, meaning that caregivers will overcome perceived barriers if they believe the child is in less than very good health (Weathers, Minkovitz, O'Campo, & Diener-West, 2003).

In children living along the U.S.–Mexico border, recent studies have found that more than half of the health care for children was received in Mexico. Possession of health insurance was not predictive of country of care, whereas perceived quality of care, accessibility, and cost were cited as reasons for medical care in Mexico (Seid, Casteneda, Mize, Zivkovic, & Varni, 2003).

An investigation of the prevalence of mental health problems and the utilization of mental health services by migrant and seasonal worker families in North Carolina found that 64% of the children evidenced clinical levels of problem behaviors (Martin, Kupersmidt, & Harter, 1996). The severity of the children's mental health problems was not related to the use of school support services (special education, counseling, remedial education). The only variable related to the use of school services was the mother's country of birth. The mother's command of English and ability to negotiate the school culture may be affecting the delivery of services to migrant children. A recent study of South Texas high school students reported that migrant youth may be at greater risk for substance abuse and work-related injuries than nonmigrant youth (Cooper, Weller, Fox, & Cooper, 2005). These children also are more likely to work before school on weekday mornings.

School itself represents an additional cultural shock for many of these students with its locker assignments, bells, and schedules. Because these youth represent only a small percentage of students, few schools have programs to assist them in adapting to and benefiting from school. Programs that provide appropriate assistance find that these students can make dramatic progress.

Homeless Children

Millions who need low-cost housing cannot locate it. The National Low-Income Housing Coalition reported that even full-time work at minimum wage is inadequate to afford adequate housing in every state, and there are increasing shortages of housing for extremely and very low-income families (Pelletierre & Wardrip, 2008). Families with children represent approximately 50% of the homeless population, meaning that every year, more than 600,000 families with 1.35 million children are homeless at some point during the year (National Alliance to End Homelessness, 2007). Requests for emergency shelter by homeless families with children increased by an average of 5% between 2004 and 2005, with requests up 28% in Boston on the high end, and a minor decline in Kansas City, Philadelphia, and Phoenix. The average stay by families in homeless shelters is about 8 months and

ranged from 1 month in Los Angeles to almost 2 years in Trenton, New Jersey (U.S. Conference of Mayors, 2006).

In 1987, popular pressure was growing for the federal government to address the increasing problem of homelessness in the United States. The McKinney-Vento Homelessness Act was the result, having been passed by large bipartisan majorities in both houses of Congress and signed into law by Ronald Reagan. It has been amended several times, most recently in 2004, but it is still the overriding federal measure to help the homeless in the United States. In the act, a homeless child or youth is defined as:

> (A) an individual who lacks a fixed, regular, and adequate nighttime residence; and (B) includes—
> (i) children and youths who are sharing the housing of other persons due to loss of housing, economic hardship, or a similar reason; are living in motels, hotels, trailer parks, or camping groups due to the lack of alternative adequate accommodations; are living in emergency or transitional shelters; are abandoned in hospitals; or are awaiting foster care placement; (ii) children and youths who have a primary nighttime residence that is a public or private place not designed for or ordinarily used as a regular sleeping accommodation for human beings; (iii) children and youths who are living in care, parks, public spaces, abandoned buildings, substandard housing, bus or train stations, or similar stations; and (iv) migratory children who qualify as homeless for the purposes of this part because the children are living in circumstances described in clauses (i) through (iii). (42 U.S.C. § 11434a)

These youth and their families are at risk of psychological, emotional, and health problems. They lack adequate food, clothing, and supportive environments. Many of these children live in an environment in which violence, crime, and prostitution are prevalent. The impact of these conditions on their educational development is devastating. Escalating homelessness in our society has been attributed to industrial changes (e.g., downsizing), lack of jobs, decreases in availability of low-income housing, cuts in public assistance, and the erosion of spending power for those in entry-level positions earning minimum wage.

The initial act made educational services, school breakfast and lunch programs, and informal assessments of homeless children possible. Following the No Child Left Behind initiatives, all states are now required to address the needs of homeless children as students and create equal access and education opportunities for these children.

However, homelessness presents a host of challenges for children. Some barriers to homeless children's academic achievement include the following: school mobility (changing schools), transportation, guardianship, immunization, faculty knowledge about homelessness, access to special education, lack of English proficiency, and scarce resources (U.S. Department of Education, 2002). According to Rafferty, Shinn, and Weitzman (2004), children who have experienced homelessness have an overall poorer academic experience than their counterparts. The students who were formerly homeless have reported a high level of school mobility (having changed schools on an average of 4.2 times since kindergarten) and high grade retention rates. School mobility and grade retention had a high association with each other, while age was controlled. Although there were some academic differences between those who have experienced homelessness and those who have not, over 90% of both groups reported that an education is "very important" and had goals to pursue further degrees (Rafferty et al., 2004). The 2001 legislation was established to combat each of these differences, providing funding to state institutions to alleviate the disparities in areas such as transportation, outreach, and school enrollment (U.S. Department of Education, 2002).

Adolescent Parents

The incidence of adolescent pregnancy has been declining since the early 1990s, with a 24% decline in teenage pregnancy (15–19 years old) between 1996 and 2003 and a 9% change in the incidence of sexual intercourse in that same period. The pregnancy rate among sexually experienced females in this age group declined by 17%

from 189 to 157 pregnancies per 1,000 sexually experienced females between 1996 and 2003 (Ventura, Abma, Mosher, & Henshaw, 2008).

The birth rate among women 15 to 19 years old fell 34% between 1991 and 2005, to 40.5 per 1,000 (see Figure 8.2). For teenagers between ages 15 and 17, the rate fell to 21.4 births per 1,000 women, which is the lowest rate ever recorded. The rate for the youngest group, 10 to 14 years old, was unchanged from 2004 to 2005, at 0.7 per 1,000. Between 1991 and 2005, the birth rate for non-Hispanic Black teenagers fell by almost half, and the rate for non-Hispanic Whites, American Indian/Alaska Natives, and Asian/Pacific Islanders declined almost 40% in each group. The rate for Hispanic teenagers decreased 22% in this period (Martin et al., 2007).

Initiation of sexual activity is associated with several variables or factors, including the norms of the peer group, use of drugs and alcohol, poor school performance, perceived risk of a sexually transmitted disease or HIV, and perceived barriers to condom use. Being a Black male and being poor also increased the likelihood of early sexual activity (Santelli et al., 2004).

We know that certain environmental conditions contribute to the other variables that are highly associated with risk for becoming pregnant during the adolescent years. Adolescent females from low-income areas make up 73% of all pregnant teens (Advocates for Youth, 2004). This group of adolescents is less likely to use contraceptives or have the proper knowledge of how to use contraceptives (Breheny & Stephens, 2004). When it comes to prenatal care, adolescent mothers are less likely to seek care on time (Aruda, McCabe, Burke, & Litty, 2008) or to be consistent with prenatal care (Chen et al., 2007). The babies born to adolescent mothers are more likely to be preterm and have low birth weight (Chen et al., 2007).

Sexual abuse is strongly linked with adolescent pregnancy. Children who report familial abuse are the least likely to engage in risk behaviors associated with adolescent pregnancy and pregnancy involvement, and those who report both familial and nonfamilial abuse are the most likely. Males who are abused are four times more likely

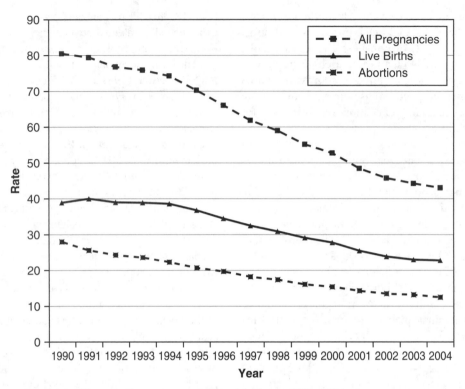

FIGURE 8.2 Teenage Pregnancy and Abortion Rates, 1990–2004 *Source:* Ventura et al. (2008) Table 2.

to be involved with a pregnancy than males who were not abused, and females are about twice more likely than their counterparts (Saewyc, Magee, & Pettingell, 2004).

The research on predictors of adolescent pregnancy has been summarized in two words: disadvantage and discouragement (Luker, 1996, in Children's Defense Fund, 1997).

In the early 1990s, a longitudinal study (Underwood, Kupersmidt, & Coie, 1996) found that fourth-grade peer sociometric measures predicted adolescent pregnancy as well as a variety of other adolescent problem behaviors. Girls who received more peer nominations as aggressive (i.e., says mean things, starts fights, hits or kicks other children) were twice as likely to bear children in adolescence. The authors noted that peer ratings of aggression are almost

as stable as IQ scores and consistently predict other outcomes. This implies that pregnancy prevention should begin in elementary school by providing children with appropriate social and problem-solving skills. Another interesting finding of this study is that controversial girls, those well liked by some and strongly disliked by others, are at the highest risk of pregnancy. This was the first time that a controversial peer sociometric status has been linked with a negative outcome. More recently, in an attempt to nail down the exact factors involved in this correlation, it has been found that the "popular" girls are more likely to engage in all forms of risk behavior than girls who are not labeled as popular by their peers (Allen, Porter, McFarland, Marsh, & McElhaney, 2005; Rose, Swenson, & Waller, 2004). In addition, the link between popularity and risk behaviors seems to be stable for boys as well as girls (Mayeaux, Sandstrom, & Cillessen, 2008). The authors hypothesized that these girls, who possess both prosocial and antisocial behaviors, probably become the group that others have referred to as competent adolescent mothers. They may also pose the greatest challenge to pregnancy prevention programs.

We also know that school attendance reduces adolescent sexual risk-taking behaviors. Youth who have dropped out of school are "more likely to initiate sexual activity earlier, fail to use contraception, become pregnant, and give birth" (Office of the Surgeon General, 2001, p. 7). Other protective factors for those in school include involvement in athletics and other school activities, which lead to less sexual risk-taking, later age of initiation of sex, and lower frequency of sex, pregnancy, and childbearing. Schools can provide an opportunity for positive peer learning that can influence social norms and create an environment that discourages unhealthy risk-taking (Office of the Surgeon General, 2001).

Though the adolescent male plays a critical role in determining the sexual behavior of the adolescent female, too little research and intervention have specifically targeted him (Allen-Meares & Roberts, 1994). Both adolescent parents are less likely to complete their schooling, increasing their risk for sporadic employment and/or welfare dependency. Premature parenthood preempts the educational, vocational, and social experiences that are required for adulthood. Moreover, the baby is at risk of developmental delays, premature birth, and lower birth weight. However, with adequate support and assistance, these negative consequences can be buffered or minimized (see Figure 8.3). Recent research suggests that many adolescent parents have an increased interest in completing high school and perhaps going to college to provide a stable and successful life for the child (SmithBattle, 2007). Many young parents who continue their schooling do so with considerable struggle. Arranging child care, coordinating transportation and doctor appointments, playing multiple roles (e.g., mother, student, daughter, and in some cases, wife) contribute to their educational failure and/or underachievement. It is essential that we recognize the heterogeneity of this target group. In 1972, the commissioner of the U.S. Office of Education stated: "Every girl in the United States has a right and need for the education that will help her prepare herself for a career, for family life, and for citizenship. To be married or pregnant is not sufficient cause to deprive her of an education and the opportunity to become a contributing member of society" (Howard & Eddinger, 1973, p. 29). Title IX of the Education Amendment of 1972 (which became effective July 12, 1975) prohibits schools that receive federal funds from excluding students solely on the basis of pregnancy or a pregnancy-related condition.

Comprehensive Sex Education. According to a poll by National Public Radio (NPR), the Henry Kaiser Family Foundation, and the Kennedy School of Government at Harvard University, less than 7% of Americans believe that sex education should not be taught in schools, and 87% believe that information on how to obtain and use contraceptives should be part of the sex education curriculum, though 39% believe that giving teens information about how to obtain and use contraceptives encourages them to have sex earlier than they would have without the information (NPR, 2004).

A recent review of 16 randomized controlled trials of school-based sex education compared abstinence-only programs to abstinence-plus contraceptive education programs (Bennett & Assefi, 2005). The abstinence-only programs reviewed failed to produce any overall changes in adolescent sexual behavior. However, contrary to popular belief, the review of abstinence-plus programs found an overall decline in the frequency of sexual activity. In regard to initiation of sexual activity, the reviews by Aarons et al. (2000) and Eisen, Zellman, and McAllister (1990) reported a delayed initiation of sexual activity in both females and males in the students who participated in abstinence-plus programs, respectively.

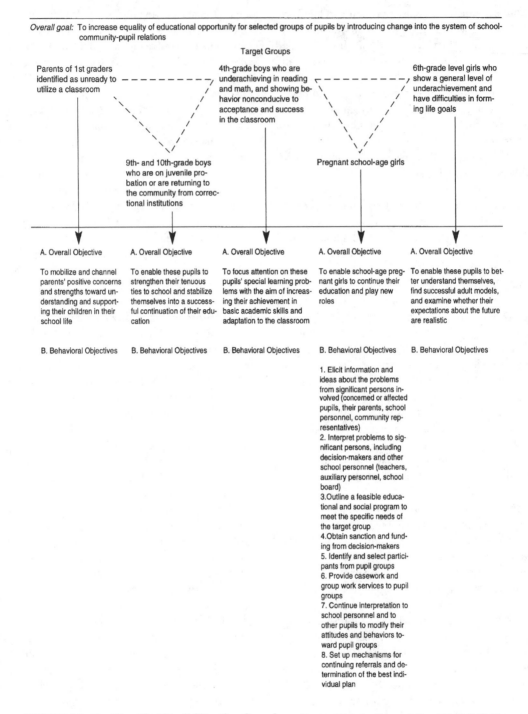

FIGURE 8.3   An Identified Pupil Situation Complex   *Source:* Printed with permission of Lela B. Costin, Professor Emeritus, School of Social Work, University of Illinois, Urbana-Champaign.

9. Work with community groups to develop supportive out-of-school programs and services
10. Institute systematic recordkeeping for interpreting outcome

C. Measurable Outcomes   C. Measurable Outcomes   C. Measurable Outcomes   C. Measurable Outcomes   C. Measurable Outcomes

1. Extent of sanction and support
2. Amount of funding and its adequacy
3. Number of girls who continued in school
4. Number of girls who made adequate plans for care of the baby
5. If baby was kept, number of girls who were able to play traditional maternal role
6. Number of girls who completed education
7. Number of girls who moved into labor market or higher education
8. Decrease in recidivism

FIGURE 8.3   Continued

This method of sex education also consistently documented that adolescents came away with improved contraceptive use and knowledge. In addition, Kohler, Manhart, and Lafferty (2008) reported that adolescents who received contraceptive education are 50% less likely to be involved in a teenage pregnancy than those who receive an abstinence-only education and 40% less likely than those who received no sex education. Santelli, Kindberg, Finer, and Singh (2007) reported that 77% of the overall decline in teen pregnancy can be attributed to improved contraceptive use, whereas the rest of the decline is attributable to the decline in sexual activity.

Though many youth complain about the content and relevance of sex education, when technical information is augmented with discussions about relationships and responsible sexual behavior, opinions change for the better (Scott-Jones, 1993). Sex education programs should not be limited to school-based health clinics or the health curriculum; churches and community-based agencies should also provide this content.

Career Planning and Personal Development. Research reports suggest that those youth with career and/or educational plans are more likely to forestall pregnancy (Driscoll, Sugland, Manlove, & Papillo, 2005). There is also some evidence that intensive service learning programs provide some protective factors for youth, even though the programs do not address sexual activity or pregnancy directly (Kirby, 2007). Youth need to know that they have a future and that there are opportunities for them. Social workers, coordinating their activities with other school-based staff and external agencies, can assist youth via small groups, career development workshops, and other goal-setting activities. The best way to prevent adolescent pregnancy (and many other risky and antisocial behaviors) is to instill within youth aspirations for the future.

AIDS and Youth

As stated previously, sexual activity among adolescents is often unplanned and sporadic. Report after report documents the spontaneity of the first sexual encounter and the negative consequences for the youth and their potential offspring: unplanned pregnancy, baby at risk of developmental delays, and sexually transmitted diseases, including the human immunodeficiency virus (HIV/AIDS). Pupils need accurate information concerning the consequence of intercourse and the risk for infection. This will require youth to change their sexual behaviors—a very difficult challenge indeed. AIDS prevention needs to be developed not only in schools, but within different settings as well (e.g., community, churches). Clearly a comprehensive community-based approach is required.

According to the Centers for Disease Control and Prevention (CDC), between 2003 and 2006, the numbers of new cases of HIV/AIDS diagnosed in populations between the ages of 13 and 19 remained stable, with only a slight increase from 2005 to 2006. The number of new cases among children under 13 continued to decrease in this period. In this period, more than 86% of the new cases of children under 13 were infected perinatally (Centers for Disease Control and Prevention [CDC], 2008b). It is clear that both educational and behavioral interventions are necessary to prevent the spread of this deadly virus. Other research on adolescent sexuality and pregnancy indicates that educational intervention alone has not influenced behavioral change. Many youth believe that it cannot happen to them—that they are invincible or lucky or it cannot happen "this one time." Between 1991 and 2005, the increase of the percentage of sexually active youth who used condoms at last sexual intercourse has increased dramatically from 46% to 62% (CDC, 2008a).

Nationally, about 90% of students have received HIV/AIDS education in school. White students (91%) and Black students (90%) were more likely than Hispanic (85%) students to have received HIV/AIDS education at school (CDC, 2008a).

HIV/AIDS education belongs not only in the health education curriculum, but also wherever discussions focus on sexuality, health, and prevention and other situations in which this education can help young people make informed decisions (Kirby, Laris, & Rolleri, 2007). According to the NPR study mentioned earlier, 68% of people believe that sex education classes in school are at least somewhat effective in helping teens avoid getting HIV/AIDS and other sexually transmitted diseases. Ninety-eight percent believe that HIV/AIDS is an appropriate topic for sex education programs (NPR, 2004). Schoolwide HIV/AIDS interventions that begin in the elementary school are essential. School social workers can organize discussions with small groups of parents, teachers, and/or students. The small-group context allows for more intimate sharing and feedback, as well as an opportunity to role-play responses to situations that could lead to the risk of an infection. The school social worker, in consultation with others (school-based health personnel), could be instrumental in planning and organizing in-service training for school staff, parents, and community leaders. If there is a school-based health clinic, it should work with other support staff and the school's administration to formulate guidelines and/or policies to allow infected youth who are physically and emotionally capable to attend school. Instruction on minimizing risk should be a central aspect of the educational intervention (e.g., use of gloves when handling any body fluids). The emphasis should be on promoting safe behavior, and the intent should take into consideration the developmental readiness of the pupils. School social workers are also in a unique position to meet the needs of HIV-affected children (those whose family members died of or are ill with HIV or AIDS, but are not infected themselves), who have been shown to be more likely than their peers to engage in substance use and other deviant activities (Gilbert, 2001; Rosenblum et al., 2005).

Gay and Lesbian Youth

Students who identify (or are perceived) as lesbian, gay, bisexual, or transgender (LGBT), as well as youth whose dress or behavior does not conform to gender expectations, are at high risk of victimization. Most states do not have anti-harassment policies and practices that include protection on the basis of sexual orientation or gender identity and expression. The National

School Climate Survey, conducted biennially by the Gay, Lesbian, and Straight Education Network (GLSEN), reported that 64% of students surveyed (LGBT students in grades 7 to 12) felt unsafe at school due to their sexual orientation, and 41% felt unsafe due to their gender expression (Kosciw & Diaz, 2006). Gay, lesbian, bisexual, and transgender youth encounter verbal insults with startling frequency, 64% due to sexual orientation, and 46% due to gender expression. Thirty-eight percent of these students report being physically harassed (pushed, shoved, etc.) due to their sexual orientation, and 18% reported that they had been physically assaulted (punched, kicked, injured with a weapon, etc.) due to their sexual orientation in the past year. Two thirds of the students reported sexual harassment in the last year, and 41% were the victim of cyberbullying (Kosciw & Diaz, 2006).

Twenty-nine percent of students feel so unsafe that they have missed classes or whole days of school. This contrasts with the national average of about 5%. More than half of the students who have been harassed or assaulted have not reported the incident(s) to anyone. The reasons for not reporting are varied, but most revolve around a belief on the part of the student that nothing would be done to address the situation or a fear of negative repercussions. There is also a belief that the members of the school staff are homophobic or, in fact, the student has heard the staff members make biased remarks about sexual orientation or gender expression, which contributed to the lack of reporting. Among students that did report an incident of harassment or abuse, a third said that the intervention by the school staff was not at all effective (Kosciw & Diaz, 2006).

The physical and emotional abuse that LGBT students receive takes its toll on these youth. According to Advocates for Youth (2005), adolescents who experience abuse like this are at risk for "truancy, dropping out of school, poor grades, and having to repeat a grade" (n.p.). It is estimated that more than 30% of lesbian, gay, and bisexual youth attempt suicide (Silenzio, Pena, Duberstein, Cerel, & Knox, 2007). Research has found that LGBT youth are at greater risk if they have disclosed their sexual orientation more completely or have experienced the loss of friends due to disclosure. A recent study found that the sucidality of LGBT students is mediated by the rate of at-school victimization (Bontempo & D'Augelli, 2002). It has also been found that students who experience high rates of at-school victimization due to their sexual orientation are more likely to have high levels of suicidality, and those who reported low rates of victimization had levels of suicidality comparable to their heterosexual counterparts. Youths who self-identified as bisexual were at highest risk (five times more likely) of attempting suicide more than once. More discussion of this group takes place in Chapter 9.

Abused and Neglected Children

Another target group of children that comes to the attention of school social workers consists of those who are physically or sexually abused and/or neglected by their parents or significant others. Often, these children come from homes characterized as having multiple problems. For example, the father may be unemployed for an extended period; there may be marital discord; the child may live with several other siblings in a single-parent household; the child may live in a middle-class or upper-middle-class home where more attention is devoted to obtaining material goods and services than to satisfying the needs of the child; the child may have a learning or physical disability; the child may have been left in the care of a babysitter who was unstable; the child may have been unwanted from birth or born to a mother who was ill-prepared to provide proper nurturing; and the parent may have a mental health or personal problem.

Each state is responsible for providing its own definitions of child abuse and neglect within the civil and criminal context of that state. Federal guidelines from the Child Abuse Prevention and Treatment Act (CAPTA) provide that child abuse and neglect are "at a minimum, any recent act or failure to act on the part of a parent or caretaker, which results in death, serious physical or emotional harm, sexual abuse or exploitation, or an act or failure to act which presents an imminent risk of serious harm" (42 U.S.C. § 5106g).

Sexual abuse is "(A) the employment, use, persuasion, inducement, enticement, or coercion of any child to engage in, or assist any other person to engage in, any sexually explicit conduct or simulation of such conduct for the purpose of producing a visual depiction of such conduct; or (B) the rape, and in cases of caretaker or interfamilial relationships, statutory rape, molestation, prostitution, or other form of sexual exploitation of children, or incest with children" (42 U.S.C. § 5106g).

Abuse and neglect have been increasing in this decade, and unfortunately the outcomes have become more severe as overtaxed social systems are unable to respond with enough services to protect America's children. U.S. Department of Health and Human Services (DHHS; 2008a) reported that an estimated 3.6 million children were investigated by Child Protective Services in 2006, which is an increase from 43.8 per 1,000 children in 2002 to 47.8 per 1,000 children in 2006. Of these children, about one quarter were determined to have been abused or neglected, approximately 905,000 children. Girls were slightly more likely than boys to be victims (51.5% versus 48.2%). The youngest children, newborn to 1 year, had the highest rate of victimization, 24.4 per 1,000; children 1 to 3 years had a victimization rate of 14.2 per 1,000 children, and children 4 to 7, 13.5 per 1,000.

In 1962, California became the first state to require by law the reporting of child abuse. By 1979, 43 states and the District of Columbia had statutes that required medical personnel and educators to report suspected cases of child abuse. Following the reauthorization of CAPTA in 1996, all 50 states have implemented laws requiring the reporting of child abuse because the funding allocated by the new version of CAPTA would not be available to states that do not have a mandatory reporting law (U.S. DHHS, 2008a). The law also states that persons who report suspected child abuse or neglect "in good faith" are immune to criminal or civil action resulting from their report (42 U.S.C. § 5106a).

In many areas, child protection workers are overburdened by the number and complexity of the cases to be investigated. The number of children entering foster care continues to exceed the number of children leaving foster care. In 2006, 510,000 children were reported to be in foster care on September 30 of that year (U.S. DHHS, 2008b). The 1996 reauthorization of the Child Abuse Prevention and Treatment Act includes grant money for demonstration projects to promote innovative interagency responses to abuse and neglect that enlist and involve public and private partnerships, including schools, religious organizations, and private agencies. For example, cities in seven states have programs modeled after New Zealand's Family Group Decision Making. The goal of this program is to assist families in altering their behaviors as they maintain responsibility for their children. Families who agree to this program participate in family conferences that include extended family workers, clergy, nurses, teachers, and others whom the family and child designate as helpful. The group determines how the child can be kept safe and presents a plan to the child protection agency. If the agency disagrees with the plan, the court makes the decision.

As stated earlier, the etiology of child abuse is multiple and interactional. Some researchers argue that the forces are sociological. For example, poverty and social change place considerable stress on a family: When the family has no one to turn to, a crisis can result with which they are unable to cope. The parents' substance abuse (drugs and/or alcohol), depression, and poor nurturing during their own childhood can also contribute to child abuse. There are also contributing environmental conditions, such as the lack of social services and other community-based services required to help high-risk parents, lack of parental knowledge of normal child development and appropriate expectations of children, the escalating cost of medical services, high unemployment, inflation, and complicated bureaucratic procedures as well as cultural values that prevent people from seeking help.

Neglected Children. It is much easier to identify and to prove the physical abuse of children than it is to prove neglect. A child who comes to school dirty, ill-fed, lacking adequate rest, dressed in soiled clothing and who otherwise shows signs of the absence of parental care can be considered neglected. In addition, these children often have poor concentration and low self-esteem. They will tend to either seek attention inappropriately or avoid it; there are few half-measures with these children (Howe, 2005). With the cutbacks in government aid and the low buying power of minimum wage, families can be overwhelmed with trying to provide even the most basic care. The private sector struggles to try to help provide safety nets, but private sources also are overburdened by the numbers seeking care. In addition, substance abuse by parents or mental illness may prevent parents from providing adequate care for their children.

Parents who do not take an interest in the child's academic progress, fail to support the child's efforts in school, and fail to work cooperatively with the school administration may be considered neglectful; however, sometimes this is the result of an ignorant or neglectful school system. Most teachers do not receive training in how to involve families in school or in important cultural differences and good communication skills with parents. The Harvard Family Research Project (Shartrand, Weiss, Kreiger, & Lopez, 1997) reported that the majority of states do not even mention family involvement in their teacher certification requirements, and most teacher education programs do not offer substantial training in family involvement. Shartrand et al. described the overall picture of teacher preparation for involving families as dismal. Unfortunately, the lack of home and school collaboration frequently results in a child who fails to develop and to achieve.

Social workers can help teachers to develop skills in working with families as well as assist in identifying necessary resources for families. In-service workshops and ongoing consultation can help teachers to learn important skills in working with families. Drawing on the theorists Joyce Epstein, Moncrieff Cochran, Luis Moll, and James

Coleman, the Harvard Family Research Project proposed four philosophical approaches to training teachers for family involvement: functional, cultural competence, parent empowerment, and social capital. Table 8.5 offers examples of attitudes, knowledge, and skills that would be addressed by each of these models (Shartrand et al., 1997).

Sexually Abused Children. The 2006 data from the Administration for Children and Families report *Child Maltreatment* indicate that an estimated 78,000 children were sexually abused, approximately 9% of all reported cases of maltreatment that year (U.S. DHHS, 2008a). The majority were females. Victims of sexual abuse exhibit a wide range of behaviors (e.g., sexual play, excessive masturbation, seductive sexual behavior, poor performance in school, and involvement in delinquency and substance abuse).

These children can find themselves in court offering testimony about the perpetrator and the actual incident or events. Today, the courts consider these victims to be competent witnesses. Social workers in the child and family service and the court system may work with school social workers to prepare a child to give testimony. Identification, reporting, and preventive intervention are the tasks of the school social worker in such cases. These children also need emotional support, guidance, and an advocate. The social worker can work with the police department, the child protection agency, and community agencies to assist the family and the child. In-service training for teachers should include such topics as how to identify these children, teachers' legal responsibility to report abuse, and the kind of assistance the child will need to meet the educational expectations of the school. The school environment may need to be assessed for areas that need additional supervision for children to be safe. Establishing schedules for monitoring hallways, bathrooms, and any identified areas of risk will help in preventing victimization of students by others, that is, older or stronger students. Social workers may be helpful in developing or implementing programs to teach children to safely

TABLE 8.5   Models for Teacher Training in Family Involvement

Functional Approach

Knowledge about benefits and goals of family involvements.

Skills in involving parents of all backgrounds in school.

Respect for different family structures, lifestyles, and cultural beliefs.

Knowledge of family functions.

Communication skills that are effective in dealing with frustrated, angry parents, defensive behaviors, distrust, and hostility.

Skills in parental involvement in children's learning outside the classroom and in sharing teaching skills with parents.

Skills in ways to involve parents in school.

Knowledge about consultation, interprofessional collaboration, referral procedures, and ways in which schools can support families.

Skills in sharing and transferring leadership to parents; sharing information that aids parents in making decisions; interacting with parents on an equal basis.

Cultural Competence

Skills in developing culturally appropriate theses in the curriculum.

Awareness of personal assumptions, value systems, and prejudices that may affect interactions with families.

Knowledge of cultural differenced in influences on childrearing, expectations, development, and communication.

Skills in incorporating family "funds of knowledge" into curricular projects involving families and communities in an active contribution to learning.

Understanding of the constraints (e.g., time, financial) that may prevent more active involvement in the school program.

Skills in discovering potential contributions and creating opportunities for involvement.

Sensitivity toward different families' perceptions of help and reciprocity.

Incorporation of parental preferences into family and school involvement activities.

Parent Empowerment

Respect for the family's role in nurturance and education of children and faith that all parents want what is best for their children.

Attitude that parents are first and most important teachers and that the most useful knowledge about raising children is found within the community; teachers seek to understand parents' views and needs rather than control them.

Knowledge of power differences and the historical influences on disenfranchised groups.

Focus on strengths rather than deficits and support rather than blame.

Skills in developing activities that build parental skill and confidence in home learning activities; provide helpful constructive feedback to families.

Skills in effective communication and developing partnerships with parents incorporating parents' self-identified needs and goals into the programs and activities offered.

Empower parents through adult education and parent education courses; including parents in governance roles and allowing their voices to be heard in meetings.

Invitations to parents to share their expertise in the school and classroom as well as at home.

Social Capital

Understanding of the concept of social capital.

Knowledge of differences and similarities in values and norms.

Skills in conflict negotiation, consensus building, trust building, and home visiting.

Skills in motivating families and communities to become involved in home learning and educational activities.

Skills in fostering parental and family investment in their child's program through attendance at school events, volunteering, fundraising.

Skills in utilizations of community resources.

Reciprocal exchanges between schools and families.

Adapted from a model in Shartrand, A. M., Weiss, H. B., Kreider, H. M., & Lopez, M. E. (1997). *New skills for new schools: Preparing teachers in family involvement.* Cambridge, MA: Harvard Family Research Project. Developed with contractual support from the U.S. Department of Education. (Reprinted with permission.)

assert their rights and protect themselves from all kinds of abuse. The establishment of parent education classes to teach appropriate techniques of discipline and the provision of parent effectiveness training can be considered as both preventive and remedial strategies. On the community level, the establishment of preventive programs and the development of community awareness are also appropriate roles for the school social worker.

Kinship Care

In 1996, the Personal Responsibility and Work Opportunity Reconciliation Act emphasized that the states should consider giving preference to relatives as caretakers of children eligible to receive foster care benefits. It is believed that kinship care preserves family ties that are often broken in nonkinship foster care, provides the child with much needed cultural and community consistency, and helps to reduce the trauma of separation from the parents (Strozier, Elrod, Beiler, Smith, & Carter, 2004). Statistics on this group are sparse, but the Children's Defense Fund (2005) estimated that more than 2.5 million children are living in households headed by a relative other than their parents without a parent present, and they often live in poverty (one in five). This rate is higher than for children living in nonrelative foster care (Fuller-Thomson & Minkler, 2000). Children in kinship care are more likely to be African American, and their caregivers tend to be less educated and of a lower socioeconomic status than children in nonkinship foster care (Gebel, 1996). Many studies have shown that kinship foster families receive less training, fewer services, and less support than nonkinship foster families, though it is unclear why this is the case. There is some evidence that child welfare workers do not feel that the same level of service is necessary in the two groups (Cuddeback, 2004).

To compound the obstacles faced by these families, a large portion of kinship care is informal and is not reported to any related agency. This makes it difficult to assess the problems faced by these families and what services they may need. Because of this, it is often necessary

for the schools to recognize these families and ensure that the children are receiving the support they need to meet school expectations.

Even with these hurdles, there is evidence that children placed in kinship care have more stable, longer placements than children in nonkinship foster care and that they are less likely to reenter care. The research regarding reunification and permanency is mixed regarding the differences between kinship care and nonkinship foster care (Cuddeback, 2004). Because the families involved in kinship care are related to the birth parents of the children, often the foster family feels more stress related to reunification and permanency than families in nonkinship foster care (Coakley, Cuddeback, Buehler, & Cox, 2007). This stress needs to be assessed when questions of the long-term goals for the children are addressed.

A 2004 intervention titled Kinship Care Connection (KCC), used a school-based intervention to "increase children's self-esteem and to mediate kin caregiver burden" (Strozier, McGrew, Krisman, & Smith, 2005, p. 1011). The intervention included mentoring and tutoring of the children by an unrelated adult, mutual support groups for the caregivers, and case management services. The study reported significant increases in caregiver self-efficacy and child self-esteem. The researchers posited that if any one of the elements had been missing, the changes would not have been so significant (Strozier, McGrew, Krisman, & Smith, 2005).

Gang Violence and Delinquent Behaviors

Gang violence is a complicated and multifaceted social problem. Whereas 75% of deaths in 15- to 19-year-olds were due to natural causes in 1933, 80% of deaths in that same age group were due to homicide and unintentional injury 60 years later (McNeil, 2002). The change in mortality rates was caused by violence, and the mortalities were typically gang-related. Adolescents who are members of minority groups and live in high-poverty areas are often the victims or perpetrators of violent crimes. More male adolescents die from gunshots than any other cause. According to a survey conducted by the National Youth Gang Center (NYGC) in 2004, approximately 29% of all city and county jurisdictions experience youth gang problems. Broken down by size, that is 82% of larger cities (population over 50,000), 42% of suburban communities, 27% of small cities (population between 2,500 and 49,999), and 14% of rural counties. Based on the results of this survey, NYGC estimates that there are approximately 760,000 gang members nationwide (Egley & Ritz, 2006).

The Carnegie Council on Adolescent Development (1995) has taken an active role in identifying risk factors of violence (e.g., being male, unemployed, poor, minority, residing in an urban environment, having poor conflict-management skills, and with ready access to weapons), as well as preventive interventions. But in recent years, gangs have expanded beyond low-income urban neighborhoods to working- and middle-class suburban areas, as evidenced by the statistics cited earlier. Media coverage of gangs has compounded the problem.

Schools, too, have become one of the battlegrounds for gang warfare and violence. Interventions must address the individual, interpersonal, and social and systems levels if we are going to reduce and prevent violence (Tolan, Gorman-Smith, & Henry, 2003). Social workers employed in schools should lead in the development of peer mediation programs and skills; family and community groups should be engaged in the formulation of solutions; and because churches play a critical role in many minority groups, they should be considered partners in this effort. The efficacy of these suggestions still needs to be proven. However, we do know that family and behavior interventions have shown efficacy and effectiveness for reducing such behaviors. Suppression strategies dominated early attempts at intervention (Vigil, 2004). However, a shift in intervention strategies might be necessary due to recent research that has shown how the community environment may play an important mediating role on parenting practices and peer deviancy, both of

which have been associated with adolescent male violence (Tolan et al., 2003). Child safety on the bus and playground, Internet access and use, gang prevention, classroom management, and anti-bullying policies are all important parts of a comprehensive approach to reducing violence in schools (Callahan, 2008). According to the National Youth Violence Prevention Resource Center (2001), substance use/abuse has been correlated to adolescent delinquent behaviors associated with gang violence and is another area in which interventions could be focused. Additional discussion on violence in schools takes place in Chapter 6.

Nonattenders

The first compulsory attendance laws were enacted in Massachusetts in 1852, and by 1918 every state had such laws. However, many children who enter schools never complete the 12 years of academic preparation. Education is a basic requirement for survival in a society that is growing more and more technical. Also, education teaches character and the duties of citizenship, two other requirements essential for survival in society. Yet, every day, large numbers of pupils fail to report to school. There are no national statistics on nonattenders, but some school districts report as many as 15% of children are absent on any given day. Some of these children have legitimate excuses, but in some cases as many as 60% of them are truant (National Center for School Engagement, 2005).

Dropouts and truant children often have a disorganized home life and parents who may not value education and have poor academic skills. Other problems of this population are low grades, reading failure, a history of behavioral problems (including suspension and/or expulsion from school), emotional and financial inability to participate in extracurricular activities, and negative relations with teachers and other authority figures. Some children experience so much failure at school, both academically and socially, that it is amazing that they are able to attend as often as they do. School and teacher attitudes that place the locus of the problem in the student rather than recognizing structural inequalities and social disadvantage may further impede both motivation and achievement (Hudley, 1997). In addition, for some children, schools are not safe environments. Eight percent of students reported that they had been threatened or injured by a weapon while at school (CDC, 2008a). It was also noted that youth are likely to stay away from school due to personally feeling unsafe in school. As mentioned earlier, LGBT youth are at particular risk of victimization.

Table 8.6 identifies some typical problem areas that are of concern to teachers in public schools. When student tardiness, student absenteeism, and cutting class are combined for public secondary schools, nonattendance becomes a major problem. These problems are not as prevalent in the private secondary institutions, where family involvement is stronger and where schools foster a sense of community.

For children, the consequences of truancy are devastating. They are unable to compete in the labor market and, embittered by their school experience, have difficulty functioning in society. Social workers, particularly those who work at the elementary level, can identify early patterns of nonattendance that suggest which pupils are at risk of becoming chronic attendance problems. They should also act as liaison with home, school, and community agencies to help these children and their families. They can help the school to develop communities of learners who are supportive of one another and provide relationships that facilitate active positive involvement in schools. Programs on social problem solving and creating school climates in which bullying and aggressive behavior are not tolerated may also be needed. Further,

TABLE 8.6 Teachers' Perceptions about Serious Problems in their Schools

Problem Area	1994–1994	1999–2000	2003–2004
Student Tardiness	10.5	10.2	13.8
Student Absenteeism	14.4	13.9	13.2
Teacher Absenteeism	1.5	2.2	1.1
Students Cutting Class	5.1	4.7	5.6
Physical Conflicts Among Students*	8.2	4.8	12.1
Robbery or Theft*	4.1	2.4	3.7
Vandalism of School Property*	6.7	3.4	3.6
Student Pregnancy	7.3	3.7	2.4
Student Use of Alcohol*	9.3	7.4	3.1
Student Drug Abuse*	5.7	6	4.5
Student Possession of Weapons*	2.8	0.8	0.5
Verbal Abuse of Teachers*	11.1	—	11.8
Student Disrespect for Teachers*	18.5	17.2	21.6
Students Dropping Out	5.8	4.6	3.3
Student Apathy	23.6	20.6	16.6
Lack of Parental Involvement	27.6	23.7	21.6
Poverty	19.5	19.2	21.4
Racial Tension*	5.1	—	2.4
Students Come Unprepared to Learn	28.8	29.5	26.8

* Questions were changed in the 2003–2004 survey to "To the best of your knowledge how often do the following types of problems occur with students at this school?" Number listed is percentage who responded "Happens daily."
Source: U.S. Department of Education, National Center for Education Statistics. (2008). *Digest of Education Statistics, 2007* (NCES No. 2008-022): Table 68, Teachers' perceptions about serious problems in their school: by control and level of school: 1993–1994, 1999–2000, 2003–2004.

social workers may help teachers in understanding the societal, cultural, and social influences on a child's learning. Appropriate tutoring that allows them to build on and track their successes is necessary for many of these children. The establishment of alternative schools or innovative in-school programs for pupils who find learning in the "traditional" school difficult can be another course of action. Evaluation of the educational environment, including the staff's attitude toward different pupil groups and its willingness to modify learning materials and expectations, should be a target of intervention. Development of extracurricular activities that are appealing to potential dropouts is one means of facilitating identification between them and the school.

The School of Social Work at the University of North Carolina worked with Communities-in-Schools (CIS—the nation's largest dropout prevention program) representatives to develop an instrument for planning and monitoring success (Bowen, Wooley, Richman, & Bowen, 2001). They provided a framework for thinking about and developing multifaceted interventions. Stability, load balance, and participation are examined at the family, school, peer group, and community level. Stability refers to the availability of stable supportive relationships. Load balance involves an understanding of how well the capabilities of the child match the demands of the environment (e.g., if a child's home is noisy and chaotic, how capable is the child at filtering stimuli when attempting to attend to homework?). Participation refers to the meaningful involvement in the environments that constitute the child's microsystems. Developing social relationships and involvement decreases anomie and gives life meaning and the student reasons for caring (Richman, Bowen, & Woolley, 2004). The goal of interventions in these areas is to increase the student's social competence, sense of purpose, autonomy, and problem-solving abilities.

Drug and Alcohol Users

Substance abuse is becoming an increasingly serious problem for adolescents. The CDC's Youth Risk Behavior Surveillance (2008a) reported that in 2007, 75% of high school students had experimented with alcohol at least once in their lives. Forty-five percent of students had at least one drink in the month preceding the survey, and just over one quarter had an episode of heavy drinking (five of more drinks) in the month preceding the survey. About two of every five students had used marijuana at least once in their life, whereas half of those had used marijuana at least once in the last month. Nationally, about 8% of students tried marijuana before age 13. About 20% of students were current tobacco users, meaning that they had used tobacco at least once in the preceding month. Between 2 and 13% of students had used other drugs in their lifetime, with the variation caused by the type of drug (2% had used injected drugs, and 6% used ecstasy, whereas 13% used inhalants). Also, about a quarter of students reported being offered, sold, or given an illegal drug while on school property within the last year (CDC, 2008a).

Some attribute the growth of this problem to the acceptability of alcohol by the adult culture and the widespread use of drugs in society. The reasons why youths and adults become dependent on alcohol and drugs are complicated. Like other problem behaviors, the risk factors for alcohol and drug abuse occur at a number of levels. It is important to note that although societal attitudes toward alcohol and drug use have fluctuated, the risk factors for substance abuse have remained stable for the past 20 years (Jenson, 1997). Residential mobility, school transitions, low neighborhood attachment, and neighborhood disorganization (i.e., high population density, high crime areas) are neighborhood variables associated with substance abuse. Family factors include parental substance abuse, poor family management practices (lax supervision or very severe or inconsistent discipline), poor family communications, and weak parent–child relationships. School-level risk factors include lack of attachment to school and lack of commitment to education. Adolescent substance abusers are more likely to be truant and to perform poorly (Roebuck, French, & Dennis, 2003). Involvement with peers who use drugs or participate in other deviant activities is one of the strongest predictors of adolescent substance abuse. Attention deficit disorders and poor impulse control are predictors of age of onset of drinking and drug use. Children who are aggressive at age 5 have an increased likelihood of deviant behaviors, including substance abuse, as adolescents. Early onset of drug use increases the likelihood of subsequent drug use and involvement in deviant behaviors. Youths may drink or use drugs to emulate the adult figures in their lives, to defy their parents and society, to be accepted by peer groups, to avoid dealing with reality, and to escape emotional problems.

Warning signals that one should be alert to include impulsive behavior, lack of perseverance, not caring about other people, nervous tremors, sudden changes in mood, inability to cope with frustrations, irritability with family members and friends, rebelliousness (McDermott, 1984), and a decrease in short-term memory skills.

Adolescent substance abusers encounter numerous difficulties in attempting to satisfy the expectations of their families and school. When confronted, their response is generally denial. Because the school is the one institution that almost every youth has some contact with, it must play an important role in identifying adolescent substance abusers, educating youths concerning the harmful effects of drugs and alcohol, and helping to provide protective conditions for youth, such as developing social bonds with teachers, parents, and prosocial peers, participation in prosocial activities, and increased commitment to school. The involvement of school social workers can include referring abusers to appropriate treatment centers, providing in-service training to school staff members and parents on how to identify these youths, and developing a preventive substance abuse curriculum that can be used in health education classes.

To create an effective school-based substance abuse intervention program, the needs of the student population must be considered. Recent research has found that programs that are specific to student groups generate better results. For example, Kulis et al. (2005) found that culturally grounded intervention programs produced more positive results for Mexican-American adolescents. This study investigated three different versions of the Keepin' it REAL substance abuse program for Mexican-American adolescents. The program is presented in one of three ways: (1) Latino-based, using Mexican and Mexican-American values; (2) based on European-American and African-American values; and (3) based on multicultural values, including half Latino values and half non-Latino values. The study found that the version geared specifically toward the population's culture, the Latino version, produced more positive results in the reduction of alcohol and marijuana use (Kulis et al., 2005). Later research on this exemplary program showed that the program's efficacy was the same for both boys and girls in their drug use, but was more effective in increasing the boys' antidrug norms. There was more variation when acculturation was taken into account. The program has been shown to be more effective on both use and norms when given to a less acculturated group of Latinos (Kulis, Yabiku, Marsiglia, Nieri, & Crossman, 2007). Another example has been found with chronic marijuana users. This group of adolescent substance abusers is more likely to be truant and drop out of school. Though cognitive behavior therapy has proven useful in treating marijuana use in adults, it alone is less effective in adolescents (Copeland, 2004). Special community collaborative efforts might be needed to reach this population (Roebuck et al., 2003).

Gifted and Talented Youth

According to the U.S. Department of Education (2008), approximately 3.2 million students were classified talented and gifted in 2004, which is about 6.7% of the student population. This group of students has been found to have the lowest academic gains compared to all other students. Because of the recent emphasis on minimal proficiency, many students that are already performing to those standards are left to flounder while the focus of the staff is on the students who need intensive instruction to reach those goals (Sanders, 2000). They are also the special-needs group that receives the lowest amount of funding on average (DeLacy, 2004). Programs for gifted and talented youth have been affected by decreased use of categorical funds, concerns about equity, and the belief of some that gifted and talented programs represent a form of tracking (Oakes, 2005). Some observers contend that the challenge offered to gifted and talented youth should be available to all. Indeed, many enrichment programs and thinking skills curricula developed for gifted and talented youth are now being utilized in regular classrooms. However, the national struggle between equity and excellence fails to recognize that we achieve equity when we strive for personal excellence for each student in programs that are more inclusive.

Minorities have been underrepresented in gifted and talented programs due, in part, to the narrow admissions policies of some school districts. Heavy reliance on nationally standardized tests as admissions criteria deters the inclusion of many minority children in these programs. These tests are often biased toward a majority middle-class culture (Pfeiffer, 2001). Increased recognition of multiple intelligences has helped to decrease the narrow definition of giftedness.

Students who are gifted or talented are defined as "students, children, or youth who give evidence of high achievement capability in areas such as intellectual, creative, artistic, or leadership capacity, or in specific academic fields, and who need services or activities not ordinarily provided by the school in order to fully develop those capabilities" (20 U.S.C. § 7801(22)).

Current best practices with gifted and talented youth emphasize use of appropriately differentiated instruction within classrooms that use flexible grouping, offer student choice in classes, and utilize gifted and talented resource specialists. Advocates for gifted and talented youth warn against heavy use of cooperative learning strategies, contending that these heterogeneous learning groups result in gifted and talented children performing as assistant teachers and limit the challenge to these students (Pfeiffer, 2001; Robinson, 1990). To provide adequate intellectual challenge and the opportunity to learn together with other exceptionally bright students, while not creating separate classrooms for them, experts

recommend cluster grouping. Cluster grouping involves placing talented children in groups of less than 10 together in classrooms. This arrangement allows the teacher to more easily attend to the special needs of this group of children (need for increasing challenge) and offers children the opportunity to understand their learning differences as they explore them with others of similar ability, but avoids some of the dangers of tracking by avoidance of permanent grouping arrangements for students of more limited ability levels (Winebrenner & Devlin, 1996).

Best practices in regular and gifted education highlight many similar beliefs and values: theme-based, integrated curriculum; student choice and interest; self-understanding; student involvement in assessment; critical thinking development; group interaction; establishing communities of learners; family involvement; school–community connections; curriculum built on student interest and relevance to the learner, including inquiry- or problem-based approaches that utilize the study of significant problems in the child's realm of experience (Tomlinson, 2001). Differentiated instruction in mixed-ability classrooms allows children to exhibit what they know in a variety of ways and is principle- or concept-focused, with advanced learners offered the opportunity to apply key concepts and explore some areas in greater depth or breadth. Learning contracts, learning centers, computer programs, multiple sources of information, complex instruction, multiple intelligence orientation, and negotiated criteria may all be part of a differentiated instruction classroom that meets children at their own level and challenges them in growth-producing ways (Tomlinson, 2001).

Children with exceptional talents may need assistance in understanding their feelings and developing social networks. They may experience increased sensitivity and be frustrated when others are unable to perceive what, to them, seems so obvious. Perfectionism in themselves is another concern for very bright children. According to Renzulli and Park (2002), gifted and talented students are at risk for dropping out of school when they feel isolated and have an overall negative attitude toward school. They also found that half of the gifted and talented students who drop out are from the lowest quartile socioeconomic group.

Teachers may refer gifted and talented children for psychological assessment, expressing concern that they have attention deficit hyperactivity disorder (ADHD). Most of the behaviors listed in the diagnostic criteria for ADHD may also be exhibited by children with exceptional abilities (e.g., blurts out answers to questions, fidgets, talks excessively; American Psychiatric Association, 2000; Hartnett, Nelson, & Rinn, 2004). As stated previously, although a gifted child may also have an attention deficit, not every gifted child has ADHD. Hartnett et al. (2004) found that unless diagnosis options were presented with a case, half of the participating counseling graduate students misdiagnosed a 7-year-old boy with ADHD. When the option of talented and gifted was presented with the case vignette, the counselors were more likely to diagnose them as such. A key determinant is the context in which the behaviors occur. For gifted and talented children, the presence of problematic behaviors fluctuates greatly from one setting to another, according to the amount of structure and challenge. Although the activity level of some gifted children is often quite high (about 25% require less sleep), their activity is more focused and directed than that of children with ADHD. Unlike the inconsistent performance of ADHD children, when appropriately challenged and interested, children who are gifted maintain high performance and effort and may be intensely focused (Webb & Latimer, 1993). If the tasks assigned are repetitive or below the level of intellectual challenge, the gifted and talented child may appear to have ADHD. It is important to evaluate all the possible causes of behavior, including consideration of a mismatch between the child's abilities and the classroom curriculum and instruction. Evaluations that include assessment of intelligence, emotional problems (e.g., anxiety and depression), and appropriateness of curriculum and instruction, and that collect information from a variety of contexts and significant individuals in the child's life (i.e., teachers, parents), are most apt to provide adequate information to determine whether a child's exceptional talents are a contributor to the observed behaviors or if ADHD is present (Webb & Latimer, 1993).

Conclusion

The goal of social work that cuts across these different pupil groups is to increase equal educational opportunity for all children and youth by introducing and facilitating change in the systems in which they function—the school, the community, the home, and the pupil group itself. The earlier the intervention, the more likely positive outcomes result (see Figure 8.3). A national study of 18 schools that were effective in serving at-risk youth identified two broad conditions typically present in these successful schools: (a) a strong sense of community and (b) characteristics similar to high-reliability organizations that provide whatever level of support is necessary to attain success 100% of the time (Irmsher, 1997). Elements involved in the creation of community included shared vision and purpose: shared values; participation by families; an ethos of caring; trust; incorporation of diversity-inclusiveness; teamwork; good communication among staff, students, and families; recognition; extended roles for staff; and respect for all (Irmsher, 1997; Royal & Rossi, 1997). High-reliability organizations are also characterized by a shared mission, and they maintain the belief that failure to achieve core tasks represents disaster. High-reliability organizations incorporate flexible hierarchies with clearly defined roles and responsibilities that utilize collegial decision making when appropriate and empower all staff members to cross traditional boundaries in responding to emergencies to avoid failure. Reliance on, and continuing development of, the professional judgment of all staff members contributes to the success of the organization.

Mike Rose (1998) traveled around the United States for 3½ years visiting public schools that had promising practices. He visited urban, rural, and suburban schools. His account concentrates largely on the promising practices found in schools that served high-risk populations. He summarized the commonalties across these successful schools: (a) sense of safety: a climate of physical and emotional safety including the safety to take risks; (b) respect: fair treatment, respect for the culture, language, and history of people; (c) teacher's authority came from multiple sources: knowledge, respectful consideration of others, caring—rather than solely from role or age, and authority was distributed even in traditional classrooms; (d) classrooms were places of expectation and responsibility supported by mechanisms to aid in involvement and achievement; and (e) creation of a vital public space: children learning, doing, making contributions, generating knowledge; places of challenge and reflection, quiet work, and public presentation. Teachers created collaborative relationships among themselves that served to nourish each other so that they in turn could nourish their students. These teachers believed in the value of their work and were able "to affirm in a deep and comprehensive way the capability of the students in their classrooms" (Rose, 1995, p. 422).

Research on resilience, the ability to succeed even in very negative environmental circumstances, indicates that three major areas of protective factors enable children to circumvent negative life experiences. These areas are (a) caring and supportive relationships, at least one, who was often a teacher when the family was highly dysfunctional; (b) positive and high expectations, with the belief that success is attainable; and (c) opportunities for meaningful participation in education, employment, growth, and achievement (Bernard, 1995; Fraser, Kirby, & Smokowski, 2004; Werner & Smith, 1992). These factors can be encouraged by increasing the students' senses of autonomy, purpose, and social competence, as wells as their problem-solving skills and achievement motivation (Morrison & Allen, 2007).

The National Association of Secondary School Principals (1997) called for personalization of the high school as a key challenge for reform. Research supports the premise that a strong sense of community among staff enhances instructional efforts and a sense of personal well-being, as well as fostering a collaborative climate and student cooperation (Royal & Rossi, 1997). Social workers have the knowledge and skills to assist in the development of community, particularly in encouraging the involvement of families in the school community, but also in helping staff to develop a shared vision and collaborative relationships and to recognize and use resources flexibly to achieve their goals.

For Study and Discussion

1. Review the characteristics of each target group of pupils discussed in this chapter. Identify additional characteristics and discuss intervention strategies.
2. Identify other target groups of pupils in the school who might come to the attention of the school social worker. Specify what might be the nature of the intervention. What aspects of the school environment could cause these children difficulty?
3. Numerous demands are made on the time of social workers in schools; they must serve many different pupil groups. Discuss how you as a professional would respond to these demands. What roles would take on more importance and how would you define "practice"?
4. Obtain a copy of your state's child abuse reporting act. Analyze it for clarity, weaknesses, and implications for reporting abuse found in the schools. How would a school district implement it?
5. Interview school social workers, teachers, and school administrators. Ask them to identify the pupil groups in their schools who are most vulnerable. Ask them to elaborate on their intervention and the type of assistance they provide these pupils and their families. What insights do they have regarding the etiology of pupils' situations?
6. Devise a strategy for identifying vulnerable pupil groups who are at risk.
7. Review the Identified Pupil Situation Complex chart (Figure 8.3). Then discuss the specific goals (i.e., B. Behavioral Objectives; C. Measurable Outcomes) that you would want to accomplish for the remaining four pupil groups identified in the chart.

8. Visit the Council for Exceptional Children Web site on gifted and talented children, www.cec.sped.org, and explore resources there or join the TAGFAM (Families of talented and gifted) listserv. Find out what issues are important for families of gifted and talented children.

Additional Readings

Allen-Meares, P., Colarossi, L. C., Oyserman, D., & DeRoos, Y. (2003). Assessing depression in childhood and adolescence: A guide for social work practice. *Child and Adolescent Social Work Journal, 20*(1), 5–20.

Allen-Meares, P., & Fraser, M. (2004). *Intervention with children & adolescents: An interdisciplinary perspective* (2nd ed.). Needham Heights, MA: Allyn & Bacon.

Altshuler, S. J., & Schmautz, T. (2006). No Hispanic student left behind: The consequences of "high stakes" testing. *Children & Schools, 28*(1), 5–14.

Butler, M., & Smith-McKeever, C. (2003). Harlem Dowling—West side center for children and family services: A comprehensive response to working with HIV-affected children and families. In D. J. Gilbert & E. M. Wright (Eds.), *African American Women and HIV/AIDS: Critical Responses.* Westport, CT: Praeger.

Clancy, J. (1995). Ecological school social work: The reality and the vision. *Social Work in Education, 17*(1), 40–47.

Coleman, J. C. (Ed.). (1987). *Working with troubled adolescents: A handbook.* San Diego: Academic Press.

Evans, G. W. (2004). The environment of childhood poverty. *American Psychologist, 59*(2), 77–92.

Freeman, E. M., Franklin, C. G., Fong, R., Shaffer, G. L., & Timberlake, E. M. (Eds.). (1998). *Multisystem skills and interventions in school social work practice.* Washington, DC: NASW Press.

Hernandez-Jozefowicz, D. M., & Allen-Meares, P. (2002). Poverty in schools: Intervention and resource building through school-linked services. *Children & Schools: Special Issue, 24*(2), 123–136.

Hernandez-Jozefowicz, D. M., & Israel, N. (2001). Services to homeless students and families: The McKinney-Vento act and its implications for school social work practice. *Children & Schools, 28*(1), 37–44.

Kransdorf, M., Doster, B., & Alvarez, A. (2002). Interactions between preservice teachers and school social work interns in an urban school setting. *Urban Education, 37*(4), 497–532.

Lindsay, D. (2003). The *Welfare of Children.* Oxford: Oxford University Press.

Morrow, D. F. (2004). Social work practice with gay, lesbian, bisexual, and transgender adolescents. *Families in Society, 85*(1), 91–99.

Rienzo, B. A., Button, J. W., Sheu, J., & Ying, L. (2006). The politics of sexual orientation in American schools. *Journal of School Health, 76*(3), 93–97.

Robin, L., Dittus, P., Whitaker, D., Crosby, R., Ethier, K., Mezoff, J., et al. (2004). Behavioral interventions to reduce incidence of HIV, STD, and pregnancy among adolescents: A decade in review. *Journal of Adolescent Health, 34*(1), 3–26.

Smith, E. P., Gorman-Smith, D., Quinn, W. H., Rabiner, D. L., Tolan, P. H., Winn, D. M., et al. (2004). Community-based multiple family groups to prevent and reduce violence and aggressive behavior: The GREAT families program. *American Journal of Preventive Medicine, 26*(1), 39–47.

Teasley, M. (2004). School social workers and urban education report with African American children and youth: Realities advocacy, and strategies for change. *School Community Journal, 14*(2), 19–38.

Whitted, K. S., & Dupper, D. R. (2005). Best practices for preventing or reducing bullying in schools. *Children & Schools, 27*(3), 167–174.

9

Securing Equal Educational Opportunity: Language, Race, Gender, and Sexual Orientation

SANDRA KOPELS

University of Illinois at Urbana-Champaign

All children living in our democracy have certain inalienable rights. One is the opportunity to experience and to use to their fullest capacity the educational program offered by our American schools.[1]

—*Alma Laabs*

Introduction

Court cases and legislation have greatly affected educational policies and practices. As you have seen in Chapter 5 on student rights and the control of behavior, in the past, schools had unfettered authority over the education of students. It was not until challenges were filed in courts and courts began to recognize that students had constitutionally protected rights in the educational environment that schools had to weigh their actions against the rights of students. Chapter 7, on special education, describes how children with disabilities had been denied their fair share of "public education." Again, it took court challenges and the passage of groundbreaking federal legislation before children with disabilities finally were granted the right to attend public school with their nondisabled peers.

The Education of All Handicapped Children Act of 1974, commonly known as IDEA, drastically altered school policies and practices, thus opening educational opportunities for students who previously had been excluded from education. Children with disabilities are not the only students who have been denied equal educational opportunities. Children whose primary language is not English, children who are ethnic and racial minorities, female students, and students who are gay/lesbian, bisexual, or transgendered have also been denied access to certain programs offered by schools. Discrimination and other unfair policies, either covert or overt, have often placed these student groups into educational tracks that deny them equal educational opportunities. In this chapter, we again use a legal lens to examine the unique status of non-English-speaking children, members of ethnic and racial minorities, and the

---

222

role of sexism, gender discrimination, and sexual orientation discrimination in education. We look at problems for groups of students who are denied equal educational opportunities under the law. We then look at the roles that school social workers can play in bringing forth awareness of issues of cultural diversity and incorporating them into the school environment to truly provide educational opportunities for children that are equal.

Bilingual and Bicultural Education

The ethnic composition of the United States has changed and will continue to change greatly over the next few decades. The early immigrants to the United States were primarily of European descent. Today, people come to the United States from all parts of the world. Data from the 2000 Census indicates that 28.4 million people in the United States were not U.S. citizens at birth, about 10% of the population. Among the foreign-born, persons from Latin America, composed of Central America, South America, and the Caribbean, constituted 51% of the population, 25.5% were born in Asia, 15.3% were born in Europe, and 8% came from other regions of the world. The population from Central America, including Mexico, constitutes about one third of the total persons born outside the United States who reside in the United States (Lollack, 2001). These new immigrant groups are less familiar racially, culturally, and linguistically than previous immigrant groups (McMullen & Lynde, 1997).

No matter what country they originate from, many people immigrate to the United States because they see it as a land of opportunity and freedom. This hope for a new and better future has been held since the Pilgrims left Europe for the United States on the Mayflower in the early 1600s. However, although the Statue of Liberty is the beacon that symbolizes to immigrants "Give me your tired, your poor,/Your huddled masses yearning to breathe free" (Lazarus, 1883), the United States' recent message has become less welcoming and

more exclusionary. For example, the U.S. federal government passed welfare reform legislation known as The Personal Responsibility and Work Reconciliation Act of 1996. This legislation affects immigration to the United States because of the ineligibility of immigrants to receive food stamps and SSI benefits for the first 5 years after entry into the country.

Other restrictions exist as well. For example, there are increasing limitations placed on the numbers of persons that can immigrate to the United States from different countries, with certain countries bearing heavier restrictions. Additionally, after the terrorist attacks of September 11, 2001, persons from specific countries, especially those that are considered Middle Eastern or Arabic, are finding increased scrutiny of their backgrounds. University students must account for their whereabouts once they enter the United States and obtain employment or leave the U.S. within a certain amount of time after completing their education.

Independent of these events, there has been a movement in a great number of states, some of which have large non-English-speaking populations, such as California and Arizona, to draft official state policies that reflect English as the official language of the state. More troubling, however, is the English-only movement that, if adopted, would make all government publications, documents, Web sites or other written material available only in English.

Although many immigrants enter the United States legally based on the quotas allotted for their countries, a significant number enter the country illegally. States such as California, Florida, and Texas have opted to increase the amount of money they spend on keeping illegal immigrants out of their states. Some states claim that illegal immigrants are costing taxpayers billions of dollars in health and educational services. As a result, California voters approved Proposition 187, which denied most public services to illegal immigrants. This proposition prohibited undocumented immigrants from receiving education, social services, and nonemergency medical care and required public officials, including social workers, to report persons who entered the United States illegally (Hiratsuka, 1995). Numerous court challenges were filed against the measure, and it has not yet been enforced, despite its passage.

The 2000 Census reported that 18% of the population, or 47 million people, aged 5 and above, spoke a language other than English in their homes. These figures were up from 14% (31.8 million people) in 1990 and 11% (23.1 million people) in 1980 (Shin & Bruno, 2003). After English and Spanish, Chinese was the language most commonly spoken at home (2.0 million speakers), followed by French (1.6 million speakers) and German (1.4 million speakers). Spanish speakers grew by about 60%, and Spanish continued to be the non-English language most frequently spoken at home (Shin & Bruno, 2003). The Chinese language, however, jumped from the fifth to the second most widely spoken non-English language, as the number of Chinese speakers rose from 1.2 to 2.0 million people (Shin & Bruno, 2003).

Persons born outside the United States are more geographically concentrated and more likely to live in central cities of metropolitan areas than those born in the United States. For example, immigrants from Mexico and Central America have settled primarily in the western and southern United States, those from South America and the Caribbean have settled in the Northeast and South, and almost half the persons from Asia have settled in the West (Lollack, 2001).

Eight states had over 1 million non-English-language speakers in 2000, led by California (12.4 million), with more than twice the number of any other state. Texas had the second-largest number of non-English-language speakers (6.0 million), followed by New York (5.0 million), Florida (3.5 million), Illinois (2.2 million), New Jersey (2.0 million), Arizona (1.2 million), and Massachusetts (1.1 million; Shin & Bruno, 2003). Nearly half of the limited-English-proficient children live in California, Texas, or New York which has significant implications for the educational system (Borden, 2001).

The schools are ill prepared to respond: A shortage of bilingual educators and programs, an unclear understanding of how special educational services might assist those students who need services, and distance between the home/community and school all interact to undermine educational success for linguistically different students. Chapter 7 discusses issues concerning the assessment of students needing special education assistance. The assessment and development of intervention strategies for language-minority students presents still another challenge. Communicating the results of these assessments to parents of limited-English-proficient children, whose English is often worse than that of their children, is a further challenge.

The public school system, as an institution, has been geared toward the middle class. Socioeconomic status is one of the single largest determinants of a student's school performance (Borden, 2001). Children who are racial minorities and children who are non-English-speaking tend to come from families occupying a lower socioeconomic position. Their parents are often poorly educated and somewhat mystified by the educational process and all its special programs. Moreover, their parents may not have a command of the English language and may lack the financial resources to afford money for books, tutoring, or extracurricular activities. These children generally find entry into the public school difficult because they lack the family resources and experiential background that usually lead to successful achievement.

Antecedent Language Movements in the United States

In the 18th and 19th centuries, non-English and bilingual instruction was typical in many parts of the United States. During the early 1700s, school instruction throughout Pennsylvania, Maryland, Virginia, and the Carolinas gave importance to German, often to the exclusion of English. In a school district in Wisconsin, funds were specified for German texts, and in other school districts in the state, the school board could hire only German-speaking teachers. In California, private schools were composed mainly of descendants of Spaniards, and thus study of the Spanish language was required. As late as 1884, a law was passed in New Mexico requiring that reading and writing be taught in either Spanish or English or both. By the end of the 19th century, about a dozen states had passed laws requiring schools to instruct students in more than one language; in other parts of the country, many localities provided bilingual instruction without state sanction, in languages as diverse as Norwegian, Italian, French, Polish, and Czech (National Bilingual Education Association, 1998). During that same period, the Cherokee Indians had an educational system that used bilingual materials and produced a population that was 90% literate in its native language.

At that time, it appeared that respect was paid to the concept of cultural diversity, although that term was not yet coined. What happened to this early commitment that recognized a child's heritage and his or her specific language needs? Mandatory school attendance laws, elimination of public funding for church-related schools, and the beginnings of an isolationist policy in the United States led the way toward English becoming the only accepted language for classroom instruction. Some states even outlawed the use of languages other than English, except when used in foreign-language classes.

The Move to Americanize Immigrant Children

The trend toward making the United States a one-language nation seemed to begin in the early 1900s. Theodore Roosevelt, who was committed to this notion, took the position that any person entering the United States must adopt the institutions of the United States and therefore must adopt the language that was the people's native tongue. He felt that it would be not merely a misfortune but a crime to perpetuate differences of language in this country (Roosevelt, 1919). Roosevelt believed that the United States should

provide the means for every immigrant to learn English in schools, for the young during the day and night schools for adults. If 5 years passed without the immigrants learning English, then they should be sent back to the lands from which they came (Roosevelt). From a governmental perspective and considering the age of the nation and the desire for national unity, cultural and linguistic homogeneity was a priority. It was assumed that different languages would further divide the nation and make it difficult to develop a national philosophy and a unified government.

Leibowitz (1983) suggested that the reason for this restrictive view may have its roots far deeper in the foundation of the nation's ideology and may have manifested social and institutional racism known to operate throughout society. Further, he maintained that an analysis of the historical records during this period indicates that official acceptance or rejection of bilingualism in U.S. schools was dependent on whether the group involved was considered politically and socially acceptable. The decision to impose English as the exclusive language of instruction in the schools reflected the popular attitudes toward the particular ethnic group and the degree of hostility evidenced toward that group's development. One study indicated that, after World War I, 23 states passed laws restricting the teaching of foreign languages, especially German, in response to postwar anti-German sentiment (Wexler, 1996). If a group was viewed as different in some way (color, religion) or alien, the United States imposed harsher restrictions on its language practices.

The Reemergence of Bilingual Education

The cry for assimilation had dominated the way of thinking for so long in the United States that educators had lost sight of the child's need to his or her cultural identity. During the 1960s, a confluence of factors occurred. The civil rights movement and the passage of the Civil Rights Act of 1964 helped focus the nation on equality. The

1965 Immigration Act changed immigration laws and allowed large numbers of Asians and Latin Americans to enter the country, causing demographic shifts in the population. As more of these children appeared in the classroom, bilingual instruction was needed to teach them (Ovando, 2003). Additionally, as Cuban exiles fled Castro's regime for Florida, they expected their stay in the United States to be short-lived. Accordingly, they wanted their children to retain their language and culture for their return home (Ovando, 2003). All these factors contributed to the realization that children should be encouraged to preserve their cultural and linguistic identity. As this idea gained popularity in the mid-twentieth century, a movement toward bilingual and bicultural education emerged.

Definition of Bilingual and Bicultural Education

Before we discuss the legal framework of bilingual and bicultural education, it is essential to understand what is meant by these and related terms.

The intent of bilingual and bicultural education is to develop an educational system that will develop the intellectual abilities of each child adequately by utilizing the child's native language to enable him or her to acquire proficiency in English. Another aim of this type of education is to attend to the cultural needs of the child and his or her community by using English and the languages that reflect the makeup of the community in instruction. Not only do bilingual and bicultural education programs promote mastery of the English language, but they also foster native language proficiency and preserve the child's cultural heritage (Moran, 1988).

The instructional form of bilingual and bicultural education programs has varied. Several types have been identified: transitional programs, bilingual maintenance programs, culturally pluralistic programs, and bicultural and bilingual restorationist programs. These programs differ in their emphasis on such factors as involvement of

families and parents, focus on history of language, inclusion of students of different languages and cultural identities, and how the staff is trained.

Some specific terms used to define teaching approaches or program models of bilingual and bicultural education are defined by Crawford (1997) as follows:

- Transitional bilingual education (TBE) is a model in which the primary goal is to mainstream students to all-English classrooms; it uses native language instruction to help students keep up in their other subjects, phasing in English instruction as soon as possible.
- Developmental bilingual education (DBE) is a model in which the goals include fluent bilingualism as well as academic excellence; English is typically phased in more gradually than in TBE and continues to develop students' skills in the native language after they have become fully English proficient.
- Two-way bilingual education or bilingual immersion is a model that combines DBE for language-minority students and foreign language immersion for students who are English proficient; it includes peer tutoring and seeks to enable each group to learn the other's language while also meeting high academic standards.

The Beginning Legal Framework of Bilingual and Bicultural Education

Before 1968, no federal legislation existed regarding the need for children with limited English proficiency to be able to speak English. The Bilingual Education Act of 1968 endeavored to aid students to acquire English language skills by instructing them in both their native languages and in English. By 2002, when the No Child Left Behind Act (NCLB) was passed, there seemed to have been serious retrenchment in the federal government's interest in teaching students whose primary language was not English. By examining the history of bilingual education legislation and its goals carefully, we will see that although the methods of teaching English to students with limited English language skills has varied, the only real emphasis in federal legislation has been to teach students to speak English. Little emphasis has ever been focused on cultural education.

Passed in 1968, the addition of Title VII to the Elementary and Secondary Education Act (ESEA) can be considered the first legislation aimed at linguistically different children. In fact, Title VII, known as the Bilingual Education Act, can be considered a major breakthrough for this group of children. The act provided grants to school districts that implemented programs aimed at increasing English proficiency but allowed school districts to retain discretion in developing bilingual programs and in applying for funds (McMullen & Lynde, 1997). Although the act did not mandate districts to provide bilingual education, it did improve state and local bilingual education policy. Prior to 1968, no state had enacted bilingual educational provisions. By 1973, at least six states had created such provisions, whereas a number of other states repealed their statutes making English the exclusive language of instruction (McMullen & Lynde).

Because the Bilingual Education Act authorized funding only until 1973, hearings were held before Congress for the act's reauthorization. These hearings noted studies showing that schools were still failing to meet the needs of limited-English-proficient children. The Bilingual Education Act of 1974 provided stronger support for bilingualism and biculturalism than the 1968 act. The policy declaration of the act recognized that these children had distinctive cultural heritages and that their native languages and heritages were the primary means for instruction. Congress recognized that schools could meet the needs of these children through bilingual education programs that used multiple languages and cultural resources. The 1974 amendments authorized higher levels of funding from 1974 to 1978 than did the 1968 act, but also put more limits on the types of bilingual education programs that could qualify for funding (Moran, 1988).

In 1978, the Bilingual Education Act was amended again. The amended act emphasized that a child's native language was to be used "to the extent necessary to allow a child to achieve competence in the English language" (P.L. 95-561). However, the act made it far clearer that the primary goal of bilingual instruction was for English acquisition. The amendments also addressed concerns about segregation. To promote limited-English-proficient children's acquisition of English and to prevent segregation from other children, the act explicitly permitted English-speaking children to participate in bilingual education classes, not to exceed 40% of the class. Elective classes, such as music, physical education, and art, could not be segregated (Moran, 1988).

In 1984, the Bilingual Education Act expanded the definition of acceptable instructional techniques and enlarged the state's role in the grant and policy-making processes. The act recognized the usefulness of programs that relied heavily on native-language instruction but also placed increased importance on "special alternative instructional programs," that is, programs that used structured English-language instruction and other special services to allow a child to achieve competence in the English language rapidly and to meet grade-promotion and graduation standards.

In 1988, Congress again reauthorized the Bilingual Education Act. Studies presented to Congress concluded that the federal government's own research consistently had understated the benefits of programs that relied heavily on native-language instruction and overstated the potential benefits of alternative techniques that used more English-language instruction. Despite these findings, Congress gave greater discretion to educators in their choice of instructional methods by raising the cap on funds for special alternative instructional techniques to 25% of total program grant appropriations. To justify the increase in funding for special alternative instruction programs, legislators cited reports indicating that a significant number of school districts served a broad array of small language groups rather than a large number of children from a single language group. Because local school districts did not have sufficient ability to handle large numbers of limited-English-proficient students of many diverse languages, no one teaching approach could fit all situations. Congress felt it was necessary to give discretion to each school district to decide what was appropriate to fit the needs of its district (Moran, 1988).

In 1994, Congress reauthorized the Bilingual Education Act for the fifth time as Title VII of the Improving America's Schools Act (P.L. 103-382). Section 7102 of the law contained the findings, policy, and purposes underlying the passage of the act. A comprehensive statement, incorporated into the law, helped explain the federal government's commitment to bilingual education (Crawford, 1997). Among the 16 enumerated findings in the Improving America's Schools Act, Congress found that limited-English-proficient children faced a number of problems in receiving an education. These problems included segregated education programs, disproportionate and improper placement in special education and other special programs due to the use of inappropriate evaluation procedures, limited English-proficiency of parents hindered their ability to fully participate in the education of their children, and a shortage of teachers and other staff who were professionally trained and qualified to serve such children.

In the Improving America's Schools Act, Congress also found that the use of a child's native language and culture in classroom instruction promoted self-esteem and contributed to academic achievement and learning English by limited-English-proficient children and youth, benefited English-proficient children and youth who also participated in such programs, and developed the nation's national language resources, promoting the nation's competitiveness in the global economy. Other important Congressional findings included that language-minority Americans speak virtually all world languages plus many that are indigenous to the United States, and that a growing number of children had a cultural heritage that differed from that of their English-proficient peers.

The inclusion of the Bilingual Education Act as part of the Improving America's Schools Act indicated Congress's commitment to high educational standards for limited-English-speaking children as part of a broader goal of school reform. As part of this improvement, Congress recognized the importance that children's native language and culture played in their own self-esteem and academic achievement as well as the benefits that other languages and cultures could have for other students and the nation's global competitiveness. Yet, this commitment lasted only until the next iteration of bilingual education and school reform. The No Child Left Behind Act (NCLB) of 2001 (2002) is the federal government's most recent attempt to improve schooling for America's children. Congress's current attempt at improving education includes no mention whatsoever of children's culture.

The No Child Left Behind Act

In January 2002, President George W. Bush signed the No Child Left Behind Act (the NCLB), which had bipartisan Congressional support. The NCLB was touted as the most sweeping reform of the Elementary and Secondary Education Act (ESEA) since its enactment in 1965. The NCLB redefined the federal role in kindergarten through high school education and is hoped to close the achievement gap between disadvantaged and minority students and their peers by placing performance expectations and ongoing accountability measures in place throughout the year 2014. The NCLB is based on four basic principles: stronger accountability for results, increased flexibility and local control, expanded options for parents, and an emphasis on teaching methods that have been proven to work.

Title III of the NCLB relates to bilingual education. The NCLB consolidated 13 bilingual and immigrant education programs into a state formula program and significantly increased flexibility and accountability. Title III is designed to maintain the previous legislative focus on assisting school districts in teaching English to limited-English-proficient students while also requiring these students to meet the same challenging state standards required of all other students. The NCLB expects schools to teach limited English-proficient students to learn English through scientifically based teaching methods, although the term *scientifically based* is undefined.

According to Section 3102 of the No Child Left Behind Act, the purposes of the act include

- Ensuring that children who are limited English proficient, including immigrant children, attain English proficiency and develop high levels of academic attainment in English
- Assisting all limited-English-proficient children to achieve at high levels in the core academic subjects
- Developing high-quality language instruction educational programs
- Promoting parental and community participation in language instruction educational programs for the parents and communities of limited-English-proficient children
- Streamlining language instructional programs into a formula grant program
- Holding state and local educational agencies accountable for increases in English proficiency of limited-English-proficient children each year.

Although the goals of the No Child Left Behind Act are laudable—educating the nation's children, using scientifically based and proven methods to do so, holding schools accountable for failures and successes, and ensuring that teachers are highly qualified—the act had been criticized before it even went into effect. Around the time of the NCLB's passage, critics wrote about negative changes that were anticipated to occur in bilingual education. For example, Crawford (2002) wrote an obituary for the Bilingual Education Act and its quiet expiration, at age 34, with the passage of the NCLB Act. Ramirez (2001) called the new act "single-minded" in that limited-English-proficient students would receive English-only instruction rather than two-way bilingual immersion education programs. Ramirez noted that the consolidation of funding for different programs for the immigrant, foreign language, and Title VII children into one block grant to address the needs of limited-English-proficient students would profoundly negatively affect all three populations. Krashen (2001) criticized the 3-year time limitation for attaining English fluency, stating that there was no evidence that children languished for excessive periods of time in bilingual education, that English immersion was faster, or that continued instruction in the primary language hurt English language development. Criticism has been leveled against the actual effects that NCLB has had on bilingual education as well. For example, Altshuler and Schmautz (2006) discussed the high stakes that discriminatory testing under NCLB has on all minority populations, but especially Hispanic children. Other studies, looking at preliminary data, show that NCLB has not improved the gaps in reading and mathematical achievement scores, especially for poor, Black, and Hispanic children (Lee, 2006). The study also revealed that the NCLB will not meet its goals if the trends of the first several years continue (Lee, 2006).

The Courts and Bilingual Education

The previous discussion described the primary legislative efforts of the federal government to establish programs for bilingual education and to provide funding for those programs. When parents have been dissatisfied with the quality of bilingual education programs for their children, or in some cases, the complete absence of such programs, they usually resort to the courts to seek redress. Under a variety of legal theories, when these cases have been successful, courts have found that children have been deprived of equal educational opportunity to language under the law.

The U.S. Supreme Court and Bilingual Education

In 1974, the U.S. Supreme Court weighed in on its first and, to date, only decision on bilingual education. *Lau v. Nichols* (1974) was a class action lawsuit brought by non-English-speaking Chinese students against the officials responsible for the operation of the San Francisco, California, public schools. Because of previous litigation against the school district on its racial segregation of Black students, the district reorganized. As a result, there were 2,856 students of Chinese ancestry who spoke little or no English. Although 1,000 of these students were given supplemental courses in the English language, at least 1,800 students did not receive any such instruction. The plaintiffs claimed that the absence of bilingual programs designed to meet the needs of Chinese students violated both Title VI of the Civil Rights Act of 1964 and the Equal Protection Clause of the Fourteenth Amendment to the Constitution. They argued that equality in education went beyond providing the same building and books to all students and included intangible factors. Because these students had not mastered standardized English and could not understand the instruction provided, they were denied or deprived of their rights to even a minimally adequate education; consequently, they received an education inferior to that of other children. Both the U.S. Court and the Ninth Circuit Court of Appeals disagreed with the students' position, ruling that the students' rights to an equal educational opportunity had been satisfied because the same education was made available on the same terms and conditions to the other students in their school district.

Unrelated to this case, in 1970, the Department of Health, Education and Welfare (HEW) had issued a memorandum that determined that Title VI of the Civil Rights Act of 1964 required schools to provide special educational assistance to students not proficient in English. HEW's director mandated that school districts receiving federal funds must take affirmative steps to rectify the language deficiencies of non-English-speaking students. The Department of Health, Education and Welfare, concerned about the impact of the lower courts' decisions on bilingual education policies, was granted permission to argue in support of the petitioners as amicus curiae when the U.S. Supreme Court accepted the students' appeal.

The department's interpretation of Title VI was upheld by the U.S. Supreme Court. The Court noted that California law required English as the basic language of instruction in California schools. The Court further noted that its education laws required the mastery of English by all students. The Education Code provided that no student could receive a diploma of graduation from grade 12 if he or she were not proficient in English as well as other subjects. The Supreme Court reasoned that under these "state-imposed standards there is no equality of treatment merely by providing students with the same facilities, textbooks, teachers, and curriculum; for students who do not understand English are effectively foreclosed from any meaningful education" (*Lau* at 566). Because the Court reasoned that basic English skills are at the core of what the public schools teach, requiring that before a child could meaningfully participate in the educational program, the child must have already acquired those basic skills would make a mockery of public education.

The *Lau* decision did not specify the types of educational programs to be provided to the Chinese students. The students' family did not urge the Supreme Court to order any specific remedy, and the Court did not choose one. Instead, the Court stated that teaching English to the students of Chinese ancestry who do not speak the language, giving instruction to them in Chinese, or using other methodologies were all choices within the discretion of the school district. In his concurrence, Justice Blackmun emphasized that his agreement with the result in the case was based only on the large number of Chinese students who were being deprived of meaningful schooling. He stated that if another case concerned only a very few youngsters or a single child who spoke a language other than English, he would not find the Court's interpretation of the HEW guidelines or the decision in the *Lau* case to require the same outcome. His concurrence demonstrated his implicit acceptance that other ethnic groups in America have had to overcome language barriers with their own efforts and not rely on governmental help.

Other Court Involvement and Bilingual Education

Congress codified the *Lau* decision by enacting the Equal Educational Opportunities Act (EEOA) of 1974. Section 1703(f) of this act states that "no State shall deny equal educational opportunity to an individual on account of his or her race, color, sex or national origin, by ... the failure by an educational agency to take appropriate action to overcome language barriers that impede equal participation by its students in the instructional program." By enacting this legislation, Congress effectively dealt with Justice Blackmun's comments that he may not have reached the same result in another case if only a small number of language minority students were not receiving instruction in English; the EEOA prohibits the state from denying educational opportunity to an individual. Although state and local school authorities maintain a great deal of discretion in the area of bilingual education, courts have upheld the affirmative obligation that schools have to provide some special language instruction to non-English-speaking students (McMullen & Lynde, 1997).

Even English-speaking children may be considered to have a language barrier that impedes their equal participation in the instructional program. In *Martin Luther King, Jr., Elementary School Children v. Ann Arbor School District Board* (1978), the question before the court was whether schools had to take affirmative action to overcome a language barrier when children were unable to use English effectively. In this case, the children were a class of Black, economically disadvantaged children, living in a housing project who spoke a vernacular of English, referred to as "Black English." They claimed that this language was so different from the English spoken in the public schools that it constituted a language barrier that impeded their equal participation in the school's instructional programs. The school argued that because the children already spoke English, the school should not have to provide them English language services. The judge ruled that the students' use of "Black English" was a language barrier that impeded them from equally partaking in the educational system, entitling them to English language instruction.

Most commonly, court challenges based on school districts' failure to take appropriate action to overcome language barriers deal with languages other than English. Most commonly, the plaintiffs allege that the school districts' choices of educational methodologies (e.g., immersion vs. transition, the number of years of bilingual educational services provided) are unsound or flawed. *Casteneda v. Picard* remains as current today as when it was decided in 1981 because it created the test by which courts decide whether the actions school districts have taken are "appropriate."

In *Casteneda,* the plaintiffs were Mexican-American children and their parents who sued a Texas school district. They claimed that the school district's bilingual education and language remediation programs were educationally deficient and unsound because the program's goals were to teach limited-English-speaking children to read and write in both English and Spanish at grade level. The plaintiffs believed that these goals improperly overemphasized the development of English language skills to the detriment of the children's overall cognitive development. The plaintiffs also took issue with the tests the district employed to identify and assess limited-English-speaking children as well as the qualifications of the teachers and staff involved in the district's language remediation program.

On appeal, the Fifth Circuit Court of Appeals observed that at the time of the passage of the EEOC, Congress also passed the Bilingual Education Act. The court reasoned that Congress could not have intended to require local educational authorities to adopt any particular type of language remediation program because bilingual programs were still at the experimental stages; programs and techniques had to be tried before it could be determined what was effective; the Department of Education was charged with the development of model bilingual education programs; and state and local educational agencies were not required to adopt a particular instructional method to be awarded funding under the law.

The *Castaneda* (1981) court noted that Congress had provided almost no legislative or interpretive guidance to assist courts in determining whether a school district's language remediation efforts were considered appropriate action under the EEOC. Accordingly, the court created a three-prong test to make this determination. First, the court must determine that the school district has selected a program based on sound educational theory. Next, the court examines whether the district has implemented the theory effectively through its choice of programs and practices. Finally, the court must evaluate whether the district has carefully monitored the program's results and modified them as necessary.

Almost all of the cases that applied the *Castaneda* standard found that the schools' choices of methodologies were appropriate. For example, in *Teresa P. v. Berkeley Unified School Dist.* (1989), the Berkeley, California, school district had 571 limited-English-proficient children who spoke 38 languages other than English. Some of these languages were spoken by only one to three of the district's children. The plaintiffs filed a class action against the school district, alleging that the district's testing and procedures for identification and assessment of the district's limited-English-proficient students were inadequate; the exit criteria and procedures used to determine when special language services for individual students were no longer necessary were inappropriate; the district failed to allocate adequate resources to its special language services for limited-English-proficient students; and that it failed to ensure that teachers and other instructional personnel had sufficient qualifications and skills to provide effective services. The students also argued that the district had not provided them with adequate English language development and adequate native tongue instruction and support.

The *Teresa P.* court applied the *Castaneda* test, concluded that the district's policy was educationally sound, and decided that there was no violation of the EEOC. The court's reasoning was consistent with most court decisions, both before

and after *Teresa P.* Courts do not believe that it is within their role to substitute their thoughts about educational values and theories for the educational and political decisions of those with actual training on the subject. They believe these decisions are properly reserved to local school authorities and to the expert knowledge of educators. Accordingly, it is extremely difficult to prove that a school district is not providing appropriate action to overcome language barriers under the three-prong *Castaneda* test.

In 2008, a court in Texas *did* determine that the Texas Education Agency, the state agency overseeing local school districts, had not taken appropriate action to overcome language barriers faced by schoolchildren in Texas (*United States v. Tyler,* 2008). It took the courts 37 years to reach that conclusion.

The background of the *Tyler* case is extremely complex, both factually and procedurally, and still remains unfinished. As a result of a lawsuit involving nine, all-black school districts, the U.S. District Court issued a comprehensive order in 1970 concerning the responsibilities of the Texas Education Agency (TEA) over all Texas school districts. These responsibilities included monitoring the provision of English-language instruction for limited English speakers. The court retained jurisdiction over the enforcement of its order. In 1975, a lawsuit was filed on behalf of Mexican-American children (the intervenors) against the TEA to enforce their rights to English-language instruction. This case had not yet been decided, due to numerous appeals, when, in 1981, the Fifth Circuit Court of Appeals rendered its decision in *Castaneda.* The *Castaneda* decision allowed the TEA to assert that the denial of equal educational opportunity to the intervenors could not be proven at *that point* in the *Tyler* litigation. Instead, the TEA claimed that the three prongs of the *Castaneda* test must be applied to the *Tyler* situation, which would then allow the TEA time to prove, through its choice of programs and practices, that it had carefully monitored its program and modified its results, as necessary. The TEA argued that before it could be evaluated for success or failure and before the intervenors could prove that they were entitled to appropriate action to overcome language barriers, the TEA's chosen methodology must be given a chance to work.

Fast-forward to 2006. The intervenors filed a motion claiming that the TEA had abandoned monitoring, enforcing, and supervising school districts to ensure compliance with Texas's bilingual education programs and that the TEA had failed to provide equal educational opportunity to limited-English-proficient children beyond the elementary school level. The *Tyler* court made detailed findings of facts on a range of issues, which included the TEA's performance-based monitoring analysis system, the TEA's administration of the limited English-proficiency programs, and an examination of achievement, dropout, and retention rates of limited-English-proficient students. The court also compared the passage and failure rates of limited English-proficient students against English-proficient students.

After reviewing all of the data, and applying it to each of the three prongs of the *Castaneda* test, the *Tyler* court found that although limited-English-proficient children were making adequate progress at the primary level, children at the secondary level were not. The court ruled that the TEA had violated their rights under the Equal Educational Opportunity Act due to TEA's failure to take appropriate action to overcome language barriers. Because part of TEA's failure was due to the inadequacy of its monitoring system, the court strongly criticized the system, stating it "does not fulfill TEA's requirement to effectively implement the [limited English proficiency] program. This failure does not excuse failing results on the secondary level. After a quarter century of sputtering implementation, Defendants have failed to achieve results that demonstrate they are overcoming language barriers for secondary LEP students. Failed implementation cannot prolong the existence of a failed program in perpetuity" (*Tyler* at 782). The court noted that under the EEOA, it is unjust to perpetually fail to provide the resources and necessary programs to ensure that limited English-proficient students catch up to their English-speaking peers. The court stated that "[t]he palpable injustice is equivalent

whether it comes from depriving non-LEP students or from depriving LEP students" (*Tyler* at 782).

Because the court determined the students' rights were, in fact, violated under the EEOC and used extremely forceful words such as "sputtering implementation," "perpetuity," and "palpable injustice," one would expect that the order directing the defendant to comply with its ruling and finally provide the necessary services that would allow limited-English-proficient students to overcome their language barriers to be equally as strong. Instead, the court issued a ruling that is simply underwhelming in its force and its expectations. The court ruled: "Defendants must soon rectify the monitoring failures and begin implementing a new language program for secondary LEP students. . . . The Court recognizes the difficult position of Defendants and the ongoing nature of this task. The Court will defer to Defendants and their course of action as much as possible, but the Court must ensure the rights of LEP students under the EEOA. With this in mind, demonstrations of good faith by Defendants will be looked upon favorably" (*Tyler* at 782).

Given the fact that it took 37 years for the court to rule that equal educational opportunity had been denied to certain Mexican-American children on the basis of language, one can only wonder how long it will take for the TEA and the school districts to "soon rectify the monitoring failures and begin implementing a new language program" for high school students. It is probably safe to assume that any children who attend high school in the affected districts will not overcome their language barriers before they graduate. Hopefully, future children in these districts will not suffer the same problems and that limited-English-speaking children will finally be provided with equal educational opportunity.

Courts and the No Child Left Behind Act

Typically, and because of very complicated constitutional rules, states do not sue the federal government for the legislation it creates, especially when the legislation provides states with the choice of participating and provides states with money for complying with the requirements that the federal legislation imposes. In 2005, Connecticut became the first state to file a lawsuit against the federal government because of the No Child Left Behind Act. The basis of Connecticut's lawsuit was that the federal government required states to comply fully with the interpretations of the U.S. Department of Education (DOE) regarding NCLB without providing states with adequate funds to do so. In its lawsuit, Connecticut alleged that certain NCLB requirements for students who were not English proficient (e.g., testing must be conducted yearly and conducted in English after 3 years) took away its instructional flexibility and forced it to divert money that could be better used for bilingual programming to be spent on mandated testing. The lawsuit further alleged that if states do not comply with the DOE's requirements, they are threatened with cuts to their funding, violating the Spending Clause of the U.S. Constitution, because the DOE does not have constitutional authority to coerce states into administering educational policies (Pendell, 2008). That case is still pending.

In the same year, another lawsuit filed by various school districts and education associations from around the country, including the National Education Association (NEA), the nation's largest teachers' union, also challenged whether each NCLB requirement needed to be followed without the DOE providing the concomitant funding. The government argued that by accepting federal educational funding, states agreed to comply with all the requirements of the NCLB Act. In *Pontiac v. Spelling* (2008), the Sixth Circuit Court of Appeals ruled that the language of the NCLB Act was not written clearly enough so that states would know that they would have to comply with the act's requirements, regardless of federal funding. This case is on appeal.

In late 2008, a federal appeals court ruled that parents cannot sue school districts to force them to comply with the No Child Left Behind Act. Parents had sued the Newark, New Jersey, school district for failing to notify them of their right to transfer their children out of a school that was graded as low performing under the NCLB standards. The federal appeals court ruled that the enforcement of the NCLB is left to state educational agencies and that parents cannot sue districts to force them to comply with the NCLB provisions ("Parents can't sue," 2008).

Whereas the effect of the NCLB and the lawsuits challenging it is unknown, it does indicate the trend to erode the statutory protections for bilingual and bicultural education. Borden (2001) argued that zealous advocacy is needed to protect the plight of minorities that have limited English proficiency. For them to have a meaningful chance to succeed in society, students need to have a substantially equal education.

Background of Desegregation–Integration Efforts

Non-English-speaking children tend to be unfairly handicapped in schools by their inability to speak structured English. Some children bear skin color as a characteristic that sets them apart from the majority and that has unfairly subjected them to discriminatory treatment. In the United States, access to education is critical to achieving success in other economic and social opportunities. Horace Mann (1848/1958) defined education as the great equalizer—the balance wheel of the social machinery.

Blacks are most often identified as the victims of segregation in the United States. However, Latinos now comprise a greater percentage of the national school-age population than do African Americans, with this trend expected to continue. Typically, school segregation and desegregation efforts have been viewed as a Black versus White issue. The Latino role in the legal history of school desegregation is often left in the shadows of the *Brown* decision and the civil rights movement. Bowman (2001) argued that the Latino history of educational segregation is often overlooked and that desegregation efforts included Latinos as if they had the same history and oppression as

Blacks. Scott (2008) pointed to the disjointed strategies of Latino education advocates as they attempted to navigate the complexity of racial segregation and language concerns within a larger civil rights environment that was dominated by the Black–White dynamic. Today, the educational situation of Latinos is further complicated by societal resentments toward the minority of Latinos who have entered the United States illegally.

Although there is a growing awareness that Latinos have been victims of segregation in the United States, desegregation of the public schools in the United States has a long and bitter history and has primarily involved discrimination against African-American children. Before 1954, states could establish policies regarding which public schools students could attend. In *Plessy v. Ferguson* (1896), the Supreme Court enunciated the "separate, but equal" doctrine in a case that involved separate transportation systems for Blacks and Whites. So long as the facilities were equal, there was no violation of constitutional law. Relying on this decision, states argued that if they provided separate educational facilities for Blacks and if the educational facilities were equal, they were fulfilling their constitutional obligations. In reality, the facilities provided Blacks were usually of inferior quality.

The Challenge: *Brown v. Board of Education of Topeka*

Brown v. Board of Education of Topeka (I) (1954) was the consolidation of a number of cases that asked the U.S. Supreme Court to determine the meaning of equality in the public schools. In this landmark decision, the Court recognized that education is perhaps the most important function of state and local governments. Four separate cases had originated in Kansas, South Carolina, Virginia, and Delaware, all of which denied Black elementary and high school students' admission to public schools attended by White children under laws requiring or permitting segregation by race. In all four cases, evidence was presented by the school districts to show that Black and White schools had been or were being equalized with respect to buildings, curricula, and qualifications and salaries of teachers. In a unanimous decision, the U.S. Supreme Court ruled in *Brown v. Board of Education* that by the very reason of segregation, these individuals (Blacks) were being deprived of the equal protection of the laws guaranteed by the Fourteenth Amendment. The Court stated that "in the field of public education, the doctrine of separate but equal has no place. Separate educational facilities are inherently unequal" (*Brown* at 495). Opportunity for an education, where the state has undertaken to provide it, must be made available to all on equal terms. Thus, the Court ruled that state-mandated public school segregation on the basis of race is inherently unequal and therefore unconstitutional.

The ruling was especially notable because it pointed out the negative effects of segregation on public education and, specifically, the detrimental effects of segregation on minority children. Segregation that has the sanction of law officially denotes inferiority of the minority group; a sense of inferiority affects the child's motivation to learn. To be different physically and then educated in separate facilities, and to interact daily with persons who view minority children as not being a part of the mainstream, must affect children's self-worth. This momentous decision not only outlawed school segregation but also provided a legal basis for attacking racial segregation in virtually every aspect of society.

Because this decision was expected to have an enormous effect on schools and on the whole of society and was expected to be met with extreme resistance, the U.S. Supreme Court did not hand down its implementation decree until a year later. *Brown v. Board of Education of Topeka (II)* (1955), popularly known as "*Brown II,*" called for good-faith compliance by the states. In another unanimous opinion, the Court gave local school districts the major responsibility for desegregation. The only relief afforded by the Court was for desegregation of schools to take place "with all deliberate speed."

Implementation of the *Brown* Decision

The lower courts interpreted the phrase "with all deliberate speed" to mean that school boards be allowed time to consider the problems involved in desegregating so that they could develop appropriate plans. Unfortunately, this interpretation only intensified delays. At the time of the *Brown II* decision, southern educators were aware that the location of public schools was an important factor in maintaining segregated school attendance patterns.

Throughout the 1950s, southern cities made considerable investments in new school facilities, and almost every school constructed was located in a racially homogeneous residential area. In some areas where the Black population was growing, more schools were added to keep that population isolated rather than allowing the races to mix.

Also, the districting of a state or local area—where both Blacks and Whites lived—in some cases made it impossible to have totally integrated schools. In the 10 years after *Brown,* the southern segregated school system remained largely intact. By 1964, only 1 out of 50 southern Black children attended integrated schools (Orfield, 1996b). The major problem was the outright rejection of any type of school integration policy throughout the South. Many states passed laws to thwart school integration by closing public schools or setting up rigid eligibility requirements for Blacks who wanted to attend White schools (Armor, 1995). In Prince Edward County, Virginia, the county board of supervisors did not levy taxes or appropriate funds for desegregated schools, resulting in the exclusion of Black children from public schools. Another attempt to circumvent the law was the selective assignment of Black students within a school. Black children were separated from White students in segregated classrooms. The school could claim it was integrated while all of its Black children remained separated from and segregated in a "desegregated" school. Such practices were eventually challenged in court and forbidden.

This manipulation and the delay in achieving integration of public schools led to further court and congressional involvement. In *Green v. County School Board of New Kent County* (1968),

the U.S. Supreme Court identified five factors—facilities, staff, faculty, extracurricular activities, and transportation—that were to be used to gauge a school system's compliance with the mandate of desegregation. In 1969, in *Alexander v. Holmes County Board of Education* (1969), the U.S. Supreme Court declared that "all deliberate speed no longer is constitutionally permissible" and "the obligation of every school district is to terminate dual school systems at once and to operate now and henceforth only unitary schools" (*Alexander* at 320).

The Neighborhood School

Historically, in the United States, as people arrived in this country from their countries of origin, they settled in areas to be close to those who were familiar to them. Many racial and ethnic groups clustered together because of the familiarity of shared culture and identity. Another important issue that emerged during the struggle to integrate public schools was how to desegregate schools in areas where persons of certain economic, racial, and ethnic groups had clustered together to form neighborhoods. The neighborhood school can be defined as a school (particularly an elementary school) located in the center of a population cluster, which was often the one institution that bound together most of the area residents. The courts' response to the legitimacy of neighborhood schools that were composed of persons of only one race was initially reluctance. The neighborhood school was generally thought of as a product of segregated housing and/or the gerrymandering of school districts (the division of geographical areas and political units to give special advantages to one group). In the case of school desegregation, gerrymandering meant maintaining White schools as "white" and redrawing community and district boundaries to maintain Black schools as "black."

Busing Students and Racial Balance: A Legal and Political Issue

The fact that Blacks and Whites were segregated as a result of community living patterns led to the idea of busing children to achieve racial balance. This, in turn, aroused considerable controversy, which escalated following the U.S. Supreme Court decision in *Swann v. Charlotte-Mecklenburg Board of Education* (1971)—the first "busing" case.

In the particular school district involved in the *Swann* case, assignment of children to the school nearest their grade would not have resulted in an effective dismantling of the dual educational system. Accordingly, the Court held that desegregation could not be limited to walk-in schools and approved the busing order. In a companion case, *North Carolina Board of Education v. Swann* (1971), the Court declared unconstitutional a North Carolina statute that prohibited the use of racial assignment of students for busing or the use of race as a factor to create racial balance. The Court held that a ban on racial assignment would deprive school authorities of the one tool absolutely essential to fulfillment of their constitutional obligation to eliminate existing dual school systems. The Court also concluded that the ban on busing was invalid because bus transportation had long been an integral part of all public educational systems. Thus, it was unlikely that an effective remedy could be devised without continued reliance on busing. The Court further suggested the assignment of students according to race to promote integration and the use of mathematical ratios as a starting point in devising remedies.

An extremely important part of the *Swann* decision was the Court's distinction between de jure and de facto segregation, holding that only de jure segregation was unconstitutional. De jure segregation concerns actions that are officially intended or mandated by law. De jure segregation is done deliberately or occurs with intent. De facto segregation is inadvertent and caused not by actions of the state, but rather by social, economic, or other factors. In other words, de facto segregation just happens naturally. As we will see, the distinction between these types of segregation is crucial in later cases in which resegregation is at issue.

Before a court mandates desegregation in a school district, the court must make a finding that there is de jure segregation. After the court makes this finding, a federal court will require the school board to propose a plan to desegregate. If the court does not find the district's plan acceptable, it will create and implement its own plan to remedy the segregation. Once the plan is entered by a district court, the school district is bound by the provisions of the plan until the district has achieved unitary status, that is, until it removes the vestiges of state-sanctioned segregation and creates a district that is not segregated by race, no longer considered dual, and is now unitary (Teitlebaum, 1995).

In 1974, Congress passed the Equal Educational Opportunities Act of 1974 (P.L. 93-380), which declared the policy of the United States to be "that all children enrolled in public schools are entitled to equal educational opportunity without regard to race, color, sex, or national origin and that the neighborhood is the appropriate basis for determining public school assignment." Transportation of students—busing—was considered to be harmful to students as demonstrated by Congress's findings that:

- The maintenance of dual school systems in which students are assigned to schools solely on the basis of race, color, sex, or national origin denies to those students the equal protection of the laws guaranteed by the 14th Amendment.
- For the purpose of abolishing dual school systems and eliminating the vestiges thereof, many local educational agencies have been required to reorganize their school systems, to reassign students, and to engage in the extensive transportation of students.
- The implementation of desegregation plans that require extensive student transportation has, in many cases, required local educational agencies to expend large amounts of funds, thereby depleting their financial resources available for the maintenance or improvement of the quality of educational facilities and instruction provided.
- Transportation of students which creates serious risks to their health and safety, disrupts the educational process carried out with respect to such students, and impinges significantly on their educational opportunity is excessive.

■ The risks and harms created by excessive transportation are particularly great for children enrolled in the first six grades.

■ The guidelines provided by the courts for fashioning remedies to dismantle dual school systems have been, the Supreme Court of the United States has said, "incomplete and imperfect," and have not established a clear, rational and uniform standard for determining the extent to which a local educational agency is required to reassign and transport its students in order to eliminate the vestiges of a dual school system. (20 U.S.C. § 1702)

Congress set out a priority of remedies for courts to use when a court determined that a denial of equal educational opportunity had taken place under the EEOA and that court-ordered desegregation should occur. These remedies included assigning students to the schools closest to their places of residence that provided the appropriate grade level and type of education for such students; taking into account school capacities and/or natural barriers; permitting students to transfer from a school in which a majority of the students were of their race, color, or national origin to a school in which a minority were; creation or revision of attendance zones or grade structures without requiring transportation; construction of new schools or the closing of inferior schools; and the construction or establishment of magnet schools. Busing of students was just one of many remedies courts could take in fashioning court orders to desegregate school districts. What remains very clear was that Congress, as the elected representatives of the voting public, did not prefer busing as the method to achieve integration.

The Major Question Raised by the Busing Controversy

Busing of students challenged the idea of the neighborhood schools. Children were going to be taken from the local schools in their neighborhoods and placed in other schools in different neighborhoods. Unfortunately, the neighborhoods that all children lived in were not equal. They were affected by many economic and social factors, including the quality of the schools as well as conditions such as housing, poverty, crime, and safety. If the schools that Black children attended were, in fact, inferior, then should White children be forced to attend inferior schools in Black neighborhoods? Would that be fair? Or, should Black children be bused to attend the schools in the better White neighborhoods? Would it be fair to only require busing of Black and not White students? How would appropriate racial balances be determined, and how would the individuals who would be bused be selected?

At the outset, whether busing should be used to achieve equal educational opportunity depended on the extent that pupils' aspirations and achievements were related to the educational backgrounds and performance of other pupils in the same schools. Coleman's 1964 study of the status of school desegregation resulted in a report entitled, *Equality of Educational Opportunity,* popularly known as the Coleman Report (Coleman et al., 1966). This report has been the topic of considerable controversy. Coleman's aim was to investigate the effects of a mandate (desegregation) that suddenly changed the entire complexion of a school district. His findings were used as a basis for the recommendations of the U.S. Commission on Civil Rights, contained in *Racial Isolation in Public Schools* (1967), and as underpinnings for critical litigation to bring about desegregation of schools. The main findings of the Coleman Report were that Blacks were by far the most segregated group in the United States and that this segregation was extensive not only in the South but also in the urban North, Midwest, and West. The report also noted that inadequate educational facilities and resources seemed related to low academic achievement; that schools provided no opportunity for most Blacks to overcome initial deficiencies; that quality of teachers showed a strong relationship to pupil achievement; and that Black children tended to have less access to the physical facilities that seemed to be related to high academic achievement.

The Coleman Report supported the notion that busing was the only available remedy for dismantling segregated educational systems in large cities. Proponents of busing argued that integrating the nation's schools was crucial to the effort to create an integrated society in which social interaction could overcome racism; thus, educational benefits or losses were incidental to the ongoing attempts to integrate schools. Opponents of the Coleman report argued that if children's achievement scores, particularly in reading achievement, could not be clearly shown to have improved through racial integration, busing should be ended, and there should be a return to neighborhood schools along naturally occurring, residential boundaries. Although the Coleman Report may seem outdated because it was written in the 1960s, these same arguments continue today. In fact, arguments that favor integration as a compelling societal benefit were made again in front of the U.S. Supreme Court in the 2007 case of *Parents Involved in Cmty. Sch. v. Seattle Sch. Dist. No. 1.*

School Desegregation and "White Flight"

When the Supreme Court ordered busing as a remedy, it did so because, until that point, nothing else had worked to integrate the schools. Despite its orders that schools comply in good faith and that desegregation occur with all deliberate speed, school officials were actively involved in efforts to avoid integrating schools. The Supreme Court may not have considered that individual citizens also would take steps to thwart integration efforts. The Court in *Swann* did not address the issue of community opinion and possible flight from the public schools, nor did it consider the possibility that opposition to the Court's policies could undermine their effectiveness and create resegregation between a city and its suburbs or between public and private schools (Armor, 1995).

Coleman's research in the decade following the 1966 study led him to renounce his earlier conclusion that massive busing programs would improve the quality of education (1975). In analyzing the stability of racial and white groups in the largest central-city districts from 1968 to 1973, Coleman found that as cities became more

integrated, Whites either abandoned these areas for the suburbs or transferred their children to private schools. He concluded that urban school desegregation leads to "white flight," the consequences of which are disastrous for the long-term integration of society because they exacerbate the Black city/White suburb racial separation.

The term "white flight" is often used to describe when middle- or working-class White people move out of cities and into suburbs to "get away" from the encroaching minorities. White flight has been associated with desegregation because it is assumed that as schools were forced to include Blacks, Whites moved away to avoid them or fled to private schools. It must be noted that "white flight" cannot be attributed solely to school desegregation. A number of other factors also occurred in society at the same time as integration and busing, some of which would also influence the rate at which people moved away from the cities. These factors included the increase in highways, which led to a decrease in travel time between suburbs and cities, the increase in the numbers of suburbs, the numbers of children born after the baby boom, which led to the need for newer houses with more bedrooms, and the decline of cities. The factors just mentioned have nothing to do with any racial animus, but can also lead to white flight. These confounding variables are not controlled for in the studies described.

According to Armor (1995), for the first 5 or 6 years after *Swann,* nearly all desegregation plans emerging from federal courts or federal governmental actions involved the mandatory reassignment of students through busing to attain a fairly high degree of racial balance. In smaller school districts, racial balance was attained by redrawing school attendance boundaries, sometimes accompanied by carefully chosen school closures. In larger school districts, however, racial balance usually required cross-district busing of both White and Black students, known as *mandatory busing plans.* Armor claimed that mandatory busing frequently led to significant white flight and in some cases to resegregation. He reviewed the research on white flight and the effectiveness of court-ordered remedies for desegregation and concluded that the most important causal link between a desegregation plan and changes in school enrollment were the opinions, attitudes, and behaviors of the parents and students involved. He argued that the relationship between desegregation plans and enrollment trends in schools is determined by the responses to a desegregation program by parents, who must decide whether to support, oppose, participate in, or withdraw from the plan. If community and parental support are lacking, this leads to loss of public support for school funding, loss of White and middle-class students, long-term enrollment instability, and resegregation.

In contrast, Orfield (1996a) argued that the huge changes in the racial composition of American public schools were a consequence of basic changes in birthrates and immigration patterns, rather than a consequence of white flight from the public to private schools. He examined data from the National Center for Education Statistics and the U.S. Census Bureau and found no significant redistribution between public and private school enrollment. Between 1984 and 1991, public school enrollment increased by 7%, whereas private school enrollment dropped 9%. This was the reverse of falling public and rising private school enrollment from 1970 until 1984. During this same time period, the number of Black students in public schools in the United States increased 3% from 1972 to 1992, which were the first two decades of widespread busing plans. In contrast, Latino enrollments soared 89%, and white enrollments fell 14%. Orfield argued that these trends led to incorrect claims that Whites were abandoning public education because of resistance to integration. The decline was not the result of Whites leaving public schools but, instead, was due to a dramatic drop in the White birthrate.

Continued U.S. Supreme Court Involvement in Desegregation Efforts

During the 1970s, the Supreme Court dealt with a number of complex legal issues involving the definition of desegregation, the nature of remedies, the obligations of school districts, and the remedial powers of the lower court as the South began to dismantle its dual system in the aftermath of the *Swann* decision (Armor, 1995). As this was occurring, there was also increased litigation directed at desegregation of schools in large, Northern school systems. These cases were different, however, in that the segregation generally resulted from segregated housing patterns, rather than because of state laws that had denied equal educational opportunities to children because of race.

Keyes v. Denver School District No. 1 (1973) was the first U.S. Supreme Court ruling concerning a case that arose from outside the South, where there was no de jure segregation—that is, no state laws requiring segregation. In this case, the parents argued that the Denver School Board manipulated student attendance zones, school-site selections, and neighborhood school policies throughout the school district so the entire school district needed to be desegregated. The Denver School Board argued that the segregation was de facto because of housing patterns and economic conditions in certain areas of the district. The federal court judge found that the Denver school board used rezoning tactics and constructed schools in racially isolated neighborhoods to intentionally segregate one area of the Denver schools. On appeal, the Court emphasized that where school authorities have been found to have practiced purposeful segregation in part of a school system, they bear the burden of showing that other segregated actions in their district were not purposefully and intentionally discriminatory. The Supreme Court ruled that if the school board intentionally segregated one part of its district, the entire district was presumed to be segregated illegally.

Milliken v. Bradley (1974) was the first major Supreme Court decision since *Brown* that looked at the question of whether, to achieve a racial balance that would integrate its schools, a school district could involve the local areas that surrounded the district. In *Milliken,* the lower court had decided that it was impossible to desegregate the Detroit school system without involving the predominately White suburbs around it; there were not enough White children that attended school in the Detroit public school system to achieve racial integration. The lower court's decision was to draw students from the heavily White surrounding suburbs to overcome segregation. The U.S. Supreme Court ruled that cross-district remedies were prohibited unless it could be shown that discriminatory action by the state or suburban communities created the pattern of all White suburbs and heavily Black city schools. Detroit would have to desegregate by mixing its own small White enrollment with its huge and rapidly growing Black enrollment.

The U.S. Supreme Court and Resegregation

Most of the school desegregation cases that occurred during the 1980s were decided in the federal trial and appellate levels. During that time, the U.S. Supreme Court did not issue any significant decisions concerning school desegregation. However, the 1990s and 2000s demonstrated the U.S. Supreme Court's departure from the desegregation focus of the *Brown* case. To be fair, it is not that the Supreme Court has abandoned the promise of equal education created by *Brown*. Instead, the Supreme Court's more recent interpretations of constitutional mandates has more narrowly focused the court on what it views as courts' proper roles in fashioning desegregation remedies. Unfortunately, the effect of these decisions has led to a return to much of the country becoming resegregated.

In *Board of Education v. Dowell* (1991), desegregation litigation began in 1961 in Oklahoma City, Oklahoma. A desegregation plan was implemented in 1972 and resulted in a substantially integrated school system. Upon finding that the school board had successfully eliminated all vestiges of de jure segregation, the district court granted the school board's request for unitary status and ordered the case terminated in 1977. In 1984, the plaintiffs wanted to reopen the case for a new desegregation plan because of demographic changes that had taken place in the school

district. The trial and appellate courts disagreed as to whether the courts still retained jurisdiction and could become involved again when the previously dual system had already been declared unitary. When the case reached the U.S. Supreme Court, the Court stated that judicial supervision ends when the school board complies in good faith with the desegregation decree and vestiges of past discrimination have been eliminated to the extent practicable. A court-supervised district that had never been declared unitary is obligated under the law to avoid actions that create segregated and unequal schools. However, after a declaration of unitary status, any actions that created racially segregated schools were presumed to have occurred innocently, unless a plaintiff proved that the school officials intentionally intended to discriminate.

In *Freeman v. Pitts* (1992), the DeKalb, Georgia, school system (DCSS) had voluntarily agreed to a 1969 court desegregation plan. Throughout the years, both sides agreed that the DCSS had substantially complied with the plan, modifying it when necessary. In 1986, DCSS asked to be released from the litigation and returned to unitary status. The question before the Supreme Court was whether a federal district court could relinquish its supervision over those aspects of a school system that complied with a desegregation order if other aspects of the system remained in noncompliance.

When DCSS asked to be released from court supervision, the respondents (schoolchildren and parents) were concerned with the racial imbalance present in the various schools of DCSS. They presented evidence in the federal district court that during the 1986 to 1987 school year, 47% of the students attending DCSS were Black; 50% of the Black students attended schools that were over 90% Black; 27% of White students attended schools that were more than 90% White; of the 22 DCSS high schools, 5 had student populations that were more than 90% Black, whereas 5 other schools had student populations that were more than 80% White; and of the 74 elementary schools in DCSS, 18 were over 90% Black, whereas 10 were over 90% White. The respondents argued that this racial imbalance in student assignment was a vestige of the dual system, rather than being caused by independent demographic forces.

DCSS argued that part of the complication in the case was that over the course of the nearly 30 years of litigation, remarkable changes in the racial composition of the county presented DCSS with a student population in 1986 far different from the one it set out to integrate in 1969. DCSS presented evidence that in 1969, the federal district court had ordered the desegregation of a school system that was comprised of 5.6% Black students; by 1986, the percentage of Black students was 47%. To compound the difficulty of working with these radical demographic changes, the northern and southern parts of the county also had experienced much different growth patterns. During the relevant period, the Black population in the southern portion of the county experienced tremendous growth while the White population did not, and the White population in the northern part of the county experienced tremendous growth while the Black population did not. The district court noted that from 1976 to 1986, enrollment in elementary schools declined overall by 15%, whereas Black enrollment in elementary schools increased by 86%. During the same period, overall high school enrollment declined by 16%, whereas Black enrollment in high schools increased by 119%. These effects were even more pronounced in the southern portion of DeKalb County. Because of these demographic factors, the district court did not find that DCSS had acted in a discriminatory fashion in student assignment. Yet, the district court believed that vestiges of discrimination occurred in certain other areas, ordered DCSS to take measures to address those problems, and maintained the ongoing desegregation order.

On appeal, the U.S. Supreme Court reaffirmed a federal district court's ability to exercise broad discretion over desegregation cases. In *Freeman,* the Court stated that the duty and responsibility of a school district once found to have engaged in de jure segregation is to take all steps necessary to eliminate the vestiges of such a system to ensure that the principal wrong, the injuries and stigma inflicted on the race disfavored by the violation, is

no longer present. In supervising desegregation plans, federal courts have the authority to relinquish supervision and control of school districts in incremental stages where compliance has been achieved, limiting further judicial supervision to the parts of the operations that are not yet in full compliance with the court decree.

In 1995, the Supreme Court decided the case of *Missouri v. Jenkins.* In 1977, Kansas City, Missouri, implemented a desegregation plan that reassigned students within the school district and attempted to affect a minimum of 30% minority enrollment in every Kansas City school. The plan changed school boundary lines, created attendance zones, and transferred minority students from schools with large minority enrollments to schools with low minority enrollments and vice versa. By 1985, the plan had failed because of white flight to private and suburban Kansas City schools. The federal district court fashioned a court-imposed remedial desegregation plan that consisted of multiple components that strove to integrate schools and improve student achievement. The focal point of the court's plan involved magnet schools and massive capital improvement programs to attract students from outside the district and from private schools. These remedies provided Kansas City with facilities and opportunities not available anywhere else in the country. In 1992, the school district presented the court with its proposed budget for the eighth year of the plan. The State of Missouri objected to the budget and asked for a finding that the school district deserved unitary status, which would then release it from court oversight (LaVine, 1995).

The Supreme Court began its analysis of the desegregation plan by defining the limits on a district court's power to fashion a proper desegregation remedy. According to the Court, factors that do not stem from school segregation should not guide judicial remedies—numerous external factors independent of de jure segregation can potentially affect both racial composition of schools and minority students' academic achievement. The Supreme Court criticized the trial and appellate courts in *Jenkins* because they had consistently promoted a remedy focused on "desegregative attractiveness" coupled with "suburban comparability," instead of focusing on eliminating desegregation to the extent practicable. In this case, the proper response by the district court should have been to eliminate the vestiges of prior de jure segregation within the Kansas City schools. The Supreme Court instructed that, when the case is returned, the district court must bear in mind that its end purpose is not only "to remedy the violation" to the extent practicable, but also to restore state and local authorities to the control of a school system that is operating in compliance with the Constitution.

The Supreme Court and the Voluntary Use of Diversity Criteria

During the early 2000s, the U.S. Supreme Court heard two cases that attacked the use of race as a factor in admissions in higher education. Both of these cases were brought by White students who had been denied admission to the University of Michigan, at the undergraduate and at the law school levels. They alleged that they had been unfairly denied admission because the races of underrepresented minority applicants such as Hispanics, Native Americans, and African Americans were used as bonus factors in the admissions' decisions. The undergraduate admissions policy automatically gave minority applicants a 20-point bonus based on their race. This process was struck down in *Gratz v. Bollinger* (2003). The law school's admission policy, which did not give an automatic point bonus but did consider race, was upheld in *Grutter v. Bollinger* (2003). In *Grutter,* the law school's admissions policy required that the applicant's entire file be examined beyond test scores and grades to give consideration as to whether the applicant will help provide diversity to the student body. In race-based classifications, courts strictly scrutinize the constitutionality of the classification under the Equal Protection Clause of the 14th Amendment. The Supreme Court differentiated the two cases by how race was used in each admissions policy and whether its use was narrowly tailored to reach a compelling state interest.

In *Parents Involved in Cmty. Sch. v. Seattle Sch. Dist. No. 1,* (2007), the U.S. Supreme Court consolidated two cases in which school districts voluntarily adopted student assignment plans that used race to determine which public schools certain children could attend. The Seattle, Washington, school district classified children as White or nonwhite to allocate slots in oversubscribed high schools. The Jefferson County, Kentucky, school district used Black or "other" to make certain elementary school assignments and to rule on transfer requests. In each case, the school district relied on an individual student's race in assigning that student to a particular school, so that the racial balance at the school fell within a predetermined range based on the racial composition of the school district as a whole. Parents of students who were denied assignment to particular schools under these plans solely because of their race brought suit, contending that allocating children to different public schools on the basis of race violated the 14th Amendment's guarantee of equal protection of the laws.

The U.S. Supreme Court believed that both cases presented the same underlying legal question—whether a public school that had not operated legally segregated schools or had not been found to be dual could choose to classify students by race and rely on that classification in making school assignments. The Seattle school district had never operated segregated schools nor had it ever been subject to court-ordered desegregation. It nonetheless employed racial tiebreakers in an attempt to address the effects of racially identifiable housing patterns on school assignments to facilitate integration. The Jefferson County public schools were previously segregated by law and were subject to a desegregation decree entered in 1975, but dissolved in 2000, when it eliminated the vestiges associated with its former policy of segregation and achieved unitary status. Could these districts use race as a factor in school admissions, even if the use of race would be to achieve integrated schools?

The Supreme Court examined its prior cases to determine when racial classifications in the school context would be considered sufficiently compelling to justify its use. The first of these situations can be when race is used to remedy the effects of past intentional discrimination. However, the Supreme Court noted that the Seattle public schools had not shown that they were ever segregated by law and were not subject to court-ordered desegregation decrees nor did Jefferson County rely on an interest in remedying the effects of past intentional discrimination in defending its present use of race in student assignments.

The second government interest that the Supreme Court recognized as compelling for purposes of strict scrutiny is the interest in student body diversity in higher education that it upheld in *Grutter.* The Supreme Court did not view the Seattle and Jefferson County school districts' use of race for student body diversity similar to that of the Michigan law school's in *Grutter.* The Court noted that the parties and their amici (including NASW, the NAACP, the NEA, and over 500 social scientists) dispute whether racial diversity in schools has a marked impact on test scores and other objective yardsticks or achieves intangible socialization benefits. The Court stated that in design and operation, the plans were directed only to achieve racial balance, pure and simple, an objective that the Court had repeatedly condemned as illegitimate. Therefore, the Supreme Court ruled in the *Seattle* case that individual students may not be assigned or denied an assignment to school on the basis of race. The Court stated, "Before *Brown,* schoolchildren were told where they could and could not go to school based on the color of their skin. The school districts in these cases have not carried the heavy burden of demonstrating that we should allow this once again—even for very different reasons. . . . The way to stop discrimination on the basis of race is to stop discriminating on the basis of race" (*Seattle* at 2768).

A Return to Racial Isolation

Since the decision in the *Jenkins* case and through the *Seattle* case discussed earlier, the Supreme Court's rulings are considered to be a profound step backward in the effort to desegregate the nation's schools (Orfield, 1996b, Orfield & Lee, 2007). Lower courts have used the Supreme Court's more recent holdings to sharply curtail broad desegregation remedies. It appears that as long as school districts temporarily maintain some aspects of desegregation for several years and do not express the intention to discriminate, courts will approve state plans. Rather than upholding the spirit of the *Brown* decision to eliminate segregation and the damage that racial segregation causes, these cases demonstrate the Court's goals of minimizing judicial involvement in education and restoring power to local and state governments. Schools that are under court orders to desegregate may still use race to make race-conscious decisions that will end the vestiges of discrimination. However, schools that choose to embrace diversity as an educational value or as a means to teach students about social justice in vivo or that try to select their student bodies on the basis of race cannot use race as a pivotal decision-making factor.

Conditions for Successful Desegregation

Little data exist regarding the nation's engagement with school desegregation. Heise (1996) provided information on a survey that reported that 960 school districts attempted to desegregate between 1968 and 1986. In 1990, the Department of Education's Office of Civil Rights reported that 256 school districts, with a total combined student enrollment exceeding two million, operated under court supervision in school desegregation cases brought by the Justice Department (Heise, 1996). Parker (2000) conducted studies that covered 192 school districts. She concluded that although a large proportion of very large school districts had been released from judicial oversight of their desegregation efforts, a greater number of school desegregation lawsuits continue.

In addition to court-ordered remedies, parents and communities can play a large part in efforts to desegregate. Certain school districts had attempted to provide racial balance in their schools by using race-conscious measures such as transferring children to other schools in the district and by using magnet schools. In some cases, African-American, Asian-American, and White parents had worked together to challenge these race-conscious student assignment practices as not being in their children's best interest (Parker, 2000). Some parents had challenged the use of these policies after their children were excluded from programs that used quotas or other devices to achieve ethnic and racial balance (Parker, 2000). However, the Supreme Court's decision in the *Seattle* case makes clear that the use of race in any voluntary program is not allowed.

Districts that are not subject to an existing desegregation order are permitted to consider race under certain circumstances. They may use race when they develop new school sites, draw and adjust attendance lines, recruit a diverse group of students and faculty, use special programs to attract a racially integrated student body (i.e., magnet schools), and in tracking and disaggregating enrollment and student performance ("One year later," 2008). Districts may take other legally permissible options, which include the consolidation of several school districts into one larger, more diverse district; school pairing plans that merge neighboring educational facilities to produce more diversity, and renovating and expanding existing school sites to attract greater student body diversity ("One year later," 2008). Finally, only after carefully documenting that race-neutral alternatives—like socioeconomic status or language background—alone would fail to produce satisfactory integration levels, school districts may consider an individual student's race as one of several factors in school assignments plans. These options, used singly or in combination with one another, are still capable of producing student body diversity. ("One year later," 2008).

Is the Country Desegregated?

According to the Civil Rights Project, resegregation is now occurring in all sections of the country and is accelerating most rapidly in the South (Orfield & Lee, 2007). Given the fact that the South was the source of *Brown* and the desegregation movement

and the South had been the most resistant and least segregated region for Black students, this shift is both chilling and ironic. After desegregation implementation efforts took effect, the South was the least segregated region for Black students for three decades. Data from 2005 show that the South has now lost that distinction and that the South joins the rest of the nation in being resegregated (Orfield & Lee, 2007). Whether schools are segregated, desegregated, or resegregated is not what really matters, however. Instead, the trends in the Civil Rights Project report show that throughout the country, students are experiencing increasing isolation and profound inequality in their education.

Gender and Educational Opportunity

So far in this chapter, we have talked about the attempt to have equal educational opportunity for all children in the area of language acquisition and by the elimination of racial segregation. In the United States, historically, girls have received a lesser education than have boys, although not nearly as restrictive as the education that girls in some other countries have received. More recently, with an increase in feminism and the passage of legislation that guarantees certain rights, the playing field has been much more equalized, although it may still be argued that girls are not receiving an equal education to boys. The fairness of opportunities between the sexes is often referred to as gender equity.

According to the landmark study of the American Association of University Women (AAUW) Education Foundation, sex and gender make a difference in the nation's schools, and the needs of girls were not being met (AAUW, 1992). Although research suggests boys are overrepresented in special education classes, girls face challenges by not being offered encouragement or gaining equal access to educational opportunities.

According to one report, girls are of equal ability to boys when they enter school but fall behind boys in academic areas such as math and science and suffer greater loss of self-esteem (*Gender Equity in America's Schools,* 1992). The school as a primary institution has much to contribute to the sex-role development of its students, particularly because interpretations of sex roles drastically change over time. However, the learning of these behaviors occurs long before formal entry into school. At the child's birth, parents assign a gender label and respond differently to the labels "boy" and "girl" in accordance with their own sex-role ideal. In addition, by their own words and actions, parents provide the child with models of sex-typed behavior (beliefs and behaviors defined by one's culture as being appropriate for a given sex). Also, peers as early as 3 years of age play a role in social learning through modeling expectations and selective reinforcement. Children contribute to their own acculturation. They selectively assimilate in accordance with their own label, and they generally consolidate sex-role identity as part of their self-concept. By the time most children enter school, they are well acculturated but still open to new influences.

Throughout the 1970s, feminists defined gender equity in terms of formal equality (Salomone, 2000). Because girls and boys were identical in intelligence and abilities, they theorized that any differences in interests must therefore be the result of social conditioning. They fought to make schools gender-neutral. But in the 1980s, some educational theorists began to view sex differences through a new lens. The discussion turned to the different experiences of women and men, which have resulted in different moral and intellectual perspectives about education and gender (Salomone, 2000).

The Systematic Relationship Between Sex-Role Development and Educational Practices

A primary task of the school is to serve the educational needs of both girls and boys without favoring either group. Teachers may have well-defined sex-role expectations and preferences and may communicate them to their pupils. Levitin and Chananie (1972) found that student teachers and first- and second-grade teachers have well-defined sex-role expectations; they defined their preferred student as being orderly, conforming, and dependent. Further, they found that teachers tend to distinguish rather sharply between their preferred student role and their perception of the male sex role.

Sadker and Sadker (1994) reported that boys dominated classroom discussions and were more likely to be praised, corrected, helped, and criticized by teachers, all of which may foster student achievement. Salomone (2002) reported that during the 1990s, the AAUW issued a series of reports on how schools unintentionally shortchanged girls, noting that girls disproportionately lost self-esteem and interest in math and science as they approached adolescence, that women were underrepresented in the school curriculum, that teacher behavior and tests tended to favor boys, that girls lagged seriously behind boys in math and science, that girls experienced widespread sexual harassment in public schools, and that they faced social and institutional challenges as they formed identities and negotiated the middle-school environment (Salomone, 2000).

In another study on gender differences (AAUW, 1998), the AAUW reviewed over 1,000 articles and studies about girls in kindergarten through 12th grade. Although the study confirmed that public schools are making progress providing equitable treatment of boys and girls, serious concerns remained. Some of the problems are ongoing, such as academic tracking in which girls are encouraged to take fewer science and math courses than boys. The study found that although the gap has diminished between the numbers of boys and girls taking math and science classes, boys tend to take more advanced courses and take all three core science courses (biology, chemistry, and physics) by the time they graduate. On the other hand, girls outnumber boys in subjects like sociology, psychology, foreign languages, and fine arts and enroll in fewer computer science and computer design classes.

The AAUW believes the impact of technology in the schools is significant because computer access may eventually bridge the educational gap between rich and poor students.

Some of the other problems reported in the Gender Gaps study (AAUW, 1998) were of more recent origin. Girls have serious threats to their health and education including being at risk of depression, delinquency, substance abuse, and pregnancy. Girls are more vulnerable than boys because they confront widespread sexual violence and harassment within the family and within the school that interfere with their ability to learn. They also reported that although boys repeat grades and drop out of school more often than girls, girls who repeat grades are more likely than boys to drop out of school and that girls who drop out are less likely to return and complete school. The study also reports that Hispanic girls have especially high dropout rates; in 1995, 30% of the Hispanic females over age 16 had dropped out of school and had not yet passed a high school equivalency examination. At the same time, dropout rates for Hispanic males and African-American females had declined.

In a study published 10 years later by the AAUW (Corbett, Hill, & St. Rose, 2008), it noted that overall, both girls and boys were performing better on national assessments since the 1970s, especially in math. Traditional gender differences seemed to persist, with boys generally outscoring girls on math tests by a small margin and girls outscoring boys on reading tests by a larger, but still relatively small margin. Increasing percentages of both girls and boys are performing at a proficient level in math, whereas in reading, the percentages of girls and boys who achieved proficiency have remained about the same (Corbett et al., 2008).

Legal Provisions: Sex Discrimination in Public Schools

Educational practices, such as the restriction of girls from woodworking or auto mechanics class and boys' athletics on the basis of sex rather than on the basis of individual capability, have been challenged successfully since 1972. Title IX of the 1972 Education Amendments is a clear statement of federal policy against sex discrimination in areas previously untouched by legislation. This legislation is significant in that it provides support at the national level for abolishing the sexist practices that permeate educational institutions in the United States.

Title IX is the first comprehensive federal law to prohibit sex discrimination in the admission and treatment of students by educational institutions receiving federal assistance. Sex discrimination in the employment policies and practices of educational institutions is also prohibited. The law reads in part:

> No person in the United States shall ... on the basis of sex be excluded from participation in, be denied the benefits of or be subjected to discrimination under any education program or activity receiving federal assistance. (20 U.S.C. § 1961(a))

The implementing regulations for the legislation were issued by the Department of Health, Education, and Welfare in June 1975. Their provisions can be grouped into five major sections: (a) general provisions, which outline procedures for ensuring nondiscrimination and compliance with the legislation; (b) coverage provisions, which identify the educational institutions, programs, and activities covered by the regulations; (c) admissions provisions, which prohibit discrimination in the recruitment and admission of students; (d) provisions pertaining to the standards of nondiscrimination in student educational programs; and (e) employment provisions, which establish the requirements for nondiscrimination in employment (U.S. Department of Health, Education, and Welfare, 1975).

Violations of Title IX. Some rules, regulations, and policies that are violations of Title IX are

> requiring different courses for males and females; allowing boys but not girls to be crossing guards; sponsoring special school programs for male students only; awarding academic credit

to males, but not to females who participate in interscholastic athletics; providing an after-school bus for boys who participate in after-school athletics but making girls walk; and requiring higher grades for admission from girls than from boys. (U.S. Department of Health, Education, and Welfare, 1978)

According to Representative Dick Swett, in 1990, 37% of school district administrators had not complied with Title IX, and some saw no need to address the issue of equity between the sexes (*Gender Equity in America's Schools,* 1992). He recommended that school districts report their compliance with Title IX on a regular basis to the Office of Civil Rights (OCR) in the Department of Education. He also recommended that OCR receive full funding so that it could monitor race and gender discrimination in the public schools. As of 2005, not only had OCR not received full funding to monitor compliance, but in 2000 it initiated only six complaints at the high school and college level, and in 2001 it initiated only two complaints (Lopiano, 2005).

Title IX was designed to protect individuals from sex discrimination by denying federal financial assistance to educational institutions that had sexually discriminatory practices. Lawsuits based on Title IX have primarily challenged discriminatory practices in admission policies and athletic programs; the only remedy available to those who successfully challenged the practices would be the denial of federal financial assistance to the offending educational institutions. The very fact that public schools now have women's and girls' sports teams, like soccer or basketball, owes its origins to Title IX legislation and the lawsuits that have successfully challenged certain practices. Title IX requires that schools treat boys and girls equally with respect to three distinct components of athletics; participation opportunities, athletic scholarships, and treatment of male and female teams. Opportunities for girls and women in athletics have increased exponentially since the passage of Title IX. Before Title IX, only 294,015 girls participated in high school athletics; in 2006,

that number was nearly 3 million, a 904% increase (Lopiano, 2005).

Sex Discrimination and Pregnancy

Title IX also prohibits schools that receive federal funds from discriminating against females who are pregnant teens and teen mothers. Although outright exclusion of pregnant students from regular classrooms no longer occurs, pregnant students are likely to face more subtle forms of discrimination (Brake, 1994). This may include coercive counseling to attend separate education programs and the withholding of information about educational options. Moreover, pregnant teens and teen mothers often face a number of other requirements that are not directed against others with medical conditions. These actions include requiring pregnant students to submit a doctor's certificate to stay in school and continue to participate in activities; revoking membership in the National Honor Society after the girl becomes pregnant; requiring a medical clearance to return to school after having given birth; requiring a pregnant student to sign a waiver of liability; not providing accommodations that are provided for students with medical conditions, such as unlimited use of the bathroom, access to an elevator, or extra time between classes to travel; failing to provide makeup work for a student who misses school to give birth; not giving credit for the work done before leaving school to give birth; and failing to provide home instruction for those who need to stay home for pregnancy-related reasons (Brake, 1994).

Adolescent pregnancy and parenting are correlated negatively with educational achievement. The economic and social costs of dropping out of school for pregnant teens and teen mothers include higher rates of poverty and welfare dependence and higher rates of academic failure for the children of unwed teen mothers. Pregnancy is the most common reason for young women to drop out of school (U.S. Department of Education, 1991). The benefits of pregnant teens continuing their education is substantial. Teen mothers who are enrolled in school during pregnancy and immediately after childbirth are more likely to complete high school and delay subsequent pregnancies (Brake, 1994). To break the cycle of poverty associated with teen parenthood, young mothers must obtain the educational skills necessary to become financially self-sufficient. Pregnant students have the right to remain in their regular education programs and activities throughout their pregnancies, and that right can be limited only in the same manner that other students with medical conditions are prohibited from engaging in such activities. The demands of pregnancy and raising a child, coupled with the demands of being a full-time student, can be extremely difficult. The most subtle forms of discrimination may be enough to preclude pregnant and parenting students from the classroom. School social workers must be aware of the Title IX protections afforded to these students.

Most recently, Title IX challenges have been directed against single-sex schools and classrooms for teaching girls or boys only. The philosophy behind this movement has been discussed in this chapter. In other words, because the public schools are failing at addressing the special needs of girls, or of boys, certain programs that contain only one gender in the classroom will better address the self-esteem, sexual harassment, high pregnancy rates, and gender inequities in the public classroom. When classrooms are restricted to members of only one sex, then the sex of the other gender is the only basis for the exclusion. In some cases, there may be sound educational reasoning behind the decision to restrict a classroom to one sex. In other cases, the decision may be discriminatory.

The U.S. Supreme Court has addressed single-sex education with respect to military institutes that only admit men and found the policy unconstitutional (*United States v. Virginia,* 1996). However, the case of the military institution concerned a challenge to a men-only policy in higher education; the Supreme Court has not had the opportunity to decide a case that has challenged single-sex education in public schools. There may be opportunities for cases to wind their way through the court systems, however, as unwise school districts adopt new single-sex policies. The NCLB Act gives discretion to local educational agencies to support same-gender schools and classrooms, if they so choose. Additionally, the Department of Education changed Title IX regulations in 2006 to expand authorization for single-sex classrooms (*Title IX at 35,* 2008). In late 2008, outraged parents learned that an Alabama school system segregated the entire student body of a middle school by sex for the 2008 to 2009 school year without notifying the parents nor providing for any coeducational option. Not only does the program segregate the students for all academic subjects, but it also punishes the boys and girls who are caught speaking to each other in the hallways. The parents have contacted the American Civil Liberties Union about the Title IX violation and are considering a lawsuit ("ACLU Warns Alabama," 2008).

Sexual Harassment and Title IX

Sexual harassment is considered to be a form of sex discrimination. The Equal Employment Opportunity Commission (EEOC) defines sexual harassment as "unwelcome sexual advances, requests for sexual favors, and other verbal or physical conduct of a sexual nature...when (1) submission to or rejection of such conduct by an individual is made either explicitly a term or condition of an individual's employment, (2) submission to or rejection of such conduct by an individual is used as the basis for employment decisions affecting such individual, or (3) such conduct has the purpose or effect of unreasonably interfering with an individual's work performance or creating an intimidating, hostile, or offensive working environment" (29 C.F.R. §1604.11). Although much of the law on sexual harassment derives from the workplace situation under Title VII of the Civil Rights Act of 1964, recent cases have looked at sexual harassment in the school setting as being a form of sex discrimination under Title IX. Since 1992, Title IX has been used in an altogether different manner, serving as a basis to financially compensate victims of sexual harassment in the school setting (Kopels & Dupper, 1999).

In 1992, the U.S. Supreme Court decided the case of *Franklin v. Gwinnett County Public Schools* (1992). In *Franklin,* a high school student alleged that she had been sexually assaulted and harassed by her teacher. She claimed that not only was the school district aware of the teacher's conduct, but it took no action to stop the harassment and discouraged the student from pressing charges. The student also alleged that the school district dropped its own investigation of the matter when the teacher agreed to resign from school. The student claimed that she had been subjected to sex discrimination and was entitled to monetary recovery under Title IX. The U.S. Supreme Court ruled that Title IX places on the schools the duty not to discriminate on the basis of sex. The Supreme Court drew an analogy to sexual harassment in the workplace, which is covered under Title VII of the Civil Rights Act of 1964. The Court reasoned that when a supervisor sexually harasses a subordinate worker because of the subordinate's sex, then the supervisor is discriminating on the basis of sex. The Court believed that the same rules should apply when a teacher sexually harasses and abuses a student. The Supreme Court ruled that because Congress had enacted Title IX to prohibit sex discrimination in schools, Congress would not intend to financially support schools that engaged in such discriminatory actions. Therefore, the Court ruled that the student was entitled to recover monetarily under Title IX for the school district's intentional conduct in failing to stop the teacher's known sexual harassment of the student. Because of the ruling in this case, school districts that have knowledge or should have knowledge of their employees' sexual harassment of their students must take action to stop the conduct or they may incur financial liability (Kopels & Dupper, 1999).

Although the *Franklin* case concerned teacher–student harassment, lawsuits have been filed against school districts for their failure to stop sexual harassment of students by other students. Sexual harassment between students, also called peer sexual harassment, has been experienced in a large number of instances. A study by the American Association of University Women (1993) found that 85% of girls and 76% of boys experience some form of sexual harassment in schools. The most common form of harassment, reported by 65% of girls and 42% of boys, was being the target of sexual comments, jokes, gestures, or looks. The second most common form of harassment was being touched, pinched, or grabbed in a sexual manner (AAUW, 1993). Another survey reported that for 39% of respondents, sexual harassment occurred on a daily basis; other results indicated that two thirds of harassing incidents occur with other persons present (Stein, 1993). Peer sexual harassment affects the school performance of a number of victims, especially girls; repeated sexual harassment may lead to high rates of truancy and have a detrimental impact on school achievement (AAUW 1993). After the *Franklin* decision in 1992, lawsuits were filed throughout the country attempting to obtain monetary compensation for children who were harassed by their peers. By 1996, several of these peer sexual harassment cases had reached the federal appellate level (Kopels & Dupper, 1999).

One of these cases, *Davis v. Monroe County Board of Education* (1996), imposed liability on a school board under Title IX for its knowing failure to respond to peer sexual harassment. A fifth-grade student alleged that another fifth-grade student fondled her breasts and vaginal area; directed offensive, explicit remarks to her; and rubbed against her sexually. After each incident the student told her mother and reported the harassing student to her teachers. Her mother repeatedly called school officials to see what actions could be taken to protect her daughter from these behaviors. The school district never disciplined the offending student. The 11th Circuit Court of Appeals ruled that when an educational institution knowingly fails to take action to remedy a hostile environment caused by one student's sexual harassment of another, the harassed student has been denied the benefits of, or has been subjected to, discrimination under that education program in violation of Title IX (*Davis v. Monroe,* 1996).

In another case, in a factually analogous situation, the Fifth Circuit Court of Appeals reached a contrary result. In *Rowinsky v. Bryan Independent School District* (1996), the court disagreed with the analogy to the workplace situation, believing that unwelcome sexual advances of one student to another did not carry the same coercive effect or abuse of power as that made by a teacher, employer, or coworker. In *Rowinsky,* the court ruled that to hold a school district liable for peer sexual harassment, a student must show that the school district responded differently to sexual harassment claims based on the sex of the complainant. If a student could demonstrate that school officials treated claims of sexual harassment of boys more seriously than claims that affect girls, then the school would have impermissibly discriminated under Title IX.

To resolve the differences between the *Davis* and *Rowinsky* cases, as well as other federal appellate cases that had ruled on peer sexual harassment, the U.S. Supreme Court agreed to hear the appeal of the *Davis* case. In a 5–4 decision, the Court ruled that Title IX could be used to sue school districts for monetary damages for peer sexual harassment. The Court stated that school districts may be held liable only when "they are deliberately indifferent to sexual harassment, of which they have actual knowledge, that is so severe, pervasive, and objectively offensive that it can be said to deprive the victims of the access to the educational opportunities or benefits provided by the schools" (*Davis v. Monroe County Board of Education,* 1999). Although the Supreme Court did not define the kinds of behaviors it was limiting, it stated that sexual harassment claims will depend on a variety of factors that include the ages of the harasser and the victim and the number of individuals involved. The court recognized the need for school officials to have flexibility in how they want to respond to peer sexual harassment. The Court stated that all that is necessary is that school officials respond to known peer harassment in a reasonable manner in light of the known circumstances. Clearly, this standard will invite future lawsuits to delineate its terms.

Kopels and Dupper (1999) suggested that the use of lawsuits as a primary intervention strategy in peer sexual harassment cases is inadequate, providing a remedy for students only after they have been harmed. They suggested actions that school social workers and other personnel can take to prevent or minimize peer sexual harassment. These include prevention efforts beginning in middle schools, ensuring that school districts have policies that define and prohibit peer sexual harassment, sensitizing school personnel and students to peer sexual harassment, establishing a grievance procedure, and familiarizing themselves with the Office of Civil Rights Title IX guidelines on peer sexual harassment. A number of school districts have implemented policies that prohibit certain offensive physical behaviors and the use of certain words and name-calling to reduce the incidents of sexual harassment and bullying between students (see Chapter 5 for more information).

Sexual Orientation and Equal Educational Opportunity

Children who are lesbian, gay, bisexual, or transgendered (LGBT) have a much greater chance than children who are heterosexual of having trouble in the school environment. Their difficulties center primarily on issues of safety, health concerns, and poor school performance. Studies have shown that LGBT students are more likely to have been abused and victimized, abuse substances, prostitute themselves, attempt suicide, and be homeless than straight youth (Schwartz, 1994; Uribe & Harbeck, 1992). Many of these children fear violence and harassment from their peers, and their constant anxiety inhibits their ability to learn. Twenty-eight percent of gay students will drop out of school, which is more than three times the national average for heterosexual students (National Mental Health Association, n.d.). According to the National School Climate Survey (2001), LGBT students in 48 states and the District of Columbia completed a survey regarding their experiences in high school. Of the respondents, 84% reported hearing homophobic remarks like "faggot" or "dyke"; 23% reported that these kinds of comments came from faculty or school staff; 81.8% stated that even when staff are present when homophobic remarks are made that staff failed to intervene; and 41.9% of LGBT students reported being shoved, pushed, punched, kicked, or subjected to other physical assaults. In a follow-up survey in 2003, 91.5% of LGBT students reported hearing homophobic remarks frequently or often at school, and 82.9% reported that faculty never or only sometimes intervened when they overheard such remarks being made (Kosciw, 2004).

Courts have begun to respond to cases that relate to peer harassment of students who are harassed on the basis that they are not heterosexual. In a peer sexual harassment case involving a gay high school student, he alleged that from 7th grade when he realized he was gay, until he dropped out of school in 11th grade, he was subjected to ongoing harassment and abuse from other students. He was called names, struck, spat upon, and subjected to a mock rape while 20 students watched and laughed. When he complained to the school principal in charge of discipline, she replied that "boys will be boys" and that if he were going to be so openly gay, he should expect such behavior. In 9th grade, he was assaulted and urinated on; no actions were taken against the offending students. Instead, the official responses throughout his school career were to ignore his complaints, make false promises of aggressive action, and tell him that he deserved the treatment because he was gay. Although his sexual harassment claim was based on an alternative legal theory to Title IX, in *Nabozny v. Podlesny* (1996), the Seventh Circuit Court of Appeals ruled in his favor, believing he was denied the equal protection of the law in his claim of sex and sexual orientation discrimination. The court found it impossible to believe that school personnel would have responded in such a cavalier fashion if a female student had complained about a mock rape; the court ruled that he was entitled to the equivalent level of protection as given to female students. The court also found no justification for

the school's allowing one of its students to assault another based on the victim's sexual orientation. The case was settled in the student's favor for $900,000 (Kopels & Dupper, 1999).

In a very recent case, *Donovan v. Poway Unified School District* (2008), two gay teenagers sued their school district under Title IX and the California Education Code for the harassment that they each received from their peers. The harassment was ongoing for 3 years and peaked during their junior years. The harassment included death threats, being spit on, physical violence and threats of physical violence, vandalism to personal property, and being subject to antigay epithets such as "fag," "faggot," "dyke," and worse. Both students completed their senior year through an independent study program offered by the district. Each complained about their treatment to a number of school administrators, but nothing was done to alleviate the problem. They filed a lawsuit against the school district, and a jury awarded them $300,000. The district appealed, and the California appellate court affirmed in favor of the students. The court ruled that the plaintiffs must show that (1) they suffered "severe, pervasive and offensive" harassment, which effectively deprived them of the right of equal access to educational benefits and opportunities; (2) the school district had "actual knowledge" of that harassment; and (3) the school district acted with "deliberate indifference" in the face of such knowledge. Because the appellate court ruled that the students were able to prove each of these factors, the judgment was affirmed.

Dyson (2004) posits that the reasons that LGBT teenagers are harassed, victimized, and disrespected can be answered from cultural, religious, and social perspectives. He stated that some antigay proponents often justify their views through the Bible or religion, firmly believing that these sources condemn homosexuality. From a cultural standpoint, homosexual stereotypes, fear, and misunderstanding of AIDS are also reasons that gays are harassed (Dyson, 2004). Moreover, other antigay proponents argue that homosexuality will doom the human race to extinction because of the lack of procreation (Dyson, 2004).

In the education context, one of the reasons for shying away from gay-related issues in the classroom is the idea that discussing the issues or making resources available that deal with homosexuality is tantamount to recruiting homosexuality as a way of life or condoning it. Other justifications in education are that homosexuality is an adult issue, that teens' sexual identities are not established yet, or the misconception that homosexuality is a choice (Dyson, 2004).

In 1984, Congress passed the Equal Access Act (EAA) to both guarantee and protect the rights of public high school students. The EAA was passed by wide, bipartisan majorities in both chambers of Congress. Its purpose was to counteract perceived discrimination against content-based religious speech in public high schools. Under the EAA, if a public school that receives federal financial assistance creates a limited open forum, it is unlawful for that school to deny equal access to or to discriminate against any students who wish to conduct a meeting within such limited open forum on the basis of the religious, political, philosophical, or other content of the speech at such meetings. A "limited open forum" is created whenever a school grants an offering to, or opportunity for, one or more noncurriculum-related student groups to meet on school premises during noninstructional time.

In some schools, gay and straight students have created organizations to promote understanding and acceptance for gay youth. However, these gay rights groups have received opposition from those who believe that schools should condemn homosexuality or oppose such clubs that send an inappropriate message on school grounds. Given these concerns, most schools choose not to sponsor controversial student groups at all. Instead, they encourage meetings only of those specific groups believed to have educational value. Some gay student organizations have challenged their schools' refusal to allow their organizations to meet on school grounds. For example, in *Boyd County High Sch. Gay Straight Alliance v. Bd. of Educ.* (2003), a Gay Straight Alliance (GSA) was formed in a Kentucky school district for the purpose of providing students with a safe

haven to talk about antigay harassment and to work together to promote tolerance, understanding, and acceptance of one another, regardless of sexual orientation. When the organization was approved, opponents of the organization staged an on-campus protest and a boycott. The board held an emergency meeting and voted unanimously to suspend all clubs, both curricular and noncurricular, at the school for the remainder of the school year. However, many student organizations continued to use the school's facilities during noninstructional time, despite the suspension. The GSA filed for a preliminary injunction, which was granted by the federal district court. The school district was ordered to give the GSA and its members equal access to those activities of other non-curriculum-related student groups.

California recently enacted a statute that specifically prohibits harassment in schools based on sexual orientation (Eisemann, 2000). In addition, a few states have nondiscrimination educational statutes that include sexual orientation as well as hate crime statutes that could protect gay students from violence in schools (Eisemann, 2000). As mentioned earlier in the discussion about sexual harassment between peers, some states and school districts have also included sexual orientation nondiscrimination in their antibullying or sexual harassment policies. Nevertheless, most states do not specifically protect gay students from harassment in their schools. In those states, gay students have to convince a court that their school's response to antigay harassment should be treated the same as indifference toward peer sexual harassment under Title IX.

Because of the unique problems faced by LGBT students, the Harvey Milk School, a 4-year fully accredited high school program, was created in 1985 as a collaboration between the New York City Department of Education's Career Education Center and the Hetrick-Martin Institute (HMI). According to the school, the Harvey Milk School offers an alternative education program for youth who often find it difficult or impossible to attend their home schools due to continuous threats and experiences of physical violence and verbal harassment (Hetrick-Martin Institute, n.d.; see

Chapter 6 on school violence). The Harvey Milk School believes that all young people, regardless of sexual orientation or identity, deserve a safe and supportive environment in which to achieve their full potential. Hetrick-Martin Institute also creates this environment for LGBT and questioning youth between the ages of 12 and 21 and their families (Hetrick-Martin Institute, n.d.). Although the idea of a separate school for gay students that fosters acceptance and protects them from violence may be appealing, the school is not without its critics. In August 2003, a New York senator and a conservative legal group filed a lawsuit charging that a public high school for LGBT students violates laws on discrimination on sexual orientation (*Suit Challenges Gay High School in New York,* 2003). Moreover, the lawsuit argued that it was unjust for New York City to spend millions of dollars on a school that served only 100 students (Colapinto, 2005). Others argued that segregating homosexuals from their straight peers promotes an unacceptable return to the "separate but equal" educational system (Colapinto, 2005).

Equal Educational Opportunity: Social Work Values and Practices

In some of the desegregation cases I discussed, it took more than 20 years to accomplish the desegregation goals. Once reached, segregation may then occur again, naturally, because of changing societal conditions. In other cases, it has taken more than 20 years for courts to finally determine that the school district did not make sufficient efforts to overcome language barriers that deprived children of their equal educational opportunities. Some change is legislative. Some change is attitudinal. Some change doesn't come easily, if it comes at all.

Much needs to be done to secure equal educational opportunities for the groups of children discussed in this chapter. The values of social work are founded on such principles as encouraging persons to develop to their maximum potential and acting as advocate on behalf of groups that

are not receiving their fair share of society's wealth, opportunities, and resources. Even though the goal for equal educational opportunity is supported by the values held by the social work profession, the profession's commitment to its achievement and record of accomplishment is not what it should be. In our work to advance equity, it is essential that social workers attempt to influence change in educational institutions as well as in those systems that support them. It is our professional obligation to create new policies, programs, attitudes, and approaches that promote equal educational opportunity.

To bring about these changes, I advocate a broad perspective of social work practice—one that allows social workers to intervene in large-scale, complex social systems at several levels (governmental agencies and legislative policy-making bodies at the local, state, and national levels), as well as in small groups and in the social systems within the school and the community.

The larger perspective, which serves as an umbrella for intervention, is ecological. Social work roles that may emerge as workers attempt to promote equal educational opportunity for all groups of pupils are

1. Consciousness training of teachers via in-service programs that focus on such issues as how they interact with certain groups of pupils, their hidden expectations, selection of nonbiased curriculum material, and enhancement of pupil self-esteem

2. Analyzing the curriculum to remove culturally biased, racist, and homophobic materials; serving on a school or districtwide committee established for that purpose

3. Working with parent groups to enable them to help remove language, race, and sex barriers to equal educational opportunity

4. Understanding the requirements of laws such as Title IX and, where indicated, acting as advocate for an individual pupil or for groups of pupils

5. Serving as the Title IX grievance officer for a school district

6. Testifying at public hearings on equal educational opportunity
7. Supporting legislation that promotes equal educational opportunity through membership in professional associations and other appropriate groups
8. Providing direct services (casework and/or group work) to children who are experiencing difficulties
9. Developing human relations activities and programs that bring children and the educational staff together for the purpose of promoting amicable relationships and better understanding
10. Working with the administration to establish and implement policies that promote equal educational opportunity
11. Mediating between the school and community when it is appropriate
12. Reducing barriers to students' receipt of equal educational opportunities

Equal educational opportunity is a value that applies to every pupil regardless of language, race, gender, or sexual orientation. Legislation and court decisions have played a major role in bringing issues of equality of educational opportunity to the forefront. The law has had significant impact at several levels, such as providing direction for states and protecting the individual rights of each student. Unfortunately, there is still much to be done to achieve equality. The goal of eliminating barriers to equal education has yet to be achieved. Social workers in schools are in a strategic position to identify such barriers and can work to remove them. Inequality in educational opportunity and educational resources reinforces and promotes a caste system, organized on the basis of language, race, gender, and sexual orientation. Inequality in education can lead to poverty, underachievement, and impaired intellectual growth.

For Study and Discussion

1. Identify several reasons why some educators and parents would be against bilingual programs.
2. Obtain a copy of your state's position on bilingual educational programs. Then discuss the strengths and weaknesses of the document, as well as potential roles for social workers in such programs.
3. Identify how social workers can assist a neighborhood parents group to create integrated and culturally diverse schools when race cannot be used as a factor for admission. What other methods could be used?
4. What would be the pros and cons of creating single-sex schools for girls or boys or creating safe learning environments for children who are LGBTQ? When do concerns for the learning needs of a group or creating safe learning environments become a cover for segregation and isolation?

10

The Design of Social Work Services

MARY BETH HARRIS

University of Southern California

CYNTHIA FRANKLIN

University of Texas at Austin

CHRISTINE LAGANA-RIORDAN

University of Texas at Austin

Introduction

Designing social work interventions in schools requires an understanding of individual and family issues, as well as knowledge about larger contextual factors that have a great impact on students' school experiences. The planning of social work service delivery cannot be separated from the larger family, school, and community context because services must always be responsive to the needs of students, families, and school systems. This contextual view of service delivery is consistent with the ecological theory covered in Chapter 4. This chapter addresses designing school social work services from the perspective of ecological assessment. Issues of individual students, school factors such as organization and political context, community context, and parent and family sociodemographic trends must be assessed in designing effective services delivery in a school. In addition, social workers and their personal contexts must be assessed when thinking about designing the services in a school. Issues such as self-awareness, cultural competencies and professional competencies, professional values and ethics, and philosophy of interventions must be addressed. This chapter summarizes each of these areas in relation to designing services.

Finally, this chapter provides information on evidence-based programs that can be implemented in a school and addresses accountability in services delivery. Evidence-based practices, standards, and accountability measures and tools and well-documented services plans are extremely important in current school-based services delivery. These trends shape the practices of school social workers and reflect the current governmental policies and management trends in school-based practice.

Individual Context

Approximately 13.3% of children and adolescents meet the diagnostic criteria for mental health disorders each year, according to epidemiological studies (Costello, Mustillo, Erkanli, Keeler, & Angold, 2003). Between 2002 and 2003 there was a rise in juvenile involvement in violent crimes such as homicide, rape, and aggravated assault for both victims and perpetrators (Federal Interagency Forum on Child & Family Statistics, 2005). Suicide is the third leading cause of death for adolescents (National Center for Health Statistics, 2007). It is important for school social workers to assess the major psychosocial problem areas faced by individual youths in the schools in which they serve. For example, social workers must be aware if students are at risk for suicide, need substance abuse prevention programs, or have other diagnoses. Mental health diagnoses have implications for classroom management, school achievement, and school safety issues. The diagnoses of conduct disorder and oppositional defiant disorder may be especially difficult for schools. Chapter 11 discusses services delivery with youth who have conduct disorder. Later sections of this chapter also address other programs for children with social and mental health issues.

Preventing school failure and increasing academic success for children with various mental health and learning deficit diagnoses have become a priority for schools under policy mandates such as the No Child Left Behind. One option for school social workers is to adopt a strengths-based, disease-prevention model approach to helping youths with mental disorders. Using this type of approach, the school social worker can use school records to assess the populations within the school based on social, health, and mental health needs. This data, coupled with interviews of school personnel, will help inform the social work services delivery that is needed. For instance, school social workers might target students receiving special education services or students who have received office referrals for behavior problems. Sometimes school social workers target entire student bodies for whole-school interventions such as character development, behavior management, or to address issues such as poverty and racism. Once the main populations are identified, the social worker can prioritize the issues for their schools. This should be done with a team that includes members such as the school nurse, the psychologist, and the principal. Parents and other community leaders may also be important people

to provide input into the services that are needed. Programs can be planned based on needs, resources, and urgent priorities. Academic success for children with health, social, and mental health concerns may be influenced by a diverse range of factors that include community, neighborhood, school, peer group, family, and individual characteristics. The School Success Profile is a measure that measures risk and protective factors in all these areas and helps practitioners select evidence-based interventions that best meet the needs of a group of students. Chapter 11 provides a detailed description of the School Success Profile. Assessment of community issues is also covered in more detail later in this chapter, as well as specific evidence-based programs that work with various social and mental health challenges.

School Organizational Context

A school is a complex organizational structure with multiple processes and entities. Arum (2000; cited in Bowen & Richman [2002]) discussed a neoinstitutional perspective of school–community relationships. From this viewpoint, both schools and communities are "situated in larger, nonlocal, institutional contexts" known as organizational fields (p. 68; see Chapter 3). These organizational fields influence school policy and practice through policies at the state and national levels and mechanisms for financing programs. Some organizational fields that influence schools are federal and state welfare policy, health and social services programs, the court system, education agencies, and state boards (Bowen & Richman, 2002).

Organizational skills are as important to school social workers as clinical practice skills. Most school organizational structures are hierarchical in nature, and learning how the social worker fits into the organizational hierarchy is important. To be accepted and accommodated, the social worker must gain some understanding of the school's organizational culture and neoinstitutional context and assume a role protocol that supports organizational norms (Austin, 2002).

Needs and Sociopolitical Demands of Multiple Stakeholders

Unlike some social work arenas, the education system is continually at the center of public attention, reflected in political, religious, and media activity. In addition to constituency groups within the institution, community and societal stakeholders with diverse agendas continually interact with public education, looking to influence policy and programs according to their own priorities.

Perhaps the most obvious indication of the public's investment in education is the school board, an elected body from the community. As such, the school board is expected to reflect the general values and concerns of the community in the policies and functions that drive school programs and operations. In some communities this may mean that the school board takes a leadership role in expanding services and responses to diverse student needs. For others it can mean that the board upholds traditional values in the schools. Thus, it is helpful for school social workers to understand the values and political climate of the community as well as demographics such as age, cultural identity, and professional background of board members.

As a constituency group, parents may be perceived as a consumer group with an important voice in the discourse about school programs and priorities. On the other hand, parents, especially those outside the mainstream culture, may be an underrepresented constituency group whose value to student learning and well-being is underutilized. As discussed in Chapter 5, parents have rights under the Family Educational Rights and Privacy Act of 1974, as well as a history of successful court cases regarding their children's education. However, parents receive varying degrees of sanction across the country regarding safety and quality of education for their children (e.g., parents' rights as defined in Chapter 864, Statutes of 1998, Education Code, 1998).

Some community groups not involved directly with the school, nevertheless, influence programs and policies. Among the most visible are religious groups and community health constituencies, both concerned with issues like sex education and abortion information (Weaver, Smith, & Kippax, 2005). Although these and other groups may not have direct connections to the schools, their issues often stir the interest of the media, which can have important consequences for social and health services.

Administrative Style

A principal's leadership style can shape the school's culture, which can have a great impact on student achievement. As an organization, every school has its own personality, the climate dominated by the administrative style of the school principal. Through the 1990s, most school principals were considered *instructional* leaders, whose main function was to make curriculum decisions for their schools. After major school reform movements, however, the leadership roles of the school principals were conceptualized in new ways. The *transformational* principal is one who inspires other members of the school system and encourages innovation. These leaders bind the school community together in an effort to reach lofty organizational goals such as empowerment, ethical behavior, and justice. The *transactional* administrator focuses on the interactions between members of the school community and observes all transactions as being motivated by self-interest. This type of leader seeks to maintain the status quo of a school environment and encourages stability over creativity (Bogler, 2001).

Political Dimensions in the Organization

Knowledge of political dimensions is implicit in understanding school organizational culture. For example, school social workers need to understand who has formal and informal power within a school and how they use their power. Following the principle that influencing the right people is the key to achieving results, social workers can learn who the key players are through knowing who influences school policy (Streeter & Franklin, 1993). They should also determine who may help or hinder work with officials, teachers, students, or families (Pawlak & Cousins, 1999). This knowledge of formal and informal power allows school social workers to understand why certain people have a lot more influence than others in the local school or school district and learn how to use informal power. School social workers must be able to "sell" themselves and their services in a setting that may not know or appreciate social work practice, which requires that they be visible, accountable, and perceived by the organization as effective and supportive of school agendas.

Developing a Relationship of Trust with School Personnel

Good interpersonal skills as well as awareness and respect for the concerns and priorities of other staff are essential to developing relationships with other school personnel. Understanding potential barriers to these relationships is important. Some relationship barriers are as unique as the local school culture and personalities involved, whereas others are universal.

Several potentially conflictual issues are common between social work services and the roles and functions of other school personnel. A primary factor is that programs and services staffed by social workers are being established with greater frequency. In a random sampling of public schools in a western state, for example, 80% of the schools reported the presence of one to five social service providers at the school site (Melaville & Blank, 1991). With this growing trend, school counselors may voice concerns about being replaced by social workers, competing for limited resources, and having differing ideas about appropriate student interventions (Porter, Epp, & Bryan, 2000). Similarly, school social workers have higher job satisfaction when they have little role discrepancy, when they feel little competition with school counselors, and when they feel valued by school counselors (Agresta, 2006). A connection of equal importance for social workers is with teachers, who may view social work services as unnecessary or stigmatizing. They many resist having students pulled from their academic classes to receive services (Porter et al.,

2000). Because teachers have more contact with students than other staff and control a large part of students' daily schedules, their support for social work activities is vital. Moreover, the relationship between teachers and students affects students' academic performance and behavior profoundly. Studies have found that teachers' beliefs about student abilities often contribute to their likelihood of succeeding in school (Ferri & Connor, 2005), and poor interactions with teachers are a risk factor for student failure (Reis, Colbert, & Hebert, 2005).

The following example demonstrates the importance of teacher support for school-based services:

> Ellie was 6 months pregnant and a sophomore in high school. At the beginning of the semester, Ellie was invited by the school social worker to participate in a weekly lunchtime group for pregnant and parenting young women in her school. The social worker told Ellie that the group would help her with skills to pass in school and be able to graduate. Lately, she had missed several days of school for medical and social service appointments and was falling behind. Although a memo had circulated asking teachers to excuse group participants for the first minutes of their class after group, Ellie's teacher stopped the class after her first group meeting to ask *why* she was late. When she told him she had been in a group, he replied that she needed to be in class more than in some group. When the teacher responded similarly after the second group session, Ellie told the social worker that she was going to drop out of the group. She feared failing the class due to her teacher's irritation with her being late each week. When the social worker spoke personally with Ellie's teacher about the value of the group for Ellie, the teacher reluctantly agreed to allow Ellie's participation without penalty. Near the end of the group 2 months later, the teacher sent a note with Ellie to the social worker saying, "Ellie's performance in my class has improved tremendously this semester in carrying out assignments from her group. Give us more like this!"

Involving and informing teachers and other staff in the planning phase of social services diminishes conflicts of priorities and enhances the possibility of much-needed support. Conferring with other staff personally shows respect for their priorities and reduces the possibility of misunderstandings and oversights. A relationship of trust can develop when the social worker demonstrates competence and a willingness to be an active team player in addressing the concerns of the school.

School social workers can also gain teacher support by listening to teachers' concerns about their classrooms and students. With the advent of the No Child Left Behind Act of 2001, teachers may feel stress about helping their students to pass required state tests (Costigan, 2002). In many cases, teachers' performance evaluations are based on the percentage of their students who pass these tests. Social workers can lend support to teachers who are feeling overwhelmed by asking them about their needs and the type of support that could be offered. For instance, a teacher might spend a large portion of the day addressing behavior problems in the classroom. The school social worker could implement a behavior management system in the classroom or even schoolwide to help reduce behavior problems and allow teachers to focus more of their time on academic tasks. An example of a schoolwide character education model focused on preventing problem behaviors is presented later in the chapter.

Interprofessional Practice

In planning for school social work services, we must recognize the inevitability of the interprofessional team, as well as the power of a collective voice advocating for the needs of children and youth. A collaborative system that evolved from the 1970s multidisciplinary approach in the health field, the interprofessional team "involves the interaction of various disciplines around an agreed-upon goal to be achieved *only* through a complex integration or synthesis of various disciplinary perspectives" (Schmitt, 1982, p. 183, cited in Casto et al., 1994, p. 36). Interprofessional practice in schools is a collaboration expanded beyond traditional "teaching," to recognize and address issues that affect the student's whole ecology. In this context, the school social

worker is required not only to collaborate on services with other professionals, but also to understand the perspectives and priorities of other professions in negotiating common goals and objectives for the school. For example, since the passing of No Child Left Behind, school guidance counselors have begun to play a central role in identifying students who are at risk of low performance on state tests. In addition, guidance counselors often have up-to-date information about student academic progress and how they are faring in each of their classes. For these reasons, it is essential for counselors and school social workers to work together to identify students who are struggling and to plan interventions for these students.

The following is an example of an interprofessional team in action.

When Pete, a 16-year-old high school student, began skipping school and performing poorly on graded assignments in several classes, his guidance counselor referred him to the school-based health center. After receiving the referral, the school social worker met with the guidance counselor and several of Pete's teachers to review the counselor's concerns. The team decided that the social worker should first meet with Pete to discuss the situation. In the meeting, Pete disclosed that his family had recently lost their home and was living with relatives in a crowded apartment. Pete had difficulty studying in the new environment and felt very concerned about his family's future. In addition, Pete reported that he was having difficulty maintaining his hygiene in the cramped quarters and was being bullied about his hygiene by several students in his math class. After meeting with Pete and with his permission, the school social worker, nurse, guidance counselor, and Pete's math teacher collaborated to create an intervention plan. The school social worker agreed to help Pete's family by providing information about local resources that could help to get them into their own apartment as soon as possible. The guidance counselor suggested that Pete join an after-school study hall where he could complete his school work in a quiet space. Pete's math teacher agreed to collaborate with Pete's other teachers to create a plan for him to make up the assignments he had missed. The school nurse agreed to provide Pete with basic hygiene items and offered to let Pete discreetly do his laundry and shower in the nurse's office before school. Finally, the social worker agreed to conduct a peer-mediation session with Pete and the students who had been bullying him. As members of a cohesive intervention team, the school social worker, nurse, guidance counselor, and teacher were able to address a multitude of problems to help Pete be successful at school, despite his difficult family situation. Without this type of interdisciplinary collaboration, many of the team members may have been unaware of Pete's difficulties, and he would not have received the multifaceted intervention needed to help him reach his potential.

Streeter and Franklin (2002) suggested that school social workers go beyond interprofessional practice and adopt transdisciplinary team models to enhance their work with diverse professionals. Transdisciplinary team models are consistent with the philosophy guiding interprofessional practice described earlier. Professionals commit to teaching-learning-working with other service providers across traditional disciplinary boundaries. As a team comprised of different professional disciplines, transdisciplinary teams seek to expand the common core of knowledge and competency of each team member systematically through a focused attempt to pool and exchange information, knowledge, and skills across disciplines. This type of boundary spanning requires a number of strategies, including planned individual study, one-to-one instruction among team members, and a planned and systematic team teaching-learning process.

Research on the Effects of School Culture and Collaboration

Research indicates that a school culture in which staff at multiple levels work together and share a common vision results in positive student outcomes (Harris & Hopkins, 2000; Hofman, Hofman, & Guldemond, 2001; Keys, Sharp, Greene, & Grayson, 2003). Using positive, simple rules developed collaboratively with students and demonstrating respect for student differences are strategies associated with reduced school violence (Erickson, Mattaini, & McGuire, 2004). Viggiani, Reid, and Bailey-Dempsey (2002) found that interventions in which social workers and teachers collaborate in resolving student difficulties were associated with fewer absences and increased improvements in classroom behavior. In their review of school-based mental health interventions, Roans and Hoagwood (2000) found that many effective interventions included components that worked to promote better collaboration among teachers or increased communication between the school staff and parents. Being effective in today's school settings requires sharing knowledge, working with those from other disciplines, and respecting the skills of other school professionals (Streeter & Franklin, 2002).

School-Wide Positive Behavior Supports (PBS) is a collaborative *character education* model for evaluating and alleviating problem behaviors in schools. PBS strives to alter the school environment to make it more responsive to student needs (Clonan, McDougal, Clark, & Davison, 2007). This model requires all members of the school community to participate in the active teaching and reinforcement of positive behaviors, including teachers, social workers, counselors, administrators, and support staff. The PBS program operates on three intervention levels: primary, secondary, and tertiary intervention. On the primary intervention level, schools adapt the school environment for all students in all settings. For instance, schools decide on simple and positively stated school rules and post these rules in hallways, classrooms, lunchrooms, and stairwells. All students receive classroom instruction regarding behavioral expectations and are reinforced for positive behavior (George, White, & Schlaffer, 2007). Secondary interventions target a small number of students for whom schoolwide interventions are less effective. These interventions include tutoring, social skills groups, or team-building exercises (Clonan et al., 2007) and are usually delivered to individuals or small groups (Eber, Sugai, Smith, & Scott, 2002). Finally, tertiary interventions aim to help the student population with chronic and persistent emotional and behavioral problems. These students receive highly individualized functional behavioral assessments by a multidisciplinary team comprised of teachers, social workers, and behavior specialists (George et al., 2007). In the past 10 years, research examining the effectiveness of the PBS model in schools has emerged. Many of these studies have reported fewer schoolwide problem behaviors and discipline referrals after the implementation of PBS (Clonan et al., 2007; George et al., 2007; Lassen, Steele, & Sailor, 2006; Netzel & Eber, 2003). Others have specifically shown reductions in problem behaviors in nonclassroom settings (Kartub, Taylor-Greene, March, & Horner, 2000; Lewis, Colvin, & Sugai, 2000; Lewis & Garrison-Harrell, 1999; Oswald, Safran, & Johanson, 2005; Todd, Horner, Anderson, & Spriggs, 2002). In addition, PBS has been effective in decreasing the number of suspensions and the frequency of seclusion and physical restraint among elementary school students (George et al., 2007; Netzel & Eber, 2003).

Conducting an Assessment of School Culture

Because the school environment plays an important role in student success, researchers are working to define and measure organizational factors that affect students. One such measure is the School Success Profile-Learning Organization (SSP-LO) developed by Gary Bowen (see Chapter 3 and www.schoolsuccessprofile.org for more information). A learning organization is defined as a school or any other community organization that uses information from staff and key stakeholders to plan, implement, and evaluate practices that help students achieve desired outcomes. Actions and sentiments help define

whether a school is a learning organization. In assessing staff actions, the SSP-LO measures the following six dimensions: team orientation, innovation, involvement, information flow, tolerance for error, and results orientation. Staff sentiment is measured through another six dimensions: common purpose, respect, cohesion, trust, mutual support, and optimism (www.schoolsuccessprofile.org).

A System of Integrated Services

Osborne and Collison (1998) offered a team model from the perspective of the school counselor. This model, as well as others (e.g., Casto et al., 1994), recognizes that although most human service professionals are prepared in academic programs that emphasize separateness rather than collaboration, the concepts and assumptions in consultation theory and group theory contain the needed framework for developing collaborative work relationships across professional boundaries.

Osborne and Collison (1998) presented five processes in the model: (a) a school counselor convenes the group, the rationale being that the counselor is the person specifically prepared and licensed to work in the schools; (b) the group articulates its reason for working cooperatively in serving its mutual clients more effectively; (c) the group begins by providing a goal and rationale statement to the school administrator containing recommendations for organizational structure and operational procedures that lead to client services; (d) the group identifies shared goals and makes those goals public throughout the school; and (e) leadership is on a rotating basis, and the group identifies the strengths and contributions that each individual or agency brings to the team.

Although parts of this model reflect issues of ownership of the program by traditional school personnel, it shows respect for the diversity of strengths and perspectives represented by different disciplines. It also gives social workers an integrated networking system for interpreting program priorities and values with other school staff. The possible barriers to effective working relationships discussed earlier would have a considerable chance for resolution within this sanctioned collaborative structure.

An Ecosystems Model

A frame for interprofessional collaboration developed by Brandis and Philliber (1998), though similar to the system of integrated services model, recommends a broader system, which involves service professionals in the school, as well as those who provide services for students and their families in the community outside the school. The ecosystems approach on which this model relies heavily advocates for enlarging the system of community resources and investment in the initial planning phase, as well as in ongoing collaboration. Chapter 4 describes the approach in more detail.

The roles of professionals and organizations in the community, because they are not involved directly in school-based services, are to serve as mediators and contributors to a broader perspective and program concept without the motivation of self-gain. Although it may be optimistic to expect that programs and agencies not involved directly in school programs would make such a commitment, it may be worth the effort to recruit those who would agree to participate.

Community Context

The school social worker has clear and compelling reasons for maintaining good working relationships in the community and for knowing how to assess those relationships. The simple truth is that the school cannot do all that needs to be done for the community's youth. This is a job for which the community must be equipped and willing to share. The community must be continually informed and developed because the spirit of willingness may not come easily, especially in the current time of fewer resources and competing priorities. Prevention education programs and active community coalitions concerned with specific problems confronting children and youth can be powerful sources of change and support for children and adolescents in school.

When problems and distressed students are identified, the school social worker can take the lead in obtaining the necessary services. Accessing resources for students and families in distress is often complex and requires sophisticated knowledge of community systems. The continual change in eligibility requirements and alliances among service systems can make this process like detective work, time-consuming and tedious. "Any commitment to vulnerable children places the school in the difficult and unwanted position of having to interact with community agencies in complex planning efforts" (Kordesk & Constable, 1999). The role of learning and engaging with community service systems on behalf of students or their families is most often filled by the school social worker. The appendices at the end of this text give examples of school social work services in two communities. Appendix I is an example of school social work practice in a rural community, and Appendix II highlights urban school social work practice. Both appendices give detailed analyses of the community and school environment, outline a plan for social work services including goals and objectives, and reveal the outcomes associated with the services.

Wraparound services, the result of recent community collaboration trends and managed care, may be of considerable benefit for obtaining services for children who need them. "Wraparound services emphasize the development of comprehensive, interagency community based systems of care in which professionals and parents work together collaboratively to serve children . . ." (Duchnowski, Kutash, & Friedman, 2002, p. 21). Wraparound services were designed to provide intensive support to children with mental illness and their families with the intention of preventing psychiatric hospitalization. Children and families would receive intensive services, such as counseling and respite care, in their homes and schools. These services enabled many children who would have been placed in special education classrooms to remain in mainstream classrooms (Furman & Jackson, 2002). Essential elements of the wraparound process include community-based services, team leadership involving natural supports, child agencies, and families working together to develop and implement individual service plans. Services are strengths based and promote the continuance of children in a community setting as contrasted to being sent to a residential or more institutional setting. Wraparound has flexible ways of operating, including using monies to buy needed services. It uses both formal and informal support systems, implementing all plans through a collaborative process. Established outcomes track services to ensure effectiveness (Burchard, Bruns, & Burchard, 2002).

In communities where wraparound services exist, it is important for school social workers to establish the school as a team member of the wraparound process. Being a part of the wraparound services will ensure quicker and better services for children in need. An assessment instrument, Communities That Care (CTC), provides a needs assessment for youth in a community and informs the process of choosing practices to improve community supports for youth. School social workers might find this a helpful tool to use in their work in wraparound services and other community interventions involving the schools. This measure allows users to learn about programs and policies that are likely to meet the particular needs of their community. The system works like a computer operating system and allows users to select programs that are consistent with their goals (Hawkins, 1999; Richman, Bowen, & Woolley, 2004). The CTC system includes the following five phases:

1. Defining the community; assessing activities and programs already in use; identifying community priorities that may affect implementation of the CTC and new prevention programs;
2. Introducing CTC to key stakeholders in the community and engaging them in the planning process;
3. Using the CTC to develop a profile of the community's strengths and needs; a limited number of risk factors are targeted for intervention;

4. The CTC planning group defines desired outcomes for each of the risk areas and develop specific, measurable outcomes that will indicate whether they are achieving outcomes; the group reviews research-based promising programs that are designed to achieve the targeted outcomes; and
5. Implementing promising programs and identifying necessary resources for implementation (Hawkins, 1999).

Assessing Sociopolitical Dynamics of School and Community

The need for effective collaboration and integration of school with other community resources has clearly intensified in response to the increasing number of children and youth vulnerable to school failure and future employment limitations. Because collaboration is a planned process that creates opportunities for people to work together, gaining knowledge of the demographics and sociopolitical dynamics of the community is valuable.

Demographic data about the community can be obtained readily from sources such as census tracts, city and county records, and national data. Meaningful knowledge of the culture and dynamics of the community is gained through interactions and observations over time. One way that social workers enhance their familiarity with the sociopolitical dynamics of the community is by attending city council and school board meetings and tracking members' positions and activities. Another way is by participating in community organizations where they become familiar with community needs, conflicts, and alliances. Table 10.1 gives questions that are helpful in assessing community educational system dynamics.

These are some good sources of data for such an assessment:

■ Interviews or conversations with people in the community about needs and problems, which should include a diversity of citizens ranging from children to the elderly, varied professionals and business owners, and service providers.

TABLE 10.1   Analysis of Community Educational System Dynamics

A. How do federal education policies such as No Child Left Behind impact community schools? Have the schools received sanctions? Is there significant pressure on the students to perform well? Are there high-stakes consequences for students and teachers?

B. What kind of leadership exists in the community educational structure? Who holds the greatest power or influence? What are the roles of the school districts and local school board? Are the teachers and administrators in the community unified or do power struggles exist?

C. How do parents and community members view the quality of community schools and teacher qualifications?

D. How do schools in the community address student health and mental health concerns? Do the schools have school-based health centers? Are mental health services available in school-based health centers or through linked services? How is sex education delivered?

E. How are the rights of students addressed in the community? Do students have a voice in decision-making processes?

F. How do schools in the community address school violence? Are the schools generally considered "safe"? Do schools use physical safety measures such as metal detectors and security guards? Do community schools have evidence-based violence prevention programs in place?

G. What kinds of relationships do community schools have with parents and other community members? Do community schools have low or high levels of parent involvement? What is the role of local Parent-Teacher Associations and how much power do they have?

H. What kinds of relationships do local businesses have with community schools? Are there any school-to-work or internship opportunities in the community? Do local businesses support school fundraisers?

 I. What is the general ethnic and socioeconomic make-up of the community and of schools in the community? Do schools seem to be integrated or segregated based on student ethnicity and socioeconomic status? Is there conflict between groups?

J. How do local religious groups interact with the school? Which religious holidays does the school recognize by closing?

K. Does the community offer a school voucher program, school choice, or charter schools? Which students do these programs target? Are there any controversies in the community regarding school financing, school reform, school choice, vouchers, or charter schools?

L. Do schools in the community have policies regarding multicultural education? Is bilingual education permitted?

Source: Adapted from Fellin, P. (2001). *The community and the social worker* (3rd ed.). Belmont, CA: Brooks/Cole.

- Current census records provide demographic data, such as education level, races and cultures, income, and other useful facts about the population. These are often available on the city or county Web site.
- The chamber of commerce has information about social and health resources such as clinics, hospitals, mental health services, churches and synagogues, social service agencies, recreational facilities and services, and civic organizations.
- The chamber of commerce and the United Way have information about foundations and other

public or private funds designated for use in the community.

Family and Parents Context

Today's school social worker must be prepared to assess and design social work services in multicultural families and to be competent with people from widely diverse cultural and ethnic backgrounds. Dimensions of race and culture are shifting among school populations. An important cultural shift resulting from a surge of immigration from South and Central America, Cuba, the

Middle East, Vietnam, and other Asian countries (Hernandez, 2004) has brought challenges of language and acculturation to urban schools. In the United States today, more than one fifth of the nation's children are growing up in immigrant homes (Annie E. Casey Foundation, 2008). Language and cultural barriers are cited as the main obstacles when children of minority cultures do not achieve in school. When Wright, Taylor, and Ruggiero (cited in Franklin & Soto, 2002) studied the problems encountered when the cultures of the student and the system vary, they found that minority language offered the most robust explanation for why students could not obtain the information needed to do well in school. This is vital information for public education when the number of Hispanic students almost doubled between 1990 and 2006 and by 2050, Hispanic school-aged children will outnumber non-Hispanic White school-aged children (Fry & Gonzales, 2008).

According to the U.S. Department of Education, National Center for Education Statistics (2008), Hispanic youths are the most at-risk group for dropout. While the dropout rate is 5.8% for White youth and 10.7% for African-American youth, the rate for Hispanic youth is 22.1%. For those youth born outside the United States, the dropout rate for Hispanics is an astounding 38% compared to 10.5% for other foreign-born youth (KewalRamani, Gilbertson, Fox, & Provasnik, 2007). Advocacy roles may become more important as schools struggle to equalize services for diverse groups.

Franklin and Soto (2002) cited an example of how a teacher got involved in advocating for a group of Hispanic youths who were not allowed to participate in advanced math classes due to their language proficiency:

> Ms. Mellor, a middle-aged Pennsylvania Quaker, relocated to a farmworker town in the central valley of California. She taught advanced math. She was amazed to find that in a school of 51% Latino students, her advanced math class was entirely white, like her. She asked the administration why there were no Hispanic students in her class and

was told that they didn't speak English well enough to take her class. The Latino students explained to her that they were not allowed to enroll in honors English class, either, because Latinos were not college-bound. One student explained that, "as a Mexican you're supposed to be humble."

> Mellor refused to accept the situation. She plucked promising Latino children from her other classes and installed them with the other advanced students. She pushed the students to work hard and told them they could succeed. (p. 5)

In this example, the teacher's efforts resulted in academic and career success for numerous students. Advocacy interventions are often needed when working with multicultural and language-minority students.

Socioeconomic Family Trends

Some researchers believe that socioeconomic status explains the differences in school achievement more than race or ethnicity (Richman et al., 2004; Rumberger, 2004). The United States maintains the highest poverty rate for children of all economically advanced countries (Jozefowicz-Simbeni & Allen-Meares, 2002; UNICEF, 2007). The overall poverty rate for children in the United States is reported at 18%, and in four states it is more than 25%. For African-American children the poverty rate is 35%, and 27% of all Latino children live in poverty (Annie E. Casey Foundation, 2007). This suggests that school social workers must use local demographic data to help raise awareness of these issues and to foster support for programs to remove the barriers to education that students from poverty may face.

Poverty is not limited to inner-city schools. A dramatic withdrawal of economic and social resources from urban and rural communities over the past few decades has changed the context of community for families and the school. Disengagement from the urban neighborhood out of fear has become a norm (Bowen & Van Dorn, 2002). These problems all point to more students entering school with basic physical, social, and emotional needs that must be met if they are to be able to learn. The scope of problems demands social and mental health services ranging from prevention to treatment. They stretch public education resources in a time when other interests are competing for federal dollars in a struggling economy and a conservative political environment. With the current emphasis on testing and possible sanctions as a result of No Child Left Behind, resources for social and mental health purposes are becoming even more scarce.

To effectively plan the services for socioeconomically challenged students requires more than statistics. The school social worker must make the school staff aware of the types of issues experienced by families that have few economic resources. For example, they may not have money to buy backpacks or may have to move frequently from residence to residence because of lost jobs or eviction. Poverty is also associated with violence and violent crime. Violence is challenging for schools, and juvenile access to guns has increased in both urban and rural communities to the point that witnessing violence, identified as *covictimization,* is now associated with a sense of hopelessness and a vendetta mentality in children and youth (Brill, Fiorentino, & Grant, 2001; Fick & Thomas, 1995; Kuther, 1999). Schools with large percentages of students that live below the poverty line need social workers who can assist them in creating schools/communities with positive expectations and hope to counter the life experiences surrounding poverty. Students and families must be linked with resources and interventions aimed at building school and community resources if schools are going to be successful with children that live in poverty (Jozefowicz-Simbeni & Allen-Meares, 2002). In this way, the assessment of the socioeconomic status of students, families, and communities guides the services delivery offered within a school, and those services must involve the whole school context, as well.

Family Diversity

Family trends also indicate that children entering school today come from diverse family compositions, including intact, single-parent, blended families, cohabitating families, and gay and lesbian families (see Chapter 8). There is also a family trend toward grandparents raising their grandchildren. The American Association of Retired Persons (2007) reported, for example, that over 8% of U.S. children under the age of 18 live in grandparent-headed households (4.5 million) or with other family members (1.5 million). Families from diverse compositions without adequate financial resources often lack food, appropriate housing, health care, and stimulating in-home materials to promote the cognitive and developmental growth of children (Jozefowicz-Simbeni & Allen-Meares, 2002). In addition, an estimated 6 to 14 million children live with gay or lesbian parents in the United States. Gay and lesbian families face many social stresses, including stigma, homophobia, and outright discrimination (Adams, Jaques, & May, 2004).

Working with School and Family

Parents are the experts on their children, and the family's resources and needs are of crucial consideration in the child's school achievement. Parental involvement is often necessary to even begin serving students in schools. Although laws and guidelines vary by state, district, and individual schools, many schools require parental *permission to serve* before mental health professionals are permitted to assess, counsel, or intervene with a student (Knauss, 2001). Without this permission, school social workers often cannot address the needs of students, no matter how great they may be. Consequently, school social workers must first form a relationship with and gain the trust of parents before addressing the students in need of services. The need is clear for families and schools to work in partnership around their children, although too often this is not the case. As Constable and Walberg (1999) discussed,

> The family and school, two critical institutions in the ecology of childhood, have long maintained a studied disregard for each other, paying cautious inattention to the extent of their real interdependence. Such cautious and strategic inattention works well when the family and school are in implicit agreement, when the pupil is succeeding in school and when the family is in control of the socialization processes outside of school hours.
>
> However, assumptions that such an ideal picture of family life is usual are no longer valid for a great many pupils. Changes in the structure of families and fragmentation and atomization of communities have increased the incidence of vulnerable children and pupils at risk in the educational process. (p. 226)

Assessing and intervening between school and family as separate entities with different, often conflicting, needs and demands can be confusing and challenging for the social worker. An ecosystems approach may be helpful, where families and the school are viewed as vital systems linked together around the child's growth, development, and learning (see Chapter 4 for more information). The following example demonstrates such an approach.

> The staff at this mid-western suburban high school was concerned about the high absenteeism and general lack of integration of the 23 student refugees from El Salvador who had entered the school during the previous year. Leo, the school's social worker, understood the difficulties faced by these students and their families. Not only was language a large barrier for them, but they had witnessed and experienced atrocities that most Americans had never seen and had endured months of survival existence in refugee camps. They needed the school to reach out to them, but raising sufficient awareness throughout the school on the realities of these students seemed an insurmountable task.
>
> After Leo presented this ongoing concern at a quarterly meeting of community service providers to the school, he received a call from the community theatre representative. The theatre received a grant each year to perform short dramatic presentations in the schools related to issues of consequence to students, such as bullying, HIV, and drugs. They believed that presenting dramatic vignettes of the El Salvadorian families' experiences to small groups at the school, followed by discussions with the students and family members themselves, could provide a forum for enhancing the school's understanding and response to these students.
>
> Leo visited with several of the El Salvadorian families, then brought them to meet with the school project director from the community theatre. The director and Leo gained their involvement and leadership in the project, and the school provided space for the group to write and rehearse. With the director's guidance and the theatre arts teacher acting as a liaison to the school, six El Salvadorian parents and four students ultimately developed three 20-minute dramatic presentations. The first presentation focused on how they had become refugees from their country, the second was about their experiences in refugee camps, and the third highlighted their challenges of acculturation in their new country. The families not only plunged into conceptualizing and writing the vignettes, but some were also enthusiastic about acting in the productions.
>
> At the end of the school year the vignettes had been performed and discussed numerous times in classes, at a PTA meeting, and at a faculty in-service. Leo reported important changes among the El Salvadorian students and their families. The students' average attendance had increased from 70% at the first grading period to over 90% at the end of the year. The school saw an increase in the presence and participation of El Salvadorian parents at the school, occasionally serving as speakers and resources in sociology, economics, and other classes. Finally, Leo reported that the El Salvadorian students' grades were up, and they were becoming more socially involved in clubs, sports, and, not surprisingly, the school's theatre arts program.

The guiding assumption from this perspective is that when parent systems and school systems find ways to be involved together in children's education, children are more likely to be successful in school and in life. It becomes important to help families and the school to develop skills and motivation for involving and participating with one another. Toward this goal, the school social worker can identify at least three objectives:

1. Educating school personnel toward understanding the psychosocial strengths and needs of families, and supporting school staff relationships with vulnerable families.
2. Offering relevant program interventions for parents and families based on an ongoing and current needs assessment.
3. Helping the interprofessional team, the PTA, and school staff to develop avenues for parent involvement in the operations and programs of the school.

Given the goal of creating a stronger family and school partnership, program interventions should take place in the school and involve other school personnel whenever possible. Programs may include parenting classes and support groups, literacy programs, acculturation classes, Parents Anonymous groups, and others that respond directly to the needs of parents and families. Curricula for many such interventions are available from community family agencies and national organizations. The Child Welfare League of America located in Washington DC, for example, provides publications, programs, and other supports for families in such areas as child mental health, domestic violence, children with incarcerated parents, and foster care. The Web site where these programs and supports are listed is www .cwla.org.

Working with children whose parents are divorcing presents unique challenges for school mental health professionals. Divorce can bring many emotional and financial hardships, stress, and depression and is often associated with behavior problems in children. Children's adjustment during and after divorce can be greatly affected by the extent the parents are able to maintain a respectful, cooperative relationship (Janzen, Harris, Jordan, & Franklin, 2006). Assessments that may be helpful in working with families affected by divorce include the

Dyadic Adjustment Scale, a 32-item instrument that measures the quality of a couple's relationship (Hunsley, Best, Lefebvre, & Vito, 2001), and the Child Behavior Checklist, which measures strengths and behavior problems in children (Achenbach, 1991). The Family Assessment Measure (FAM) provides an assessment of family functioning in seven dimensions: affective involvement, control, task accomplishment, role performance, communication, affective expression, and values and norms (Franklin, Hopson, & Ten Barge, 2003; Skinner, Steinhauer, & Sitarenios, 2000). These measures are useful for families affected by divorce as well as for families experiencing early stages of conflict and communication difficulties.

Assessing Oneself in Preparation for Services Delivery

Working within the cultural, racial, and socioeconomic diversity of a school environment may present a challenge for some social workers. Assessing our fit with such an environment, as well as our practice competence for school social work, requires that we examine ourselves from at least three perspectives:

1. Our values and beliefs from our own cultural and racial context
2. Our attitudes and expectations about persons from other cultures and races
3. Our knowledge and practice competence with other cultures and races

Examining our own values and beliefs requires a close look at the cultural and racial context in which they are embedded. Some questions we might ask ourselves: Are my life experiences laced with racial or cultural discrimination and alienation, or conversely, with power and privilege? When do I find myself judging, patronizing, or resenting the lifestyles, beliefs, and values of people racially and culturally different from myself? How do these thoughts and attitudes affect my behavior and interactions with others? These are difficult questions, but they are essential for developing the self-awareness and insight that a social worker needs to work effectively in a diverse school environment.

Culturally Competent Assessment

No social worker can claim awareness of all nuances of cultures that differ from their own. Even so, it is important to gain knowledge and familiarity with culturally based values, worldviews, and environmental systems of students and families in the local school and community. In discussing the relevance of ecological theory in assessing children in schools, Allen-Meares (2008) stated, "A child's ability to function at one age, on one day, and in one setting, cannot be evaluated without also considering the people and places with which he or she comes in contact, as well as the effects of society at large" (p. 309) Inherent in this statement is the assumption that social workers must seek authentic understanding of the cultural, racial, and socioeconomic context—ecology—of the children and youth they serve. As social workers, we base our practice decisions on knowledge and beliefs about particular characteristics of clients and their problems, as well as the environments in which they live. In building our perspectives for working with culturally diverse children and families, we draw on specific cultural knowledge and familiarity, as well as our own values and beliefs. Without cultural knowledge and understanding of the ecological context, using only generic social work and personal values and beliefs, our perspectives can be biased, and our work with clients can be ineffective (Williams, 2006).

It is a fact that ethnic minority children are overrepresented in special education (Allen-Meares, 2008). African-American children, for example, are twice as likely as White children to be labeled mentally retarded in 39 states (Allen-Meares, 2008, citing Osher, Sims, & Woodruff, 2002). These alarming facts lead to the question of validity in school-based child assessments. Allen-Meares (2008) proposed that school social

workers can be leaders in establishing a norm of cultural competence in child assessment in schools. Foremost is the social worker's use of ecological theory to assess children through the lens of their cultural context. This involves not only choosing assessment instruments that are demonstrated culturally sensitive (Allen-Meares, 2008), but also integrating and reflecting the students' culturally circumscribed environmental systems and their adaptive behavior in the context of those systems.

The following example illustrates this practice principle:

> Eileen had been a school social worker on the East Coast for 6 years when she moved to a southwestern city on the Mexican border. She began working in the dropout recovery program of a local school district, where she provided services to students and their families. Eileen became discouraged after several home visits with Mexican-American families, where she felt her time in the home was more social than problem solving. She perceived the families as more interested in small talk and serving her refreshments than in dealing with the issues at hand. These behaviors were puzzling to Eileen, and she saw them as time consuming and a form of resistance. Eileen's supervisor, herself a Mexican-American social worker, explained to Eileen that she was being received into these homes with great respect, indicated by the families treating her as they would treat a friend rather than as a stranger on a professional visit. Allowing time for customary social rituals and for families to become familiar with her was a culturally linked key to establishing the relationships that Eileen and the families needed for their work together.

Assessing Professional Values and Ethics

The school is a host setting where education values, above social work values, are the norm. As "owner" of its mental health and social services, the school district may endorse services that support its priorities, but restrict services that appear to conflict with its policy position or the values of its constituency. The following experience of school social workers in one district demonstrates this point:

> The social workers in our district had been concerned for some time about the rising dropout rate among the pregnant and parenting students in our six high schools. A community agency provided case management services for many of them, but we had very little for them at school. There was no budget for program, so we turned again to the community for help. Within 2 months we had a commitment from three organizations to provide services at the schools for teen parents. The county health department would provide mother–baby clinics once a month, a family counseling agency would provide parenting classes each semester, and the nurses' association would provide counseling and referrals for family planning 1 day a month. Since the schools only needed to provide space and an occasional hour out of class for the students, we hoped they would all go for the programs. In the end, they all went for the parenting classes and mother–baby clinics, but only two out of the six would let students out of class to meet with the nurses about family planning.

Differences between social work and education priorities can present ethical dilemmas related to client rights and service needs. The size of client load and constraints on time, frequency, and facilities for program interventions, for example, can affect quality of service. To deal effectively with such priority conflicts, social workers first need to be clear about where they can and cannot compromise on service delivery conditions and then be prepared to negotiate for conditions that support quality services.

The *philosophy of intervention* is a major difference between education and social work that affects the climate of school social work. Schools relate to children and adolescents as students, whereas social workers view them as client consumers. In the hierarchy of school organization, student stakeholders have the least power and participation in determining their own outcomes. As social work clients, the same children and adoles-

cents have more input into their own intervention and significant options in decision making and responses.

In the education culture, the "student at-risk" model, generally seen as a deficits model by education and other social sciences (e.g., Sagor & Cox, 2004), has been dominant in explaining school failure (Ronda & Valencia, 1994; Schnoor & Ware, 2001). The model assumes that poor school performance is rooted in students' personal cognitive and motivational deficits and in pathologies in their social environments. With these assumptions, it contains descriptive, explanatory, and predictive elements that have shaped educational policy and practice. This model is contrary to the strengths perspective used by social workers, which posits that the strengths and resources of people and their environment, rather than their problems and pathologies, should be the central focus of the helping process (Saleeby, 2002). Unlike the at-risk model, the strengths perspective places the client in the role of partner with the worker to achieve desired goals. Partnering with students and families as social services clients in an environment where the dominant theory and philosophy can minimize their personal and environmental/cultural strengths requires clear vision and strong command of social work skills.

Assessing Professional Competency

The breadth of knowledge and skills needed to work effectively in schools is more than any one individual may possess. Although social work education provides a sound conceptual foundation for practice, the increasing range of problems such as bullying, substance abuse, homelessness, child abuse, and school dropout makes it important for school social workers to be current in these specific areas. An important professional task is to acquire expertise in one or more of these areas through professional reading and specialized training.

It is beneficial to examine our skills and interests periodically in light of these expectations and issues confronting school social workers. This allows us an ongoing awareness of whether this field of practice continues to be a good match for our professional growth and satisfaction.

Designing Empirically Supported Interventions Around Needs of the School

Matching Interventions to Diverse Client Groups and School Needs

Statistics show us that children of color and children living in poverty are more vulnerable to school failure than White children and children of middle- or high-income families (Planty et al., 2008). It is logical to conclude from this that all children do not have an equal opportunity to succeed in school. We can assume that most school organizations fit with the needs and abilities of White, middle- and upper-income students more than lower-income students and/or children of color (Blanchett, Mumford, & Beachum, 2005; Shealey, 2006). Although education institutions across the country are in the midst of an enormous shift toward multiculturalism in education, the needs are many, and social workers can play an important role.

Although diversity is reflected in schools in numerous ways, the lack of fit between the school and children who are not White and/or from middle- to upper-income families may be the school social worker's greatest challenge in program design and services delivery. Social workers know that multicultural education goes beyond the inclusion of curricular content about various cultures. It includes instructional methods and interpersonal relationships in the classroom, as well as approaches to discipline, family interactions, and outcome goals throughout the school. In an organizational environment that has been based traditionally on White, mainstream cultural skills and expectations, the school social worker can model cultural competence skills to school staff, students, and families. We can continue to

inform ourselves of the specific cultural values and traditions of families and children in our schools and stress the meaning and importance of this to our colleagues in the school. We can develop culturally sensitive services for students and families and interpret the basis for these with administrators and staff. We can help bridge the gap between school and family by engaging with families in culturally informed and culturally responsive ways.

Reconciling School and Social Work Outcome Priorities

Austin (2002) described social work as interested in private outcomes for students such as healthy support systems and a good sense of self, whereas education is interested in public outcomes such as high test scores and high-school graduation. Outcomes that concern social work and education mutually are problems such as school violence and teen pregnancy, which social workers view as barriers to life quality and schools perceive as barriers to educational outcomes. Chapter 6 provides resources on addressing violence in schools. It is in this and other arenas of mutual concern that school social workers have more flexibility to address immediate needs of students and their families with the sanction and support of the school. Clarifying connections between private and public outcomes in funding proposals and including public outcome measures in social service evaluations are two effective ways to bridge different priorities.

Evidence-Based Programs That Work

Over the past several decades our knowledge of "what works" in school-based prevention and intervention programs has increased dramatically. However, the list of evidence-based programs for a wide range of school-based social and health problems continues to grow and can be accessed with a bit of Internet or library research (e.g., Franklin, Harris, & Allen-Meares, 2006;

www.teenpregnancy.org). Many reputable organizations have begun to create databases or lists of evidence-based programs and practices available to school social workers via the Internet. For instance, the Campbell Collaboration (www.campbellcollaboration.org) has a library of systematic reviews of the research literature in education, social welfare, and crime and justice. School social workers can access and download these the reviews to stay up-to-date on rigorously researched interventions. Similarly, the Cochrane Collaboration (www.cochrane.org/) has a similar database of systematic reviews on the effects of health-care interventions. The Substance Abuse and Mental Health Administration (SAMHSA) has recently introduced the National Registry of Evidence-Based Programs and Practices (www.nrepp.samhsa.gov/). This user-friendly database lists and describes specific interventions that have shown positive effects. The database allows users to search specifically for interventions used in schools and to select particular areas of interest such as suicide prevention, violence prevention, or alcohol/drug use. These are just some of the resources available to help school social workers to research and select evidence-based programs to implement in their schools.

Substance abuse, bullying, gang involvement, and mental illness in schools are only a few of many social problems that have escalated in recent years. Many school social workers are asked to address these problems in their schools. Using Internet resources such as SAMHSA's National Registry of Evidence-Based Programs and Practices can help school social workers to select promising interventions that are appropriate for their school populations. SAMHSA lists and describes the following evidence-based programs that have been tested, replicated, and demonstrated effective with school conflict and violence (see Chapter 6, "Violence in Schools"):

All Stars is a middle-school program designed to prevent and delay high-risk behaviors, including violence. It is delivered over multiple years and has classroom, small-group, individual, and parent components.

Caring School Community is a schoolwide program for elementary students designed to improve peer relationships and create a caring school culture. Components include classroom interventions, helping students of different ages to form relationships, home–school communication, and whole school community building.

Early Risers "Skills for Success" is a developmental program for elementary school students at risk of early substance abuse and conduct disorder. The program utilizes an assigned family advocate, summer camp program, in-school groups, school support, parent education, and family support.

Incredible Years targets children ages 2 to 12 years old to prevent and decrease behavioral and emotional problems. The student component focuses on skills such as anger management, behavior management, and social skills, whereas the parent component focuses on improving parent involvement in school.

Lions Quest Skills for Adolescence is a schoolwide and classroom program for middle schoolers to encourage healthy lifestyles. Components include skill-building sessions and encouragement for families, communities, and educators to promote social competencies.

Multisystemic Therapy for Juvenile Offenders targets youths who have already exhibited antisocial behavior to avoid in-patient treatment or incarceration. This multidimensional program uses a variety of case management and therapy techniques to empower families.

Project Toward No Drug Abuse is a drug abuse prevention program for high school students that also affects other high-risk behaviors such as weapons carrying. The curriculum, taught by teachers or health educators, can be implemented with at-risk students or the general student population.

Promoting Alternative Thinking Strategies (PATHS) is a program for elementary school students that focuses on skills such as self-control, self-esteem, and the reduction of aggression and other behavior problems. Classroom teachers typically deliver the curriculum.

Responding in Peaceful and Positive Ways (RiPP) is a middle school violence prevention program that helps students learn to deal with conflict in nonviolent ways. A prevention specialist typically delivers the curriculum in the classroom.

Second Step is a social skills program for students from preschool to ninth grade. Components include parent training, classroom curriculum, and skill development.

Strengthening Families Program is a program that aims to strengthen families for students from preschool age through 10th grade. It consists of children skills sessions, parenting skills sessions, and family skills sessions.

Too Good for Drugs is a schoolwide drug use prevention program that also targets decision making and students from kindergarten to 12th grade. Components include school staff development, a series of lessons, and follow-up lessons infused into the general curriculum.

These school-based programs incorporate individual and school change strategies that reflect a social work perspective and utilize social work skills. The school social worker can advocate and implement such programs that show promise for the needs of local schools. See Chapter 11 for other evidence-based intervention programs for children and adolescents.

Selecting an Evidence-Based Program That Fits

The importance of matching any model program to the local community, school, school staff, and cultural group cannot be stressed enough. Even if a program is demonstrated effective with many other groups, this does not ensure its fit and effectiveness in the local school and community. Although the following tips for selecting a school-based program (Solomon & Card, 2004) were directed at selecting programs for the prevention of teen pregnancy, they give good guidance for achieving goodness-of-fit with any model program.

1. Talk with community members such as teachers, parents, local clergy and politicians, health-care providers, and students who have an investment in the program. Inquire about their preferences and values around (the program issue), including their views on anything controversial, such as sex education and contraception. Use what you learn from these stakeholders to aim for programs that have been found effective in achieving goals and objectives that are relevant and acceptable to your school and community.

2. Engage with your school's administrators and interdisciplinary mental health team about initiating a prevention program, so that all of you have investment in its operation and success. Of prime consideration is the availability of resources such as space, staff, and especially funding.

3. Look for programs that were effective with youth who are as similar to your target group of students as possible. Some important characteristics are age, gender, ethnicity, acculturation, language, incarceration status, drug and alcohol use, and literacy level. All of these characteristics can influence participants' interest in the program and ability to benefit from it.

4. Once program selections are narrowed to two or three, determine which of these has replication kits or treatment manuals. It is more difficult to present a program if the original program materials are not available in a user-friendly format. PASHA (www.socio.com/pasha.htm), for example, offers replication kits for 17 different teen pregnancy prevention programs and provides sources for additional programs that it identifies as effective.

Services Evaluation and Reporting

Standards and Accountability

Accountability in public education is here to stay (see Chapter 12). The enactment of the No Child Left Behind Act of 2001 (NCLB) shifted the focus of public education in the United States to accountability for student outcomes and a reduction in the achievement gap between White, economically advantaged students and ethnic minority students and those with lower incomes. NCLB requires that schools test students regularly and report on their progress with the goal of improving student performance so that 100% of American students meet predetermined standards in reading and math by the 2013 to 2014 school year (Hursh, 2005; Orlich, 2004). In addition, schools must report separate scores for specific at-risk subgroups such as ethnic minority students, students from low-income families, students for whom English is a second language, and students with disabilities. Schools that fail to make adequate progress for the entire student population or for any at-risk subgroup are subject to administrative and financial sanctions (Hursh, 2005).

With the focus on academic achievement and the threat of financial sanction, schools are bound to account for every public tax dollar they receive. In this time of fiscal conservatism, schools also compete for private grants and foundation money to provide for programs that traditional funds no longer support. School social workers must demonstrate that social work interventions lead to improved educational achievement and that public and private funds supporting school social work are well spent.

At the local school level, decisions for selecting personnel are based on accountability and effectiveness, which are closely tied to performance objectives (Streeter & Franklin, 1993). Without hard data to support the effectiveness of social services, administrators and school board members do not always make a direct association between school effectiveness and social work services. Data that substantiates the volume and results of social work services should be reported regularly to administrators and other stakeholders in the local school, school district, and community.

Social workers not only must describe what they do but also show the impact of their interventions using specific *outcome measures*. Evaluation should be built into the design of social work services, defined by up-front goals and objectives for every service. Outcome measures should include issues that both social work and education consider important, such as attendance, grades, behavior, and retention. The credibility of social

workers' roles in the school partly depends on clear documentation that services make a difference to students and their families and to the achievement of the school's goals. Developing service goals and objectives and using outcome measures and other observations to evaluate services is discussed fully in Chapter 12.

Social Work Services Plan

A plan for social work services is the primary tool for organizing, monitoring, and evaluating our services. The plan should be guided by the results of community and school assessments and remain sensitive to the dynamics operating within both entities. The plan should be clearly presented and easy to read and understand. It should include every social work service in the school, both those identified formally and those done spontaneously or by immediate request. Service priorities identified in the plan can draw on a number of school social work roles and tasks, including facilitator, consultant, collaborator, mediator, advocate, broker, home–school–community liaison, educator, program director, clinician, community organizer, and cultural diversity specialist. These roles are discussed more fully in Chapter 11.

Reporting School Social Work Services

Periodic progress reports for stakeholder groups during the year are vital to local sanction and support. Administrators are responsible for what happens in their schools and need to be kept informed of activities and progress with students and families. Additionally, school district personnel as well as private and public funding sources expect regular feedback on the volume of services and the extent of impact. Yet informing diverse constituencies in ways that reflect their own interests and accessibility requires careful thought. For example, although periodic reports containing detailed data on outcome objectives are essential for informing school administrators, teachers may be more receptive to a brief verbal report and fact sheet during a faculty meeting or in-service.

The school board may respond positively to successful case vignettes and other client-specific examples, as well as hard data. The media, its own powerful constituency, can also be used effectively to inform outside community groups with periodic (school-approved) stories about positive results from social work services. Stakeholders such as parents, community service providers, and potential or current funding sources should be identified and provided with reports or information using the same individualized approach.

Conclusion

This chapter covered the design of school social work interventions from the viewpoint that services delivery must be responsive to the ecological context of schools and their constituents. Such a view requires an understanding of individual and family issues as well as knowledge about larger contextual factors that have a great impact on students' school experiences. Issues of individual students, school factors such as organization and political context, community context, and parent and family sociodemographic trends were suggested as important issues to assess in designing effective services delivery in a school. In addition, it is important for social workers to assess themselves and their personal context when thinking about designing the services in a school. Issues such as self-awareness, cultural and professional competencies, professional values and ethics, and philosophy of interventions are areas that must be addressed. Finally, this chapter provided information on evidence-based programs that can be implemented in a school and addressed accountability in services delivery. Evidence-based practices, standards and accountability measures and tools, and well-documented services plans are extremely important in current school-based services delivery and shape the practices of school social workers.

For Study and Discussion

1. Identify barriers that may deter school social workers from developing social work services seen as controversial in your community's schools.
2. What activities might school social workers undertake to overcome these barriers?
3. Large caseloads and restrictions on time and facilities are identified as challenges to service quality in schools. Discuss some ways that social workers can maintain service integrity with such conditions.
4. Create and discuss a specific school practice situation in which the at-risk model and the strengths perspective could conflict for intervention planning.
5. A group of Haitian refugees has been relocated in the local community, bringing a number of newly immigrated Haitian students into the school district over the past months. Assess your readiness for working with these students and their families. What are some ways that you can go about gaining knowledge that you may need?
6. As a school social worker, your practice expertise is in drugs and alcohol. You have recently moved to a school district challenged with school violence. Design a plan for preparing yourself to work with this problem that is relatively new to you.
7. You are proposing a gang intervention program at your school. Identify outcome objectives that will satisfy both a social work focus on private outcomes and the school's focus on public outcomes.

Additional Readings

Epstein, J. L., Sanders, M. G., Simon, B. S., Salinas, K. C., Jansorn, M. R., & Van Voorhis, F. L. (2002). *School, family, and community partnerships: Your handbook for action* (2nd ed.). Thousand Oaks, CA: Corwin.

Family Resource and Youth Service Centers. Downloaded on November 12, 2008, from http://chfs.ky.gov/dfrcrs/frysc/

Fong, R. (Ed.). (2004). *Culturally competent practice with immigrant and refugee children and families.* New York: Guilford.

Franklin, C., Harris, M. B., & Allen-Meares, P. (2006). *The school services sourcebook: A guide for school professionals.* New York: Oxford University Press.

Franklin, C., Hopson, L., & Ten Barge, C. (2003). Family systems. In C. Jordan & C. Franklin (Eds.), *Clinical assessment for social workers: Quantitative and qualitative methods* (pp. 255–311). Chicago: Lyceum Books.

Harris, M. B., & Franklin, C. (2008). *Taking charge: A school-based life skills program for adolescent mothers.* New York: Oxford University Press.

Horton, C. B., & Cruise, T. K. (2001). *Child abuse and neglect: The school's response.* New York: Guilford Press.

Lum, D. (Ed.). (2003). *Culturally competent practice: A framework for understanding diverse groups and justice issues* (2nd ed.). Pacific Grove, CA: Brooks/Cole-Thomson Learning.

Schonfeld, D. J., Lichtenstein, R., Pruett, M. K., & Speese-Linehan, D. (2002). *How to prepare for and respond to a crisis.* Alexandria, VA: Association for Supervision and Curriculum Development.

Taylor, L., & Adelman, H. S. (2004). Advancing mental health in schools: Guiding frameworks and strategic approaches. In K. Robinson (Ed.), *Advances in school-based mental health: Best practices and program models* (pp. 2-1–2-20). Kingston, NJ: Civic Research Institute.

Tower, K. (2000). Image crisis: A study of attitudes about school social workers. *Social Work in Education, 22*(2), 83–107.

Wasik, B. H., & Bryant, D. M. (2001). *Home visiting: Procedures for helping families* (2nd ed.). Thousand Oaks, CA: Sage.

11

The Delivery of School Social Work Services

CYNTHIA FRANKLIN
University of Texas at Austin

MARY BETH HARRIS
University of Southern California

CHRISTINE LAGANA-RIORDAN
University of Texas at Austin

Introduction

This chapter focuses on the delivery of school social work services and addresses practice knowledge and skills that are needed to work in a school setting. Several trends that are affecting practices are covered, such as expanded school mental health services, school-linked programs, and emerging evidence-based practices. Controversies and issues facing school social workers in service delivery are also summarized in relationship to the changing climate of school-based services. This chapter further presents practice roles and intervention skills needed to be effective in school practice. The new roles of school social workers in school-linked expanded school mental health services are highlighted, as are several examples of the intervention roles that school social workers routinely perform in their jobs. Practice roles and intervention skills are illustrated with case examples. Finally, specialized intervention skills, such as those necessary to work with individual students, families, groups, classrooms,

and school systems are discussed. Because space limitations do not permit the presentation of detailed information about practice interventions, an annotated bibliography of books and materials is provided at the end of the chapter.

Expanded School Mental Health and School-Linked Services

School services delivery is being affected by expanded mental health and school-linked services solutions for helping students with health, mental health, and social services needs. Ten million or more school-age youth are in need of mental health intervention, and over 70% rely on public school as the place where they can receive mental health care. Unfortunately, the reality on school campuses is that less than one in five children in need of mental health services is receiving treatment (U.S. Department of Health and Human Services, 2000), and this need has contributed to more mental health professionals working on school campuses. Expanded school mental health services and school-based health centers have been a national movement and have greatly contributed to mental health professionals from diverse disciplines working on school campuses (Franklin & Gerlach, 2006; Lynn, McKay, & Atkins, 2003; Weist & Paternite, 2006). The emphasis in the 1990s on funding collaborative-based services in the human services, and school-linked services programs in particular, has added to a plethora of clinical professionals working in schools, including clinical social workers. Keeley and Wiens (2007) described the difference between school-based and school-linked services

> School-based mental health services are typically provided within the school environment, whereas school-linked mental health services refer to services that are in coordination with the school but not necessarily provided on school grounds (i.e., may be provided at off-site buildings). School-based and school-linked mental health services are different from more typical clinical services in the extent to which they provide consultation to, and are integrated with, the school. (p. 110)

Proponents of school-linked services exist across services systems and often refer to the school as a central hub for the delivery of human services because it is a place where the services can converge that also has the maximum access for children. The President's New Freedom Commission on Mental Health, created in 2002, supported the need for children to have mental health care access through schools. In addition, the American Academy of Pediatrics made an official statement of support for school-based mental health services in 2004 (Brener, Weist, Adelman, Taylor, & Vernon-Smiley, 2006).

A recent national survey, the School Health Policies and Programs Study (SHPPS), conducted by the Centers for Disease Control and Prevention (CDC), has confirmed the expansion of school mental health and social services (Brener et al., 2006). Interestingly, the survey describes the essential functions of school mental health and social services as including "a range of services including assessment, case management, therapy, and prevention to all students through partnerships between schools and community

agencies" (Brener et al., 2006, p. 488), and these roles are very similar to those performed by school social workers. Nationwide, almost 30% of school districts reported at least one school-based mental health center. However, the survey indicates that a large number of school mental health and social services are being offered from outside the school by mental health providers who work in school-linked health centers or who have contractual arrangements or memorandums of agreements with school districts. More than one third (35.6%) of states had adopted a policy stating that districts or schools will have these types of arrangements, and 62.2% of districts had such arrangements (Brener et al., 2006, p. 491). Overall, over 70% of school districts had either a school-based mental health center or school-linked mental health services.

To illustrate the expanded school mental health services trend, Franklin and Gerlach (2006) offered a concrete example of how many mental health professionals have come onto school campuses through a nonprofit organization called Communities in Schools (CIS). This agency serves as a school assistance program with 200 programs in some 3,250 schools and education sites across 27 states. CIS serves approximately two million students per year with the goal of preventing school dropout and enhancing student mental health (www.cisnet.org).

Resources for Expanded School Mental Health Services

As a part of the expansion of mental health services, a number of community and national resources have also been developed to support the school-based health and mental health service centers (Brener, Martindale, & Weist, 2001; Franklin & Gerlach, 2006; Lynn, McKay, & Atkins, 2003; Streeter & Franklin, 2002; Weist & Paternite, 2006). For example, there are more than a dozen national training and technical assistance centers for school-based mental health services. Two well-respected centers are housed in universities and have been operating since 1995. The UCLA School Mental Health Project, Center for Mental Health in the Schools, is operated by the UCLA Department of Psychology (www.smhp.psych.ucla.edu/), and the Center for School Mental Health is operated by the University of Maryland School of Medicine (http://csmh .umaryland.edu/). These centers have been funded in response to a national mental health crisis with children and adolescents. They provide tremendous support to mental health professionals who are coming from outside agencies to provide services on school campuses. The technical centers also provide literature, training, and support aimed at helping outside and inside mental health professionals, such as school social workers, collaborate.

Consequences for School Social Work Services Delivery

The practice trends being discussed result in two groups of social workers in schools. First are those who are direct employees of the school district, and second are those who are school-based service providers employed by community-based organizations contracting with the school districts (Franklin & Gerlach, 2006). These trends have been influenced by related services provisions and demands of the Individual with Disabilities Education Improvement Act (IDEA; Faircloth, 2004), the vanishing autonomy of private practice, and the school-linked services movement (Dryfoos & Maguire, 2002; Franklin & Gerlach, 2006; Streeter & Franklin, 2002).

Expanded school mental health services and school-linked services programs are quickly evolving into community-linked services where community systems are more involved in planning and providing the services on school campuses than school-based personnel. Varied projects have emphasized community linkages across the country aimed at increasing the schools' involvement with community-based services, and "statewide initiatives were established in California, Florida, Kentucky, Iowa, Missouri, New Jersey, Ohio, and Oregon, among others" (Taylor & Adelman, 2006). One implication of this trend is for schools to move toward outsourcing or contracting with community practitioners

to provide their mental health, social services, and other youth development programs. An immediate implication for school social workers is that there is an increasing need to coordinate and plan services on school campuses.

Controversies for School Social Work Services Delivery

The expanded school mental health movement and community-linked services alternatives on school campuses have created controversies within school social work practice. As has been conveyed in Chapter 2 of this book, school social work is a specialized profession with over 100 years of experience serving the needs of public schools. This book has further provided the history of school social work as an independent profession and a very important group among the larger social work profession. School social workers have specialized credentials and expertise to work in schools and have been trained to understand school systems and the unique mission and challenges of educating youth. Expanded school-based mental health services and other school-linked programs have raised questions about the best way to deliver services on school campuses. In response to these questions, school social workers consider the quality of services and the best interests of school systems.

These questions and other concerns have caused the school social work profession to take a new look at itself in relationship to current trends in school services delivery. Many issues have to be evaluated, including the school social workers' relationships with other service providers, such as clinical social workers, who are increasingly working on school campuses (Streeter & Franklin, 2002). One concern is that the traditional school social work practice may be replaced with these newer school-linked and expanded mental health services models. The community-linked movement that co-locates more services on the school campuses has been driven by economic and public policy trends, and school social workers watch these trends to see if they will benefit school systems. For example, the mental health professionals who offer services on school campuses may not understand school systems or represent the interests of the educators. This could lead to inappropriate or ineffective services being delivered.

Two distinct views for responding to the diversity in school-based services delivery have been debated among school social work practitioners and researchers. One view suggests that history tells us that there are distinct advantages for schools to employ their own school social workers and that social workers must guard this advantage in the changing times. Historically, school social workers have followed a similar direction to the school psychologist, who is certified and licensed for school-based practice, but may not be involved in work within other fields of practice (e.g., clinical, counseling). Thus, the areas of specialization are kept more separate and fall along the lines of the systems of care in which one works (e.g., schools, mental health clinics, hospitals). This distinctive view is perhaps best illustrated by the positions and definitions of school social work upheld by the School Social Work Association of America (SSWAA). This professional organization for school social workers defines them as professionals employed by educational systems. As independent school-based professionals, school social workers should not be some type of transplant from the community or mental health field. Both SSWAA and the National Association of Social Workers (NASW) provide considerable infrastructure for training and advancement for school social work as a distinct profession and protect the professional roles of school social work as a group of distinct professionals who serve educational systems.

The second view comes from the academic literature, where writers have suggested that there may be a political and economic advantage to moving beyond the historic field of practices distinctions within social work (e.g., mental health, school, child, and family; Streeter & Franklin, 2002). In fact these distinctions are thought to be outdated given the way practice is operating in the 21st century. Funding for school services, for example, comes from a broad array of sources, and many revenues for funding school social work positions may be tied back to health and mental health funding such as Medicaid and behavioral health

care. Education, on the other hand, has shrinking budgets for school-support services. In addition, mental health and social services have been controversial areas for schools, and there is continued tension about educational systems funding school social work and other school-support positions, even though the services are desperately needed. Furthermore, the majority of social workers in the United States already work in the health and mental health services, and they are the major providers of mental health services in the United States. This fact, coupled with the current trend in schools to outsource and link with mental health and health services, could mean that it is advantageous for school social workers to broaden their vision of themselves to incorporate these changing definitions and roles within schools. For example, why not embrace the social workers that work within schools and are being co-located from community settings and define them as a type of school social worker too?

In day-to-day practice of schools, it is important to make the most of current trends and issues that are affecting school social work practice. Therefore, it may be important to embrace both perspectives discussed earlier. It is certainly necessary to protect the historic roles of school social workers, but it may also be advantageous to expand services definitions and roles as school social workers work on campuses that include expanded school mental health services and school-linked programs. School social workers may also find ways that schools can also recover from these trends and controversies, while creating new roles for themselves on campus.

Emerging Roles of School Social Workers Within Expanded School Mental Health and School-Linked Services

The CDC survey mentioned earlier (Brener et al., 2006) suggests that there are many different renditions for how school mental health and social services are provided. Several models exist, including student assistance programs, school-based health centers, and comprehensive expanded school mental health programs designed to reach all students. Anecdotal experience points to the complex relationships that these types of services are bringing to the school campuses and the need for better collaboration between the different services providers (Franklin, 2001). It is important to note, also, that the increase in mental health service delivery is not always viewed as an effective means of educating children from the viewpoint of educators. Fast (1999) reported, for example, a satirical cartoon that appeared in the educational journal *Phi Delta Kappan,* which communicates skepticism about the expanding services approach in education. The cartoon's heading was "The School of the Future," and it depicted a building with many wings labeled Detox Center, Day Care Center, Child Development Center, etc. One small addition in the back was labeled "Education Wing" (p. 100). It is important for school social workers to identify strongly with public school interests and to focus on the mission of the school, which is education. It is equally important to ensure that the diverse services delivery does not detract from children's learning and to ensure that each and every child receives a quality education.

Franklin (1999, 2000, 2001) and Streeter and Franklin (2002) discussed the increasing competition in services delivery, and these authors suggested that expanded models of services may be requiring school social workers to find better ways to work with outside mental health professionals who are delivering services on school campuses. In some cases it has also become important for school social workers to define the importance of their job roles more explicitly and find ways to compete or cooperate with professionals who occupy similar positions. Fortunately, however, school social workers have the right skills to work with diverse service providers and help the schools manage and optimize the school–community programs that are being offered. Some of the practice interventions needed to help schools with community-linked programs are

1. Resource mapping
2. Coordination
3. Case management
4. Transdisciplinary teamwork and collaboration

These are not new skills, but generalist practice skills that have served school social workers well in school systems, and these practice skills are needed now more than ever.

Ethics in School Social Work Practice

Schools are unique environments with their own set of ethical challenges. School social workers must abide by the NASW code of ethics (see also Chapter 4) while balancing the needs of multiple stakeholders such as students, parents, teachers, guidance counselors, and school administrators. For instance, school social workers need to respect the rights of parents, while also advocating for the needs of a student (Mattison, 2006). This can become difficult when a parent does not agree to an intervention plan suggested by the social worker, forcing the social worker to either further advocate for the plan or compromise the plan to meet the parent's wishes. School social workers also have to navigate various standards and guidelines set forth by the school, school district, and their employing agency (if applicable), even when they might not be complementary (Mattison, 2006). For example, many states now have abstinence-only policies regarding sex education. Although a social worker might believe that a student who is already sexually active would benefit from a discussion on safe sex practices, it could be illegal for the social worker to present this material. Consequently, the social worker must find other routes to helping the student obtain this information, such as referring the student to a local clinic or health department. The NASW (2002b) has put forth specific standards for school social work services. These include standards for professional practice, standards for professional preparation and development, and standards for administrative structure and support. The standards for professional practice are

1. A school social worker shall demonstrate commitment to the values and ethics of the social work profession and shall use NASW's Code of Ethics as a guide to ethical decision making.
2. School social workers shall organize their time, energies, and workloads to fulfill their responsibilities and complete assignments of their position, with due consideration of the priorities among their various responsibilities.
3. School social workers shall provide consultation to local education agency personnel, school board members, and community representatives to promote understanding and effective utilization of school social work services.
4. School social workers shall ensure that students and their families are provided services within the context of multicultural understanding and competence that enhance families' support of students' learning experiences.
5. School social work services shall be extended to students in ways that build students' individual strengths and offer students maximum opportunity to participate in the planning and direction of their own learning experience.
6. School social workers shall help empower students and their families to gain access to and effectively use formal and informal community resources.
7. School social workers shall maintain adequate safeguards for the privacy and confidentiality of information.
8. School social workers shall advocate for students and their families in a variety of situations.
9. As leaders and members of interdisciplinary teams and coalitions, school social workers shall work collaboratively to mobilize the resources of local education agencies and communities to meet the needs of students and families.
10. School social workers shall develop and provide training and educational programs that address the goals and mission of the educational institution.
11. School social workers shall maintain accurate data that are relevant to planning, management, and evaluation of school social work services.
12. School social workers shall conduct assessments of student needs that are individualized and provide information that is directly useful for designing interventions that address behaviors of concern.
13. School social workers shall incorporate assessments in developing and implementing intervention and evaluation plans that enhance students' abilities to benefit from educational experiences.
14. School social workers, as systems change agents, shall identify areas of need that are not being addressed by the local education agency and community and shall work to create services that address these needs.
15. School social workers shall be trained in and use mediation and conflict-resolution strategies to promote students' resolution of their nonproductive encounters in the school and community and to promote productive relationships. From: National Association of Social Workers. (2002). *NASW standards for school social work services*. Washington DC: Author (pp. 10–16).

Confidentiality is a major concern for school social workers. Although team collaboration can be a strength of mental health service delivery in school settings, it also poses challenges to confidentiality. School settings require an extensive amount of information sharing among school professionals, but the social work value of confidentiality can sometimes prohibit school social workers from sharing information with others. School social workers need to distinguish between information that might be essential for planning effective services for students and families and information that is unrelated to service provision and should be kept private (Cuevas, 2006). Social workers can overcome these obstacles by discussing the teaming process with families, reminding them of the benefits of sharing information with students' professional teams, and by asking permission to share specific information with the members of the team when it benefits the student. Other professionals on the team should also agree to confidentiality throughout the teaming process to further protect the students.

Evidence-Based Practice

Evidence-based practice is another national movement that has implications for defining the directions of school social work practice (Allen-Meares, 2006). Huang, Hepburn, and Espiritu (2003, cited in Allen-Meares, 2006) state that

> Evidence-based practice is an emerging concept and reflects a nationwide effort to build quality and accountability in health and behavioral health care service delivery. Underlying this concept is (1) the fundamental belief that children with emotional and behavioral disorders should be able to count on receiving care that meets their needs and is based on the best scientific knowledge available, and (2) the fundamental concern that for many of these children, the care that is delivered is not effective care. (p. 1)

Chapter 10 discusses in some detail the evidence-based practice (EBP) process and how school social workers can become more evidence-based in their practices. Franklin and Hopson (2004) reviewed how evidence-based practices are becoming a standard for school mental health services and instructional areas in education and as these EBP are used more in education, it becomes important for school social workers to understand how to improve their work using the best scientific knowledge and clinical decision making. To aid in identifying scientific practices, the Department of Education, founded the What Works Clearinghouse (ies.ed.gov/ncee/wwc/), which focuses on the dissemination of evidence-based practices in education. Criteria for evidence-based practices in education are set by the Institute for Educational Sciences, which is the research arm for the Department of Education, in consultation with a technical services group of distinguished researchers. Their criteria for evidence-based studies include

a. rigorous study design [randomized control or quasi experimental design] with:
   1. appropriate outcome measures
   2. advanced statistical analysis
b. extent to which relevant people, settings, and measure timings were included;
c. extent to which the study allowed for the testing of the intervention's effect within subgroups;
d. statistical reporting   (http://ies.ed.gov/ncee/ wwc/references/iDocViewer/Doc.aspx?docId =2&tocId=1)

Other organizations also advance evidence-based practices in schools and offer training to school practitioners on the best scientific practices. One of these organizations, founded by Dr. Peter Jensen and colleagues, is The REsource for Advancing Children's Health (The Reach Institute, http://www.thereachinstitute.org/SchoolMental HealthAlliance.html). In 2003, The Reach Institute staff (then at Columbia University) held a summit called "Approaches to School Mental Health Evidence-Based Partnerships: Key Obstacles and Strategic Opportunities." The summit brought together experts in the field of children's mental health for the purpose of: (a) identifying obstacles to the implementation of evidence-based school mental health programs, and (b) reaching consensus about effective strategies to overcome these obstacles. Following the summit, the School Mental Health Alliance (SMHA) was formed to help put the summit recommendations into action. Several important initiatives resulted from the summit, including a tool kit that helps local educational authorities integrate evidence-based mental health services within school systems (Hunter et al., 2005).

Twenty-five key organizations make up the School Mental Health Alliance that is dedicated to implementation of best school practices. A position paper that emerged from The School Mental Health Alliance has since been distributed to Congress, and this group, as a partner with The Reach Institute, continues to promote identification and dissemination of evidence-based practices in schools (Hunter et al., 2005).

Preparing for EBP

Preparation for implementing evidence-based practices involves learning the best practices for addressing student and family issues (e.g., ADHD, education of dropouts, immigrant students, substance abuse, parental involvement, facilitating teams). Evidence-based practices also focus practitioners on thinking about the importance of outcomes. However, there is disagreement in the research literature about how to define and identify evidence-based practices. Consequently, many programs are labeled "evidence-based," but it is difficult to determine the strength of the research base for each of them. Some scholars and practitioners consider independent organizations that conduct systematic reviews, such as the Campbell Collaboration (http://www.campbellcollaboration.org/) and the Cochrane Collaboration (http://www.cochrane.org/), to be the gold standard for identifying evidence-based practices. Others, however, believe that federal agencies that have set their own criteria for evidence-based practices (such as the What Works Clearinghouse and the Substance Abuse and Mental Health Services Administration's National Registry: http://www.nrepp.samhsa.gov/) are just as valid (Franklin & Hopson, 2007). For these reasons, we will refer to the programs and practices outlined in this chapter as "empirically supported" to denote that there exists different types of intervention knowledge and that all interventions must be evaluated with particular clients in mind. Chapter 10 discusses the evidence-based practice process and how school social workers can proceed to make the best clinical judgments about their work. Practitioners must evaluate both the needs of their clients and the available literature regarding empirically supported practices to choose the most appropriate interventions. Table 11.1 offers selected examples of empirically supported interventions for a few populations that may be seen in school-based practices. These practices have been compiled from a number of sources such as the Campbell Collaboration library, the Cochrane Collaboration library, and the What Works Clearinghouse. Programs listed

as evidence based by SAMHSA or effective by the National Institute on Drug Abuse (NIDA, 2003) are noted as well. It is also important to note that information about empirically supported practices can be obtained from other sources such as meta-analyses and systematic reviews in scholarly journals related to school social work such as *Children & Schools, School Social Work Journal, Social Work,* and *Research on Social Work Practice.*

Practice resources are emerging that help the practitioners identify empirically supported practices in school social work (Franklin, Kim, & Tripodi, in press). The What Works Clearinghouse offers reviews of empirically supported practices for salient practice issues for education and provides evidence screens for existing practices. The *Children & Schools* journal (2004) published a special issue highlighting evidence-based practices for a number of problems faced in school social work practice. Franklin, Harris, and Allen-Meares (2006) further provided a comprehensive volume on practices with empirical support for school social workers. As far as the issue of practitioners' abilities to learn the evidence-based practices, research indicates that reading practice manuals is not as effective as in-service training, and training is not as effective as supervision and consultation models (Franklin & Hopson, 2007). Training and supervision on evidence-based practices, however, are often extremely expensive. Increasing training budgets and funding sources for effective training and supervision in schools represents an ongoing resource challenge for school social work practice (Franklin & Hopson, 2007).

For school social workers to successfully implement empirically supported practices, it is also important to learn new and briefer models of intervention, such as those associated with cognitive-behavioral, brief, solution-focused, and brief consultation models. Practice knowledge and skills of differing evidence-based practices are also believed to follow certain core components. If practitioners are not trained in the core components, then it is difficult to learn the practices. Once a practitioner learns these components, it may be easier to read practice manuals and

TABLE 11.1 Selected Empirically Supported Practices for Children and Adolescents

Empirically Supported Interventions	Program Goals	Program Outcomes	Population	Cost	Training Requirements	Implementation Requirements	Source
Dropout prevention Accelerated Middle Schools	To reduce the risk of dropout for middle school students who are academically behind grade level	Lower dropout rate; increase in the number of school years completed	Middle school students	Unavailable	Unavailable	Alternative program (in home school or alternative school) that covers several years of material within only 1–2 years; offers few electives to focus on core academics; focus on hands-on instruction; additional social supports offered	What Works Clearinghouse (http://ies.ed.gov/ ncee/wwc/pdf/ do_tr_09_ 23_08.Pdf)
ALAS (Achievement for Latinos through Academic Success) (http://www .ndpc-sd .org/documents/ Evidence_Based_ Practices/ALAS_ Model_Description .pdf)	To prevent school dropout and recover students who have already dropped out	Lower dropout rate; increase in the number of school years completed	Middle school students with focus on low-income, urban, Latino students	Unavailable	Required for parent and student trainers and teachers	Multicomponent intervention: 1. Students receive counseling and problem-solving and social skills training; 2. Schools focus on teacher feedback to parents and students, attendance monitoring, and positive recognition of students; 3. Parent training to increase parent–school involvement; 4. Links to community and social services	What Works Clearinghouse

Career Academies (http://ncacinc.com/)	To reduce the risk of dropout for high school students	Lower dropout rate; increase in the number of school years completed	High schools students	Unavailable	Unavailable	Small learning communities within a school focused on future career goals; partnerships with local businesses	What Works Clearinghouse
Check and Connect (http://ici.umn.edu/checkandconnect)	To promote school engagement and decrease dropout rates	Decrease in dropout rates, increase in accrual of credits	Middle school students with focus on urban students with behavioral challenges	$545 per person	2-day introductory training; Intensive on-site workshop recommended before implementing (see Web site)	Students receive individual mentor who monitors attendance, behavior, and academic performance; conducts outreach with the family; and links family to social services	What Works Clearinghouse
Character education							
Positive Action (www.positiveaction.net/google/character_education/)	To improve academic success and behavior and to foster character development	Improved behavior (reduction in discipline and violence) and academic achievement	K–12	$1200 for training, $700 for travel, and travel expenses; Self-training kits start at $200	1-day onsite training; Self-training	15 minute lessons, several times per week; covers 6 value-based units	What Works Clearinghouse SAMHSA (http://www.nrepp.samhsa.gov/)

(continued)

TABLE 11.1 Continued

Empirically Supported Interventions	Program Goals	Program Outcomes	Population	Cost	Training Requirements	Implementation Requirements	Source
Too Good for Drugs and Violence (http://www.mendezfoundation.org/)	To reduce risk factors related to drug, alcohol, and tobacco use	Positive impact on knowledge, attitudes, and values (i.e., intention to drink, attitudes toward violence, peer norms)	High school	$795 $2,500 per day plus travel expenses $300 per person per day	Self-training: Can purchase starter kit Onsite training Regional core curriculum training sessions (1–2 days)	14 one-hour lessons that address topics regarding drugs and violence; 12 infusion lessons incorporated into regular classes	What Works Clearinghouse
Too Good for Violence (http://www.mendezfoundation.org/)	To reduce the risk of violence in schools and to help students have peaceful relationships	Positive impact on knowledge, attitudes, and values (i.e. improved communication and conflict resolution)	K–8	$100–$130 for a grade level kit (varies by grade) $2,500 per day plus travel expenses $300 per person per day	Self-training: Can purchase starter kit Onsite training Regional core curriculum training sessions (1–2 days)	Seven 30–60 minute lessons for each grade level K–5; Nine 30–45 minute lessons for each grade level 6–8	What Works Clearinghouse SAMHSA

	Goal	Outcome	Target	Cost	Training	Dosage	Source
Project Towards No Drug Abuse (http://tnd.usc .edu/)	To reduce drug use and weapons carrying and increase coping skills	Reduced drug use at follow-up when compared to students who received curriculum-based instruction; not effective for alcohol use	9–11th graders	One day training: $1200–1400 plus travel expenses; Two-day training: $1900–2100	1–2 day training on-site or at training location	Three 50-minute sessions per week for 3 consecutive weeks	Cochrane Collaboration meta-analysis (Faggiano, Vigna-Taglianti, Versino, Zambon, Borraccino, & Lemma, 2002) SAMHSA NIDA (http:// www.nida.nih .gov/Prevention/ examples.html)
Cognitive-Behavioral Therapy	To prevent and reduce drug use among adolescents	Reduced generic drug use	6th graders	Varies	Varies	40-minute sessions once per week for 12 weeks	Cochrane Collaboration meta-analysis (Faggiano, Vigna-Taglianti, Versino, Zambon, Borraccino, & Lemma, 2002)

(continued)

TABLE 11.1 Continued

Empirically Supported Interventions	Program Goals	Program Outcomes	Population	Cost	Training Requirements	Implementation Requirements	Source
Drug Abuse Prevention Curriculum	To prevent and reduce drug use among adolescents	Reduced drug use at follow-up	7th graders	Unavailable	Unavailable	15-session psychosocial program taught in regular classrooms. Sessions include direct instruction, behavioral exercises, and video-tapes	Cochrane Collaboration meta-analysis (Faggiano, Vigna-Taglianti, Versino, Zambon, Borraccino, & Lemma, 2002)
STARS (Start Taking Alcohol Risks Seriously) (http://druged .nimcoinc.com/ productDetails .asp?product_id= NIM-153-1-CW)	To postpone alcohol use until adulthood	Decreased heavy alcohol use at 30-day follow-up	Middle school students	One day: $1500 plus travel expenses; Two day: $2000 plus travel expenses $299 for manual	1–2 day training	First year: one-on-one consultation with nurse and 10 pre-vention postcards mailed to parents; Second year: follow-up consultation with nurse and four take-home packets for family	Cochrane Collaboration meta-analysis (Foxcroft, Ireland, Lowe, & Breen, 2002) SAMHSA
Culturally focused substance abuse interventions	To decrease the frequency and amount of drinking	Decrease in weekly drinking for Native American youth	3rd–5th grade children	Unavailable	Unavailable	Not available	Cochrane Collaboration meta-analysis (Foxcroft, Ireland, Lowe, & Breen, 2002)

Program	Objective	Focus	Population	Cost	Training	Description	Source
Strengthening Families Program (http://www.strengtheningfamilies.org/html/programs_1999/06_SFP.html)	To reduce the risk of substance abuse, depression, aggression, delinquency, and school failure in high-risk children	Prevention of alcohol use and misuse	High-risk children ages 6–12	Two-day training: $2,700 plus travel expenses; Three-day training: $3,700 plus travel expenses	2–3 day training	7 family sessions once per week averaging approximately 2 hours per session (or 14 one-hour sessions)	Cochrane Collaboration meta-analysis (Foxcroft, Ireland, Lowe, & Breen, 2002) NIDA SAMHSA
Aggressive/ Disruptive Behavior							
Social Information Processing Programs (universal programs)	To prevent aggressive and disruptive behavior for all students in the school environment	Decrease in aggressive and disruptive behavior	K–12	Varies by program	Varies by program	Lessons directly teach skills such as problem-solving skills or how to interpret social situations; emphasize cognitive skills; use of structured tasks. Programs that teach frequent lessons (several per week) are most effective.	Campbell Collaboration (Wilson & Lipsey, 2006–Part I)
Social Information Processing Programs (pull-out programs for selected students)	To prevent aggressive and disruptive behavior for students at risk for these behaviors	Decrease in aggressive and disruptive behavior	K–12	Varies by program	Varies by program	Students typically pulled out once or twice per week	Campbell Collaboration (Wilson & Lipsey, 2006–Part II)

(continued)

TABLE 11.1 Continued

Mental Health

Empirically Supported Interventions	Program Goals	Program Outcomes	Population	Cost	Training Requirements	Implementation Requirements	Source
Cognitive-Behavioral Therapy	To reduce symptoms and improve functioning for children and adolescents with anxiety disorders	Decrease in anxiety symptoms, increase in anxiety disorder remission rates	Children ages 6–18 with anxiety disorders	Unavailable	Unavailable	Treatment ranges from 7.5 hours to 27 hours total	Cochrane Collaboration (James, Soler, & Weatherall, 2005)
Adolescent Coping with Stress Course (abbreviated version) (http://www.kpchr.org/public/acwd/acwd.html)	To prevent symptoms of depression in at-risk children	Reduction in depression symptoms and diagnosis of depression	Children at-risk of depression ages 13–18	Free	Treatment manual can be downloaded online	15 one hour group sessions with 6–10 participants; groups held 2–4 times per week	Cochrane Collaboration (Merry, McDowell, Hetrick, Bir, & Muller, 2004)
Behavioral Therapy and Cognitive Behavioral Therapy	To reduce symptoms and improve functioning for children and adolescents with OCD	Reduction in OCD risk and improved behavioral functioning	Children with OCD ages 7–18	Varies	Varies	Treatment ranged from 12–20 sessions of 60–90 minutes	Cochrane Collaboration (O'Kearney, Anstey, & von Sanden, 2006)

deliver evidence-based practices. Some of the core components include the following:

1. Conducting brief group and family sessions instead of individual sessions.
2. Working with a limited number of contacts usually no more than 4 to 15 sessions.
3. Interventions on multiple levels such as child, family, and teacher interactions.
4. Parent and family approaches that have a foundation in cognitive-behavioral, structural, and strategic therapies.
5. Interdisciplinary cooperation including the use of psychopharmacology and allied professionals to help clients obtain rapid improvement.
6. Problem-solving skills and communication training as well as approaches in training other skills.
7. Empowerment and strengths focus in the delivery of interventions.
8. Behavioral therapy skills such as role-playing and feedback, contingency contracting, specific goal setting, and targeting specific behaviors for change.
9. Tailoring interventions to the needs of diverse populations such as Hispanic youth and families.

These core components complement the ecological perspective and the historic role of school social workers.

Assessment and Outcome Measurement within Evidence-Based Practice.

School social workers can equip themselves for the demands of evidence-based practices by giving attention to learning assessment methods and outcome measures. (See Chapter 12 for detailed information on evaluating school social work practice.) Bowen and colleagues have developed an excellent measurement tool that every school social worker should learn—*The School Success Profile* (SSP) (Bowen, Richman, & Bowen, 2002)—a comprehensive tool for evaluating and monitoring the effects of interventions in school settings. This measure is especially useful for school-based practice. The SSP assesses youth in the social environment

and considers both risk and protective factors in the social environment and the individual that can lead to school success or failure. (See Box 11.1 for a list of areas assessed by the measure.) The SSP is available online, can be administered in both English and Spanish, and has a detailed manual to assist with administration. A new and expanded version of the SSP will be available in 2009. Powers, Bowen, and Rose (2005) illustrated how to evaluate school practice and pointed out some of the positives and negatives that a school social worker can encounter when taking on such an approach as the use of the SSP.

Many other measures are available for performing assessment and monitoring the effectiveness of practice interventions. Chapter 12 describes methods for assessing and monitoring social work practice, as well as the process for choosing an appropriate measurement instrument. Fischer and Corcoran (2007), Corcoran (2000), and Jordan and Franklin (2003) reviewed and illustrated several assessment measures that can be used with children and families. Table 11.2 describes several assessment and outcome measures that may be used in school-based practice.

The process of choosing empirically supported practices and evaluating these practices is somewhat complicated by the wide array of roles that school social workers are often expected to fill in schools. School social workers rarely assume a narrowly defined role within a school. Instead, school social workers are expected to move seamlessly from one role to another or to fulfill several roles simultaneously. What this means practically is that school social workers often do not act independently in their work so they may not be able to be solely responsible for deciding on the use of a measurement instrument or a practice program. These decisions might be made in consultation or with input of others within the school such as the student support services team, the principal, or even parents. School social workers also find themselves in a position to offer consultations to a number of school personnel. The consultation role and other key roles that school social workers play in a school are discussed next.

BOX 11.1 • *Measurement Dimensions of the School Success Profile*

ABOUT YOU-REFERENCE INFORMATION
Basic Demographics (6 items)

SOCIAL ENVIRONMENT PROFILE

NEIGHBORHOOD (23 items)
Neighborhood Support
Neighborhood Youth Behavior
Neighborhood Safety

SCHOOL (30 items)
Learning Climate
School Satisfaction
Teacher Support
School Safety

FRIENDS (21 items)
Friend Support
Peer Group Acceptance
Friend Behavior

FAMILY (38 items)
Family Togetherness
Parent Support

Home Academic Environment
Parent Education Support
School Behavior Expectations

INDIVIDUAL ADAPATATION PROFILE

***PERSONAL BELIEFS
AND WELL-BEING (27 items)***
Personal Beliefs and Well-Being
Social Support Use
Physical Health
Self-confidence
Adjustment

SCHOOL ATTITUDES AND BEHAVIOR
(17 items)
School Engagement
Trouble Avoidance
Grades

School Success Profile, Copyright 2005, Gary Bowen, Ph.D. & Jack Richman, Ph.D., School of Social Work, The University of North Carolina at Chapel Hill, North Carolina 27599-3550 (919) 962-6542.

Current Intervention Roles

Consultant

Research provides convincing evidence that consultation services are effective at the client, consultee, and system levels (Sabatino, 1999). A recent study found that 85% of school social workers' client cases involved teacher consultation and collaboration (Jonson-Reid, Kontak, Citerman, Essma, & Fezzi, 2004). Consultation is a method of intervention that takes place between a professional consultant and a consultee who has responsibility for direct service to another person in a voluntary relationship aimed at solving a job-related problem through a shared problem-solving process (Mannino & Shore, 1975; Medway & Updyke, 1985). It is important for the consultee to feel comfortable, accepted, and respected. Social

work consultation may occur with teachers, principals, other school personnel, or community members. School social workers provide information, education, and support and help consultees develop a plan of action. The plan may focus on an individual child, a family, or the classroom; policies or procedures; or services and programs. Teachers frequently want advice and education on working with a student with classroom behavior problems. The consultant makes short-term educational and supportive interventions aimed at helping teachers feel competent in making changes. A strengths perspective is assumed. Consultations help to alleviate the student's current problem, while giving the other team members the skills needed to solve similar problems in the future. Albers and Kratochwill (2006) provided the stages of an effective problem solving consultation process (Table 11.3).

TABLE 11.2 Selected Outcome Measures

Measure	Outcomes Measured	No. of Items	Completed by	Time Required	Target Population	Developer/Source
YOQ 2.0	Treatment progress in 6 domains	64	Parent	5–10 minutes	4–17-year-olds	www.carepaths.com
YOQ-30 parent rated version	Measure of psychological disturbance	30	Parent	5 minutes	4–17-year-olds	www.carepaths.com
YOQ-30 self-report version	Measure of psychological disturbance	30	Child	5 minutes	12–17-year-olds	www.carepaths.com
Carepaths Assessment Center	System uses a battery of standardized instruments to assess client progress	Variable	Clinician interviewing child and/or parent	Variable	Variable	www.carepaths.com
The Child & Adolescent Functional Assessment Scale (CAFAS)	Assessment of functioning	315	Clinician interviewing child and/or parent	10 minutes	7–17-year-olds	Functional Assessment Systems: Kay Hodges (hodges@provide.net)
Brief Impairment Scale	Interpersonal relations, school functioning, self-care	23	Clinician/layperson interviewing parent	3–5 minutes	4–17-year-olds	H. R. Bird; Bird et al. (2005)
Brief Psychiatric Rating Scale for Children	Behavior problems, thinking disturbance, anxiety, depression, excitability, withdrawal	21	Clinician/layperson interviewing child and/or parent	5 minutes	3–18-year-olds	J. E. Overall; Overall & Pfefferbaum (1982)
Behavioral and Emotional Rating Scale (BERS)	Measures emotional and behavioral strengths	52	Adult familiar with child	10 minutes	5–18-year-olds	M. H. Epstein & J. M. Sharma (1998)
Columbia Impairment Scale	Global impairment	13	Clinician/layperson interviewing child and/or parent	5 minutes	Children under 9	H. R. Bird et al. (1993)

(continued)

TABLE 11.2 Continued

296

Measure	Outcomes Measured	No. of Items	Completed by	Time Required	Target Population	Developer/Source
Children's Global Assessment Scale (C-GAS)	A broad range of data about child's behavior and functioning	1	Clinician interviewing child	5 minutes	6–17-year-olds	D. Shaffer et al. (1983)
McMaster Family Assessment Device (FAD)	Six dimensions of family functioning	60 items	A member of the family		Families members of various ages	Epstein, Baldwin, & Bishop. 1983).
Family Adaptability and Cohesion Evaluation Scales (FACES-IV)	Assess 16 family styles of interaction	24 items	A member of the family	5–10 minutes	Families members of various ages	Olson et al., 1979, 1983
Family Assessment Measure	Family, dyadic, and individual functioning	42–50 items	Family members 10 years and older	20–45 minutes	10-year-olds and above	Skinner et al., 1995
School Success Profile	Students' self-assessment of their beliefs about their social environment, health, and school performance	220 items	Middle and high school students	30–40 minutes	Fourth-grade reading level	Bowen et al, 2001
Behavior Assessment System for Children (BASC)—Parent Rating Scales (PRS)	Adaptive and problem behaviors in the community and home setting	134–160 items	Parent/caregiver	10–20 minutes	Ages 2–21, fourth-grade reading level	Cecil R. Reynolds & Randy W. Kamphaus
Behavior Assessment System for Children (BASC)—Teacher Rating Scales (TRS)	Adaptive and problem behaviors in the school setting	100–139 items	Teacher	10–20 minutes	Ages 2–21	Cecil R. Reynolds & Randy W. Kamphaus
Behavior Assessment System for Children (BASC)—Self-Report of Personality (SRP): Child	Insight into a child's thoughts and feelings		Child (ages 8–11)	30 minutes	Ages 8–11	Cecil R. Reynolds & Randy W. Kamphaus

Instrument	Description	Items	Respondent	Time	Ages	Author
Behavior Assessment System for Children (BASC)—Self-Report of Personality (SRP): Adolescent	Insight into an adolescent's thoughts and feelings		Adolescent (12–21)	30 minutes	Ages 12–21	Cecil R. Reynolds & Randy W. Kamphaus
Behavior Assessment System for Children (BASC)—Self-Report of Personality (SRP): College	Insight into a young adult's thoughts and feelings		College student (18–25)	30 minutes	Ages 18–25	Cecil R. Reynolds & Randy W. Kamphaus
Child Behavior Checklist (CBCL/6–18)	Children's competencies & behavioral/emotional problems	140 items	Parent or guardian	Approx. 10 minutes	Ages 6–18	Thomas Achenbach
Teacher's Report Form for Ages 6–18 (TRF)	Children's academic performance, adaptive functioning, and behavioral/emotional problems	Appr. 118 items	Teacher	Approx. 10 minutes	Ages 6–18	Thomas Achenbach
Youth Self-Report for Ages 11–18 (YSR)		112+ items	Student	Approx. 10 minutes	5th grade reading skills or read to student, ages 11–18	Thomas Achenbach
Child Behavior Checklist/1½–5 (CBCL/1½–5/LDS)	Children's competencies & behavioral/emotional problems	100+items	Parent or guardian	Approx. 10 minutes	Ages 1.5–5	Thomas Achenbach
Caregiver-Teacher Report Form/1½–5 (C-TRF)	Children's academic performance, adaptive functioning, and behavioral/emotional problems	100 items	Teacher	Approx. 10 minutes	Ages 1.5–5	Thomas Achenbach

Source: Franklin, C., Hopson, L., & Judd, L. (2008). The University of Texas at Austin. School of Social Work.

TABLE 11.3   The Problem-Solving Consultation Process

Stages of Consultation		Typical Activities
Stage 1	Development of consultative relationship	■ Establish rapport and organize materials ■ Plan initial meeting/collect background information
Stage 2	Problem identification	■ Determine whether discrepancy exists ■ Provide a clear, objective definition of the problem ■ Collect additional information ■ Summarize the meeting
Stage 3	Problem analysis	■ Identify what the problem is/what the problem is not ■ Identify what factors are contributing to the problem ■ Have the consultee specify what he or she would like to see ■ Generate possible interventions
Stage 4	Plan implementation	■ Determine how to evaluate outcomes ■ Makes sure the consultee has the skills to implement the plan ■ Implement the plan and monitor progress
Stage 5	Plan evaluation	■ Evaluate the progress and process ■ If effective, plan for maintenance and follow-up ■ If not effective, revert back to earlier stage

Source: Albers, C.A., and Kratochwill, T.R. (2006). Teacher and principal consultations: Best practices. In C. Franklin, M. B. Harris, & P. Allen-Meares (Eds.), *The school services sourcebook: A guide for school-based professionals* (pp. 971–976). New York: Oxford University Press. By permission of Oxford University Press, Inc.

Practice Example.   A school social worker in a high school often served in the role of consultant to administrators and teachers on social functioning and mental health issues. The ninth-grade teachers were concerned because this year there was a large population of students who had recently emigrated from El Salvador due to a change in school district boundaries. Previously, the school population had been mostly made up of White students and teachers. Most of the teachers had little experience teaching students from cultures different than their own. The teachers worried that the students were "getting lost," were misplaced in their classrooms, and had concerns about communicating with families. The school social worker attended the ninth-grade team meeting to consult with the teachers about this problem. She discussed particular problems that the teachers were experiencing in the classroom and how these difficulties might be related to cultural differences. She spoke with the teachers about culturally competent teaching and provided

them with some suggestions for incorporating multiculturalism into their lessons. She also provided the teachers with some guidelines for contacting parents and made them aware of resources in the community that might be able to help them. At the end of the meeting, each teacher had made a list of strategies for helping the new students to feel comfortable in their classrooms and for solving the problems they had faced during the first few weeks of school.

Clinical Interventionist

In a study of social work services, Jonson-Reid et al. (2004) found that traditional clinical services such as individual and group counseling were the focal point of school social workers in a school district. Agresta (2006) surveyed school social workers, asking them about their current roles. The results of this survey confirmed that school social workers devote the largest portion of their time to counseling, and they wanted to do more counseling.

There is no doubt that the delivery of counseling and clinical services is an important role for school social workers. Some school social workers shy away from the word *clinical* because they associate it with diagnosis, the medical model, and psychiatric practice. School social work is certainly not limited to those activities. Over the years, however, the meaning of the term *clinical* has expanded from a narrow definition of social workers involved in psychiatric social work or providing long-term therapeutic services to mean any type of direct services intervention delivered to individuals, families, and small groups (Simpson, Williams, & Segall, 2007). According to Simpson et al., this includes services such as crisis management, case management, assessment, and individual and group therapy, all of which can be performed by social workers. School social workers provide a number of clinical and counseling services to children and their parents. Clinical services are often delivered in the role of home–school–community liaison where a school social worker is trying to address a child's difficulties in school and finds it necessary to involve parents and other social agencies. Social workers in clinical interventionist roles work to bring forth both psychosocial change and change in social systems. They may conduct counseling sessions with students and parents or run small, clinically oriented support groups to help students and families change.

Practice Example. A 15-year-old adolescent girl who was truant from school was referred to a school social worker. In an individual counseling session it was discovered that the child was clinically depressed. In addition, there were extreme family circumstances involved with the case. The mother left town 2 months prior with her boyfriend. The girl did not know the whereabouts of her mother since that time. The father was a man with obsessive-compulsive disorder and a drinking problem. The social worker used clinical interventions to help the girl. She made a referral and helped her get on medication for her depression. The social worker saw both the girl and father in counseling sessions in the school that focused on resolution of their mental health problems. The school social worker also helped the father get into further treatment at a mental health agency. The girl joined the social worker's weekly support group that focused on grief issues to help her cope with the loss of her mother.

Enabler and Facilitator

Central to the role of facilitator is assisting the student, parent, or staff member in the use of various techniques to accomplish a defined change (Radin, 1988). This empowerment function establishes an inner locus of control to meet present and future challenges. An old adage of practice wisdom in social casework practice demonstrates the role of the enabler or the facilitator: "Never do anything for clients 'that they can do for themselves.' " The facilitator works within the capacities of clients and enables them to help themselves.

Practice Example. At the beginning of the school year, a group of parents approached the school principal about the school's lack of resources. They noted that the school had not had new textbooks in many years and that the students often lacked essential school supplies. The principal asked the school social worker to serve as the parent group coordinator and assist them with the development of strategies to overcome the problems with which they were concerned. Within this role, the social worker encouraged one of the parents, who emerged as an internal leader, to assume the leadership of this group. The social worker directed the parent leader toward resources such as local nonprofits that routinely helped students secure school supplies, and the parent sought this group out on her own. After several weeks, the parent group had organized a school supply drive with the help of the local nonprofits, had planned several fund-raising events with the PTA, and had petitioned the local school board for additional resources. Each time the parent made strides in moving the group forward, the social worker praised and reinforced this self-initiative.

When the parent leader tried to defer to the social worker, the social worker was quick to give the parent leader the credit for the progress of the group, pointing out all the group's achievements. The social worker also denied that she had done anything to help, but attributed responsibility for the success of the program to the parent leader and the group members.

Collaborator

The role of collaborator differs from that of consultant in that it denotes the development of partnerships and networks in which participants have different but equally valuable contributions to make at various times and under various circumstances (Alter, 2000). Although the roles of collaborator and consultant often complement each other, "collaborator" denotes an exchange of information that results in joint problem-solving efforts. The ability of team members to link their unique contributions to those of other professionals is essential to interdisciplinary practice (Pugach & Allen-Meares, 1985).

Collaboration allows for personal development while working with other persons toward the attainment of a common goal. It helps to build relationships by recognizing and encouraging the strengths and contributions made by others. A collaborative relationship allows for stimulation of more ideas, approaches, and solutions than any one person can generate independently. In the continuous process of feedback and support, successes are reinforced, and the team is strengthened. The higher the level of collaboration, the greater the strength the group will have for collective action and commitment to the goals that have been developed. Finally, a collaborative relationship encourages the many talents available in the professional staff, thus multiplying resources in an organization. In today's school environment, building collaborative relationships with many other service providers is absolutely necessary to effective school practice. Waxrnan (cited in Streeter & Franklin, 2002) offered the following suggestions for ways that school social

workers and other mental health professionals can enhance collaborations among diverse professional groups.

1. Being positive, affirming, and receptive to collaborations
2. Setting up school teams and assuming leadership and coordination of roles on interagency teams
3. Working with agencies and collaborators to overcome barriers that prevent them from getting along
4. Serving as mediators in resource conflicts and disputes
5. Taking the initiative in leading efforts at mapping and coordinating resources
6. Working with the school and agency to develop formal agreements and formal mechanisms for maintaining programs and relationships
7. Working to help other mental health professionals to achieve outcomes that are academic as well as behavioral in nature

Adelman and Taylor (2002) provided other papers on effective practices, and practice guidelines for working with diverse professionals in school settings are found at the Web site of the Center for Mental Health in the Schools.

Practice Example. Social workers often set up collaborative meetings between teachers and students for helping students with behavior problems. Ms. Johnson was at her wit's end in dealing with John, who was a class clown and a constant disruption in her classroom. Sending him to the principal, Mr. Peterson, had not worked, and John quickly returned to her classroom. The school social worker was asked to collaborate on the case. The school social worker called a collaborative meeting between John, Ms. Johnson, John's parents, and his outside therapist to come up with solutions. In that meeting the worker focused on John's strengths and times that he does better in the classroom. Other participants gave similar input about times when John is mature and goal directed. The teacher and John worked out a special cue for settling down and a reward system that would motivate John.

Educator

In the role of educator, the social worker provides specific information, imparts knowledge, and deepens comprehension in work with pupils, teachers, and families. The teaching role is a way of sharing knowledge that others need to fulfill their responsibilities. Social workers provide workshops for parents and teachers in areas such as parenting, values clarification, and communication skills. Skills training interventions, like parenting training and social skills training, are some of the most popular approaches in which school social workers fulfill their role as "educator." Skills training is based on psychoeducational, social learning and behavioral models of change, which assume that clients lack certain behavioral skills for performing prosocial or competent behaviors. Social skills training, problem-solving training, anger control training, parent training, and life skills training are a few examples of the types of skills training programs that are useful in schools. Goldstein (1980, 1984; Goldstein & McGinnis, 1984) has developed several curricula for social skills training that are useful. These teaching methods may be used in skills training regardless of the content the school social worker is delivering.

1. Present the information the client needs to know didactically (e.g., steps of problem solving).
2. Model for the skills presented (e.g., to have a student come up with a problem and the social worker demonstrate how to go about problem solving while the client watches).
3. Practice the skills being taught through role-play (e.g., to have the student role-play solving a problem with the social worker).
4. Provide feedback to the client about their performance in practicing the skills. Be sure to provide both positive and corrective feedback (e.g., a student role-plays a problem-solving process about Johnny bullying at his locker in the hall. The social worker notes he did a good job in generating different options for how to handle the situation, but had difficulty evaluating the options and selecting one. The social worker shows him how to correct his actions).
5. Practice in the real world (social worker asks student to practice with problem situations).
6. Evaluate (social worker schedules time with the student to evaluate the real-world outcomes, and the steps start over to enhance learning).

Practice Example. Over the course of several weeks, three students at a large suburban high school were assaulted by peers on school property after school hours. Each of the students identified as being gay, lesbian, or bisexual. In addition, graffiti with hate slurs toward gay and lesbian students had appeared on the exterior walls of the school and on individual student lockers. The school mental health team was asked to arrange a series of workshops for students and parents to educate them about the rights of gay, lesbian, bisexual, and transgendered students. The team arranged an all-school assembly to discuss the recent incidents and the school's reaction to them. In addition, the mental health team held workshops in classrooms at each grade level to discuss topics such as tolerance and acceptance. The workshops used videos to promote student empathy, as well as adult guest speakers who discussed how their experiences of high school violence due to prejudice had affected their lives. Two free parent workshops were held in the evening hours with transportation, refreshments, and child care provided. The mental health team was responsible for covering several topics such as, "Keeping Your Child Safe at School," "Helping Your Child to Understand Differences," and "How to Support Your Gay, Lesbian, Bisexual, or Transgendered Child."

Mediator

The role of mediator places the social worker in a position between clients and their environment, providing a problem-solving service to both parties. Because of school violence, models for conflict resolution have been developed as a preventive measure to deter violence. Social workers are active in teaching this skill to others and use it themselves to mediate conflict between peers, between and among students and teachers/administration, and between parents and teachers. The severity of situations ranges from children fighting on the playground to random or planned violence that results in physical injuries or death. Mediation balances concern for the needs of students with the needs of the institution effectively, which provides a format for addressing problems that have a disruptive and negative effect on students' daily lives (Drolet, Paquin, & Soutyrine, 2007).

Practice Example. A teacher at a rural elementary school contacted the school social worker because she had not been able to reach the parents of one of her students by phone despite multiple attempts. The teacher explained that every time she called the student's house and introduced herself, the parents would hang up on her without explanation. The teacher hoped that the social worker could help with this problem because the social worker saw the student for weekly counseling sessions. The social worker had conducted home visits with the family in the past and agreed to visit the family and discuss this problem with them. During the home visit, the parents described their mistrust of the teacher due to a poor experience their older son had with her in the past. The parents and teacher agreed to attend a mediation session conducted by the school social worker to resolve their conflict and improve home–school communication.

Advocate

Advocacy differs from mediation in that the goal of the mediator is to achieve dispute resolution through compromise on both sides, whereas the goal of the advocate is to win for the client. The social worker becomes the speaker for the client and will argue, debate, bargain, negotiate, and manipulate the environment on behalf of the client (Compton & Galaway, 1984). This role is particularly important in supporting the rights of vulnerable populations (the developmentally disabled, the unmarried pregnant student, parents with limited resources, and minority students) when it is not possible to empower them to advocate for themselves.

Advocacy is particularly important at individual educational planning committee meetings, when the parents and/or students require support.

Advocacy on behalf of student populations can take place on several different levels. A social worker may use advocacy skills, for example, in school and community committees, at the state and national levels (advocating the rights of high-risk pupil groups), and within the school and community systems (identifying inadequate services and unfair policies and practices).

Practice Example. A child with behavior problems was repeatedly expelled from school and/or put into in-school suspension. The mother (an African-American woman of low socioeconomic status) was concerned that the student had a learning disorder, but due to resource restraints and lack of support from a teacher who said that this is just a "bad kid" and that learning problems were not indicated, the school would not test the child or consider him for special education placement. The social worker's assessment indicated that a learning disorder was a possibility. The social worker sided with the mother and educated her concerning her rights to have her son tested and educated. The social worker also used the policy mandates of the IDEA to educate the school district on their legal obligations to act and to provide an appropriate educational placement for this child. Through these advocacy efforts the child was tested and found to have a learning disorder, as well as another psychiatric disorder, that qualified him for special education placement.

Diversity Specialist

Schools work with an extremely culturally diverse and heterogeneous group of students (see Chapter 10 for additional discussion). Many cultural conflicts turn into problems between schools, parents, and students. A new role that the school social worker might assume in the 21st century is that of cultural specialist or specialist in diverse lifestyles. The key to being effective in this role is helping others develop knowledge and skills for effectively interacting with others.

Learning about diverse cultures is a must, and the school social worker might arrange in-service trainings and panel groups to discuss various cultural preferences and lifestyles. Mediating cultural differences and conflicts is another way that the school social worker might serve in this role.

Practice Example. The Mexican celebration of the Mayan festival starts well before Christmas and ends days into the New Year. In Mexico, the festival serves to unite the people and to reestablish ties. Hispanic children, however, are taken out of school by their parents so that the family can travel home to Mexico to join in the celebrations and feel rejuvenated in the Mexican traditions. The time missed at school was creating a problematic situation for the school. Only about half of the Mexican children, for example, were returning in time for class, and some were 1 to 2 weeks late. A school committee on which the social worker served wanted to pass a policy that required parents to sign an agreement stating that they will return from Mexico in time for students to attend classes. The school social worker knew, however, that this policy would further alienate the parents, who were very invested in the participation in the cultural tradition with their families. The school social worker was able to help the committee think about the cultural conflict and implications of this policy resulting in an alternative plan. A group of Mexican parents was asked to join the committee to discuss the issue, and they came up with the following resolution: the parents would make sure that no child was more than 1 week late for their classes, and they would get the schoolwork assignments before the holidays so that their children could complete the work before returning to school. Each child would also be asked to give a report on their experiences in Mexico to their classes so that the missed class time could become an enriched learning experience for all.

Manager

Every social worker in a school is a manager. The design and delivery of social work services in a school requires management skills: planning, negotiating, implementing, and evaluating a service.

A management role, however, may become more formalized, and social workers may even assume administrative duties, such as being the lead social worker in charge of a unit of school social workers in a school district. Management may also include the role of coordinator, which requires the ability to comprehend and conceptualize relationships between a client and multiple services and among various school, community, and agency resources (Sheafor, Horejsi, & Horejsi, 2000). Today, many school social workers coordinate the work of the individualized educational planning committee or act as case managers of prereferral intervention teams. School-linked service programs provide additional opportunities for management and coordination of social and mental health services on the school campus.

Practice Example. In a school district fostering school-linked programs, the roles involving management increased for the school social worker as the service providers moved onto campus. For example, the presence of several social and mental health agency personnel required the full-time attention of the pupil services team, who were being bombarded with a diversity of programs and professionals. This required some adjustment in job functions for the school social worker in that the clinical and counseling services she was offering were also being offered by social workers and other therapists working as a part of mental health teams. The school social worker found a new administrative role in coordinating the clinically oriented school-linked programs, and the principal supported her in this new role.

Case Manager and Broker

The case management and broker role provides a link between the problem situation and the resources that are support sources. Community agencies have been the most common resource used, but many other resources are available in the community and school, sometimes in the most unlikely places. Case management is necessary, for example, to track students involved in the myriad services being received on campus. School-linked services programs foster the need for more complex case management and new roles such as social services coordinator.

Practice Example. After an increase in the number of teen pregnancies and suicides, a medium-sized school district began to solicit help from the community and recruited a number of youth-serving agencies. Several mental health and social service providers offered services as diverse as substance abuse counseling, mentoring, sex education, self-esteem groups, parenting groups, and anger control training. Unfortunately, the school did not have a process for referring students at risk of pregnancy or mental health problems or for assigning referred students to needed services. In addition, once students began to receive services, there were no policies regarding follow-up procedures. Someone needed to coordinate the efforts by the diverse services and track the progress of students in those services. Under direction of the assistant principal, the school social worker became a case manager and assumed this function.

Community Intervention

Social workers have long been valued by schools for their extensive knowledge of community resources and their skill in helping pupils and their families use those resources. Their participation on agency boards and councils has enhanced this knowledge and has resulted in pupils receiving agency services that match their individual needs. In some instances, the social worker in the school has been responsible for identifying a social need and taking steps to mobilize forces within the community to establish a new service, such as a shelter for runaways, crisis-line service, or a quiet supervised place to study in a noisy apartment building (see Chapter 4).

Communities that have a low income and that place a low value on education require interventions that will increase positive attitudes about education and encourage the school to reach into the community and provide services responsive to community need. The development of bilingual education programs, preschool child-care programs that are part of the high school curriculum, and after-school care programs that involve school personnel are of mutual benefit to the school and the community.

Practice Example. There are times when the community requires the school's assistance. One city was condemning property while expanding its cultural center, which threatened the existence of the school. The low-income families had established roots in the community and had a compatible relationship with the school. Under the leadership of the school social worker, the faculty joined the community members in establishing a school–community collaborative that developed enough power to engage the city in negotiations for a compromise of the demolition plan. Through the joint efforts of the school and community, the community was saved, with only minor property loss.

Policy Initiator and Developer

School social workers influence, initiate, and develop policy that affects the social and emotional development of children and youth within the school and community. Through participating in policy-making committees, writing grants, and as members of professional organizations, they are active in creating programs that benefit the educational process. The knowledge of when and how to use political "know-how" is an essential skill for this role.

Practice Example. A school social worker became frustrated with her state's testing policies for students with special needs. All the students at her school were required to take state-mandated tests at their assigned grade level, regardless of their ability. For instance, although a student was reading at a third-grade level due to a severe cognitive disability, he was required to take the eighth-grade test because of his chronological age. The student had become very frustrated with the test and had acted out behaviorally. The student's parents complained to the social worker and asked why their child had to be tested on algebra when he had not yet mastered his multiplication tables. After researching the No Child Left Behind Act of 2001 (NCLB), the social worker realized that this problem was not unique to her school, but that many schools around the state were experiencing similar problems due to the way the state had chosen to implement the NCLB legislation. Because the social worker had learned that NCLB would soon be coming up for reauthorization, she organized school social workers, teachers, and parents in her school district to begin a letter writing campaign to their state board of education. The social worker hoped to have the state testing policies changed, which would protect students with special needs from unnecessary mental anguish and ensure that the students would be tested with more appropriate subject matter.

Specialized Intervention Skills

Schools provide a natural environment in which to use the full range of practice methods. In ecological practice, an intervention is one component of a larger plan requiring intervention techniques that join and link systems in the change process (Freeman & Pennekamp, 1988). In Chapter 12, Thyer and Jayarante discuss in more detail school social work interventions grounded in both evidence and ecological validity.

Intervention with Individual Students

Skills in assessment of individual dynamics, interviewing and counseling techniques, consultation, and linking and joining with other systems are required to intervene effectively with individual students. Counseling services range from individual counseling, providing temporary support, crisis intervention, and operating specific intervention programs such as grief support programs, transition programs, and violence prevention, to preparation of the client for referral to outside resources. This includes assistance to students returning to their home-school

following hospitalization or confinement in a juvenile facility or special education program. Sometimes a student's need for individual counseling and support can be met by a well-trained volunteer such as a senior citizen or peer counselor (Pryor, 1992).

Interventions that empower individual pupils to cope with life situations should occur simultaneously in all systems affected by or exacerbating the presenting concern. For example, consider situations involving sensitive counseling of gay or lesbian students. Individual counseling may be helpful to the gay or lesbian student, but he or she still faces a hostile environment. Initiatives directed toward acceptance of different sexual orientations by the school and community are necessary for the healthy development of all adolescents in the future (Elze, 2006; Marks, 1987).

Crisis Intervention

Even though a nationwide survey of school social workers' job tasks and skills indicates that school social workers prefer doing preventative work, they provide most interventions in the context of crisis intervention (Allen-Meares, 1994). Crisis situations occur throughout the normal life span of individuals, families, groups, communities, and nations. A crisis demands immediate short-term help. Crisis situations frequently addressed by school social workers may be created by a suspension, a failing grade, the divorce or death of parents, the death or injury of a friend, attempted suicide, drug use, a change to a physically disabling state, or an unwanted pregnancy.

Child abuse is a situation that requires immediate attention. Service is required for both the child and the abuser and requires the involvement of a child protection agency. Because of violence in neighborhoods and schools, social work services have been made available to the victim, as well as to other students and staff who have been traumatized by the incidents (Jimerson, Brock, Woehler, & Clinton-Higuita, 2006). Each school district has developed a plan for crisis intervention, and social workers need to be prepared to respond appropriately at the time of a crisis. For example, hypothetically, a first-grade teacher was shot and killed by her estranged husband in front of her class. A crisis team of social workers was immediately formed to assist the parents, students, and teachers to come to terms with the trauma and grief they experienced.

Working with Emotionally and Behaviorally Disturbed Students

Social workers frequently provide service to severely emotionally disturbed students in general education, those who work in special education classrooms, or day treatment programs for emotionally disturbed children. These practitioners should seek training in the best evidence-based practices for specific diagnosis and supervision, consultation, or collaboration with other mental health professionals with expertise in these areas. Table 11.1 offers guidance in programs for some specific problem areas. Support to learn about evidence-based practices is sometimes available within the program, but may have to be obtained from an outside source also (sources of support may come from both inside and outside the program; it varies from school to school). See Chapter 12 for additional information about monitoring and evaluating school social work practices.

School social workers often get involved in working with children with special needs and need ongoing training to know how to effectively intervene. Youths who have severe behavior problems and conduct disorder, for example, may commit violent acts against others and violate others' rights. Work with such youth requires considerable expertise to develop effective practice skills and programs. To move beyond the generalist level to offer in-school intervention, even more expertise and advanced training is required. It is unlikely that every school social worker can become an expert in helping aggressive youth with a conduct disorder. School social workers refer many students to other school professionals and experts in the community. Aggressive, disruptive, and antisocial behaviors are responsible for most of the referrals to clinic and

agency settings (Kazdin, 1996). Also, one of the most worrisome behaviors for schools today is the aggressive acts committed by these children in school, including fighting, assaults, and even murder (Dinkes, Cataldi, & Lin-Kelly, 2007). An example of the types of the specialized knowledge and skills needed for working with children with severe behavior problems and conduct disorder is described next.

Severe Behavior Problems and Conduct Disorder

Children with conduct disorder exhibit behaviors such as aggressive acts, theft, vandalism, fire setting, lying, truancy, and running away. The prevalence rate of conduct disorder is between 1 and 4% (U.S. Department of Health and Human Services, 1999). Children with conduct disorder also are likely to have academic problems, poor grades, and learning disorders (American Psychiatric Association, 2000). They are a constant challenge to the school, which often does not know how to manage children with such severe learning and behavior problems. Thus, schools desperately need the help of school social workers in their work with these children.

Helping Individual Students with Conduct Disorder

Helping students with conduct disorder has also been a constant challenge to school social workers and other helping professionals. Children with conduct disorder show a variety of cognitive errors related to their cognitive processes (perceptions, self-statements, attributions, and problem-solving skills) concerning themselves and others. Examples of the errors in cognitive processing include social cognitive skills such as cognitive problem-solving skills and misattributions of hostile intent to others (Kazdin, 1996, 2005).

The pervasiveness and intensity of conduct disorder demands a multimodal response from school practitioners. To manage the behavior of conduct-disordered children, school social workers must intervene with parents, teachers, and students. Parent training is a particularly useful intervention (Kazdin, 2005). Several parent and teacher training models have been developed to help children with conduct disorder. Webster-Stratton (1996), for example, has developed parent and teacher training programs for use in schools, as well as curricula and programs for students. These multimodal programs include curricula, videotapes, and teaching modules. This program is called the *Incredible Years* and is highlighted in Chapter 10 in the list of violence and conflict prevention programs.

Interventions with Bullying and Aggressive Behaviors

Recent years have seen an outbreak of school violence, and school social workers have taken on leadership roles in the prevention of violence (Klein, 2002; NASW, 2002a). Chapter 6 discusses research on the current rates of bullying in U.S. schools. One of the behavior problems that places children at risk for violent behaviors is bullying. Bullying is the type of aggressive responding that occurs over time, is threatening and intimidating, and is meant to disturb or harm others. An imbalance of power also exists between bully and victim such that the bully is larger and has more power than those being bullied (Garrett, 2001). Like other children who propose a threat of school violence, bullies often come from family and community situations in which they have witnessed or been victims of violence themselves. As individuals, they possess aggressive and impulsive characteristics and tend to lack inhibitions about using physical hitting or intimidation as a means of solving problems or controlling others. They also tend to be poor students and to have difficulty in their relationships with others. School social workers help schools stop bullying by identifying bully behaviors and developing policies of nontolerance on school grounds.

It is also important to educate all school staff, including bus drivers and other school personnel, so that they have the skills to monitor children closely to make sure that aggressive behaviors are not tolerated. Schools have to have firm policies that ensure careful monitoring and supervision of children on playgrounds, bathrooms, and halls to stop bullying (Astor, Behre, Wallace, & Fravil, 1998). Teachers can also use classroom time to help children learn conflict management and appropriate social skills. Role-plays to teach children how to respond to bullies and psychoeducation materials that send a strong message that bullying is inappropriate behavior may also be used in the classroom. For other sources of information on stopping bullying, see Garrett (2001) or the NASW's practice guidelines on bullying in youths (NASW, 2002a). Chapter 6 also describes promising programs to prevent and reduce bullying in schools.

Violence Prevention

Even though children are statistically more likely to be murdered in their own home or neighborhood, there has been increasing concern over incidences of school violence (Dwyer, Osher, & Warger, 1998; see Chapter 6 on school violence). The highly publicized school shootings that occurred in the late 20th century and early part of the current century have pointed to the need for schools to have violence prevention and crisis intervention policies and plans. Policies and interventions for the prevention of acts of violence are most important, in particular, the identification of at-risk youths (Klein, 2002). The identification of at-risk youths, however, is a difficult task for schools because there are so many risk factors, and violence-prone youths often have overlapping characteristics with other troubled youths who may not be violence prone (Klein, 2002). Eisenbraun (2007) summarized the research on how to identify youths at risk for violent acts. The following early warning signs are to serve as "red flags" to school personnel:

1. Social withdrawal
2. Excessive feelings of isolation or being alone
3. Excessive feelings of rejection
4. Being a victim of violence
5. Feelings of being picked on and persecuted
6. Low school interest and academic performance

7. Expression of violence in writings or drawings
8. Uncontrolled anger
9. Sudden changes in school attendance
10. Hypervigilence
11. Inability to set goals
12. Drug use and alcohol use
13. Affiliation with gangs
14. Inappropriate access to, possession of, and use of firearms
15. Serious threats of violence
16. Timidity when expressing personal opinions
17. Sudden mood changes
18. Intolerance of differences
19. Minority ethnic group (Eisenbraun, 2007, p. 462)

Chapter 6 offers additional warning signs and interventions for school violence.

One of the roles of school social workers is to help educators respond to risk factors such as those named and to help assess and intervene with youths before a violent act is committed. School social workers can also help schools not stereotype and jump into wrong conclusions about youths. They can focus schools on violence prevention policies and interventions that both protect and preserve the rights of individual students and families. Some of the effective school programs that can be put into place are comprehensive mental health services, special education programs, and day treatment and alternative school programs with intensive clinical services, instead of punitive alternatives or simple removal programs (Klein, 2002). Also see Chapter 6 for examples of promising practices to combat school violence.

Practice Example. A 16-year-old Euro-American ninth grader, Julian was referred to the school social worker because he wrote a letter about wanting to kill a classmate (Joey) who had been picking on him in the halls. Julian was withdrawn and had few friends. He wore an unusual black coat with red markings but did not belong to any particular gang or cult. He was mostly known as a loner and a "real quiet boy." He had been sent to the principal's office two times the previous school year for fighting and conflicts with other students but had not been in fights this year. He

had been known in younger years to bully some of the younger kids during middle school and to have a younger peer group than his age. He was a marginal student and had failed fifth grade because his mother was getting a divorce and moving around with her new boyfriend. Consequently, he missed too much school and could not catch up in time to be promoted. Further, family history indicated that Julian has observed violent incidents between his mother and stepfather and that there was much history of family conflict.

Julian currently lived with his father in a rural setting, and visited his mother, who lived about 30 minutes away in the next town. When the school social worker asked him about the letter, he said that he was mad at the student for picking on him and had written the letter to scare the student so that he would stop calling him names in the hall. The school social worker worked with the pupil services team to do a more thorough mental health evaluation of Julian. He was found to be a depressed and anxious boy with much anger toward his parents because of the divorce and the hardships it had caused. His father was called in for family work, and the school social worker discussed the risk factors and the importance of keeping guns away from Julian. His father agreed to keep his hunting guns under lock and key and to work with the school on getting Julian help. Julian's mother was called but failed to show up at the school for a meeting. Julian was referred to mental health services and a support group for children who had witnessed violence. It was also agreed that Julian would limit his visits with his mother to times that his stepfather was not present and that these meetings would not take place in her home. The school social worker also alerted hall monitors to keep Joey away from Julian. Joey was also reprimanded for his behavior by the assistant principal, and his parents were called.

Intervention with Families

Research has shown that children who have parents that are involved in their education perform better academically and socially (Englund, Egeland, & Collins, 2008; Miedel & Reynolds,

1999; Westat & Policy Studies Associates, 2001). Epstein (2001) outlined six different approaches that schools often use to engage parents: (a) offering services, such as parenting classes, to students' families; (b) teaching parents to assist students with activities related to their class work and create home environments that foster learning; (c) creating effective communication between the school and home; (d) recruiting parents to volunteer in schools; (e) encouraging parents to become involved in school decision making and student advocacy; and (f) creating collaborations between school and the community to improve education.

School social workers can play an integral role in improving parent participation in the school environment and thus improving student outcomes. Ward, Anderson-Butcher, and Kwiatkowski (2006) suggested seven steps that school social workers should take to engage parents by addressing their needs:

1. Assess parent and family needs
2. Addressing identified needs
3. Building relationships
4. Viewing parents as experts
5. Having parents as leaders
6. Creating spaces for parents
7. Creating meaningful and engaging activities (Ward et al., 2006, pp. 643–645).

Also see Chapter 12 for more information about performing family needs assessments.

Many families function under oppressive conditions. Substance abuse, violence, economic instability, homelessness, and fear for safety drain energy from child-nurturing tasks. School social workers involve themselves in providing ongoing support to families in need and help them with their oppressive conditions. An important issue for schools also is the degree of family disruption a child may have experienced or is still experiencing. Divorce, for example, is a common experience of children in American society, and school social workers need to be able to address divorce adjustment. Children experiencing disrupted family life may develop behavior problems, and school social workers are often involved in the aftermath of these family disruptions.

Fortunately, in recent years several empirically supported family treatments have emerged that address family life. Janzen, Harris, Jordan, and Franklin (2006) covered evidenced-based interventions for divorce, blended families, and myriad other populations. Family interventions are also especially efficacious for those who are violence prone, delinquent, and may also have substance abuse problems. Two of these programs are Brief Strategic Therapy (Szapocznik, Hervis, & Schwartz, 2003) and Multidimensional Family Therapy, the family-based preventative program developed by Hogue and Liddle (1999). Brief Strategic Therapy is short-term, problem-focused family intervention for treating child and adolescent behavior problems. These interventions target maladaptive family interactions to improve family relationships, promote strength and resiliency in children, and decrease the risk of substance abuse and conduct or behavior problems. They also place emphasis on culture and ethnicity and how they relate to the relationship change process. Hogue and Liddle's program also targets risk factors and provides family-based treatment alternatives for youths who might otherwise be incarcerated. Table 11.1 on empirically supported practices also describes other family-based programs such as Strengthening Families and STARS. Some of these programs are described in more detail in Franklin, Harris, & Allen-Meares (2006), and this reference provides information for how to implement them in a school-based program, as well as many other evidence-based school programs.

Practice Example. Mrs. Erickson, her two young daughters, and her 15-year-old son, John, a developmentally disabled student in a wheelchair, were evicted from their rented home and were living in a shelter for the homeless. The mother and part-time father had been substance abusers over the years and had worn out their families with their constant demands for help. John not only suffered from the loss of home, car, and attention, but he was also afraid of losing his classmates' friendship if they learned of his homeless status. His grief and embarrassment became a focus in counseling with the social worker. Based on an ongoing relationship with Mrs. Erickson, the social worker responded to the immediate crisis by mobilizing her resources to assist the family in locating suitable housing. They would need to be on the first floor to accommodate John's wheelchair. Because little support or assistance was available from the shelter, the social worker contacted the county housing authority and, with the mother, combed newspaper ads for leads. Although an afternoon of following up on some of the ads with the mother was not immediately successful, it did mobilize John's mother to continue the search on her own. Support and continued contact with John eased some of the pain he was experiencing until the family was able to move from the shelter.

Foster Families and Children

Astor (2005) used the term "public foster care schools" to describe public schools where almost an unbelievable proportion (20 to 60%, or more) of students are foster children. This trend is indicative of the need to define families with a broad definition and to understand how family disruption may affect the schooling of children. These trends require both skills for working with foster families and systems of care such as group homes in which many of these children receive custodial care. Astor discussed how foster children are housed in schools not equipped to handle their specialized needs. He questioned whether it is a good idea to have large proportions of foster children in large urban public schools. Most are children of color and are disproportionately attending large, urban inner-city schools. The fact that there are so many foster children in public schools is a symptom of a larger issue within children's services and indicates that children are not being appropriately placed in loving homes, and their care is often not satisfactory. Because of these trends in schooling of foster children, there is an opportunity for school social workers to help schools respond to the needs of these families who are involved in the foster care system and that subsequently need help with these children.

Public schools certainly need help educating these children who often have a variety of emotional and behavioral issues, including high incidences of conduct disorder. One empirically based practice for foster families is known as the Treatment Foster Care (Chamberlain, 2002). In this approach, children who have more serious emotional disturbances such as antisocial behavior are helped in the context of foster families instead of residential treatment. Many of these children may have been in the juvenile justice system. Schools become partners in the Treatment Foster Care approach, and the community-based practitioners using this approach make use of a daily report card to be filled out by teachers and sent home, for example. School social workers may be involved as treatment liaisons with community practitioners implementing this model to facilitate the interventions within the school.

According to Astor (2005), school social workers might be able to help schools be more effective with foster children if they facilitated the design of effective methods for communicating with foster parents and community agencies to improve the academic and behavioral outcomes of foster children in school settings. Resource development may also be an important practice skill. More resources are needed to have adequate interventions for schools to effectively instruct foster children. Astor mentioned resources such as community mentoring programs, extra tutors, after-school programs, vocational education, and an excellent staff that have specific training in classroom management techniques and academic issues with foster children.

Practice Example. A school social worker named Sue was hired in a large urban middle school whose population included 40% foster children. The school personnel were not trained to work with these children. Many incidences of violence and classroom disruptions happened every day. The principal wanted to install metal detectors and take out lockers due to the violence. The school social worker began researching various strategies for addressing school violence. She consulted several reputable Web sites, including the What Works Clearinghouse and the Substance Abuse and Mental Health Services Administration. These sites led her to several recent research studies on empirically supported practices to prevent and reduce school violence. She found that the use of metal detectors had mixed results in the research literature and had, in some circumstances, actually let to increased violence. The social worker presented these results to the principal, and he agreed to allow her to try a different approach to the problem.

The school social worker worked with the local juvenile justice agency and foster care agencies to provide in-service training for teachers on how to work with foster children. She developed a weekly parent support group and monthly parent–teacher luncheon to facilitate communication between foster parents and the school. Select children were assigned to a special after-school program and provided a mentor from the community to help with tutoring. She further worked with foster care professionals to institute the daily report card system with high-risk, antisocial youths.

Immigrant Families

Immigrant families often find themselves in culturally conflicting situations with schools that can require interpretation and mediation. Adjustment problems, misunderstandings of a cultural nature, and lack of follow-through on medical care for the handicapped child may require interpretation of customs of Western culture to the immigrant family and the culture of the family to school personnel or health-care providers. Adjustment for immigrant families is often stressful. Many children of immigrants, especially adolescents, experience pressure for conformity by their peers and friction in their relationships with their parents on adherence to traditional gender roles and values as defined in their cultures. At the same time, parents have a strong need for their children to maintain their heritage and often find it difficult themselves to accept American culture. Differences in dress, foods, recreation, social expectations, gender roles, and language all create stress.

Practice Example. Ray, an 11-year-old sixth grader of mixed ethnicity (Hispanic/Anglo), was referred to a school social worker, due to his inability to make decisions for himself and his passive behavior in class, such as not turning in his work. Ray was initially assessed to determine the need for special education services when he was in the fifth grade, which was the most recent evaluation. At that time, he was found to demonstrate a significant academic deficit in math calculation and a significant behavioral deficit in peer relationships. It was determined that he met the eligibility criteria for the handicapping condition of Other Health Impaired. He had been placed in regular classrooms and had been performing well until the last 6 weeks. The school social worker visited the parents for a consultation on Ray's behavior. Ray lived with his multiethnic parents. His father was a Mexican who had immigrated to the United States 3 months ago. The family had been going through a tremendous amount of transition with the father looking for work. He currently worked as a sharecropper, and it was feared that unless he got another job, he might have to leave the family to follow the crops, and the family may have to go with him. The mother did not want to leave her job, and she did not want to work in the fields like the father. The situation had created discord in the family. In speaking to Ray, the social worker determined that he was not getting much sleep due to the parental arguments. He also was worried about his father leaving. The school social worker held two problem-solving sessions with the family and referred the father to an employment agency that helped him obtain a different job. Ray's passive and indecisive behavior began to improve.

Interventions with Groups

The school is an organization composed of many groups: teachers, parents, classrooms, and students (Johnson, 1991). Most activities take place within a group context: classrooms, committee meetings, assemblies, lunchroom, sports, and other activities. Groups are particularly useful when development of socialization skills is indicated, when activity is desirable, and when natural groups can reinforce change (Johnson, 1983). The objectives also include exchanging information, clarifying value orientations, and diverting antisocial behaviors into productive channels.

With the advent of managed behavioral health care, groups are becoming a preferred method of treatment in different practice settings. Groups are believed to be an efficient and cost-effective method for intervention. Groups may be used for treatment and education, but there are also groups in which students and teachers work together to accomplish various tasks and goals. A differentiation can be made between a task group and an intervention group. An example of a task group is a committee formed to study a problem in a school and come up with a set of solutions. An intervention group is aimed at resolving the social problems and difficulties of students, parents, or teachers. For example, social workers may form parent groups to help parents learn how to respond to the drug problems of their children or a parenting skills group to help parents learn to be better parents. Groups may also be formed to help students with various problems such as grief, death of a friend, ADHD, or family problems.

Volumes have been written about group dynamics, the uses of groups, and the skills needed to lead them. One type of group structure and process that appears to be helpful for schools is the task-centered group, which was originally developed by Reid (1992, 2000). Task-centered group work is a behaviorally focused group that is usually formed to help youths solve various problem issues. Harris and Franklin (2003) recently found the task group process to be helpful when helping pregnant and parenting adolescents stay in school and improve their grades. Table 11.4 describes the group structure and process for task-centered groups.

School social workers are involved in a tremendous amount of school and community committee work. As members of or consultants to curriculum committees, social workers are in a position to influence thoughtful consideration of cultural and mental health content. Social workers also lead many different types of prevention groups to accomplish goals and objectives of helping students. Examples of prevention groups

---

TABLE 11.4   Task Group Model Process

(1) Problem Specification: The focus is on determining the problems the client wishes to work on. This is expected to take place in the first one to three sessions. During this phase, a contract is developed, written or verbal, which delineates the problems, goals, and duration of treatment. Focus is on what the client wants and not on what the practitioner thinks the client may need. The practitioner may engage with the client in a mutual process of deliberation in which the practitioner contributes her or his own knowledge and perception, arriving at an explicit agreement on the identified problems.

(2) Task Planning and Implementation: The focus is on formulating, planning, and evaluating tasks to resolve target problems. A task is an action that the participant agrees to take toward resolving the problem. Group leaders and participants define the task in a highly structured way, thus increasing chances that the task will be accomplished. This process usually happens over 6 to 10 sessions. The model offers specific strategies to assist the participant during this phase of intervention. One of these is assessing whether the group member has the knowledge and skills to perform as she desires, and if not, how to develop them. Another strategy, especially if the problem involves a formal organization, is for the practitioner to act as an advocate on behalf of the client to the organization. Leader activities as a strategy has evolved, as preferred over clinical techniques such as encouragement, direction, and explanation, and express the collaborative spirit of the model—what the practitioner and client do together to achieve common ends.

(3) Termination: Progress is reviewed and summarized, and plans are made to increase lasting results from intervention gains. The last one to two sessions are assigned to this phase.

Source: Harris, M. B. & Franklin, C. (2007). *Taking charge: A school-based life skills program for adolescent mothers.* Oxford University Press. By permission of Oxford University Press, Inc.

include those focused on preventing HIV infection and pregnancy, value education, and substance abuse prevention. For information on evaluating group work, see Chapter 12.

Practice Example. A school social worker employed in a high school was asked to develop groups that focused on the prevention of HIV infection and pregnancy. Sex education curricula are often used in these types of groups in schools, and thousands of curricula have been developed by school districts. The school social worker was concerned about finding out what were the best curricula in use, and she read the professional literature to identify an effective curriculum. She found there were many resources to help her choose a program that would meet the needs of her school. For example, Harris and Allgood (in press) summarized various empirically supported curricula that affect adolescent sexual behavior appearing on five well-respected effective program lists (Advocates for Youth, 2003; Kirby, 2007; Manlove et al., 2001, 2002; National Campaign to Prevent Teen Pregnancy, 2008; PASHA, 2002). Table 11.5 presents a summary of these recommended curricula, based on Harris and Allgood's work. Each of the programs in Table 11.5 has been selected as an effective program by the National Campaign to Prevent Teen Pregnancy, as well as at least two other lists of effective programs.

Intervention with Classrooms

School social workers often work with classrooms of students and their teachers. Teachers may become collaborators or cofacilitators in this process. One area of concern for classrooms is the integration of new students. New students change the group dynamics of the classroom. It takes time and often assistance before a new classroom equilibrium is established. Equilibrium is also disturbed when a class member leaves to attend another school or program or dies or when a class member or members are suspended or expelled. Each circumstance may require different approaches by the teacher and

others. The social worker can play a major role in this process by identifying the need to pay attention to these issues and by providing consultation and support as requested.

The transition of a new student entering the classroom may be made easier, for example, if the social worker and the teacher work together to prepare the class to accept the new student. The new student may not speak English, may be suspended from another school, might be a former special education student who is now being included in the general education program, or is possibly a homeless child or a child from a military family or from another state due to company reassignments or job changes (Bloomfield & Holzman, 1988).

Practice Example. In an elementary school that practiced mainstreaming for students with disabilities, a school social worker cofacilitated a classroom group with the teacher to prepare for a new student with cerebral palsy who would be joining the class. After completing an icebreaker activity about "differences," the students were broken into small groups to discuss how they could make their new classmate feel welcome and comfortable in the classroom, in the hallway, and at lunch and recess. The groups then put their ideas into action by participating in role-plays. The teacher and social worker reinforced students when they showed compassion and excitement in their discussions and role-plays and corrected students who seemed likely to make fun of the new student based on their behavior during the class exercises. The social worker agreed to sit in on the class on the new student's first morning of school to help students to remain positive in their interactions with the new student.

Intervention with the School

The school is the second most important influence (after the family) on the behavior and accomplishments of the children, and Allen-Meares (1985) listed some of the important qualities schools model for children:

TABLE 11.5   Nine Recommended Sex Education Curriculums

Curriculum	Focus of Intervention	Implementation	Theoretical Orientation	Impact
Be Proud! Be Responsible! (Select Media: http://www .selectmedia.org/)	Reducing the rates of HIV in inner city, African-American communities	Program consists of six culturally appropriate, hour-long modules	Cognitive-behavioral	Higher rates of condom use
Becoming a Responsible Teen (ETR Associates: http://pub.etr.org/)	Reducing the rates of HIV in African-American adolescents ages 14–18	Program consists of eight sessions, 1.5 to 2 hours each. Teens are encouraged to "spread the word" about HIV risk to their peers.	Social learning theory and self-efficacy theory	Delay in sexual initiation; improved contraceptive use
Making a Difference: An Abstinence Approach to STD, Teen Pregnancy, and HIV/AIDS Prevention (Select Media: http://www .selectmedia.org/)	Reducing the rates of adolescent pregnancy, HIV, and other STDs through abstinence	Program consists of eight 60-minute modules	Social cognitive theory, theory of reasoned action, and theory of planned behavior	Delay in sexual initiation at 3 month follow-up, but not at 6 or 9 month follow-up Improved contraceptive use at 12 month follow-up, but not at 3 or 6 month follow-up
Making Proud Choices: A Safer Sex Approach to HIV/STD and Teen Pregnancy Prevention (Select Media: http://www .selectmedia.org/)	Reducing the rates of adolescent pregnancy, HIV, and other STDs through contra-ceptive use	Program consists of eight 60-minute modules	Social cognitive theory, theory of reasoned action, and theory of planned behavior	Improved contraceptive use
Reducing the Risk (ETR Associates: http://pub.etr.org/)	Preventing adolescent pregnancy, HIV, and STDs	Program consists of 16 lessons, 45 minutes in length	Social learning theory, social influence theory and cognitive-behavioral theory	Delay in sexual initiation and improved con-traceptive use for adolescents who were sexually inexperienced before program

Curriculum	Focus of Intervention	Implementation	Theoretical Orientation	Impact
Safer Choices: A School-Based HIV Prevention Program (ETR Associates: http://pub.etr.org/)	Preventing HIV and STDs	Program consists of multiple components including: school health promotion council, 20 sessions of classroom curriculum taught over two years, staff training, peer resources, parent education, and school–community linkages.	Social cognitive theory, social influences theory, and models of school change	Delay in sexual initiation for Latino students only Improved contraceptive use
Children's Aid Society—Carrera Program (http://www .stopteenpregnancy .com/)	Reduction in adolescent pregnancy with a focus on urban, economically disadvantaged, African-American and Hispanic youth ages 13–15	Intensive, year-round, holistic program consists of multiple components including: daily after-school activities for 3–5 hours, summer program, health care, family involvement, and access to social services	Not available	Delay in sexual initiation, improved contraceptive use, and reduced teen pregnancy in girls only
Reach for Health Community Youth Services (Sociometrics: http://www.socio .com/)	To reduce early and unprotected sex for urban, African American and Hispanic 7th and 8th graders	Combines classroom teaching (35 weekly lessons in 7th grade and 30 weekly lessons in 8th grade) and community service activities (3 hours per week for both school years).	Not available	Delay in sexual initiation

(continued)

TABLE 11.5   Continued

Curriculum	Focus of Intervention	Implementation	Theoretical Orientation	Impact
Teen Outreach Program (The Wyman Center: http://www.wymancenter.org/teenoutreach.htm)	To reduce the rates of teen pregnancy, school dropout, and academic failure	The 9-month curriculum targets improvement in self-image, life management skills, and goal development. Components include classroom lessons and volunteer community service.	Not available	Reduced teen pregnancies

Adapted from: Harris, M.B. & Allgood, J. (in press). Adolescent pregnancy prevention: Choosing an effective program that fits. *Children and Youth Services Review* and National Campaign to Prevent Teen Pregnancy. (2008). *What works 2008: Curriculum-based programs that prevent teen pregnancy.* Washington, DC: Author.

Its atmosphere and academic expectations; quality and consistence of the teacher interaction; resourcefulness of the teacher and the educational program; its responsiveness to children of different ethnic, socio-economic, and status backgrounds; its willingness to reach out to parents and work together to resolve conflicting points of view and/or support each other; and the degree of humanness and flexibility that exists in policies and educational programs. (p. 103)

Facilitating a nurturing climate in the school may include recognizing efforts and achievements of teachers, staff, and volunteers. Some schools have an annual teacher appreciation day. In one school, the social workers developed a list of ways in which students and classes could show their appreciation.

Practice Example.   Middle school students were moved from a new urban middle school to an old elementary school building that still contained furniture and fixtures used by its previous tenants. During the first month, students broke windows, hurled furniture down the stairs, and scrawled graffiti on walls. Teachers found that little energy was being spent on learning and that the students were restless. The school administrators viewed the students' behavior as deviant. With each escalation in disciplinary measures, the situation became worse. After talking with students, teachers, and parents, the social worker concluded that the students were expressing a strong resentment toward the change in school buildings. She sat down with the principal and engaged him in an assessment of the situation, resulting in a plan of action that involved the pupils in creating a school environment that was more appropriate for their age group. The word *elementary* was removed from the sign on the front of the building, appropriately sized furniture was ordered from the supply department, and members of the art department worked with students to paint attractive murals on the walls. In addition, programs were developed in the school to build school spirit, and teachers, through in-service training, learned alternative ways of allowing the students to vent their anger about school conditions. Within a few weeks, the vandalism ceased, and the students were back to work.

Conclusion

In today's schools the delivery of school social work services has evolved into an array of services and interventions. This chapter addressed practice knowledge and skills that are needed to work in a school setting. Several trends that are affecting practices were covered, such as expanded school mental health services, school-linked programs, and emerging evidence-based practices. Controversies and issues facing school social workers in service delivery were also reviewed in relationship to the changing climate of school-based services and what is needed for school social workers to cooperate and form relationships with diverse mental health professionals. This chapter further presented practice roles and intervention skills needed to be effective in school practice. The new roles of school social workers in school-linked expanded school mental health services were highlighted, as well as several examples of the intervention roles that school social workers routinely perform in their jobs. Practice roles and intervention skills were illustrated with case examples. Finally, specialized intervention skills, such as those necessary to work with individual students, families, groups, classrooms, and school systems, were discussed. Issues such as conduct disorder, violence, and working with diverse families were covered in some detail.

For Study and Discussion

1. Camille is a Hispanic student who is failing language arts and social studies. As a school social worker, you have been asked to contact her parents about the problem. The parents do not speak English and do not have a telephone. What types of intervention skills would you use in working with this family and helping Camille with her school problems?

2. Five-year-old Kendra Beal was referred to a school social worker by her kindergarten teacher because of destructive behavior in the classroom and for acts of self-mutilation. During the first interview, Mrs. Beal revealed that she has a terminal illness and wants to find a good home for her three daughters. She was receiving help from other social workers representing three different agencies (health facility, family agency, and DSS); each gave conflicting advice. She is confused. What steps would you take to assist Mrs. Beal and Kendra?

3. An African-American student's parents show up at the school frantic because their 14-year-old daughter, Lynda, has been skipping school and leaving with an 18-year-old boy. The last incident of leaving school, which occurred 2 days before, resulted in her staying out all night in a hotel and being returned by the police. The parents are in a crisis and are asking for help. They are especially worried that their daughter may become pregnant or contract HIV. As a school social worker, how would you proceed with this family?

4. The population of the school is multicultural. What role can or should the social worker assume to maintain harmonious cultural relationships?

5. A 12-year-old boy is committing violent acts such as fighting and destroying school property. He has been expelled or served time in in-school suspension several times. Other students say he brags about torturing animals and owning guns. One student expresses to a school counselor that she is afraid of him because "he gives her the creeps" when he repeatedly asks her to come to his house, even though she has declined his offer on several occasions. The teachers are worried about his violent tendencies. As a school social worker what roles and intervention skills would you use to help this student?

Additional Readings

Allen-Meares, P. (1996). School social work services in the schools: A look at yesteryear and the future. *Social Work in Education, 18,* 202–209.

Ashman, K. K., & Hull, G. H. (2001). *Generalist practice with organizations and communities* (2nd ed.). Pacific Grove, CA: Brooks/Cole.

Brooks, J. E. (2006). Strengthening resilience in children and youths: Maximizing opportunities through schools. *Children & Schools, 28*(2), 69–76.

Brunk, M. (2000). *Effective treatment of conduct disorder.* Juvenile justice Fact Sheet. Charlottesville, VA: Institute of Law, Psychiatry, & Public Policy, University of Virginia.

Burns, B. J., & Hoagwood, K. (2002). *Community treatment for youth.* New York: Oxford University Press.

Center for Mental Health in Schools. (1999, Winter). *Addressing barriers to learning: New ways to think, Better ways to link.* Los Angeles: Author.

Center for Substance Abuse Prevention. (2003). *Building a successful prevention program.* Retrieved June 20, 2005, from http://casatunr.edu/bestpractices/alpha-list.php

Clarke, G. N., Hornbrook, M., Lynch, F., Polen, M., Gale, J., Beardslee, W., et al. (2001). A randomized trial of a group cognitive intervention for preventing depression in adolescent offspring of depressed parents. *Archives of General Psychiatry, 58*(12), 1127–1134.

Columbia University. (2003). *Guidelines for Child and Adolescent Mental Health Referral* (2nd Ed.). New York: Columbia University, Department of Child and Adolescent Psychiatry. Retrieved June 20, 2005, from www.promotementalhealth.org/downloads/Guidelines.pdf

Corcoran, J. (2000). *Evidence-based social work practice with families: A lifespan approach.* New York: Springer.

Delva-Tauili'ili, J. (1995). Assessment and prevention of aggressive behavior among youths of color: Integrating cultural and social factors. *Social Work in Education, 17,* 83–91.

Diehl, D., & Frey, A. (2008). Evaluating a community-school model of social work practice. *School Social Work, 32*(2), 1–20.

Early, T. J., & Vonk, M. E. (2001). Effectiveness of school social work from a risk and resilience perspective. *Children & Schools, 23,* 9–31.

Eddy, M., Reid, J., & Fetrow, B. (2000). An elementary school-based prevention program targeting modifiable antecedents of youth delinquency and violence: Linking the Interests of Family and Teachers (LIFT). *Journal of Emotional and Behavioral Disorders, 8,* 165–176.

Essex, E. L., & Massat, C. R. (2005). Preparing school social workers for their wider role: Policy as practice. *School Social Work Journal, 29*(2), 25–39.

Fischer, J., & Corcoran, K. (2000). *Measures for clinical practice.* New York: Free Press.

Franklin, C., Biever, J. L., Moore, K., Clemons, D., & Scamardo, M. (2001). The effectiveness of solution-focused therapy with children in a school setting. *Research on Social Work Practice, 11*(4), 411–434.

Franklin, C., Harris, M. B., & Allen-Meares, P. (2006). *The school services sourcebook: A guide for school-based professionals.* New York: Oxford University Press.

Franklin, C., & Hopson, L. (2004). Into the school with evidence-based practices. *Children & Schools, 26*(2), 67–70.

Franklin, C., & Hopson, L. (2005). *Selected outcome measures.* Austin: The University of Texas at Austin. School of Social Work.

Fraser, M. (Ed.). (2002). *Risk and resiliency in childhood: An ecological perspective* (2nd ed.). Washington, DC: NASW Press.

Fraser, M., Nash, J. K., Galinsky, M. J., & Darwin, K. M. (2000). *Making choices: Social problem solving skills for children.* Washington, DC: NASW Press.

Frey, A. J., & Dupper, D. (2005). Towards a 21st century model of school social work practice. *Children & Schools, 26*(2) 33–44.

Harris, M. B. & Franklin, C. (2007). *Taking charge: A school-based, life skills program for adolescent mothers.* New York: Oxford University Press.

Garrett, K. J. (2001). Reducing school-based bullying. *Journal of School Social Work, 12,* 74–90.

Gingerich, W. J., & Wabeke, T. (2001). A solution-focused approach to mental health intervention in schools. *Children & Schools, 23,* 33–48.

Goldhaber, D. D. (1999). School choice: An examination of the empirical evidence on achievement, parental decision making, and equity. *Educational Researcher, 28*(9), 16–25.

Greenberg, M. T., Weissberg, R. P., O'Brien, M. U., Zins, J. E., Fredericks, L., Resnik, H., & Elias, M. J. (2003). Enhancing school-based prevention and youth development through coordinated social, emotional, and academic learning. *American Psychologist, 58,* 466–474.

Henggeler, S. W., Schoenwald, S. K., Borduin, C. M., Rowland, M. D., & Cunningham, P. B. (1998). *Multisystemic treatment of antisocial behavior in children and adolescents.* New York: Guilford Press.

Hogue, A., & Liddle, H. A. (1999). Family-based preventive intervention: An approach to preventing substance abuse and antisocial behavior. *The American Journal of Orthopsychiatry, 69,* 278–290.

Jordan, C., & Franklin, C. (2003). *Clinical assessment for social workers. Quantitative and qualitative methods.* Chicago: Lyceum Books/Nelson Hall Books.

Kazdin, A. E. (2005). *Parent management training for oppositional, aggressive and anti-social children and adolescents.* New York: Oxford University Press.

Kelly, M. S. (2008). *The domains and demands of school social work practice.* New York: Oxford University Press.

Kelly, M. S., Kim, J. S., & Franklin, C. (2008). *Solution-focused brief therapy in schools.* New York: Oxford University Press.

Kleiner, B., & Chapman, C. (2000). Youth service learning and community service among 6th-through 12th grade students in the United States: 1996 and 1999. *Education Statistics Quarterly, 2*(1). Retrieved November 27, 2008, from http://nces.ed.gov/programs/quarterly/vol_2/2_1/

Linares, O. L., Rosbruch, N., Stern, M. B., Edwards, M. E., Walker, G., & Abikoff, H. B. (2005). Developing cognitive-social-emotional competencies to enhance academic learning. *Psychology in the Schools, 42*(4), 405–417.

Martin, E. J., Tobin, T. J., & Sugai, G. M. (2002). Current information on dropout prevention: Ideas from practitioners and the literature. *Preventing School Failure, 47*(1), 10–18.

McMahon, R. R., & Forehand, R. L. (2003). *Helping the noncompliant child.* New York: The Guilford Press.

National Association of Social Workers. (2002). *Standards for school social work practice.* Washington, DC: NASW Press.

Newsome, W. S. (2005). The impact of solution-focused brief therapy with at-risk junior high school students. *Children & Schools, 27*(2), 83–90.

Office of Juvenile Justice and Delinquency Prevention's Model Programs Guide. (2004). *Office of juvenile justice and delinquency prevention.* Retrieved June 30, 2005, from www.dsgonline.com/mpg_nonflash/Web Form4-Supplemental-Template.aspx?OrderBy="Title"

Prevatt, F., & Kelly, F. D. (2003). Dropping out of school: A review of intervention programs. *Journal of School Psychology, 41,* 377–395.

Prodente, C. A., Sander, M. A., & Weist, M. D. (2002). Furthering support for expanded school mental health programs. *Children's Services: Social Policy, Research, and Practice, 5*(3), 173–188.

Pruett, M. K., Davidson, L., McMahon, T. J., Ward, N. L., & Griffith, E. E. H. (2000). Comprehensive services for at-risk urban youth: Applying lessons from the community mental health movement. *Children's Services: Social Policy, Research, and Practice, 3*(2), 63–83.

Raines, J. C. (2004). Evidence-based practice in school social work: A process in perspective. *Children & Schools, 26*(2) 71–85.

Raines, J. C. (2004). To tell or not to tell: Ethical issues regarding confidentiality. *School Social Work Journal, 28*(2), 61–78.

Roberts, A. L (2009). *Social workers desk reference* (2nd ed.). New York: Oxford University Press.

Rumberger, R.W. (2004). Why students drop out of school. In G. Orfield (Ed.), *Drop outs in America: Confronting the graduation rate crisis* (pp. 131–155). Cambridge, MA: Harvard Education Press.

Schargel, F. P., & Smink, J. (2001). *Strategies to help solve our school dropout problem.* Larchmont, NY: Eye on Education.

Schinke, S. P., Tepavac, L., & Cole, K. C. (2000). Preventing substance use among Native American youth: Three-year results. *Addictive Behaviours, 25*(3), 387–397.

Shaffer, G. L. (2006). Promising school social work practices of the 1920s: Reflections for today. *Children & Schools, 28*(4), 243–251.

Spoth, R. L., Redmond, C., & Shin, C. (2001). Randomized trial of brief family interventions for general populations: Adolescent substance use outcomes 4 years following baseline. *Journal of Consulting and Clinical Psychology, 69*(4), 1–15.

Substance Abuse and Mental Health Services Administration. (2005). *SAMHSA model programs.* Retrieved June 30, 2005, from http://modelprograms.samhsa.gov/ template cf.cfm?page=model list#Model Matthew R.

Theide, C. E. (2005). A macro approach to meet the challenge of No Child Left Behind. *School Social Work Journal, 29*(2), 1–24.

Weisz, J. R., & Jenson, P. S. (1999). Efficacy and effectiveness of child and adolescent psychotherapy and pharmacotherapy. *Mental Health Services Research, 1,* 125–157.

Werch, C. E., Pappas, D. M., Carlson, J. M., Edgemon, P., Sinder, J. A., & Di-Clemente, C. C. (2000). Evaluation of a brief alcohol prevention program for urban school youth. *American Journal of Health Behavior, 24*(2), 120–131.

Williams, E. G., & Sadler, L. S. (2001). Effects of an urban high school-based child care center on self-selected adolescent parents and their children. *Journal of School Health, 71*(2), 47–52.

Wilson, D. B., Gottfredson, D. C., & Najaka, S. S. (2001). School-based prevention of problem behaviors: A meta-analysis. *Journal of Quantitative Criminology, 17,* 247–272.

Annotated Bibliography for Social Work Intervention with Pupils, Small Groups, Classrooms, Schools, Families, and Communities

Alexander, R., & Curtis, C. M. (1995). A critical review of strategies to reduce school violence. *Social Work in Education, 17,* 73–82. Reviews literature and reports interventions being used to reduce school violence.

Astor, R. A., Behre, W. J., Wallace, J. M., & Fravil, K. A. (1998). School social workers and school violence: Personal safety, training and violence programs. *Social Work, 43,* 223–232. Reports findings from a national survey that questioned school social workers on violence.

Chavkin, N. F. (Ed.). (1993). *Families and schools in a pluralistic society.* New York: SUNY Press. Presents information on working with multicultural families in a school context.

Dupper, D. R. (1994). Preventing school dropouts: Guidelines for school social work practice. *Social Work in Education, 15,* 141–149. Provides information on the problems facing schools concerning dropouts and provides practice guidelines for how to reduce the dropout problem in schools.

Dupper, D. R., & Poertner, J. (1997). Public schools and the revitalization center of impoverished communities: School-linked family resource centers. *Social Work, 42,* 415–422. Discusses how school-linked family resources can be used to make community interventions. Provides helpful guidelines for developing such centers.

Dwight, L. (1992). *We can do it.* New York: Checkerboard Press. A positive support book for upper elementary children with spina bifida, Down syndrome, cerebral palsy, and visual impairments. Excellent photographs of children engaging in many activities.

Ewalt, P. L., Freeman, E. M., Kirk, S. A., & Poole, D. L. (1996). *Multicultural issues in social work.* Washington, DC: NASW Press. A large book of case readings and intervention strategies on working with multicultural clients.

Flick, G. L. (1998). *ADD/ADHD behavior change resource kit.* West Nyack, New York: The Center for Applied Research in Education. A comprehensive resource guide and intervention manual for work in schools with children with ADHD. Provides step-by-step directions and resources for classroom and other behavioral management issues. Also, discusses work with parents and how to collaborate with other professionals for behavior change.

Franklin, C. (2001). Establishing successful relationships with expanded mental health services. *Children in Schools, 23*(4), 194–197. Points to the need for school social workers to find ways to collaborate with expanded mental health services.

Franklin, C., & Jordan, C. (1999). *Family practice: Brief systems methods for social work.* Pacific Grove: CA: Brooks/Cole. Provides overviews of several different brief practice models for families. Includes transcripts of cases and case studies illustrating different methods for family practice.

Franklin, C., Grant, D., Corcoran, J., Mill, E. O., & Bultman, L. (1997). Effectiveness or prevention programs for adolescent pregnancy: A meta-analysis. *Journal of Marriage and the Family, 59,* 551–567. Synthesizes the studies on the primary prevention of adolescent pregnancy for community-based and school-based programs. Discusses the state of the art in effective interventions.

Friedrich, M. J. (1999). Twenty-five years of school-based health centers. *Journal of the American Medical Association, 28,* 781–881. Speaks to statistics and experiences in establishing health clinics in the schools. Offers information on funding issues.

Gibelman, M. (1993). School social workers, counselors and psychologists: A shared agenda. *Social Work in Education, 15,* 45–54. Reviews the roles of related services professionals and highlights similarities and collaboration.

Henggeler, S. W, Schoenwald, S. K., Borduin, C. M., Rowland, M. D., & Cunningham, P. B. (1998). *Multisystemic treatment of antisocial behavior in children and adolescents.* New York: Guilford Press. Treatment manual that teaches practitioners how to do multisystemic therapy. A step-by-step guide with case studies.

Hogue, A., & Liddle, H. A. (1999). Family-based preventive intervention: An approach to preventing substance abuse and antisocial behavior. *The American Journal of Orthopsychiatry, 69,* 278–290. Journal

article illustrating an evidenced-based, family-based, intervention program.

Jordan, C., & Franklin, C. (1995, 2003). *Clinical assessment for social workers. Quantitative and qualitative methods.* Chicago: Lyceum Books/Nelson Hall Books. Provides information on different methods for assessing children and families and provides measurement tools for assessment.

McNeece, C. A., & DiNitto, D. M. (2002). *Chemical dependency: A systems approach* (3rd ed.). Boston: Allyn and Bacon. Introduces students to the broad range of topics necessary for a basic understanding of professional practice with alcohol and other drug abusers.

McWhirter, I. J., McWhirter, B. T., McWhirter, A. M., & McWhirter, E. H. (1993). *At-risk youth: A comprehensive response.* Pacific Grove, CA: Brooks/Cole. Present information on how to intervene with youth across several areas of concern, including youth suicide, adolescent pregnancy, family problems, and academic problems.

Moe, J., & Ways, P. (1991). *Conducting support groups for elementary children K–6.* Minneapolis: Johnson Institute. This book provides the professional with an educational strategy that engages students in the affective. Support groups provide a way for many hurting children to get help.

Morgan, G. (n.d.) *Finding your 15 percent: The art of mobilizing small changes to produce large effects.* Imaginization Website www.imaginiz.com/provocative/concept/fmd.html. Provides information on setting up collaborations and interprofessional teams.

National Assembly on School-Based Health Care, www.nasbhc.org/. Web site for school-based health clinics statistics and information.

National Crisis Prevention Institute, 3315-K North 124th Street, Brookfield, Wisconsin 53005. CPI has developed a number of products and services to train staff in nonviolent crisis intervention.

Pryor, C. B. (1996). Techniques for assessing family-school connections. *Social Work in Education, 18,* 85–94. Reviews eight techniques for assessing family–school connections.

Reinecke, M. A., Dattilio, E M., & Freeman, A. (1996). *Cognitive therapy with children and adolescents.* New York: Guilford. Presents a casebook of information on how to help children with diverse problems using cognitive therapy.

Taylor, L. (2000). Achieving coordinated mental health programs in schools. *Journal of School Health, 70*(5), 169. Provides information on how to work well with outside mental health professionals.

Taylor, L., & Adelman, H. (2000). Toward the end of marginalization and fragmentation of mental health in schools. *Journal of School Health, 70*(5), 210. Advocates a comprehensive and collaborative approach to school mental health services.

Waxman, R. P., Weist, M., & Benson, D. M. (1999). Toward collaboration in the growing education–mental health interface. *Clinical Psychology Review, 19,* 239–253. Sets forth important principles for working with diverse professionals in a school setting.

Weist, M. D., Myers, C. P., Hastings, E., Ghuman, H., & Han, Y. (1999). Psychosocial functioning of youth receiving mental health services in the school vs. community mental health centers. *Community Mental Health Journal, 35*(1), 69–81. Study that compares mental health services offered in school-based clinics with community mental health clinics. Schools were just as effective and offered greater access to the services.

Catalogues

Table 11.6 lists a few catalogues that address mental health needs through games and books and professional literature.

TABLE 11.6 Professional Catalogues for School Social Workers

Company	Web site	Description
ABC School Supply	http://www.abcschoolsupply.com/	Provides a wide variety of toys, games, manipulatives, and educational materials.
Pearson AGS Globe	http://www.pearsonschool.com/	Provides a wide variety of books and games for middle school and high school students to address life skills and psychological and behavioral issues.
Childwork/Childsplay	http://childswork.com/	Offers a large selection of therapeutic resources including play therapy tools and training programs.
Child Therapy Toys.Com	http://www.childtherapytoys.com/store/aboutus.html	Provides a variety of noncompetitive games, toys, and puppets designed for use in therapy sessions.
Childcraft	https://www.childcrafteducation.com/	Offers a variety of toys and games designed for use in schools.
Research Press	http://www.researchpress.com/	Publishes professional books and intervention manuals on topics of sociopsychological concern to school social workers.

12

Evaluating School Social Work

BRUCE A. THYER

Florida State University

SRINIKA D. JAYARATNE

University of Michigan

The need for systematic evaluation of practice and programs and for professional accountability is not an academic issue, but a service delivery and management reality. The conduct of systematic evaluation, however, is part politics, part knowledge, and part skill. An evaluator must be able to design and implement an evaluation of school social work that can withstand the criticism of detractors, as well as meet the needs of schools. This chapter will address key concepts, principles, and practices related to the development, design, implementation, and write-up of evaluation studies of the services of school social workers. Attention will be paid to the value and utility of understanding context and the ethical responsibilities of the evaluator.

Introduction

Organizations and practitioners engage in some form of evaluation explicitly or implicitly at virtually all levels of functioning. Evaluating social work programs and practices in schools is no different. The efficacy of a school and its programs is judged by the school board and administrators, parents, students, and indirectly by the community. Social work services within the larger milieu of a school system may constitute a

unit or department, albeit small in many instances. In other instances, social workers may be contract workers external to the school system. The centrality of school social work to the overall functioning of the school lies in its ability to demonstrate the need for and effectiveness of services provided, just as a corporate manager must demonstrate the value and utility of products and product lines. Thus, responsibility for demonstrating the functional value of social work practice rests primarily with the practitioners themselves. In the absence of evidence, it may not be too cynical to say that a school system might eliminate school social workers just as corporations eliminate low-performing product lines. It is in this context that school social workers must brace themselves for systematic evaluations of their practice and programs. The influence of the evidence-based practice (EBP) movement is also penetrating the world of school social work, which we believe is generally a good thing (see Franklin & Hopson, 2004), as is the adoption of practice guidelines (see Cherry, Staudt, & Watson, 2005). EBP is making inroads into the training and practice of school psychologists (Kratochwill, 2007), and school social workers must similarly become prepared for this new and influential model of practice.

Program and Practice Evaluation: Meaning and Context

The focus of an evaluation study can be an individual student, a group of students, one or more families of students, specific programs provided by school social workers, or an organization itself. Textbooks on evaluation research are generally dichotomous, in that those that reference the evaluation of programs and organizations generally use the term "program evaluation" (see, for example, Berk & Rossi, 1999; Rossi & Williams, 1972; Royse, Thyer, & Padgett, 2010; Weiss, 1972). In contrast, evaluation texts that focus on individuals, groups, and families typically identify themselves as "practice evaluation" (see, for example, Alter & Evens, 1990; Bloom, Fischer, & Orme, 2006; Shaw & Lishman, 1999; Thyer & Myers, 2007). In effect, the former emphasize "macro" assessments, whereas the latter focus on the individual practitioner and practice interventions. This distinction aside, both utilize similar research concepts, principles, methods, and strategies.

Why Evaluate Programs?

This is perhaps a rhetorical question in that societal expectations, budget allocation models, and consumers all expect some information or evidence to justify the existence of programs and services. Formal evaluation of programs is seen as a vehicle to move from a reactive or crisis-oriented approach in the delivery of services to a more guided and disciplined strategy to provide needed services, the logic being that certain programs, if evaluated, would turn out to be more "effective" and "efficient" than other programs. Once we identify these "effective and efficient" programs, then indeed one could justify their existence and continuation and the elimination of others. As simplistic as this logic may appear, this is the political reality of many funded programs. In fact, some have argued that evaluation is useful only to the extent that it produces timely results that would help decision makers in their deliberations

(see, for example, Patton, 1978; Smith & Glass, 1987). Tripodi (1983) stated that "evaluative research should not be conducted if its results cannot be utilized" (p. 14).

As will become apparent later, what is considered effective and efficient may depend on the eyes of the beholder. Stakeholders, individuals, and groups who have a vested interest in a program and presumably its evaluation, will influence decisions, as well as the methods of evaluation. Thus, the relative simplicity of program evaluation is, by default, encumbered by ideology, values, and politics at all levels (e.g., No Child Left Behind). The potential objectivity of an evaluation is subjected to goals and objectives of stakeholders. Everything from theory, to design, to analysis, to interpretation and dissemination may all be prone to conjuncture and debate. Thus, not only the characteristics of the program, but also the context of practice becomes relevant and critical to the evaluation of a program.

Why Evaluate Practice?

In contrast to the evaluation of programs, the evaluation of practice has somewhat of a different history, one that is more deeply rooted in the profession of social work. The question is perhaps all too simple: How do we know that we are doing what we think we are doing, and how do we know what we are doing has a demonstrable effect? Mary Richmond (1917, p. 230) raised these issues when discussing social workers' involvement in schools, as presented in her classic textbook *Social Diagnosis,* observing:

> The elements with which social work has to deal are so many and so intermingled that any tests of the results of the work itself are applied with difficulty.

It is important, for evaluation purposes, to specify the process, nature, and character of the interventions being utilized in a given situation. For a practitioner to say, "I am doing group work," is meaningless from the perspective of process evaluation. On the other hand, to say that in Session 1 of a 14-session program, we engaged in an assertiveness training exercise designed to help the group members feel comfortable in expressing their opinions freely, is more informative. But, to also say that the exercise consisted of certain specific activities would provide far more specification about the intervention. Such details provide information on planned activities that are purposefully designed to bring about change in a situation or to reach some goal. One resource we recommend in this regard is the recent *Handbook of Evidence-based Treatment Manuals for Children and Adolescents,* edited by social worker Craig LeCroy (2008). In this volume you will find a wide array of detailed treatment manuals that address the specifics of helping youth with various psychosocial problems. Among those covered are interventions focused on school refusal, dating violence, HIV prevention, anger management, coping with divorce, and other issues often encountered by school social workers. However, it is certainly possible to empirically examine the outcomes of school social work services *without* being able to describe in great detail exactly what was done. It is just that when you can provide such details, it is more likely your professional colleagues will be able to learn from your effective services.

It is also very important to make use of outcome measures, often some assessment of the student's presenting problem, that lend themselves to being used by others. This will also help you determine if the goals of intervention were achieved. As with the specification desired of intervention, clarity and specificity in the definition of problems and goals would enhance the likelihood of demonstrating the effects of intervention. To say that the student is more assertive in communicating with peers would be considered a weak measure of outcome. If, on the other hand, the practitioner is able to demonstrate that the student has engaged in certain assertive behaviors in defined situations, and furthermore, the frequency with which such behaviors occur has increased compared to preintervention levels, then we may have a demonstrable effect. If, in addition to the behavioral measure, the practitioner had

administered a valid "assertiveness scale" before intervention and again at termination, and the scale score shows a higher level of assertiveness, then we have even more evidence to demonstrate a positive outcome.

These recommendations are also in accord with the view expressed by Mary Richmond amid the earliest days of professional social work when she stated, "To state that we think our client is mentally deranged is futile; to state the observations that have created this impression is a possible help" (1917/1935, p. 362).

These issues, being able to adequately describe what social work intervention consists of and being able to measure the effects of social work intervention, were addressed in the very beginnings of professional social work practice and regained momentum in the 1970s and 1980s under the rubrics of "empirical clinical practice" or "practitioner-researcher" (see, for example, Briar, 1980; Jayaratne & Levy, 1979; Thomas, 1975). This is not merely an exercise in professional growth and development, but something fundamental to good practice. As Alter and Evens (1990) pointed out, "Today's need for accountability to clients, organizations and communities requires that we be able to evaluate our practice; the push for legitimacy and full professional status requires that social work services be effective; and competition for scarce resources requires that social work services be efficient" (p. 1). It is important to note, in this regard, that the *Code of Ethics* of the National Association of Social Workers (NASW) states that "social workers should monitor and evaluate policies, the implementation of programs, and practice interventions" (5.02(a); NASW, 1999).

Politics of Context

It should be clear by now that evaluation is rarely free of politics. Regardless of the form of evaluation, the purposes will always be defined by some as having a political motive. We have discussed the why of program and practice evaluation and, in so doing, have emphasized the importance of specificity and definition so that those in decision-making roles can then use the data appropriately. But sometimes, as Cohen (1970) pointed out, "decision-making, of course, is a euphemism for the allocation of resources—money, position, authority, etc." (p. 214). Thus, perceived or real, the very act of evaluation may begin with presuppositions of bias and fear of change.

What makes the context of evaluation politicized are the potentially disparate goals of stakeholders. Regardless of the outcome, some will favor the continuation of a program, and others may be more skeptical. School districts and boards may ask for information on whether or not a program should be continued. Principals and program heads may be tuned in to relative effectiveness and cost/benefits of different types of services within a program. The direct service social workers may be more concerned with how best to deliver services. Teachers may want to know how the services provided will result in better learning or less disruptive behavior on the part of a child. And parents and community advocates may want to have a greater say in the types of services and how services are provided. It will be difficult if not impossible for a single evaluation study to address all these dimensions. Thus, an effective evaluator must be someone who is sensitive to the vagaries of politics and multiple constituencies, and at the same time have the knowledge and stature to ensure the implementation of the best evaluation design possible under the circumstances.

As a concrete example, many school districts are under great pressure to do *something* about the program of alcohol and other drug abuse. A widely known and respected program is called DARE (Drug Abuse Resistance Education). It has a standardized curriculum and is taught by uniformed police officers in classrooms. DARE's favorable reputation and the urgency of the program has lead many school systems to purchase the DARE program, despite the fact that well-crafted program evaluations have shown that, to date, the program has little effect on deterring drug use (see Lynam et al., 1999). It takes a very brave school superintendent or principal to drop the DARE program on the grounds that it does not seem to work, in the face of strong parental support for such programs.

In this context, the political demands on program evaluation will presumably be more contentious than in practice evaluation. At least in theory, practice evaluation should be more idiosyncratic and driven by the particulars of the given situation. However, to the extent that a program is being judged by the sum of its components, success of a program may be viewed as the sum of successful cases. Under this scenario, the definition of "success" may become critical to the various stakeholders because that becomes synonymous with the program outcome. At this juncture, the distinction between program evaluation and practice evaluation becomes blurred and artificial. As Tripodi, Fellin, and Epstein (1978) noted, "Naive evaluators without political sophistication may draw up evaluation plans that are irrelevant and unrealistic" (p. 19).

Embedding the Evaluation in Culture. Whether a particular evaluation and measurement strategy is valued and accepted, whether the results of an evaluation are viewed with trust and confidence, and whether the findings have credibility and transferability may be affected by the perceived cultural competence of the evaluators. One of the authors once heard a radio announcement for the Peace Corps, which said something like this: "You are working in a remote village in India. There is no well, no school, and no bridge. It is *your* decision to help the people in the village to do one of these things." This simple announcement characterizes the essence of what an evaluator must *not* do.

Lincoln and Guba (1985), in discussing the helpfulness of qualitative data, argued that ensuring *trustworthiness and confidence* in the reliability, validity, and objectivity of data is an essential component of usefulness. From a pragmatic perspective, if the evaluators or the evaluation process is viewed with suspicion by those who are likely to be affected, one may cautiously argue that this has been an exercise in futility. Many of the components of trustworthiness resonate with any type of evaluation when considered in the context of cultural relevance. The elements of trust, as articulated by Varjas, Nastasi, Moore, and Jayasena (2005) are presented here as critical to the understanding and acceptance of an evaluation and its results.

Credibility.   Has the evaluation been conducted in a manner that has legitimacy among stakeholders? Has the process been "checked out" with relevant parties? Do the stakeholders believe that the evaluators have been around long enough to have a good understanding of the context? Do the participants understand that the evaluators have in-depth understanding of issues? Are multiple sources of data and information being used in the evaluation?

Transferability.   Is there sufficient information to justify the transferability of findings from one location of evaluation to another location? Has there been sufficient documentation on contextual similarities to justify the transferability of data? Have the consumers of the results been informed about any contextual differences?

Dependability and Confirmability.   Is there a detailed description of design, instrumentation, data collection procedures, and logic of analysis? Is there a record of decision points and the logic or rationale undergirding substantive decisions? Is there enough detailed information to allow for replication?

Affirmative answers to these questions will increase the probability that evaluation has taken into consideration culture and context. For example, do the outcome measures make sense for the population and context? Do the language and style of interventions reflect cultural sensitivities? To what extent are the providers of service and the evaluators "different" from those receiving services? In other words, the most powerful randomized design will have little practical value unless the evaluators take into consideration the elements of culture and context.

School social workers may need to take on the role of an advocate when engaging in evaluation studies. Many evaluators, especially those brought in to the system, may be most likely to engage with those who hired them because they will represent the primary stakeholder. They may be less sensitive to broader contextual issues and perhaps even disinterested in proposing comprehensive evaluation models, which are likely to be more expensive. The social workers in the relevant schools can and must play a significant role in ensuring that relevant stakeholders are at the table. After all is said and done, the social workers will be the ones facing the community and answering the questions. Taken in this light, advocating for the "right" evaluation is not a choice, it is a responsibility.

Role of the Evaluator

Given political and fiscal necessities, evaluation has now become big business. Unfortunately, however, many evaluators are hired or brought into the picture only after program activities have gone on for some time, typically, when someone sees an opportunity for a grant or questions are being asked about the efficacy of the program. The net result is that the evaluator is usually faced with assessing unclear programmatic practices, ill-defined outcomes, and systemic problems that make evaluation difficult at best. Regardless, evaluation is increasingly a way of organizational life, and as a result perhaps, private entities with the defined purpose of hiring themselves out as "external evaluators" are now quite commonplace. Several large for-profit and nonprofit organizations are now almost synonymous with evaluation, for example, Research Triangle Institute, RAND Corporation, and National Opinion Research Center. In addition, more and more large human service agencies are developing the capacity to conduct evaluations of their programs by employing "internal evaluators," individuals trained in the art and science of evaluation, who are a part of an evaluation unit within the agency. The reality, however, is that quite often, the political and policy debates dictate whether or not the evaluation will be conducted by an internal or external evaluator.

An external evaluator, someone who is not a part of the organization being evaluated, is hired to go into an organization and conduct an evaluation of a part or the entire organization. For example, a teachers' union may hire an evaluator to examine the effectiveness of substitute teachers, or a school district might hire an evaluator to determine whether social workers are providing needed services in a school system. Such evaluators are perceived as being more independent and, thereby, more objective and less prone to influence by organizational politics. They typically report findings to a funding body, committee, or some entity that has oversight over the organization. By definition then, what the external evaluator will study will be determined to a large extent by the expectations of this group. Thus, an evaluator hired by a school board to determine whether needed services are being provided by social workers will take their cue from the board, with goals being specified in the form of a contract. The extent to which the study includes various stakeholders (families, teachers, social workers, etc.) may truly depend on the predilections and goals of the school board.

However, it is the responsibility of the evaluator to present to the board an evaluation design that can withstand controversy and criticism. If the evaluator fails to include relevant stakeholders, resistance and skepticism is likely—after all, it is possible that the evaluator is merely helping the school board meet its agenda. If an evaluator is viewed as independent, they may be provided with unsolicited and unedited information because they are perceived as independent. But, if you don't *know* the program, you cannot evaluate it well, and the only way to learn it is to meet with the program participants. Thus, the time taken to learn must be built into the time of an external evaluator. The fact of the matter is that an external evaluator must first learn the organization and its culture. In general, an evaluation conducted by an external evaluator is likely to cost more than one conducted by an internal evaluator on the payroll.

Internal evaluators are employees of the organization with reporting responsibility to management. They are far more likely than external evaluators to know program details. But knowing the program could be a double-edged sword in this instance. The very fact of knowing may result in bias and an unwillingness to ask the hard questions because there is the potential of having to deal with issues such as collegiality and possible job losses of coworkers. However, they are also more likely to have access to less obvious information and possibly a higher level of trust from the participants. To the extent that an individual has a defined title and office, as opposed to an ad hoc role as an appointed evaluator, there may be greater legitimacy attached to actions and findings. Thus, on balance, it may appear that using an outside evaluator is more compelling. But, as you will see, the practice of good evaluation requires commitment and effort on the part of the whole program. "Good" programs will build in evaluation so that it is a part of organization culture, just as the "good" practitioner systematically assesses their practice.

In a school setting, a program evaluation may likely involve the school board, administrators, teachers, social workers, counselors, parents, and possibly students, depending on the nature of the questions being addressed. It is incumbent on the evaluator to seek input from all identified stakeholders prior to embarking on the evaluation. Such input will not only help address the appropriate questions, but it will also help develop a design, measures, and outcomes that will maximize the acceptance of findings after the fact.

Evaluability Assessment

Just because someone says a program *needs* to be evaluated does not mean the program *can* be evaluated at that time. For example, a program designed to increase social work services to adolescents by increasing the number of hours spent by social workers in a school cannot be readily evaluated without further specification on what kinds of services or a better understanding of the need for services. As such, evaluability assessment is viewed as a process for determining the goals and objectives of the program, the components of the program itself, the extent to which appropriate measures of the goals and objectives are in place, and the potential utility of evaluation data (see, for example, Berk & Rossi, 1999; Rossi & Freeman, 1993; Smith, 1989; Wholey, 1987).

Evaluability assessment is an oft-overlooked but well worthwhile procedure. Berk and Rossi (1999) have identified several criteria for establishing evaluability. First, is it possible to clarify program goals? This is a time-consuming process that typically requires interviews with stakeholders and an analysis of written documents. Second, is it possible to specify the content of the program, that is, what is the intended intervention? This again is a task that may require interviews with direct service providers, administrators, consumers, and others who may be in a position to specify the nature and character of interventions intended, interventions delivered, and interventions received. Third, is it possible to measure the impact of the program? This may require inquiry in to the availability of prepost measures, comparison groups, time-series data, and so forth. And finally, is there evidence of resource commitment and stakeholder buy in? If the resources are limited, or if there is inadequate time to develop stakeholder ownership, the utility of an evaluation may be questioned. In effect, this is time and money well spent lest we end up with a study that is open to a wide range of criticism.

Process and Outcome Evaluation: Compatibility and Purpose

The purpose of process evaluation, also referred to as formative evaluation, is primarily to generate information that would be useful for revising and refining practice or a program. In contrast, the purpose of outcome evaluation, also referred to as summative evaluation, is to generate information about the relative success or failure of a program. In theory, process and outcome evaluations could be conducted independently, and they often are. In practice, the conduct of a formative evaluation is usually viewed as a strategy to increase program efficacy and is usually supported by practitioners and program administrators. The conduct of a summative evaluation, in contrast, is often considered when there is a question of program continuation and typically requested by funders and sponsors. This is an unfortunate dichotomy in evaluation research because both elements of evaluation, formative and summative, are essential to effective practice.

Process Evaluation

Process evaluation and treatment monitoring are intended to operationally define and establish the fact that the specifics of a particular intervention are in fact being delivered. In other words, this is a method for confirming the nature of the independent variable. If the purpose of an evaluation is to find out whether X (independent variable) had an effect on Y (dependent variable), the more we know about X, the greater the likelihood we can in fact establish a relationship between X and Y, everything else held constant.

In general, program monitoring is important for several reasons. First, it allows us to establish whether or not the program is being delivered as intended. Such information would allow administrators to modify the program, establish ways to ensure the delivery of all components of the program, and even determine which aspects of the program are essential to keep and which may be harmful or ineffective. Second, in the absence of process evaluation, we have a much weaker case in establishing cause and effect as noted earlier. Finally, monitoring will allow for replication and diffusion. If program components can be described with a high degree of specificity, then it is much more transferable. By knowing the "elements" of intervention in the program, an evaluation plan could be put in place that actually determines the extent to which the planned activities occurred. The relationship between the intended activities of an intervention and the activities actually delivered is referred to as "treatment integrity" or "treatment fidelity." As

McGrew, Bond, Dietzen, and Salyers (1994) noted, treatment fidelity means not only conforming to the prescribed elements of a program but also ensuring the absence of nonprescribed elements. The greater the integrity or fidelity of the program, the greater its "testability," as well as transferability and potential utility. Consider the following study:

Peer-led, school-based nutrition education for young adolescents: Feasibility and process evaluation of the TEENS study (Story, Lytle, Birnbaum, & Perry 2002):

> Peer education has become a popular strategy for health promotion interventions with adolescents, but it has not been used widely in school-based nutrition education. This paper describes and reports on the feasibility of the peer leader component of a school-based nutrition intervention for young adolescents designed to increase fruit and vegetable intake and lower fat foods. About 1,000 seventh grade students in eight schools received the intervention. Of these, 272 were trained as peer leaders to assist the teacher in implementing the activities. Results ... based on peer leader and classroom student feedback, direct classroom observation, and teacher ratings and interviews are presented. Results show that peer-led nutrition education approaches in schools are feasible and have high acceptability among peer leaders, classroom students, and teachers. (edited abstract, p. 121)

This study reports on the feasibility of one component of the *Teens Eating for Energy and Nutrition at School* (TEENS) intervention program using peer leaders to deliver a structured curriculum across ten 40- to 45-minute classroom sessions. The peer leaders were trained, and each session was reviewed and rehearsed. In addition, each received a manual detailing session activities. The interventions are described in detail. For example, a specific knowledge development exercise is described as a "race for labels, a relay-race type activity where students divide into teams and compete to count fat grams in food packages" with the goal being to "teach students how to use food labels to make healthy changes" (p. 122).

The authors then delineated a set of process evaluation measures:

a. Attendance at training sessions to assess knowledge of training
b. Peer leader and student feedback to assess self-perception and helpfulness as peer leaders
c. Classroom observation to assess fidelity to intervention protocols
d. Teacher ratings on how well the peer leaders conducted the tasks
e. Teacher interviews to assess the effectiveness of the peer leaders

A systematic effort was made by the authors to assess the extent to which the defined interventions were being delivered as planned. One could certainly argue about the adequacy and/or appropriateness of the measures; for example, does an attendance log provide information about knowledge acquired? Yet, the variety of measures and different sources of information contributes to the strength of this process evaluation. Both the details provided on the intervention program and the multiple evaluation measures allow for a reasonable assessment of the extent to which the intervention was being implemented as designed.

Outcome Evaluation

Outcome evaluation is intended to operationally define and measure the impact of an intervention, that is, the extent to which a program is meeting its stated goals. In conducting an outcome evaluation, one must specify what changes are expected, devise methods of assessing change, and design methods for the collection of data. Typically, one measures several outcomes, gathers data from more than one source, and attempts to get more than one type of data. The greater the specificity in the definitions of intended outcomes, the higher the probability of obtaining "good" indicators of outcome. Consider the following example:

Does mentoring work? An impact study of the Big Brothers/Big Sisters program (Grossman & Tierny, 1998):

> Our random assignment evaluation found that this type of mentoring had a significant positive effect

on youth ages 10 to 16. Over the 18-month follow-up period, youths participating in Big Brothers/Big Sisters Programs were significantly less likely to have started using illegal drugs or alcohol, hit someone, or skipped school. They were also more confident about their school performance and got along better with their families. Mentors were carefully screened, trained, and matched with a youth whom they met, on average, three or four times a month for approximately a year. (edited abstract, p. 403)

The authors hypothesized that this program, which pairs unrelated adult volunteers with youths from single-parent families, would lead to a reduction in antisocial behaviors, show positive changes in academic attitudes, behavior, and performance, would carry over to other peer relationships, as well as family, and positively affect self-concept. They operationalized "antisocial behavior," for example, as alcohol or drug use and delinquent behavior. Similarly, they measured "self-concept" by administering instruments measuring global self-worth, social acceptance, and self-confidence. By identifying a set of outcome variables and systematically measuring them before and after the Big Brother/Big Sister (BBBS) matching, they were able to assess whether or not change occurred on each of the expected dimensions. By gathering prepost data, as well as relatively discrete measures, the authors were in a position to establish with some degree of accuracy the nature and quantity of change as hypothesized. Thus, from the perspective of evaluability assessment, one may conclude that this meets the standard as far as outcome criteria are concerned. However, from the perspective of process measurement, there is little information about the actual activities that occurred in the BB/BS relationships.

Therefore, this study may meet the criteria for outcome evaluation, but it essentially fails in meeting the criteria for process evaluation. Although the specified outcomes may have been achieved, we are in no real position to say why. Because each BB/BS pair did whatever they did, we have no sense of critical components, and as such, there is no way to test or monitor the fidelity of intervention.

Process and Outcome:
One without the Other

It is an accurate and unfortunate representation of evaluation to say that outcome evaluation holds sway when it comes to program evaluation. Most program funders, as well as administrators and consumers, are comforted by data indicating the effectiveness of a program, however ill-defined. The bottom line, so to speak, is whether problems are being ameliorated and goals being met. If they are, little attention may be paid to the specifics of the interventions that constitute the program. As a result, program evaluation studies tend to use broad indicators of service such as number of interviews, time spent, and reported delivery of services. For example, the BB/BS study imputes positive outcomes to the mentoring relationships, but we know very little about the nature of the activities. But, as Grinnell (2001) has pointed out, "We cannot be certain, however, that any change was caused by the program's activities unless we know precisely what these activities were" (p. 498).

Interestingly, the conduct of process evaluation is often confined to practice effectiveness studies because of a narrow definition of practice. This is mostly a result of increasing pressure placed on practitioners to demonstrate the effectiveness of their interventions. The scientist–practitioner and evidenced-based practice movements reflect the degree of attention being paid to the dimensions of intervention. The TEENS study clearly addresses the issue of whether or not a particular part of a program is being implemented as planned. However, we do not know whether the overall program was successful, a situation perfectly amenable to practice evaluation, but somewhat at odds with the expectations of program evaluation.

What should be abundantly clear by now is that an evaluation effort must pay close attention to *both* process and outcome. Failure to address one and not the other merely results in partial answers and, usually, more questions. Thus, an evaluability assessment must address the evaluation potential of both the intervention and the outcome. It is, of course, important to note that the utility of any evaluation study will be only as good as its design and methodology.

Consider the two following studies:

Effects of a cognitive-behavioral, school-based group intervention with Mexican-American pregnant and parenting adolescents (Harris & Franklin, 2003):

The authors evaluated a cognitive-behavioral school-based group intervention for Mexican-American pregnant and parenting adolescent girls, using a randomized experimental design, pretest, posttest, and 30-day follow-up. There were 85 participants and a variety of standardized measures and school grades and attendance were used as indicators of outcome. At posttest, those who received the intervention had statistically better scores than those who did not receive the intervention on all measures, and these differences were maintained at the 30-day follow-up time. "The cognitive-behavioral intervention shows promise as an effective method for helping Mexican-American pregnant and parenting adolescent mothers work toward high school graduation. (edited abstract, p. 71)

This study examines the impact of a task-centered cognitive-behavioral approach titled "Taking Charge." What is most important to note is that the authors not only utilized a manualized intervention program, but they also tried hard to establish "treatment fidelity" (the extent to which the intervention delivered is in fact the intervention designed). This degree of specificity not only allows for replication, but also clearly strengthens any arguments supporting the relationship between an intervention and measured outcomes. It is also noteworthy that the authors not only used validated measures in the study, but also took care to assess the internal reliability of these measures within the study sample. This effort is particularly important when using instruments that may raise questions about relevance and utility in a cross-cultural context. Thus, by using a powerful research design, established outcome measures, and a well-developed intervention program, the authors have demonstrated the feasibility and desirability of an evaluation in which there is a focus on both process and outcome. By clearly describing the interventions, they not only

allow others to replicate the interventions, but also allow others to understand *why* they did what they did, given the specifics of the situation.

Promoting school completion of urban secondary youth with emotional or behavioral disabilities (Sinclair, Christenson, & Thurlow, 2005):

An experimental research design was used to examine the effectiveness of a targeted, long-term intervention to promote school completion and reduce dropout among urban high school students with emotional or behavioral disabilities. African Americans (67 percent) and males (82 percent) composed a large portion of the sample, all of whom were ninth grade students. One hundred and forty four students were randomly assigned to a treatment or control group. The intervention used was titled "check & connect," which is a detailed and tested intervention. The participants were followed for a period of four years, with outcomes including lower dropout rates, higher rates of attendance, and more comprehensive transition or IEP (Individualized Education Program) plans. (edited abstract, p. 465)

The authors were interested in testing the efficacy of the seven-element "check & connect" model of intervention designed for use with urban high school youth. In the model, "check" refers to continuous assessment, and "connect" refers to defined interventions based on the continuous feedback received from family members, community workers, and school personnel. What is immediately evident is the comprehensive and grounded approach to intervention. As an additional fact, the authors present numerous references, which in turn allow the interested reader to further examine the efficacy of other studies utilizing the "same" intervention. The intervention components are carefully articulated, and the role of a key player, the "Monitor," is detailed by the authors. Thus, sufficient information is provided to replicate the intervention.

The authors paid a great deal of attention to the specification of outcomes. To some extent, the identified outcomes are relatively concrete and hence more easily objectified. For example, one outcome measure was *mobility,* referring to the "number of educational settings a student attended within a year" (Sinclair et al., 2005, p. 473). When such discrete measures are used in conjunction with a powerful design, it is difficult to contest the findings in an evaluation study. From the perspective persuasiveness and polity of evaluation, exemplars of individual students and perhaps a personal story would have made an already strong study even stronger in the context convincing stakeholders.

Needs Assessment

Needs assessment studies, which are conducted to determine whether a program or components of a program are needed, are usually categorized under the rubric of evaluation research. The questions addressed by a needs assessment vary from determining the existence of a problem, to determining the nature of desired services, to identifying sources of resistance, and to determining the character of available resources. Practically, this means finding out whether or not particular services are needed, and if they are, how best to deliver them. In theory, a needs assessment is something that should be done well before a program is implemented. On the other hand, a needs assessment is also justified if existing program services are being underutilized, and there are realistic questions about the need to continue a given program.

Strategies for conducting a needs assessment can be complex (see, for example, Krueger, 1993; Warheit, Bell, & Schwab, 1977). The cardinal rule, however, is to identify stakeholders. It should also be kept in mind that stakeholders for needs assessment may not necessarily include the primary beneficiaries of service, as would be the case with services for children. Here, the gamut could run from teachers and parents to professional organizations and advocacy groups. Sensitivity to the perceptions of these various parties is critical to the conduct of a useful needs assessment. We will simply identify some of the principle strategies used in needs assessment studies and urge the reader to go to primary sources for more detailed practices.

- *Stakeholder survey*—a simple survey could be done among identified stakeholder groups to gather preliminary information about program needs. For example, it may be useful to conduct a survey among students, teachers, and parents to obtain a sense of the need for an after-school math tutoring program.
- *Key informant study*—key informants are individuals in the community, who by virtue of their job, training, or experience are viewed as experts. Once identified, these individuals could be interviewed to gather information on the question under consideration. For example, math teachers could provide critical information about the need for an after-school tutoring program. University faculty in a school of education may provide good information about programs that worked and relevant research.
- *Focus groups*—by getting together a small number of individuals in a group representing different attributes (student, teacher, parent), a facilitator can conduct a session in which questions are posed in a structured manner. The dialog that emanates from these structured discussions could help define the needs and elements of a program. For example, parents might prefer that the program be immediately after school, and students may prefer one later in the evening.

A "best practice" for a needs assessment study would be to incorporate a variety of methods in one study. If conducted properly, needs assessment will increase the likelihood of stakeholder buy in and thereby, increase the probability of program success. Consider the following example:

Parent involvement: A needs assessment (Neely-Barnes, 1999):

A needs assessment of parent involvement was conducted at two elementary schools. There are many reasons why parent involvement is important to children's education. . . . Parents' level of involvement, barriers to involvement, and values concerning their children's education were measures at two elementary schools in a large

Midwestern city. . . . Parents who said that work or other conflicts made it difficult for them to come to school were less likely to communicate with their children's teachers and less likely to participate in school activities. Findings suggest that staff at these two elementary schools should be sensitive to parents' work schedules when planning activities. (edited abstract, p. 29)

This straightforward study illustrates the practical utility of a needs assessment. The author defined "parent involvement" as "talking to children about their school experience, helping with homework, attending school events, and talking to teachers" (p. 32). In one elementary school, 15 children were chosen randomly from each grade, whereas at the other school, "the principal chose one classroom at each grade, and the entire classroom was surveyed." They then proceeded to survey parents to determine the extent to which parent involvement occurred, was valued by the parents, and the barriers to such involvement. The survey instrument contained 17 questions. The survey was distributed by teachers to the students to take home and resulted in a 24% response rate. Although the study design has numerous weaknesses (different selection strategies in the two schools, low response rate, etc.), it provides potentially useful information and direction to decision makers.

Designing and Implementing Evaluation Studies

As with any good research, the design of an evaluation should be guided by the research questions. At some level, implicitly or explicitly, every program is being evaluated, and every practitioner is assessing the impact of their work. Such information, however, may be gathered quite informally and unsystematically. By formalizing the evaluation, we systematize the process and presumably bring it consistency and legitimacy. Presented next are implementation steps with illustrative examples from three different types of evaluation studies to elucidate the meaning of each step (see, for example, Thomas, 1984; Tripodi, 1983).

Validating school social work: An evaluation of a cognitive behavioral approach to reduce school violence (Whitfield, 1999):

This study evaluated the effectiveness of anger control training with conduct-disordered male adolescents at a day treatment program. A multiple baseline single-subject design . . . combined with visual analyses and groups comparison methods were used in the assessment. The experimental students significantly improved in their weekly self-reports of using better anger control and experiencing more positive management and expression of anger. The experimental students also significantly improved in their use of self control as shown by a pretest through six-month follow-up assessment. (edited abstract, p. 399)

Evaluating a sexual assault and dating violence prevention program for urban youth (Weisz & Black, 2001):

A sexual assault and dating violence program presented in an urban middle school was evaluated to assess its influence on the knowledge and attitudes of an intervention group of 46 and a comparison group of 20 African-American seventh graders. A quasi-experimental pretest, posttest, follow-up groups design was used to evaluate the program s effectiveness. . . . Results support the need for early prevention programming among youths in the inner-city schools. (edited abstract, p. 89)

Evaluation of an alternative discipline program (Andrews, Taylor, Martin, & Slate, 1998):

Students who misbehave tend to perform poorly in school and tend to be absent frequently from school. . . . This has led researchers to examine the relationship of school suspension to attendance and achievement, and further the relative impact of suspensions in school (ISS) and out of school (OS). One stated purpose of this study was to compare the effects of a lunch detention versus an out of school suspension program for secondary school students. Students were assigned to one of the two conditions, and the frequency of suspensions was monitored. Results showed that lunch detention was associated with a statistically significant and meaningfully lower frequency of suspension than after school detention. (edited summary of article)

Now, let us consider the evaluation implementation steps for each of the preceding studies:

a. The Purpose of the Evaluation Must Be Established

> *Whitfield:* Identified the study purpose as "evaluating the effectiveness of a cognitive behavioral intervention (i.e., anger control training) with explosive and conduct disordered male adolescents in reducing school violence" (p. 400).
>
> *Weisz & Black:* Identified the study purpose as an evaluation of "a sexual assault and dating violence prevention program ... The study sought to evaluate both the short-term and intermediate effects on the knowledge and attitudes of participants" (p. 91).
>
> *Andrews et al.:* "The purposes of this study were threefold: (1) What is the effect of a school lunch detention versus an out-of-school suspension program on the suspension frequencies of secondary school students? (2) How do school policies affect the suspension frequencies of secondary school students? And (3) what is the perception by the school community of the effectiveness of alternative discipline programs?" (p. 210).

By reading these statements, we know the overall purpose of the evaluations. All three studies purport to evaluate the effectiveness of a particular intervention program. We also know that Whitfield and Andrews hope to change behavior, whereas Weisz and Black hope to affect knowledge and attitudes. All three could be construed as focusing on outcome, but we do not know the specifics about outcome in two—what is meant by "violence" in the Whitfield study or "knowledge and attitudes" in the Weisz and Black study. These are questions that must be answered as we move forward with implementation.

b. The Goals Must Be Made Clear, Specific, and Measurable

> *Whitfield:* "... the student receiving Anger Control Training would have higher Anger Control scale scores and lower anger

expression scale scores relative to control students' self-reports for these two measures" (p. 406).

> *Weisz & Black:* "Program goals included increasing knowledge about the extent and causes of teenage sexual assault and dating violence, including knowledge of community resources; increasing intolerance for sexual assault and teenage dating violence ..." (p. 92).
>
> *Andrews et al.:* These authors essentially stated their goals for the study in presenting the purpose listed earlier. However, one could say their goal is to compare the effects of school lunch detention versus an out-of-school suspension on the suspension frequencies of secondary school students and, in addition, to gather information on the perception of these alternative discipline programs from the larger school community.

These statements tell us specifically what it is that the authors intended to evaluate. Whitfield specified the goals in terms of expected changes in scale scores, a hypothesis. Weisz and Black want to examine changes in knowledge and attitude and further want to see whether these changes will be maintained over time. Andrews et al. not only want to look at a change in behavior within one population (students), but are also interested in what one group of stakeholders may think about the program.

The second step in the process further clarifies program objectives. These statements help us understand the specific purpose of the evaluations. What we don't know up to now is how the attainment of these objectives will be monitored or measured, a question that must be answered in the next step of the process.

c. Valid and Reliable Goal Attainment Measures Must Be Identified

> *Whitfield:* Employed "two self-report measures and a behavioral count or measure of acting-out behaviors" (p. 404). The self-report

measures are *The State-Trait Anger Expression Inventory* and the *Self-Control Rating Scale*. A behavioral count was obtained through *The Staff Daily Report.*

Weisz & Black: The authors developed four instruments to measure knowledge, attitudes, behavior, or anticipated behavior and incidence. The authors noted that they "adapted questions from instruments developed for older youth . . ." (p. 93).

Andrews et al.: "The dependent variable under investigation was the frequency of suspension. For each student in the study, school files and system computer records were used as the source of information regarding the discipline infraction and subsequent punishments" (p. 211).

Both Whitfield and Weisz and Black relied on measures of self-report, although Whitfield also used an observational measure completed by a designated staff member. In contrast, Andrews used the frequency of occurrence data from the school's administrative database.

We have now reached a point in the evaluation design and implementation process when the study design has to be considered. Given the purpose of the study and the goals, and given the "best" measures of goal attainment, what would be the best design to use? This question is addressed in the next step of the process.

d. Choose and Implement an Appropriate Research Design

> *Whitfield:* "I used a single-subject, multiple baseline design across subjects as the main research design" (p. 403).
>
> *Weisz & Black:* Although the authors don't state it as such, they used a "nonequivalent control group design." For the treatment group, seventh-grade "students voluntarily chose to participate in the program. . . . The comparison group consisted of seventh grade students from the same charter school who were not enrolled in the program" (p. 91).
>
> *Andrews et al.:* ". . . a quasi-experimental design was used to evaluate the effectiveness

of the alternative discipline program." The students suspended during the first and second 6 weeks of school were in out-of-school detention, whereas the students suspended during the fourth and fifth 6-week periods were placed in lunch detention. . . . The qualitative research design included surveys of . . . administrators and selected teachers (as well as student volunteers) (p. 211).

Along with the choice of design comes the decision on data collection. Because the decisions have already been made about instrumentation in the previous step, the implementation phase requires a decision on when and how the data are to be gathered. More often than not, these decisions are made concurrently, but we have separated them because they are important decisions in of themselves.

> *Whitfield: The State-Trait Anger Expression Inventory* was completed weekly by the students, whereas *The Staff Daily Report* was also completed weekly by program staff. In contrast, the *Self-Control Rating Scale* was administered at pretest, at posttest, and 6 months after the program.
>
> *Weisz & Black:* utilized a pre-post strategy in their evaluation of the violence prevention program. They "administered pretest and posttest questionnaires during the sessions on the initial and final day of the program and again six months later" (p. 92).
>
> *Andrews et al.:* "Specifically, the numbers of students referred to detention during the time periods of the study and the numbers of students suspended for failure to serve detention during those time periods were tabulated from the computer data." To address the question regarding community perception, "open-ended survey questions related to the two forms of detention under investigation were completed by school personnel and students" (p. 211).

The design and the measures together constitute the methodology of the study in conjunction with the study subjects. As should be self-evident, methodology is dictated by the study questions and constrained by the context of practice. In examining the steps of design and implementation, it is important to note that more often than not, compromises have to be made. Realistically, perfect designs with ideal measures are rarely within the realm of possibility in evaluation research. This is due to a lack of control over the context of evaluation, the demands of stakeholders, the ethics of providing human services, and the very real fact that there are no "perfect measures" for the complex problems encountered in the service arena. As Rossi and Freeman (1993) noted, "Evaluations may be justifiably undertaken that are 'good enough' for answering relevant policy and program questions even though from a scientific standpoint they are not the best possible designs" (p. 30). However, it is the obligation of the evaluator to come as close to the ideal as possible.

e. Analyzing, Interpreting, and Reporting Data

Analysis and interpretation is necessarily guided by the methodology and the level of measurement. Thus, time-series data from single-case studies are unlikely to be analyzed statistically, but rather, they are more likely to be visually examined for trend and direction. In contrast, evaluations that compare groups of subjects should undergo statistical analyses, and the resulting statistics would help interpret the impact of interventions.

Whitfield: "In summary, patterns of improvement with this self-report data were evident with four anger control training clients. One student displayed a negative pattern of change from baseline to intervention phase and three students' data patterns were ambiguous or unchanged" (p. 407). No statistical analyses were conducted.

Weisz & Black: Compared the "students' pretest and posttest scores to determine any immediate effects" and compared the "intervention and comparison group students at follow-up six months after the program ended" (p. 95). The authors used t-tests and ANOVA statistics for these analyses across groups.

Andrews, et al.: To compare the frequency of suspensions under the two conditions, the authors conducted a CM-Square analysis. No statistical analyses were conducted with the survey data. The authors simply presented percentage distributions across the various questions.

In sum, these studies illustrate the tremendous variations that exist in evaluation studies. What we wish to emphasize is the importance of the stepwise process in that it will guide the evaluator through the questions that need to be answered prior to implementation of an evaluation study.

Measurement Issues

"Measurement is controversial" (Smith & Glass, 1987, p. 82). Yet, along with selecting a study design, no other evaluation question is as important as determining the appropriate outcome measures. Although measurement has been defined as "nothing more than a systematic procedure to assign numbers to objects" (Berk & Rossi, 1999, p. 16), the practical questions of selection are far less elegant. Measurement is not an end to itself; it must serve a purpose helping the decision process in an evaluation. As with research design, there is a rich literature on measurement and related issues, including some excellent volumes on collections of instruments (see, for example, Fischer & Corcoran, 2007; Lake, Miles, & Earler, 1973; Miller, 1991; Nugent, Sieppert, & Hudson, 2001; Robinson, Shaver, & Wrightsman, 1991; Sederer & Dickey, 1996).

Berk and Rossi (1999) suggested that a " 'good' measure is, in commonsense terms, one that is likely to measure accurately what it is supposed to measure" (p. 16). We will add to that a good measure will be even better if it will accurately measure what it is supposed to measure over and over again. In other words, the better the validity and reliability of a measure, the greater the probability of a better evaluation. With this caveat in mind, and reminding the reader to go to the various resources on measurement, we will highlight some critical issues related to the selection of a measurement strategy.

In deciding on a measure or measurement strategy, four basic questions need to be answered (see Jayaratne & Levy, 1979):

What do you measure? Typically references variables (outcome, process, or both), that need to be monitored.

When do you measure? A decision needs to be made about the points at which measurement should occur.

Who does the measuring? Refers to the fact that a determination has to be made about the sources of information?

With what do you measure? Once a decision has been made about what to measure, another decision has to be made about the selection of appropriate instrumentation.

Radin (1988) identified a number of different ways to measure variables for the purposes of evaluating school social work practice. Any given evaluation may utilize one or a number of these modalities as measurement strategies. Among these approaches are the following:

■ *Hard Data*—references objective reports of events such as attendance, grades, police reports, and dropout rates. Such measures are indirect and unobtrusive, and the data may be collected for reasons other than the study in question. However, it is possible that the nature of the problem being evaluated allows for the use of such indicators. The proliferation of management information systems and centralized databases have resulted in literally volumes of data at the individual, family, organization, community, state, and federal levels, much of which are ready for analyses. However, because these data were not necessarily gathered for the primary purpose of evaluating the specific problem or goal under consideration, they may be more indirect in their measurement of attributes. In the realm of research, such data sets are referred to as "secondary data," but within the context of evaluation, they

could indeed play a much more direct role. Consider the following examples:

> Implementation was considered a series of stochastic steps. Measures included (a) number of schools (of seven) to enlist a school staff person to serve as the student ASB group staff advisor; (b) number of schools that organized a drug-abuse focused ASB; (c) number of schools that established a student chair, co-chair, publicity chair, videotape person, and events organizers . . . (Sussman et al., 1997, p. 100)

> For each student in the study, school files and system computer records were used as the source of information regarding the discipline infraction and subsequent punishments. Specifically, the numbers of students referred to detention during time periods of the study and the number of students suspended for failure to serve detention during those time periods were tabulated from the computer data. (Andrews et al., 1998, p. 211)

■ *Tests*—This usually refers to standardized measures such as the SAT, Beck Depression Inventory, final examination score, IQ, etc. There is a presumption of objectivity and fairness that is attributed to such tests, but this has been brought into question by researchers. Within the practice arena, however, psychological testing is commonplace and frequently used as an assessment device for purposes of diagnosis or problem presence. Consider the following examples:

> Data on self-esteem, empathy, communication skills . . . were collected using paper and pencil tests. Self-esteem was measured by the 25 item Short Form of the Coopersmith Self-Esteem Inventory, and . . . Empathy was measured by the 10 item empathy subscale of the Social Skills Rating System. (Westhues, Clarke, & Watton, 2001, p. 483)

> At the beginning of the 1998–09 school year, the principal of the Carmen School announced that the school would be re-engineered if standardized test scores did not improve. In order to avoid dismissal of the teaching and administration staff 25 percent of the student population must perform at grade level on the ITBS (Iowa Test of Basic Skills). (Terzian, 2002, p. 282)

■ *Observations*—This requires identifying a specific behavior or group of behaviors, training someone to identify these behaviors, designating the location or locations for the observation, and identifying time periods for *observation.* This process, therefore, is sometimes referred to as structured observation. In theory, this strategy could lead to relatively objective information if the behaviors are sufficiently defined and the behaviors are being observed unobtrusively by more than one person. In practice, however, observational data are often gathered from parents about their children and teachers about students in a class, for example. In addition, participant observation is also a common practice in which participants in a group session, for example, may provide information on other group members. These latter types of behavioral assessment are more likely to result in biased data, although they have the potential to be validated. Consider the following examples:

> The Staff Daily Report was another weekly repeated measure.... Essentially, the SDR was a behavioral count of the aggressive episodes and the specific instances of rules violations. In calculating these scores, the severity of the offense was not being rated but whether a specific problem occurred or not. (Whitfield, 1999, p. 405).

> The direct observations were conducted using the Student Teacher Interaction Profile (STIP).... The STIP requires the observer to code the student's behavior for 15 seconds and then code the teaching staff's behavior for the next 15 seconds. Student behaviors were coded in to categories including appropriate behavior, off-task behavior, mildly disruptive behavior, severely disruptive behavior, and other behaviors. (Gerdtz, 2000, p. 101)

■ *Rating Scales*—refer to self-reports or reports by others on the intensity, frequency, or magnitude of specific behaviors and feelings. These types of indicators are widely used to, for example, have a student self-rate their level of anxiety on a 1 to 10 scale or in studies using peer ratings of popularity. Sometimes these are

not standardized and validated measures but rather serve the function of providing self-reported, observed, or perceived changes in some client characteristic in a specific manner. Consider the following:

> Parent involvement was measured through the use of a survey.... There were four questions measuring the parents' level of involvement. These questions asked how often parents communicated with teachers, participated in school activities, talked to their children about school, and helped their children with homework. Responses were on a six-point scale ranging from "every day" to "a few times a year. (Neely-Barnes, 1999, p. 33)

> The extent to which ... school-related behaviors and attitudes had changed as a result of being mentored was measured by the administration of the Child Behavior Checklist ... completed by foster parents, and the School Attitude Measure ... and a mentee satisfaction questionnaire completed by the mentees. (Altshuler, 2001, p. 19)

■ *Questionnaires*—typically respondents answer a series of questions about a variety of topics in questionnaires, which may be self-administered or administered by another. In general, survey questions have no right or wrong answers but are used to obtain information about respondents' feelings, beliefs, values, etc., in given areas. This is perhaps the most common method of collecting data in the evaluation of school social work. Done well, questionnaires provide exceedingly useful data. Done poorly, they can provide misleading and erroneous information. Consider the following examples:

> A survey instrument was used to obtain students' perceptions of various prevention strategies. Students gave each strategy letter grades (consistent with the grading system used in their schools) and quantified on a Likert-type scale for statistical analyses. (Lisnov, Gibb, & Safer, 1998, p. 303)

> After project implementation, 15 of 16 health educators evaluated their role as linking agent by completing an open-ended questionnaire that

addressed three main evaluation questions. The first question assessed support activities provided by the researchers. The second question evaluated time spent on the project and the advantages and disadvantages of participation. (Dijkstra, de Vries, & Parcel, 1993, p. 340)

■ *Interviews*—Personal interviews may be conducted with students, teachers, parents, and others to examine observed changes in behavior, feelings, and thoughts. These interviews may be open ended, where the individual is free to express their answers about the questions asked as they see fit, or they may be more structured, where the response options are generally guided. In either case the clients have the opportunity to express their views, and the evaluators have the opportunity to design the questions and obtain information directly from relevant parties. Consider the following examples:

> Within two weeks after the curriculum was completed, classroom teachers who taught the curriculum were interviewed at school by a trained TEENS evaluation staff member to assess their perceptions of the curriculum, including effectiveness of peer leaders and responsiveness of the students. (Story et al., 2002, p. 124)

> To obtain mentees' perspectives with respect to their expectations regarding the program and their relationship with their mentors, individual audiotaped interviews employing a standardized set of open-ended questions were conducted in a community meeting room. (De Anda, 2001, p. 99)

■ *Self-Reports*—Once a problem or goal is defined, changes may be monitored and measured through daily logs, behavior checklists, or questionnaires. The particular measures may be individualized or previously published and validated instruments. By definition, self-report requires the individual to report about himself or herself or to report their observations of others and therefore have the distinct advantage of being able to gather data in the natural environment. Although it is indeed possible to collect such information systematically, this method too

is subject to bias, subjectivity, and idiosyncratic judgment. However, self-reports are widely used and increasingly employed in evaluation studies as one type of outcome measure. Consider the following examples:

> At the end of the TEENS curriculum, peer leaders completed an evaluation form to assess their perception of being a peer leader. The form listed 16 attitudinal and behavioral statements (with which the students expressed the degree of agreement or disagreement). (Story et al., 2002, p. 123)

> In focus groups and interviews, stakeholder perceptions about four topics of interest were investigated. (1) Positive aspects of the program, (2) suggestions for improving services, (3) how to reach youth in need of mental health services (e.g., the "hard to reach student"), and (4) ideas for measuring treatment outcomes. (Nabors, Reynolds, & Weist, 2000, p. 4)

■ *Simulations and Graphics*—Simulations present hypothetical situations to a client and solicit responses to these situations. For example, a student may be asked how she would respond to a situation where there is a physical attack by one student on another in the playground, and there is no adult present. Graphics use a model or picture to generate information about feelings related to another person's situation. Graphics as assessment devices are typically used with younger children. For example, a child may be presented with a picture of scene in a family and asked to describe his feelings about the picture. His responses are recorded by him on a line-drawn face as either a smile, frown, or neutral expression. These types of assessment devices are less common and are more prone to alternative interpretations.

Selection of Instruments

Within the categories of measurement noted earlier, the utility of a particular instrument or strategy will depend on (a) its relevance and appropriateness to target group or situation;

(b) ease of administration; (c) ease of interpretation; (d) reliability and validity; (e) sensitivity to change; and (f) cost (see, for example, Royse et al., 2010). The "golden rule" is to measure the same concept (problem or goal) in more than one way using valid and reliable measures as much as possible. By using a multiple measurement strategy, one can increase the likelihood of obtaining better quality and more accurate data. For example, Gerdtz (2000) described the following multiple measurement strategy he used in evaluating an autistic child: "The descriptive analysis had the following components: direct observations of RS in a number of different classrooms during the school day, interviews with RS, interviews with teachers and other teaching staff, and review of school records" (p. 101). This type of assessment is likely to result in a more complete and better report on how the child is doing than any one of these reports alone would have achieved.

As a social worker assesses a client and evaluates practice, he or she must integrate a subjective intimate knowledge of the client and his or her environment with an objective grasp of the critical variables. For example, the social worker first can use qualitative methods to achieve a grounded, subjective understanding of the client's situation and then determine which aspects must be measured quantitatively.... Then, the social worker can draw on quantitative methods to provide the data baseline necessary to gain an understanding of the frequency and occurrence of selected variables. These data help shape and guide the intervention. Finally the social worker may return to either qualitative or quantitative data-collection techniques to asses the effects of intervention. Each step of the social work process requires specific knowledge and data requirements that could fall into either or both of the paradigms. (Allen-Meares & Lane, 1990)

One of the key tasks to be considered when one is conducting an evaluation is selecting the most appropriate instrument. "It is measurement of the client's problem that allows feedback on the success or failure of treatment efforts.... It helps standardize and objectify both research

and practice.... Because formal measurement procedures provide some of the best bases for evaluating what we do, they are essential components of responsible, accountable practice."

Several principles underlie sound measurements. A good measurement instrument is one that is reliable—meaning that it consistently measures the same entity in the same way, over time. It is valid, meaning that it accurately assesses the phenomenon that it is designed to assess. For example, a self-concept scale should measure self-concept and not depression or another phenomenon. Many of the instruments used to evaluate clinical practice, in particular, are not completely reliable or valid; therefore, it is prudent for the practitioner to review the data and/or information on the development of the measurement/instrument to ascertain its degree of validity and reliability and any unique aspect that would bear on its use in the practice.

When Goals or Outcomes Are Not Achieved

Examination of the process *used* is one avenue to follow in identifying why the outcome was not achieved. Some of the following possibilities may also be involved.

1. A common error in writing the goals and outcomes is to describe the intervention to be used instead of identifying the change desired. For example, if the social worker wants to increase parenting skills and the parent's knowledge of available resources, the objective is correctly stated if written, "To increase parenting skills and knowledge of available resources," rather than wording the objective, "To provide programs to parents for their education," which reflects the intervention to be used.

2. Is the objective realistic and attainable? For example, Johnny was referred for social work services by his third-grade teacher because his reading level remained low despite the use of various teaching techniques. Social work assessment of Johnny showed ability to

achieve academically, but identified low self-esteem as a major barrier. The social worker believed that once Johnny felt better about himself, his reading would improve and designed interventions accordingly. Responding to the teacher's referral, the social worker wrote the following: "To increase Johnny's reading score to grade level by the end of the semester." At the end of the semester, not only has his reading ability not changed, but self-reports from Johnny and tests and observation of the teacher indicated that Johnny was depressed. Specifying the *goal* to increase reading level by the next school year with the *outcome* stated, "To reduce depression," would provide an achievable step toward the larger goal.

3. Would a different intervention or combination of interventions be more appropriate? There are times when the objective is clear, but the intervention chosen is just not the right one to do the job.

We do note the increasing use of standardized outcome measures by members of related disciplines. A national survey of psychologists found that over one third routinely used some form of formal outcome measure in practice, for initial assessment purposes, of course, but also for evaluating individual client changes over the course of treatment (see Hatfield & Ogles, 2004). The more commonly used measures included rapid assessment instruments to appraise anxiety, depression, behavior, health, and structured clinical interviews used to help arrive at a formal diagnosis. Social workers, too, are being told that incorporating such measures into their practice can be a very useful undertaking, and it certainly facilitates for formal evaluation of the outcomes of school social work (see Jayaratne & Levy, 1979; Thyer & Myers, 2007).

Having presented something of the general principles of measurement and evaluation, we will next provide an overview of some of the more common types of research designs that school social workers can adopt in appraising the outcomes of their services.

Selected Types of Single-System Designs Useful in Evaluating School Social Work Services

Single-system designs that are useful for evaluating the outcomes of school social work practice have really only two requirements. The first is that you be able to locate and apply some outcome measure related to the student's functioning that is both reliable and valid. The second requirement is that you be able to apply this outcome measure (e.g., assess the client's functioning) repeatedly over time. If you can meet these two requirements, then the door is open for you to evaluate your own practice.

The section of one or more proper outcome measures is the essential first step, and you have really only three options: to measure the client's observable behavior; to measure client self-reports of behavior, thinking, or feelings; or to measure some aspect of the client's physiological functioning (e.g., drug screens). For most problems, measuring the observable actions of the client possesses an appealing sense of "face validity." Coming to school is a compelling indicator of the success or failure of intervention aimed at promoting school attendance. Academic performance as assessed by the student's grades is another. Disciplinary referrals should decrease if the presenting problem is classroom misbehavior and you are trying to help the student achieve greater self-control. Direct observations are the most compelling, but practicality dictates that we sometimes rely on surrogates or make use of indirect measures, as in teachers' or parents' reports on the student's conduct.

Whenever the student's overt behavior is a part of the presenting issue, then serious consideration should be given to directly assessing behavior, preferably in its natural environments (e.g., the classroom, the playground, at home). A little searching will disclose a rather large literature on various methods for reliably and validly assessing client behavior (Fischer & Gochros, 1975; Gambrill, 1987; Hudson & Thyer, 1987; Polster & Collins, 1993) and the informed school social worker will want to learn of these methods. Technological advances can assist in this process. Parents can keep track of their child's whereabouts via computer-assisted GPS tracking linked to the child's cell phone or automobile, for example. Unobtrusive camera monitoring systems can record events occurring within the house (teenage parties?) while the parents are away, and two-way interactive cameras attached to laptop or person computers permit visual contacts with youth in ways not imagined several decades ago.

The measurement of clients' reports of their attitudes, feelings, beliefs, and thoughts is challenging, but if properly carried out, it is immensely valuable as a measure of evaluating one' practice. Fischer and Corcoran (2007) provided us with hundreds of examples of previously published scales by which we can undertake such measurement across a very wide array of practice problems, including, among many others, constructs such as self-control, trauma, loneliness, depression, eating and weight concerns, self-esteem, self-concept, suicidality, child–parent relationships, and so on. In general it is not a good idea for the individual school social worker to try to develop a formal scale or questionnaire from scratch, if a satisfactory one already exists somewhere in the literature.

The assessment of physiological measures is not usually a part of school social work practice, but there may be selected circumstances where this is valuable. The widespread availability of low-cost urine tests for drug use that can be a valuable adjunct to substance abuse counseling efforts is one example. Social workers can make use of biofeedback as a therapy that can record brain wave activity, skin responsivity, and muscle tension as potentially useful indicators of client functioning. Such biofeedback therapies are being provided (ahead of the evidentiary curve, it must be admitted) by social workers to treat youthful problems such as attention-deficit disorder, hyperactivity, and anxiety.

Once you have chosen your outcome measure(s) (it can be a good idea to have more than one), the next step is to actually apply the outcome measure with your client repeatedly over time.

Doing this only twice is not usually considered an adequate number of times for your evaluation to be truly considered an SSD, but there are no rules set in stone as to how many data points you need. Generally, the more the better. Making a determination of client change is a function not only of the numbers of data points, but also of the validity of the outcome measure you have chosen and of the quality of the data you have obtained. Some measures are inherently more labile than others, being highly influenced by social desirability factors, the student's desire to please the school social worker, or their generally unreliable nature. Others measures are made of sterner stuff, so to speak. Direct measures of performance or behavior are generally more credible than client self-reports, as in demonstrated ability to solve math problems as opposed to self-reported confidence in solving math problems.

Designs for Evaluation

Fitz-Gibbon and Morris (1987) defined an evaluation design as "a plan which dictates when and from whom measurements will be gathered during the course of an evaluation" (p. 9). Presumably, if you go through the stepwise procedures stated earlier, you should have a good sense of when and how data should be gathered. Although there are many designs to choose from, and many that are desirable given the questions you want answered, only two or three will probably work in a particular situation. Numerous books describe the different designs and their relative strengths and weaknesses (see, for example, Alter & Evens, 1990; Bloom et al., 1999; Campbell & Stanley, 1963; Cook & Campbell, 1979; Royse et al., 2010; Thyer & Myers, 2007; Weiss, 1998; Yegidis & Weinbach, 2005). Readers are strongly advised to look at these and other resources prior to designing and implementing an evaluation study because issues around validity of designs, generalizability of information, selecting subjects, and so on will be addressed in most of these texts on evaluation research. As such, this chapter will not go into the details of all of these designs and will introduce only those that are considered to be of pragmatic value within the general context of evaluation.

Next we describe the general features of some of the more common single-system designs and outline how some of these have been used in actually evaluating school social work services and programs.

The B Design. The B design consists of selecting a reliable and valid outcome measure of client functioning and to begin measuring client functioning at the same time treatment begins. In single-system terminology, the treatment period is called a B phase. This concurrent process of assessment and treatment continues until school social service services are discontinued, although measurements may be retaken to assess follow-up status. By displaying the data on a simple line graph, it is generally easy for the social worker, the student, and others to see if the outcome measure is improving, degrading, or not really changing. This is an excellent design in that it is relatively simple to use, intrudes minimally into the interventive process, and can provide very clear information, supplementing the school social worker's clinical narrative of the process and progress of treatment. A limitation is that you do not know if the student's issue (problem, strength, skill, ability) is already improving or maybe getting worse, before you begin intervention. Thus, if the client improves, it is possible they were getting better already at the time you began intervention. Social worker William Butterfield used this B design to evaluate the outcomes of a tutoring program to help a 14-year-old culturally deprived Hispanic youth acquire better reading skills (see Staats & Butterfield, 1965). Over the course of 4½ months of simple reinforcement-based intervention, the student learned 430 new words, increased his reading skills 2½ grade levels, and misbehavior dropped from a very high rate to zero. The results were dramatic, easy to understand, and plausibly linked to the services he received.

Social worker Alice Sluckin also used a B design to evaluate behavioral treatment provided to a 10½-year-old girl who was referred due to secondary nocturnal enuresis. The referral was elicited due, in part, to voiding problems occurring while the client attended school. Treatment consisted of some simple psychoeducation content and the parent's use of a bell-and-pad nighttime enuresis alarm. Treatment and data collection of nighttime enuresis began concurrently. The first week the student wet the bed at night three times, the second week only once, and none at all for weeks 3 to 6, after which formal treatment was discontinued. The data were displayed in a simple line graph and provided a nice visual supplement to the social worker's narrative description of the case (see Sluckin, 1989).

The A-B Design. The A-B design consists of similarly selecting a reliable and valid outcome measure of client functioning, but in delaying treatment a bit so that some pretreatment measures of functioning can be obtained. In this way you can see if there is any preexisting tendency of the outcome measure to be improving or deteriorating, prior to beginning treatment. This pretreatment period of assessment is called a baseline phase of a single-system design and is also known as an A phase, hence the A-B design refers to taking a formal baseline prior to beginning treatment. This approach was used by Roderick, Pitchford, and Miller (1997) to evaluate aggressive playground behavior of elementary schoolchildren. A 5-day baseline of playground aggression (defined as kicking and hitting) was taken, then a schoolwide raffle system was introduced and explained to the children, whereby children who played cooperatively without fighting would receive a raffle ticket after every play period and at the end of the school term all tickets would be entered into a bin and one randomly selected to win a prized toy. Raffle tickets were distributed by teachers. Data were collected postintervention, after the raffle program was put into place, for the 5 days at the end of the term. Observed kicks per day dropped 75%, from 49 to 12, and hits were reduced by 47%, from 17 to 9.

A series of A-B designs was completed by Franklin, Biever, Moore, Clemons, and Scamardo (2001) to evaluate the outcomes of providing solution-focused therapy to children in a school setting, students with learning disabilities and classroom behavior problems. Students were referred to the school social worker and following a series of baseline assessments, the students were provided with 5 to 10 sessions of solution-focused brief treatment. There were clear, observable, and positive changes in five of the seven students, suggesting the potential effectiveness of this approach for use by school social workers.

A useful variation of the prospective use of gathering baseline data for an A-B study is to take advantage of existing data that are sometimes available to construct a retrospective baseline. Existing student records may provide legitimate information on attendance, tardiness, disciplinary referrals, academic progress, and so on. If one or more of these variables is useful as an outcome measure of school social work services, they can be used and possess the advantage of not requiring any delay in beginning formal intervention.

The A-B-C Design.   The A-B-C design tacks on a third phase of evaluation, with C representing another treatment condition, something completely different from B, which is discontinued at the end of the B phase. B and C could represent two legitimate approaches to intervention, or B could represent a placebo-type treatment, if one wished to see if treatment C was any more effective than a placebo intervention. For example, a B phase may involve one-to-one tutoring, which could be subsequently compared with student progress using a computer-assisted learning program (the C phase).

The A_1-B_1-A_2 Design.   This design is used in an attempt to determine one of two things: "Did any treatment gains observed during the B phase maintain during the second A phase?" or "Did any treatment gains observed during the B phases deteriorate during the second A phase?" The first outcome (gains maintained in the absence of treatment) is very good to find out from a clinical perspective. After all, we would like to see clients remain improved following the discontinuation of

social work intervention. The second outcome is, perhaps perversely, useful to find out because it enhances the likelihood that the treatment gains observed during the B phase were really, after all, truly caused by the social work intervention. In this circumstance, the internal validity (plausibility of concluding that treatment caused any improvements) of the A_1-B_1-A_2 design is superior to that of the A-B design. This is because we have two demonstrations of an apparent functional relationship between treatment and clinical change. The first is when treatment is introduced and the client improves. The second is when treatment is halted, and the client regresses. This is bad clinically, but good in terms of enhancing our confidence that B was responsible for those improvements.

This design was used by Moffitt, Chorpita, and Fernandez (2003) to treat a 12-year-old multiracial girl with school refusal, a serious problem often encountered by school social workers (see Thyer & Sowers-Hoag, 1986). Following a comprehensive assessment, cognitive behavior therapy was begun. In the 4 weeks prior to treatment, the girl had attended only 19% of her classes. After 5 weeks she was attending 45% of her classes. During the second A phase, after which treatment had been discontinued, she was attending 76% of her classes. "Therapy" involved only seven actual sessions, combined with intensive phone contact with the family and school. Another example of using this design can be found in the evaluation of the clinical outcomes of teaching social skills to two adolescents with severe disabilities, attending an integrated school setting (see Nientimp & Cole, 1992).

The A_1-B_1-A_2-B_2 Design.   By now you should be able to figure out what the A_1-B_1-A_2-B_2 single-system design consists of. Following a regular A-B design, the first B phase is discontinued, and the baseline condition (A) is reinstated to see if client functioning relapses. If it does, this provides greater evidence that B truly caused any improvements seen during the first B phase. If, when B is reinstated during the second B phase, the client improves again, then you have very

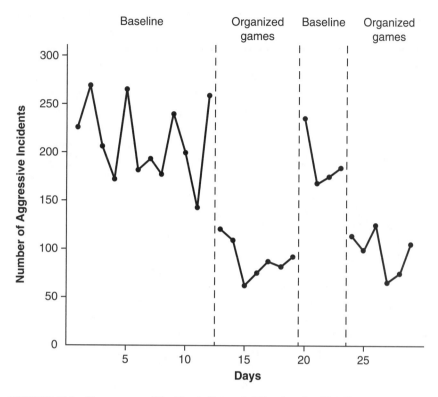

FIGURE 12.1 Frequency of Incidents Recorded During the 20-Minute Morning Observation Periods in the Playground. Murphy et al. (1983). Behavioral school psychology goes outdoors: The effect of organized games on playground aggression. *JABA, 16,* 29–35. Reprinted with permission.

plausibly provided evidence not only that the client improved, but that the treatment B *caused* this improvement. This is a very nice position for a school social worker to be in. This design was used at one school to try to help deal with a perennial problem, that of school bullying. Baseline measures of bullying behavior were taken over 12 days via directed structured and unobtrusive observations of schoolchildren during free time at recess. Child-to-child aggression was very high. This was followed by the deliberate introduction of an intervention it was hoped would reduce bullying, namely structured games (e.g., racing, jumping rope), organized by a college student aide. This first B phase lasted 7 days. Aggression plummeted. The games were discontinued for a 4-day baseline period (the second A phase).

Aggression dramatically increased, and then following reinstatement of a second B phase lasting 6 days, aggression dramatically dropped again. The data for this study are depicted in Figure 12.1, and it is clear that the simple introduction of structured games dramatically reduced bullying, relative to that observed during free time. See Murphy, Hutchison, and Bailey (1983) for further details of this study.

The B_1-A-B_2 Design. Once you understand the fundamentals of single-system designs, you can adapt them to practice circumstances pretty readily. The B_1-A-B_2 can be used to evaluate an existing program. Measures are taken of some outcome measure while the existing program is in place, the B_1 phase, then the program is discontinued while the outcome measures continued to be assessed (the A phase). If big changes occur (the situation gets worse) during the A phase relative to the B_1 phase, it is tempting to believe that this proves that B is helpful. But to be certain, you can reinstate B (the B_2 phase) and see if things improve. If they do, then you have much stronger grounds for believing that B is a helpful intervention. This design was used by Bushell, Wrobel, and Michaelis (1968) with 12 young children in summer school. The outcome measure was the percentage of time the kids were engaged in studying during 20 consecutive days of 75-minute classes. The behavioral observations were structured and reliable. The "normal" practice of the teacher was to permit the children to participate in a "special event" (a short movie, trip to a park, a gym class, etc.) after class, *if* the children had earned sufficient tokens for study behavior during class. It was an open question whether this token system was really needed to maintain the kids' studying. Data were recorded for 9 days, with percentage time spent studying as the outcome measure, across all 12 children, under the "normal" condition of earning tokens for studying well and gaining access to the special event after class if a given child had sufficient tokens. Study behavior was pretty high, occurring about 67% of the time. This was followed by a 7-day period in which the children got to participate in the special event regardless of their studying. During this A phase, studying declined to about 42% of the time. Then, the original condition was reestablished, again requiring the children to earn sufficient tokens via studying to attend the special event, a B_2 phase lasting 4 days, during which period the percentage of time spent studying increased on average to 64%, close to that observed during the B_1 phase. The visually graphed data was pretty compelling (see Figure 12.2), leading one to conclude that making access to the special event contingent on studying really did promote studying.

The Multiple-baseline Across Subjects Design.

The multiple-baseline (MBL) across subjects design is useful in practice circumstances where the effects of intervention can be presumed to be irreversible. Some school social work interventions such as insight-oriented counseling, tutoring, social skills training, memorization exercises, and teaching academic skills are liable to produce changes that are pretty durable, even when the intervention is discontinued, thus an A-B-A-B design, which depends on client relapse to establish whether or not treatment caused any observed improvements, is not very useful in this circumstance. The MBL can be then considered. It requires at least two clients (students?) with a *similar* problem who are referred for treatment at the same time. Appropriate outcome measures are selected, and a baseline is begun with both students (call them Mary and Paula). When both baselines are stable, intervention is begun with Mary, but not Paula. If Mary improves, after some time (the exact period is dictated by the stability of the kids' data and the urgency for intervention), the *same* intervention is provided to Paula. The logic is something like this. Both students' baselines are stable. Mary (but not Paula) is given treatment, and she improves. Paula does not change. This continues for a while, then Paula is given the same intervention as was Mary, and then, *and only then*, does Paula improve. In such circumstances, it is plausible to argue that treatment caused the changes in both Mary and Paula. This design can be diagrammed as follows:

Mary   A A A A A B B B B B B B B B B

Paula   A A A A A A A A A B B B B B B

The experimental logic of this design depends on having a staggered baseline and of only seeing improvements when treatment B is implemented. If you use baselines of the same length, you do not have a multiple-baseline design; you simply have two A–B designs, which provide less grounds for claiming that treatment caused any observed improvements.

A variation of the multiple baseline across subjects design was used by social worker Karen Sowers to evaluate the effectiveness of a schoolwide safety-belt use curriculum. Conducted in a state that, at the time, did not require that age-appropriate children wear safety belts while being driven in a car, Karen developed a safety belt training curriculum suitable for elementary students attending a private school. Following unobtrusive observations

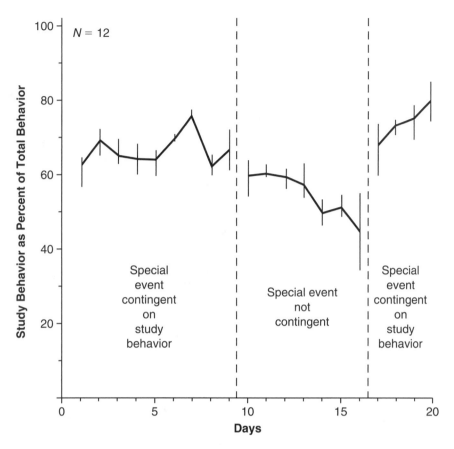

FIGURE 12.2 Mean Percent of 12 Children's Study Behavior Over 20 School Days. Vertical Lines Indicate the Range of Scores Obtained by the Four Observers Each Day.   Bushell et al. (1968). Applying "group" contingencies to the classroom study behavior of preschool children. *JABA*, *1*, 55–61. Reprinted with permission.

of the children's use of seat belts, 16 kids were determined to *never* wear their safety belts when being picked up after school by the parents. These consistent nonusers were the focus of Karen's evaluation. The 16 kids were divided into two groups of eight each, and following a baseline period, the first group received the safety belt use curriculum, whereas the second group did not. Safety belt use increased dramatically for Group 1 as assessed by the kids' unobtrusively observed (adults monitoring student pickups did this) buckling up behaviors after school when being driven home. Safety belt use also increased somewhat in Group 2. (Turns out that two of the children with different last names were actually siblings living together, but were randomly assigned to the two

different groups. When the child in the first group got trained, her changed behavior apparently influenced her brother!) After some time, Group 2 was trained, and they too evidenced dramatic increased in safety belt use. The program was phased out and discontinued, but follow-up assessments a couple of months later revealed consistent and high safety belt use. The data for this multiple-baseline design are presented in Figure 12.3. Look it over carefully and see if you can understand how it is portrayed. Note that the outcome measure is the *percent* of the children in each group who used their safety belts each day, not the numbers of kids (which would vary from day to day). See Sowers-Hoag, Thyer, and Bailey (1987) for more details on this study.

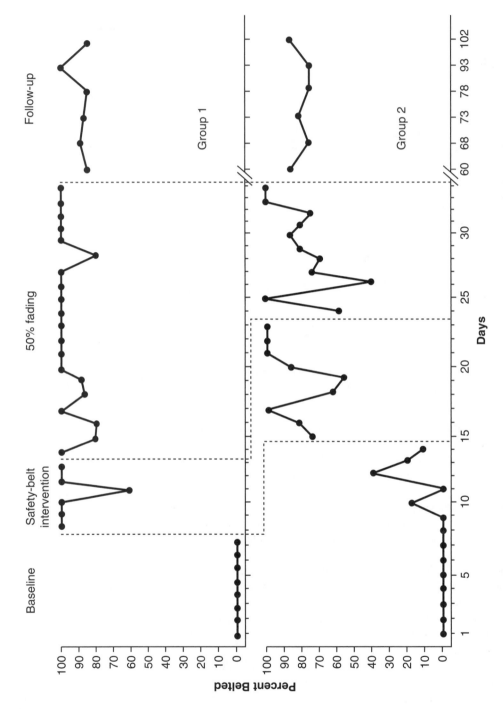

FIGURE 12.3   Percentage of Safety Belt Use of Eight Children in Group 1 and by Eight Children in Group 2.   Sowers-Hoag et al. (1987). Promoting automobile safety belt use by young children. *JABA, 20,* 133–138. Reprinted with permission.

Whitfield (1999), previously cited in this chapter, innovatively used a series of multiple-baseline designs across clients to evaluate a cognitive-behavioral approach to reducing school violence. The previously published and validated intervention consisted of 12 one-hour individually conducted training sessions completed one to two times per week and was provided to eight schoolchildren who were referred to the school social worker because of apparent problems with self-control.

A multiple baseline design across two students provides for greater internal validity than does an SSD involving only one student. A MBL using three students, each with the same problem treated in the same manner, provides potentially even higher confidence in our concluding that treatment was causally responsible for client improvements. There are other variants of the MBL design, such as the MBL design across problems and the MBL across settings, but these are beyond the scope of this chapter. See Bloom et al. (2006) for illustrations.

Combined Single-System Designs. There are few rules relating to creating single-system designs. Although some writers contend that all SSDs must begin with a baseline phase, this is obviously not true, as demonstrated by the descriptions of the B and B_1-A-B_2 designs noted earlier. One flexible standard is that to maximize internal validity, that is to try to be able to isolate the "real" effects of treatment, you should only change one element at a time when shifting phases. For example, if you implement two interventions at the same time, following a baseline phase, this could be diagrammed as a A-(BC) design, with B and C representing two discrete interventions (say 1-1 counseling, plus academic tutoring) applied at the same time. This can be desirable clinically, but if you see any improvements, it is not usually possible to say whether they were caused by intervention B alone, by C alone, or by the combination of (BC). This compromises the study's internal validity. Another flexible standard is to have an A phase inserted between two consecutively applied treatments. For example, if you conduct an A-B-C study, whatever was observed during the C phase

may have been the result of an interaction with the prior B treatment experienced by the client. If you instead used an A-B-A-C design, this potential confounding interaction is reduced.

In general, the construction of an SSD is best guided by the clinical demands of the situation, not by any stringent principles of research design. This will keep the use of this method of evaluation driven by client concerns, which is a good thing, in our opinion.

Selected Group Research Designs for Evaluating School Social Work Practices

Like SSDs, group research designs require the use of one or more reliable and valid outcome measures appropriate to the assessment of your client's functioning. These designs are appropriate when you have enough clients to support the use of simple inferential statistics to analyze your data, with a rough guide being that at least 15 participants per group are necessary. You will recall that SSDs used some abbreviations to diagram those types of designs, with A indicating a baseline phase, B indicating a treatment phase, C indicating a treatment different from B, etc. Group research designs have their own simple abbreviations, with O representing a pretest, or assessment of client functioning, and X indicating the clients' receipt of social work intervention. Y can be used to indicate a treatment different from X, etc. Next we outline some of the more common GRD that can be useful in evaluating school social work programs.

The Pretest-Posttest Design $(O_1\text{-}X\text{-}O_2)$

This design involves having a group of students participate in some sort of assessment process (e.g., filling out a scale, staff recording children's grades, or attendance) before applying a school social work interventive program, and then obtaining the same measures again when the program is completed. This evaluation design was used by social worker Denise Burnette (1998) to evaluate the outcomes of a school-based support group provided to grandparents raising their own grandchildren. An increasing proportion of children are being primarily cared for by their grandparents, older individuals often not anticipating parenting responsibilities later in life. These individuals are often in need of some support to help cope with the demands of parenting, and sometimes school social workers are in a good position to offer some assistance. In this study, a school social worker recruited 11 grandparents of minority children attending elementary school in Brooklyn, New York. The grandparents were, on average, rearing three grandchildren, with one child having special needs. The children's biological parents were often unable to care for their offspring due to problems with substance abuse, HIV-AIDS, or incarceration. In some instances the biological parents had died. The average age of the children was 9 years. The intervention was a series of 90-minute psychoeducational, coping-with-stress and supportive therapy sessions held weekly for 8 weeks. Groups were held at the school during the school day. At the beginning of the first group therapy session, the grandparents completed two previously published and validated outcome measures, one related to general health and the other related to ways of coping. They completed these measures again at the end of the last group session. Simple statistical tests demonstrated that the grandparents' average level of depression had improved as did their sense of social support and several other variables. This was a novel study, reportedly the first to examine the outcomes of a school-based social support group for grandparents raising their own grandchildren. It is important to recognize that the school social worker had no grounds to claim that the social support group *caused* the observed improvements; she could only note that improvements *did* occur. We suggest that the addition of a simple group design like this greatly enhanced the credibility of what the school social worker did. She could buttress her subjective impressions and clinical anecdotes about client improvements with supplemental quantitative data to support her claims. It was relatively easy to administer, score, and analyze the outcome measures, so the design did not place an undue burden on the social worker.

Salloum (2008) provides us with another practical example of using this design, as used to evaluate changes in posttraumatic stress disorder (PTSD) symptomatology experienced by children affected by homicide and other violence. A total of 102 children participated in 21 different therapy groups, provided in 10 different schools located in New Orleans, Louisiana. Children completed a standardized and previously validated measure of PTSD at the beginning of their group work and again when it was concluded. Both statistically significant and clinically meaningful improvements were found following group therapy. Although the author could not claim that group therapy caused these improvements, any time you have clients getting demonstrably better following treatment, this is a hopeful indicator of effectiveness.

Yet another illustration of the O_1-X-O_2 design can be found in Abel and Greco (2008). These social workers developed a school-based abstinence-oriented sex education program intended to promote positive attitudes toward sexual abstinence, self-esteem, ability to resist peer pressure, and attachment to parents. The program was delivered via an 8-week group therapy format and after-school program. A total of 130 children in grades 5 through 9 participated, and completed various assessment measures at the beginning of the program and again at its completion. Positive and statistically significant improvements were found on all measures, comparing pretreatment scores with posttreatment.

Diehl and Frey (2008) improved on the basic pretest/posttest by adding follow-up assessments at 3 and 6 months after the intervention began. The intervention was the students' referral to a community–school program and was focused on ameliorating problematic behavior via the provision of MSW-delivered case management and direct intervention to students and their families. The project involved 12 schools and 11 different social workers (one served two schools), as well as 154 individual students. A previously published and validated behavior rating scale was a major outcome measure, as were scales assessing parent and teacher concerns over the student, and students' concerns for their families. It was found that the parents and teachers reports of the students' behavior problems significantly decreased in the six months following the initiation of school social work services, as did the intensity of their concerns over the student.

The Pretest-Posttest Group Research Design is very widely used. It is an excellent way to answer the question, "Did the students who received school social work services improve following their receipt of those services?" It is not a very good way to try to demonstrate that the students improved *because* of school social work intervention. But sometimes administrators are content with a simple demonstration that students improved, not on proving why they may have gotten better.

The Pretest-Posttest Comparison Group Design

This design is something of an improvement compared to the Pretest-Posttest Design described earlier due to the addition of a comparison group. Using such comparison groups elevates the design to the group of studies called quasi-experiments. It may be diagramed as follows:

Treatment Group $\quad O_1 - X - O_2$

No-Treatment Group $\quad O_1 \quad\quad O_2$

You can see that the O_1 again represents an assessment made of clients prior to beginning the intervention, with O_2 being the same assessment readministered. The dashed line is conventionally used to indicate that the groups were *not* constructed using random assignment procedures. If random assignment methods were used to create two or more groups, the study could be called a true experiment. But if the school social worker used other ways to obtain comparison groups (naturally occurring differences in classrooms or schools, for example), the study is classified as a quasi-experimental outcome study. By examining the demographic variables and pretreatment scores of the two groups, we can see if they are roughly comparable at the point in time before the treatment group gets intervention. Looking at the set of scores, after treatment for the first group, and after an equivalent period of time for

the no-treatment control group, we can see if the treatment group improved more relative to those not receiving treatment and if its posttreatment scores were better than its pretreatment scores.

This approach to evaluating a program was conducted by Viggiani, Reid, and Bailey-Dempsey (2002) to try to ascertain the effectiveness of a task-centered approach to promoting social worker–teacher classroom collaboration. The program was intended to improve the children's attendance, behavior, and grades. Four classes were selected for participation in the project, two kindergarten classes and two third-grade classes, located in the same inner-city elementary school in Albany, New York. One class of each grade was assigned to receive the intervention, whereas the other two did not receive it. The intervention (details in the article) was provided 2 days a week for the second half of the school year. The treatment group demonstrated improved attendance and improvements on 4 of 14 behavioral variables, relative to the no-treatment control group. Subject grade changes, however, did not favor the treatment group.

Franklin, Streeter, Kim, and Tripodi (2007) also used this design in their evaluation of a solution-focused public alternative school aimed at preventing school dropout and retrieving students who had stopped coming to school. Forty-six students attending the alternative school's program were compared with a comparison group of 39 students who did not attend the special program, but who were equally vulnerable on a wide array of dimensions. Outcome measures included attendance, credits earned, and graduation rates. Although comparable at the beginning of the study, students participating in the solution-focused program earned more credits than the comparison group and graduated at a higher rate (90% vs. 62%) A Pretest-Posttest Comparison Group Design was also used by Newsome, Anderson-Butcher, Fink, Hall, and Huffer (2008) in a study involving five secondary schools. Seventy-four children received the experimental school social work intervention and were matched with 71 similar students who did not receive the program. A variety of reliable and valid outcome measures were used to measure risk factors related to poor school performance, and absenteeism was recorded as well, pre-and posttreatment. Posttreatment the students receiving the school social work program demonstrated significant improvements on 4 of 12 measured risk factors, improvements greater than those observed in the control group students. There was no evident impact of school social work intervention on absenteeism itself. Although it was not the hoped-for outcome, it is surely better to know that your program is not working than to remain in ignorance of that fact.

The Randomized Controlled Clinical Trial (RCT)

This design is one of the strongest available in terms of being able to make a compelling claim that school social work services *did* cause any observed improvements. A large group of students are *randomly* assigned to receive a given treatment or to a no-treatment control group condition. Careful assessments are made of client functioning before the intervention is applied and again some time later for both groups. This design can be diagrammed as follows:

$$R \qquad O_1 \ X \ O_2$$
$$R \qquad O_1 \ \ O_2$$

The R before each group indicates that group assignment was made on the basis of some sort of system to ensure randomized allocation, with the top group getting treatment X, and the bottom group not receiving treatment, and both groups being assessed at about the same points in chronological time, roughly pre- and post- the top group receiving treatment. This design can control for the passage of time alone, the possibility of something else in the natural environment happening that affected all the kids (think 9/11), the possibility that kids got a bit better simply because they entered the program in a state of crisis, and can control to some extent for the possible effects of being assessed, absent any formal treatment. The ability to control for or to account for these variables is what makes this design one of the stronger ones to use in program evaluation studies.

The RCT design as described above was used by social worker Juanita Hepler (1994) to evaluate

an 8-week social skills building curriculum provided by social workers and psychologists in a school setting. Twenty-four children with deficiencies in social skills received the formal program, and 20 children were randomly assigned to the no-treatment control group. Four different outcome measures were used to assess the kids' social skills at the beginning of the program and again at its conclusion. Children receiving the program demonstrated a number of improvements in social skills not seen among the control group child immediately posttreatment.

School social worker Rufus Larkin also used a modification of the RCT design to evaluate the outcomes of a cognitive-behavioral treatment group therapy program provided to behaviorally disruptive elementary school students, aimed at improving their self-esteem, self-control, and classroom behavior. Fifty-two children referred to him were randomly assigned to either receive group therapy immediately or later on (Mr. Larkin could not treat all children right away, so a delayed treatment option was not a problem, ethically). His evaluation design looked as follows:

Immediate Treatment
Group ($N = 31$)   R O_1 X O_2 O_3

Delayed Treatment
Group ($N = 21$)   R O_1 O_2 X O_3

Can you follow the logic and design of the preceding diagram? Kids were randomly assigned to the two conditions, and all were assessed (O_1). The first group received group therapy right away (X), whereas the second group had to wait. When group therapy was completed for the first group, both groups were assessed again (O_2). Then the second group received the same group therapy program as did the first group. When this delayed treatment group completed their treatment, both groups were again assessed as before (O_3), permitting an estimate of the immediate improvements of the second group and also to see if the first group's improvements, if any, were maintained at follow-up, after treatment for them had concluded. Roughly speaking, the first group got better after participation in group therapy, whereas the second (delayed treatment) group did not improve. Then the second group also then improved, but only after they in turn received group therapy. At follow-up, the first group's treatment gains had been maintained. Using a delayed treatment group as a control, and then providing them with the same treatment, is a feature called a cross-over design. All in all, this is a pretty powerful approach, permitting the conclusion that the school social work intervention was indeed causally responsible for the improvements in the children's behavior, self-esteem, and self-control (see Larkin & Thyer, 1999, for further details). Other examples of RCTs being used to evaluate school programs offered by social workers include Leslie Tutty's (2000) evaluation of a sexual abuse prevention program, with 231 elementary school children randomly assigned to receive the curriculum, or to a waiting list condition. Letendre, Henry, and Tolan (2003) described a rather large-scale experimental study of the effects of prosocial skill building groups provided to 794 schoolchildren in Chicago, in terms of their effects on reducing aggression.

Another example is found in Harris and Franklin (2003), who were able to randomly assign 85 pregnant or parenting Mexican-American girls to a cognitive-behavioral group intervention or to a control group (regular case management services) to evaluate whether or not the experimental treatment could help improve school attendance, problem-solving skills, grades, and adolescent coping skills. Group treatment was provided via eight weekly 1-hour sessions, and measures were obtained pretreatment, posttreatment, and at 6 weeks follow-up. Participants in the experimental treatment group had statistically and substantively greater improvements, compared to those students receiving regular case management services.

Preparing an End-of-the-Year Summary Report

Another approach to evaluating the processes and outcomes of school social work services is to create an end-of-year report. An end-of-the-year report can serve several purposes by "assessing effectiveness of one's interventions" and "interpreting the effectiveness of social work service to administrators of the local education agency and other appropriate persons" (NASW, 1992). Such a report provides valuable data about client characteristics and changes achieved, all of which lays the groundwork for the development of a plan of work for the next year. In addition, when a summative report is submitted to administration, the contribution of social work service is substantiated. In times of financial retrenchment, when jobs are on the line, social workers often scramble to defend their worth. Evaluating outcomes of social work interventions and presenting them to administration or the public not only increases the understanding of social work services, but also enhance the image of the school.

The social worker evaluates the plan of service developed at the beginning of the year, which includes IEP, end-of-the-year, and service reports that map the progress of special education clients (see Table 12.1). A summary report of the data and information regarding individual clients can provide the administrator with information about reasons for referrals, patterns of service requests, effective interventions, and any other types of information that may be relevant. The section headed "Outcome Evaluation of Individual Referrals" in Table 12.1 illustrates this work. The same recording system used in developing IEPs also provides an appropriate format for recording the progress of both special and general education students and any changes in program or home situation. Outcome evaluations of these services are determined by the use of the various evaluation frameworks discussed previously. As mentioned earlier, gathering data and writing these reports are less tedious and time consuming with the aid of computer technology to record data and analyze results.

Each school social worker or administrative unit develops its own format for an end-of-the-year report. The social worker's report depicted in Table 12.1 organized her summary in five parts: (1) introduction; (2) report of outcome evaluation of the service plan developed at the beginning of the year; (3) indirect outcome summary; (4) outcome of evaluation of individual referrals; and (5) recommendations for the next school year.

TABLE 12.1   Sample of an End-of-Year-Report for School Social Work Services—Epsilon School

Introduction: By the fourth week of the school year a social work service plan was prepared based on recommendations from the previous year. The plan, which was designed to contribute to the accomplishment of goals of Epsilon school, was developed by the social worker and principal and accepted by the School-Based Management Team. The following report shows the outcome of this work with recommendations for next year. Social work services were provided by the building school social worker (2 days a week) and two graduate social work interns (2 days a week each).

Report of Outcomes of Epsilon School Social Work Service Plan
Target #1

Objective
To increase coping ability of students moving from one school or educational program to another by facilitating the transition process.

Intervention
1. Developed, trained, and monitored a welcoming committee of student volunteers who also served as "buddies" throughout the semester.
2. Discussed the program at three faculty meetings.
3. Conducted four class meetings in the receiving school.
4. Consultation with teachers.
5. Prepared pamphlet for parents on ways to support child at the time of a move.

Data Collection
1. Observation reports of teachers.
2. Self-reports of students.
3. Rating scale on entrance to school or program and at end of first marking period completed by current teacher.

Outcome
1. Only 5% of students in transition program required continued support.
2. Fewer referrals of students due to inability to cope with change in program.

Target #2

Objective
To increase student afternoon "on-task" behavior of students referred for disruptive behavior by 75%.

Intervention
1. Recruited university fraternity to provide activities during lunchtime.
2. Monitored the program with the principal.

Data Collection Methods
1. Reports of teachers re: behaviors of students in p.m.
2. Overall program evaluation: (see program evaluation report).

Outcome
There was a significant change in behavior of 85% of the referred disruptive students. The remaining 15% required additional service.

Target #3

Objective
To increase completion of homework by referred students living in X apartment house by 75%.

Interventions
1. Arranged with the apartment manager to provide a room for students to do homework.
2. Recruited five parents to supervise.
3. Met with parents and teachers to discuss ways to help students with homework.

Data Collection Methods
Teacher's records of completed homework of participating students.

Outcome
Objective was surpassed. All students turned in homework 80% of the time, with half exceeding that amount.

Target #4

Objective
To increase positive relationships among program for teachers on teachers, students, and parents.

Interventions
1. Developed in-service program for teachers on interviewing skills.
2. Arranged for a graduate credit university course on classroom management.
3. Acted as member of planning committee for the week at camp for fourth and fifth graders.

Data Collection Methods
1. Questionnaires completed by teachers, parents, and students and informal interviews.
2. Evaluation of camp program by school.

Outcome
1. Increased parent participation at open house in spring and attendance at parent–teacher conferences.
2. Principal reported an increase in home visits by teachers.
3. Pupil school attendance increased by 10%.

Target #5

Objective
To increase age-appropriate verbal communication skills among six siblings of the Johnson family.

Interventions
1. Twice a week meetings with sibling group for 12 weeks.
2. Collaboration with classroom teachers of the siblings to discuss ways in which they could increase positive verbal interaction and decrease physical interaction.
3. Conferences with Mrs. Johnson to support her to encourage verbal interaction.
4. At termination time, the siblings invited their parents to a lunch they had prepared for them.

Data Collection Methods
1. Time-series design of each sibling in classroom and on playground every 4 weeks.
2. Interview with mother and father re: any changed behaviors. Periodic diagrams of verbal interactions during group sessions.
3. Periodic diagrams of verbal interactions during group sessions.

Outcome
1. One of the twins refused to participate, saying she did not have a problem.
2. Other siblings showed marked improvement in communication skills.
3. The teacher of the kindergarten student felt she was well prepared to succeed in first grade.

Indirect Outcomes
Secondary benefits emerged from the evaluations:

1. Student volunteer mentors (see Target 1) reported increased ability to provide leadership, and the four mentors who were clients achieved objectives previously set with the social worker. Both teachers and student mentors reported more positive relationships with each other.
2. By increasing student afternoon "on-task" behavior (Target 2), not only did the students benefit, but also teachers and the lunchroom aides reported less stress. In addition to providing lunchtime activities, the university students served as role models for the students, and some friendships developed.

(continued)

TABLE 12.1 Continued

3. More homework was completed through the study room in the apartment house (Target 3), and the program also provided opportunity for building a closer working relationship with some of the parents.

4. As positive relationships among teachers, students, and parents increased (Target 4), there was evidence of some increase in parents and teachers volunteering in both school and community projects.

5. Not only did verbal communication skills increase for members of the sibling group (Target 5), but four of the six siblings increased a grade in at least one subject.

6. As the social worker, I feel better accepted in the school and community.

7. The planning, implementation of the plan, and evaluation of outcomes provided a valuable practice experience for the two graduate social work interns.

Outcome Evaluation of Individual Referrals
During the year 75 individual students were referred for social work service; some were identified as requiring additional service through the lunchtime program and the transition program. Assessments of each referred student were processed and recorded utilizing the same format as the Individual Educational Plan requires for special education students. Following the initial assessment process, 15 students were referred to the Special Education Department, and 20 students were referred to child welfare and community agencies. Of the remaining 40 students, the presenting problems focused mainly on underachievement, aggressive behavior, poor social skills, and low self-esteem. As reported earlier, many of these clients benefited from programs in the service plan. Additionally, interventions designed to meet the objectives of each individual included consultation and collaboration with parents and teachers and individual and group counseling. Outcome evaluations showed that 75% of the 150 objectives identified for 40 students had been met within the agreed time limits.

Recommendations for Next School Year
1. Based on the outcome evaluation of the transition program, it is recommended that a student mentor group composed of "experienced" and new mentors be used again next year. Training material is already developed, and the school faculty is familiar with the plan. Social work services would be used to support the mentors and continue as a coordinator of the program. The parent booklets received a favorable response, and changes recommended by teachers and parents will be incorporated.

2. The evaluation of the lunchtime program indicated sufficient benefits to both students and faculty that the faculty requested continuation of the program. There is uncertainty that the same fraternity will be able to provide the service next year. There is a need to explore alternative sources. What about the active Senior Citizen club in the neighborhood? A parent group? In any case recruitment, planning, and monitoring are important tasks for this project to continue.

3. Teachers have identified a number of students with homework problems other than those benefiting from the X apartment house study room. The program was brought before the last meeting of the school–community collaborative seeking additional study room resources. The Boys Club is interested and will be explored as a potential resource by the school social worker and the principal.

4. Continue to support any effort that builds on work accomplished to date to encourage positive, trusting relationships among teachers, students, and parents.

5. Maintain supportive contact with members of the Johnson family.

6. Review of the objectives not accomplished will be made in the fall and incorporated in services provided in the new school year.

A design for service for the next school year will be presented to the School Site-Based Management Team by the fourth week in September. It will be based on the preceding recommendations and additional service needs identified in initial weeks of the fall semester.

Although the sample service report in Table 12.1 sounds glowing, the social worker reported many discouraging events during the school year. Crisis situations that occurred interrupted several of the programs. The university fraternity, at the last minute, hesitated following through on developing the program, and there were times when some members failed to show and there was a scramble to rearrange activities. There were, as is common, those students who did not respond to interventions, and all parent contacts weren't positive, especially in several of the child abuse and neglect situations.

Ethical and Human Subjects Issues in Evaluation

As Babbie (1998) has noted, "Ethics and evaluation are intertwined in many ways" (p. 360). In fact, it is fair to say that evaluation research in the human service arena by its very nature is ripe with ethical dilemmas and issues of human subjects. For services to be evaluated, ethical guidelines must be followed, both by virtue of law and by professional standards. The moment data are collected by a researcher about an individual and that individual has the potential to be identified, we have encountered a situation where that individual has now become the "subject" of inquiry. Before that moment occurs, protocols for the protection of human subjects must be put in place. Broadly speaking, such protocols must include procedures for (a) obtaining voluntary informed consent, (b) protecting subjects from physical or mental harm, (c) ensuring confidentiality, and (d) the provision of information about the nature of interventions, purpose of the study, what will happen to the data, and any known risks and benefits.

Most school districts will have formally constituted human subjects institutional review boards that can provide consultation and assistance in the ethical design of proposed evaluation studies. If your local school board does not have an IRB, the one at your local university may be available to help you. You should note that evaluations on the effectiveness of educational innovations conducted internally and with no intent to publish the results in a journal or to present the findings at a conference may be exempt from IRB review. But you should never assume any proposed evaluation is exempt—always check with the IRB.

Some evaluation strategies are more likely to engender ethical concerns than others, for example, those involving the use of deception, placebo-treatment control groups, unobtrusive observation of students, or the withholding of intervention, may be viewed with particular concern. After all, is it not better to provide some service than none at all? Not necessarily, because some interventions can actually harm clients (see Lilienfeld, 2007). Evaluations of school-based sex education or drug abuse prevention programs may also raise flags of concern, given the sensitive nature of the information being collected. On the other hand, relatively simple evaluations such as a B-design single system study, where behavior monitoring using self-report procedure is employed, may draw little or no attention and, in fact, will be viewed as an example of good practice, as would posttest only or pretest-posttest evaluations of standard educational programs. Needless to say, it is the responsibility of the evaluator to carefully assess the pros and cons of all procedures and to receive the necessary human subjects' approval prior to embarking on the evaluation study.

By definition, evaluation in schools is particularly sensitive, given the participation of minors. The implementation of the *Family Privacy Act* requires explicit written consent from parents or guardians before children can participate in studies where sensitive information (e.g., sexual behavior, psychological problems) is requested. This requirement, in turn, may affect the quality and accuracy of information collected from children. There are, of course, other issues about the very notion of children as subjects, with concerns being raised about labeling and fear of parental reprisals (Gensheimer, Ayers, & Roosa, 1993).

It is an ethical responsibility of the evaluator to present findings to relevant stakeholders in a manner that is comprehensive and comprehensible. As has been noted earlier, evaluation efforts are usually used because someone wants information for decision making. However, it is not uncommon for evaluation results to be downplayed and not have an impact on practice. First, the findings may not always be presented in an understandable manner. The typical consumer will not be a researcher, therefore, to present "path models," and "t-tests" may impress some, but may have little practical impact until these findings are "translated into English." Second, the evaluation findings may contradict or bring into question some fundamental beliefs and attitudes. If someone believes that sex education in school results in greater promiscuity, data to the contrary may have little impact on this individual. To the extent that this individual holds sway over the situation, questions will emerge about "quality of the evaluation" or the "adequacy of the measures." In other words, values will rule the day. Third, the degree of vested interest in a program will make any contrary information unpalatable. It would be very difficult for someone who has invested the time to develop and implement a program and, perhaps, has been told by some participants that is successful to deal with contrary evidence from a more systematic and comprehensive evaluation. Fourth, the entire evaluation, including its defined purpose and methodology, may be brought into question by those with a different agenda. This is most likely to occur in situations where the evaluators did not do their homework and failed to involve relevant stakeholders in the process. Thus, an evaluator must present data as objectively as possible. Decisions will be made, and programs may be changed either as a result or despite the evaluation data.

Conclusion

We hope that this review of relatively simple single-system and group research designs and end-of-year summary reports has illustrated for you their relative value in helping evaluate school social work clinical services and programs. Most evaluation designs can be flexibly adapted to meet the varying demands of practice and can often be undertaken without the need for external funding. School social work is a challenging field. The types of student problems social workers encounter can sometimes be dishearteningly, overwhelming, and seemingly intractable. But then there are times when we are capable of exerting genuinely effective services that markedly improve student well-being and that have positive ramifications throughout the person-in-environment matrix involving teachers, administrators, parents, and other caregivers. The systematic evaluation of school social work services as described in this chapter can be a useful way to augment the clinician's subjective impressions of treatment outcome, can be a way to help modify and improve social work services and programs, and can help provide evidence to stakeholders of the value of the services we perform. By building an accumulation of outcome studies like this, with reasonably solid research designs and with positive results, the evidentiary foundations of school social work practice will become more firmly established, and the credibility of the entire field will be enhanced.

For Study and Discussion _____

1. Design a single-system study to evaluate the outcomes of school social work services provided to an individual student. Chose an outcome measure and describe how data will be collected. Also describe the services provided and the expected results. Draw a simple graph portraying a positive outcome.

2. Design a pre-experimental group research study to evaluate the outcomes of a school social work program provided to an entire grade of students at a particular school. Chose an outcome measure and describe how data will be collected. Also describe the program and the expected results.

3. Describe a quasi-experimental or experimental group research study to use in evaluating the outcomes of a school social work program provided to about half the students in a given grade within one particular school. The other half of the students are not to receive the program. Chose an outcome measure and describe how data will be collected. Also discuss how students will be selected to receive the program or not. Describe the expected results.

4. Separately interview a school social worker and a school administrator, and ask them to identify any concerns they have about social work services in the school. How would you go about confirming these concerns and remedying the conditions?

5. Using a common database such as PsycINFO or Web-of-Science, locate an outcome study on school social work practice published during the past 5 years. Identify the intervention, the outcome measures, the research design, and the results.

Annotated Bibliography of Evaluation Resources

Altschuld, J. W., & Witkin, B. R. (2000). *From needs assessment to action: Transforming needs into solution strategies.* Thousand Oaks, CA: Sage. An introduction to needs assessment strategies is followed by a straightforward discussion on tactics, analysis, and most important, application. This book offers the reader numerous examples of how to conduct needs assessments using mixed methods. The variety of illustrative examples provided offer good ideas on how needs assessments may be conducted in complex settings.

Bloom, M., Fischer, J., & Orme, J. G. (2006). *Evaluating practice: Guidelines for the accountable professional* (5th ed.). New York: Allyn & Bacon. This is perhaps the most comprehensive book currently available on how to evaluate practice using single system research designs. It walks the reader through the various steps in practice evaluation from formulating goals, to developing measures, to the application of a design and evaluating results. The book provides both breadth and depth and would be of singular importance to both administrators and practitioners who wish to evaluate programs as well as practice.

Bowen, G. L., Rose, R. A., & Bowen, N. K. (2005). *The reliability and validity of the school success profile.* Philadelphia, PA.: Xlibris Corporation. This monograph offers a comprehensive measurement tool with broad applicability in a variety of school settings. It contains a series of standardized measures, which together offer a comprehensive assessment instrument. It is a technical manual in the best sense of the word, providing the user both empirical documentation and practical implementation and analytic strategies. It would be most useful to practitioners in search of indicators of school success.

Fischer, J., & Corcoran, K. (2007). *Measures for clinical practice and research* (4th ed.). New York: Oxford University Press. This two-volume compendium contains a wide array of measures that could be used in research and evaluation. The authors present relevant data on reliability and validity when available and also comment on other attributes of scales. As a single source of information on available scales, these two volumes stand out.

Nugent, W. R., Siepperc, J. D., & Hudson, W. W. (2001). *Practice evaluation for the 21st century.* Belmont, CA: Brooks/Cole-Thomson Learning. The authors provide an introduction to the single-case methodology, but spend most of the time introducing and discussing issues related to case aggregation. A major emphasis is on measurement tools and relevant statistical procedures. This book will serve as a good reference for time-series measures that can be used in practice evaluation.

Royse, D., Thyer, B. A., & Padgett, D. (2010). *Program evaluation: An introduction* (5th ed.). Belmont, CA: Cengage. This is a basic introductory text to program evaluation. It provides basic definitions and a good overview of evaluation methodology, instrumentation, and relevant issues. It provides coverage of needs assessments, formative and summative evaluation methods, how to locate assessment measures, the ethics of evaluation research, group research designs, and single system methodology.

Thyer, B. A., & Myers, L. L. (2007). *A social worker's guide to evaluating practice outcomes.* Alexandria, VA: Council on Social Work Education. This provides social work practitioners with an easy-to-follow guide to selecting measures useful in evaluating the outcomes of social work practice and in applying these in the context of simple group or single-system research designs.

Appendix I

An Example of Rural Practice

The following example of practice illustrates the development and implementation of a design for social work service for a rural school district. Due to less density and smaller population, the organization of the school system tends to be less complex than an urban or even many suburban school systems. With fewer levels of administration, there tend to be fewer rules and regulations. It is easier to know upper administration and for them to know you. The same is true in relation to community resources. Drawbacks include scarcity of professional supervision, isolation, and often a paucity of resources.

Identifying Data

Alpha is a small school district with a student enrollment of approximately 740 students. There is one elementary school, grades K–6, and one high school, grades 7–12. The two school buildings are located on one campus, with a play area for the elementary school and a medium-sized athletic field with bleachers for spectators at the fall football games and other athletic events. There is a new superintendent who is enthusiastic and a strong proponent of accountability. The elementary-school principal is young and has taught in the school district for the past five 5 years. He is highly respected in the community. This is his first year as principal. The high-school principal is also a young man who was previously a vocational education teacher. He has been principal for five 5 years. Half of the elementary-school

teachers are new to the school system due to retirements and an increase in student population. The high-school teachers have taught in the system for an average of five 5 years. The home economics teacher is new to the system. A special education classroom in the elementary school is used as a resource for students with various learning impairments. A new course in the high school, developed by the high-school counselor the previous year, provides achieving students the opportunity to tutor elementary-school students who are having difficulty in reading. A woman from the community was hired as coordinator of the parents' program under Chapter 1/Title I funds. A part-time librarian and full-time school counselor are employed in the high school. Additional services such as the teacher of speech and language impaired, reading consultant, and school psychology and school social work services are provided by the Intermediate School District (ISD). Nursing services are provided by the county health department. The community supports the educational program in millage campaigns.

A small business community of eight stores is within walking distance of the schools. The financial support of the community comes from farming, tourist trade, and a small sawmill. The county seat (where medical, mental health, and social services and the court system are located) is 30 miles away. Thirty percent of the population receives some form of government supplement, either financial assistance or surplus food. The population is approximately 3,000 (larger in the summer because of summer residents) and consists largely of white, Anglo-Saxon Protestants. There is a small Native American population of 20—all are members of the same family.

All members of the school community have expressed feelings of isolation, especially during the long winter months. Alcoholism is prevalent among adults and teenagers. Child abuse and incest are commonly expressed concerns. These concerns contribute to family dysfunction and were expressed by members of the Chapter 1/Title I parents' group. The principal and teachers of the elementary school identified concerns about their newness and wondered if they could work together to avoid the effects of isolation. The principal realized that he would lose teachers the next year if they were unable to find satisfaction in their professional lives. He was also concerned about the inexperience of the new teachers and wanted to help them increase their knowledge and skills in working with children. The high-school principal and teachers did not specify any problems with staff relations, but each identified three ninth-grade girls whose behavior was disrupting the whole school. The building administrators and the program coordinator asked for some support from the social worker with the parents' group.

Figure A.1, an ecomap, shows the stress being experienced within the Alpha School District community. There is stress between the girls' group and the high-school teachers, pupils, school administrators, and the business community. The social worker has not yet been able to establish working relationships with any of the systems. There is intermittent tension between the minority population and the business community and between that population and both the elementary school and high school. Intermittent tension is also evident between parents (both Chapter 1/Title I and others) and both schools. There is intermittent tension between the high-school students and the elementary-school students. As shown by the solid lines, there are a number of positive relationships existing within this school district. Reasons for the tensions shown in the figure will become clear later in the discussion.

Making a Contract for Service

The social worker developed the following goals and objectives for social work service for the year based on the information that she had gathered in the initial phase of her work. The goals were discussed and accepted by the school district administrators and the superintendent of the Intermediate School District, who was also the supervisor of the social worker.

The goal focused on the concern about the effect of isolation on the total community. If the feeling of isolation could be reduced among all members of the school community, the quality of life could be improved. The goal was stated as follows:

> To increase positive social interaction among children, adolescents, their families, and school personnel.

Objectives, intended to achieve the above preceding goal by the end of the school year, were:

1. To provide a satisfying professional experience for new elementary-school teachers
2. To strengthen the coping abilities of Chapter 1/Title I families
3. To increase the social functioning of three high-school girls referred for disruptive behavior in the classroom.

The objectives served as the boundaries for service for the school year. If information and circumstances changed, these objectives would be modified.

Design of Social Work Service to Meet Objectives

Objective 1. To Provide a Satisfying First-Year Professional Experience for the New Elementary-School Teachers

Interventions (Activities).

1. Supporting the principal to establish groups of teachers to work on tasks. (The principal

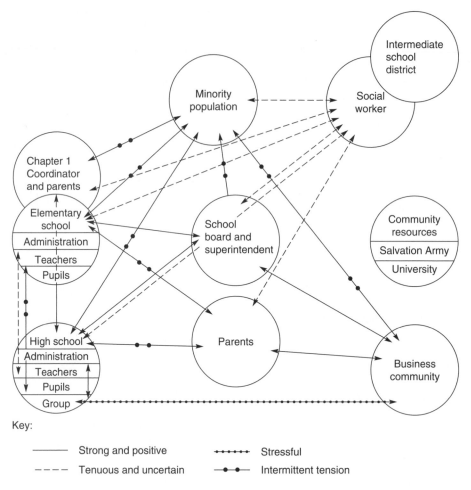

Key:

———— Strong and positive   •••••• Stressful

– – – – Tenuous and uncertain   —•—•— Intermittent tension

FIGURE A.1   Ecomap of the Assessment of Relationships in the Alpha School District

established teacher groups to write down curriculum learning objectives.)

2. Teaching at the school a university extension course on classroom management for elementary teachers. (The course also provided needed postgraduate credits for teacher certification. Eighty percent of the elementary-school teachers enrolled and 10 percent of elementary-school teachers from nearby school districts enrolled.)

3. Developing two in-service education sessions for all of the teachers on interviewing techniques to use in parent–teacher interviews.

4. Participating in the school's open house, during which some of the parent–teacher conferences involved children whom the social worker was serving

5. Collaborating and consulting with teachers and principal about classroom and individual behavior concerns.

Outcome. Every elementary-school teacher signed a contract for the next year, indicating a degree of satisfaction with the past year's experience. The staff became a cohesive group. The emphasis on group process in the university course not only developed their awareness of group dynamics in their classrooms, but also provided them with some insight into their interactions with each other. The teachers and principal learned to trust and respect one another, and the social worker was accepted as a member of the school staff. Communication between parents and teachers was increased as a result of the in-service training sessions on interviewing techniques. The positive relationships that developed between the teachers and the building administrator, the teachers and the social worker, and the building administrator and the social worker are shown in the Alpha school community ecomap (Figure A.2).

Objective 2. To Strengthen the Coping Abilities of Families

Background Information. The elementary school was receiving Chapter 1 funding. During the year, the purpose of the project was to increase the reading level of the elementary-school pupils through the establishment of a commercial reading program and the involvement of parents in the educational process. A mother who had worked as a paraprofessional in another community was hired to coordinate the parent segment of the program. The parents had met

several times during the previous year. They were informed about the reading program, saw a demonstration, and were encouraged to read with their children at home. Mrs. Brown, the coordinator, asked the social worker to help her accomplish the program goals. Mrs. Brown and the social worker developed a working relationship by identifying roles and boundaries. The Chapter 1/Title I parents' group consisted of between 30 and 40 mothers and some fathers. The school's goal was to involve the parents in their child's education; the social work goal was to increase positive family interaction. The following interventions and results show how both goals were accomplished.

Interventions (Activities).

1. Making a presentation at the November parent meeting, which focused on toys that educate and encourage family interaction. A booklet of toys for different age groups was developed and distributed, and samples of toys were demonstrated and passed among the parents.

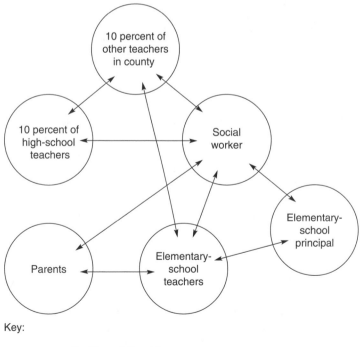

Key:

———— Positive relationships

FIGURE A.2 Ecomap of the Outcome of Work on Objective One

The question raised by one parent was: "Can we make some of these toys for our children?"

2. Establishing Christmas toy workshops. (Used toys donated by a service group were repaired, and new toys, such as blocks, puzzles, and games, were made with materials bought with funds from the Salvation Army.)

3. Inviting teachers and administrators to an open house to see the display of toys prepared by the parents. (Cookies baked with ingredients from the surplus foods were served.)

4. Focusing meetings on concerns of the parents. (In January the program centered on "living within a budget." Mothers said they did not know how to use some of the surplus foods they received. Also, their experience of dressing dolls for Christmas led the mothers to ask for instruction in sewing and other tips related to home management. Sewing machines and kitchen equipment in the Home Economics Department of the high school were made available to the parents.)

5. Involving the minority population. (As spring approached, the parents, mostly mothers, wanted to make baskets for their children. Mrs. Simpson, the Native American grandmother in the community who made baskets for sale, was paid a consultant's fee to teach the parents how to weave their own baskets. This project became complicated because black ash trees in the nearby national forest had to be cut down, with permission, and the wood dried, split, and dyed before the baskets could be made.)

6. Encouraging the development of a toy library. (Toys could be borrowed just as books are borrowed from the library. The project was begun by teachers who lent classroom games and materials to children to take home for a specified period.).

Outcomes.   Providing consultation to Mrs. Brown was a fruitful use of the social worker's time. Mrs. Brown worked directly with the parents, although the social worker also attended meetings and visited projects. The parents' Christmas tea for the teachers provided an opportunity for the teachers to know the parents' strengths and promoted communication between them. Comments in the teachers' lounge indicated that the teachers had a new respect for parents, whom they had previously viewed as inadequate. As the mothers learned new skills and received support from each other, stress in many of the homes lessened. There were fewer reports of abuse, and teachers reported that many of the children seemed more relaxed. Hiring Mrs. Simpson as a consultant and instructor improved the image of the Native American population in the community. It was a beginning. The ecomap (Figure A.3) shows the changes that took place in relationships over the year.

Objective 3. To Increase the Social Functioning of Three High-School Girls Referred for Disruptive Behavior in the Classroom

Background Information.   Sandy, Ellen, and Helen had much in common. They were friends largely because their antisocial behavior had alienated them from their peers. Each girl would turn 16 before the end of the school year. As eighth graders, they were two years behind grade and did not plan to continue school beyond their 16th birthday. Ellen had been born in this community and lived with her mother, stepfather, a 14-year-old brother Frank (also in the eighth grade), and an 18-year-old brother, who was a senior in the high school. There was constant conflict among family members. Helen lived with her father in a cabin partially destroyed by fire. Her father entertained a variety of women, and Helen was expected to be the housekeeper. Sandy lived with her mother in their summer cottage. She had experienced difficulty in the urban school district where she and her mother formerly lived. Her father was a chauffeur for a company and could not leave that community. Sandy was given the alternative of leaving the community or being sent to a juvenile facility. The mother had taken Sandy to the Alpha community hoping that the new environment would make a difference. Testing indicated that Sandy and Helen possessed average ability, but were underachieving academically. Ellen's tests indicated a learning disability and a

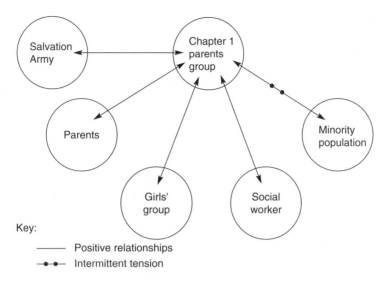

Key:

——— Positive relationships

–•–•– Intermittent tension

FIGURE A.3   Ecomap of the Outcome of Work on Objective Two

need for special education services. All three girls were discouraged about school and said that they would quit when they were 16. In one of the social worker's early meetings with the group, the girls confided that they felt dumb and not valued by anyone. They said they were expected to have deviant behavior and did not know why they should disappoint anyone. Because their families had limited incomes, the girls had little spending money. The result was that they could not participate in some of the community activities with peers, and they were bored. Behaviors of the girls that the teachers reported as offensive included not completing work, making loud noises in class, and swearing at classmates and teachers. Ellen was excluded from her home economics class because she used profane language when her teacher told her that she would have to tear out the stitching in a pair of slacks and start over. The three were restricted to the school grounds during the lunch hour because they had been caught shoplifting from seven of the eight shops on Main Street during lunch hour.

The social worker and the girls identified three objectives to achieve during the school year: (1) to gain status among peers and teachers, (2) to increase spending money, and (3) to decrease isolation and boredom.

Interventions (Activities).

1. Arranging for Ellen to have individual tutoring by the special education resource teacher. (This followed her being certified as learning disabled and the development of an Individualized Education Program.)

2. Inviting teachers to meet with the girls individually, so they could discuss their concerns. (Some agreements were made between the girls and the teachers. Some issues were raised and some were not, but communication was improved.)

3. Broadening the scope of the tutoring program, which provided high-school credit, and had been developed the year before by the counselor and the parents' group coordinator to include achieving high-school pupils as tutors. (Each girl received an assignment appropriate to her interests and abilities. The social worker arranged in-service training sessions for all of the tutors and established feedback sessions that included the tutors, Mrs. Brown, the social worker, and the counselor. Each girl received an "A" in the course. This was the first "A" Ellen or any member of her family had ever received.)

4. Helping the parents' groups make gifts for their children. (Ellen designed a drawstring purse and made it from a donated deerskin. She did such an excellent job that when she

showed her work to her home economics teacher, she was readmitted to the class.)

5. Forming a group patterned after a junior Achievement Club. (Group members decided to make items that could be sold to friends as well as tourists during the tourist season. The owner of the crafts store, the one shop from which the girls had not shoplifted, agreed to sponsor the venture. He not only sold them materials and advised them on profitable items to make, but also placed the items in his shop for sale and gave them the profits. There were ups and downs in this experience, but the girls worked together for a common cause. They gained an awareness of their abilities and limitations, and in the process of displaying and selling their items, they gained some respect from their teachers and peers. There was a small profit—not enough to meet all their financial requirements—but they felt that the effort had been worthwhile.)

6. Holding counseling interviews with the families throughout the year.

Outcomes. At the end of the school year, the three girls evaluated their year's work together. They said that they felt better about themselves and felt that others viewed them differently than before. They decided not to drop out of school although they were now 16 years old. They had some new interests and enjoyed the tutoring and craft projects. They had developed positive relationships with the storekeeper and with some of their teachers. They still felt bored in the evenings and still did not have spending money, but they now knew there were opportunities and they could be rewarded for their efforts. Helen returned to live with her mother in another town as a result of a plan that she and the social worker had developed with her father and the juvenile authorities. There were still some incidents in the school, and the girls' grades, although improved, were marginal; however, teachers and the principal reported significant changes in the behavior of each girl.

The outcomes are shown in the ecomap (Figure A.4). The areas of intermittent tension

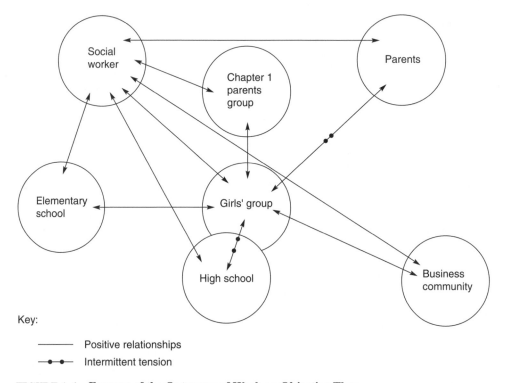

FIGURE A.4   **Ecomap of the Outcomes of Work on Objective Three**

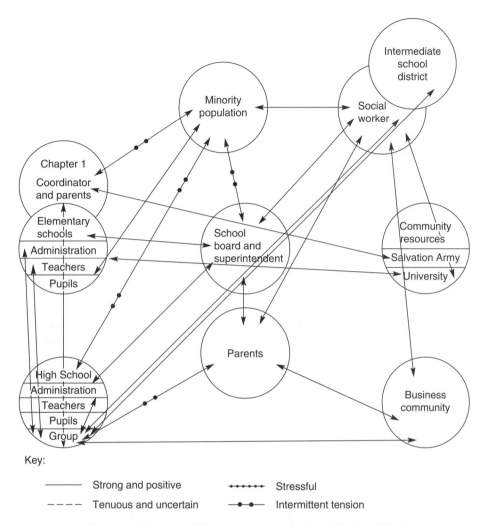

Key:

——— Strong and positive   •••••• Stressful

– – – Tenuous and uncertain   —•—•— Intermittent tension

FIGURE A.5   Ecomap of Results of Interventions in the Alpha School District

remain, but if the girls receive continued support, the tension need not increase. Compare Figure A.5 with Figure A.1 and note the changes in interactions among the various systems following social work intervention.

Additional Readings

Hartman, A. (1978, October). Diagrammatic assessment of family relationships. *Social Casework, 59,* 465–476.

Lauffer, A. (1982). *Assessment tools for practitioners, managers, and trainers.* Beverly Hills, CA: Sage.

Johnson, L. (1983). *Social work practice: A generalist approach.* Boston: Allyn & Bacon.

Appendix II

An Example of Urban Practice

The following example of practice illustrates the development and implementation of a design for social work service for an inner-city elementary school in a large metropolitan school district. In this example, the school social worker is a member of the school's newly formed site-based management team.

Identifying Data

The School

Located in the center of the city, Epsilon public school serves 500 kindergarten through fifth-grade children. The building and playground fill one city block and overlook an expressway on the east side. Across the street on the south side of the school there is a complex of buildings that once housed TB and mentally ill patients. Utilizing about half of the facility, the complex now provides outpatient physical and mental health services, department of vital statistics, and adult education programs. On the west side, across from the school, there is a fire station. A small fenced-in playground is behind the school. The school was built in the 1920s and has wide hallways and high ceilings. It has been well maintained. The rooms were recently painted, and there are decorative bulletin boards in each room. The art teacher has worked with her fourth- and fifth-grade classes to design and paint murals on the walls in the hall depicting the accomplishments of

various Americans. The teaching staff consists of classroom teachers for the kindergarten through third grade. There are English, social studies, science, music, and art classroom teachers for the fourth- and fifth-grade students. Fourth- and fifth-grade classrooms have scheduled use of a computer laboratory. A staff person is responsible for this curricular area. There is a resource room and teacher for high incidence special education students. She not only instructs students on a scheduled basis, but also provides classroom teachers with appropriate teaching material when special education students are mainstreamed or included in a general education classroom. Support team services are provided to students based on needs of the student and classroom situation.

The school is at full capacity of 500 elementary students, with an average class size of 30 students. There are two kindergartens, each with a morning and afternoon session. The first-through third-grade students are in self-contained classrooms, whereas the curriculum of fourth and fifth grades are on a platoon system where the students as a class move to music, art, science, and computer classrooms. Classrooms share bathroom facilities. All students stay for lunch and are supervised by two school aides. The cultural composition of the student population is 60 percent African American, 20 percent Hispanic, 5 percent Native American, 10 percent Asian, and 5 percent White.

The teachers have an average of five years teaching experience. Most of the teachers take university courses toward continued certification or an advanced degree in education. The principal, an African-American female, is a seasoned educator with a strong commitment to meet the educational and socioemotional needs of her students. She is open to any programs that will assist her in achieving the goals of the school.

During the previous year, the school district, in its search for new ways to restructure the educational program to achieve more effective educational outcomes, elected to use a site-based management approach. Under this management system, a team of school staff, parents, and students is empowered with the authority to tailor its educational program to the needs of their students. The management team consists of the principal, two teachers, parents, students, and community leaders elected or appointed by their group, plus a member of student support services, which in this school is the school social worker. The site-based management team developed a school mission statement and established goals for the year. Through the efforts of the management team, a crisis plan was revised, and on the recommendation of the school social worker, the services of the district Student Assistant Program (SAP) were requested.

The Epsilon school social worker, who is an African-American female, has an MSW degree and has been a practicing social worker for 10 years. She previously worked with children and youth in a private, multiservice agency and has been with this school system for the past 5 years; however, this is her second year in this building. She is assigned to the building Monday and Thursday mornings and Friday afternoons. She has two second-year graduate social work interns, a White male and female, both in their thirties. They are assigned to Epsilon school all day on Thursdays and Fridays. The social worker has a pager, which makes her accessible any time when there is a question or concern requiring her attention. The social workers in this school system are under the supervision of a department head, and the social workers' plans for service are reviewed by the department supervisor, as well as by the site-based management team.

Other physical and mental health support services include the school psychologist, who is available from the psychology department of the school district for testing students referred for special education, and a school nurse from the public health department. Although all of the social workers in the district have training in crisis intervention, district teams are available when a crisis of magnitude occurs. There is an extensive preschool program (Head Start, a state program for high-risk preschool children, and a program for preprimary impaired children) in the school district that employs a staff of social workers, who in addition to their other duties, are responsible for facilitating the transition of preschool children to the kindergarten. The district SAP, staffed by social workers, provides a comprehensive substance abuse prevention and intervention program for students that is available to individual schools on request. A special education districtwide social work staff collaborates with the school psychologist to make decisions about eligibility for and placement in a special education program and inclusion decisions and re-reevaluations of students who are in the program.

The Community

Housing in the community consists of small apartment buildings, duplexes, and a few single-family dwellings. Although most of the property is adequately maintained, the community is dotted with vacant, deteriorating buildings. City services are minimal. Trash is sometimes not picked up for weeks, and streetlights are undependable. Unemployment runs 40 percent, with 50 percent of the residents on some form of welfare. There is a homeless shelter in the neighborhood and several group homes for the mentally retarded. Fifteen percent of the residents are retired, supported by Social Security. There is a senior citizen's club in the community operated through the department of recreation. A Boys Club is the only recreation facility in the community with the exception of summer programs operated by the department of recreation. As in many inner-city communities where poor economic conditions spawn crime and discontent, the majority of households own some type of weapon. Iron bars are on first-floor windows and doors to provide protection from intruders. Five unattended children died in a fire when the bars prevented them from escaping the building. Three of the children attended Epsilon. Because of the increase in youth violence and substance abuse–related crimes, a community collaborative is in the process of development. At this point it is composed of representatives of city departments such as the Youth Division of the Police, Department of Parks and Recreation, Housing Department, Department of Social Services, Health Department, and Department of Public Safety. Representatives of the Boys Club and the Neighborhood Service Organization are active members. The churches and community are represented by their leaders. The three public schools within the boundaries of this collaborative or coalition of services to the community are represented by an administrator and interdisciplinary team member from each school. The collaborative is in the process of assessing social needs of the community and developing an action plan to promote a stronger, healthier, and safer community.

Plan for Social Work Services Based on a Needs Assessment

The following design for service is the result of program decisions made by the Epsilon site-based management team. The plan is social work's contribution to Epsilon's goals to maintain a safe and nurturing environment and to improve social and academic skills of the students. These two goals are implementation goals of the school district's overall goal: "To Promote Student Success." The activities outlined evolved from an assessment of the Epsilon school and community using outlines detailed in Chapter 11, Tables 11.2 and 11.3. Transactions between and among various systems were examined and evaluated with a view to minimizing stress factors and increasing coping abilities of students, utilizing the resources of administration, school staff, support services, families, and community. In addition to implementing the plan, the school social worker carried other responsibilities, such as responding to crisis situations, consultation, coordination with school and the various social work staff members, supervision of the two graduate social work interns, and attention to X number of referrals.

School Social Work Service Plan for Epsilon School for the School Year of 200_

Objective	Presenting Problem	Interventions	With Whom?	Evaluation Criteria
1. To increase coping ability of students moving from one school or educational program to another by facilitating the transition process.	Increase in student turnover during the school year. Last year there were a number of preventable incidents involving teachers and students who were not prepared for new members of the class. At the same time, students transferring to other schools because of family moves or returning from mental health or correctional facilities or being mainstreamed from special education programs showed signs of stress due to the absence of preparation for the move.	1. Develop a welcoming committee composed of student volunteers. Provide a training program and monthly progress report meeting. Include a buddy mentor system. 2. Report to teachers at a faculty meeting on progress and discuss ways in which new students can feel welcome and those leaving feel support for the move. 3. Conduct a class meeting to discuss the part classmates play to help the new student succeed when a special education student is integrated into the general education class. 4. Provide support services to assist the teacher when requested. 5. Prepare a small pamphlet for parents on ways in which they can support their child at the time of a transition.	Social worker and one intern will take responsibility for implementing plan in cooperation with teachers and the principal.	Observation report. Self-reports of students at the end of a semester.
2. To increase "on-task" behavior of 40 students referred for disruptive behavior in afternoon classes.	Many teacher referrals indicated a pattern of behavior problems in the afternoon. Due to recent budget cuts only two aides are available to supervise the 500 students who stay for lunch. To prevent fights and disruption students are not permitted to talk or engage in any physical exercise during the 60-minute lunch hour. For 30 minutes, 250 students are in gym with hands on head while the other 250 eat lunch. At the end of 30 minutes the two groups are reversed. Consequently, pent-up energy is expressed in acting-out behavior in afternoon classes.	1. Locate outside resource to organize lunchtime activities. A possibility is the African-American fraternity at the nearby university that is looking for a project in the urban school system. If not available, identify other possibilities. 2. Monitor the program by providing feedback sessions with those leading activities and make changes if necessary.	Planning committee: Principal, university fraternity leadership, lunchroom aides, and social worker as chairperson. Social worker and principal coordinate and supervise group that provides the lunchroom activity program.	Reports of teachers. Reduction in referrals with same concerns.

(continued)

School Social Work Service Plan for Epsilon School for the School Year of 200_   (Continued)

Objective	Presenting Problem	Interventions	With Whom?	Evaluation Criteria
3. To increase positive relationships between teachers, students, and parents.	Conversation in teachers' room frequently focuses on desire to increase positive relationship with parents and students. Questionnaires to teachers indicated the same desire.	1. Develop in-service program for teachers focused on interviewing skills with parents at parent–teacher conferences. 2. Arrange for course from university (with credits for teacher certification) on managing a classroom as a group. 3. Suggest to teachers and principal that fifth- and sixth-grade students and teachers spend a week at the city camp together.	Social worker as in-service leader. Social worker as liaison with the university. Social worker as consultant and social work interns as camp counselors for the week.	Questionnaire and sample interviews with teachers, parents, and students.
4. To increase completion of homework by referred students living in X apartment house.	Pattern of incomplete homework by the ten students who all live in the same apartment building.	1. Contract with apartment manager to see if space is available to use as a study room. 2. Recruit at least five parents willing to supervise according to a schedule developed by them. 3. Meet with parents and teachers identifying ways to help students with homework. 4. Include students in final planning.	Social worker to take main responsibility for developing the program. Social work interns will take responsibility for periodic meetings with parents and apartment manager, with parents and teachers, and with parents, teachers, and students. Interns will conduct support sessions for the parent tutors.	Teacher records of completed homework of participating students.

| 5. | To increase age-appropriate communication skills among six siblings of the Johnson family. | Six of the Johnson's 12 children were in Epsilon school. Each of them was referred by his or her teacher because of a lack of verbal communication skills. Instead of asking another child for something, they hit them. Hitting was not an angry act but in place of the verbal word. They were each able to talk but had developed a pattern in the family that spilled into the school. The children ranged in age from 5 to 12 with one set of twins in the third grade. The father worked two jobs to make expenses meet, and the mother was overwhelmed by her responsibilities. The children did household chores in isolation. For example, 12-year-old Yolanda was responsible for washing dishes for 14 people every night by herself. Testing indicated average ability of each of the children and each had passed each grade, but teachers were worried about their inappropriate communication skills. | 1. Develop intervention plan following an assessment of each child and the family.
2. Twice a week lunch time group meetings of a sibling group. Use parallel activities and gradually increase activities which require interaction.
3. Collaborate with the classroom teachers of the siblings to discuss ways in which they could increase positive verbal interaction and decrease physical interaction.
4. Conferences with Mrs. Johnson to support her coping abilities. She was eager for assistance.
5. Culminating activity at the end of the school year such as an invitation to parents to lunch prepared by the sibling group. | Social worker and both interns. | Three interrupted time series measurements of each sibling in classroom and on playground.
Three interviews with parents on change in verbal interactions and physical interactions.
Use of an ecogram at every third group meeting. |

Appendix III

Assessment of Adaptive Behavior and Individual Education Program

Practice Illustration

The case of Maggie illustrates the process as it is prescribed by the federal law, including the procedural steps and the ways in which social work services can become an integral part of the educational decision-making process.

Background

Maggie, aged 14 years and 7 months, has been in the EMH program for several years. She was assigned to a full-time special education class when she was identified as needing special education services in the fourth grade. She is now a ninth grader, and she has been referred by her special education teacher for a reevaluation, to ascertain whether modifications should be made in her instructional program.

Maggie comes from a large family. There is no father present, and the mother is employed as an unskilled laborer outside the home. No known physical problems or traumatic life experiences account for Maggie's handicap. A recent physical examination revealed that she is developing according to the pattern of other children in her age group. Her mother is very concerned that Maggie should acquire skills to enable her to be self-sufficient and that she have more interaction with nonhandicapped students before entering high school.

Assessment Data

The social worker completed and updated information about Maggie's home situation and conducted an assessment of her adaptive behavior. The American Association of Mental Deficiency Scale, Public School Version, was used to ascertain information about her adaptive behavior. This scale showed Maggie to be above average in independent functioning, economic activity, language development, vocational activity, self-direction, assumption of responsibility, and socialization. The final scores indicated that she exhibited appropriate adaptive behaviors in the environment outside the school. She was responsible and took care of herself and others without a lot of supervision. She initiated tasks and worked until they were completed.

The psychometric tests administered by the psychologist showed that Maggie was performing as follows:

Weschsler Intelligence Scale for Children (Revised):

Verbal IQ	68
Performance IQ	63
Full Scale IQ	63
Median Verbal Test	Age 8–10
Median Performance Test	Age 6–7

374

Wide Range Achievement Test (1978 Norms):

	Standardized		
	Grade	Score	Percentile
Reading (Level II)	5.7	83	23
Spelling (Level II)	4.8	78	7
Arithmetic (Level I)	4.5	—	—

Note: Level I Arithmetic was administered because of the level of difficulty of Level II. She performed 3-digit addition, 2-digit multiplication, and 2-digit subtraction. No fraction problems were completed.

A projective test (on the subject of "How I Feel about School") was also administered. The results indicated that she was rather reticent in responding; she offered no spontaneous conversation and did not elaborate in giving answers. She found math and reading very difficult but did not know why. Most important, she thought she was liked by others, and most of the time she liked being in school.

The psychologist concluded that Maggie needed help in the following areas:

1. Expressive and receptive vocabulary development
2. Attention to visual information
3. Learning units of measurements
4. Reading comprehension.

Multidisciplinary Staff Meeting

A staff meeting was called following the collection of information obtained from parent, student, and teacher interviews; social development study; psychometric testing; and an assessment of adaptive behavior. Participants included the school social worker, psychologist, Maggie's special education teacher, the invited regular education staff, a school administrator, Maggie's mother, and Maggie.

Each participant shared the information that he or she had collected and gave a recommendation. Both the mother and Maggie had an opportunity to share information and to participate in the discussion and final recommendation. In other words, a consensus was reached.

The final recommendations were:

1. Maggie is still eligible for special education classes (EMI-1).

2. More emphasis needs to be placed on vocabulary and reading comprehension.
3. Maggie should be integrated into regular classes (such as home economics, art, physical education, and music) as much as possible.
4. When Maggie enters high school, she and her parent should consider enrollment in a vocational education program.

Individual Educational Program

These recommendations were then translated into instructional goals and included in Maggie's Individual Education Program (IEP), which was later signed by all who participated in the meeting. Examples of the instructional goals are:

Goal 1: To improve reading comprehension and vocabulary skills in order to be able to answer literal questions after reading a chapter or story.
Criterion of successful performance: Student will achieve a 90 percent correct response rate.
Goal 2: To define a word verbally from a unit.
Criterion of successful performance: She will achieve a score of 85 percent or better on written vocabulary tests.
Goal 3: To match words with their meanings.
Criterion of successful performance: She will achieve an accuracy rate of 75 percent or better on tests.

The school social worker's role will be to support the student during the transition from a specialized classroom to a part-time special class assignment. Further, he or she will consult and collaborate with the special education teacher, regular teacher, and mother, for facilitating the transition. Specifically, the school social worker's major annual goal will be

Goal 1: For Maggie to increase positive social relations (that is, number of positive interactions) with nondisabled peers through interaction experiences in a group with the social worker. The group will consist of both special education and regular education students.
Criterion of successful performance: Maggie's interaction (the number of times that she speaks) with a nondisabled group member will increase by 50 percent during the life of the group experience.

References

Aarons, S. J., Jenkins, R. R., Raine, T. R., El-Khorazaty, M. N., Woodward, K. M., & Williams, R. L. (2000). Postponing sexual intercourse among urban junior high school students: A randomized controlled evaluation. *Journal of Adolescent Health, 27*(4), 236–247.

Abbott, E., & Breckinridge, S. (1917). *Truancy and non-attendance in the Chicago schools: A study of the social aspects of the compulsory education and child labor legislation of Illinois.* Chicago: University of Chicago Press.

Abel, E. M. & Greco, M. (2008). A preliminary evaluation of an abstinence-oriented empowerment program for public school youth, *Research on Social Work Practice, 18,* 223–230.

Aber, J. L., Brown, J. L., Chaudry, N., Jones, S. M., & Samples, F. (1996). The evaluation of the resolving conflict creatively program: An overview. In K. E. Powell & D. F. Hawkins (Eds.), *Youth violence prevention: Descriptions and baseline data from 13 evaluation projects* (pp. 82–90). Supplement to *American Journal of Preventive Medicine, 12*(5).

Achenbach, T. M. (1991). *Manual for the Child Behavior Checklist/4-18 and 1991 Profile.* Burlington, VA: University of Vermont Department of Psychiatry.

ACLU warns Alabama school district that its mandatory sex segregation program is illegal and discriminatory. (2008, November 12). Retrieved December 1, 2008, from http://www.aclu.org/womensrights/edu/37738prs20081112.html

Adams, J. L., Jaques, J. D., & May, K. M. (2004). Counseling gay and lesbian families: Theoretical considerations. *The Family Journal, 12*(1), 40–42.

Adelman, H. S., & Taylor, L. (2002). *So you want higher achievement scores? It's time to rethink learning supports.* UCLA School Mental Health Project. Retrieved June 20, 2005, from http://smhp.psych.ucla.edu/summit2002/schoolboard.pdf

Advocates for Youth. (2003). *Science and success: Sex education and other programs that work to prevent teen pregnancy, HIV, and sexually transmitted infections.* Washington, DC: Author. Accessed online November 12, 2004, at http://www.advocatesforyouth.org/publications/ScienceSuccess.pdf

Advocates for Youth. (2004). *Adolescent pregnancy and childbearing in the United States.* Retrieved May

16, 2008, from http://www.advocatesforyouth.org/publications/factsheet/fsprechd.htm

Advocates for Youth. (2005). *GLBTQ youth.* Retrieved May 22, 2008, from http://www.advocatesforyouth.org/publications/factsheet/fsglbt.htm

Agresta, J. (2006). Job satisfaction among school social workers: The role of interprofessional relationships and professional role discrepancy. *Journal of Social Service Research, 33*(1), 47–52.

Aguilar, M. A. (1995). Promoting the educational achievement of Mexican American young women. *Social Work, 18*(3), 145–156.

Albers, C. A., & Kratochwill, T. R. (2006). Teacher and principal consultations: Best practices. In C. Franklin, M. B. Harris, & P. Allen-Meares (Eds.), *The school services sourcebook: A guide for school-based professionals* (pp. 971–976). New York: Oxford University Press.

Alderson, J. J. (1952). Specific content of school social work. *Bulletin of the National Association of School Social Workers, 27,* 3–13.

Alderson, J. J. (1972). Models of school social work practice. In R. C. Sarri & F. Maple (Eds.), *The school in the community* (pp. 151–160). Washington, DC: National Association of Social Workers.

Alderson, J., & Krishef, C. H. (1973). Another perspective on tasks in school social work. *Social Casework, 54,* 591–600.

Alexander v. Holmes County Board of Education, 396 U.S. 19 (1969).

Alexander, K., & Alexander, M. D. (1998). *American public school law* (4th ed.). St. Paul, MN: West.

Allen, J. P., Porter, M. R., McFarland, F. C., Marsh, P., & McElhaney, K. B. (2005). The two faces of adolescents' success with peers: Adolescent popularity, social adaptation, and deviant behavior. *Child Development, 76,* 747–760.

Allen, M., Elliott, M., Kataoka, S., Morales, L., Hambarsoomian, K., & Schuster, M. (2007). The contributions of family and acculturation-related stress to Latino adolescents' mental health: A social network approach. *Journal of Adolescent Health, 40*(2), S45.

Allen-Meares, P. (1977). Analysis of tasks in school social work. *Social Work, 22*(3), 196–201.

Allen-Meares, P. (1981). Educating social workers for specialization. *Social Work in Education, 3,* 36–51.

Allen-Meares, P. (1985). Children with behavioral disorders: An eclectic approach for social workers. *Social Work in Education, 7,* 100–114.

Allen-Meares, P. (1987). A national study of educational reform: Implications for social work services in schools. *Children and Youth Services Review, 19*(2), 207–219.

Allen-Meares, P. (1994). Social work services in schools: A national study of entry-level tasks. *Social Work, 39,* 560–565.

Allen-Meares, P. (2006). Where do we go from here? Mental health workers and the implementation of an evidence-based practice. In C. Franklin, M. B. Harris, & P. Allen-Meares (Eds.), *The school services sourcebook: A guide for school-based professionals* (pp. 1189–1194). New York: Oxford University Press.

Allen-Meares, P. (2008). Assessing the adaptive behavior of youths: Multicultural responsivity. *Social Work, 53*(4), 307–316.

Allen-Meares, P., & Lane, B. (1983). Assessing the adaptive behavior of children and youths. *Social Work, 28,* 297–301.

Allen-Meares, P., & Lane, B. (1987). Grounding social practice in theory. *Social Casework, 68*(9), 519.

Allen-Meares, P., & Lane, B. (1990). Social work practice: Integrating qualitative and quantitative data collection techniques. *Social Work, 35,* 453–454.

Allen-Meares, P., & Lane, B. A. (1982). A content analysis of school social work literature, 1968–1978. In R. T. Constable & J. P. Flynn (Eds.), *School social work: Practice and research perspectives* (pp. 49–72). Homewood, IL: Dorsey Press.

Allen-Meares, P., Lane, B., & Oppenheimer, M. (1981). *Assessing the adaptive behavior of children and youth.* Second National Conference on School Social Work, Washington, DC.

Allen-Meares, P., & Roberts, E. (1994). Associations of social integration variables with prenatal care use by adolescents and young adults. *Journal of Social Service Research, 19*(1), 23–47.

Allen-Meares, P., Washington, R. O., & Welsh, B. (1986). *Social work services in schools.* Englewood Cliffs, NJ: Prentice Hall.

Allington, R. L. (August, 2005). Urgency and instructional time. *Reading Today, 23*(1), 17.

Alter, C. F. (2000). Interorganizational collaboration in the task environment. In R. J. Patti (Ed.), *The handbook of social welfare management* (pp. 283–302). Thousand Oaks, CA: Sage.

Alter, C., & Evens, W. (1990). *Evaluating your practice: A guide to self-assessment.* New York: Springer Publishing Company.

Altshuler, S. J. (2001). When is mentoring not helpful for students living in foster care? *School Social Work Journal, 26,* 15–29.

Altshuler, S. J., & Kopels, S. (2003). Advocating in schools for children with disabilities: What's the new I.D.E.A.? *Social Work, 48*(3), 320–329.

Altshuler, S. J. & Schmautz, T. (2006). No Hispanic child left behind: The consequences of high stakes testing. *Children and Schools, 28*(1), 5–14.

American Association of Retired Persons. (2007). State fact sheets for grandparents and other relatives raising children. Retrieved September 27, 2008, from http://www.grandfactsheets.org/state_fact_sheets.cfm

American Association of University Women (AAUW). (1992). *How schools shortchange girls.* Washington, DC: Author.

American Association of University Women (AAUW). (1993). *Hostile hallways: The AAUW survey on sexual harassment in America's schools.* Washington, DC: Author.

American Association of University Women (AAUW). (1998). *Gender gaps: Where schools still fail our children.* Washington, DC: Author.

American Psychiatric Association. (2000). *Diagnostic and statistical manual of mental disorders* (4th ed.). Arlington, VA: American Psychiatric Association.

American Psychiatric Association. (2000). *Diagnostic and statistical manual of mental health disorders* (4th ed, text revision). Washington, DC: Author.

American Psychological Association. (1993). *Violence and youth: Psychology's response* (Vol. 1). Washington, DC: Author.

Americans with Disabilities Act (28 CFR Part 36). *Federal Register.* July 26, 1991.

Amos, J. (2008). *Dropouts, diplomas, and dollars: U.S. high schools and the nation's economy.* Washington, DC: Alliance for Excellent Education.

An interview with Daniel Yankelovich. (1992, Summer). *Family Affairs, 5*(1–2), New York: Institute for American Values.

Anderson, J. J. (1974). Introducing change in school-community-pupil relationships: Maintaining credibility and accountability. *Journal of Education for Social Work, 19*(1), 3–8.

Anderson, R. J. (1968). *Procedures and problems in referring school children to mental health clinics.* Unpublished Doctoral Dissertation, Illinois State University, Normal, IL.

Anderson-Butcher, D. (2004). Transforming schools into 21st century community learning centers. *Children & Schools, 26,* 248–252.

Andrews, S. P., Taylor, P. B., Martin, E. P., & Slate, J. R. (1998). Evaluation of an alternative discipline program. *The High School Journal, 81*(4), 209–217.

Annie E. Casey Foundation. (2005). *Kids count databook: State profiles of child well-being 2005.* Baltimore: Author.

Annie E. Casey Foundation. (2007). *Kids count database: Children in poverty, by race: 2007.* Retrieved October

6, 2008, from http://www.kidscount.org/datacenter/compare_results.jsp?i=191

Annie E. Casey Foundation. (2008). *Kids count database: Children in immigrant families: 2000–2002–2006.* Retrieved October 6, 2008, from http://www.kidscount.org/datacenter/trend.jsp?i=750&yr=&yra=&yrb=&va=&m=3&cr=1&x=28&y=8

Antell v. Stokes, 287 Mass. 103, 191 N.E. 407 (1934).

Apter, S. J. (1982). *Troubled children—troubled systems* (Rev. ed.). Elmsford, NY: Pergamon Press.

Areson, C. W. (1923). Status of children's work in the United States. *Proceedings of the National Conference Of Social Work.* Chicago: University of Chicago Press.

Argyris, C. (1992). *On organizational learning.* Malden, MA: Blackwell Business.

Armor, D. J. (1995). *Forced justice: School desegregation and the law.* New York: Oxford University Press.

Artiles, A., & Trent, S. (1994). Overrepresentation of minority students in special education: A continuing debate. *The Journal of Special Education, 27,* 410–437.

Aruda, M. M., McCabe, M., Burke, P., & Litty, C. (2008). Adolescent pregnancy diagnosis and outcomes: A six-year clinical sample. *Journal of Pediatric and Adolescent Gynecology, 21*(1), 17–19.

Arum, R. (2000). Schools and communities: Ecological and institutional dimensions. *Annual Review of Sociology, 26,* 395–418.

Ash, P., Kellermann, A., Fuqua-Whitley, D., & Johnson, A. (1996). Gun acquisition and use by juvenile offenders. *Journal of the American Medical Association, 275,* 1754–1758.

Astor, R. (1998). Moral reasoning about school violence: Informational assumptions about harm within school sub-contexts. *Educational Psychologist, 33,* 207–221.

Astor, R., Benbenishty, R., Marachi, R. & Pitner, R. (2008). Evidence-based violence prevention programs and best implementation practices. In A. R. Roberts (Ed.) *Social workers' desk reference* (2nd ed.) (pp. 985–1003). NYC: Oxford.

Astor, R., Meyer, H., & Behre, W. (1999). Unowned space and time in high schools: Mapping violence with students and teachers. *American Educational Research Journal, 36,* 3–42.

Astor, R., Pitner, R. O., & Duncan, B. (1996). Ecological approaches to mental health consultation with teachers on issues related to youth and school violence. *Journal of Negro Education, 65,* 336–355.

Astor, R. A. (2005, September 9). Public foster care schools. *Teachers College Record.* Retrieved September 28, 2005, from www.tcrecord.org

Astor, R. A., Behre, W. J., Fravil, K. A., & Wallace, J. M. (1997). Perceptions of school violence as a problem and reports of violent events: A national survey of school social workers. *Social Work, 42,* 55–68.

Astor, R. A., Behre, W. J., Wallace, J. M., & Fravil, K. A. (1998). School social workers and school violence: Personal safety, training, and violence programs. *Social Work, 43*(3), 223–232.

Astor, R. A., & Benbenishty, R. (2005). Zero tolerance for zero knowledge. *Education Week, 24*(43), 52.

Astor, R. A., Benbenishty, R., & Estrada, J. (2008). School violence. In T. Mizrahi & L. E. Davis (Eds.), *The encyclopedia of social work.* Washington, DC: NASW Press; New York: Oxford University Press.

Astor, R. A., Benbenishty, R., & Meyer, H. A. (2004). Monitoring and mapping student victimization in schools. *Theory into Practice, 43*(1), 39–49.

Astor, R. A., Benbenishty, R., Meyer, H. A., & Rosemond, M. (2004). Adolescent victimization and weapon-use on school grounds: An empirical study from Israel. In T. Urdan & F. Parjes (Eds.), *Educating adolescents: Challenges and strategies* (pp. 109–130). Greenwich, CT: Information Age.

Astor, R. A., Benbenishty, R., Pitner, R. O., & Meyer, H. A. (2004). Bullying and peer victimization in schools. In P. A. Meares & M. W. Fraser (Eds.), *Intervention with children & adolescents: An interdisciplinary perspective* (pp. 471–448). Boston: Allyn & Bacon.

Astor, R. A., & Meyer, H. (1999). Where girls and women won't go: Female students', teachers', and school social workers' views of school safety. *Social Work in Education, 21,* 201–219.

Astor, R. A., & Meyer, H. (2001). The conceptualization of violence prone school subcontexts: Is the sum of the parts greater than the whole? *Urban Education, 36,* 374–399.

Astor, R. A., Meyer, H. A., Benbenishty, R., Marachi, R., & Rosemond, M. (2005). School safety interventions: Best practices and programs. *Children & Schools, 24*(1), 17–32.

Astor, R. A., Meyer, A., & Pitner, R. O. (1999). Mapping school violence with students, teachers and administrators. In L. Davis (Ed.), *Working with African American males: A practice guide* (pp. 129–144). Thousand Oaks, CA: Sage.

Astor, R. A., Pitner, R. O., Meyer, H. A., & Vargas, L. A. (2000). The most violent event at school: A ripple in the pond. *Children & Schools, 22,* 99–116.

Astor, R. A., Rosemond, M., Pitner, R. O., & Marachi, R. (2006). An overview of best violence prevention practices in schools. In C. Franklin, M. B. Harris, & P. Allen-Meares (Eds.), *School social work and mental health worker's training and resource manual* (Chapter 43). New York: Oxford University Press.

Astor, R. A., Rosemond, M., Pitner, R. O., Marachi, R., & Benbenishty, R. (2006). Evidence-based violence prevention program and best implementation practices. In C. Franklin, M. B. Harris, & P. Allen-Meares (Eds.), *Social work and mental health workers training and resource manual.* New York: Oxford University Press.

Astor, R. A., Vargas, L. A., Pitner, R. O., & Meyer, H. A. (1999). School violence: Research, theory, & practice. In J. M. Jenson & M. O. Howard (Eds.), *Youth violence: Current research and recent practice innovations* (pp. 139–172). Washington, DC: NASW Press.

Auerbach, A. B. (1955). The special contribution of school social work in work with parent groups. *Bulletin of the National Association of School Social Workers, 30*, 10–19.

Austin, D. (2002). *Human services management: Organizational leadership in social work practice.* New York: Columbia University Press.

Babbie, E. (1998). *The practice of social research* (7th ed.). Belmont, CA: Wadsworth Publishing Company.

Baker v. Owen, 437 U.S. 907 (1975).

Baker, J. A. (1998). Are we missing the forest for the trees? Considering the social context of school violence. *Journal of School Psychology, 36,* 29–44.

Ballard, M. K. (2002). *Schools social policy analysis: Zero tolerance policy.* Unpublished manuscript.

Barbarin, O., Bryant, D., McCandies, T., Burchinal, M., Early, D., Clifford, R., et al. (2006). Children enrolled in public pre-k: The relation of family life, neighborhood quality, and socioeconomic resources to early competence. *American Journal of Orthopsychiatry, 76*(2), 256–276.

Barker, R. L. (1999). *The social work dictionary* (4th ed.). Washington, DC: NASW.

Barker, R. L. (2003). *The social work dictionary* (5th ed.). Washington, DC: NASW Press.

Barnett, W. S., Hustedt, J. T., Friedman, A. H., Boyd, J. S., & Ainsworth, P. (2008). *The state of preschool 2007.* Retrieved October 17, 2008, from http://nieer.org/yearbook/

Bartlett, H. M. (1970). *The common base of social work practice.* Washington, DC: NASW Press.

Barton, P. E. (2002). *Raising achievement and reducing gaps: Reporting progress toward goals for academic achievement in mathematics.* Washington, DC: National Education Goals Panel.

Batsche, G., & Knoff, A. (1994). Bullies and their victims: Understanding a pervasive problem in the schools. *School Psychology Review, 23,* 165–174.

Bausch, K. C. (2001). *The emerging consensus in social systems theory.* New York: Mower Academic/Plenum.

Beckham, J. (2000). Searches in public schools. In W. E. Camp, M. J. Connelly, K. E. Lane, & J. F. Mead (Eds.), *The principal's legal handbook* (2nd ed., pp. 3–24). Dayton, OH: Education Law Association.

Belfield, C. R., & Levin, H. M. (2005). *Privatizing educational choice: Consequences for parents, schools, and public policy.* Boulder, CO: Paradigm Publishers.

Benbenishty, R., & Astor, R. A. (2003). Cultural specific and cross-cultural bully/victim patterns: The response from Israel. In P. K. Smith (Ed.), *Violence in schools: The response in Europe* (pp. 317–331). New York: Routledge Falmer.

Benbenishty, R., & Astor, R. A. (2005). *School violence in context: Culture, neighborhood, family, school, and gender.* New York: Oxford University Press.

Benbenishty, R., & Astor, R. A. (2007). Monitoring indicators of children's victimization in school: Linking national-, regional-, and site-level indicators. *Social Indicators, 84*(3), 333–348.

Benbenishty, R., Astor, R. A., & Estrada, J. N. (2008). School violence assessment: A conceptual framework, instruments and methods. *Children & Schools, 30*(2), 71–81.

Benbenishty, R., Astor, R. A., & Zeira, A. (2003). Monitoring school violence at the site level: Linking national, district and school-level data. *Journal of School Violence, 2*(2), 29–50.

Benbenishty, R., Astor, R. A., Zeira, A., & Vinokur, A. (2002). Perceptions of violence and fear of school attendance among junior high school students in Israel. *Social Work Research, 26,* 71–87.

Benbenishty, R., Zeira, A., & Astor, R. A. (2000, June). *A national study of school violence in Israel—Wave II: Fall 1999.* Jerusalem, Israel: Israeli Ministry of Education. Sent by the Ministry of Education to every school principal in Israel.

Benbenishty, R., Zeira, A., & Astor, R. A. (2002). Children reports of emotional, physical and sexual maltreatment by educational staff in Israel. *Child Abuse and Neglect, 26*(8), 763–782.

Benbenishty, R., Zeira, A., Astor, R. A., & Khoury-Kassabri, M. (2002). Maltreatment of primary school students by educational staff in Israel. *Child Abuse and Neglect, 26,* 1291–1309.

Bennett, S. E., & Assefi, N. P. (2005). School based teenage pregnancy prevention programs: A systematic review of randomized controlled trials. *Journal of Adolescent Health, 36*(1), 72–81.

Berger v. Rensselaer Cent. School Corp., 982 F. 2d 1160 (7th Cir. 1993).

Berk, R. A., & Rossi, P. H. (1999). *Thinking about program valuation.* Thousand Oaks, CA: Sage.

Bernard, B. (1992). Fostering resilience in kids: Protective factors in the family, school, and community. *Prevention Forum, 12,* 1–16.

Bernard, B. (1995). *Fostering resilience in children.* Urbana, IL: ERIC Clearinghouse on Early Childhood Education (ERIC Document Reproduction Service No. EDO-PS-95-9).

Bernstein, J., Brocht, C., & Spade-Aguilar, M. (2000). *How much is enough? Basic family budgets for working families.* Washington, DC: Economic Policy Institute.

Berrill, K. (1990). Anti-gay violence and victimization in the U.S.: An overview. *Journal of Interpersonal Violence: Special issue: Violence against lesbians and gay men: Issues for research, practice, and policy, 5,* 274–294.

Bertalanffy, L. von. (1968). *General systems theory.* New York: Braziller.

Bethel School District No. 403 v. Fraser, 478 U.S. 675 (1986).

Bird, H. R., Canino, G. J., Davies, M., Ramirez, R., Chavez, L., Duarte, C., et al. (2005). The Brief Impairment Scale (BIS): A multidimensional scale of functional impairment for children and adolescents. *Journal of the American Academy of Child and Adolescent Psychiatry, 44*(7), 699–707.

Bird, H. R., Shaffer, D., Fisher, P., Gould, M. S., Staghezza, B., Chen, J. Y., et al. (1993).The Columbia Impairment Scale (CIS): Pilot findings on a measure of global impairment for children and adolescents. *International Journal of Methods in Psychiatric Research, 3*(3), 167–176.

Bishop v. Houston School District, 35 S.W 2d 465 (Tex.Civ. App. 1931).

Blanchett, W. J., Mumford, V., & Beachum, F. (2005). Urban school failure and disproportionality in a post-Brown era: Benign neglect of the constitutional rights of students of color. *Remedial and Special Education, 26*(2), 70–81.

Blau, J. R., Lamb, V. L., Stearns, E., & Pellerin, L. (2001). Cosmopolitan environments and adolescents' gains in social studies. *Sociology of Education, 74,* 121–138.

Bloom, B. (1976). *Human characteristics and school learning.* New York: McGraw-Hill.

Bloom, M., Fischer, J., & Orme, J. G. (2006). *Evaluating practice: Guidelines for the accountable professional* (5th ed.). New York: Allyn & Bacon.

Bloomfield, K. M., & Holzman, R. (1988). Helping today's nomads: A collaborative program to assist mobile children and their families. *Social Work in Education, 10,* 183–189.

Board of Education of Westside Community Schools v. Mergens, 496 U.S. 226 (1990).

Board of Education v. Dowell, 498 U.S. 237 (1991).

Board of Education v. Earls, 122 S. Ct. 2559 (2002).

Board of Education v. Helston, 32 Ill. App. 300 (1889).

Bogler, R. (2001). The influence of leadership style on teacher job satisfaction. *Educational Administration Quarterly, 37,* 662–683.

Bontempo, D. E., & D'Augelli, A. R. (2002). Effects of at-school victimization and sexual orientation on lesbian, gay, or bisexual youths' health risk behavior. *Journal of Adolescent Health, 30*(5), 364–374.

Boocock, S. S. (1973). The school as asocial environment for learning: Social organization and micro-social process in education. *Sociology of Education, 46*(1), 15–50.

Booth, A., & Crouter, A. C. (Eds.). (2001). *Does it take a village? Community effects on children, adolescents, & families.* New York: Erlbaum.

Borden, G. (2001). Creating an underclass through benign neglect: The plight of minorities with limited English proficiency. *Geo. Journal of Poverty Law & Policy, 8,* 395.

Botvin, G. J., Baker, E., Filazzola, D. D., & Botvin, E. M. (1990). A cognitive-behavioral approach to substance abuse prevention: A one-year follow-up. *Addictive Behaviors, 15,* 47–63.

Boulton, M. (1993). Aggressive fighting in British middle school children. *Educational Studies, 19,* 19–39.

Bowditch, C. (1993). Getting rid of troublemakers: High school disciplinary procedures and the production of dropouts. *Social Problems, 40,* 493–507.

Bowe, F. G. (1995). *Birth to five: Early childhood special education.* Albany, NY: Delmar Publishers.

Bowen, G. L., & Chapman, M. V. (1996). Poverty, neighborhood danger, social support, and the individual adaptation among at-risk youth in urban areas. *Journal of Family Issues, 17,* 641–666.

Bowen, G. L., & Richman, J. (2002). Schools in the context of communities. *Children & Schools, 24,* 67–71.

Bowen, G. L., & Van Dorn, R. A. (2002). Community violent crime rates and school danger. *Children & Schools, 24,* 90–104.

Bowen, G. L., Bowen, N. K., & Cook, P. G. (2000). Neighborhood characteristics and supportive parenting among single mothers. In G. L. Fox & M. L. Benson (Eds.), *Families, crime and criminal justice* (pp. 183–206). New York: Elsevier Science.

Bowen, G. L., Bowen, N. K., & Richman, J. M. (1998). *Students in peril: Crime and violence in neighborhoods and schools.* Chapel Hill, NC: Jordan Institute for Families, School of Social Work, The University of North Carolina at Chapel Hill.

Bowen, G. L., Bowen, N. K., & Richman, J. M. (2000). School size and middle school students' perceptions of the school environment. *Children & Schools, 22,* 69–82.

Bowen, G. L., Martin, J. A., Mancini, J. A., & Nelson, J. P. (2000). Community capacity: Antecedents and consequences. *Journal of Community Practice, 8*(2), 1–21.

Bowen, G. L., Richman, J., & Bowen, N. K. (2002). The School Success Profile: A results management approach to assessment and intervention planning. In A. R. Roberts & G. J. Greene (Eds.), *The social workers desk reference* (pp. 787–793). New York: Oxford University Press.

Bowen, G. L., Rose, R. A., & Bowen, N. K. (2005). *The reliability and validity of the school success profile.* Philadelphia: Xlibris Corporation.

Bowen, G. L., Rose, R. A., & Ware, W. B. (2006). The reliability and validity of the School Success Profile Learning Organization Measure. *Evaluation and Program Planning, 29,* 97–104.

Bowen, G. L., Rose, R. A., Powers, J. D., & Glennie, E. J. (2008). The joint effects of neighborhoods, schools, peers, and families on changes in the school success of middle school students. *Family Relations, 57,* 504–516.

Bowen, G. L., Ware, W. B., Rose, R. A., & Powers, J. D. (2007). Assessing the functioning of schools as learning organizations. *Children & Schools, 29,* 199–208.

Bowen, G. L., Woolley, M. E., Richman, J. M., & Bowen, N. K. (2001). Brief intervention in schools: The school success profile. *Brief Treatment and Crisis Intervention, 1*(1), 43–54.

Bowen, N. K., & Bowen, G. L. (1998). The mediating role of educational meaning in the relationship between home academic culture and academic performance. *Family Relations, 47,* 45–51.

Bowen, N. K., & Bowen, G. L. (1999). Effects of crime and violence in neighborhoods and schools on the school behavior and performance of adolescents. *Journal of Adolescent Research, 14,* 319–342.

Bowen, N. K., Bowen, G. L., & Ware, W B. (2002). Neighborhood social disorganization, families, and the educational behavior of adolescents. *Journal of Adolescent Research, 17,* 468–490.

Bowers, S. (1949). Nature and definition of social casework. *Social Casework, 30,* 417.

Bowes, J. M. (2004). *Children, families, and communities: Contexts and consequences* (2nd ed.). New York: Oxford University Press.

Bowles, S., & Gintis, H. (1976). *Schooling in capitalist America: Educational reform and the contradictions of economic life.* New York: Basic Books.

Bowman, B. T., Donovan, M. S., & Burns, M. S. (Eds.). (2001). *Eager to learn: Educating our preschoolers.* Washington, DC: National Academy Press.

Bowman, K. L. (2001). The new face of school desegregation. *Duke Law Journal, 50,* 1751.

Boyd County High Sch. Gay Straight Alliance v Bd. of Educ., 258 F. Supp. 2d 667 (E.D. Ky. 2003).

Boyd, W. L., & Shouse, R. C. (1997). The problems and promise of urban schools. In H. J. Walberg, O. Reyes, & R. P. Weissberg (Eds.), *Children and youth: Interdisciplinary perspectives* (pp. 141–165). Newbury Park, CA: Sage.

Bragg, R. (1997, December 3). Forgiveness, after 3 die in Kentucky shooting; M. Carneal opens fire on fellow students at Heath High School in West Paducah. *The New York Times,* p. A16.

Brake, D. (1994). Legal challenges to the educational barriers facing pregnant and parenting adolescents. *Clearinghouse Review, 28,* 141.

Brandis, C., & Philliber, S. (1998). Room to grow: Improving services for pregnant and parenting teenagers in school settings. *Education and Urban Society, 30*(5), 242–261.

Braunstein, A. (1959). The social worker and the parents. In G. Lee (Ed.), *Helping the troubled school child: Selected readings in school social work, 1935–1955.*

Washington, DC: National Association of Social Workers.

Breckinridge, S. (1914). Some aspects of the public school from a social worker's point of view. *Journal of the Proceedings and Addresses of the National Education Association.*

Breheny, M., & Stephens, C. (2004). Barriers to effective contraception and strategies for overcoming them among adolescent mothers. *Public Health Nursing, 21*(3), 220–227.

Brener, N. D., Martindale, J., & Weist, M. D. (2001). Mental health and social services: Results from the school health policies and programs study 2000. *Journal of School Health, 71,* 305–312.

Brener, N. D., Weist, M., Adelman, H., Taylor, L., & Vernon-Smiley, M. (2006). Mental health and social services: Results from the school health policies and programs study 2006. *Journal of School Health 77*(8), 486–499.

Briar, S. (1980). Toward the integration of practice and research. In C. Fanshel (Ed.), *Future of social work research.* Washington, DC: NASW Press.

Brief of Amici Curiae the National Association of Social Workers and the National Association of Social Workers Arizona Chapter, in Support of Appellant April Redding. (2008). Washington, DC: NASW. Retrieved November 9, 2008, from http://www .socialworkers.org/assets/secured/documents/ldf/brief Documents/Redding%20v.%20Safford.pdf

Brieland, D. (1977). Historical overview. *Social Work: Special Issue on Conceptual Frameworks, 22,* 338–433.

Brill, C., Fiorentino, N., Grant, J. (2001). Covictimization and inner city youth: A review. *International Journal of Emergency Mental Health, 3*(4), 229–239.

Brodsky, A. E. (1996). Resilient single mothers in risky neighborhoods. *Journal of Community Psychology, 24,* 347–363.

Bronfenbrenner, U. (1979). *The ecology of human development: Experiments by nature and design.* Cambridge, MA: Harvard University Press.

Brown v. Board of Education of Topeka (I), 347 U.S. 483 (1954).

Brown v. Board of Education of Topeka (II), 349 U.S. 294 (1955).

Bryk, A. S., & Driscoll, M. E. (1988). *The school as community: Theoretical foundations, contextual influences, and consequences for students and teachers.* Chicago: The University of Chicago Benton Center for Curriculum and Instruction.

Bryk, A. S., Lee, V. E., & Holland, P. B. (1993). *Catholic schools and the common good.* Cambridge, MA: Harvard University Press.

Burchard, J. D., Bruns, E. J., & Burchard, S. N. (2002). The wrap-around approach. In B. J. Burns & K. Hoagwood (Eds.), *Community treatment for youth* (pp. 69–90). New York: Oxford University Press.

Burcky, W., Reuterman, N., & Kopsky, S. (1988). Dating violence among high school students. *School Counselor, 35,* 353–358.

Burke, M. (2005) Sanctions on driving privileges. *Education Commission of the States.* Retrieved September 10, 2005, from www.ees.org/clearinghouse/60/10/6010.pdf

Burnette, D. (1998). Grandparents rearing grandchildren: A school-based small group intervention. *Research on Social Work Practice, 8,* 10–27.

Bushell, D., Wrobel, P. A., & Michaelis, M. L. (1968). Applying "group" contingencies to the classroom study behavior of preschool children. *Journal of Applied Behavior Analysis, 1,* 55–61.

Buysse, V., Schulte, A. C., Pierce, P. P., & Terry, D. (1994). Models and styles of consultation: Preferences of professionals in early intervention. *Journal of Early Intervention, 18*(3), 302–310.

Buysse, V., & Wesley, P. W. (2004). *Consultation in early childhood settings.* Baltimore: Paul H. Brookes.

California Education Code. Deering's California Code Annotated. Part 48200 et. seq. (2008).

Call from mother in Iraq leads to teen's suspension. (2005). *St. Louis Post Dispatch,* p. 22.

Callahan, C. (2008). Threat Assessment in School Violence. In T. W. Miller (Ed.), *School violence and primary prevention* (pp. 59–77). New York: Springer.

Callahan, R. E. (1962). *Education and the cult of efficiency; A study of the social forces that have shaped the administration of the public schools.* Chicago: University of Chicago Press.

Campbell, D. T., & Stanley, S. J. (1963). *Experimental and quasi-experimental designs for research.* Chicago: Rand McNally.

Cano, A., Avery-Leaf, S., Cascardi, M., & O'Leary, K. (1998). Dating violence in two high school samples: Discriminating variables. *Journal of Primary Prevention, 18,* 431–446.

Cantillon, D. (2006). Community social organization, parents, and peers as mediators of perceived neighborhood block characteristics on delinquent and prosocial activities. *American Journal of Community Psychology, 37,* 111–127.

Card, D., & Rothstein, J. (2007). Racial segregation and the black-white test score gap. *Journal of Public Economics, 91*(11–12), 2158–2184.

Carestio v. School Bd. of Broward Country, 79 F.Supp.2d 1347 (S.D. Fla.. 1999).

Carnegie Council on Adolescent Development. (1995). *Great transitions: Preparing adolescents for a new century.* New York: Carnegie Corporation of New York.

Carnoy, M., Jacobsen, R., Mishel, L., & Rothstein, R. (2005). *The charter school dust-up: Examining the evidence on enrollment and achievement.* New York: Economic Policy Institute and Teachers College Press.

Castaneda v. Picard, 648 F. 2d 989 (5th Cir. 1981).

Casto, R. M., Julia, M. C., Platt, L. J., Harbaugh, G. L., Waugaman, W. R., Thompson, A., et al. (1994). *Interprofessional care and collaborative practice* (pp. 35–58). Belmont, CA: Brooks/Cole.

Center for Education Reform. (2008). *Charter school laws across the states: Ranking and scoring* (10th ed.). Washington, DC: Author. (available at www.edreform.com).

Center for Social and Emotional Foundations for Early Learning. (2003). *Promoting social and emotional competence training modules.* Retrieved March 3, 2006, from http://www.csefel.uiuc.edu/modules.html#intro

Centers for Disease Control and Prevention (CDC). (2008a). *Youth risk behavior surveillance—United States, 2007* (SS No. 57-04). Surveillance Summaries. MMWR. Atlanta, GA: U.S. Department of Health and Human Services.

Centers for Disease Control and Prevention (CDC). (2008b). *HIV/AIDS surveillance report, 2006* (Volume No. 18). Atlanta, GA: U.S. Department of Health and Human Services. Retrieved from http://www.cdc.gov/hiv/topics/surveillance/resources/reports/

Chalifoux v. New Carey Indep. Sch. Dist., 976 F. Supp. 659 (S.D. Tex. 1997).

Chamberlain, P. (2002). Treatment foster care. In B. Burns, & K. Hoagwood (Eds.), *Community treatment for youth: evidence-based treatment for severe emotional and behavioral disorders* (pp. 117–138). Oxford: Oxford University Press.

Chen, X. K., Wen, S. W., Fleming, N., Demissie, K., Rhoads, G. G., & Walker, M. (2007). Teenage pregnancy and adverse birth outcomes: A large population based retrospective cohort study. *International Journal of Epidemiology, 36*(2), 368–373.

Cherry, D. J., Staudt, M. M., & Watson, M. (2005). Practice guidelines for school social workers: A modified replication and extension of a prototype. *Children & Schools, 27*(2), 71–81.

Child Abuse Prevention and Treatment Act (CAPTA). (2003). 42 U. S. C. A. §5106g.

Child Trends. (2003). Percentage of children living in unsafe neighborhoods by race and ethnicity, 2003. *Child Trends data bank.* Retrieved December 7, 2008, from http://www.childtrendsdatabank.org/

Children's Defense Fund. (1997). *The state of America's children yearbook, 1997.* Washington, DC: Children's Defense Fund.

Children's Defense Fund. (2005). *The state of America's children, 2005.* Washington, DC: Children's Defense Fund.

Children's Defense Fund. (2007). *America's cradle to prison pipeline.* Washington, DC: Children's Defense Fund.

Children's Defense Fund. (2008). *Moments in America for children.* Retrieved May 7, 2008, from http://www.childrensdefense.org/site/PageServer?pagename=research_national_data_moments

Christenson, S. L. (2004). The family-school partnership: An opportunity to promote the learning competence of all students. *School Psychology Review, 33,* 83–104.

Chubb, J. E., & Moe, T. M. (1990). *Politics, markets, and America's schools.* Washington, DC: Brookings Institution Press.

Clonan, S. M., McDougal, J. L., Clark, K., & Davison, S. (2007). Use of office discipline referrals in school-wide decision making: A practical example. *Psychology in the Schools, 44*(1), 19–27.

Coakley, T. M., Cuddeback, G., Buehler, C., & Cox, M. E. (2007). Kinship foster parents' perceptions of factors that promote or inhibit successful fostering. *Children and Youth Services Review, 29*(1), 92–109.

Cohen, D. K. (1970). Politics and research: Evaluation of social action programs in education. *Review of Educational Research, 40,* 213–238.

Colapinto, J. (2005). The controversy over the Harvey Milk School. [Electronic version]. *New York Times Magazine.* Retrieved September 4, 2005, from www.printhis.clickability.com/pt/cpt?action=cpt$title+ TheControversy+Overthe+

Coleman, J. S. (1966). *Equality of educational opportunity* (Report to the President and Congress). Washington, DC: U.S. Office of Education.

Coleman, J. S. (1975). Has forced busing failed? James Coleman offers new insights from recent research. *Phi Delta Kappan, 2,* 75–78.

Coleman, J. S. (1988). Social capital in the creation of human capital. *American Journal of Sociology, 94,* S95–S120.

Coleman, J. S. (1997). Output-driven schools: Principles of design. In J. S. Coleman, B. Schneider, S. Plank, K. S. Schiller, R. Shouse, & H. Wang with S. A. Lee (Eds.), *Redesigning American education* (pp. 13–38). Boulder, CO: Westview Press.

Coleman, J. S., Campbell, E. Q., Hobson, C. J., McPartland, J., Mood, A. M., Weinfeld, F. D., et al. (1966). *Equality of educational opportunity.* Washington, DC: U.S. Government Printing Office.

Collaborative Dissemination for Prevention Programs Group. (n.d.). *Prevention strategies that work: What administrators can do to promote positive student behavior.* Retrieved September 5, 2005, from http://cecp.air.org/preventionstrategies/prevent.pdf

Collins v. Chandler Unified School District, 644 F. 2d 759 (9th Cir. 1981).

Collins, J. (2001). *Good to great.* New York: HarperCollins.

Commonwealth of Virginia v. May, 62 Va. Cir. 360 (2003).

Compton, B., & Galaway, B. (1984). *Social work processes* (3rd ed.). Homewood, IL: Dorsey Press.

Conceptual Frameworks II: Second Special Issue on Conceptual Frameworks. (1981). *Social Work, 26*(1).

Condon, T., & Wolff, P. (1996). *School rights. A parent's legal handbook and action guide.* New York: Macmillan.

Conduct Problems Prevention Research Group. (1992). A developmental and clinical model for the prevention of conduct disorders: The Fast Track Program. *Development and Psychopathology, 4,* 509–527.

Conduct Problems Prevention Research Group. (2004). The effects of the Fast Track program on serious problem outcomes at the end of elementary school. *Journal of Clinical Child and Adolescent Psychology, 33,* 650–661.

Conoley, J., & Conoley, C. (2001). Systemic intervention for safe schools. In J. Hughes, A. Greca, & J. Conoley (Eds.), *Handbook of psychological services for children and adolescents* (pp. 439–455). New York: Oxford University Press.

Constable, R., & Walberg, H. (1999). Working with families. In R. Constable, S. McDonald, & J. P. Flynn (Eds.), *School social work: Practice, policy, and research perspective* (4th ed., pp. 226–247). Chicago: Lyceum Books.

Constable, R. T., & Flynn, J. P. (Eds.). (1982). *School social work: Practice and research perspectives.* Homewood, IL: Dorsey Press.

Cook, T. D., & Campbell, D. T. (1979). *Quasi-experimentation: Design and analysis issues for field settings.* Chicago: Rand McNally.

Cooper, B. S., & Sureau, J. (2007). The politics of home-schooling: New developments, new challenges. *Educational Policy 21*(1), 110–131.

Cooper, S. P., Weller, N. F., Fox, E. E., & Cooper, S. R. (2005). Comparative description of migrant farm-workers versus other students attending rural south Texas schools: Substance abuse, work, and injuries. *The Journal of Rural Health, 21*(4), 361–366.

Copeland, J. (2004). Developments in the treatment of cannabis use disorder. *Current Opinion in Psychiatry, 17*(3), 161–167.

Corbett, C., Hill, C., & St. Rose, A. (2008). *Where the girls are: The facts about gender equity in education.* Washington DC: AAUW Educational Foundation.

Corcoran, J. (2000). Evidenced-based social work practice with families: A life span approach. New York: Springer.

Corcoran, J., Franklin, C., & Bennett, P. (2000). Ecological factors associated with adolescent pregnancy and parenting. *Social Work Research, 24*(1), 29–39.

Corcoran, K., & Fischer, J. (2000). *Measures for clinical practice.* New York: Free Press.

Cornell, D. G. (2006). *School violence: Fears versus facts.* Mahwah, NJ: Erlbaum.

Cornfield v. Consolidated High Sch. Dist. No. 230, 991 F.2d 1316 (7th Cir. 1993).

Costello, E. J., Mustillo, S., Erkanli, A., Keeler, G., & Angold, A. (2003). Prevalence and development of psychiatric disorders in childhood and adolescence. *Archives of General Psychiatry, 60*(8), 837–844.

Costigan, A. T., III. (2002). Teaching the culture of high stakes testing: Listening to new teachers. *Action in Teacher Education, 23*(4), 28–34.

Costin, L. B. (1969a). An analysis of the tasks in school social work. *Social Service Review, 43*, 274–285.

Costin, L. B. (1969b). A historical review of school social work. *Social Casework, 50*, 439–453.

Costin, L. B. (1972). Adaptations on the delivery of school social work services. *Social Casework, 53*, 348–354.

Costin, L. B. (1975). School social work practice: A new model. *Social Work, 20*(2), 135–139.

Costin, L. B. (1978). *Social work services in schools: Historical perspectives and current directions* (pp. 1–34). Washington, DC: National Association of Social Workers.

Council for Exceptional Children. (1997). *Summary of the Individuals with Disabilities Education Act amendments of 1997.* Reston, VA: Author.

Council for Exceptional Children. (2003). *No Child Left Behind Act of 2001: Implications for special education policy and practice. Selected sections of Title I and Title IL.* Washington, DC: Author. Retrieved September 3, 2005, from www.cec.sped.org/pp/NCLBside-by-side.pdf

Council for Exceptional Children. (2004). *The new IDEA.* Washington, DC: Author. Retrieved September 3, 2005, from www.cec.sped.org/pp/IDEA-120204.pdf

Covington County v. G. W., 767 So. 2d 187 (Miss. 2000).

Craig. S. E., & Haggart, A. G. (1994). Including all children: The ADAs challenge to early intervention. *Infants & Young Children, 7*(2), 15–19.

Crawford, J. (1997). *Best evidence: Research foundations of the Bilingual Education Act.* Washington, DC: National Center for Bilingual Education.

Crawford, J. (2002). Obituary, the bilingual ed act, 1968–2002. [Electronic version]. *Rethinking schools online.* Retrieved June 1, 2002, from www.rethinkingschools.org/Archives/16_04/Bi1164.htm

Croninger, R. G., & Lee, V. E. (2001). Social capital and dropping out of high school: Benefits to at-risk students of teachers' support and guidance. *Teachers College Record, 103*, 548–581.

Crosnoe, R., Johnson, M. K., & Elder, G. H., Jr. (2004). Intergeneral bonding in school: The behavioral and contextual correlates of student-teacher relationships. *Sociology of Education, 77*, 60–81.

Crowthers, V. L. (1963). The school as a group setting. *Social work practice, 1963. Selected papers, 90th annual forum, national conference on social welfare* (pp. 70–83). New York: Columbia University Press.

Cuddeback, G. S. (2004). Kinship family foster care. *Children and Youth Services Review, 26*(7), 623–639.

Cuevas, M. C. (2006). Guidelines for confidentiality: Writing progress notes and storing confidential information. In C. Franklin, M. B. Harris, & P. Allen-Meares (Eds.), *The school services sourcebook: A guide for school-based professionals* (pp. 913–920). New York: Oxford University Press.

Culbert, J. (1916). Visiting teachers and their activities. *Proceedings of the National Conference of Charities and Corrections.* Chicago: Hildman Printing Company.

Culbert, J. (1923). *Visiting teachers in the United States.* New York: Public Education Association of the City of New York.

Cunha, F., & Heckman, J. J. (2006). Investing in our young people. Chicago: University of Chicago.

Daniel R. R. v. State Board of Education. (1989). 874 F 2d 1036 (5th circuit).

Daniels v. Gordon, 232 Ga. App. 811, 503 S.E. 2d 72 (1998).

Danziger, S., & Gottschalk, P. (1993). *Uneven tides: Rising inequality in America.* New York: Russell Sage Foundation.

Darling, N., & Steinberg, L. (1997). Community influences on adolescent achievement and deviance. In J. Brooks-Gunn, G. J. Duncan, & J. L. Aber (Eds.), *Neighborhood poverty* (Vol. 11, pp. 120–131). New York: Russell Sage Foundation.

Davies, D. (2002). The 10th School Revisited: Are School/Family/Community Partnerships on the Reform Agenda Now? *Phi Delta Kappan, 83*(5), 388–392.

Davis v. Monroe County Board of Education, 74 F. 3d 1186 (11th Cir. 1996).

Davis v. Monroe County Board of Education, 526 U.S. 629 (1999).

de Anda, D. (1999). Project Peace: The evaluation of a skills-based violence prevention program for high school adolescents. *Social Work in Education, 21,* 137–149.

de Anda, D. (2001). A qualitative evaluation of a mentor program for at-risk youth: The participants' perspective. *Child and Adolescent Social Work Journal, 18,* 97–117.

deBettencourt, L. U. (2002). Understanding the differences between IDEA and Section 504. *Teaching Exceptional Children, 34*(3), 16–23.

DeLacy, M. (2004). The "no child" law's biggest victims? An answer that may surprise you. *Education Week Commentary, 23*(41), 40.

Delva-Tauili'ili, J. (1995). Assessment and prevention of aggressive behavior among youths of color: Integrating cultural and social factors. *Social Work in Education, 17*(2), 83–90.

Department of Heath and Human Services (2005). Head Start Impact Study, 2005. Dept. of Health and Human Services: Washington, DC. Available at http://www.acf.hhs.gov/programs/opre/hs/impact_study/reports/first_yr_execsum/firstyr_sum_title.html.

Deshler, B., & Erlich, J. L. (1972). Changing school/community relations. In R. Sarri & F. Maple (Eds.), *The school in the community* (pp. 233–253). Washington, DC: NASW.

Developmental Studies Center. (2000). *Caring school community: Elementary school student questionnaire measures.* Oakland, CA: Developmental Studies Center.

DeVoe, J. E., Peter, K., Kaufman, P., Miller, A., Noonan, M., Snyder, T. D., et al. (2004). *Indicators of school crime and safety: 2004* (NCES 2005-002/NCS 205290). U.S. Departments of Education and Justice. Washington, DC: U.S. Government Printing Office.

Diaz de La Portilla, R. (2002). *The effect of Florida's tuition credits on public schools: Competition or convolution?* Unpublished master's thesis, Cornell University, Ithaca, NY.

Diehl, D., & Frey, A. (2008). Evaluating a community-school model of social work practice. *School Social Work Journal, 32*(2), 1–20.

Dijkstra, M., de Vries, H., & Parcel, G. S. (1993). The linkage approach to a school-based smoking prevention program in the Netherlands. *Journal of School Health, 63,* 339–342.

Dinkes, R., Cataldi, E. F., & Lin-Kelly, W. (2007). *Indicators of school crime and safety: 2007* (NCES 2008-021/NCJ 219553). National Center for Education Statistics, Institute of Education Sciences, U.S. Department of Education, and Bureau of Justice Statistics, Office of Justice Programs, U.S. Department of Justice. Washington, DC.

Dinnebeil, L. A., Hale, L. M., & Rule, S. (1996). A qualitative analysis of parents' and service coordinators' descriptions of variables that influence collaborative relationships. *Topics in Early Childhood Special Education, 16*(3), 322–347.

Domitrovich, D. E., Cortes, R. C., & Greenberg, M. T. (2007). Improving young children's social and emotional competence: A randomized trial of the preschool PATHS curriculum. *Journal of Primary Prevention, 28*(2), 67–91.

Donovan v. Poway Unified School Dist. (Super. Ct. No. GIC823157) (Cert. for publication, 4th. App. Dist. 2008).

Donovan, S., & Cross, C. T. (Eds.) & Committee on Minority Representation in Special Education, National Research Council. (2002). *Minority students in special and gifted education.* Washington, DC: National Academies Press.

Driscoll, A. K., Sugland, B. W., Manlove, J., & Papillo, A. R. (2005). Community opportunity, perceptions of opportunity, and the odds of an adolescent birth. *Youth & Society, 37*(1), 33–61.

Drolet, M., Paquin, M., & Soutyrine, M. (2007). Strengths-based approach and coping strategies used by parents whose young children exhibit violent behaviour: Collaboration between schools and parents. *Child & Adolescent Social Work Journal 24*(5), 437–453.

Dryfoos, J., & Maguire, S. (2002). *Inside full-service community schools.* Thousand Oaks, CA: Corwin Press.

Duchnowski, A. J., Kutash, K., & Friedman, R. M. (2002). Community-based intervention in a system of care and outcome framework. In B. J. Burns & K. Hoagwood (Eds.), *Community treatment for youth* (pp. 16–38). New York: Oxford University Press.

Duncan, G. J., & Brooks-Gunn, J. (1997). Income effects across the lifespan: Integration and interpretations. In G. J. Duncan & J. Brooks-Gunn (Eds.), *Consequences of growing up poor* (pp. 596–610). New York: Russel Sage Foundation.

Dunst C. J., Trivette C. M., & Thompson, R. (1994). Parent-professional collaboration and partnership. In C. J. Dunst, C. M., Trivette, & Deal, A. G. (Eds.), *Supporting and strengthening families. Volume I: Methods, strategies and practices* (pp. 197–212). Cambridge, MA: Brookline Books.

Dunst, C. J., Trivette, C. M., & Deal, A. G. (1994a). Enabling and empowering families. In C. I. Dunst, C. M. Trivette, & A. G. Deal (Eds.), *Supporting and strengthening families. Volume 1: Methods, strategies and practices* (pp. 2–11). Cambridge, MA: Brookline Books.

Dunst, C. J., Trivette, C. M., & Deal, A. G. (Eds.). (1994b). *Supporting and strengthening families. Volume I: Methods, strategies and practices.* Cambridge, MA: Brookline Books.

Dupper, D. R. (1994). Reducing out-of-school suspensions: A survey of attitudes and barriers. *Social Work in Education, 16,* 115–123.

Durlak, J. A., Taylor, R. D., Kawashima, K., Pachan, M. K., DuPre, E. P., Celio, C. I., et al. (2007). Effects of positive youth development programs on school, family, and community. *American Journal of Community Psychology, 39*(3–4), 269–286.

Dwyer, K., Osher, D., & Warger, C. (1998). *Early warning, timely response: A guide to safe schools.* Washington, DC: U.S. Department of Education. Retrieved June 27, 2002, from http://cecp.air.org/ guide/guide.pdf

Dyson, M. R. (2004). *Safe rules or gays' schools? The dilemma of sexual orientation segregation in public education.* 7 U. Pa. J. Const. L. 183.

Eaton, D. K., Kann, L., Kinchen, S., Ross, J., Harris, W. A., Lowry, R., et al. (2006). Youth risk behavior surveillance—United States, 2005. In *Surveillance Summaries* (MMWR) (No. SS-5). Atlanta, GA: Centers for Disease Control and Prevention.

Eber, L., Sugai, G., Smith, C. R., & Scott, T. M. (2002). Wraparound and positive behavioral interventions and supports in the schools. *Journal of Emotional and Behavioral Disorders, 10*(3), 171–180.

Education for All Handicapped Children Act, 20 U.S.C.A. § 1400 (1975). *Federal Register* (P.L. 94-142 41:46977).

Edwards v. Aguillard, 482 U.S. 578 (1987).

Egley, A., Jr., & Ritz, C. E. (2006). *Highlights of the 2004 national youth gang survey* (FS No. 200601). Washington, DC: Office of Justice Programs, U.S. Department of Justice.

Eisemann, V. (2000). Protecting the kids in the hall: Using Title IX to stop student-on-student anti-gay harassment. 15 *Berkeley Women's L.J.,* 125.

Eisen, M., Zellman, G. L., & McAlister, A. L. (1990). Evaluating the impact of a theory based sexuality and contraceptive education program. *Family Planning Perspective, 22*(6), 261–271.

Eisenbraun, K. D. (2007). Violence in schools: Prevalence, prediction, and prevention. *Aggression and Violent Behavior, 12,* 459–469.

Eisenman, J. W, & Fischer, L. (1994). *The rights of students and teachers.* New York: Harper & Row.

Elizalde, T., & Ramirez, G. (2006). Effective intervention with gangs and gang members. In C. Franklin, M. B. Harris, & P. Allen-Meares (Eds.), *The school services sourcebook: A guide for social workers, counselors, and mental health professionals.* New York: Oxford University Press.

Elze, D. E. (2006). Working with gay, lesbian, bisexual, and transgender students. In C. Franklin, M. B. Harris, & P. Allen-Meares (Eds.), *The school services sourcebook: A guide for school-based professionals* (pp. 861–870). New York: Oxford University Press.

Engle v. Vitale, 370 U.S. 421 (1962).

Englund, M. M., Egeland, B., & Collins, W. A. (2008). Exceptions to high school dropout predictions in a low-income sample: Do adults make a difference? *Journal of Social Issues, 64*(1), 77–93.

Epp, J. R., & Watkinson, A. M. (Eds.). (1997). *Systemic violence in education: Promise broken.* Albany: State University of New York Press.

Epstein, J. (2001). *School, family, and community partnerships: Preparing educators and improving schools.* Boulder, CO: Westview Press.

Epstein, M. H., & Sharma, J. M. (1998). *Behavioral and Emotional Rating Scale: A strength-based approach to assessment.* Austin, TX: PRO-ED.

Equal Access Act, 20 U.S.C. 4071(a) (1989).

Equal Educational Opportunities Act of 1974, P.L. 93-380, 20 U.S.C. 1701, et. seq.

Erickson, C., Mattaini, M. A., & McGuire, M. S. (2004). Constructing nonviolent cultures in schools: The state of the science. *Children and Schools, 26,* 102–116.

Evans, G. W. (2004). The environment of childhood poverty. *American Psychologist, 59*(2), 77–92.

Everett, E. M. (1938). The importance of social work in a school program. *The Family, 19,* 58.

Faggiano, F., Vigna-Taglianti, F., Versino, E., Zambon, A., Borraccino, A., & Lemma P. (2002). School-based prevention for illicit drugs' use. *Cochrane Database of Systematic Reviews*, 2. New York: Wiley.

Faircloth, S. C. (2004). Understanding the impact of U.S. federal education policies of the education of children and youth with disabilities. *International Studies in Educational Administration, 32*(2), 32–46.

Family Educational Rights and Privacy Act (FERPA), 20 U.S.C. § 1232(g) (1974).

Fass, S., & Cauthen, N. K. (2007). *Who are America's poor children?* Retrieved May 14, 2008, from http://www.nccp.org/publications/pub_787.html

Fast, J. (1999). Where were you fifth period? Five strategies for high school group formation in the 1990s. *Social Work in Education, 21,* 99–107.

Federal Interagency Forum on Child & Family Statistics. (2005). *America's children: Key national indicators of well-being 2005.* Retrieved September 6, 2005, from http://childsstats.gov/americaschildren/index.asp

Federal Poverty Guidelines. (2008, January 23). *Federal Register, 73*(15), 3971–3972.

Fellin, P. (2001). *The community and the social worker* (3rd ed.). Belmont, CA: Brooks/Cole.

Felner, R., Phillips, R., DuBois, D., & Lease, M. (1991). Ecological interventions and the process of change for prevention: Wedding theory and research to implementation in real world settings. *American Journal of Community Psychology, 19*(3), 379–387.

Ferri, B. A., & Connor, D. J. (2005). In the shadow of "Brown": Special education and overrepresentation of students of color. *Remedial and Special Education, 26*(2), 93–100.

Fick, A. C., & Thomas, S. M. (1995). Growing up in a violent environment: Relationship to health-related beliefs and behaviors. *Youth and Society, 27*(2), 136–147.

Figlio, D. N., & Lucas, M. E. (2004). Do high grading standards affect student performance? *Journal of Public Economics, 88*(9–10), 1815–1834.

File, N., & Kontos, S. (1992). Indirect service delivery through consultation: Review and implications for early intervention. *Journal of Early Intervention, 16*(2), 221–223.

Fischer, C. S., Hout, M., Jankowski, M., Lucas, S., Swidler, A., & Voss, K. (1996). *Inequality by design: Cracking the bell curve myth.* Princeton, NJ: Princeton University Press.

Fischer, J., & Corcoran, K. (2007). *Measures for clinical practice* (4th ed.). New York: Oxford University Press.

Fischer, J., & Gochros, H. L. (1975). *Planned behavior change: Behavior modification in social work.* New York: Free Press.

Fisher, J. K. (1966). Role perceptions and characteristics of attendance coordinators, psychologists, and social workers. *Journal of the International Association of Pupil Personnel Workers, 10,* 1–8.

Fitz-Gibbon, C. T., & Morris, L. L. (1987). *How to design a program evaluation.* Beverly Hills, CA: Sage.

Flynn, J. P. (1976). Congruence in perception of social work-related tasks in a school system. *Social Service Review, 59,* 471–481.

Foxcroft, D., Ireland, D., Lowe, G., & Breen, R. (2002). Primary prevention for alcohol misuse in young people. *Cochrane Database of Systematic Reviews, 3.* New York: Wiley.

Franklin v. Gwinnett County Public Schools, 503 U.S. 60 (1992).

Franklin, C. (1999). Grandparents as parents. Editorial, *Children & Schools, 2*(3), 131–135.

Franklin, C. (1999). Preparing for managed behavioral health care in children's services. *Children & Schools, 21*, 67–71.

Franklin, C. (2000). Predicting the future of school social work practice in the new millennium. [Editorial]. *Social Work in Education, 22*(1), 3–7.

Franklin, C. (2001). Establishing successful relationships with expanded mental health services. *Children in Schools, 23*(4), 194–197.

Franklin, C., & Gerlach, B. (2006). One hundred years of linking schools with communities: Current models and opportunities. *School Social Work Journal, 31*, 44–62.

Franklin, C., & Hopson, L. (2004). Into the schools with evidenced-based practices. *Children & Schools, 26*, 67–70.

Franklin, C., & Hopson, L. (2007). Facilitating the use of evidence-based practice in community organizations. *Journal of Social Work Education, 43*(3), 377–404.

Franklin, C., & Soto, I. (2002). Keeping Hispanic students in school. *Children & Schools, 25*, 4–7.

Franklin, C., Biever, J., Moore, K., Clemons, D., & Scamardo, M. (2001). The effectiveness of solution-focused therapy with children in a school settting. *Research on Social Work Practice, 11*, 441–434.

Franklin, C., Harris, M. B., & Allen-Meares, P. (Eds.). (2006). *The school services sourcebook: A guide for school-based professionals.* New York: Oxford University Press.

Franklin, C., Hopson, L., & Tenbarge, C. (2003). Family systems. In C. Jordan & C. Franklin (Eds.), *Clinical assessment for social workers: Quantitative and qualitative methods.* Chicago: Lyceum Books, Inc.

Franklin, C., Kim, J. S., & Tripodi, S. J. (in press). A meta-analysis of published school social work practice studies: 1980–2007. *Research on Social Work Practice.*

Franklin, C., Streeter, C., Kim, J. S., & Tripodi, S. (2007). The effectiveness of a solution-focused public alternative school for dropout prevention and retrieval. *Children & Schools, 29*, 133–144.

Fraser, M. W. (Ed.). (2004). *Risk and resilience in childhood: An ecological perspective* (2nd ed.). Washington, DC: NASW.

Fraser, M. W., Kirby, L. D., & Smokowski, P. R. (2004). Risk and resilience in childhood: An ecological perspective. In M. W. Fraser (Ed.), *Risk and resilience in childhood: An ecological perspective* (pp. 13–66). Washington, DC: National Association of Social Workers.

Freeman v. Pitts, 503 U.S. 467 (1992).

Freeman, E., & Pennekamp, M. (1988). *Social work practice: Toward a child, family, school, community perspective.* Springfield, IL: Charles C Thomas.

Freeman, E. M. (1995). School social work overview. In R. L. Edwards (Ed.), *Encyclopedia of social work*

(19th ed., Vol. 3, pp. 2087–2099). Washington, DC: NASW.

Fry, R., & Gonzales, F. (2008). *One-in-five and growing fast: A profile of Hispanic public school students.* Washington DC: Pew Hispanic Center. Accessed October 15, 2008, from http://pewhispanic.org/files/reports/92.pdf

Fryer, R. G., & Levitt, S. D. (2007). *Testing for racial differences in the mental ability of young children.* Unpublished manuscript, Harvard University, Cambridge, MA.

Fuller-Thomson, E., & Minkler, M. (2000). African American grandparents raising grandchildren: A national profile of demographic and health characteristics. *Health & Social Work, 25*(2), 109–118.

Furman, R., & Jackson, R. (2002). Wraparound services: An analysis of community-based mental health services for children. *Journal of Child & Adolescent Psychiatric Nursing, 15*(3), 124–131.

Furstenberg, F. E., Jr., & Hughes, M. E. (1997). The influence of neighborhoods on children's development: A theoretical perspective and a research agenda. In J. Brooks-Gunn, G. J. Duncan, & J. L. Aber (Eds.), *Neighborhood poverty* (Vol. II, pp. 23–47). New York: Russell Sage Foundation.

Furstenburg, E. F., Jr., Cook, T. D., Eccles, J., Elder, G. H., Jr., & Sameroff, A. (1999). *Managing to make it: Urban families and adolescent success.* Chicago: University of Chicago Press.

Gaither v. Barron, 924 F. Supp.134 (M.D.Ala.1996).

Gambrill, E. (1999). Evidence-based practice: An alternative to authority-based practice. *Families in Society: The Journal of Contemporary Human Services, 80*, 341–350.

Gambrill, E. (2001). Social work: An authority-based profession. *Research on Social Work Practice, 11*(2), 166–175.

Gambrill, E. D. (1987). *Behavior modification: Handbook of assessment, intervention and evaluation.* San Francisco, CA: Jossey-Bass.

Garbarino, J. (1990). The human ecology of early risk. In S. J. Meisels & J. P. Shonkoff (Eds.), *Handbook of early childhood intervention* (pp. 78–96). New York: Cambridge University Press.

Garcia, S., & Ortiz, A. (1988). Preventing inappropriate referrals of language minority students to special education. *New Focus, 5,* 1–3.

Garrett, K. J. (2001). Reducing school-based bullying. *Journal of School Social Work, 12,* 74–90.

Gebel, T. J. (1996). Kinship care and nonrelative family foster care: A comparison of caregiver attributes and attitudes. *Child Welfare, 75*(1), 5–18.

Geierstanger S. P., & Amaral G. (2005). School-based health centers and academic performance: What is the intersection? April 2004 Meeting Proceedings. White Paper. Washington, DC: National Assembly on School-Based Health Care.

Gender equity in America's schools. 101st Cong., 2d Sess. (1992) (testimony of Dick Swett).

Gensheimer, L. K., Ayers, T. S., & Roosa, M. W. (1993). School-based prevention interventions for at-risk populations. *Evaluation and Program Planning, 16,* 159–167.

George, M. P., White, G. P., & Schlaffer, J. J. (2007). Implementing school-wide behavior change: Lessons from the field. *Psychology in the Schools, 44*(1), 41–51.

Georgia girl's Tweety Bird chain runs afoul of weapons policy. (2000, September 28). Retrieved June 1, 2002, from www.cnn.com/2000/US/09/28/wallet .suspension.02/

Gerdtz, J. (2000). Evaluating behavioral treatment of disruptive classroom behaviors of an adolescent with autism. *Research on Social Work Practice, 10,* 98–110.

Germain, C. B. (1979). Ecology and social work. In C. B. Germain (Ed.), *Social work practice: People and environment* (pp. 1–22). New York: Columbia University Press.

Germain, C. B. (Ed.). (1979). *Social work practice: People and environments.* New York: Columbia University Press.

Germain, C. B. (2006). An ecological perspective on social work in the schools. In R. Constable, C. R. Massat, S. McDonald, & J. P. Flynn (Eds.), *School social work: Practice, policy, and research* (6th ed., pp. 29–39). Chicago: Lyceum Books.

Germain, C. B., & Gitterman, A. (1995). Ecological perspective. In R. Edwards (Ed.), *Encyclopedia of social work* (19th ed., pp. 817–825). Washington, DC: NASW Press.

Gershoff, E. T., & Bitensky, S. H. (2007). The case against corporal punishment of children: Converging evidence from social science research and international human rights law and implications for U.S. public policy. *Psychology, Public Policy, and Law, 13,* 231–272.

Gibbs, L. E. (2003). *Evidence-based practice for the helping professions.* Canada: Thompson Brooks/Cole.

Gilbert, C. B. (1999). We are what we wear: Revisiting school dress codes. *1999 B.Y.U. Education & Law Journal, 3.*

Gilbert, D. J. (2001). HIV-affected children and adolescents: What school social workers should know. *Children and Schools, 23*(3), 135–142.

Gilgun, J. (1996). Human development and adversity in ecological perspective, part I: A conceptual framework. *The Journal of Contemporary Human Services, 77*(7), 395–402.

Gill, B. P., Timpane, P. M., Ross, K. E., & Brewer, D. J. (2001). *Rhetoric versus reality: What we know and what we need to know about vouchers and charter schools.* Santa Monica, CA: Rand.

Gilliam, W. S. (2005). *Prekindergarteners left behind: Expulsion rates in state prekindergarten systems.* Retrieved October 18, 2008 from http://www.med .yale.edu/chldstdy/faculty/pdf/Gilliam05.pdf

Gioia, D. (2007). Using an organizational change model to qualitatively understand practitioner adoption of evidence-based practice in community mental health. *Mental Health, 3,* 1–16.

Gitterman, A., & Shulman, L. (Eds.). (2005). *Mutual aid groups, vulnerable & resilient populations, and the life cycle.* New York: Columbia University Press.

Gladieux, L. E., & Swail, W. S. (1998). Financial aid is not enough: Improving the odds of college success. Reprinted from *The College Board Review, 185,* 1–11.

Goldstein, A. (1996). *The psychology of vandalism.* New York: Plenum Press.

Goldstein, A. P. (1980). *Skill streaming for adolescents.* Champaign, IL: Research Press.

Goldstein, A. P. (1984). *The prepared curriculum.* Champaign, IL: Research Press.

Goldstein, A. P. (1998). *The peace curriculum: Expanded aggression replacement training.* Erie, CO: Research Press, Center for Safe Schools and Communities, Inc.

Goldstein, A. P., & McGinnis, E. (1984). *Skill streaming for elementary school children.* Champaign, IL: Research Press.

Gordon, W. (1962). A critique of the working definition. *Social Work, 7*(1), 3–13.

Gorman-Smith, D., Tolan, P. H., Henry, D. B., Quintana, E., Lutovsky, K., & Leventhal, A. (2007). Schools and families educating children: A preventative intervention for early elementary school children. In P. H. Tolan, J. Szapocznik, & S. Sambrano (Eds.), *Preventing youth substance abuse: Science-based programs for adolescents and children* (pp. 113–135). Washington, DC: American Psychological Association.

Gormley, W. T. J., Phillips, D., & Gayer, T. (2008). Preschool programs can boost school readiness. *Science, 320,* 1723–1724.

Goss v. Lopez, 419 U.S. 565 (1975).

Gottlieb, B. H., & Gottlieb, L. J. (1971). An expanded role for the school social workers. *Social Work, 16,* 12–21.

Government Accounting Office. (2000a). *Charter schools: Limited access to facility financing* (HEHS-00-163). Washington, DC: U.S. Government Printing Office.

Government Accounting Office. (2000b). *Title I program: Stronger accountability needed for performance of disadvantaged students* (HEHS00-89). Washington, DC: U.S. Government Printing Office.

Grant, G. (1973). Shaping social policy: The politics of the Coleman Report. *Teachers College Record, 75*(1), 17–54.

Gratz v. Bollinger, 539 U.S. 244 (2003).

Gray, C. (2000). *The new social story book* (2nd ed.). Philadelphia: Jessica Kingsley.

Gray, C. (n.d.). *What is a social story?* Retrieved September 5, 2005, from www.thegraycenter.org/page.asp? catID=3&sctID==25

Gray, C., White, A. L., & McAndrew, S. (2002). *My social stories book* (2nd ed.). Philadelphia: Jessica Kingsley.

Gray, D. (1991). *The plight of the African American male: An executive summary of a legislative hearing.* Detroit, MI: Council President Pro Tem Gil, the Detroit City Council Youth Advisory Commission.

Green v. County School Board of New Kent County, 391 U.S. 430 (1968).

Green, P. E. (2003). The undocumented: Educating the children of migrant workers in American. *Bilingual Research Journal, 27*(1), 51–71.

Greenberg, M. T., Kusche, C., & Mihalic, S. E. (1998). *Blueprints for violence prevention, book ten: Promoting alternative thinking strategies (PATHS).* Boulder, CO: Center for the Study and Prevention of Violence.

Greenspan, S., with Benderly, B. L. (1997). *The growth of the mind and the endangered origins of intelligence.* Reading, MA: Addison-Wesley.

Greif, G. L., & Lynch, A. A. (1983). The ecosystems perspective. In C. H. Meyer (Ed.), *Clinical social work in the eco-systems perspective* (pp. 35–71). New York: Columbia University Press.

Grinnell, R. M. (2001). *Social work research and evaluation* (6th ed.). Itasca, IL: F. E. Peacock.

Grossman, D. C., Neckerman, H. J., Koepsell, T. D., Liu, P. Y., Asher, K. N., Beland, K., et al. (1997). Effectiveness of a violence prevention curriculum among children in elementary school: A randomized controlled trial. *Journal of the American Medical Association, 277,* 1605–1611.

Grossman, J. B., & Tierney, J. P (1998). Does mentoring work? An impact of the Big Brothers Big Sisters program. *Evaluation Review, 22,* 403–426.

Grutter v. Bollinger, 539 U.S. 306 (2003).

Gun-Free Schools Act. 20 U.S.C.§§8921-8926 (1994). 20 U.S.C. 7151 (2002).

Guralnick, M. J. (Ed.). (1997a). *The effectiveness of early intervention.* Baltimore: Paul H. Brookes.

Guralnick, M. J. (1997b). Organizing themes in early intervention. *Infants & Young Children, 10*(2), v–vii.

Guralnick, M. J. (1997c). Second generation research in the field of early intervention. In M. J. Guralnick (Ed.), *The effectiveness of early intervention* (pp. 3–22). Baltimore: Paul H. Brookes.

Hall, G. E. (1936). Changing concepts in visiting teacher work. *Visiting Teacher Bulletin, 12.*

Hammond, C., Linton, D., Smink, J., & Drew, S. (2007). *Dropout risk factors and exemplary programs.* Clemson, SC: National Dropout Prevention Center, Communities in Schools, Inc.

Hammond, W. R., & Yung, B. (1991). Preventing violence in at-risk African American youth. *Journal of Heath Care for the Poor and Underserved, 2,* 358–372.

Hammond, W. R., & Yung, B. (1993). Psychology's role in the public health response to assaultive violence among young African-American men. *American Psychologist, 48,* 142–154.

Hanft, B. E., Rush, D. D., & Shelden, M. L. (2004). *Coaching families and colleagues in early childhood.* Baltimore: Paul H. Brookes.

Hansen, W., & Tanglewood Research, Inc. (2004). *All Stars Core: Version 2.4.* Greensboro, NC: Tanglewood Research, Inc.

Harris v. Joint Sch. Dist. No. 241, 821 F. Supp. 638 (D. Idaho, 1993).

Harris, A., & Hopkins, D. (2000). Introduction to special feature: Alternative perspectives on school improvement. *School Leadership and Management, 20*(1), 6–14.

Harris, L. H. (1981). Goal attainment scaling on the treatment of adolescents. *Social Work in Education, 5*(1), 7–18.

Harris, M. B., & Allgood, J. (in press). Adolescent pregnancy prevention: Choosing an effective program that fits. *Children and Youth Services Review.*

Harris, M. B., & Franklin, C. G. (2003). Effects of cognitive-behavioral, school-based, group intervention with Mexican American pregnant and parenting adolescents. *Social Work Research, 27*(2), 71–83.

Harrison, P. L., & Oakland, T. (2000). *Adaptive behavior assessment system.* San Antonio, TX: The Psychological Corporation.

Harry, B. (1992a). *Cultural diversity, families, and the special education system communication and empowerment.* New York: Teachers College Press.

Harry, B. (1992b). Developing cultural self-awareness: The first step in values clarification for early interventionists. *Topics in Early Childhood Special Education, 12*(3), 333–350.

Harry, B. (1998). Leaning forward or bending over backwards: Cultural reciprocity in working with families. *Journal of Early Intervention, 21*(l), 62–72.

Harry, B., Allen, N., & McLaughlin, M. (1995). Communication versus compliance: African-American parents' involvement in special education. *Exceptional Children, 61*(4), 364–377.

Harry, B., Kalyanpur, M., & Day, M. (1999). *Building cultural reciprocity with families: Case studies in special education.* Baltimore: Paul H. Brookes.

Hart Research Associates. (1995). Valuable views: A public opinion research report on the views of AFT teachers on professional issues. Washington DC: American Federation of Teachers, 1995, 1–24.

Hartnett, D. N., Nelson, J. M., & Rinn, A. N. (2004). Gifted or ADHD? The possibilities of misdiagnosis. *Roeper Review, 26*(2), 73–76.

Harvard Project. (2000). *Opportunities suspended: The devastating consequences of zero-tolerance and school discipline policies.* Report by the Advancement Project and The Civil Rights Project. Retrieved June 1, 2002, from www.law.harvard.edu/civilrights/conferences/zero/zt-report2.html

The Harwood Group. (1999). *Community rhythms: Five stages of community life.* Washington, DC: The Harwood Group and the Charles Stewart Mott Foundation.

Haskins, R. (2004). Competing visions. *Education Next, 4*(1), 26–33.

Hatfield, D. R., & Ogles, B. M. (2004). The use of outcome measures by psychologists in clinical practice. *Professional Psychology: Research and Practice, 35,* 485–491.

Hawkins, J. D. (1999). Preventing crime and violence through Communities that Care. *European Journal on Criminal Policy and Research, 7,* 443–458.

Haycock, K., & Huang, S. (2001, Winter). Are today's high school graduates ready? *Thinking K–I 6, 5*(1), 3–17.

Hays, K. (1998, April 26). Boy held in teacher's killing. *The Detroit News & Free Press,* p. 5A.

Hazelwood School District v. Kuhlmeier, 484 U.S. 260 (1988).

Heaviside, S., Rowand, C., Williams, C., & Farris, E. (1998). *Violence and discipline problems in US public schools: 1996–1997* (NCES 98-030). Washington, DC: U.S. Department of Education, National Center for Education Statistics. (ERIC Document Reproduction Service No. 417 257).

Hehir, T. (2002). IDEA 2002 reauthorization: An opportunity to improve educational results for students with disabilities. *A timely IDEA: Rethinking Federal Education Programs for Children with Disabilities* (pp. 4–13). Washington, DC: Center on Education Policy. Retrieved September 5, 2005, from www.cep-de .org/specialeducation/timelyidea2002.htm

Heise, M. (1996). Assessing the efficacy of school desegregation. *Syracuse Law Review, 46,* 1093.

Henault, C. (2001). Zero-tolerance in school. *Journal of Law & Education, 30,* 547.

Hepler, J. (1994). Evaluating the effectiveness of a social skills program for preadolescents. *Research on Social Work Practice, 4,* 411–435.

Hernandez, D. J. (2004). Demographic change and the life characteristics of immigrant families. *Future of Children, 14*(2), 17–47.

Herrnstein, R., & Murray, C. (1994). *The bell curve: Intelligence and class structure in American life.* New York: Free Press.

Hetrick-Martin Institute (n.d). *FAQs.* Retrieved September 13, 2005, from www.hmi.org/HOME/Article/ Params/articles/1311/pathlist/s1036_01222default.as px#iteml311

Hiatt-Michael, D. B. (2001). Schools as learning communities: A vision for organic school reform. *The School Community Journal, 11,* 113–127.

Hines ex rel. Oliver v. McClung, 919 F.Supp.1206 (N.D. Ind. 1995).

Hiratsuka, J. (1995, January). Immigration cost, compassion collide. *NASW News, 5.*

Hobson v. Hansen, 269 ESupp. 401. (D.D.C. 1967), cert. Dismissed 393. U.S.801(1968), *aff'd* in part, rev'd in part sub nom. *Smack v. Hobson* 175 (D.D.C. 1969). 408 F2d.

Hofman, R. H., Hofman, W. H. A., & Guldemond, H. (2001). The effectiveness of cohesive schools. *International Journal of Leadership in Education, 4*(2), 115–135.

Hogue, A., & Liddle, H. A. (1999). Family-based preventive intervention: An approach to preventing substance abuse and antisocial behavior. *The American Journal of Orthopsychiatry, 69,* 278–290.

Honig v. Doe, 484 U.S.305 (1988).

Horn, W. E., & Tynan, D. (2001). Time to make special education "special" again. In C. E. Finn, A. J. Rotherham, & C. R. Hokanson, Jr. (Eds.), *Rethinking special education for a new century* (pp. 23–52). Dayton, OH: Thomas B. Fordham and the Progressive Policy Institute. Retrieved March 3, 2006, from www .cep-dc.org/specialeducation/timelyidea 2002.htm

Hourihan, J. (1952). *The duties and responsibilities of the visiting teacher.* Unpublished Doctoral Dissertation, Wayne State University, Detroit, MI.

Hourihan, J. (1965). Social work in the schools: New developments in theory, knowledge, and practice. Paper presented at *The NASW Tenth Anniversary Symposium on Social Work Practice and Knowledge,* Atlantic City, NJ.

Howard, M., & Eddinger, L. (1973). *School-age parents.* Syracuse, NY: National Alliance Concerned with School-Age Parents.

Howe, D. (2005). *Child abuse and neglect: Attachment, development, and intervention.* New York: Palgrave Macmillian.

Hoy, W. K., & Clover, S. I. R. (2007). Elementary school climate: A revision of the OCDQ. In W. K. Hoy & M. F. DiPaola (Eds.), *Essential ideas for the reform of American schools* (pp. 27–48). Charlotte, NC: Information Age Publishers.

Hoy, W. K., & Feldman, J. A. (2007). Organizational health: The concept and its measure. In W. K. Hoy & M. F. DiPaola (Eds.), *Essential ideas for the reform of American schools* (pp. 49–62). Charlotte, NC: Information Age Publishers.

Hsu by and through Hsu v. Roslyn Free School District No. 3, 85 F. 3d 839 (2nd Cir. N.Y., 1996).

Hudley, C. A. (1997). Teacher practices and student motivation in a middle school program for African-American males. *Urban Education, 32*(2), 304–319.

Hudley, C., Britsch, B., Wakefield, T., Demorat, M., & Cho, S. (1998). An attribution retraining program to reduce aggression in elementary school students. *Psychology in the Schools, 35,* 271–282.

Hudson, W. W., & Thyer, B. A. (1987). Research measures and indices in direct practice. In A. Minahan (Ed.), *Encyclopedia of social work* (pp. 487–498). Washington, DC: National Association of Social Workers.

Human Rights Watch. 2008. *A violent education: Corporal punishment of children in U.S. public schools.* Retrieved November 11, 2008, from http://www.hrw .org/reports/2008/us0808/index.htm

Hunsley, J., Best, M., Lefebvre, M., & Vito, D. (2001). The seven-item short form of the Dyadic Adjustment Scale: Further evidence for construct validity. *American Journal of Family Therapy, 29*(4), 325–335.

Hunter, L., Hoagwood, K., Evans, S., Weist, M., Smith, C., Paternite, C., et al. (2005). Working together to promote academic performance, social and emotional learning, and mental health for all children. New York: Center for the Advancement of Children's Mental Health at Columbia University.

Hursh, D. (2005). The growth of high-stakes testing in the USA: Accountability, markets and the decline in educational equality. *British Educational Research Journal, 31*(5), 605–622.

Hyman, I. A., & Perone, D. C. (1998). The other side of school violence: Educator policies and practices that may contribute to student misbehavior. *Journal of School Psychology, 36*, 7–27.

Hyman, I. A., & Snook, P. A. (2000). Dangerous schools and what you can do about them. *Phi Delta Kappan, 81*, 488–501.

Hyman, R. T., & Rathbone, C. H. (1993). *Corporal punishment in schools: Reading the law.* Topeka, KS: NOLPE.

Illinois School Code, 105 ILCS 5/26-1 (2008).

Illinois School Student Records Act. 105 ILCS 10/1 et. seq. (2008).

Improving America's Schools Act of 1994, P.L. 103-382 (1994).

In Re S.S., 452 Pa. Super.15, 680 A. 2d 1172 (1996).

Individuals with Disabilities Education Act (IDEA). (1991). *Congressional Information Service Annual Legislative Histories for U.S. Public Laws* (P.L. 101–476).

Individuals with Disabilities Education Improvement Act of 2004. H. R. 1350.

Ingraham v. Wright, 430 U.S. 651 (1977).

Insel, T. R. (2005, January). NIMH: Renewing priorities and organizational structure. *SRCD Developments, 48*(1), 1 & 9–10.

Iowa Annotated Statutes, 280.28(2)(c) (2008).

Irmsher, K. (1997). *Education reform and students at risk* (ERIC Digest No. 112). Eugene, OR: ERIC Clearinghouse on Education Management.

Issacs, M. (1992). *Violence: The impact of community violence on African-American children and families: Collaborative approaches to prevention and intervention.* Arlington, VA: National Center for Education in Maternal and Child Health.

Isaacs, M. L. (2003). Data-driven decision making: The engine of accountability. *Professional School Counseling, 6*, 288–296.

Jacobs, L. A. (1999). Equal opportunity, natural inequalities, and racial disadvantage: The Bell Curve and its critics. *Philosophy of the Social Sciences, 29*(1), 121–145.

James, A., Soler, A., & Weatherall, R. (2005) Cognitive behavioural therapy for anxiety disorders in children and adolescents. *Cochrane Database of Systematic Reviews, 4.* New York: Wiley.

Janesick, V. J. (1995). Our multicultural society. In E. L. Meyen & T. M. Skrtic (Eds.), *Special education & student disability: An introduction-Traditional, emerging, and alternative perspectives* (pp. 713–727). Denver, CO: Love Publishing Company.

Janzen, C., Harris, O., Jordan, C., & Franklin, C. (2006). *Family treatment in social work practice* (4th ed.). Itasca, IL: F. E. Peacock.

Jayaratne, S. D., & Levy, R. (1979). *Empirical clinical practice.* New York: Columbia University Press.

Jencks, C. (1972). *Inequality; A reassessment of the effect of family and schooling in America.* New York: Basic Books.

Jencks, C., & Phillips, M. (1998). *The black-white test score gap.* Washington, DC: Brookings Institution Press.

Jenson, J. M. (1997). Risk and protective factors for alcohol and other drug use in childhood and adolescence. In M. W. Fraser (Ed.), *Risk and resilience in childhood: An ecological perspective* (pp. 117–139). Washington, DC: National Association for Social Workers.

Jimerson, S. R., Brock, S. E., Woehr, S. M., & Clinton-Higuita, A. (2006). Immediate school-based intervention following violent crises. In C. Franklin, M. B. Harris, & P. Allen-Meares (Eds.), *The school services sourcebook: A guide for school-based professionals* (pp. 559–566). New York: Oxford University Press.

Johnson, A. K. (1998). The revitalization of community practice: Characteristics, competencies, and curricula for community based services. *Journal of Community Practice, 5*(3), 37–62.

Johnson, J. (1991). The no-fault school: Understanding groups-understanding schools. In R. T. Constable, J. E. Flynn, & S. McDonald (Eds.), *School social work: Practice and research perspectives* (2nd ed., pp. 290–310). Chicago: Lyceum.

Johnson, K., Bryant, D., Strader, T., Bucholtz, G., Berbaum, M., Collins, D., & Noe, T. (1996). Reducing alcohol and other drug use by strengthening community, family, and youth resiliency: An evaluation of the creating lasting connections program. *Journal of Adolescent Research, 11*(1), 36–67

Johnson, L. (1972). *Definition of model social work practice: A syllabus and book of readings.* Iowa City: University of Iowa Press.

Johnson, L. (1983). *Social work practice: A generalist approach.* Boston: Allyn and Bacon.

Jones v. Clear Creek Independent School District, 977 F. 2d 963 (5th Cir. 1992).

Jones, J. B. (1997). Conditions at school as excusing or justifying nonattendance. 9 A.L.R. 4th ed. 122.

Jonson-Reid, M., Kontak, D., Citerman, B., Essma, A., & Fezzi, N. (2004). School social work case characteristics, services, and dispositions: Year one results. *Children & Schools, 26*(1), 5–22.

Jordan, C., & Franklin, C. (2003). *Clinical assessment for social workers.* Chicago: Lyceum.

Jordan, D. (2001). *Functional behavioral assessment and positive interventions: What parents need to know.* Minneapolis, MN: Families and Advocates Partnership for Education. Available at: www.fape.org

Jozefowicz-Simbeni, D. M. H. (2008). An ecological and developmental perspective on dropout factors in early adolescence: Role of school social workers in dropout prevention efforts. *Children and Schools, 30*(1), 49–62.

Jozefowicz-Simbeni, D. M. H., & Allen-Meares, P. (2002). Poverty and schools: Intervention and resource building through school-linked services. *Children & Schools, 24,* 123–136.

Kachur, P., Stennies, G., Powell, K., Modzeleski, W., Stephens, R., Murphy, R., et al. (1996). School-associated violent deaths in the United States, 1992 to 1994. *Journal of the American Medical Association, 275,* 1729–1733.

Kaestle, C. (1983). *Pillars of the republic: Common schools and American society. New* York: Hill & Wang.

Kagle, J. D., & Kopels, S. (2008). *Social work records* (3rd ed.). Buffalo Grove, IL: Waveland Press.

Kaiser, D., & Abell, M. (1997). Learning life management in the classroom. *Teaching Exceptional Children, 30*(1), 70–75.

Kalyanpur, M., & Harry, B. (1999). *Culture in special education: Building reciprocal family–professional relationships.* Baltimore: Paul H. Brookes.

Kam, C., Greenberg, M., & Walls, C. (2003). Examining the role of implementation quality in school-based prevention using the PATHS curriculum. *Prevention Science, 4*(1), 55–63.

Kann, L., Kinchen, S., Williams, B., Ross, J., Lowry, R., Hill, C., et al. (1998). Youth risk behavior surveillance—1997. *Morbidity and Mortality Weekly Report Surveillance Summary, 48* (SS-3), 1–89.

Karr v. Schmidt, 460 F. 2d 609 (5th Cir. 1972).

Kartub, D. T., Taylor-Greene, S., March, R. E., & Horner, R. H. (2000). Reducing hallway noise: A systems approach. *Journal of Behavioral Disorders, 9*(3), 161–171.

Kaufman, P., Chen, X., Choy, S., Chandler, K., Chapman, C., Rand, M., et al. (1998). *Indicators of school crime and safety, 1998.* U.S. Departments of Education and Justice. NCES 98-251/NCJ-172215. Washington, DC.

Kaufman, P., Chen, X., Choy, S., Ruddy, S., Miller, A., Fleury, J., et al. (2000). *Indicators of school crime and safety, 2000.* U.S. Departments of Education and Justice. NCES 2001-017/NCJ-184176.

Kazdin, A. E. (1996). Problem solving and parent management in treating aggressive and antisocial behavior. In E. D. Hibbs & P. S. Jensen (Eds.), *Psychosocial treatments for child and adolescent disorders* (pp. 377–408). Washington, DC: APA.

Kazdin, A. E. (2005). *Parent management training for oppositional, aggressive and anti-social children and adolescents.* New York: Oxford University Press.

Kean, J. M. (1970). The impact of head start: An evaluation of the effects of head start on children's cognitive and affective development by Victor G. Cicirelli. *Childhood Education, 46*(8), 449–452.

Keeley, M. L., & Wiens, B. A. (2007). Family influences on treatment refusal in school-linked health services. *Journal of Child and Family Studies, 17*(1), 109–126.

Kenny v. Gurley, 208 Ala. 625, 95 So. 34 (1923).

Kettner, P. M. (1975). A framework for comparing practice models. *Social Service Review, 49,* 629–642.

KewalRamani, A., Gilbertson, L., Fox, M., & Provasnik, S. (2007). *Status and trends in the education of racial and ethnic minorities* (NCES 2007-039). Washington DC: National Center for Education Statistics, Institute of Education Sciences, Department of Education. Retrieved October 5, 2008, from http://nces.ed.gov/pubs2007/2007039.pdf

Keyes v. Denver School District No. 1, 413 U.S. 189 (1973).

Keys, W., Sharp, C., Greene, K., & Grayson, H. (2003). *Successful leadership of schools in urban and challenging contexts: A review of the literature.* Nottingham: National College for School Leadership. Retrieved March 10, 2004, from www.ncls.org.uk/literaturereviews

Khoury-Kassabri, M. Benbenishty, R., Astor, R. A., & Zeira, A. (2004). The contribution of community, family and school variables on student victimization. *American Journal of Community Psychology, 34,* 187–204.

Kirby, D. (2007). *Emerging answers 2007: New research findings on programs to reduce teen pregnancy.* Washington, DC: National Campaign to Prevent Teen Pregnancy.

Kirby, D. B. (2007). *Emerging answers: Research findings on programs to reduce teen pregnancy and sexually transmitted diseases.* Washington, DC: The National Campaign to Prevent Teen and Unplanned Pregnancy. Retrieved from http://www.thenationalcampaign.org/EA2007/EA2007_full.pdf

Kirby, D. B., Laris, B. A., & Rolleri, L. A. (2007). Sex and HIV education programs: Their impact on sexual behaviors of young people throughout the world. *Journal of Adolescent Health, 40*(3), 206–217.

Klein, J. (2002). *NASW policy statement on school violence.* Washington, DC: NASW.

Klein, J. (2002, March). School violence: Public and professional policies. *NASW News,* p. 6.

Klingner, J. K., & Harry, B. (2006). The special education referral and decision-making process for English language learners: Child study team meetings and staffings. *Teachers College Record, 108,* 2247–2281.

Knauss, L. K. (2001). Ethical issues in psychological assessment in school settings. *Journal of Personality Assessment, 77*(2), 231–241.

Knoff, H. M., & Batsche, G. M. (1995). Project ACHIEVE: Analyzing a school reform process for at-risk and underachieving students. *School Psychology Review, 24,* 579–603.

Knoff, H., & Batsche, G. (2001). *The stop and think social skills program.* Longmont, CO: Sopris West.

Kodluboy, D. (1997). Gang-oriented interventions. In A. Goldstein (Ed.), *School violence intervention: A practical handbook* (pp. 189–214). New York: Guilford Press.

Kohler, P. K., Manhart, L. E., & Lafferty, W. E. (2008). Abstinence-only and comprehensive sex education and the initiation of sexual activity and teen pregnancy. *Journal of Adolescent Health, 42*(4), 344–351.

Kopels, S. (1992). Confidentiality and the school social worker. *Social Work in Education, 14*(4), 203–205.

Kopels, S. (1998). Wedded to the status quo: Same-sex marriage after *Baehr v. Lewin. Journal of Gay and Lesbian Social Services, 8*(3), 69–81.

Kopels, S., & Dupper, D. R. (1999). Peer sexual harassment in schools. *Child Welfare, 78*(4), 435–460.

Kopels, S., & Lindsey, B. (2006, Summer). The complexity of confidentiality in schools today: The school social worker context [Special Issue]. *School Social Work Journal,* 63–78.

Kordesk, R. S., & Constable, R. (1999). Policies, programs, and mandates for developing social services in the schools. In R. Constable, S. McDonald, & J. P. Flynn (Eds.), *School social work: Practice, policy, and research perspectives* (4th ed.). Chicago: Lyceum Books.

Kosciw, J. G. (2004). *The 2003 National School Climate Survey: The school-related experiences of our nation's lesbian, gay, bisexual and transgender youth.* New York: Gay, Lesbian, and Straight Education Network.

Kosciw, J. G., & Diaz, E. M. (2006). *The 2005 National School Climate Survey: The experiences of lesbian, gay, bisexual and transgender youth in our nation's schools.* New York: Gay, Lesbian, and Straight Education Network.

Kowalski, R. M., & Limber, S. P. (2007). Electronic bullying among middle school students. *Journal of Adolescent Health, 41,* 22–30.

Kozol, J. (1967). *Death at an early age.* Boston: Houghton Mifflin.

Kozol, J. (1991). *Savage inequalities: Children in American schools.* New York: Crown.

Kozol, J. (1995). *Amazing grace: The lives of children and the conscience of a nation.* New York: Crown.

Krashen, S. (2001). Bush's bad idea for bilingual ed [Electronic version]. *Rethinking Schools Online.* Retrieved June 1, 2002, from www.rethinkingschools.Org Archives/1504/Biedl54.htm

Kratchowill, T. R. (2007). Preparing psychologists for evidence-based school practice: Lessons learned and challenges ahead. *American Psychologist, 62,* 829–843.

Krueger, R. A. (1993). *Focus groups: A practice guide for applied research.* Newbury Park, CA: Sage.

Kuche, C. A., & Greenberg, M. T. (1995). *The PATHS curriculum.* Seattle, WA: Developmental Research and Programs.

Kulis, S., Marsiglis, F. F., Elek, E., Dustman, P., Wagstaff, D. A., & Hecht, M. L. (2005). Mexican/Mexican American adolescents and keepin' it REAL: An evidence-based substance use prevention program. *Children & Schools, 27*(3), 133–145.

Kulis, S., Yabiku, S. T., Marsiglia, F. F., Nieri, T., & Crossman, A. (2007). Differences by gender, ethnicity, and acculturation in the efficacy of the keepin' it REAL model prevention program. *Journal of Drug Education, 37*(2), 123–144.

Kuther, T. L. (1999). A developmental contextual perspective on covictimization by community violence. *Adolescence, 34*(136), 699–714.

Labaree, D. (1997). Public goods, private goods: The American struggle over educational goals. *American Educational Research Association, 34*(1), 39–81.

Ladd, H. F., Chalk, R., & Hansen, J. S. (1999). *Equity and adequacy in education finance: Issues and perspectives.* Washington, DC: National Academy Press.

Lake, D. G., Miles, M. B., & Earler, R. B. (1973). *Measuring human behavior.* New York: Columbia University Press.

Lander v. Seaver, 32 Vt. 114 (1859).

Larkin, R., & Thyer, B. A. (1999). Evaluating cognitive-behavioral group counseling to improve elementary school students' self-esteem, self-control, and classroom behavior. *Behavioral Interventions, 14,* 147–161.

Larry P. v. Riles, 343 E Supp. 1306, affd., 502 F. 2d 963, *Further proceedings,* 495 F, Supp. 926 *affd.,S02 F.* 2d 693 (9th Cu. 1984).

Larson, J. (1998). Managing student aggression in high schools: Implications for practice. *Psychology in the Schools, 35,* 283–295.

Lassen, S. R., Steele, M. M., & Sailor, W. (2006). The relationship of school-wide positive behavior support to academic achievement in an urban middle school. *Psychology in the Schools, 43*(6), 701–712.

Latkin, C. A., & Knowlton, A. R. (2005). Micro-social structural approaches to HIV prevention: A social ecological perspective. *AIDS Care, 17*(4), 102–113.

Lau v. Nichols, 414 U.S. 563 (1974).

Lauterbach, S. (Ed.). (2005). *Society & values: The United States in 2005, who we are today.* Washington, DC: U.S. Department of State.

LaVine, J. A. (1995). The Supreme Court's latest rendition of equality in education: Examining the traditional components of success in *Missouri v. Jenkins. Villanova Law Review, 40,* 1395.

Lazarus, E. (1883). "The new colossus."

LeCroy, C. W. (Ed.). (2008). *Handbook of evidence-based treatment manuals for children and adolescents.* New York: Oxford University Press.

Lee v. Weisman, 505 U.S. 577 (1992).

Lee, G. (Ed.). (1959). *Helping the troubled school child: Selected readings in school social work.* Washington, DC: National Association of Social Workers.

Lee, J. (2006). *Tracking achievement gaps and assessing the impact of the NCLB on the gaps. An in-depth look into national and state reading and math outcome trends.* Cambridge, MA: The Civil Rights Project at Harvard University.

Lee, J.-S., & Bowen, N. K. (2006). Parent involvement, cultural capital, and the achievement gap among elementary school children. *American Education Research Journal, 43,* 193–218.

Lee, V. E., & Burkham, D. E. (2002). *Inequality at the starting gate: Social background differences in achievement as children begin school.* Washington, DC: Economic Policy Institute.

Lee, V. E., Dedrick, R. F., & Smith, J. B. (1991). The effect of the social organization of schools on teachers' efficacy and satisfaction. *Sociology of Education, 64,* 190–208.

Lee, V. E., & Smith, J. B. (1999). Social support and achievement for young adolescents in Chicago: The role of school academic press. *American Educational Research Journal, 36,* 907–945.

Leibowitz, A. (1983). *Immigration law and refugee policy.* New York: Matthew Bender.

Leithwood, K., Jantzi, D., & Steinbach, R. (1998). Leadership and other conditions which foster organizational learning in schools. In K. Leithwood & K. S. Louis (Eds.), *Organizational learning in schools* (pp. 67–90). Lisse, NL: Swets & Zeitlinger.

Lemon v. Kurtzman, 403 U.S. 602 (1971).

Lerner, R. M. (1995). *America's youth in crisis: Challenges and options for programs and policies.* Thousand Oaks, CA: Sage.

Lesaux, N. K. (2006). Building consensus: Future directions for research on English language learners at risk for learning difficulties. *Teachers College Record, 108,* 2406–2438.

Letendre, J., Henry, D., & Tolan, P. H. (2003). Leader and therapeutic influences on prosocial skill building in school-based groups to prevent aggression. *Research on Social Work Practice, 13,* 569–587.

Leventhal, T., & Brooks-Gunn, J. (2000). The neighborhoods they live in: The effects of neighborhood residence on child and adolescent outcomes. *Psychological Bulletin, 126,* 309–337.

Levitin, T. E., & Chananie, J. D. (1972). Response of female primary school teachers to sex-typed behaviors in male and female children. *Child Development, 43,* 1309–1316.

Lewin, K. (1951). *Field theory in social science.* New York: Harper & Brothers.

Lewis, T. J., Colvin, G., & Sugai, G. (2000). The effects of pre-correction and active supervision on the recess behavior of elementary students. *Education and Treatment of Children, 23*(2), 109–121.

Lewis, T. J., & Garrison-Harrell, L. (1999). Effective behavior support: Designing setting specific interventions. *Effective School Practices, 17*(4), 38–46.

Lick, D. W. (2006). A new perspective on organizational learning: Creating learning teams. *Evaluation and Program Planning, 29,* 88–96.

Lide, P. (1959). Historical influences on function of school social workers. In G. Lee (Ed.), *Helping the troubled school child: Selected readings in school social work* (pp. 18–33). Washington, DC: National Association of Social Workers.

Lieberman, L. M. (2001, January 17). The death of special education. *Education Week, 201*(18), 60, 40. [On-line] Available: www.edweek.org

Lilienfeld, S. O. (2007). Psychological treatments that cause harm. *Perspectives on Psychological Science, 2,* 53–70.

Limber, S. P. (2006). The Olweus bullying prevention program: An overview of its implementation and research basis. In S. R. Jimerson & M. J. Furlong (Eds.), *Handbook of school violence and school safety: From research to practice* (pp. 293–308). Mahwah, NJ: Erlbaum.

Lincoln, Y. S., & Guba, E. G. (1985). *Naturalistic inquiry.* Beverly Hills, CA: Sage.

Lisnov, L., Gibb, C., & Safer, L. A. (1998). Adolescent perceptions of substance abuse prevention strategies. *Adolescence, 33*(130), 301–311.

Livingston, A., & Wirt, J. (Eds.). (2004). *The condition of education, 2004 in brief.* Washington, DC: National Center for Education Statistics.

Lollack, L. (2001). *The foreign-born population in the United States. Population characteristics.* March 2000, Current Population Reports, P20-534. U.S. Census Bureau, Washington, DC: Author.

London v. Directors of DeWitt Pub. Schs., 194 F. 3d 873 (8th Cir. 1999).

Lopiano, D. (2005). *Title IX. Q & A.* Retrieved December 1, 2008, from http://www.womenssportsfoundation .org/Content/Articles/Issues/Title%20IX/T/Title%20I X%20Q%20%20A.aspx

Losen, D. J., & Edley, C. (2001). The role of law in policing abusive disciplinary practices: Why school discipline is a civil rights issue. In *2001: A Legal Odyssey: 2001 conference papers, topic outlines* (pp. 82–103). Dayton, OH: Education Law Association.

Lynam, D., Milich, R., Zimmerman, R., Novak, S., Logan, T. K., Martin, C., et al. (1999). Project DARE: No effects at 10-year follow-up. *Journal of Consulting and Clinical Psychology, 67,* 590–593.

Lynch, E. W., & Hanson, M. J. (Eds.). (1998). *Developing cross-cultural competence: A guide for working with children and their families* (3rd ed.). Baltimore: Paul H. Brookes.

Lynn, C. J., McKay, M. M., & Atkins, M. S. (2003). School social work: Meeting the mental health needs of students through collaboration with teachers. *Children & Schools, 24*(4), 197–209.

Lyons v. Penn Hills Sch. Dist., 723 A.2d 1073 (Pa. Comm. Ct., 1999).

Malnak v Yogi, 592 F. 2d. 197 (3rd Cir. 1979).

Mancini, J. A., Martin, J. A., & Bowen, G. L. (2003). Community capacity and social organization: The role of community in the promotion of health and the prevention of illness. In T. Gullotta & M. Bloom (Eds.), *Encyclopedia of primary prevention and health promotion* (pp. 319–330). New York: Kluwer Academic/Plenum.

Mandel, S. (2007). *The parent-teacher partnership: How to work together for student achievement.* Chicago: Zephyr Press.

Mangum v. Keith, 145 Ga. 603, 95 S.E. 1 (1918).

Manlove, J., Terry-Humen, E., Papillo, A. R., Franzetta, K., Williams, S., & Ryan, S. (2001). Background for community-level work on positive reproductive health in adolescence: Reviewing the literature on contributing factors. Washington, DC: Child Trends. Retrieved online November 23, 2004, at www.childtrends.org/PDF/KnightReports/KRepro.pdf

Manlove, J., Terry-Humen, E., Papillo, A. R., Franzetta, K., Williams, S., & Ryan, S. (2002). *Preventing teenage pregnancy, childbearing, and sexually transmitted diseases: What the research shows.* Washington, DC: Child Trends. Retrieved November 22, 2004, at www.childtrends.org/PDF/Knightreports/K1Brief.pdf

Mann, H. (1848/1958). Twelfth annual report—Secretary of Massachusetts State Board of Education. In H. S. Commanger (Ed.), *Documents of American history* (6th ed.). New York: Appleton-Century-Crofts.

Mannino, F., & Shore, M. (1975). The effects of consultation: A review of empirical studies. *American Journal of Community Psychology, 3,* 1–21.

Marks, J. A. (1987). Stresses on gay and lesbian adolescents. *Social Work in Education, 9*(3), 169–180.

Martin Luther King, Jr., Elementary School Children v. Ann Arbor School District Board, 451 F. Supp. 1324 (E.D. Mich. 1978).

Martin, E. W., Martin, R., & Terman, D. L. (1996). The legislative litigation history of special education. *The Future of Children, 6*(1). Retrieved September 5, 2005, from www.futureofchildren.org/pubs-info2825/pubs-info_show.htm?doc_id=72440

Martin, J. A., Hamilton, B. E., Sutton, P. D., Ventura, S. J., Menacker, F., Kimeyer, S., et al. (2007). *Births: Final data for 2005* (NVSR No. 51–06). Hyattsville, MD: National Center for Health Statistics. Retrieved from http://www.cdc.gov/nchs/data/nvsr/nvsr56/nvsr56_06.pdf

Martin, S. L., Kupersmidt, J. B., & Harter, K. S. M. (1996). Children of farm laborers: Utilization of services for mental health problems. *Community Mental Health Journal, 32*(4), 327–340.

Martin, W., & Swartz-Kulstad, J. L. (Eds.). (2000). *Person-environment psychology and mental health: Assessment and intervention.* Mahwah, NJ: Erlbaum.

Maslow, A. (1954). *Motivation and personality.* New York: Harper Collins.

Mattison, M. (2006). Professional ethical codes: Applications to common ethical dilemmas. In C. Franklin, M. B. Harris, & P. Allen-Meares (Eds.), *The school services sourcebook: A guide for school-based professionals* (pp. 921–927). New York: Oxford University Press.

Mayeaux, L., Sandstrom, M. J., & Cillessen, A. H. N. (2008). Is being popular a risky proposition? *Journal of Research on Adolescence, 18*(1), 49–74.

Mayer, M. J., & Leone, P. E. (1999). A structural analysis of school violence and disruption: Implications for creating safer schools. *Education and the Treatment of Children, 22,* 333–356.

McCarney, S, B. (1995). *Adaptive behavior evaluation scale, revised.* Columbia, MO: Hawthorne Educational Services.

McCarthy, J. D., & Hoge, D. R. (1987). The social construction of school punishment: Racial disadvantage out of universalistic process. *Social Forces, 65,* 1101–1120.

McCarthy, M. (2000). Devotional activities in public schools. In W. E. Camp, M. J. Connelly, K. E. Lane, & J. E. Mead (Eds.), *The principal's legal handbook* (2nd ed., pp. 293–312). Dayton, OH: Education Law Association.

McCarthy, M. (2002). Anti-harassment policies in public schools: How vulnerable are they? *Journal of Law and Education, 31,* 52.

McCarthy, M. (2008). Anti-harassment provisions revisited: No bright-line rule. *Brigham Young University Education and Law Journal, 8,* 225–249.

McDermott, D. (1984). The relationship of parental drug use and parents' attitude concerning adolescent drug use. *Adolescence, 19*(73), 89–97.

McDonnell, L. M., McLaughlin, M. J., & Morison, P. (Eds.), and Committee on Goals 2000 and the Inclusion of Students with Disabilities, Board on Testing and Assessment, Commission on Behavioral and Social Sciences and Education National Research Council. (1997). *Educating one and all: Students with disabilities and standards-based reform.* Washington, DC: National Academy Press.

McFadden, A. C., Marsh, G. E., Price, B. J., & Hwang, Y. (1992). A study of race and gender bias in the punishment of school children. *Education and the Treatment of Children, 15,* 140–146.

McGinnis, E., & Goldstein, A. P. (1997). *Skillstreaming the elementary school child* (Rev ed.). Champaign, IL: Research Press.

McGinnis, E., & Goldstein, A. P. (2003). *Skillstreaming in early childhood* (Rev. ed.). Champaign, IL: Research Press.

McGrew, J. H., Bond, G. R., Dietzen, L., & Salyers, M. (1994). Measuring the fidelity of implementation of a mental health program model. *Journal of Consulting and Clinical Psychology, 62,* 670–678.

McKinney-Vento Homeless Education Assistance Improvements Act of 2001. 42 U.S.C. §11431 et. seq.

McLaughlin, M. J. (2002). Issues for consideration in the reauthorization of Part B of the Individuals with Disabilities Education Act. In *A timely IDEA: Rethinking Federal Education Programs for Children with Disabilities* (pp. 24–42). Washington, DC: Center on Education Policy. Retrieved September 5, 2005, from www.cep-dc.org/specialeducation/timelyidea2002.htm

McMullen, L. A., & Lynde, C. R. (1997). The "Official English" movement and the demise of diversity: The elimination of federal judicial and statutory minority language rights. *Land and Water Law Review, 32,* 789.

McNeil, D. (Ed.). (2002). *Youth and violence: What we can do about it.* Marina del Rey, CA: Josephson Institute of Ethics.

Medway, F. J., & Updyke, J. F. (1985). Metaanalysis of consultation outcome studies. *American Journal of Community Psychology, 13,* 389–405.

Melaville, A. I., & Blank, M. J. (1991). *What it takes: Structuring interagency partnerships to connect children and families with comprehensive services.* Washington DC: Education and Human Services Consortium.

Merry, S., McDowell, H., Hetrick, S., Bir, J., & Muller, N. (2004). Psychological and/or educational interventions for the prevention of depression in children and adolescents. *Cochrane Database of Systematic Reviews, 2.* New York: Wiley.

Metzger v. Osbeck, 841 F. 2d 518 (3d Cir. 1988).

Meyer, J. W., Scott, W. R., Strang, D., & Creighton, A. L. (1988). Bureaucratization without centralization: Changes in the organizational system of U.S. public education, 1940–80. In L. G. Zucker (Ed.), *Institutional patterns in organizations: Culture and environments* (pp. 139–168). Cambridge, MA: Ballinger.

Midol suspension ends: Honor student returns to class. (1996, October 3). Retrieved June 1, 2002, from www.cnn.com/US/9610/03/midol.suspension/index.html

Midwest Center Satellite Consortium for Planned Change in Pupil Personnel Programs for Urban Schools in Indiana. (1974). *A final report from the Jane Addams school of social work.* Urbana: University of Illinois, School–Community Pupil Training Programs.

Miedel, W. T., & Reynolds, A. J. (1999). Parent involvement in early intervention for disadvantaged children: Does it matter? *Journal of School Psychology 37*(4), 379–402.

Miller, D. (1991). *Handbook of research design and social measurement* (5th ed.). Newbury Park, CA: Sage.

Milliken v. Bradley, 418 U.S. 717 (1974).

Mills v. Washington, DC, Board of Education, 348 F. Supp. 866 (D. DC 1972); *contempt proceedings.* EHLR 551:643 (D.DC 1980).

Milwaukee Board of School Directors. (1993). *An evaluation of the Second Step Violence Prevention Curriculum for elementary students.* Milwaukee, WI: Author.

Miner, C. A., & Bates, P. E. (1997). Person-centered transition planning. *Teaching Exceptional Children, 30*(1), 66–69.

Minersville School Dist. v. Gobitis, 310 U.S. 586 (1940).

Missouri v Jenkins, 515 U.S.70 (1995).

Mitchell, K. J., Ybarra, M., & Finkelhor, D. (2007). The relative importance of online victimization in understanding depression, delinquency, and substance use. *Child Maltreatment, 12*(4), 314–324.

Moffitt, C. E., Chorpita, B. F. & Fernandez, S. N. (2003). Intensive cognitive-behavioral treatment of school refusal behavior. *Cognitive and Behavioral Practice, 10,* 51–60.

Monkman, M. M. (1978). A broader, more comprehensive view of social work practice. *School Social Work Journal, 2*(2), 89–96.

Monkman, M. M. (2006). The characteristic focus of the social worker in the public schools. In R. Constable, C. R. Massat, S. McDonald, & J. P. Flynn (Eds.), *School social work: Practice, policy, and research* (6th ed., pp. 40–59). Chicago: Lyceum Books.

Moore, K. M. (2007). Visible through the veil: The regulation of Islam in American law. *Association for the Sociology of Religion, 68*(3), 237(15). Retrieved October 26, 2008, from http://www.lexis.com/research/retrieve?_m=0f8acee80f85a5a5ab4f426f12*753f30&docnum=3&_fmtstr=FULL&_startdoc=1&*wchp=dGLbVlz-zSkAB&_md5=ef1558709c94e42453f0d6cbbf151b63&focBudTerms=Hearn%20and%20headscarf&focBudSel=all

Moran, R. F (1988). The politics of discretion: Federal intervention in bilingual education. *California Law Review, 76,* 1249.

Morris v. Nowotny, 323 S.W 2d 302 (Tex.Civ.App. Austin, 1959).

Morrison, G. M., & Allen, M. R. (2007). Promoting student resilience in school contexts. *Theory into Practice, 46*(2), 162–169.

Morse v. Frederick, 127 S. Ct. 2618 (2007).

Murphy, H. A., Hutchison, J. M., & Bailey, J. S. (1983). Behavioral school psychology goes outdoors: The effect of organized games on playground aggression. *Journal of Applied Behavior Analysis, 16,* 29–35.

Nabors, L. A., Reynolds, M. W., & Weist, M. D. (2000). Qualitative evaluation of a high school mental health program. *Journal of Youth and Adolescence, 29*(1), 1–13.

Nabozny v. Podlesny, 92 F. 3d 446 (7th Cir.1996).

Nadel, H., Spellman, M., Alvarez-Canino, T., Lausell-Bryant, L., & Landsberg, G. (1996). The cycle of violence and victimization: A study of the school-based interventions of a multidisciplinary youth violence prevention program. In K. E. Powell & D. F. Haskins, *Youth violence prevention: Descriptions and baseline data from 13 evaluation projects* (pp. 109–119). Supplement to *American Journal of Preventive Medicine, 12*(5).

Nansel, T., Overpeck, M., Pilla, R., Roan, W., Simons-Morton, B., & Scheidt, P. (2001). Bullying behaviors among U.S. youth: Prevalence and association with psychosocial adjustment. *Journal of the American Medical Association, 285,* 2094–2100.

Nash, J. K. (2002). Neighborhood effects on sense of school coherence and educational behavior in students at risk of school failure. *Children & Schools, 24,* 73–89.

NASW Taskforce on Specialization. (1978). *Specialization in the social work profession.* Washington, DC: National Association of Social Workers.

National Advisory Committee on Civil Disorders. (1968). *The Kerner report.* Washington, DC: Government Printing Office.

National Alliance to End Homelessness. (2007). *Family homelessness.* Retrieved from http://www.endhomelessness.org/content/article/detail/1525

National Assembly of School-Based Health Centers (2008). *Census of School Based Health Centers, 2007–2008.* NASBHC: Washington, DC. Available at http://www.nasbhc.org/

National Association of Bilingual Education. (1998, Spring). History of bilingual education. *Rethinking Schools Online, 12*(3). Retrieved November 17, 2008, from http://www.rethinkingschools.org/archive/12_03/langhst.shtml

National Association of Secondary School Principals. (1997). *Breaking ranks.* Washington, DC: National Association of Secondary School Principals.

National Association of Social Workers (NASW) Committee on Education. (1991). *Fact sheet: School social work and NASW* (pp. 1–7). Washington, DC: National Association of Social Workers.

National Association of Social Workers (NASW) Steering Committee. (1997). *The section correction* (pp. 1–23). Washington, DC: National Association of Social Workers.

National Association of Social Workers (NASW). (1973). *NASW manpower policy statement.* Washington, DC: National Association of Social Workers.

National Association of Social Workers (NASW). (1978). *Summary of the preliminary report on the survey of social workers in the schools* (pp. 1–11). Washington, DC: National Association of Social Workers.

National Association of Social Workers (NASW). (1992). *Standards for social work services in the schools.* Washington, DC: NASW Press.

National Association of Social Workers (NASW). (1999). *Code of ethics.* Washington, DC: NASW Press.

National Association of Social Workers (NASW). (2001, October). *Confidentiality and school social work: A practice perspective.* Retrieved June 1, 2002, from www.socialworkers.org/practice

National Association of Social Workers (NASW). (2002a). *Bullying among school-age youths.* Washington, DC: Author.

National Association of Social Workers (NASW). (2002b). *NASW standards for school social work services.* Washington DC: Author. Retrieved July 28, 2008, from www.socialworkers.org/sections/credentials/school_social.asp

National Association of Social Workers (NASW). (2005). *Social work profession: General fact sheets.* Retrieved July 28, 2008, from www.socialworkers.org/pressroom/features/general/profession.asp

National Association of Social Workers (NASW). (n.d.). *Certified school social work specialist: Information booklet with application and reference forms.* Retrieved July 28, 2008, from www.naswdc.org/credentials/applications/c-ssws.pdf

National Association of State Boards of Education (NASBE). (1992). *Winners all: A call for inclusive schools.* The report of the NASBE Study Group on Special Education. Alexandria, VA: NASBE.

National Campaign to Prevent Teen Pregnancy. (2008). *What works 2008: Curriculum-based programs that prevent teen pregnancy.* Washington, DC: Author.

National Center for Education Statistics. (2001a). *Digest of Education Statistics,* Table 167. Washington, DC: U.S. Government Printing Office.

National Center for Education Statistics. (2005). *Condition of education.* Washington, DC: U.S. Government Printing Office. Available at http://nces.ed.gov/programs/coe/list/index. Asp

National Center for Education Statistics. (2007). *Mapping 2005 state proficiency standards onto the NAEP scales* (NCES 2007-482). U.S. Department of Education. Washington, DC: Author.

National Center for Education Statistics. (2008). *Digest of Education Statistics.* Washington, DC: U.S. Government Printing Office.

National Center for Health Statistics. (2007). Health, United States, with chartbook on trends in the health of Americans. Hyattsville, MD. Retrieved on October 15, 2008, from http://www.cdc.gov/nchs/data/hus/hus07.pdf#032

National Center for School Engagement. (2005). *OJJDP truancy reduction demonstration evaluation.* Paper presented at the Washington State Truancy Conference, Seattle, WA.

National Coalition Against Corporal Punishment in Schools (NCACPS). Retrieved November 12, 2008, from www.stophitting.com

National Commission on Excellence in Education. (1983). *A nation at risk: The imperative for educational reform.* Washington, DC: U.S. Department of Education.

National Council on Disability. (2000, January 25). *Back to school on civil rights: Letter of transmittal.* Washington, DC: Author.

National Institute on Drug Abuse (NIDA). (2003). *Preventing drug use among children and adolescents: A research-based guide for parents, educators, and community leaders* (2nd ed.). Washington DC: Author.

National Mental Health Association. (n.d.). *Bullying in schools: Harassment puts gay youth at risk.* Retrieved September 13, 2005, from www.nmha.org/pbedu/backtoschool/bullyingGayYouth.pdf

National Migrant and Seasonal Head Start Association. (n.d.). *About us.* Retrieved May 14, 2008, from http://www.nmshsa.org/About%20Us

National Public Radio, The Henry Kaiser Family Foundation, & The Kennedy School of Government at Harvard University. (2004). *Sex education in America: General Public/Parents survey.* Washington, DC: National Public Radio.

National School Climate Survey. (2001). The GLSEN 2000 National Climate Survey: The school related experiences of our nation's lesbian, gay, bisexual and transgender youth. [Electronic version]. Retrieved June 1, 2002, from www.glsen.org/templates/news/recordhtml

National Scientific Council on the Developing Child, Young Children Develop in an Environment of Relationships. (2004). *Working Paper No. 1.* Retrieved October 17, 2008, from www.developingchild.net/pubs/wp/environment_of_relationships.pdf

National Youth Violence Prevention Resource Center. (2001). *Teen substance abuse and violence facts.* Retrieved May 23, 2008, from www.safeyouth.org/scripts/faq/substabuse.asp

National. Research Council and Institute of Medicine. (2002). *Community programs to promote youth development.* J. Eccles & J. A. Gootman (Eds.), Board on Children, Youth, and Families, Division of Behavioral and Social Sciences and Education. Washington, DC: National Academy Press.

Neal v. Fulton County Bd. of Educ., 229 F.3d 1069 (11th Cir. 2000).

Nebo, J. C. (1955). Interpretation of school social welfare services to educators and other professionals who serve the schools. *Bulletin of the National Association of School Social Workers, 30,* 1–55.

Neely-Barnes, S. L. (1999). Parent involvement: A needs assessment. *School Social Work Journal, 24*(1), 29–43.

Nelson, G. M. (2000). *Self-governance in communities and families.* San Francisco: Berrett-Koehler.

Netzel, D. M., & Eber, L. (2003). Shifting from reactive to proactive discipline in an urban school district: A change of focus through PBIS implementation. *Journal of Positive Behavior Interventions, 5*(2), 71–79.

Neuhaus v. Federico, 12 Or. App. 315, 505 P. 939 (1973).

New Hampshire Revised Statutes Annotated 189:35-a (2008).

New Jersey v. T.L.O., 469 U.S. 325 (1985).

Newsome, W. S., Anderson-Butcher, D., Fink, J., Hall, L., & Huffer, J. (2008). The impact of school social work services on student absenteeism and risk factors related to school truancy. *School Social Work Journal, 32*(2), 21–38.

Nieberl, H. R. (1972). Breaking out of the bind in school social work practice. In R. C. Sarri & F. Maple (Eds.), *The school in the community* (pp. 151–160). Washington, DC: National Association of Social Workers.

Nientimp, E. G., & Cole, C. L. (1992). Teaching socially valid social interaction responses to students with severe disabilities in an integrated school setting. *Journal of School Psychology, 30,* 343–354.

No Child Left Behind Act of 2001, PL. 107-110, 115 Stat. 1425. Jan. 8. 2002.

Noguera, P. A. (1995). Preventing and producing violence: A critical analysis of responses to school violence. *Harvard Educational Review, 51,* 546–564.

North Carolina Board of Education v. Swann, 402 U.S. 43 (1971).

North Carolina General Statutes §115C-381 (2008).

Nugent, W. R., Sieppert, J. D., & Hudson, W. W. (2001). *Practice evaluation for the 21st century.* Belmont, CA: Brooks/Cole-Thomson Learning.

O'Kearney, R. T., Anstey, K. J., & von Sanden, C. (2006). Behavioural and cognitive behavioural therapy for obsessive compulsive disorder in children and adolescents. *Cochrane Database of Systematic Reviews, 4.* New York: Wiley.

Oakes, J. (2005). *Keeping track: How schools structure inequality* (2nd ed.). New Haven, CT: Yale University Press.

Oberti v. Board of Education. (1993), 995 F 2d 1204.

Office of Head Start. (2005a). *Biennial report to Congress: The status of children in head start programs.* Washington, DC: Administration for Children and Families. Retrieved from http://www.acf.hhs.gov/programs/hsb/about/biennial_report_2005.pdf

Office of Head Start. (2005b). *Head start impact study: First year findings.* Washington, DC: Administration for Children and Families.

Office of Head Start. (2007). *Head start program fact sheet.* Retrieved May 7, 2008, from http://www.acf.hhs.gov/programs/hsb/about/fy2007.html

Office of Planning, Research, and Evaluation. (2002). *Making a difference in the lives of infants and toddlers and their families: The impacts of early head start.* Washington, DC: Administration for Children and Families.

Office of the Surgeon General. (2001). *The surgeon general's call to action to promote sexual health and responsible sexual behavior.* Washington, DC: U.S. Department of Health and Human Services.

Ogbu, J. U. (1978). *Minority education and caste: The American system in cross-cultural perspective.* New York: Academic Press.

Olweus, D. (1993). *Bullying at school.* Oxford, UK: Blackwell.

Olweus, D., Limber, S., & Mihalic, S. E. (1999). *Blueprints for violence prevention, book nine: Bullying prevention program.* Boulder, CO: Center for the Study and Prevention of Violence.

One year later: The Civil Rights Project at UCLA reflects on the anniversary of the Supreme Court's voluntary integration decision. (June 27, 2008). Retrieved November 28, 2008 from, http://www.civilrightsproject.ucla.edu/policy/court/voltinit-anniversary.php

Oppenheimer, J. (1925). *The visiting teacher movement with special reference to administrative relationships* (2nd ed.). New York: Joint Committee on Methods of Preventing Delinquency.

Orfield, G. (1978). *Must we bus? Segregation and national policy.* Washington: Brookings Institution Press.

Orfield, G. (1996a). The growth of segregation. In G. Orfield & S. E. Eaton (Eds.), *Dismantling desegregation: The quiet reversal of Brown v. Board of Education* (pp. 53–71). New York: The New Press.

Orfield, G. (1996b). Turning back to segregation. In G. Orfield & S. E. Eaton (Eds.), *Dismantling desegregation: The quiet reversal of Brown v. Board of Education* (pp. 1–22). New York: The New Press.

Orfield, G., Bachmeier, M. D., James, D. R., & Fide, T. (1997). *Deepening segregation in American public schools.* [Electronic version]. Harvard Project on School Desegregation. Retrieved June 1, 2002, from www.bamn.com/resources/97-deepingseg.htm

Orfield, G., & Eaton, S. E. (1996). *Dismantling desegregation: The quiet reversal of Brown v. Board of Education.* New York: New Press.

Orfield, G., & Lee, C. (2007). Historic reversals, accelerating resegregation, and the need for new integration strategies. A report of the Civil Rights Project/ *Proyecto Derechos Civiles,* UCLA. Retrieved November 27, 2008 from http://www.civilrightsproject.ucla.edu/research/deseg/reversals_reseg_need.pdf

Organisation for Economic Co-operation and Development. (2004). *Learning for tomorrow's world: First results from PISA 2003.* Retrieved September 11, 2005, from www.pisa.oecd.org/document/55/0,2340, en_32252351_32236173339173031I1I,00.html

Orlich, D. C. (2004). No Child Left Behind: An illogical accountability model. *Clearing House, 78*(1), 6–12.

Orthner, D. K., & Bowen, G. L. (2004). Strengthening practice through Results Management. In A. R. Roberts, & K. R. Yeager (Eds.), *Evidence-based practice manual: Research and outcome measures in health and human services* (pp. 897–904). New York: Oxford University Press.

Orthner, D. K., Cook, E., Sabah, Y., & Rosenfeld, J. (2006). Organizational learning: A crossnational pilot-test of effectiveness in children's services. *Evaluation and Program Planning, 29,* 70–78.

Orthner, D. K., Cook, P. G., Rose, R. A., & Randolph, K. (2002). Welfare reform, poverty, and children's performance in school: Challenges for the school community. *Children & Schools, 24,* 105–121.

Osborne, J., & Collison, B. (1998). School counselors and external providers: Conflict or complement. *Professional School Counseling, 1*(4),7–11.

Oswald, K., Safran, S., & Johanson, G. (2005). Preventing trouble: Making schools safer places using positive behavior supports. *Education and Treatment of Children, 28*(3), 265–278.

Ovando, C. (2003). Bilingual education in the United States: Historical development and current issues. [Electronic version]. Retrieved November 29, 2008 from *Bilingual Research Journal,* http://findarticles.com/p/articles/mi_qa3722/is_200304/ai_n9181273

Overall, J. E., & Pfefferbaum, B. (1982). The Brief Psychiatric Rating Scale for Children. *Psychopharmacology Bulletin, 18*(2), 10–16.

P.B. v. Koch, 96 F. 3d 1298 (9th Cir. 1996).

Page, R. (1997). Helping adolescents avoid date rape: The role of secondary education. *High School Journal, 80,* 75–80.

Pahwa, B. A. (2003). Technology and school social work services: Introducing technology in an alternative school. *Journal of Technology in Human Services, 21*(1/2), 139–160.

Palmaffy, T. (2001). Special education history and issues. In C. E. Finn, A. J. Rotherham, & C. R. Hokanson, Jr. (Eds.), *Rethinking special education for a new century* (pp. 233–257). Dayton, OH: Thomas B. Fordham Foundation and the Progressive Policy Institute. Retrieved September 5, 2005, from www.edexcellence.net/doc/special-ed_inal.pdf

Parents can't sue to enforce No Child left behind Act, federal court rules. (2008, November 20). Retrieved November 23, 2008, from http://www.dallasnews.com/sharedcontent/dws/news/nation/stories/112108dnnatnochild

Parents involved in Cmty. Sch. v. Seattle Sch. Dist. No. 1, 127 S. Ct. 2738$ $(2007).

Parents' rights as defined in chapter 864, Statutes of 1998, Education Code. (1998). Retrieved May 23, 2002, from www.cde.ca.gov/iasa/parntrts.html

Parker, W. (2000). The future of school desegregation, *94 N W UL. Rev.* 1157.

Parks, C. (1995). Gang behavior in the schools: Reality or myth? *Educational Psychology Review, 7,* 41–68.

PASHA Programs Table. (2002). Retrieved October 17, 2008, from http://www.socio.com/newpasha/pasha tablebox1.htm

Patchin, J. W., & Hinduja, S. (2006). Bullies move beyond the school yard: A preliminary look at cyberbullying. *Youth Violence and Juvenile Justice, 4*(2), 148–169.

Patton, M. Q. (1978). *Utilization focused evaluation.* Beverly Hills, CA: Sage.

Pawlak, E. J., & Cousins, L. (1999). School social work: Organizational perspectives. In R. Constable, S. McDonald, & J. P. Flynn (Eds.), *School social work: Practice, policy, and research perspectives* (4th ed., pp. 150–165). Chicago: Lyceum Books.

Pelletierre, D., & Wardrip, K. (2008). *Housing at the half: A mid-decade progress report from the American community survey.* Washington, DC: National Low

Income Housing Coalition. Retrieved from http://www.nlihc.org/doc/Mid-DecadeReport_2-19-08.pdf

Pendell, M. J. (2008). How far is too far? The spending clause, the tenth amendment, and the education state's battle against unfunded mandates. *71 Alb. L. Rev.* 519.

Pennsylvania Association for Retarded Citizens [PARC] v. Commonwealth of Pennsylvania, 334 F Supp. 1257, 343 F Supp. 279 (B. D. Pa. 1971, 1972).

People v. Dilworth, 169 Ill. 2d 195, 661 N.E. 2d 310 (1996).

People v. Overton, 24 N.Y. 2d 522, 242 N.E. 2d 366 (1969).

Personal Responsibility and Work Opportunity Reconciliation Act of 1996. P.L. 104-193, 110 Stat. 2105 (1996).

Pfeiffer, S. I. (2001). Professional psychology and the gifted: Emerging practice opportunities. *Professional Psychology: Research and Practice, 32*(2), 175–180.

Phillippo, K., & Stone, S. (2006). School-based collaborative teams: An exploratory study of tasks and activities. *Children & Schools, 28,* 229–235.

Phillips, M. (1997). What makes schools effective? A comparison of the relationships of communitarian climate and academic achievement and attendance during middle school. *American Educational Research Journal, 34,* 633–662.

Phoenix Elem. Sch. Dist. No. 1 v. Green, 189 Ariz. 476, 943 P. 2d 836 (1997).

Pierce v. Soc'y of Sisters, 268 U.S. 510 (1925).

Pitner, R. O., Astor, R. A., Benbenishty, R., Haj-Yahia, M. M., & Zeira, A. (2003). The effects of group stereotypes on adolescents' reasoning about peer retribution. *Child Development, 74*(2), 413–425.

Pittel, E. (1998). How to take a weapons history: Interviewing children at risk for violence at school. *Journal of the American Academy of Child & Adolescent Psychiatry, 37,* 1100–1102.

Planty, M., Hussar, W., Snyder, T., Provasnik, S., Kena, G., Dinkes, R., KewalRamani, A., & Kemp, J. (2008). *The condition of education 2008* (NCES 2008-031). Washington DC: National Center for Education Statistics, Institute of Education Sciences, U.S. Department of Education. Retrieved October 1, 2008, from http://nces.ed.gov/pubs2008/2008031.pdf

Plessy v. Ferguson, 163 U.S. 537 (1896).

Polster, R. A., & Collins, D. (1993). Structured observation. In R. M. Grinnell (Ed.), *Social work research and evaluation* (4th ed., pp. 244–261). Itasca, IL: F. E. Peacock.

Poole, F. (1949). An analysis of the structure and practice of school social work today. *Social Service Review, 23,* 456.

Porter, G., Epp, L., & Bryan, S. (2000). Collaboration among school health professionals: A necessity, not a luxury. *Professional School Counseling, 3*(5), 315–322.

Powell, A. G., Farrar, E., & Cohen, D. K. (1985). *The shopping mall high school: Winners and losers in the educational market place.* Boston: Houghton Mifflin.

Powers, J. D. (2005). *Evidence-based practice in schools: Current status, potential barriers, and critical next steps.* Unpublished doctoral dissertation, School of Social Work, The University of North Carolina at Chapel Hill.

Powers, J. D., & Bowen, G. L. (2006). Coping with isolation: Guidelines for developing a professional network. In C. Franklin, M. B. Harris, & P. Allen-Meares (Eds.), *The school services source book: A guide for school-based professionals* (pp. 1157–1164). New York: Oxford University Press.

Powers, J. D., Bowen, G. L., & Rose, R. A. (2005). Using social environment assets to identify intervention strategies for promoting school success. *Children & Schools, 27*(3), 177–185.

Princiotta, D., & Bielick, S. (2006). *Homeschooling in the United States: 2003,* (NCES 2006-042) U.S. Department of Education. National Center for Education Statistics, Washington, DC: 2005. Available at http://nces.ed.gov/pubs2006/2006042.pdf.

Prothrow-Stith, D. (1987). *Violence prevention curriculum for adolescents.* Newton, MA: Education development Center, Inc.

Prothrow-Stith, D., & Weissman, M. (1991). *Deadly consequences.* New York: HarperCollins.

Pryor, C. B. (1992). Peer helping programs in school settings: Social workers report. *School Social Work Journal, 16*(2), 16–25.

Pugach, M., & Allen-Meares, P. (1985). Collaboration at the preservice level: Instructional and evaluational activities. *Journal of Teacher Education and Special Education, 8*(1), 3–11.

Pugsley v. Sellmeyer, 158 Ark. 247, 250 S.W 538 (1923).

Radin, N. (1975). A personal perspective on school social work. *Social Casework, 56,* 605–613.

Radin, N. (1988). Alternatives to suspension and corporal punishment. *Urban Education, 22*(4), 24.

Radin, N. (1988). Assessing the effectiveness of school social workers: An update focused on simulations, graphics, and peers. In J. G. McCullaugh & P. Allen-Meares (Eds.), *Conducting research: A handbook for school social workers* (pp. 77–78). Des Moines, IA: Iowa Department of Education.

Rafferty, Y., Shinn, M., & Weitzman, B. C. (2004). Academic achievement among formerly homeless adolescents and their continuously housed peers. *Journal of School Psychology, 42,* 179–199.

Raines, J. C. (2004). Evidence-based practice in school social work: A process in perspective. *Children & Schools, 26,* 71–85.

Ramirez, D. (2001). *No child left behind: A blueprint for education reform. Testimony given to the United States Commission on Civil Rights.* Retrieved June 1, 2002, from www.clmer.csulb.edu/ramireztestimony.html

Rando v. Newberg Public School Board, 23 Or. App. 425, 542 E 2d 938 (1975).

Rappaport, J. (1977). *Community psychology: Values, research, and action.* New York: Holt, Rinehart, and Winston.

Raver, C. C. (2002). Emotions matter: Making the case for the role of young children's emotional development for early school readiness. *Social Policy Report, 16*(3), 1–20.

Ravitch, D. (2000). *Left back: A century of failed school reforms.* New York: Simon & Schuster.

Redding v. Safford Unified Sch. Dist. # 1, 531 F. 3d 1071 (9th Cir. 2008).

Redmond, M. E. (2003). School social work information systems (SSWIS): A relational database for school social workers. *Journal of Technology in Human Services, 21*(1/2), 161–175.

Reid, W. J. (1992). *Task strategies: An empirical approach to social work practice.* New York: Columbia University Press.

Reid, W. J. (2000). *The task planner.* New York: Columbia University Press.

Reid, W., & Epstein, L. (1972). *Task-centered case-work* (pp. 7–8). New York: Columbia University Press.

Reis, S. M., Colbert, R. D., & Hebert, T. P. (2005). Understanding resilience in diverse, talented students in an urban high school. *Roeper Review, 27*(2), 110–120.

Renzulli, J. S., & Park, S. (2002). *Giftedness and high school dropouts: Personal, family, and school-related factors* (RM No. 02168). Storrs, CT: The National Research Center on the Gifted and Talented, University of Connecticut.

Reschly, D. J. (1995). *IQ and special education: History, current status, and alternatives.* Washington, DC: National Research Council, Commission on Social Sciences and Education, Board of Testing and Assessment.

Reschly, D. J. (1996). Identification and assessment of students with disabilities. *The Future of Children, 6*(1), 40–53. Reprinted with permission of the Center for the Future of Children of the David and Lucille Packard Foundation.

Respect for all. (2008). Retrieved on December 8, 2008, from http://schools.nyc.gov/RulesPolicies/Respectfor All/default.htm

Reynolds, B. C. (1935). Social casework: What is it? What is its place in the world today? *The Family, 16*, 238.

Richardson, V., Casanova, U., Placier, P., & Guilfoyle, K. (1989). *School children at risk: Schools as communities of support.* Philadelphia: Falmer Publishers.

Richman, J. M., Bowen, G. L., & Woolley, M. E. (2004). School failure: An eco-interactional developmental perspective. In M. Fraser (Ed.), *Risk and resilience in childhood: An ecological perspective* (2nd ed., pp. 133–160). Washington, DC: NASW Press.

Richmond, I., & Ayoub, C. C. (1993). Evolution of early intervention philosophy. In D. M. Bryant & M. A. Graham (Eds.), *Implementing early intervention: From research to effective practice* (pp. 1–17). New York: Guilford Press.

Richmond, M. (1917/1935). *Social diagnosis.* New York: Russell Sage Foundation.

Rigby, K. (1996). *Bullying in schools: And what to do about it.* Melbourne, VIC: Australian Council for Educational Research.

Rinaldi, C., & Samson, J. (2008). English language learners and response to intervention: referral considerations. *Teaching Exceptional Children, 40*(5), 6–14.

Roans, M., & Hoagwood, K. (2000). School-based mental health services: A research review. *Clinical Child and Family Psychology Review, 3*(4), 223–241.

Robinson, A. (1990). Cooperation of exploitation: The argument against cooperative learning groups for talented students. *Journal for the Education of the Gifted, 14*(1), 9027.

Robinson, J. P., Shaver, P. R., & Wrightsman, L. S. (Eds.). (1991). *Measures of personality and social psychological attitudes.* San Diego, CA: Academic Press.

Roderick, C., Pitchford, M., & Miller, A. (1997). Reducing aggressive playground behaviour by means of a school-wide "raffle." *Educational Psychology in Practice, 13,* 57–63.

Roebuck, M. C., French, M. T., & Dennis, M. L. (2003). Adolescent marijuana use and school attendance. *Economics of Education Review, 23*(2), 133–141.

Ronda, M. A., & Valencia, R. R. (1994). "At risk" Chicano students: The institutional and communicative life of a category. *Hispanic Journal of Behavioral Sciences, 16*(4), 363–395.

Roosevelt, T. (1919). *The foes of our household.* New York: George Doran.

Rose, A. J., Swenson, L. P., & Waller, E. M. (2004). Overt and relational aggression and perceived popularity: Developmental differences in concurrent and prospective relations. *Developmental Psychology, 40,* 378–387.

Rose, L. C., & Gallup, A. M. (2001). The 33rd Annual Phi Delta Kappa/Gallup Poll of the public's attitudes toward the public schools. *Phi Delta Kappan, 83*(1), 41–58.

Rose, M. (1995). *Possible lives: The promise of public education in America.* New York: Penguin Books.

Rose, M. (1998). Taking control of teacher quality. *American Teacher, 83*(1), 6–10.

Rosenblum, A., Magura, S., Fong, C., Cleland, C., Norwood, C., Casella, D., et al. (2005). Substance use among young adolescents in HIV-affected families: Resiliency, peer deviance, and family functioning. *Substance Use & Misuse, 40*(5), 581–603.

Rossi, P. H., & Freeman, H. E. (1993). *Evaluation: A systematic approach.* Newbury Park, CA: Sage.

Rossi, P. H., & Williams, W. (1972). *Evaluating social programs: Theory, practice and politics.* New York: Seminar Press.

Roth, J., Brooks-Gunn, J., Linver, M., & Hofferth, S. (2003). What happens during the school day? Time diaries from a national sample of elementary school teachers. *Teacher's College Record, 105*(3), 317–343.

Rowen, R. (1965). The function of the visiting teacher in the school. *Journal of the International Association of Pupil Personnel Workers, 9*, 3–9.

Rowinsky v. Bryan Independent School Dist., 80 F. 3d 1006 (5th Cir. 1996).

Rowley v. Board of Education. (1982). 458 U.S. at 203, 102 5. Ct. at 3049.

Royal, M. A., & Rossi, R. J. (1996). Individual level correlates of sense of community: Findings from workplace and school. *Journal of Community Psychology, 24*, 395–416.

Royal, M. A., & Rossi, R. J. (1997). *Schools as communities* (ERIC Digest No. 111). Eugene, OR: ERIC Clearinghouse on Education Management. (ED 405157).

Royse, D. D., Thyer, B. A., & Padgett, D. K. (2009). *Program evaluation: An introduction.* Belmont, CA: Cengage.

Rumberger, R. W. (2004). What can be done to prevent and assist school dropouts? In P. Allen-Meares & M. W. Fraser (Eds.), *Intervention with children and adolescents: An interdisciplinary perspective* (pp. 311–334). Boston: Allyn & Bacon.

Rury, J. L. (2005). *Education and social change* (2nd ed.). Mahwah, NJ: Erlbaum.

Sabah, Y., & Orthner, D. K. (2007). Implementing organizational learning in schools: Assessment and strategy. *Children & Schools, 29*, 243–246.

Sabatino, C. A. (1999). School social work consultation and collaboration. In R. Constable, S. McDonald, & J. P. Flynn (Eds.), *School social work: Practice, policy, and research perspectives* (4th ed., pp. 334–355). Chicago: Lyceum Books.

Sacramento City Unified School District, Board of Education v. Rachel H. (1994). 12 E3d 1398 (9th circuit).

Sadker, M., & Sadker, D. (1994). *Failing at fairness: How schools shortchange girls.* New York: Scribner's.

Saewyc, E. M., Magee, L. L., & Pettingell, S. E. (2004). Teenage pregnancy and associated risk behaviors among sexually abused adolescents. *Perspectives on Sexual and Reproductive Health, 36*(3), 98–105.

Sagor, R., & Cox, J. (2004). *At-risk students: Reaching and teaching them* (2nd ed.). (2004). Larchmont NY: Eye on Education.

Saleeby, D. (Ed.). (2002). *The strengths perspective in social work practice* (3rd ed.). Boston: Allyn & Bacon.

Salloum, A. (2008). Group therapy for children after homicide and violence: A pilot study. *Research on Social Work Practice, 18*, 198–211.

Salomone, R. (2000). Education and the Constitution: Shaping each other and the next century: Rich kids, poor kids, and the single-sex education debate. *Akron L. Rev., 34*, 209.

Sampson, R. J. (2001). How do communities undergird or undermine human development? Relevant contexts and social mechanisms. In A. Booth & A. C. Crouter (Eds.), *Does it take a village? Community effects on children, adolescents, & families* (pp. 3–30). New York: Erlbaum.

Sampson, R. J., Raudenbush, S., & Earls, F. (1997). Neighborhoods and violent crime: A multilevel study of collective efficacy. *Science, 277*, 918–924.

San Antonio Independent School District v. Rodriguez, 411 U.S. 1 (1973).

Sanders, W. L. (2000). Value-added assessment from student achievement data: Opportunities and hurdles. *Journal of Personnel Evaluation in Education, 14*(4), 329–339. Retrieved from http://www.sas.com/govedu/edu/opp_hurdles.pdf

Santa Fe Independent School District v. Doe, 530 U.S. 290 (2000).

Santelli, J. S., Kaiser, J., Hirsch, L., Radosh, A., Simkin, L., & Middlestadt, S. (2004). Initiation of sexual intercourse among middle school adolescents: The influence of psychosocial factors. *Journal of Adolescent Health, 34*(3), 200–208.

Santelli, J. S., Kindberg, L. D., Finer, L. B., & Singh, S. (2007). Explaining recent declines in adolescent pregnancy in the United States: The contribution of abstinence and improved contraceptive use. *American Journal of Public Health, 97*(1), 150–156.

Sarri, R., & Maple, F. (Eds.). (1972). *The school in the community.* Washington, DC: National Association of Social Workers.

Saxe v. State College Area School Dist. (SCASD), 240 F. 3d 200 (3rd Cir. 2001).

Saylor v. Board of Educ., 118 F. 3d 507 (6th Cir. 1997).

Sch. Dist. of Pontiac v. Spelling, Sec'y of the United States Dep't of Educ., 512 F. 3d 252 (6th Cir. 2008).

Schafer, M., & Smith, P. (1996). Teacher's perceptions of play fighting and real fighting in primary school. *Educational Research, 38*, 173–181.

Schein, E. H. (1985). *Organizational culture and leadership.* San Francisco: Jossey-Bass.

Schimmel, D. M., & Eiseman, J. (1982, Fall). *School discipline, round two. Update on law—related education.* Chicago: American Bar Association.

Schnorr, D., & Ware, H. W. (2001). Moving beyond a deficit model to describe and promote the career development of at-risk youth. *Journal of Career Development, 27*(4), 247–263.

School Dist. of Abington Twp., Pennsylvania v. Schempp, 374 U.S. 203 (1963).

Schwartz, W. (1994). *Improving the school experience for gay, lesbian, and bisexual students.* New York: ERIC Clearinghouse on Urban Education. Digest No. 101.

Schweinhart, L., Barnes, H., & Weikart, D. (1993). Significant benefits of the High/Scope Perry preschool study through age 27. *Monographs of the High/Scope Educational Research Foundation (No. 10).*

Scott, M. C. (2008). Resegregation, language, and educational opportunity: The influx of Latino students into North Carolina public schools. *Harvard Latino Law Review, 11*, 123.

Scott-Jones, D. (1993). Adolescent child-bearing: Whose problem? What can we do? *Phi Delta Kappan, 75*, 1–12.

Seal v. Morgan, 229 F. 3d 567 (6th Cir. 2000).

Sederer, L. I., & Dickey, B. (Eds.). (1996). *Outcomes assessments in clinical practice.* Baltimore: Williams & Wilkins.

Seid, M., Casteneda, D., Mize, R., Zivkovic, M., & Varni, J. (2003). Crossing the border for health care: Access and primary care characteristics for young children of Latino farm workers along the U.S.-Mexico border. *Ambulatory Pediatrics, 3*(3), 121–130.

Senge, P., Cambron-McCabe, N., Lucas, T., Smith, B., Dutton, J., & Kleiner, A. (2000). *Schools that learn: A fifth discipline fieldbook for educators, parents, and everyone who cares about education.* New York: Doubleday.

Senge, P., Kleiner, A., Roberts, C., Ross, R., Roth, G., & Smith, B. (1999). *The dance of change: The challenges to sustaining momentum in learning organizations.* New York: Doubleday/Currency.

Serrano v. Priest, 5 Cal. 3d 584 (1971).

Shaffer, D., Gould, M. S., Brasic, J., Ambrosini, P., Fisher, P., Bird, H., et al. (1983). A children's global assessment scale (CGAS). *Archives of General Psychiatry, 40*(11),1228–1231.

Sharp, S., & Smith, P. (1994). *Tackling bullying in your school: A practical handbook for teachers.* London: Routledge.

Shartrand, A. M., Weiss, H. B., Kreiger, H. M., & Lopez, M. E. (1997). *New skills for new schools: Preparing teachers in family involvement.* Cambridge, MA: Harvard Family Research Project.

Shaw, I., & Lishman, J. (Eds.). (1999). *Evaluation and social work practice.* Thousand Oaks, CA: Sage.

Shaw, M. C. (1967). Role delineation among guidance professions. *Psychology in the Schools, 4,* 3–13.

Sheafor, B. W., Horejsi, C. R., & Horejsi, G. A. (2000). *Techniques and guidelines for social work practice* (5th ed.). Boston: Allyn and Bacon.

Shealey, M. W. (2006). The promise and perils of "scientifically based" research for urban schools. *Urban Education, 41*(1), 5–19.

Sherman, A. (1997). *Poverty matters: The cost of child poverty in America.* Washington, DC: Children's Defense Fund.

Shin, H. B., & Bruno, R. (2003). *Language use and English speaking ability: 2000. Census 2000 Brief.* Washington. DC: U.S. Department of Commerce, Economics and Statistic Administration, U.S. Census Bureau.

Shonkoff, J. E., & Phillips, D. A. (Eds.). (2000). *From neurons to neighborhoods: The science of early childhood development.* Washington, DC: National Academy Press.

Shore, R. (1997). *Rethinking the brain: New insights into early development.* New York: Families and Work Institute.

Shouse, R. (1997). Academic press, sense of community, and student achievement. In J. S. Coleman, B. Schneider, S. Plank, K. S. Schiller, R. Shouse, & H. Wang with S. A. Lee (Eds.), *Redesigning American education* (pp. 60–86). Boulder, CO: Westview Press.

Shouse, R. C. (2002). School effects. In D. L. Levinson, P. W. Cookson, & A. Sadovnik (Eds.), *Education and sociology: An encyclopedia* (pp. 519–524). New York: Routledge Falmer.

Sikkema, M. (1949). An analysis of the structure and practice of school social work today. *Social Service Review, 23,* 447–453.

Sikkema, M. (1953). *Report of a study of school social work practice in twelve communities.* New York: American Association of School Social Workers.

Silberman, C. (1970). *Crisis in the classroom.* New York: Random House.

Silenzio, V. M. B., Pena, J. B., Duberstein, P. R., Cerel, J., & Knox, K. L. (2007). Sexual orientation and risk factors for suicidal ideation and suicide attempts among adolescents and young adults. *American Journal of Public Health, 97*(11), 11–14.

Simon, P. (1955). Social group work in the schools. *Bulletin of the National Association of School Social Workers, 30.*

Simpson, G. A., Williams, J. C., & Segall, A. B. (2007). Social work education and clinical learning. *Clinical Social Work, 35*(1), 3–14.

Simpson, R. E., Jr. (2001). Limits on students' speech in the Internet Age. *Dickinson Law Review, 105,* 81.

Sinclair, M. F., Christenson, S. L., & Thurlow, M. L. (2005). Promoting school completion of urban secondary youth with emotional behavioral disabilities. *Exceptional Children, 71,* 465–482.

Sipple, J. W., McCabe, L. M., & Ross-Bernstein, J. (2007). Assessing capacity: Early childhood education in rural New York State. Albany, NY: Unpublished report for the Rural Education Advisory Committee.

Sipple, J. W., McCabe, L. M., Ross-Bernstein, J., & Casto, H. G. (2008). Educational services for preschool children in rural New York State: Links among community-based organizations, pre-kindergarten programs, and school districts. Albany, NY: Unpublished report for the Rural Education Advisory Committee.

Skinner, H. A., Steinhauer, P. J., & Sitarenios, G. (2000). Family assessment measure and process model of family functioning. *Journal of Family Therapy, 22,* 190–210.

Sluckin, A. (1989). Behavioral social work treatment of childhood nocturnal enuresis. *Behavior Modification, 13,* 482–497.

Smalley, R. (1947). School social work as a part of the school program. *Bulletin of the National Association of School Social Workers, 22.*

Smalley, R. (1955). School counseling as social work. *Bulletin of the National Association of School Social Workers, 30,* 21–34.

Smith v. Board of Education, 182 Ill. App. 342 (1913).

Smith, J. R., Brooks-Gunn, J., & Klebanov, P. K. (1997). Consequences of living in poverty for young children's cognitive and verbal ability and early school achievement. In G. J. Duncan & J. Brooks-Gunn (Eds.), *Consequences of growing up poor* (pp. 132–189). New York: Russel Sage Foundation.

Smith, M. F. (1989). *Evaluabililty assessment: A practical approach.* Boston: Mower Academic.

Smith, M. L., & Glass, G. V. (1987). *Research and evaluation in education and the social sciences.* Englewood Cliffs, NJ: Prentice Hall.

Smith, P., & Sharp, S. (1994). *School bullying.* London: Routledge.

SmithBattle, L. (2007). "I wanna have a good future": Teen mothers' rise in educational aspirations, competing demands, and limited school support. *Youth & Society, 38*(3), 348–371.

Snyder, H. N., & Sickmund M. (1999). *Juvenile offenders and victims: 1999 national report.* Washington, DC: Office of Juvenile Justice and Delinquency Prevention.

Solomon, J., & Card, J. J. (2004). *Making the list: Understanding, selecting, and replicating effective teen pregnancy prevention programs.* Retrieved on August 24, 2005, from www.teenpregnancy.org

Soriano, M., Soriano, F. I., & Jimenez, E. (1994). School violence among culturally diverse populations: Sociocultural and institutional considerations. *School Psychology Review, 23*(2), 216–235.

Sowers-Hoag, K. M., Thyer, B. A., & Bailey, J. S. (1987). Promoting safety belt use by young children. *Journal of Applied Behavior Analysis, 20,* 133–138.

Special Issue on Conceptual Frameworks. (1977). *Social Work, 22*(5).

Spencer, M. B., Fegley, S., Harpalani, V., & Seaton, G. (2004). Understanding hypermasculinity in context: A theory driven analysis of urban adolescent males' coping responses. *Research in Human Development, 1*(4), 229–257.

Spitzer, K., & Welsh, B. (1969). A problem-focused model of practice. *Social Casework, 50,* 323–329.

Sroufe, A. (1996). *Emotional development: The organization of emotional life in the early years.* New York: Cambridge University Press.

Staats, A. W., & Butterfield, W. H. (1965). Treatment of non-reading in a culturally deprived juvenile delinquent: An application of reinforcement principles. *Child Development, 36,* 925–942

Stanley v. Northeast Independent School District, 462 F. 2d 960 (5th Cir. 1972).

State ex rel. Barno v. Crestwood Bd. of Educ., 134 Ohio App. 3d 494 (1998).

State of Florida v. J.A., 679 So. 2d 316 (1996).

State v. Self, 155 S.W. 3d 756 (Mo. 2005).

Staudt, M., & Alter, C. (1993). Practice evaluation in social work. In J. Clark (Ed.), *Best practice guidelines for school social work practice.* Des Moines, IA: Iowa Department of Education.

Stein, N. (1995). Sexual harassment in the school: The public performance of gendered violence. *Harvard Educational Review, 65,* 145–162.

Stein, N. D. (1993). *Secrets in public: Sexual harassment in our schools.* Wellesley, MA: Wellesley College Center for Research on Women.

Steinberg, L. (1996). *Beyond the classroom: Why school reform has failed and what parents need to do.* New York: Simon & Schuster.

Stone v. Graham, 449 U.S. 39 (1980).

Story, M., Lytle, L. A., Birnbaum, A. S., & Perry C. L. (2002). Peer-led, school-based nutrition education for young adolescents: Feasibility and process evaluation of the TEENS study. *Journal of School Health, 72*(3), 121–127.

Streeter, C. L., & Franklin, C. (1993). Site-based management in public opportunities and challenges for school social workers. *Social Work in Education, 15,* 71–81.

Streeter, C. L., & Franklin, C. (2002). Standards for school social work in the 21st century. In A. R. Roberts & G. J. Greene (Eds.), *Social workers desk reference* (pp. 612–618). New York: Oxford University Press.

Strizek, G. A., Pittsonberger, J. L., Riordan, K. E., Lyter, D. M., & Orlofsky, G. F. (2006). *Characteristics of schools, districts, teachers, principals, and school libraries in the United States: 2003–2004* (NCES No. 2006-313). U.S. Department of Education. Washington, DC: National Center for Education Statistics. Retrieved from http://nces.ed.gov/pubs 2006/2006313.pdf

Strozier, A., McGrew, L., Krisman, K., & Smith, A. (2005). Kinship care connection: A school-based intervention for kinship caregivers and the children in their care. *Children and Youth Services Review, 27*(9), 1011–1029.

Study of Personnel Needs in Special Education. (2002). *SPeNSE fact sheet: Paperwork in special education.* Retrieved from www.spense.org.

Sugai, G., Horner, R. H., Dunlap, G., Hieneman, M., Lewis, T. J., Nelson, C. M., et al. (2000). Applying positive behavioral support and functional behavioral assessment in schools. *Journal of Positive Behavior Interventions, 2,* 131–143

Suit challenges gay high school in New York. (2003). Retrieved August 16, 2003, from http://news.findlaw .com/scripts/printer_friendly.pi?page=/ap/6/1110.../ 20030814033005_16.htm

Sussman, S., Dent, C. W., Galaif, E. R., Stacy, A. W., Newman, T., Moss, M. A., et al. (1997). Implementation and process evaluation of a student "school as-community" group: A component of a school-based drug abuse prevention program. *Evaluation Review, 21*(l), 94–123.

Suzuki, L. A., Short, E. L., Pierterse, A., & Kugler, J. (2001). Multicultural issues and the assessment of aptitude. In L. A. Suzuki (Ed.), *Handbook of multicultural assessment: Clinical, psychological, and educational applications* (2nd ed., pp. 359–382). San Francisco: Jossey-Bass.

Sviridoff, M., & Ryan, W. (1997). Community centered family service. *Families in Society: The Journal of Contemporary Human Services, 78,* 128–139.

Swann v. Charlotte-Mecklenburg Board of Education, 402 U.S. 1 (1971).

Swap, S. (1978). The ecological model of emotional disturbance in children: A status report and proposed synthesis. *Behavioral Disorders, 3,* 186–196.

Swartz, J., & Martin, W. (Eds.). (1997). *Applied ecological psychology for schools within communities: Assessment and intervention.* Mahwah, NJ: Erlbaum.

Szapocznik, J., & Williams, R. A. (2000). Brief strategic family therapy: Twenty-five years of interplay among theory, research and practice in adolescent behavior problems and drug abuse. *Clinical Child and Family Psychology Review, 3*(2), 117–134.

Szapocznik, J., Hervis, O. E., and Schwartz, S. J. (2003). Brief strategic family therapy for adolescent drug abuse (NIH Publication No. 03–4751). NIDA Therapy Manuals for Drug Addiction. Rockville, MD: National Institute on Drug Abuse.

Taft, J. (1923). The relation of the school on the mental health of the average child. *Proceedings of the National Conference of Social Work* (p. 398). Chicago: University of Chicago Press.

Tanton v. McKenney, 226 Mich. 245, 197 N.W. 510 (1924).

Task Force on Children Out of School. (1970). *The way we go to school.* Boston: Beacon Press.

Taylor, L., & Adelman, H. S. (2006). Want to work with schools? What is involved in successful linkages? In C. Franklin, M. B. Harris, & P. Allen-Meares (Eds.), *The school services sourcebook: A guide for school-based professionals* (pp. 955–970). New York: Oxford University Press.

Teitlebaum, J. (1995). Issues in school desegregation: The dissolution of a well-intended mandate. *Marquette Law Review, 79,* 347.

Teresa P. v. Berkeley Unified School Dist. 724 F. Supp. 698 (N.D. Cal. 1989).

Terzian, S. (2002). On probation and under pressure: How one 4th-grade class managed high-stakes testing. *Childhood Education, 78,* 282–284.

Thomas, E. J. (1975). Uses of research methods in interpersonal practice. In N. A. Polansky (Ed.), *Social work research* (pp. 254–283). Chicago: University of Chicago Press.

Thomas, E. J. (1984). *Designing interventions for the helping professions.* Beverly Hills, CA: Sage.

Thyer, B. A., & Myers, L. L. (2007). *A social worker's guide to evaluating practice outcomes.* Alexandria, VA: Council on Social Work Education.

Thyer, B. A., & Sowers-Hoag, K. M. (1986). The etiology of school phobia: A behavioral approach. *School Social Work Journal, 10,* 86–98.

Tice, P., Princiotta, D., Chapman, C., & Bielick, S. (2007). *Trends in the use of school choice: 1993 to 2003* (NCES No. 2007-045). U.S. Department of Education. Washington, DC: National Center for Education Statistics. Retrieved from http://nces.ed.gov/pubs 2007/2007045.pdf

Timberlake, E. M., Sabantino, C. A., & Hooper, S. N. (1982). School social work practice and P.L. 94–142. In R. T. Constable & J. P. Flynn (Eds.), *School social work: Practice and research perspectives* (pp. 49–72). Homewood, IL: Dorsey Press.

Time (2001). Is homeschooling good for America? August 27, 2001.

Timpane, M., & Reich, B. (1997, February). Revitalizing the ecosystem for youth: A new perspective for school reform. *Phi Delta Kappan,* 464–470.

Tinker v. Des Moines School Dist. 393 U.S. 503 (1969).

Title IX at 35: Beyond the headlines. A report of the national coalition for women and girls in education. (2008). Retrieved December 1, 2008, from http://www.ncwge.org/PDF/TitleIXat35.pdf

Todd, A. W., Horner, R. H., Anderson, K., & Spriggs, M. (2002). Teaching recess: Low-cost efforts producing effective results. *Journal of Positive Behavior Interventions, 4*(1), 46–52.

Todd, P. E., & Wolpin, K. I. (2007). The production of cognitive achievement in children: Home, school, and racial test score gaps. *Journal of Human Capital, 1*(1), 91–136.

Tolan, P., & Guerra, N. (1994). Prevention of delinquency: Current status and issues. *Applied and Preventive Psychology, 3,* 251–273.

Tolan, P. H., Gorman-Smith, D., & Henry, D. B. (2003). The developmental ecology of urban males' youth violence. *Developmental Psychology, 39*(2), 274–291.

Tolan, P. H., Gorman-Smith, D., & Henry, D. B. (2004). Supporting families in a high risk setting: Proximal effects of SAFEchildren preventative intervention. *Journal of Consulting & Clinical Psychology, 72*(5), 855–869.

Tomlinson, C. A. (2001). *How to differentiate instruction in mixed-ability classroom* (2nd ed.). Alexandria, VA: Association for Supervision and Curriculum Development.

Towle, C. (1936). Discussion of "changing concepts in visiting teacher work." *Visiting Teacher Bulletin, 12,* 15–16.

Tripodi, T. (1983). *Evaluative research for social workers.* Englewood Cliffs, NJ: Prentice Hall.

Tripodi, T., & Epstein, I. (1980). *Research techniques for clinical social workers.* New York: Columbia University Press.

Tripodi, T., Fellin, P., & Epstein, I. (1978). *Differential social program evaluation.* Itasca, IL: F.E. Peacock Publishers Inc.

Trohanis, P. L. (1994). Early intervention—a national overview. *The Exceptional Parent, 24,* 18–20.

Turnbull, A. P. (1994). *Group action planning for families with infants and toddlers.* Richmond, VA: Zero to Three.

Turnbull, A. P., & Turnbull, H. R. (1996). *Families, professionals, and exceptionality.* Columbus, OH: Merrill/Prentice Hall.

Turnbull, A. P., Turnbull, H. R., Shank, M., & Leal, D. (1995). *Exceptional lives: Special education in today's schools.* Columbus, OH: Merrill/Prentice Hall.

Turnbull, R., Turnbull, A., Shank, M., & Smith, S. J. (2004). *Exceptional lives: special education in today's schools. Fourth edition.* Upper Saddle River, NJ: Pearson Education, Inc.

Turner, J. B. (1998). Foreword. In P. L. Ewalt, E. M. Freeman, & D. L. Poole (Eds.), *Community building: Renewal, well-being, and shared responsibility* (pp. ix–x). Washington, DC: NASW Press.

Tutty, L. M. (2000). What children learn from sexual abuse prevention programs: Difficult concepts and developmental issues. *Research on Social Work Practice, 10,* 275–300.

Tyack, D. B. (1974). *The one best system: A history of American urban education.* Cambridge, MA: Harvard University Press.

Tyack, D. B., & Cuban, L. (1995). *Tinkering toward utopia: A century of public school reform.* Cambridge, MA: Harvard University Press.

U.S. Bureau of the Census. (2000). *Statistical abstract of the United States.* Washington, DC: U.S. Department of Commerce.

U.S. Commission on Civil Rights. (1967). *Racial isolation in public schools: A report.* Washington, DC: Author.

U.S. Conference of Mayors. (2006). *Hunger and homelessness survey.* Washington, DC: Sodexho.

U.S. Department of Agriculture. (2007). *Household food security in the United States, 2006* (ERR No. 49).

U.S. Department of Education, National Center for Education Statistics. (1998). *Digest of education statistics, 1997* (NCES No. 98-015). Washington, DC: Government Printing Office. Retrieved from http://nces.ed.gov/pubs97/98015.pdf

U.S. Department of Education, National Center for Education Statistics. (2006). *Common core of data dataset 2004–2005.*

U.S. Department of Education, National Center for Education Statistics. (2007). *The condition of education 2007* (NCES 2007-064). Washington, DC: U.S. Government Printing Office.

U.S. Department of Education, National Center for Education Statistics. (2008). *Digest of education statistics, 2007* (NCES No. 2008-022). Washington, DC: Government Printing Office. Retrieved from http://nces.ed.gov/pubs2008/2008022.pdf

U.S. Department of Education, National Center for Education Statistics. (2008). *The condition of education 2008: Fast Facts* (NCES 2008-031). Washington DC: Author. Retrieved October 5, 2008, from http://nces.ed.gov/FastFacts/display.asp?id=16

U.S. Department of Education, Office of Special Education Programs. (n.d.) *Data Analysis System (DANS).* Data retrieved September 2, 2008, from www.ideadata.org

U.S. Department of Education, Planning and Evaluation Service. (2002). *The education for homeless children and youth program: Learning to succeed, volume I* (Doc. No. 2000-13).

U.S. Department of Education. (1991). *Teenage pregnancy and parenthood issues under Title IX of the Education Amendments of 1972.* Washington, DC: U.S. Government Printing Office.

U.S. Department of Education. (2000). *Fall 1998 elementary and secondary school civil rights compliance report: National and state projections.* Washington, DC: Author.

U.S. Department of Education. (2000). *Twenty-second annual report to Congress on the implementation of the Individuals with Disabilities Education Act.* Washington, DC: Author. Retrieved September 1, 2005, from www.ed.gov/about/reports/annual/osep/2000/index.html

U.S. Department of Education. (2002). *Twenty-fourth annual report to Congress on the implementation of the Individuals with Disabilities Education Act.* Washington, DC: Author. Retrieved September 1, 2005, from www.ed.gov/about/reports/annual/osep/2002/index.html

U.S. Department of Education. (2007). *Twenty-seventh annual report to Congress on the implementation of the Individuals with Disabilities Education Act, Volume 1.* Washington, DC: Author. Retrieved October 1, 2008, from http://www.ed.gov/about/reports/annual/osep/2005/parts-b-c/index.html

U.S. Department of Health and Human Services, Administration on Children, Youth and Families. (2008a). *Child maltreatment, 2006.* Washington, DC: U.S. Government Printing Office.

U.S. Department of Health and Human Services, Administration on Children, Youth and Families. (2008b). *The AFCARS report: Preliminary FY 2006 estimates* (AFCARS No. 14).

U.S. Department of Health and Human Services. (1999). *Mental health: A report of the surgeon general—Executive summary.* Rockville, MD: U.S. Department of Health and Human Services, Substance Abuse and Mental Health Services Administration, Center for Mental Health Services, National Institutes of Health, National Institute of Mental Health.

U.S. Department of Health and Human Services. (2000). *Report of the surgeon general's conference on children's mental health: A national action agenda.* Washington, DC: Department of Health and Human Services.

U.S. Department of Health, Education, and Welfare. (1975). *Title IX of the Education Act of 1972: A summary of the implementing regulation.* Washington, DC: U.S. Government Printing Office.

U.S. Department of Health, Education, and Welfare. (1978). *Taking sexism out of education: A national project on women in education.* Washington, DC: U.S. Government Printing Office.

U.S. Departments of Education and Justice. (2000). *2000 annual report on school safety.* Washington, DC.

Underwood, M., Kupersmidt, J. B., & Coie, J. D. (1996). Childhood peer sociometric status and aggression as predictors of adolescent childbearing. *Journal of Research on Adolescence, 6*(1), 2–15.

UNICEF. (2007). *Child poverty in perspective: An overview of child well-being in rich countries, Innocenti Report Card.* Florence: UNICEF Innocenti Research Centre. The United Nations Children's Fund. Retrieved October 5, 2008, from http://www .unicef.org/media/files/ChildPovertyReport.pdf

United States v. Tyler, 572 F. Supp. 2d 726 (E. D. Tex. 2008).

United States v. Virginia, 518 U.S. 515 (1996).

Urbonya, K. R. (2001). Determining reasonableness under the Fourth Amendment: Physical force to control and punish students. *Cornell J. L. & Public Policy, 10,* 397.

Uribe, V., & Harbeck, K. M. (1992). Addressing the needs of gay, lesbian, and bisexual youth. In K. M. Harbeck (Ed.), *Coming out of the classroom closet: Gay and lesbian students, teachers and curricula.* New York: Harrington Park Press.

USA Patriot Act of 2001, "Uniting and Strengthening America Act by Providing Appropriate Tools Required to Intercept and Obstruct Terrorism." P.L.107-56, 115 Stat. 272 (2001).

Valencia, R. R., & Suzuki, L. A. (2001). *Intelligence testing and minority students: Foundations, performance factors, and assessment issues.* Thousand Oaks, CA: Sage.

Van Wormer, K. S., Besthorn, F. H., & Keefe, T. (2007). *Human behavior and the social environment: Macro level: Groups, communities, and organizations.* New York: Oxford University Press.

Vargus, I. (1976). Developing, launching, and maintaining the school–community–pupil program. In D. J. Kurpiur & I. Thomas (Eds.), *Social services and the public schools* (pp. 61–73). Bloomington, IN: Midwest Center Satellite Consortium for Planned Change in Pupil Personnel Program for Urban Schools.

Varjas, K., Nastasi, B. K., Moore, R. B., & Jayasena, A. (2005). Using ethnographic methods for development of culture specific interventions. *Journal of School Psychology, 43,* 241–258.

Ventura, S. J., Abma, J. C., Mosher, W. D., & Henshaw, S. K. (2008). *Estimated pregnancy rates by outcome for the United States, 1990–2004* (NVSR No. 56-15). Hyattsville, MD: National Center for Health Statistics. Retrieved from http://www.cdc.gov/nchs/data/ nvsr/nvsr56/nvsr56_15.pdf

Vernez, G., Krop, R. A., & Rydell, C. P. (1999). *Closing the education gap: Benefits and costs.* Santa Monica, CA: RAND.

Vernonia Sch. Dist. v. Acton, 515 U.S. 646 (1995).

Viggiani, P. A., Reid, W. J., & Bailey-Dempsey, C. (2002). Social worker-teacher collaboration in the classroom: Help for elementary school students at risk of failure. *Research on Social Work Practice, 12*(5), 604–620.

Vigil, J. D. (2004). Gangs and group membership: Implications for schooling. In M. A. Gibson, P. Gandara, & J. P. Koyama (Eds.), *School connections: U.S. Mexican youth, peers, and school* (pp. 87–107). New York: Teachers College Press.

Vinter, R. D., & Sarri, R. C. (1965). Malperformance in the public schools. *Social Work, 10,* 38–48.

Wagner, M. (1995). *The contributions of poverty and ethnic background to the participation of secondary school students in special education.* Menlo Park, CA: SRI International.

Wagner, M., Newman, L., Cameto, R., & Levine, P. (2005). *National Longitudinal Transition Study 2: Changes over time in the early postschool outcomes of youth with disabilities.* Menlo Park, CA: SRI International. Retrieved March 3, 2006, from http:// www.nlts2.org/pdfs/str6completereport.pdf

Wald, L. (1915). *The house on Henry Street.* New York: Henry Holt and Co.

Walker, H. M., Golly, A., Kavanaugh, K., Stiller, B., Severson, H. H., & Feil, E. G. (2004). *First step to success.* Longmont, CO: Sopris West.

Walker, H. M., Kavanaugh, K., Stiller, B., Golly, A., Severson, H. H., & Feil, E. G. (1998). First steps: An early intervention approach for preventing school antisocial behavior. *Journal of Emotional and Behavioral Disorders, 6*(4), 243–251.

Walker, H. M., Stiller, B., Golly, A., Kavanagh, K., Severson, H. H., & Feil, E. G. (1997). *First step to success: Preschool edition kit.* Longmont, CO: Sopris West.

Waller, V. V. (1965). *The sociology of teaching.* New York: Wiley.

Ward, H., Anderson-Butcher, D., & Kwiatkowski, A. (2006). Effective strategies for involving parents in schools. In C. Franklin, M. B. Harris, & P. Allen-Meares (Eds.), *The school services sourcebook: A guide for school-based professionals* (pp. 641–649). New York: Oxford University Press.

Ward, J. V. (1995). Cultivating a morality of care in African American adolescents: A culture-based model of violence prevention. *Harvard Educational Review, 65*(2), 175–188.

Warheit, G. J., Bell, R. A., & Schwab, J. J. (1977). *Planning for change: Needs assessment approaches.* Rockville, MD: National Institute of Mental Health.

Washington, J. A., & Craig, H. K. (1992). Performances of low-income, African American preschool and kindergarten children on the Peabody Picture Vocabulary

Test-Revised. *Language, Speech, & Hearing Services in Schools, 23*(4), 329–333.

Waters, D. B., & Lawrence, E. C. (1993). *Competence, courage, and change.* New York: W. W. Norton.

Watson, T. F. (1975). An open letter to social workers in schools. *NASW News, 19.*

Weathers, A., Minkovitz, C., O'Campo, P., & Diener-West, M. (2003). Health services use by children of migratory agricultural workers: Exploring the role of need for care. *Pediatrics, 111*(5), 956–963.

Weaver, H., Smith, G., & Kippax, S. (2005). School-based sex education policies and indicators of sexual health among young people: A comparison of the Netherlands, France, Australia and the United States. *Sex Education, 5*(2) 171–188.

Webb, J. T., & Latimer, D. (1993). *ADHD and children who are gifted* (ERIC EC Digest No. E522). Reston, VA: The ERIC Clearinghouse on Disabilities and Gifted Education.

Webber, A. M. (1999, May). Learning for a change. *Fast Company.com,* pp. 178–188 (http://fastcompany.com/online/24/senge.html).

Webster, D. (1993). The unconvincing case for school based conflict resolution programs for adolescents. *Health Affairs, 4,* 126–141.

Webster-Stratton, C. (1996). Early intervention with videotape modeling: Programs for families of children with oppositional defiant disorder or conduct disorder. In E. D. Hibbs & P. S. Jensen (Eds.), *Psychosocial treatments with children and adolescents* (pp. 435–474). Washington DC: APA.

Webster-Stratton, C. (n.d.) *The incredible years.* Retrieved October 17, 2008, from http://www.incredibleyears.com/index.asp

Webster-Stratton, C., Reid, M. J., & Stoolmiller, M. (2006). *Preventing aggression and improving social, emotional, and academic competence: Evaluation of Dina Dinosaur classroom curriculum in high-risk schools.* Unpublished manuscript.

Weiss, C. H. (1972). *Evaluation research: Methods of assessing program effectiveness.* Englewood Cliffs, NJ: Prentice Hall.

Weiss, C. H. (1998). *Evaluation* (2nd ed.). Upper Saddle River, NJ: Prentice Hall.

Weiss, H. B., Kreider, H., Lopez, M. E., & Chatman, C. M. (Eds.). (2005). *Preparing educators to involve families: From theory to practice.* London: Sage.

Weist, M. D., & Paternite, C. E. (2006). Building an interconnected policy-training-practice-research agenda to advance school mental health. *Education and Treatment of Children, 29*(2), 173–196.

Weisz, A. N., & Black, B. M. (2001). Evaluating a sexual assault and dating violence prevention program for urban youth. *Social Work Research, 25*(2), 89–100.

Wells, M., & Mitchell, K. J. (2008). How do high-risk youth use the Internet? Characteristics and implications for prevention. *Child Maltreatment, 13*(3), 227–234.

Werner, B. (1959). *Objectives of the social work curriculum.* New York: Council on Social Work Education.

Werner, E. (1986). The concept of risk from a developmental prospective. *Advances in Special Education, 5*(1), 1–23.

Werner, E., & Smith, R. (1992). *Overcoming the odds: High risk children from birth to adulthood.* Ithaca, NY: Cornell University Press.

Wesley, P. W. (1994). Providing on-site consultation to promote quality in integrated child care programs. *Journal of Early Intervention, 18,* 391–402.

Wessenich, L. P. (1972). Systems analysis applied to school social work. In R. Sarri & F. Maple (Eds.), *The school in the community* (pp. 196–210). Washington, DC: National Association of Social Workers.

West Virginia State Board of Education v. Barnette, 319 U.S. 624 (1943).

West, J., Denton, K., & Germino-Hausken, E. (2000). *America's kindergartners.* [NCES 2000-070] Washington, DC: U.S. Department of Education Office of Educational Research and Improvement.

Westat & Policy Studies Associates. (2001). The longitudinal evaluation of school change and performance in Title I schools: Volume 1. Washington DC: U.S. Department of Education.

Westat Corporation. (2002). Personnel recruitment, retention, and shortage data tables: Tables 3.130, 3.146, 3.147, 5.130, 5.146, 5.147. Retrieved April 30, 2002, from www.spense.org

Westhues, A., Clarke, L., & Watton, J. (2001). Building positive relationships: An evaluation of process and outcomes in a Big Sister program. *Journal of Primary Prevention, 21,* 477–493.

Weston, D. R., Ivins, B., Heffron, M. C., & Sweet, N. (1997). Formulating the centrality of relationships in early intervention: An organizational perspective. *Infants & Young Children, 9*(3), 1–12.

Wexler, L. S. (1996). Official English, nationalism and linguistic terror: A French lesson. *Washington Law Review, 71,* 285.

Whitchurch, G. G., & Constantine, L. L. (1993). Systems theory. In P. G. Boss, W. J. Doherty, R. LaRossa, W. R. Schumm, & S. K. Steinmetz (Eds.), *Sourcebook of family theories and methods: A contextual approach* (pp. 325–352). New York: Plenum.

Whitfield, G. W. (1999). Validating school social work: An evaluation of a cognitive behavioral approach to reduce school violence. *Research on Social Work Practice, 9,* 399–426.

Wholey, J. S. (1987). Evaluability assessment: Developing program theory. In L. Brickman (Ed.), *Using program theory in evaluation.* San Francisco, CA: Jossey-Bass.

Widener v. Frye, 809 F. Supp. 35 (S.D. Ohio, 1992).

Wigoren, J. (2001, May 3). Lawsuits touch off debate over paddling in the schools. *The New York Times,* pp. Al, A22.

Williams, C. C. (2006). The epistemology of cultural competence. *Families in Society 87*(2), 209–220.

Williams, J. H., Ayers, C. D., & Arthur, M. W. (1997). Risk and protective factors in the development of delinquency and conduct disorder. In M. W. Fraser (Ed.), *Risk and resilience in childhood: An ecological perspective* (pp. 140–170). Washington, DC: NASW Press.

Williams, K., Rivera, L., Neighbours, R., & Reznik, V. (2007). Youth violence prevention comes of age: Research, training and future directions. *Annual Review of Public Health, 28*, 195–211.

Williams, R. B. (1970). School compatibility and social work role. *Social Service Review, 44*, 169–174.

Willis, J. (1969). The mental health worker as a systems engineer. In R. Sarri & F. Maple (Eds.), *The general systems approach: Contribution toward an holistic conception of social work*. New York: Council on Social Work Education.

Willis, J. W., & Willis, J. S. (1972). The mental health worker as a systems behavioral engineer. In R. Sarri & F. Maple (Eds.), *The school in the community* (pp. 141–160). Washington, DC: National Association of Social Workers.

Willower, D. J. (1991). School reform and schools as organizations. *Journal of School Leadership, 1,* 305–315.

Wilson, S. J., & Lipsey, M. W. (2006). *The effects of school-based social information processing interventions on aggressive behavior: Part I: Selected/indicated pull-out programs*. Oslo, Norway: The Campbell Collaboration.

Winebrenner, S., & Devlin, B. (1996). *Cluster grouping of gifted students: How to provide full-time services on a part-time budget* (ERIC EC Digest No. E538). Reston, VA: The Eric Clearinghouse on Disabilities and Gifted Education. Retrieved from http://www.hoagiesgifted.org/eric/e538.html

Winslow, E. B., Sandler, I. N., & Wolchik, S. A. (2005). Building resilience in all children. In S. Goldstein & R. B. Brooks (Eds.), *Handbook of resilience in children* (pp. 337–356). New York: Springer.

Winters, W., & Easton, F. (1983). *The practice of social work in school: An ecological perspective*. New York: Free Press.

Winters, W. G., & Gourdine, R. M. (2000). School reform: A viable domain for school social work practice. In J. G. Hopps & R. Morris (Eds.), *Social work at the millennium* (pp. 138–174). New York: Free Press.

Wisconsin v. Yoder, 406 U.S. 205 (1972).

Wood v. Strickland, 420 U.S. 308 (1975).

Wooster v. Sunderland, 27 Cal. App. 51, 148 P. 959 (1915).

Ybarra, M., Mitchell, K., Wolak, J., & Finkelhor, D. (2006). Examining characteristics and associated distress related to Internet harassment: Findings from the Second Youth Internet Safety Survey. *Pediatrics, 118*, 1169–1177.

Ybarra, M., & Mitchell, K. J. (2007). Prevalence and frequency of internet harassment instigation: Implications for adolescent health. *Journal of Adolescent Health, 41*, 189–195.

Ybarra, M. L., Alexander, C., & Mitchell, K. J. (2005). Depressive symptomatology, youth Internet use, and online interactions: A national survey. *Journal of Adolescent Health, 36*, 9–18.

Yegidis, B. L., & Weinbach, R. W. (2005). *Research methods for social workers* (5th ed.). Boston: Allyn and Bacon.

Youssef, R., Attia, M., & Kamel, M. (1998). Children experiencing violence II: Prevalence and determinants of corporal punishment in schools. *Child Abuse & Neglect, 22,* 975–985.

Yung, B., & Hammond, W. R. (1998). Breaking the cycle: A culturally sensitive violence prevention program for African-American children. In L. Lutzker (Ed.), *Handbook of child abuse research and treatments*. New York: Plenum Press.

Zarichney v. State Board of Agriculture, 338 U.S. 118 (1949).

Zeanah, C. H., Jr., & McDonough, S. (1989). Clinical approaches to families in early intervention. *Seminars in Perinatology, 13*(6), 513–526.

Zeira, A., Astor, R. A., & Benbenishty, R. (2002). Sexual harassment in Jewish and Arab public schools in Israel. *Child Abuse & Neglect, 26,* 149–166.

Zeira, A., Astor, R. A., & Benbenishty, R. (2004). Teachers' reports of school violence in Jewish and Arab public schools in Israel. *School Psychology International, 25*(2), 149–166.

Zelman v. Simmons-Harris, 536 U.S. 639 (2002).

Zigler, E., Gilliam, W. S., & Jones, S. M. (2006). *A vision for universal preschool education*. New York: Cambridge.

Zirkel, P. A., Richardson, S. N., & Goldberg, S. S. (1995). *A digest of Supreme Court decisions affecting education*. Bloomington, IN: Phi Delta Kappa Educational Foundation.

Index